YO-AAG-929

STRONG
WINE

STRONG WINE

The Life and Legend of Agoston Haraszthy

BRIAN McGINTY

STANFORD UNIVERSITY PRESS

STANFORD, CALIFORNIA

LIBRARY OF
WINE INSTITUTE

Stanford University Press
Stanford, California
© 1998 by the Board of Trustees of the
Leland Stanford Junior University
Printed in the United States of America

CIP data are at the back of the book

Quotation from *Vintage: The Story of Wine*
by Hugh Johnson (Simon & Schuster,
1989, first published by Mitchell Beazley,
UK) by permission of Mitchell Beazley

Frontispiece: Portrait of Agoston Haraszthy
by William Shew, San Francisco. Frank H.
Bartholomew Foundation.

"No novelist could have
invented Haraszthy.
There is a surprise
around every corner
of his life—and how
many lives have had so
many corners?"

Hugh Johnson, *Vintage:
The Story of Wine*

Acknowledgments

This book would not be complete without an expression of thanks to the many people who helped in its preparation. In Budapest, Dr. Tamás Magyarics, chairman of the Department of American Studies at Eötvös Loránd University, deserves special gratitude for translating Hungarian texts for my use, for sharing his insights into Hungarian and Hungarian-American history, and for carefully reading the finished manuscript. Dr. Tibor Frank, director of the School of English and American Studies, Eötvös Loránd University, was kind enough to read the manuscript and offer suggestions for corrections and additions. Mr. and Mrs. Gyula Lelbach welcomed me into their Budapest home and shared with me a part of their very considerable knowledge of noble life in Bács County during the nineteenth century. Melinda Kovács was a great help in locating documents in the National Archives and the National Széchényi Library and in translating Hungarian texts. The staffs of both the Archives and the Széchényi Library were helpful and, in spite of what at times seemed a formidable language barrier, courteous and friendly.

My research in Serbia was facilitated by Mrs. Voyka Askovič and Mr. Negovan Laušev, both of Novi Sad. In Slovakia, Mrs. Kamila Chudá of Bytča conducted research on my behalf, while Msgr. Emilián Foltýn, pastor of St. Mary's Church in Hearne, Texas, acted as a bridge in the correspondence I carried on with Mrs. Chudá after my return to the United States, translating my letters and hers.

Those who offered me help and assistance in the United States are so numerous that I scarcely know where to begin in expressing my appreciation. The late Theodore Schoenman of Santa Barbara made the unpublished English translation of Haraszthy's *Utazás Éjszakamerikában* (Travels in North America) that he completed with his wife, Helen Benedek Schoenman, available for my use. Zoltán Sztáray of San Bernardino offered encouragement for my project and shared some of the information he acquired during the research for his own study of Haraszthy's life, published in Hungarian in 1986. Eva T. Liptak of the Family History Library of the Church of Jesus Christ of Latter-Day Saints in Salt Lake City was a good friend in plumbing the resources of that great genealogical repository, while Dr. George Barany of the University of Denver read the Hungarian portions of my manuscript and offered corrections and suggestions for improvement. Pamela Herr, former managing editor of *American West* magazine and author of *Jessie Benton Frémont: A Biography*, read the entire manuscript, offering many good suggestions. Dr. Kevin Starr, State Librarian of California and author of the "Americans and the California Dream" series, read the book and enthusiastically recommended it to Stanford University Press.

Others who offered generous help include Brother Steve Herro, O. Praem., and Abbott Benjamin Mackin, O. Praem., of St. Norbert Abbey, De Pere, Wisconsin; Eileen Adank, secretary of St. Aloysius Church in Sauk City, and Father William Rock, pastor of St. Norbert Church in nearby Roxbury; Paul Meyer of Sauk City and Robert Wollersheim of Prairie du Sac; and William F. Heintz of Sonoma and Charles L. Sullivan of Los Gatos, California, both dedicated wine historians. Although Mr. Sullivan and I have reached different conclusions regarding important aspects of Haraszthy's life and career, I salute him as an important scholar in the field and thank him for his generosity in sharing information and insights.

Jim Barnett of Scottsdale, Arizona, deserves special thanks, for he accompanied me on many of my research trips (including the long automobile trip retracing Haraszthy's route across the Great Plains and southwestern deserts to California) and read the entire book in manuscript. My uncle, Jan James Haraszthy of Sonoma, helped in many ways, as did his wife of more than fifty years, my dear Aunt Mianna. I can never adequately express the thanks I owe

my late mother, Natalia Haraszthy McGinty. It was she who introduced me to the astonishing story of her great-grandfather, Agoston
Haraszthy, and who inspired in me a love for books and history that
sustained me through a long and oftentimes difficult task. In large
measure this book was written for her.

                                        Brian McGinty

Contents

Photographs follow pages 138 and 334.

STRONG
WINE

Introduction

More than a century and a quarter after he went to his death in a Central American jungle, Agoston Haraszthy[1] still holds a unique place in American history. For years, virtually every printed mention of Haraszthy's name was accompanied by the sobriquet "Father of California Viticulture" or "Father of Winemaking in California," to underline his pioneer role in the development of the California wine industry. Interest in Haraszthy's life and career still focuses primarily on his winemaking activities in California, despite the vigorous efforts of a generation of revisionist historians to prove that he was not the "father" of the industry. Far from destroying interest in Haraszthy's story, the revisionists have kindled a new interest in his life and achievements.

But Haraszthy's fame rests on more than his contributions to the development of the California wine industry. He was the first Hungarian to settle permanently in the United States; only the second Hungarian to write a book about the United States in his native language. He is remembered in Wisconsin as the founder of the oldest incorporated village in the state and the operator of the first steamboat to engage in regularly scheduled traffic on the upper Mississippi River. In San Diego, he is remembered as the first town marshal, the first county sheriff, and the builder of the first city jail. In San Francisco, he was the first assayer of the United States Mint, in which position he became embroiled in a heated controversy centering on the disappearance of $150,000 worth of federal gold. In the Sonoma Valley north of San Francisco, he built the first stone wineries in California, introduced more than three hundred varieties of European grapes, and planted (or helped to plant) more than a thousand acres of choice wine vineyards. He made a "grand tour" of Europe as a California state commissioner on vines and wines, and was the author of the first book on wine ever written by a Californian.[2] For a few years in the early 1860's his Buena Vista Estate just outside the town of Sonoma was widely (and perhaps accurately) advertised as "the largest vineyard in the world."

A listing of Haraszthy's many accomplishments is enough to explain the fascination that historians (particularly wine historians) have long had with his life. But telling the story of his life in anything approaching satisfactory detail has not been so easy. From his earliest days in the United States, Haraszthy concocted fanciful stories about himself and his Hungarian background. He claimed to be a Hungarian count, and to have fled his native country because of political persecution. After his death, his talented son Arpad repeated stories that his father had told him, embellishing them with implausible details. The stories that Agoston Haraszthy told about himself—and that Arpad Haraszthy repeated and later magnified—took on a life of their own, confounding the efforts of serious researchers to discover the truth. I have called these stories the Haraszthy Legend and have given them the place they deserve in this biography—for after dealing with them on a serious basis for more than six years, I have come to the conclusion that it is impossible to understand Haraszthy the man without first understanding the Haraszthy Legend.

Agoston Haraszthy did not set out to cast off the attributes of his real life and assume the identity of a person he never was and could never be. He did, however, deliberately misrepresent his background and origins with a view of making his arrival in America somehow more romantic and exciting than it was. He claimed that he was a Hungarian count, which he was not; but he *was* a Hungarian nobleman, the scion of one of the oldest families in Hungary. He was a man of enormous natural talents, well educated, energetic, and resourceful, but he was not a member of the Royal Hungarian Bodyguard, as he later claimed; he was not active in political movements to overthrow the Hapsburg monarchy that ruled Hungary from Vienna; he was never imprisoned in his native land, or sentenced to death; and he did not come to the United States as a political refugee. He left Hungary in search of economic opportunity, as millions of Europeans had done before him and would continue to do after him, hoping in the new country to achieve the kind of economic independence that the semifeudal institutions of nineteenth-century Hungary had denied him. He embellished his past, perhaps in the belief that the embellishments would help him succeed in his American enterprises—not because he wanted to deny his Hungarian past or bury his heritage, but because Americans were fascinated with European aristocrats, no matter how much they professed to deplore them.

Haraszthy was fiercely proud of his ancestral ties to the Magyar warriors who crossed the Carpathians from the steppes of Russia at the end of the ninth century and eventually established the Christian kingdom of Hungary. But to most Americans in the nineteenth century, Hungary was a mysterious land, an exotic kingdom fragrant with the mingled odors of Eastern potentates and Asiatic warriors, a country that was *in* Europe but not really *of* Europe. Perhaps it was an effort to explain his place in the hierarchy of that fascinating land that led him to call himself a count when his proper title was *tekintetes úr*, the approximate equivalent of the English "Honorable Sir." Perhaps it was an effort to lend an aristocratic cachet to the town he founded on the banks of the Wisconsin River in southwestern Wisconsin and thus draw new settlers to the place. Whatever the motivation, the pose was more an exaggeration than a misrepresentation, and it is to his credit that after he left Wisconsin in 1849 he dropped it, choosing to be known instead by the courtesy title "colonel," which reflected his military background.

Writing this book has been for me both a joy and an agony. As I have searched in the United States and in Hungary for keys to the true story of Agoston Haraszthy's life, I have discovered facts that have never before seen print. These facts, however, have not been easy to find or properly evaluate.

Since Arpad Haraszthy wrote in 1886 that his father was born in Bács County, on the southern borderlands of Hungary, Haraszthy researchers have sought in vain for any record of his birth in that county. At least two would-be biographers have traveled to the supposed site of his birthplace (now a part of Serbia) and personally searched for records of the birth in county and church records.[3] Finding none, they have thrown up their hands in frustration. I have discovered that Haraszthy was not born where his son claimed he was, but in the city of Pest on the banks of the Danube in the very heart of Hungary (before 1873, Buda and Pest were separate cities, facing each other across the historic river). I verified this discovery in the baptismal records of the Roman Catholic parish of Terézváros in Pest, an oversize volume with yellowed pages and a heavy leather binding that I examined with my own eyes on a recent visit to Hungary.[4] My discovery of Haraszthy's baptismal record has helped to uncover other key facts in his life, explaining not only why the written record of the Haraszthy family in Bács County is so thin,[5] but also why the family was in somewhat reduced circumstances during Agoston's youth and why, at the comparatively tender age of twenty-eight, he turned his back on his homeland to search for new opportunities in a strange land halfway round the world. This discovery led to another and then another, until I was able to draw something like a complete picture of Haraszthy and his life.

This book has been six years in the making, but it has been stirring in me much longer. Some years ago, I looked into the facts of Haraszthy's career at the mint in San Francisco and produced a little book about his work there and his subsequent arrest, trial, and acquittal on embezzlement charges. The book, called *Haraszthy at the Mint*,[6] found a place in libraries here and there, and brought my name to the attention of researchers who sought to know more about Haraszthy's life and career. Some of these people informed me of their wish to produce a full-length biography of Haraszthy and asked me for any advice, suggestions, or research leads that might help them with their task. I was pleased to offer what help I could, though I resisted suggestions that I undertake such a project myself. Agoston Haraszthy was, after all, my great-great-grandfather, and I knew it would not be easy for me to appraise him with the detachment that an honest biography demands. But, as it became apparent to me that the other writers had abandoned their projects, I began to think more seriously about taking on the task myself. I knew it would be hard to pierce the Haraszthy Legend, and once it was pierced it would be equally hard to make a fair and balanced assessment of Haraszthy's accomplishments and failures. But I concluded at last to attempt to do so.

I have made a serious effort throughout this book to overcome any bias that I might have brought to this subject. Of course, I have made judgments, but in every case I have made a conscious effort to lay out the facts upon which those judgments rest and, through the notes assembled at the end of the book, show the sources of each of those facts.

When it came time for me to reassess the story of Haraszthy's career at the San Francisco Mint, I reviewed the research materials I had gathered while writing *Haraszthy at the Mint*, and any other information I could get my hands on. I did not rely on my earlier conclusions about Haraszthy's arrest and trial but attempted to reassess the facts in a fresh light. I was nonetheless pleased that, on this review, my earlier conclusions seemed not only to be reaffirmed but even strengthened. I was more convinced than ever before that he was innocent of the embezzlement charges brought against him, and that the jury's verdict absolving him of responsibility for the disappearance of the mint's gold was both fair and just.

I wish I could be as pleased about some of my earlier observations about Haraszthy's life and career outside the mint. Before I wrote *Haraszthy at the Mint*, I published several articles about Haraszthy (all detailed in the Bibliography) that adhered much too slavishly to the Haraszthy Legend. In my defense, I can only say that the Legend was a tradition in my family, and that until I finished the research for this book I did not know which parts of it were true and which apocryphal. Of course, what I did was no better or worse than what dozens of other writers had done up to that point. But that does not excuse it, or ease the embarrassment I feel even now. I hope that this book will serve in some measure as an atonement for my earlier transgressions. Certainly the years of research that went into its preparation—research that took me to Hungary, to Wisconsin, across the plains from Missouri to San Diego, to San Francisco, Crystal Springs, and Sonoma—should be counted as a penance of sorts.

My research has discovered much that is new, and much that sheds new light on familiar facts. I was delighted when, in Wisconsin, I stumbled on a long diary kept by a Tyrolean priest who had been on intimate terms with the Haraszthy family during the years they lived on Sauk Prairie and recorded some very interesting impressions of them.[7] I was equally pleased when, through a circuitous trail that led from Kansas through Ohio and Wisconsin to the Bancroft Library in California, I discovered the unpublished diary of a man who had accompanied Haraszthy on his epic journey across the plains to California in 1849.[8] It was with the aid of this diary that I was able to follow the route of the Haraszthy wagon train across Iowa, Missouri, Kansas, Oklahoma, New Mexico, Arizona, and southern California, and to retrace the exact route in my car. I count it as a stroke of good fortune that, shortly before the death of the late Theodore Schoenman, I was able to obtain his very readable but unpublished English translation of Haraszthy's Hungarian book, originally published in 1844 in Pest.[9] This enabled me to follow the course of Haraszthy's travels through the United States in 1840 and 1841 and to have the benefit of his early views on American life and culture.

The month I spent following Haraszthy's trail in Hungary (including parts of the trail that wended north into Slovakia and south into Serbia) gave me many reasons to be thankful that I had at least a speaking acquaintance with the Hungarian language, the ancient and (at least to Western Europeans) very difficult mother tongue of the native peoples of Hungary.[10] But my Hungarian is too basic for serious historical research, and I was relieved when Professor Tamás Magyarics of the Department of American Studies at Eötvös Loránd University in Budapest agreed to translate into English a large body of material that would otherwise have been inaccessible to me. I am grateful to Professor Magyarics not only for his skills as a translator but also for the valuable historical insights he has offered.

No biography of Agoston Haraszthy can be complete without

touching on two questions, one quite central to the story of his life and the other tangential but nonetheless fascinating. The first is whether he is deserving of the title "Father of California Viticulture" that generations of wine writers have bestowed on him. A large bronze plaque, erected in the tree-shaded plaza of Sonoma in 1946, is tangible evidence of the title, although countless printed references—and a resolution of the California Legislature—have reaffirmed it.[11] Beginning in the 1970's, however, a new generation of wine historians began to reassess the facts upon which the title rested and determined that it was not merited.[12] These writers pointed out that wine had been produced in California long before Haraszthy arrived in the state, beginning in fact in the early days of the California missions, and that he was not the first man to import European (that is, *Vitis vinifera*) grapes into California.

These facts are, of course, indisputable, but they do not necessarily answer the question posed. It is impossible to determine whether Haraszthy deserves to be called the "Father of California Viticulture" until that term is first defined. If it means the first man to grow grapes, or the first man to produce or sell wine in California, Haraszthy clearly was not the "father." If, however, it means a man who came on a winemaking community that in the early 1850's was so tiny as to be barely recognizable as an industry and, in the course of a dozen years, built it by force of his example and preachments into one of the most important agricultural industries in California—indeed, in the whole United States—he was surely the "father." Haraszthy was the first commercial producer who recognized that a world-class industry might one day be built in California, and who set out in a conscious way to build it; the first producer who sought to publicize the potential of California as a great wine land; who sought to induce farmers to buy suitable land and plant it to wine vineyards; who used his pen to instruct would-be winemakers in the best methods of planting, cultivating, and harvesting grapes, and making those grapes into a wine that might rival the best products of Europe. He set a standard that winemakers for a generation afterward sought to emulate, and even though his own efforts to build a great "wine estate" at Sonoma ended in commercial failure, he was the first man who dared to plan and build on so grand a scale. If

Agoston Haraszthy was not the "father" of the California wine industry, then there was no "father," for no other man did as much to launch the industry in its pioneer days and induce others to help him make it prosper and thrive.

Perhaps the early writers who chose to call Haraszthy the "Father of California Viticulture" chose their words inexpertly, for the word "father" does connote a kind of primacy in time, and there is no doubt that there were winemakers before Haraszthy. Another term might have described him more appropriately. He might have been called "The First Important Commercial Winemaker in California," or "The First Pioneer of California Viticulture." A generation ago, the great food and wine writer James Beard called Haraszthy quite simply "the great name in California wine history."[13] Beard's label has the twin virtues of succinctness and aptness.

The question of whether Haraszthy was the first man to import the Zinfandel grape into California is less important than the question of his "fatherhood," but it has occupied more time and ink, at least in the last dozen years. It was Arpad Haraszthy who published the claim that his father was the first man to bring this mysterious, almost magical, grape to the Golden State, where it flourished and eventually became one of the most important wine grapes in the United States. But Arpad was not altogether clear about the dates and circumstances of his father's importation, and his written statements on the subject include some obviously inconsistent assertions. There is not a single word in Agoston Haraszthy's own hand that refers to the Zinfandel in any way—a fact that some recent historians have pointed to as evidence that he had nothing to do with the early development of the grape. But Haraszthy brought hundreds of grapes to California, experimented with scores of them, and probably used dozens of them in his wine, and did not write anything specific about any of them. It was the almost universal custom in California in the 1850's and 1860's to identify a wine by its color, type, and place of origin, and not by the grape or grapes (for many wines were blends) from which it was made. In this respect, California wine-labeling practices reflected the labeling traditions of European winemakers. Some writers have even suggested that, if Haraszthy did not bring the first Zinfandel vines into California, he could not have been the "Father of California Viticulture," and all the other claims about his early achievements must fall. Of course, this is a logical fallacy and needs no refutation. The question of the introduction of the Zinfandel into California is a separate question and entitled to its own answer. Although my research has uncovered no direct evidence either proving or disproving that Agoston Haraszthy was the first man to bring the Zinfandel into California, I have found some new and intriguing evidence that he could well have been that man. For details of that evidence—and the rest of the astonishing story of Agoston Haraszthy's life—I commend to my readers the pages that follow.

1

The Young
Noble

It was the custom among Hungarian nobles to name a child for the saint whose feast day most closely coincided with the child's birth. And so the baby that was born into the household of Károly Haraszthy and his wife, Anna Mária Fischer, in the Terézváros parish of Pest on August 30, 1812, was named Agoston, for St. Augustine of Hippo, the great fourth-century bishop and philosopher whose feast day is August 28.[1]

A good Hungarian mother, mindful of the terrible fate of babies who died without benefit of baptism, would take her child to the parish priest within a week, or at most a month, of its birth. If a child was baptized on the very day of its birth, it was often because it was born weak or unwell and the mother feared it might not survive the customary wait. The baby boy that Anna Mária Fischer brought into the world on August 30, 1812, was baptized the same day. This fact may indicate that the baby was small and weak, or simply that the church was close to his parents' house and the trip to the baptistry easy and natural. If he was weak, it was an anomaly, for in the lifetime that was to follow, Agoston Haraszthy was to show a vitality and energy beyond those of most men.

The family into which Agoston Haraszthy was born in August of

1812 was one of the oldest in Hungary. Haraszthys had distinguished
themselves in the service of king and country for a dozen or more
generations. The royal and provincial archives of the country contained many references to Agoston's warrior ancestors, some dating
as far back as the twelfth century. The most illustrious of all the men
who bore the name Haraszthy was probably Ferencz Haraszthy, a Re-
naissance landowner and warrior who held a variety of important
positions in the last years of the fifteenth and the early years of the
sixteenth century. The land archives of Hungary contain records of
scores of estates, castles, farms, and fortresses that were registered in
Ferencz Haraszthy's name.[2] He served as the *főispán* (lord lieutenant)
of the County of Arad and *bán* (viceroy) of Szörény, in the south-
central portion of the country.[3] The Hungarian *bán*s were links in
the chain of defenses that protected the Roman Catholic kingdom of
Hungary—and, behind it, the other Christian nations of Europe—
from the Balkan lands to the south that had fallen under the domi-
nation of the Muslim Turks.

Despite the wealth and power that Ferencz Haraszthy gathered
unto himself during his lifetime, he never acquired a noble title—
never won the right to be called baron or count. His descendants
were fond of recalling that the emperor had once sent an ambassador to honor Ferencz with the title of count. The *bán* received the
ambassador in his castle, saying: "I am glad to receive you. I extend
to you the hospitality of my house; but when you go back to your
master, the Emperor, say to him, that when you have said, 'Ferencz
Haraszthy,' you have said all that can be said."[4] And so the baby
boy that Károly Haraszthy and Anna Mária Fischer brought to the
Terézváros church on August 30, 1812, was heir to a long and proud
Hungarian ancestry, but not one who would bear any title other than
the *úr* (sir) or *tekintetes úr* (honorable sir) to which every male Hungarian noble was entitled.[5]

The vast estates that Ferencz Haraszthy had acquired in the late
fifteenth and early sixteenth centuries had been scattered and lost
centuries before Agoston Haraszthy's birth. The southern frontiers
of Hungary, where the bulk of Ferencz's estates were situated, were
overrun by the Turks during his own lifetime. The Battle of Mo-
hács, fought on the banks of the Danube south of Buda and Pest

in 1526, was a great victory for the Turks under Suleiman the Magnificent and an equally great defeat for the Hungarians under King Lajos (Louis) II. With the Hungarian army virtually annihilated, ten thousand foot soldiers, almost all the bishops of the realm, and the king himself were brutally slaughtered. Then the Turkish columns, turbaned, beating drums, and brandishing scimitars, marched north toward Buda and Pest. While the Turks installed a pasha in Buda, the ragtag remnants of the Hungarian army retreated to the foothills of the Carpathians in the north, the mountain fastness of Transylvania in the east, and the rolling hills west of the Danube. For nearly two centuries, the Turks occupied the heartland of the country, while Hungarian nobles dreamed of the day when they could return to Buda in triumph.

The day of triumph did not arrive until September 1686, and the last remnants of the Turkish armies were not repelled from Hungarian territory until thirteen years later. As the Turks withdrew, they left the southern frontiers of the country a wasteland, occupied by a thin sprinkling of Serbs and Croats, but virtually devoid of Hungarians and without any agriculture. And in place of the Hungarian kings who once ruled the realm, the people of Hungary had to deal with a new, German-speaking dynasty, the Hapsburgs of Austria who had acquired the right to wear the ancient symbol of the Hungarian nation, the Crown of St. Stephen. Even as the Hungarians rejoiced that they had rid themselves of the Turks, they bemoaned the advent of the Hapsburgs, and for the next two centuries they would struggle to free themselves from their rule.

The Haraszthys lost their great wealth in the long years of the Turkish occupation. After the reestablishment of a royal court in Buda, one branch of the family found a home on the plain of Ung, in the far northeastern corner of the country. There, at a place called Mokcsa, they acquired estates and built new homes.[6] These Haraszthys were not counted among the "magnates" (great landowners) of Hungary. Their estates in Ung County were modest, and they rarely received invitations to the court in Buda. Even more rarely did they venture beyond the Austrian border to the Hapsburg capital at Vienna. But they never forgot their proud heritage, never failed to point with pride to their descent from the *bán* Ferencz Haraszthy.

The Haraszthys of Ung County were enrolled in the Hungarian archives as the Mokcsai Haraszthy family, signifying that their ancestors had at one time or another owned property both at Haraszth and at Mokcsa.[7] Their coat of arms, the emblem of their nobility, consisted of a shield on which was shown an arm clad in armor and holding in its fist a drawn sword, all mounted over an advancing crown.[8] In Hungary, surnames precede Christian names instead of following them. Thus Agoston's father was called Mokcsai Haraszthy Károly (Charles Haraszthy of Mokcsa). His son was entitled to the same family names, even though he was born far from Ung County and the place called Mokcsa, and would be called Mokcsai Haraszthy Agoston (Augustine Haraszthy of Mokcsa).

Mokcsai Haraszthy Károly (whom we shall call Károly Haraszthy in this chapter) was born in 1789 in the royal free city of Szeged, on the banks of the Tisza River in the southern reaches of the huge central basin of Hungary, called the Nagy Alföld (or Great Plain). When Károly's ancestors left Ung County is not known, but it was probably sometime after 1750, for the records of the Belváros church of Szeged (now the Cathedral of St. Demetrius) reveal the names of Haraszthys going back as far as 1752; these names, however, do not include that of Károly's father, Mokcsai Haraszthy Antal (Anthony Haraszthy of Mokcsa). It can be determined on the basis of other evidence that Antal Haraszthy was born about 1760,[9] though no record has been found of the place. It is possible, perhaps even likely, that he was born somewhere in Ung County, perhaps in a village not far from his ancestors' home at Mokcsa. Károly Haraszthy's own birth is evidenced by an entry in the baptismal book of the Belváros parish church of Szeged made on November 19, 1789. Parish books in Hungary (like most official records in the kingdom) were kept in Latin, so Károly's baptismal names were recorded as Carolus Borromeus Vilhelmus.[10] The Carolus Borromeus signified that he was born around November 4, the feast day of the sixteenth-century Italian cardinal St. Charles of Borromeo. The Vilhelmus was given in honor of his godfather, Vericz Vilmos Úr (Sir William Vericz).[11] The exact date of Károly's birth has not been discovered, though it was probably October 22.[12]

The baptismal register of the Belváros church in Szeged reveals that Károly Haraszthy's mother was a woman named Barbara Schungenmajer and that she and Antal Haraszthy were the parents of at least two other children, daughters named Theresa and Barbara, baptized in the Belváros church in 1785 and 1787.[13] Barbara Schungenmajer's name suggests that she was of German, or at least partly German, ancestry. Of course, Germans were widely dispersed throughout central Europe in the eighteenth and nineteenth centuries, and it was not at all unusual to find Germans in Hungary. The ruling dynasty was itself a German-speaking family, and German-speaking settlers had entered Hungary on a regular basis since the Hapsburgs seized the Hungarian throne. The godparents of Theresa and Barbara Haraszthy suggest that the Haraszthys of Szeged were on very friendly terms with the German community of the city. The godfather to both Theresa and Barbara Haraszthy was a man named Joseph Gruber, whose name also suggests that he was of German ancestry, if not birth.

The only written evidence relating to Antal Haraszthy's occupation is a notation in the church register, in the hand of the parish priest, in a kind of shorthand Latin, reading *posae magister*, or something to that effect. The exact meaning of this entry is not clear, though it probably indicates that he was a public official, possibly in the government of the royal free city. His name was preceded by the capital letter "D," which is an abbreviation for the Latin *Dominus* (or Lord) and the equivalent of the Hungarian *úr*. Thus did the priest signify that Antal was a Hungarian noble.[14]

Why Antal Haraszthy left his family's ancestral home in Ung County is not known. Other members of the Mokcsai Haraszthy clan remained there, even through the twentieth century. The Haraszthys who stayed behind, however, were adherents of the Calvinist faith that swept much of Hungary in the sixteenth century. At the time of Agoston Haraszthy's birth in 1812, about 60 percent of the Hungarian population was Roman Catholic, while the remaining 40 percent was divided among the Calvinist, Lutheran, Orthodox, and Jewish faiths. But at one point in the sixteenth century, under the influence of the Protestant Reformation, fully 90 percent of the population claimed some religion other than that of their Catholic ancestors. The majority of the nobles returned to the Catholic fold by the end of the seventeenth century, and at the end of the eighteenth both Antal Haraszthy and his son Károly were loyal communicants of Rome.

Could it be that sectarian rivalries had driven Antal and his family out of Ung County? Or were these Haraszthys simply seeking the greater opportunities that presented themselves in the rest of the country? Under Hungarian law, a noble's estates were divided equally among his sons, so large estates had a tendency over successive generations to become very small. Nobles who accepted this result also had to resign themselves to a dilution of their wealth and social status. Nobles who resisted this kind of slow decline left the villages of their ancestors and sought new opportunities, often in the royal free cities that were beginning to blossom in the late eighteenth and early nineteenth centuries. Szeged, a thriving trading center for the Great Plain, was such a city. Pest, situated on a gently rolling plain opposite the hilly site of Buda on the Danube, was another.

When Antal Haraszthy and his family left Szeged for Pest has not been determined, but it was sometime before 1811, for on October 15 of that year Antal's son Károly married Anna Mária Fischer in the Belváros parish church of Pest. At the time of his marriage, Károly Haraszthy was twenty-two years old and a resident of Buda; his bride was twenty and a resident of Pest.[15]

Anna Mária Fischer was a native of Óbuda, an ancient village north of Buda on the west bank of the Danube. The records of the Roman Catholic parish church of Óbuda show that a baby girl named Anna was baptized on April 19, 1791, the daughter of Joannes Fischer and his wife, Theresia Blasserin. The godparents were Georgius Akerman and his wife, Anna Hirshin.[16] It would appear from the records that Anna Mária Fischer was of German descent on both sides of her family, since both her father's and her mother's names were German. This fact, coupled with the obviously German names of her godfather and godmother, indicates that the Fischers were a thoroughly German family, if not necessarily newly arrived in Hungary. Many German families had lived in Hungary for generations, and although they kept largely to their own communities, they were enthusiastic Hungarians and considered themselves loyal subjects of the Hungarian king.

Some indication of the social status of Károly Haraszthy and Anna Mária Fischer may be derived from the official witnesses at their wedding. One was a man identified in the marriage register as Spectabilis Dominus Anselmas Peláty, advocatus (the Very Honorable Sir Anselm Peláty, attorney). The other was Maximus Dominus Consiliarius Martinus Ignatius Lendvay (the Right Honorable Sir Councillor Martin Ignatius Lendvay).[17] Both the Lendvays and the Pelátys were of Magyar blood, and the Lendvays at least were a family of some prominence in the Hungarian capital. Martin Ignatius Lendvay was a member of the Court Council in Buda and had occupied the prestigious position of Director of the Archives of the Hungarian Chamber since 1801.[18]

After their marriage, Károly and Anna Mária Haraszthy set up a household in the Terézváros (Theresatown) parish of Pest, in the northeastern quarter of the city. Pest was then experiencing an explosion of growth, encouraged in part by the Napoleonic Wars, which had disrupted the traditional pattern of country life throughout central Europe and sent tens of thousands of Hungarians to the cities in search of a new urban existence. Since Pest was surrounded by mostly flat land extending south and east as far as the eye could see, it could accommodate much of the new growth, while its cross-river counterpart, Buda, hemmed in by steep, wooded hills, remained largely confined to its medieval walls. The stone-and-tile houses of Terézváros were built on narrow, cobbled streets that formed an irregular grid around the parish church. Founded in 1778, the church had held its first services in a wooden building, but the foundations of a stone sanctuary were laid in 1803, and the new edifice, dedicated to St. Theresa of Avila, was consecrated in 1809. The church was still new and only partially furnished when the infant Agoston Haraszthy was brought to the baptistry on August 30, 1812.[19]

He was baptized, in Latin, as Augustus Fredericus Antonius. These names would translate into Hungarian as Agoston Frigyes Antal and into English as Augustine Frederick Anthony. The Antonius was conferred in honor of the baby's grandfather, Antal Haraszthy, who served as his godfather. His godmother was Theresa Grossinger. We know nothing about this woman, except that she bore a German name, not a surprising fact since the baby's mother was of pure

German blood and his father was probably at least half-German. Throughout his life, the boy would be known by the Christian name of Agoston, although his family and friends would refer to him by the Magyar diminutive "Guszti."[20]

The fact that this baby, who was to achieve fame in his own country and abroad as a Magyar, was probably three-quarters German indicates the mixture of peoples in his native land at the beginning of the nineteenth century. Though it was a country peopled predominantly by Magyars, Hungary also had many Germans, Slavs, and other races mixed in. Agoston Haraszthy was not at all unique in that he was a Hungarian with German ancestors. The great pianist and composer Franz Liszt, the apotheosis of the Magyar spirit in nineteenth-century European concert halls, was himself half-German, as was Lajos (Louis) Kossuth, the lawyer, writer, and orator who, in 1848–49 assumed the political leadership of the Hungarian people in their struggle against the Hapsburgs. Kossuth, born in 1802, was ten years Agoston's senior; Liszt, born in 1811, was less than a year older.[21] Neither of these men ever doubted their right to claim a part of the ancient Magyar patrimony that was Hungary. Agoston, too, was always to speak with pride of his Hungarian ancestry, and to think of the ancient kingdom on the Danube as his spiritual home. As if to reinforce the validity of this claim, the priest who baptized him in the Terézváros church wrote the word "nobilis" in the heavy, leather-bound parish register next to the name of Károly Haraszthy, thus signifying that the baby's father — hence the baby himself — were both Hungarian nobles.[22]

Agoston Haraszthy's father, Károly Haraszthy Mokcsai, was evidently a man of intelligence and refinement. Years after he arrived in the United States, he claimed to have a military background. The claim is quite plausible, for it was traditional in Hungary for male nobles to give military service, and in the troubled years of the Napoleonic Wars, when central Europe was almost constantly under the siege of the armies of Napoleon I, the Hungarian nobles were repeatedly called on to render military service, both to their counties and to the Hapsburg monarchs. In the United States, Károly was addressed as "general," but this must be regarded as a courtesy title only. There is no reason to assume that he ever achieved that lofty military rank or that anybody with whom he came in contact reasonably believed that he had.

Károly seems to have been an unusually studious man. His grandson Arpad remembered many years later that he was "a man of great intellect and culture" and that he "wrote and read in sixteen languages and dialects and spoke twelve."[23] Although this statement undoubtedly owes something to the inflated pride of a grandson, there is other evidence to support it. An article that Károly wrote for a newspaper in California reveals his very considerable knowledge of languages, including French, German, Spanish, Italian, and Latin, in addition, of course, to his native Magyar.[24] A Norbertine priest from the Tyrol once described Károly as "exceedingly cultured,"[25] and an attorney who was well acquainted with him during the time he lived in Wisconsin wrote that he was "probably the best educated man who ever came to this country from abroad."[26] His intellectual pursuits ran to scientific and technical subjects as well as languages. His grandson recalled that he had "great inventive genius" and had secured about a dozen patents and "had enough inventions for a hundred."[27] After he came to the United States, he showed his skills as a chemist and apothecary by dispensing medicines to a frontier community that had no resident physician.[28] Later, in San Francisco, he showed his skills as a metallurgist by assaying, refining, and melting precious metals.

Agoston Haraszthy's father seems all his life to have been more of a thinker than a doer. A Hungarian who was on intimate terms with the Haraszthys during the time they lived in California once told Károly's grandson: "There is the greatest difference between your father [Agoston] and your grandfather. Your grandfather has a thousand ideas and never puts one of them in practical motion. Your father has a thousand ideas and the trouble with him is that he puts them all in motion."[29]

But unless he has the luxury of inherited wealth, even a man of ideas must have a practical side. Although the Haraszthys were nobles, they were not a rich family, and Károly almost certainly had to make a living for himself and his family. In later years, Károly recalled that he had spent most of his adult life in the wine business. In an intriguing letter he wrote for a San Francisco newspaper in 1856, he noted that he had spent time in all the important wine-producing countries of Europe, excepting only Spain and Portugal.[30] This statement probably means that he worked, at least for a while, as a wine merchant or broker, a fact that would explain his (and perhaps his father's) presence in Szeged and Pest at the end of the eighteenth and the beginning of the nineteenth centuries, for both cities were thriving centers of the Hungarian wine trade. Károly also recalled in the 1856 letter that over a period of thirty-one years he cultivated extensive vineyards of his own, with what he rather immodestly called "an unparalleled success."[31] Discounting his own evaluation of his winegrowing efforts, it is entirely reasonable to suppose that he was a successful winegrower—Hungary was, after all, one of the great wine-growing countries of Europe, and it was only natural for a man of Károly Haraszthy's background and temperament to work at making and selling wine, both to his fellow countrymen and to the foreign nations (chief among them the hundreds of independent German-speaking kingdoms, principalities, and duchies) that from time immemorial had consumed more wine than they could produce.

The ability of a Hungarian male in the early years of the nineteenth century to pursue his livelihood away from his family's ancestral home was closely related to his social and legal status, for Hungarian nobles were free to move about the country and take up residence if they chose in a city. Hungarian peasants, in contrast, were bound to specific plots or tracts of land. In the same way that ownership of land was passed down from landlords to their sons and grandsons, so the duty of working the land was passed down from peasants to their sons and grandsons. In the beginning, the peasants had traded their labor for the protection of the lord, who was obliged to take up arms in their defense if they should ever be threatened. Over the centuries, the lord's duty to provide military defense came to be more theoretical than real, since individual warriors could do little to resist the onslaughts of modern armies; but the peasants' ties to the land survived, condemning them to lives of dreary labor and providing them with escape only if they could pay their debts and scrape together enough money to begin a new life in a town or city.[32] Yet the freedom nobles had to leave their families' ancestral estates involved risks, for a noble who did not live on an estate could be mistaken for a peasant, or for a member of the indeterminate class of people who were neither nobles nor peasants but city dwellers— *Bürger*, as the Germans called them, *polgárok* as they were known to the Hungarians. By leaving the land, the Haraszthys had run the risk that they would be regarded as mere *polgárok*.

A fascinating series of documents, handwritten in Hungarian and carefully preserved in the Hungarian National Archives, reveals that the Haraszthys' nobility was indeed questioned. In 1819, while Antal Haraszthy was living in Pest, he commenced a lawsuit to prove that both he and his son Károly were "true nobles" and entitled to exercise the privileges of their class. They had been living in Pest for some years, apparently enjoying the same noble status that they had enjoyed in Szeged and that their ancestors had enjoyed in Ung County. But in that year an unnamed person or persons challenged their status as nobles. Responding to the challenge, Antal Haraszthy called on the General Assembly of Nobles of Ung County to attest to the nobility of the Mokcsai Haraszthy family. He also called on a noble named István Szabady who resided in Szeged, and the authorities of the Szeged church in which Károly was baptized in 1789, to give evidence concerning the family's noble status. The church authorities responded with a certificate showing the date and the fact of Károly's baptism, and both Szabady and the General Assembly of Ung gave written evidence that the Mokcsai Haraszthys were not only a noble family of Ung County but one of that county's oldest noble families. This evidence was examined by the county attorney in Pest and then submitted to the General Assembly in a report that found "no deficiency" in Antal's claim. Indeed, the evidence that supported it was so strong that the report concluded with the words: "And if the truth must be said, rare is the family able to trace this far its nobility." [33] Antal demanded that official certificates of nobility be issued to both him and his son, and the demand was readily complied with. The evidence and the report were read in public "on the twelfth day of the month of Saint Andrew [November in the ecclesiastical calendar] in the year 1819 at the General Assembly held in Pest." [34]

Agoston Haraszthy was just seven years old when his grandfather's lawsuit resulted in an official affirmation of his and his ancestors' noble status. The effect of this official proceeding on his

young mind can well be imagined. He must initially have been surprised—perhaps even frightened—to learn that his family's nobility
had been questioned, but then reassured by the proceedings in the
General Assembly that reaffirmed his father's and his grandfather's
(hence his own) right to call themselves nobles. There is no doubt
that the lawsuit was a serious undertaking and not an exercise in
self-flattery; in Hungary in the early years of the nineteenth century the right of a man to call himself a noble was one of the most
valuable rights any Hungarian could exercise, and any challenge to
that right had to be regarded as threatening the legal, political, and
social status not only of the man to whom the challenge was issued
but also of his descendants in perpetuity.

There were in the early years of the nineteenth century about ten
million Hungarians, but only about 5 percent—or 500,000—were
nobles.[35] Not all these nobles were titled nobles—counts or barons.
Indeed, the great majority were without title, and not surprisingly,
for almost all the noble titles were conferred by the Hapsburgs in return for services rendered to the monarchy. Literate Hungarians were
fond of pointing out that the words *gróf* (count) and *báró* (baron) were
both of German origin, and that they had been virtually unknown
in Hungary before the Hapsburgs "captured" the crown.[36] The titled
nobles were the magnates of the land, men who had acquired vast estates (often scattered widely about the country) from the same monarchs who had granted them their noble titles. These magnates were
rich and cultured men who spent much of their time in Vienna. In
contrast, the overwhelming majority of the Hungarian nobles were
not only untitled men, they were also men of very modest circumstances. Many—deprecatingly called "one-house," "half-spurred," or
"sandaled" nobles—were no better off economically than the peasants among whom they lived in conditions that often verged on
sheerest poverty. Between the magnates and the one-house nobles
was a group of intermediate nobles, often called *bene possessionati* (or
"well possessioned") because they owned estates of a few hundred
or a few thousand acres and could afford to maintain a comfortable
if not luxurious way of life. These nobles were the rough equivalents
of the class of English country gentleman called "gentry." The magnates and the *bene possessionati* spoke German as well as (in many cases

better than) their native language, while the "one-house" nobles rarely spoke any language other than Magyar. The magnates were usually Catholics (like the Hapsburgs), while the *bene possessionati* and the "one-house" nobles were usually (but not always) Protestants.[37]

Regardless of the economic, social, and religious differences that separated them, all the Hungarian nobles were the possessors of a common set of rights and privileges. These derived from the famous *Bulla Aurea* (or "Golden Bull") signed by King Andrew II in 1222. Like the Magna Carta, extracted from King John by the English barons only seven years earlier, the Golden Bull was a royal concession to the power and influence of the nobles. It guaranteed basic rights that were to inure to the benefit of every male noble in the realm (and his male descendants) in perpetuity: the right to be free from arrest and detainment, except upon conviction in a court of law; the right to own property and to transmit it to the noble's male heirs; freedom from the obligation to give military service on foreign soil, except at the king's expense; freedom from the obligation of paying taxes; and the right of resisting, by force if necessary, if the sovereign should attempt to impair or deny any other right that inured to the nobles. In the eyes of the law, it mattered not one whit whether a Hungarian was a magnate or a "one-house" noble. If he was a true descendant of one of the men to whom King Andrew directed the Golden Bull in 1222, or any other male later admitted to the ranks of the nobility by royal decree, he was entitled to exercise all the rights and privileges delineated in the bull.

The Pest in which Agoston Haraszthy was born and grew up was a thriving city and an important commercial and cultural center. In it were located many of the great institutions of the kingdom, the Hungarian National Museum, the Hungarian Academy of Sciences, and the National University, and the quays along the riverbank were crowded with colorful boats that brought goods in and out of the city.

We know little of Agoston's early life in Pest, though a few facts are uncontroverted. He was an only child, a fact that is verified not only by the later recollections of his descendants but also by the absence in the church records of Terézváros of any references to other children born to Károly and Anna Mária Haraszthy. It is possible, of course, that other children were born to the couple but did not survive to adulthood; but it appears that the family remained in Teréz-város at least until 1825, and in all that time no brother or sister of Agoston Haraszthy was brought to the church for baptism. The family's presence in Terézváros as late as 1825 is verified by an entry in the parish book of deaths revealing that Antal Haraszthy died on January 25 of that year. As if to vindicate the legal battle he fought in 1819 to reaffirm his and his family's nobility, the priest noted in the parish register that the deceased was sixty-four years of age and *nobilis* (i.e., noble).

Agoston was twelve years old when his grandfather died, old enough to have completed a good part of his education and to have given some indication of the path he wished to follow in life. It would have been usual for a boy of his station to attend one of the *gymnasia* or *archgymnasia* (high schools) with which Pest was well supplied; and, since the National University was located in the city, he could also have pursued a course of study in its halls. Law was the curriculum traditionally favored by Hungarian nobles of the middle and upper classes, not primarily because they intended to make careers as lawyers or judges, but because the study of law was deemed appropriate to men of their social and economic status. According to the Haraszthy Legend, Agoston was in fact educated "to the law." No records have been found verifying this part of his education, although it seems entirely plausible.[38]

The Legend also affirms that, at the age of sixteen, the young man became a member of the Royal Hungarian Bodyguard, one of the most prestigious organizations to which young Hungarian nobles could aspire.[39] The Bodyguard (called the *Magyar királyi testőrség* in Hungary) was established in 1760 by Maria Theresa in her capacity as Queen of Hungary to provide opportunities for outstanding young nobles to come to Vienna for four years of intimate contact with the Hapsburg court. A special palace was built in Vienna to house the young men, two of whom were elected to represent each of the Hungarian counties. In theory, it was the duty of the bodyguards to guard the person of the monarch, if necessary with their lives. In practice, however, they were rarely called on to exert themselves in defense of any of the Hapsburgs, but instead took advantage of the opportunities presented to them in Vienna to read books, acquire proficiency in the languages favored by the royal court (German and French), visit museums, and attend the theater. If the Legend is correct, Agoston's service in the Bodyguard would have commenced in 1828, the year in which he celebrated his sixteenth birthday, and would have constituted a badge of honor for the young noble.

But the records do not support the Legend in regard to the Bodyguards. Two comprehensive lists of the men who served in the Bodyguard were published late in the nineteenth and early in the twentieth centuries.[40] Based on careful examinations of the original membership rolls in Vienna, they contain the names of several thousand nobles, the counties they represented, and the dates of their membership. Agoston's name does not appear in either list. It is possible that Agoston was elected to serve in the Bodyguard but for some reason did not actually take up his duties in Vienna. Certainly it was not unprecedented for a talented young noble to be elected to membership in the Bodyguard and yet be denied the opportunity of serving for some reason totally beyond his control, such, for example, as the failure of an incumbent member to give up his place.[41] Though this possibility cannot be ruled out, it seems improbable. It is more likely that Agoston's later claim that he served in the Bodyguard was simply manufactured to lend a lustrous cachet to his background.[42]

Similarly suspect is the claim, often repeated as part of the Haraszthy Legend, that Agoston spent some time as private secretary to the Archduke Joseph, the palatine of Hungary. Since the Hapsburg monarchs resided in Vienna, they named deputies to represent them in Buda and preside over the day-to-day functions of the Hungarian government. The palatines were viceroys, with broad administrative, legislative, and judicial authority. The office of palatine had traditionally been occupied by men of aristocratic origins and executive ability who enjoyed the trust not only of the Hapsburgs but also of the Hungarian nobility. One of the most respected men to hold this important position was the Archduke Joseph, younger brother of the Emperor Francis I. Beginning in the late 1790's, Joseph lived in Buda, presiding firmly but fairly over the chancelleries and bureaucracies of the Hungarian government. Although the Hungarians did not trust the Hapsburg kings, they regarded Joseph with a mixture

of respect and even affection, and he eventually became a kind of
father figure to the Hungarian nation. If Agoston Haraszthy had
distinguished himself in the Royal Hungarian Bodyguard, he might
have been invited to serve as secretary (or perhaps one of the several secretaries) to the palatine. No records of any of the men who
entered Joseph's private service have been discovered — not surprisingly, perhaps, for the good palatine's royal headquarters in Buda
castle were subjected to sieges, sacks, fires, and bombardments in
the long succession of wars that followed his death in 1847. The
available record is simply inadequate to either affirm or deny that
Agoston was in the service of Joseph, even for a short period of time.
But other transparent discrepancies in the Legend suggest that this
claim, too, is probably false.

During the years he lived in California and Nicaragua, Agoston was almost universally addressed as "colonel." The source of this
military title was never very adequately explained. After his death,
Agoston's son Arpad claimed that it derived from his father's service
in the Royal Hungarian Bodyguard. This explanation is not persuasive. Even assuming that Agoston served for a time in that prestigious
body, he would not thereby have earned the right to call himself
colonel, for the commander of the Bodyguard was only a captain,
and his first deputy was a vice-captain.[43] Yet it does seem likely that
Agoston saw some service in the Hungarian army. After he arrived
in San Diego toward the end of 1849, he told an American attorney
that, in 1831, he raised a company of volunteer soldiers to aid the
Polish revolutionaries who rose up against their Russian overlords
in Warsaw.[44] Poland had been a large and powerful nation in the
Middle Ages, but in the closing years of the eighteenth century it
was subjected to a series of humiliating partitions that parceled out
all its territory among the Austrians, Prussians, and Russians. At the
end of 1830, the Poles in the Russian sector of the country mounted
a rebellion, and in January 1831 the Diet of Warsaw voted to strip
Czar Nicholas I of all his authority in Poland. The Poles and the
Hungarians had both suffered mightily at the hands of more powerful neighbors, so it was not surprising that a great wave of pro-Polish
sentiment swept over Hungary. When Nicholas sent his armies into
Warsaw to crush the Polish rebellion, Hungarians pleaded with their

government to send aid; when it refused to do so, individual Hungarians began to raise volunteer forces to help the Poles in defending their country against the Russians. Agoston told the American attorney that he recruited a force of 120 men and, with them, succeeded in joining the Polish army. Although he was only nineteen years old at the time, he saw combat with his soldiers and suffered at least one wound before his father caught up with him and brought him back to Hungary.[45] When the Warsaw rebellion collapsed, Hungarians warmly welcomed the throngs of Polish refugees who fled across the Carpathians onto Hungarian soil.[46]

Some time after the defeat of the Poles, Agoston apparently saw some service with the regular Hungarian army. He told the same American attorney that he was the captain of a company of Hussars (a kind of light cavalry long favored by the Hungarians) and, in this capacity, took part in a long march in Italy—the northern part of which then belonged to the Hapsburg Empire.[47] There is no particular reason to doubt the truth of these assertions, but even assuming that everything Agoston told the American attorney was true, he would not have been entitled to be called a colonel. That title (like his father's title of "general") appears never to have been any more than the kind of courtesy title that was commonly conferred on "gentlemen" with indistinct military backgrounds. Agoston became a "colonel" on the American frontier, where courtesy titles were common and almost never challenged, and there is no evidence that the title was ever applied to him in Hungary.[48]

Agoston also claimed that he had once been in the Hungarian Diet. This claim would be suspect, if for no other reason, because he was still a very young man when he left Hungary, and it would have been unusual for a man of his youth to have achieved such a high political position. In Hungary, the age of majority (that is, the age at which a nobleman could fully exercise his political rights) was twenty-four. Agoston did not reach that age until 1836, and by that time he was already married, a father, and involved in a host of other time-consuming activities. It is hardly surprising, therefore, that the membership rolls of the Diet include no reference to Agoston Haraszthy.[49] But this does not mean that he never attended any session of the legislature. Every male noble in Hungary had the right to attend sessions of the Diet, to enter personally onto the floor of the Chamber of Deputies, and by cheers or jeers to signify approval or disapproval of views expressed by the elected deputies.[50] Nobles did not customarily exercise this right, for they had other important business to attend to and relied on the elected deputies (two from each county) to look after their interests. Young nobles, however—particularly those who were just finishing their legal studies—often availed themselves of this right, if for no other reason than that they wished to observe the Diet's proceedings at close hand.

The prerogative of summoning a Diet rested solely with the Hapsburgs, and they always convened those assemblies in the medieval city of Pozsony (called Pressburg by the Germans and later renamed Bratislava by the Slovaks), on the Danube a little more than one hundred miles northwest of Buda and Pest. Although Hungarian law required that the Diet meet at least once every three years, the Hapsburgs were stingy with invitations to the assemblies. Thirteen years passed between the Diet of 1812 and the next Diet, which met in 1825, and it was another seven years before the Diet of 1832 was convened. This latter assembly, which met when Agoston was twenty years old, was notable for the large number of law students who attended and for the vigor with which the Hungarian deputies expressed their displeasure with their Hapsburg rulers. Some of the students helped Lajos Kossuth, then a young deputy from northern Hungary,[51] prepare transcripts of the debates, which were then published and circulated throughout the country; and all cheered mightily as the Transylvanian magnate Miklós Wesselényi rose on the floor of the Chamber of Deputies to demand that the Hapsburgs loosen their iron grip on Hungarian laws and institutions. Both Kossuth and Wesselényi became national heroes when the Austrians had them arrested for treason. Wesselényi's "crime" was uttering "seditious words," Kossuth's that of publishing debates that had traditionally been kept secret. The law students who attended the Diet of 1832–36 came to be called the "Dietal Youth," and in succeeding years they were to be a potent force in changing Hungarian society.

Since no records were kept of the names of the students,[52] we have no way of knowing if Agoston Haraszthy was one of the young law students who thronged to Pozsony, cheered Wesselényi, and helped Kossuth publish the deputies' debates. In later years he was to claim that he was a friend of Kossuth and that he had warmly embraced the liberal political causes of the 1830's; both claims are entirely plausible, even without a written record to authenticate them.

Kossuth, an untitled noble of modest origins but enormous natural talents, was to become a national hero during the Hungarian revolution of 1848–49, and the courageous magnate Wesselényi was to be recognized as the preeminent political leader of the 1830's. During all this time, however, the spirit of the Hungarian nation was inspired by the words and example of another man, Count István Széchenyi, born in feudal luxury in 1791 but destined eventually to lead Hungary out of its past and into the community of modern European nations.

A true magnate of the realm, Széchenyi spent most of his privileged youth in Vienna, consorting with king and princes, archdukes and counts. But he read widely, traveled in other European countries (notably England), and eventually became convinced that Hungary could achieve its true destiny only by throwing off its feudal institutions and adopting a series of thorough political and economic reforms. He wrote a series of best-selling books that expressed his ideas and exhorted his fellow countrymen to look to the future and not the past. In *Lovakrul* (On Horses), published in 1828, he argued that Hungarians should make a concerted effort to improve the breed of horses used in the country and thus enhance the efficiency of the nation's agriculture. In *Hitel* (On Credit), which appeared in 1830, he urged fundamental changes in the land tenure laws of the country so that Hungary could step out of the feudal age and into the new age of capitalism. In *Világ* (Light), published in 1831, he sought to demonstrate that Hungarians were a youthful people full of vigorous energy and capable of achieving anything if they would only develop what he called their "public intelligence and nationality." [53]

In *Világ*, Széchenyi also expressed strong opinions on the subject of Hungarian wine and winemaking. He knew, of course, that winemaking was one of Hungary's most important industries, but he recognized that Hungarian winemaking methods had lagged behind those of other European countries. In *Világ*, Széchenyi deplored the antiquated methods used by many of the country's winemakers and urged his countrymen to make use of new advances in enology and viticulture. He also called for the creation of training centers in which winemakers and viticulturists could learn the best techniques of growing vines and making wine.[54]

Hitel was Széchenyi's most important book. In it, he pointed out that the ancient law of entail, which provided that a nobleman's feudal estates would pass to his male heirs in perpetuity and could never be sold, made it virtually impossible for nobles to obtain credit. If a property owner was forbidden by law to transfer his property, no one would advance him any money on the security of that property, since a lender will lend money only if the law gives him some security for its repayment. Without credit, the Hungarian nobles were virtually powerless to modernize their farms, launch business enterprises, or do anything to develop the natural resources of the country. To Széchenyi, the lack of credit was symbolic of Hungary's backwardness, and the need to modify the law of entail only one of the dozens of ways in which Hungarian laws and institutions cried out for modernization.

To show his fellow countrymen the miracles that could be achieved in a modernized nation, Széchenyi embarked on a series of ambitious public and private projects designed to improve the nation's economy. He used blasting powder to clear huge rocks from the Danube, and then launched the first steamboats ever to navigate the Hungarian portion of that historic river. With his own money, he drained swamplands, built roads, and established the Hungarian Academy of Sciences in Pest. He invited English engineers to come to Hungary and help him make plans for a great suspension bridge across the Danube between Buda and Pest. So strong were Széchenyi's ideas, and so confident and bold his own development projects, that intelligent and thoughtful Hungarians soon began to call the age in which they lived the "Age of Széchenyi."[55] Kossuth, speaking for his countrymen, was to call the good count "the greatest of all Hungarians."[56]

Agoston Haraszthy was profoundly influenced by the ideas and example of Count István Széchenyi. For the rest of his life, he was to attempt in his own way to embody the principles of progress enunciated by the Hungarian magnate. He was to make ample use of credit (and also to abuse it). He was to become fascinated with the idea of steam power as the engine of modern industrial society, and to launch two steamboats in the United States, one on the Mississippi River and another in San Francisco Bay. He was to lay the plans for a great bridge over the Wisconsin River and to obtain legislative approval for the project, only to abandon it to others when news of the discovery of gold in California led him across the Great Plains. He was to ceaselessly seek new and better ways of growing vines and making wines, tirelessly searching for improved grape varieties and viticultural techniques. In these, and countless other ways, he was to show himself to be a spiritual and intellectual son of the great reformer of nineteenth-century Hungary, István Széchenyi.[57]

But before he could embark on an American career that would mirror in so many respects the brilliant Hungarian career of Count Széchenyi, Agoston Haraszthy had to establish himself in his own right as a credible member of the Hungarian nobility. It was one thing to be the scion of an old Magyar family, quite another to be accepted into the staid and tradition-bound Hungarian aristocracy as a man of real substance and stature. Since the Haraszthys were not a rich family, Agoston had to draw on his own natural abilities in launching his career.

Fortunately, nature had amply endowed him with the requisites of success: intelligence, energy, resourcefulness, and a bold and adventurous spirit. He had inherited from his Haraszthy ancestors a love of the land that would express itself in a veritable passion for everything that could be grown on a farm—animals, plants, trees, vegetables, fruits—and an almost uncanny ability to extract the very best from any plot of land that he worked. But he was also gifted with a fine physique and a disarmingly handsome face. When full grown, he stood five feet eight inches in height, not particularly tall by the standards of later generations, but well above the average height of his fellow Hungarians. His hair was black, his complexion dark, his eyes hazel. He had a high forehead, a round chin, and an oval face that reflected both strength and confidence. His well-formed nose was, perhaps, a little large, but not so large that young ladies were not impressed by his good looks.[58]

Like virtually all Hungarian males (except young boys and clergy-

men), Agoston's upper lip was adorned with a handsome mustache.
Before mustaches became fashionable in England or the United
States, they were de rigueur among all classes of Hungarians, from
the highest magnate to the lowliest peasant. The mustaches, which
were long and carefully trimmed, stood out on each side of the face,
as an English traveler of the time quipped, "as stiff, straight, and
black as wax could make them." Indeed, mustaches were so universal
among male Hungarians that foreign travelers whose lips were clean-
shaven were the objects of curiosity, and some children even thought
they looked like young ladies. Agoston's mustaches were grand and
black enough to assure anyone he might meet that he was no young
lady, but a real Hungarian gentleman.[59]

He was an impressive figure of a man, particularly so when he
donned the dress uniform of Hungarian nobles, a traditional costume that was one of the most cherished reflections of Hungarian
nationalism: tight pantaloons and ankle boots worn under a long
frock coat (called the *attila*) with a military collar and a fine front
decorated with gold or silver lace; a second coat (called the *mente*),
somewhat larger than the first, lined with fur, and draped loosely
over one shoulder; a high fur cap (the *kalap*), surmounted by a
feather fastened by a rich brooch; and a curved Turkish sword carried in the belt.[60]

The Turkish sword (or scimitar) was the Hungarian nobleman's
most valuable personal possession—the symbol of his feudal status
and a reminder of his ancestors' centuries-long struggle to rid the
fatherland of the scourge of the Turks. Agoston Haraszthy carried
his sword with as much pride as the greatest magnates of Hungary.
When he attended meetings of the county nobles, it was always at his
side. When he crossed the Atlantic to the United States, it was carefully packed away in his traveling trunk. When he crossed the Great
Plains to California, he guarded the sword with his life; and after he
went to his final reward in the jungles of Central America, his descendants preserved the sword as a tangible reminder of his noble
birth, adventurous life, and tragic death.[61]

2

A Little
Estate
in the South

Some time before 1833, Agoston Haraszthy and his father, Károly, acquired land on the southern frontier of the old kingdom of Hungary, in a region the Hungarians called the Bácska.[1] This part of Hungary had been held the longest and most tenaciously by the Turks, and after the invaders were ousted from the kingdom at the end of the seventeenth century, it was one of the last to be resettled by the Hungarians. Hungarian nobles in particular had avoided the Bácska, in part because the Turks were still nearby in Serbia and continued to pose a danger, in part because there was already a sprinkling of Serbs in the area and Hungarians who ventured into the region were regarded to some degree as interlopers, even though it was an undisputed domain of the Hungarian Crown.

The Bácska was an extension of the Great Plain that was the agricultural heartland of Hungary. A vast plate of flat-to-slightly-rolling land entirely surrounded by mountains, the Plain began at the base of the Carpathians in the northeastern corner of the country, spanned the Tisza River in the center of the kingdom, crossed the Danube south of Buda and Pest, and extended south almost as far as the Turkish-held fortress at Belgrade. In all, the plain occupied an area of almost five thousand square miles. It was a fertile region in which thin, sandy soil alternated with strips of rich, black earth. Grapevines grew in profusion on the hillsides that ringed the plain in both the north and south, though they were most abundant in the north-central portion of the country, around Tokaj and Eger, and in the southwest, where the plain gave way to rugged mountains that walled it off from the Adriatic and Hungary's only important seaport, the port city of Fiume.[2]

By the beginning of the nineteenth century, the Bácska was still something of a frontier, a sparsely populated country with few towns of consequence. Large sections of the region were still held outright by the Crown, although there were a few large estates that dated back to the eighteenth century or even beyond. One of the largest was Futtak, a tract of more than 34,000 acres that hugged the northern bank of the Danube about eight miles west of the town of Újvidék.[3] Futtak was owned by the Hussar general Count András Hadik in the eighteenth century, but sometime after 1800 King Francis I approved its transfer to Count József Brunswick. The principal seat of the Brunswick family was at Martonvásár, about twenty miles southwest of Buda and nearly one hundred fifty miles north of Futtak. There the Brunswicks played host to Hungarian and Austrian aristocrats, and to prominent artists and musicians of the late eighteenth and early nineteenth centuries. Ludwig van Beethoven often visited at Martonvásár, where he developed an affection for one of József Brunswick's nieces, a winsome countess who may have been the unnamed "Immortal Beloved" to whom the composer addressed his most famous love letter.[4]

Among his many other honors, Count József Brunswick held the prestigious office of Lord Chief Justice of Hungary. Brunswick was too busy with his official duties in Buda and Vienna to spend much time at Futtak, and so he commissioned a superintendent to manage the estate. After the count's death in 1827, his widow assumed control of Futtak.[5]

Sometime during this period, a nobleman named Ferencz Dedinszky became the superintendent of the estate.[6] Dedinszky saw to the day-to-day management of the property, occupying the large house that was the headquarters of the estate and sending regular reports on the property's affairs to the absent countess. It was an

important position, for Futtak was one of the richest agricultural
estates in the Bácska, producing large crops of wheat and hay, maintaining large herds of cattle, and supporting two thriving villages on
the Danube, one called Ófuttak (Old Futtak) and the other Újfuttak
(New Futtak).[7]

It is not known when or under what circumstances the Haraszthys came to the Bácska. Early-nineteenth-century land records for
this part of Hungary are no longer in existence,[8] so it cannot be
established when or from whom they derived their titles. However,
a local history published after they left for the United States records
that they held two plots of land, one in an agricultural area called Kútas, a few miles north of the village of Szenttamás, and another near
a village called Pacsér.[9] Records of the Roman Catholic parishes of
Futtak and Szenttamás for the 1830's confirm both these holdings.[10]

Szenttamás, which had a population of about 12,000, was about
twenty-two miles north of Futtak. It was conveniently located beside
the Ferencz Canal, an artificial waterway cut through the Bácska a
generation earlier to facilitate the movement of boats between the
Danube, about forty miles to the west, and the Tisza, about fifteen
miles to the east. There were about 40,000 acres of agricultural land
surrounding Szenttamás, but nearly half were undeveloped meadow-
lands and woods. Most of the land was flat to gently rolling, but a
cluster of low hills rose out of the plain about twelve miles northwest
of the village center. These hills, which formed a series of low ridges
that alternated with narrow valleys, formed the center of a district
called Kishegyes, or the "Little Hills."[11]

The Haraszthy property at Szenttamás was at the far northern
end of the district, at a place called Kútas, just east of Kishegyes.
Kútas (which means a place in which there were wells) was originally a *puszta*, or uncultivated tract, and it was still designated on
maps of the Bácska as *Puszta Kútas*, although the Haraszthys undoubtedly used their land there for crops. A gazetteer published a
few years after the family left for the United States indicated that all
the land in the Szenttamás district was part of the "free Tisza district
of the Crown."[12] Thus the Haraszthys probably held their land there
as lessees of the crown, rather than as proprietors. North and west
of Kútas, the county road continued through Kishegyes to a place

called Pacsér, where the Haraszthys cultivated another tract. Pacsér, which included about 26,000 acres of gently rolling farm land, was notable because it was the ancestral seat of some of the most prominent noble families of Bács County, the political subdivision that embraced most of the Bácska. Nobles who traced their roots to the village included the Odry, Koronai, Vojnics, Matyasovszky, Császár, and Mészáros families.

It seems unlikely that the Haraszthys acquired their property at either Kútas or Pacsér before 1825, for Agoston's grandfather, Antal Haraszthy, was still in the Terézváros parish of Pest when he died in January of that year.[13] This is only speculation, however, for many Hungarian nobles maintained residences both in the city and in the country, and Antal could well have had property in the Bácska while still maintaining a townhouse in Pest.

The earliest reference to the Haraszthys' landownership in the Bácska dates from 1833. On January 6 of that year, at the parish church in Újfuttak, Agoston Haraszthy, then twenty years old, married Eleonora, the seventeen-year-old daughter of Ferencz Dedinszky.[14] It is not known when or where the young couple met or became engaged, though it was most likely in the year 1832 and probably somewhere in the Bácska. The parish records of this marriage, written in Latin, indicate that Augustinus, son of Caroli Vilhelmi Haraszthy and Anna Fischer, of Szenttamás, married Eleonora, daughter of Franciscus Dedinszky and Theresia Csupor, of Újfuttak. Both the Haraszthys and the Dedinszkys were described as noble families. The witnesses were Franciscus Endrődy and Carolus Jablonszky.[15]

The Dedinszkys were of Polish descent, though they had lived in Hungary for six or seven centuries before Eleonora's birth in 1815 and had long since been accepted into the Hungarian nobility.[16] The family's estates were in the most northerly recess of Hungary, a steeply mountainous county called Árva tucked up in the Tatra Mountains next to the Polish border. In 1355, the Hungarian King Lajos the Great had conferred an estate on one of their ancestors at a place called Dedina in Árva County. The family took both their family name of Dedinszky and their predicate, Dedinai, from this estate, which occupied a little mountain valley just north of the Árva River. As the ancestral home of the Dedinszkys, Dedina became known as Nemes Dedina, or "Noble" Dedina, and male members of the family became prominent officials in the government of Árva County. Genealogies published in Eleonora's lifetime reveal that her grandfather was a man named Jónas Dedinszky, who was the treasurer of Árva County, but the same genealogies trace the family back for several generations before Jónas.[17] Although many members of the Dedinszky family were Lutherans, the branch of the family to which Ferencz and Eleonora belonged was Roman Catholic. In addition to Eleonora, Ferencz Dedinszky and his wife, Theresia Csupor, were the parents of at least four other children, a boy named Dienes and girls named Jusztina, Ottilia, and Emilia.[18]

Before he became the superintendent at Futtak, Ferencz himself may have had a career as a soldier. Many years later, one of his granddaughters recalled that he had been a captain in the Hungarian army and, in that capacity, took part in the war against Napoleon.[19] Nobles throughout Hungary were recruited for this great military campaign, which convulsed so much of the European continent, and Dedinszky may in fact have played a role in the struggle. There was a military tradition of sorts in the Dedinszky family, for in 1820 one of Ferencz's brothers received an appointment from Francis I to serve in the Royal Hungarian Bodyguard at Vienna. Unlike Agoston's own claim to membership in that prestigious organization, Antal Dedinszky's membership in the Bodyguard is well documented. According to the standard authority on the subject, Antal Dedinszky joined the Royal Hungarian Bodyguard on March 1, 1820, and remained with it until February 28, 1825. He later had a distinguished career as a professional soldier.[20]

The fact that Antal Dedinszky went to Vienna as a member of the Bodyguard, coupled with the fact that Ferencz Dedinszky was the supervisor of the estate at Futtak, indicates that the Dedinszkys were a family of some social prominence. Although a noble who served as superintendent of a great estate could never be treated as the social equal of the magnate he served, his position did mark him apart from the great majority of the nobles, who either held no estates or had only modest properties. In the absence of the Count or Countess Brunswick, Ferencz Dedinszky was the acting master of Futtak. When he traveled from one end of the sprawling property to the other, he was greeted with respectful bows from peasants and nobles alike. He and his family lived comfortably in the big house at Futtak, where they entertained distinguished travelers who came through the village, conferred with neighboring landowners on matters of common concern, and made plans for the annual planting and harvest of crops.

The confidence reposed in Ferencz Dedinszky by the lords of Futtak would have served him in good stead when it came to helping his friends and relatives. Both Count Brunswick and his widow spent a part of each year in Vienna, where they had access to the Hapsburg court. In Buda, where the palatine presided over the Hungarian bureaucracy, they also had more than a little influence. It is interesting to speculate whether Ferencz Dedinszky might have helped the Haraszthys obtain their properties in the Bácska, although there are no records indicating that he did so.

Aside from her good family connections, there is every reason to believe that Eleonora Dedinszky was a most desirable bride. A drawing made of her while she was still quite young reveals a young woman with dark eyes and hair, a full mouth, and slender waist, dressed in the elaborately jeweled costume of a Hungarian noblewoman. Friends who knew her after she emigrated to the United States commented on her "great beauty" and "rare accomplishments."[21] Unlike Agoston, whose complexion was dark, Eleonora was fair.

On December 27, 1833, eleven months and twenty-one days after she and Agoston were married in Futtak, Eleonora gave birth to her first child, a healthy baby boy. Born on the family's estate at Puszta Kútas, the baby was taken six days later to the parish church of Kishegyes, where, on January 2, 1834, he was baptized.[22] The baby's baptismal name was Geisa Josephus Alexander Arpadus Franciscus Carolus in Latin, and Géza József Sándor Árpád Ferencz Károly in Hungarian. Géza and Árpád are names of two of the great hero-princes of the Magyars. József and Alexander were names of the baby's two godfathers; Ferencz and Károly were the names of his grandfathers, Ferencz Dedinszky and Károly Haraszthy. For the rest of his life, the baby would be known as Géza.[23]

The parish register of Kishegyes contains some interesting information about the Haraszthys at the time of Géza's birth. The child's mother and father were listed as Spectabilis Dominus Augustinus Haraszti [*sic*] de Mokcsa and his wife, Eleonora Dedinszky. Their residence was given as Possessionis Rex Coronalis Szenttamás, or the Crown Lands of Szenttamás. The baby was represented at the baptism by two sponsors, Spectabilis Dominus Josephus Ódry de Pacsér and Spectabilis Dominus Alexandri Matyasovszky of the same place. Ódry was the *alispán* of Bács County; Matyasovszky was the vice-treasurer. Agoston himself was described as a vice-notarius (or deputy clerk). The baptism was performed by the pastor of the church.[24]

The fact that no less than six Christian names were bestowed on the baby was an indication of his parents' high social status (peasants were typically given only one name, while "half-spurred" or "sandaled" nobles were given one or two). The fact that one of his godparents was the *alispán* of the county further enforced his parents' social position, for the *alispán* was the highest county official other than the *főispán* (or lord lieutenant). However, the *főispán* (who was typically a count or other magnate chosen by the Crown) spent most of his time in Buda or Vienna, while the *alispán* (who was elected by the General Assembly of Nobles) remained at home and, for all practical purposes, was the chief executive officer of the county. The English office of sheriff is perhaps the closest equivalent of the Hungarian *alispán*, but the powers of the Hungarian officer were in fact much broader. Among other things, it was his duty to communicate with the Crown and with the county's deputies in the Diet; to execute all royal decrees in the county; to supervise the county courts; and to preside over meetings of the General Assembly of Nobles. The position of *alispán* was one of the most important in all of Hungary, for under the ancient feudal structure of the kingdom the counties were largely self-governing units; and, save for those rare occasions when the Crown interfered directly in the county affairs, the *alispán* and General Assembly of Nobles ruled their jurisdiction in the manner of semi-autonomous states.[25] As *alispán* of Bács County, József Ódry of Pacsér was probably the most powerful public official in the Bácska, and his agreement to act as godfather for Agoston's firstborn son was a mark of the close relations between the two men.

Agoston's own position as vice-notarius was not particularly important, but it was a prestigious post for a man not yet twenty-two years old. Even the fact that the baptism was performed personally by the pastor of the church was significant, for pastors often reserved their baptismal services for the upper classes, relegating peasants and lower nobles to assistant pastors.[26]

Sixteen months after her first child was baptized in Kishegyes, Eleonora Haraszthy brought a second son to the parish church in Szenttamás for baptism. Born on April 16, 1835, this child was baptized on April 20 under the Latin names of Attila Antonius Aemlius Cornelius, or Attila Antal Emil Kornél in Hungarian. The mother and father were described in the parish register as Dominus Augustinus Haraszty [*sic*] and Domina Eleonora Dedinszky, both nobles. The godparents were the *alispán*, József Ódry of Pacsér, and a man named Stephen [*sic*] Hajnal. The residence of the parents was not stated, but Agoston's official position was still that of vice-notarius.[27] Named for the great warrior king of the Huns, this second son of Agoston and Eleonora would be known throughout his life as Attila.

The fact that Agoston held a county office did not indicate that he had become a professional politician, or that most (or even a substantial part) of his time was devoted to county business. All the Hungarian county officers were, in fact, part-time officials, "gentlemen" who considered public service one of the duties (and honors) of their class. As Hungarian noblemen, they were stewards of the land that their forefathers had wrested from the wilderness and rescued from the scourge of the Turks. Although county officials received modest annual payments out of the country treasury, the payments were not intended as remuneration for their services, but only as provision for the expenses that their offices brought upon them; and it was expected that all officers, from the *alispán* down to the humblest constable, would be men of independent means.[28]

As vice-notarius of Bács County, Agoston Haraszthy's "independent means" would have been his estate at Kútas, supplemented perhaps by the family's property at Pacsér. No reasonable estimate can be made of the profitability of either of these properties, since no records have survived of the kinds of crops that were grown on them, or even the size of the estates. Agoston's own references to his Bács County properties, made some years after he left them, were sketchy and not always consistent. In the early 1840's, he referred rather modestly to his "little estate" in Bács County,[29] but twenty years later he described the same property as "my domain in Hungary."[30] In 1837, when a royal commissioner came to Bács County to investigate county affairs, Agoston gave a deposition in which he claimed to be the owner of no less than thirty-six horses.[31] Although horses were plentiful in the Bácska, a stable of three-dozen horses was hardly inconsequential, and an estate that kept so many animals employed could not have been small.

What crops did Agoston cultivate at Kútas? The absence of records again leaves us largely in the dark. It is likely that at least some of the property was dedicated to the production of grains, for the Bácska was widely known as the breadbasket of Hungary and was rich in the production of wheat, maize, and rye. Hemp, hops, and tobacco, which flourished in other parts of Bács County, may also have been grown on the property.[32] When he was traveling in Italy in 1861, Agoston recalled that he "raised silk-worms on a large scale, and in the most approved manner," on his Bácska property.[33] This would have required the cultivation of mulberry trees, for silkworms feed exclusively on the leaves of those trees. Sericulture was an industry that Maria Theresa had warmly urged upon her Hungarian subjects, and from the early years of the nineteenth century it had been an important industry in the Bácska.

Given Károly Haraszthy's extensive experience as a viticulturist, it would hardly seem necessary to question whether the Haraszthys grew grapes in the Bácska. Yet it is worth noting that in his extant writings Agoston never once described his winemaking or grape-growing activities in Hungary. He always spoke with authority about wine, and frequently spiced his descriptions of foreign lands and territories with knowledgeable comments about the local wines and vines. But he never described the methods by which he made wine in his native country; never described the kind of wine that he produced or the grapes that he grew on his home turf. It would be wrong to make too much of this, however, for none of his fairly large body of published writings was more than incidentally autobiographical, and none referred directly to his experience in Hungary. People who knew and worked with him had no reason to doubt that he was an experienced winemaker, and he never found it necessary to "show his credentials."

To be sure, the Bácska itself was never known as a great wine-producing area, in part because the soils were generally unsuited to the production of good wine grapes (some were too heavy and clayey, while others were too thin and sandy). Vineyards were nevertheless cultivated in the county, since relatively poor wines could be consumed domestically even if they were unsuited to export. There were almost 32,000 acres of vineyards in Bács County in 1826,[34] a respectable enough figure given the natural deficiencies of the terrain. Besides the poor soil, the area was very flat, almost totally devoid of the hillsides on which Hungarians had always preferred to plant their wine grapes.

Almost—but not entirely—devoid of hills. There were some good slopes in the Kishegyes area, suitable to the cultivation of wine grapes. It can hardly be regarded as a coincidence that less than ten years after the Haraszthys emigrated to the United States there were some six hundred acres of grapevines in the district where the Haraszthys had their properties.[35] If those vines were not planted directly on the Haraszthy estates, it seems likely that Agoston and Károly would have taken some part in cultivating them, making them into wine, and bringing them to the nearest market.

Of course, there were fine wine-producing areas all around the Bácska. Several of Hungary's best-known wine-producing districts were in the hills to the northwest, just beyond the southern curve of the Danube in Baranya and Tolna counties. The Villány district, which centered around the medieval castle of Siklós, had a wine-making tradition that extended back in an almost unbroken line to the Romans. The Romans had called this part of their far-flung empire Pannonia and were delighted with its Mediterranean-like climate and sunny hillsides. The Kadarka grape, originally brought to Hungary from Albania, made the red wine for which the region was famous; the Oportó, introduced by Austrians toward the end of the eighteenth century, was also widely cultivated.[36] About fifteen miles north of Villány, the Mecsek hills raised their vine-covered slopes above the ancient fortress city of Pécs. Olaszrizling (Italian Riesling) was the most popular white wine variety in the Mecsek region, although a red grape called the Cirfandli was also popular. The Cirfandli was said to yield wine with the fragrance of flowers, while its fermented juice was spicy and pleasantly acid. With quick stemming and pressing, a yellow-green wine could also be made from the red grapes of the Cirfandli.[37] Szekszárd, about thirty miles northeast of Pécs, also had a Roman winemaking tradition. Kadarka was widely planted around Szekszárd, where it produced a dark red wine that was widely exported. Franz Schubert was inspired by the wine of Szekszárd to write one of his most famous quintets, and Liszt presented some of it to the pope with the explanation that "this wine from Szekszárd protects my health and keeps up my spirits."[38]

None of the winemaking districts of Hungary was very far from the Bácska, for the country was compact, and communication between the various regions was not particularly difficult. Even the Tokaj-Hegyalja, home of the most celebrated of all Hungarian wines, was not beyond the reach of a curious young nobleman. Years after he left Hungary, Agoston was to reveal a good knowledge of the techniques for making Tokaj wine, thus indicating that he had at least visited the cellars of that fabled district.[39] The fact that his family's ancestral home at Mokcsa was only about sixty miles northeast of the Tokaj-Hegyalja may perhaps indicate that he was more than an infrequent visitor to the home of the wine that France's Louis XIV called "the King of Wines and the Wine of Kings."[40]

Another winemaking region of note was even closer to the Haraszthy properties in the Bácska. This was on the southern bank of the Danube directly opposite Futtak. The river there marked the boundary between Bács and Szerém counties, but the domain of the Brunswicks easily bridged the barrier, for the magnates also owned the estate of Cerevic on the south side of the river. Above Cerevic, a long range of mountains rose up from the river to a height of about seventeen hundred feet above sea level. In Roman times, this was the province of Syrmia, and rich and productive vineyards hugged the mountain slopes. The Hungarians called this district the Szerémség and placed a high value on its wines, which were made mostly from Olaszrizling, Kadarka, and Ezerjó grapes. The Serbs called the mountains the Fruška Gora, or "Fresh Mountains."

It is not known if the Haraszthys managed the vineyards on the

Brunswick estates. Years after he left Hungary, Károly Haraszthy recalled that he had visited all the important wine-producing countries
of Europe and had extensive experience cultivating vineyards, and
that experience might have included some time as a vineyard stew-
ard.[41] Since the Haraszthys were allied by marriage to the Dedinszkys,
it seems possible, perhaps even likely, that Ferencz Dedinszky would
have retained the Haraszthys to manage the Brunswick wine properties. And it seems probable that there was more than one property,
for in addition to the vineyards that grew on the Cerevic estate there
were nearly five hundred acres of vines at Futtak itself. Years later,
one of Agoston's sons was to remember that his mother (i.e., Eleonora) had a vineyard of her own,[42] and this vineyard may well have
been on the Futtak estate.

Lacking positive evidence on the matter, we can only speculate
about what kinds of grapes were grown at Futtak and on the Haraszthy properties farther north. Was the Zinfandel, a mysterious grape
that later became closely associated with Agoston Haraszthy's name
in California but that has never been positively identified in Hungary, one of these grapes? We do not know. Certainly it is possible
that the Zinfandel may have grown in or around the Haraszthy properties; Agoston's son Arpad was later to speculate that it may have
grown in his mother's vineyard.[43] But this speculation is not entirely
convincing. There were many grapes in Hungary in the first half of
the nineteenth century, and they grew under a bewildering variety
of names. This is hardly surprising, given the ethnically and linguis-
tically diverse character of the kingdom and the fact that it was surrounded by winegrowing lands in which grape varieties grew under a
host of strange-sounding names. Perhaps the Zinfandel was in Hungary when the Haraszthys lived in the Bácska but later disappeared,
either because it was not favored by local growers or because it succumbed to disease (the phylloxera, which devastated the vineyards
of California in the 1880's and 1890's, ravaged Hungary's vine lands
about the same time, totally destroying many varieties of grapes).

If there is no good evidence that the Zinfandel was grown in
the Bácska in the time of the Haraszthys, the evidence is quite good
that the grape's distinctive name, so unlike that of any other grape
known in California, owes at least something to Hungarian roots.

Early-day grape catalogs published in the United States contain numerous references to the "Zinfinthal," "Zeinfindall," "Zenfenthal," "Zinfindal," "Zinfindel," and "Zinthindal," all of which may reasonably be presumed to be the same as today's "Zinfandel." It was not until the 1880's that "Zinfandel" was accepted as the standard spelling in California, and as late as 1888 some winemakers still insisted that it should be "Zinfindal."[44] Before the vine came to California, its name had even more diverse and various spellings.

In Hungary, the word generally accepted as the surrogate for Zinfandel is Cirfandli. Although these two words are spelled differently, their close resemblance becomes more evident when they are spoken, for the Hungarian Cirfandli is pronounced *tseer*-fawn-dlee. Though the word has a strong Magyar flavor, etymologists speculate that it may be of German, French, or even Italian origin.[45] It was probably a variation of "Silvaner" or "Sylvaner," a much more widely known name that refers to a grape from the woods or forest (i.e., a grape that grew wild before it was brought into a vineyard and cultivated).[46] The word entered Hungarian at least as early as 1800 and between that date and 1888 went through more than a dozen Hungarian metamorphoses, including "czirifandli," "tzirifandli," "tzilifant," "cilifánt," "tzirifándli," "czilifánt," "Tzili fan," "cinifaj," "czelifántszőlő," "zierfandli," and "cirfandel."[47] (When "cirifandel" is pronounced aloud—as *tseer*-ee-fawn-dell—its resemblance to "Zinfandel" becomes striking.) In German-speaking countries, a very similar name, "Zierfandler," has gained usage. The German word probably derives from the same root as the Hungarian "Szirifandli" and "zierfandli" and may have been borrowed from the Hungarian.[48]

Although it is impossible to say with any certainty that Agoston Haraszthy cultivated the "cirfandli" in his native Hungary, the fact that the grape was grown in Hungarian vineyards during the time that he lived there, that its name had a strong Magyar flavor, and that he later showed himself to be so keenly interested in discovering and testing new grape varieties, suggests that he may well have had the grape, or at least known of it. Was the "cirfandli" the same as the grape that later grew in California under the name Zinfandel? This question cannot be answered without much more evidence than is available now. Perhaps more than one Hungarian grape

variety was grown under the name of "cirfandli." Perhaps a variety
that was later destroyed by the phylloxera originally bore the name,
and another variety later assumed its identity. Or perhaps the grape
that later became celebrated in California as "Zinfandel" originally
grew under a different name in Hungary.[49]

Whatever wine the Haraszthys produced in the Bácska would
have been put to good use, for wine was as much a part of Hungarian
culture as paprika and the csárdás and always in demand. While
many Hungarian wines were sweet and white, many others were red
table wines that did not differ much in style from table wines produced in Italy or even France. Aside from the fact that table wines
had a long tradition among the Magyar people, the popularity of
wines with meals is explained by the characteristic cuisine of the
country, which featured generous servings of beef, pork, and mutton
covered with rich sauces. The pepper, ginger, and other spices that
Hungarian cooks used so liberally in their cooking tended to make
diners thirsty, and wine was an ideal beverage with which to slake a
thirst. The Hungarian fondness for wine was also nourished by the
knowledge that water (drawn in most parts of the country from wells)
was often impure. Though a humble country wine might not please
the palate of a connoisseur, it would not give him dysentery, either.

But Hungarians did not regard wine as a mere adornment of
their tables. There was hardly any event in Magyar life that was not a
fitting occasion for opening a bottle of wine. Baptisms and confirma-
tions and weddings were all followed by toasts. When young lovers
announced their betrothals, their families joined them in celebrating with wine. When local officials were chosen, wine was poured,
and when new laws were announced, the judges drank to celebrate.[50]
When the nobles of the county gathered for their General Assemblies, the county marked the occasion with toasts. And when the results of their county elections were announced, the *főispán* returned
from Buda or Vienna to provide a table for the county nobles, complete with generous supplies of wine.[51]

Hungarian wines were not widely exported, in large part because
the Hapsburgs imposed stiff tariffs on any Hungarian products that
were exported beyond the boundaries of their empire. But good
quantities of Hungarian wine were sold in Vienna, and smaller quantities were exported to Silesia, Poland, and Russia. For a long time,

it was thought that Hungarian wines would not transport well across the ocean, but Count Széchenyi took it upon himself to disprove the theory. He sent a cask of good Hungarian wine to the East Indies and, when it came back, found that it was perfectly sound.[52]

We have little information as to Agoston's personal drinking habits, though we know that he was always an enthusiastic imbiber of wines. When he was traveling in Europe in 1861, he was quite capable of downing a full bottle of wine at a single sitting, and apparently with no untoward effects. When he was in Central America in 1868, he joked that, after a hard day's horseback ride, he "felt inclined to indulge in a bottle of wine," but added quickly: "Do not for a moment believe that I incline towards a bottle of wine only after a hard ride—by no means. I like it even after having done nothing the whole day."[53]

He told a story about a soldier who was billeted in a strange house and, before going to bed, called out to his landlord: "Landlord! wake me at night, when I get thirsty." The landlord looked at the soldier with a puzzled expression and asked, "How will I know when you are thirsty?" "By thunder," the soldier replied, "any time you wake me I'll be thirsty." "That is the case with me," Agoston added, "I am thirsty all the time."[54] This little joke does not necessarily indicate that he drank to excess. Wine has always been known as a beverage of moderation, and drunkenness is not common in any country in which wine is the everyday beverage of the people.[55] But Agoston was a winemaker who clearly believed in his own product, who enjoyed drinking wine as much as he enjoyed making it.

In Bács County, the nobles traditionally assembled in the county hall in the town of Zombor, a few miles west of the Haraszthy properties at Szenttamás and Pacsér. When Agoston went to Zombor to attend these convocations, he wore his best noble uniform, carried his Turkish scimitar, and came equipped not only with his wine cups but with his pipes. If there was anything that Hungarian nobles loved as much as their wine, it was their meerschaum pipes. Any gathering of "country gentlemen" in Hungary was hovered over by swirling clouds of smoke, some produced by domestic tobacco, others by the product of more exotic Turkish blends. If anything, the wine seemed to be enhanced by the tobacco, and the tobacco by the wine.[56]

But Hungarian nobles did not spend all their time sipping wine or smoking meerschaum pipes; they were also men of action. Hunting, in particular, was a favorite occupation of the nobility and occupied much of their leisure time. Almost every estate of consequence was equipped with a hunting lodge, located on the edge of the cultivated portions of the noble's lands and conveniently close to the woods, swamps, and meadows in which game could most conveniently be found. By his own admission, Agoston was a "passionate hunter,"[57] and he rarely lost an opportunity to mount his horse and take off into the countryside in search of the fowl and larger animals with which the Bácska was well supplied. There were wild geese, ducks, coots, and snipes in abundance in the swamps and in the lowland marshes, and quail could be found quite easily in the woods and meadows. Here and there on the plains there were roe deer, wild boars, hares, and foxes, and wildcats were sometimes encountered in the hills or on the slopes of the mountains above Cerevic.[58] If there were reports of wolves in the neighborhood, the news spread rapidly, and elaborate hunting parties were organized to seek out the fierce animals, who were both feared and despised throughout Central Europe.[59]

Hungarian nobles responded enthusiastically to every call for the county's General Assembly. Conversation in the assemblies was sometimes subdued, sometimes loud and excited, but always concerned, for the nobles treasured their hereditary rights to govern themselves through these county meetings. The election of county officials and deputies to the Diet was always important. Elections were held in the assemblies, and the votes were traditionally taken by acclamation, although a poll of the nobles could be demanded if the result was in doubt. The assemblies also directed their attention to matters of general concern to the kingdom. After the Hapsburgs ordered the arrests of Lajos Kossuth and Miklós Wesselényi, the General Assembly of Bács wavered in its attitude toward the monarchs' increasingly repressive rule in Hungary. Although many of the nobles regarded the arrests as clear violations of their traditional noble rights, others were reluctant to express open defiance of Vienna, and the resolutions of the General Assembly alternated between expressions of concern over the repressive measures of the central government and soothing protestations of loyalty to the Crown.

In 1836, the nobles of Bács County had to deal with more direct royal intermeddling in their affairs. In that year, the *főispán* of Máramaros County, in the far northeastern corner of the kingdom, was sent south by the Hapsburgs to investigate the affairs of Bács. Count Ábrahám Vay plunged into his duties as royal commissioner with what some of the nobles thought an unseemly enthusiasm. He inspected the accounts of the county treasury from 1814 through 1836 and announced that there were "important deficits," then recommended that the treasurer, Mihály Horváth, be removed from office. The *főispán* of Bács, a noble named Ferencz Győry, was so upset by Vay's recommendation that he resigned, saying that his "health" would not permit him to continue in office. The new *főispán*, József Rudics, showed his loyalty to the Hapsburgs by seizing Horváth's personal property and filing lawsuits against other important county officials.[60]

Agoston felt the sting of the royal investigation in 1837, when the deputy chief magistrate of the county informed Count Vay that the young vice-notarius was guilty of "corrupt practices in agricultural matters." Vay investigated the reports and concluded that Agoston had improperly used horses belonging to the county for his own personal purposes. Agoston vigorously denied the charges, and filed his own complaint against the deputy chief magistrate, charging him with making false accusations. He asserted that, since he had a large stable of his own horses, he had no need to use any of the county's animals. When the official investigations were concluded, Agoston seems to have been completely exonerated. Far from destroying his political career in Bács County, his brush with the royal commissioner seems to have strengthened his local standing, for his close friendship with the *alispán* József Ódry continued, and he not only kept his position as vice-notarius but was elevated to the much more prestigious office of *főbíró*, or chief justice, of the county.[61]

Despite this accomplishment, Agoston was clearly unsatisfied with his life as a country gentleman in the Bácska. The hierarchy of nobles was small, even clubby, but almost stultifyingly parochial. If Agoston's neighbors had read Count Széchenyi's stirring calls for progress and reform, they gave little evidence of it as they went about the business of managing their estates and dealing with the peasants who worked their fields. Hungarian nobles liked to think of themselves as a special class of men on whom God had bestowed special blessings, but their conservatism was almost complete. They looked with suspicion on innovations and regarded "reformers" with unconcealed horror. They steadfastly adhered to time-honored traditions, and recoiled when any man sought to advance his station in life by personal efforts. When a new idea was broached, they instinctively drew back, replying, "What was good enough for our fathers is good enough for us!"[62] In a society in which sons were expected to lead lives in the molds of their fathers, there was little place for a man who had so enthusiastically embraced the ideas of Count Széchenyi.

Agoston tried to expand his horizons beyond the Bácska. He returned to Pest seeking business opportunities. He visited Újvidék and made the acquaintance of some of the merchants who kept stores there. But he was disappointed in what he saw. Though the streets of Pest and Újvidék were crowded with fine coaches drawn by showy horses and driven by liveried servants, there was little in the way of business activity. Noblemen and their wives promenaded idly through the streets, showing off their fine clothes, and seemed almost totally uninterested in enterprise.[63] He apparently made some efforts to export Hungarian products to neighboring countries. It was a risky thing for a man of his station to do, for the hidebound nobles condemned forays into the world of "commerce" as beneath their class. Collecting the profits of an estate was the true calling of a Hungarian noble, they thought, even if the "estate" was only a few acres of tired land. And he soon learned that it was necessary to obtain royal "permission" to engage in almost any business enterprise in Hungary, whether it was the construction of a railroad, the excavation of a canal, the launching of a steamboat, or the inauguration of a factory. Those who were in a position to grant "permission" did so with a view to feathering their own nests, with the result that what little real commerce there was in the country was almost totally dominated by royally chartered companies—"blood-sucking monopolies," Agoston was later to call them.[64]

Inspired by Széchenyi's fascination with foreign countries, particularly England, Agoston began to dream of the day when he could emulate the great magnate and tour Great Britain. He sought out opportunities to meet foreigners who were traveling in Hungary and plied them with questions about travel opportunities outside the country. He frequented Mehádia, a fashionable resort at the base of the Transylvanian Alps, just north of the Danube and about 150 miles east of Futtak. The Romans had been the first to exploit the rich minerals springs at Mehádia—they called them the Baths of Hercules— and all the succeeding conquerors of the Danube basin regarded them with special fondness. King Francis I built a handsome hotel there in the early years of the nineteenth century, and this helped to draw flocks of Austrians, Serbs, and eventually Englishmen to the fashionable spa.

Agoston was an intelligent young man with polished manners and a gift for lively conversation, and he easily made friends at Mehádia. As he broadened his circle, he began to ask for letters of introduction to foreign lands—letters that he knew would help ease his passage out of Hungary when the time came for him to make his departure.[65] Sometime in the middle of 1839, he made the acquaintance of an English naval captain named Bennett and two Americans, men whom he later identified only as "Messrs. Whitlock and Hislip."[66] The four men seemed to hit it off almost immediately, and Agoston listened raptly as they recounted stories of their travels. He was fascinated by all he heard, but particularly by his new friends' tales of the United States, a faraway land that seemed at once so marvelous and so unattainable. For Agoston, as for most Hungarians, the best source of information about the United States was the travel book published in 1834 by Sándor Bölöni Farkas under the title, *Travels in North America.*[67] Farkas was a Transylvania-born Hungarian (Transylvania was then a semiautonomous principality subject to the Hungarian crown), and his was the first book about the United States ever published in Hungarian. But Agoston had read other descriptions of the United States, and those seemed to differ in some particulars from Farkas. He posed a long series of questions to Bennett, Whitlock, and Hislip, and listened carefully to all their answers. But he wanted to hear more, and at his invitation his new friends spent four weeks with him and his family at his estate in the Bácska. At the end of their visit they left Agoston a set of the letters of introduction he so craved.[68]

In subsequent years, Agoston was to give conflicting accounts of the circumstances under which he left Hungary. He claimed at one time that he was forced to leave his native land because he had had "an unhappy duel" in Vienna and was prosecuted by the authorities. To escape imprisonment, so he said, he had had to leave Hungary an exile.[69] Later, he said that he had been court-martialed while serving in the Hungarian army and that his court-martial led to a death sentence, but that the sentence was commuted to two years in Spielberg prison. According to this story, he became active in liberal politics, became a target of the authorities, and was then forced out of the country.[70]

Even later, he told an elaborate story about rescuing a Hungarian poet who had been confined in the medieval fortress of Peter Wardein, overlooking the Danube just east of Újvidék. Peter Wardein (called Pétervárad by the Hungarians) was used as a prison by the Hapsburgs and was a symbol to many Hungarians of Austrian oppression. According to Agoston's story, he learned that the poor poet, "whose only offense was that he had dared to sing of freedom and the rights of man," had been confined in a dungeon in the prison for some seventeen years. With a group of his friends, he decided to free the prisoner. The conspirators surprised the guard, took possession of the fortress, and set the poet at liberty, then disappeared in the night, confident that their crime would never be discovered. Two months later, however, Agoston received a confidential message from Vienna informing him that the Hapsburgs had learned of his participation in the escape and that an order had been sent out to have him and his fellow conspirators arrested. He said the message came from one of his uncles, who was "the Hungarian Minister at the Court of Vienna," and who wanted to give him an opportunity to escape. While his colleagues fled toward the Turkish border, the bold Agoston donned a disguise and proceeded toward Vienna, whence he made his way to Hamburg and eventual freedom in America.[71]

These stories were later to become a keystone of the Haraszthy Legend, and to be repeated in one form or another in countless stories of Agoston's life. Thus it became accepted that he was a "political exile" from his native land, a man who was forced by a cruel and repressive government to give up his comfortable life as a nobleman and begin life anew in a remote corner of the New World. But this part of the Legend, like so many others, is simply untrue.

There is no credible evidence to support Agoston's claim that he was a political exile, that he was ever imprisoned, or that an order for his arrest was ever sent out from Vienna. There is no evidence that any of his uncles was a minister at Vienna, much less a minister who might have had responsibility for overseeing affairs in Hungary.[72] In fact, Agoston was a successful member of the noble hierarchy of Bács County, a man who had held public office for the better part of a decade and, for his good services, been rewarded with the chief justiceship of the county. The gross inconsistencies in the stories he later told (was he a rash duelist, a court-martialed soldier, the instigator of a prison escape, or all—or none—of the above?) should in themselves be enough to put the lie to all of these tales.

But other facts, including his own published statements of the reasons he left Hungary in 1839, prove even more convincingly that he was not a fugitive from injustice, that he had not been implicated in political plots, and that he did not leave his native land as an exile. He left Hungary because he had grown impatient with the backward ways of a backward country and wanted to see other countries in which the progressive spirit of the modern age was flourishing. He wanted to go to England, where Count Széchenyi had gone before him, and to the United States, of which he had read and heard so much. And so, at the end of 1839, carrying letters of introduction given him by Bennett, Whitlock, and Hislip, Agoston Haraszthy made plans for a trip to England and America. He was twenty-seven years old and was about to set out on the greatest adventure of his life.

3

To

America

Before leaving Hungary, Agoston asked one of his cousins, a man named Károly Fischer, if he would like to make the trip with him. Fischer was seven years Agoston's senior, but he was still a bachelor and, unencumbered by a family, was willing to take enough time out of his life to see a new and exciting part of the world. He seems to have been sober and solid, the sort of man who would never have embarked on a long trip outside Hungary if Agoston had not suggested it, but his very sobriety and solidity made him the ideal person to look after his younger and more volatile cousin.

No record has been found of the circumstances under which Agoston left his family in the Bácska. He later wrote that he expected to be away from home for two years, and this fact alone suggests that the parting must have been wrenching, at least for his father and his wife. The close bonds that tied Agoston with Károly would surely have been strained by such a long separation, and Eleonora cannot have been pleased by her husband's plans. The parting may even have been stormy, for she was only twenty-five years old, had two little boys to care for, and was already expecting a third child. But when she realized that Agoston's decision was firm, she may have been mollified by the news that he would be traveling with Károly Fischer, whose caution and sober reflection would balance his own daring and bravado.

Agoston decided at some point to keep a written record of his trip. It probably did not amount to a daily journal, for long stretches of the journey were totally unaccounted for in the written narrative he later printed. But he took notes, recorded impressions, and searched for interesting bits of historical and statistical information as he went along, eventually accumulating a sizable body of facts and opinions about the places he and Fischer traveled through. Later, when he returned to Hungary, the notes, descriptions, and impressions he collected along the way would form the raw material from which he would fashion a very interesting book about the journey.[1]

We know from the book, *Travels in North America* (*Utazás Éjszakamerikában*) that Agoston left his home in the Bácska on March 27, 1840. He probably joined forces with Fischer in Pest, whence the two cousins headed eastward toward the Austrian border. In Vienna, they reported at once to the immigration authorities. If either of the young Hungarians had any trouble obtaining their passports, Agoston left no hint of it in his subsequent account of the journey. He says it took two days for the Austrians to process their applications, and there is no reason to suppose that this was an unusually long time. With their papers safely in hand, the travelers set out on the next leg of their journey, northward by post chaise to the Bohemian capital of Prague. From Prague they pushed on to Dresden, where they paused a few days while Agoston made arrangements to continue the trip by rail, but only as far as Leipzig, where the line ended. From Leipzig they continued their journey by post coach to the Prussian city of Magdeburg on the Elbe River, then went upriver by steamboat to the northern German city of Hamburg where, after a few days' rest, they boarded an English steamer bound for London. After an uneventful trip of thirty-six hours across the North Sea and through the English Channel, they arrived in the English capital. Agoston's excitement grew as their ship steamed up the Thames past hundreds of sailboats and almost as many steamboats. "It was as if all the boats of the world had gathered here for a celebration," he wrote. "Finally we had to slow down to get by the heavy traffic in the narrowing river; and then the capital city of the world, London, appeared in all its magnitude before us."

In London he proceeded at once to look up Captain Bennett. The Englishman was not at home the first day, but he soon returned and took delight in showing his Hungarian guests the sights of the city and the surrounding countryside. The Hungarians' visit to London lasted "a few weeks" and was interrupted by a side trip to Paris, where they visited Bennett's married sister.

Investigating the opportunities for an Atlantic crossing, Agoston pondered the comparative advantages of steamboats and sailing ships (or what he later called "packet boats"). A steamboat could make the crossing in fourteen to fifteen days; a packet would make the same voyage in thirty to forty days. Since he had allotted such a long time for his journey, saving a mere ten to twenty days made little difference. But the difference in the fares was important: a ticket on a typical steamboat was forty-five pounds sterling, whereas a first-class ticket on a packet boat could be had for only sixteen. Agoston noted that the lower cost was "a most potent argument for a Hungarian pocketbook (at least for mine)."

And so Agoston Haraszthy and Károly Fischer booked passage on the ship *Samson*, an American-owned packet boat of 484 tons capacity that sailed under the command of a Captain Sturgis. They left London bound for New York about April 30, 1840.[2] Their friends came to see them off and remained for a long time on the dock waving with their kerchiefs. "Our leave-taking was quite emotional," Agoston wrote, "as we felt great affection for our new acquaintances, an affection which was thoroughly reciprocated." It took about an hour and a half for the ship's crew to raise the anchor and get the vessel under way. The sailors slowly cranked the capstan, and a low voice sounded a farewell song. Then the *Samson* moved slowly down the Thames.

As the ship headed out to sea, Agoston began to get acquainted with the vessel and its passengers. *Travels in North America* contains a glowing description of the ship, with its gleaming mahogany doors, silver-plated doorknobs, and handsomely mirrored salons. He soon settled into an easy routine of strolling the decks, standing at the rails

to admire the ocean view, engaging the captain in friendly conversation, and, when the weather was good, playing quoits. He describes
the ship's cuisine as "rich and plentiful." There was wine—he does
not mention the varieties—but he notes that wine was not as abundant on the *Samson* as it had once been: "Formerly on these ships
anyone could get as much wine as he desired, but this custom was
discontinued because many Americans don't drink wine, yet would
have had to pay as much as those who consumed several bottles
every day. Since this was unfair, the service was stopped."

Many of the passengers suffered from seasickness during the first
few days of the voyage; Fischer was confined to his bed for two weeks.
But Agoston was not affected, and while the others suffered he used
his free time to strike up acquaintances with other hardy sailors.
One was an English colonel who was on a government mission to fix
the border between Canada and the United States; another a Polish
colonel who was a veteran of the Polish uprising of 1830 and a refugee from his long-oppressed homeland; a third a German named
Adolph Rendtorff, who had been sent to America to buy tobacco for
a wholesale merchant in Hamburg. There was also an American actor
named Thomas Rice, who was traveling with his family, and a muscu-
lar young Englishman who was going to America to buy land for his
brother, who wished to emigrate. In his book Agoston also claimed
to have become friendly with a German doctor named "Roges." But
the passenger list of the *Samson* contains no name even remotely resembling Roges, and the conclusion is inevitable that the "German
doctor" was a later invention, designed to play a minor though essential role in one of Agoston's first major fictions in America.

Agoston took time to visit the second-class passengers who were
crowded like cattle into the bow of the *Samson.* They were immigrants
from England, Ireland, Scotland, Holland, France, and Bavaria—
poor peasants who were seeking new homes in the land of freedom.
He counted 252 men, women, and children in the second-class section, huddled in conditions of "indescribable misery." "Husband,
wife and child were sick in their bunks," he wrote, "with no one to
cook for them. They had to live on cold ham and bacon when they
most needed hot and tasty food." The immigrants shared their space
with the ship's cargo and had barely enough room in which to walk,

let alone take exercise. Yet they were strictly excluded from the first-class areas of the ship. The immigrants bore their misery with equanimity, Agoston wrote, "bolstered as they were by the thought that their suffering would not last long, and that the relations on whose invitations they were coming had encountered the same conditions, and now blessed the moment of their decision to emigrate to the happy land."

Agoston and Károly had originally intended to visit Florida, a land long celebrated in European literature as an earthly paradise.[3] But a book they read aboard ship persuaded them to set another destination. Its title was *A Diary in America, With Remarks on Its Institutions*, and it had been written by Captain Frederick Marryat, a popular British novelist and essayist. Published in London in 1839, Marryat's book was an entertaining and informative account of its author's wide-ranging tour through the United States the preceding year. But it gave special prominence to a remote, far-western territory then hardly known in Europe called Wisconsin. "I consider the Wisconsin territory as the finest portion of North America," Marryat wrote, "not only from the soil, but its climate. The air is pure, and the winters, although severe, are dry and bracing; very different from, and more healthy than those of the Eastern States."[4]

Agoston and Károly Fischer were intrigued. They discussed Marryat's book with some of their fellow passengers, among them Adolph Rendtorff. Rendtorff told them that he was on his way to visit a brother who lived in Illinois, just south of Wisconsin, but he, too, was taken with Marryat's description of Wisconsin and thought he and his brother might join the Hungarians there. In the meantime, they agreed to keep in touch by mail.[5]

Week after week, the *Samson* inched slowly across the Atlantic. When, after nearly forty days at sea, the captain announced that land would come into view the next morning, the voyagers celebrated with champagne and, at dawn, lined up on deck to catch their first glimpse of land, the distant coastline of Nova Scotia. Two days later, the *Samson* approached New York harbor. A small sailboat appeared off the bow, and a pilot boarded the big ship and took its wheel. A small steamer then came alongside and took the packet in tow to lead it into the harbor.

The first stop was the quarantine station. The first-class passengers were permitted to disembark at once (the others were obliged to spend two days in quarantine). Forty-two days after leaving London, Agoston Haraszthy and Károly Fischer set foot on the Battery at the foot of Manhattan Island. They quickly made their way to the Hotel Astor, where they found comfortable rooms and then set out to explore the city.

They marveled at the busy harbor, thronged with ships from every corner of the world, and were fascinated by the crowded warehouses, packed with an incredible variety of merchandise. They admired the smart shops on Broadway, likening them to those they saw in London, and noted that they were illuminated with gas. "New York has many theaters," Agoston wrote, "all well attended. It can also boast of good actors. But opera does not seem to attract the audiences. . . . The native music is bad and earsplittingly loud, produced by huge drums and shrill pipes." They saw some splendid homes beyond the commercial district, and marveled, too, at the city's newspapers. Agoston noted that the *Herald* alone had a circulation of fifty thousand and asked in amazement, "What other paper in the world can boast so many subscribers?" Of all the physical attributes of New York, he was most impressed by the oak planks in the streets; they were durable and neat, and much quieter under horse and carriage traffic than cobblestones. Although wood was more expensive than stone, Agoston predicted that all the streets in New York would soon be covered with the material.

Agoston's first business in New York was to look up his American acquaintance Whitlock, who lived in the city. But when he called at Whitlock's home, he learned that he was at his country estate, about thirty miles distant. The journey by train took an hour and a half. Whitlock greeted the Hungarian with surprise and evident pleasure, and immediately sent for some of his friends. Agoston recalled that he and Whitlock spent a day and a half relating the events that had taken place since their last meeting, then returned to the city, where Whitlock introduced Agoston to some of his other friends. One of the most notable was a man named Hamilton Jackson. Agoston described Jackson in his book as "the brother of ex-President Jackson." This is in error: Andrew Jackson had no living brothers, indeed no male kinfolk of any degree who answered to the name of Hamilton.[6] A man named Hamilton Jackson was living in New York City in 1840, but he was certainly not a member of President Jackson's family.[7] Whether Agoston innocently misunderstood Hamilton Jackson's family connections, or deliberately misrepresented them, is not clear. Certainly he was capable of such a misrepresentation, and before his tour of the United States was over he would be guilty of many similar misstatements.

Through the efforts of his New York friends, Agoston was able to add to his already substantial collection of letters of recommendation. Before he left the city, Whitlock and Jackson regaled the affable young Hungarian with a dinner party at the Hotel Clinton. Agoston later remembered that about eighty guests attended and that "long and beautiful speeches were given." The oratory was formal, and as he was still a stranger to the English language, Agoston could understand only part of what was said; but he understood enough to know that he had made something of a hit in New York. He thanked his friends for their hospitality and promised to return with a full account of his experiences in their country. Then, with his entourage of friends in tow, he and Fischer proceeded to the Barclay Street pier, where they boarded the steamer *Trojan*, bound for Albany.

As the boat moved up the Hudson, Agoston marveled at the magnificent river. "Those who have traveled on the Rhine or the lower Danube can appreciate its beauty," he wrote, "but not its width and depth." He was excited to be traversing the river in which the great inventor Robert Fulton had made his epochal experiments with steamboats: "If his many contemporaries who doubted him when they observed his first experiments could see the triumph of this momentous invention—how great steamboats ply the innumerable rivers and lakes of the North American Free States, and how they send their spiraling columns of smoke over the Ganges, Indus, Tigris, Euphrates, Nile and Danube, and over the great oceans— they would indeed be astonished."

In Albany, Agoston and Fischer inspected the handsome New York State House, the State Library, and the Albany City Hall, then set out for Schenectady and the resort town of Saratoga Springs. (They were, after all, Hungarian noblemen.) After a stay of eight days, hobnobbing with the patrician guests, many of whom were from the South, they returned to Schenectady and headed west by train to Utica and Syracuse, following the bed of the Erie Canal. Agoston understood that much of the prosperity of New York was attributable to the canal and believed that the people of the state rightly revered its sponsor, onetime New York Governor De Witt Clinton.

The journey proceeded by water and rail: along the Erie Canal on a packet boat to Oswego, on Lake Ontario; from there on a lake steamer west to Lewiston and, a few miles beyond that, the great Niagara Falls, which Agoston found exhilarating; thence, by train, to Buffalo, at the eastern end of Lake Erie, where Agoston paid special notice to business activities. The next leg was by the steamboat *Great Western* across Lake Erie to Cleveland, Ohio, where Agoston again gathered information about local business and agriculture. He was informed that wheat was planted in Ohio, but that the crop was often damaged by the severe winters, and that there was also a burgeoning wine industry in the state. He thought the local wine was "fair"; but he was horrified to discover that the vines were not pruned but permitted to grow unrestrained in every direction, and that the wine was not made with European (*vinifera*) grapes, but with strong-tasting, almost bitter, native North American varieties. Despite the viticultural naïveté of the local winegrowers, he sensed that Ohio had the potential for producing good wine: "I do not doubt that wine comparable to our famous Hungarian wines could be made here, if cuttings were imported from Hungary and our methods of cultivation applied." His ideas on viticulture were to undergo many changes in the years to come, but he was to return again and again to the theme he first sounded in Cleveland—that a sound American wine industry could be built only on European vine stocks and proper methods of cultivation.

From Cleveland the travelers continued by steamboat to Detroit, thence across Lake St. Clair and the St. Clair River to Lake Huron, and then north to Mackinac Island and the Strait of Mackinac. On route to Mackinac, around ten o'clock at night, the boat was shaken by a "terrific collision." They rushed onto the deck and, through the darkness, managed to catch a glimpse of a sailing ship that had collided with the steamboat and was quickly sinking. The captain and

eight sailors were barely able to make it to safety aboard the steamship before the last of the sails and masts disappeared beneath the
waves of the lake. Fortunately, the *Great Western* suffered only minor
damage to the pole that protruded from its bow.

On Mackinac Island, Agoston and his cousin visited a cliff-top
fort and spent some time with Indians who camped at the base of the
cliff, carrying on a lively trade with the local whites. It was their first
significant contact with the American Indians, a people they were to
come to know more intimately in Wisconsin and that Agoston was to
encounter on an almost daily basis on the Great Plains and in California. The Indians at Mackinac were a tame sort of people who had
had several generations of contact with French, British, and American trappers, traders, and soldiers, but they were still exotic enough
to excite the curiosity of a pair of Hungarian noblemen only recently
arrived in the United States. Agoston later wrote that there were
several white merchants who had taken up residence in the area,
married into local tribes, and now carried on a thriving trade with
the Indians.

It was but a short way down Lake Michigan from Mackinac to
Milwaukee, an upstart city on the shore of the Wisconsin Territory,
one of the young republic's newest territories and the focus of a vigorous new wave of westward settlement. Explored in the seventeenth
century by French missionaries and fur traders, captured in the eighteenth century by British army officers, Wisconsin had fallen under
American control at the conclusion of the Revolutionary War. In
1836, Congress established the Wisconsin Territory, with boundaries
marked by Lake Michigan on the east, the Missouri River on the
west, the Canadian border on the north, and the state of Illinois on
the south. This vast territory embraced all the land that would later
constitute the states of Wisconsin, Iowa, Minnesota, and the Dako-
tas. Milwaukee had begun as a fur trading post in the 1790's, but
it had not amounted to much until the middle of the 1830's, when
a French trader named Solomon Juneau surveyed a townsite near
the shore of "Milwalky" Bay. A census ordered by territorial Governor Henry Dodge in 1836 showed Wisconsin's population to be only
11,683. By 1840 that number had nearly tripled to 30,945.[8]

Agoston was clearly impressed by Milwaukee. "Immigrants flock here from every corner of the earth," he wrote. "Every newcomer who arrived the very first year, and could afford to buy even a small parcel of land, can today boast of affluence. . . . The visitor is filled with admiration when he looks around and realizes that all of this was achieved in a mere four years. One wonders what will have been accomplished here in a hundred years." After a few days in Milwaukee he and Fischer set out on horseback to explore the country west of Lake Michigan. Agoston says in his book that the German "Dr. Roges," whom he met on his voyage across the Atlantic, joined them in Milwaukee and accompanied them on their westward trek. Fischer recalled only that he and his cousin hired an interpreter, at two dollars a day, and that the interpreter proved to be "nearly as green" as they.[9] Fischer's recollections are more plausible than Agoston's. "Dr. Roges," again, seems nothing more than a stage character manufactured by Agoston to lend credence to an exciting (though almost wholly fictional) tale with which he was later to regale Hungarian readers.

Their trail led westward from Milwaukee through dense forests, oak openings, and an abundance of lakes. They seemed to be wandering, enjoying the countryside, eyes on the alert for wild game and inspiring vistas. After a few days, they came to the town of Jefferson, situated at the confluence of the Rock and Crawfish rivers. Attracted by the broad Rock River, they left their horses in the care of a tavern keeper while they hired a boat and local guide for a trip down the river. Taking turns at the oars, they passed through the settlement of Fort Atkinson and then on to Lake Koshkonong, a low sheet of water about ten miles long and five miles across, where they decided to stop. In the book he later published, Agoston says little about their sojourn on the lake, allowing only that he suffered an attack of the "fever" while there but, after "a few weeks," recovered and proceeded on. The "fever" may have been malaria, spread by the swarms of mosquitoes that infested the lake in the summer.[10]

Fischer's recollections of Koshkonong are more detailed. Twenty years later, he recalled that he and his cousin made an attempt to settle some land at the head of the lake. They built a temporary hay hut and, warming to the site, purchased some ox-teams and supplies and started to gather in a winter's supply of hay.[11] But the mosquitoes were "intolerable." In the hut one night Agoston announced that he could not stand the marauding insects and, with a handful of hay, fashioned a makeshift torch to smoke them out. But the flaming torch soon set fire to the roof, and in a minute the whole hut was ablaze. Realizing that their little store of arms—six loaded pistols, three shotguns, and thirty-five pounds of powder—was in the house, the men beat a hasty retreat into a nearby ravine and listened for the expected explosion. When it came, Fischer recalled, ashes, coals, and sticks "flew beautifully."[12]

Now Agoston and his cousin began to build a log cabin. Fischer later recalled that they registered claims to some land at Koshkonong with the United States Land Office in Milwaukee, but the clerk made a mistake in the plat he gave them and they discovered that their lands had already been entered in the name of another settler. Disgusted, they set fire to their partly completed cabin, picked up what equipment they could, and left. Fischer recalled a bittersweet journey from Koshkonong through the towns of Janesville and Madison, during which his horse was lost (and then recovered), and, for a time, the travelers "had but a small respect for the land of their 'golden dreams.'" But they struggled determinedly over trails and roads until they made it at last to the Wisconsin River.[13]

In the book he later published, Agoston tells quite a different story of their movements after they left Koshkonong. His recollections, of course, were much fresher than those of Fischer, but they were also recorded for a different audience. Fischer, speaking twenty years later, was regaling friends and neighbors with tales of his early adventures in Wisconsin. Agoston, writing within two years, was penning a paean of praise to the land he had chosen to make his home. It would hardly be surprising if Agoston chose to gloss over difficulties and emphasize triumphs, to cast discouraging experiences in a bright rather than dark light.

According to Agoston, the travelers crossed a sparsely settled expanse of oak openings and prairies to Madison, then continued northward into the wilderness. He was much taken by Madison, then the territorial capital, and by its unusual site on a rise of land in the middle of a gathering of four lakes. "I do not think that any capital in the world can boast of a more beautiful vista" he wrote. "The capital building stands on the highest point, from which all four lakes are visible. These lakes are surrounded by a variety of trees, whose delightfully artistic groupings and picturesque foliage seem to be the creation of a skillful landscape gardener." Madison, founded in 1836, was still a very small town when Agoston first saw it (he counted only a hundred houses and two stores on its dusty streets), but he predicted that its healthy climate and beautiful surroundings would eventually make it into a popular residential center.

Leaving Madison, the two Hungarians traveled north. Agoston was exhilarated by the dense woods, by the natural springs that bubbled up from the black earth, and by the deer and wildfowl they found along the trail. Recalling his hunting experiences in the Bácska, he welcomed the challenge of providing meat enough to satisfy his and his companion's robust appetites. When he bagged a deer, he and Fischer prepared it in a kettle "in the true Hungarian style." Several days of travel brought them to Lake Winnebago, a shallow plate of water about thirty miles long and ten miles wide that ranked (after Lake Michigan) as Wisconsin's largest lake. Making their way along the lakeshore, they moved on to the head of Green Bay, where they visited the town of Green Bay and the nearby trading post maintained by John Jacob Astor. Then they turned to the south again, following the bed of the Fox River through a profusion of forests, hills, and prairies.

Agoston does not state that this part of their route followed the so-called "Military Road," but it probably did. This road, cut through the forest by the Army between 1835 and 1838, was little more than a horse path marked at intervals by mounds of earth and stones, but it was the best road in central Wisconsin when it was finished, and it soon became a favorite route for civilian as well as military travelers. The northern end of the road was marked by Fort Howard, adjacent to Green Bay; the southern end lay at Fort Crawford, near the confluence of the Wisconsin and Mississippi rivers. About halfway between, the road passed through Fort Winnebago, an army post built between 1828 and 1830 to defend settlers in the central part of the territory from Indian attacks.

Agoston does mention Fort Winnebago in his book, commenting graciously on the hospitality of its officers. He also comments on the unusual site on which the fort was built—the historic *portage* (or carrying-place) of the French traders. Here the Fox, which drains the northeastern quarter of Wisconsin, passes within a mile and a half of the Wisconsin, which drains the central and southwestern regions. At the portage, the French carried their canoes from one river to the other, thereby connecting the two rivers and providing a continuous water link between the French settlements in Quebec and Louisiana. Then, as now, the Fox drained toward the Great Lakes, the St. Lawrence, and the Atlantic, while the Wisconsin drained toward the Mississippi and the Gulf of Mexico. At Fort Winnebago two of the great watersheds of North America met in a spongy marsh guarded over by log palisades and glowering cannons. "When the rivers are in flood," Agoston wrote, "the waters of the Wisconsin often reach those of the Fox, and then it is possible for boats to cross from one river to the other."

Leaving Winnebago, they followed the Military Road southwestward through the lead-mining district that centered around the town of Mineral Point and thence on to the French village of Prairie du Chien, at the confluence of the Wisconsin and the Mississippi. From bluffs above Prairie du Chien, it was possible to catch a fine view to the west and south. Across the mighty "Father of Waters," the Hungarian cousins could see the green hills of the Iowa Territory, split off from Wisconsin in 1838. Fort Crawford, a U.S. Army post built in 1836, stood on high ground a few miles from Prairie du Chien, marking the southern end of the Military Road. After visiting the village and fort, the Hungarians crossed back over the river and, following its southern shore, moved eastward. Their trail led through heavy underbrush and across a seemingly endless series of streams. "We had to detour many times to avoid marshes," Agoston wrote. "Crossing the boggy ground, our horses often sank to their bellies and fell, nearly smothering us. . . . Nevertheless we were still in good spirits when, after two days of difficult and hazardous travel, we reached a high hill opposite Sauk Prairie."

Agoston was deeply moved by his first sight of the prairie that was to be his home for most of the next nine years. He spoke often enough of the occasion to convince his friends and family that he had experienced a kind of revelation when he climbed to the top of a hill overlooking the Wisconsin and gazed out over the expanse of river and grassland, ringed in the far distance by hills.

One of his friends (probably repeating one of Agoston's own stories) said that he had shouted "Eureka! Eureka!" when he first laid his eyes on the prairie, and followed those words with "Italia! Italia!"[14] Agoston's own version is slightly different but no less ecstatic. "When our eyes beheld the panorama spread out before us," he wrote in the book that he eventually published, "a veritable masterpiece of nature, all three of us exclaimed in unison, 'Oh, how magnificent!' In truth, the view was more beautiful than anything I had seen in all my travels in Europe and America. I was firmly convinced that nowhere in the world could there be a more enchanting place."

4

A "City"
on the
Frontier

Agoston says in *Travels in North America* that it took him and his companions several hours to tear themselves away from the magnificent view of the prairie, and it is not difficult to understand why, for the vista that spread out before them that summer day in 1840 was one of the most beautiful in all of Wisconsin, a fine meeting place of water and land surrounded by wooded hills and covered over by a vast expanse of sky.

Sauk Prairie is a broad sweep of gently sloping land that measures about eight miles from east to west and twelve from north to south.[1] It is bounded on the south and east by an arc of the Wisconsin River, on the north by wooded hills, and on the west by a mixed country of small valleys, ravines, and bluffs. In 1840 the prairie was carpeted with grass and wildflowers that extended almost continuously from the river's edge to the base of the circling hills.[2] The prairie was named for the Sauk (or Sac) Indians, whose principal village stood on the riverbank from the 1740's to the 1780's. The French had called the Indians "Sacs"; the English called them "Sauks" or "Saukies." The earliest American settlers used "Sac" and "Sauk" almost interchangeably, sometimes calling the grassland, in

English fashion, "Sauk Prairie" and sometimes adopting the French style, "Prairie du Sac."

Agoston cannot have missed the resemblance between the Wisconsin and the Danube. A Tyrolean priest who viewed the river from the same vantage point as Agoston just five years later was to liken the stream to the Danube at Vienna.[3] Agoston did not cite the resemblance in his book, though he did describe the Wisconsin's "surging waves" and the "many delightful little islands" that studded the riverbed.[4] Rising in a shallow lake on the border between Wisconsin and Upper Michigan, the river flows for more than four hundred miles through hills and valleys and prairies to the Mississippi at Prairie du Chien. Sauk Prairie occupies the west bank of the river, about one hundred miles from its mouth, at a point where the river measures about a quarter of a mile in width.

Agoston and Károly Fischer crossed the river by means of a crude ferry. On the opposite shore they found a small community, six families only, dwelling in cabins. They quickly made arrangements to lodge in one of the cabins, but before Agoston could settle in, he explored the riverbank and a stretch of the nearby prairie. After supper, still in a ferment, he went back to the river. He later recorded his feelings:

It was a beautiful, quiet evening. Only the lovely song of the whippoorwill disturbed the deep silence. The moon cast its silvery light on the hills across the river. I was so entranced by the magnificent scenery that I roamed about in solitude until the early hours of the morning. At last I returned to my bed, but tired as I was, could not sleep. An irresistible longing gripped my soul, and I made a firm decision to buy a small piece of land. Next morning I again reconnoitered the place, and my resolve was strengthened.[5]

This small community of pioneers—the Haney and Baxter, Fairchild and Alban, Crossman and Crocker families[6]—had come across the river in 1838 on rumors that Congress was about to conclude a treaty with the Winnebago Indians for their lands north and west of the Wisconsin. But the government had not yet opened the land for purchase, so the settlers had staked out claims, hoping they could eventually get legal title.

Determined to acquire some land on the prairie, Agoston en-

tered into negotiations with some of the local settlers and quickly
agreed to buy a section of land (a square mile, or 640 acres) for
the sum of three dollars an acre, one-third payable in cash and two-
thirds payable in merchandise. He records in his book that the merchandise consisted of woolen goods that he had brought with him
from New York for purposes of bartering, since "in the United States
everyone is a trader." Thus he became the owner "of the most desirable location on either side of the river."[7] (Fischer's recollections of
his cousin's first land purchase are somewhat different. According
to Fischer, Agoston bought a strip of land from Burk Fairchild for
$400; it had thirty rods of frontage on the river and ran back from
the water a distance of a mile.[8] If Fischer's figures are correct, Agoston's first parcel of land amounted to only sixty acres and was bought
for $6.66 an acre, a surprisingly high price in that frontier market.)[9]
Agoston then asked each of the settlers what they thought he should
do with his property. He later wrote:

They were unanimous in their advice that I should establish a city here, because all along the river's course, between the mountains and the swamps,
this was the only suitable place for a city to be built. Sooner or later steamboats would ply the mighty Wisconsin River, making it possible to ship to
the South the produce of the fertile land and the area's abundance of lead,
copper, and even iron ore. Furthermore, there were still 220,000 acres of
rich farmland available here at $1.25 an acre. I shared their opinion, but
also realized that if I wanted to found a city I would have to buy at least ten
thousand acres, and immediately build a large inn, a school, several houses,
and a gristmill, as well as a sawmill to provide the anticipated poor immigrants from Europe with lumber and other building materials.[10]

This narrative is interesting on two accounts—both for the boldness of the local settlers in suggesting that a stranger who had just
emerged from the woods should undertake to build a "city" in the
wilderness, and for the eagerness with which the stranger entertained
their suggestion. But one must always remember to read between
the lines in Agoston's account. He had clearly been puffing to the
Haneys and Fairchilds, the Baxters and Albans—planting in their
minds the idea that he was a man with the ability, if not exactly the
means, to bring civilization to the wilderness. No doubt they were
struck by his handsome face, lithe figure, and Old World manner—

and by his self-assurance, though his English was still rudimentary. If he exaggerated, embellished, or even manufactured details of his past to impress them, his enthusiasm was sincere; and if any of the settlers doubted that he really intended to build a "city" on the prairie, he was soon to remove that doubt from their minds.

The two cousins arrived on the prairie in June or mid-July.[11] Their first order of business was to build a cabin (which they probably shared) of felled logs with a wooden roof and earthen floor.[12] Fischer recalled that they went back to Milwaukee (a distance of 130 miles, or three days' travel by horse and wagon) for supplies and then spent the rest of the summer hunting.[13]

And a glorious time it must have been for hunting. In its natural state, Sauk Prairie was a wonderland of grass, trees, flowers, and wild animals. Tall timber grew along the river's edge and on the islands in the stream, and an abundance of Indian artifacts—spear points, arrowheads, and half-buried mounds—protruded here and there from the flowers and grass, bearing silent witness to its first human inhabitants.[14] There was plenty of game—rabbits, squirrels, prairie chickens, sometimes in flocks of up to fifty birds, and passenger pigeons in incredible numbers. Mammals on the prairie and in the neighboring hills included raccoons, deer, bears, some elk, an occasional lynx, and timber wolves.[15]

Both the Indians and the white settlers looked upon the wolves as a menace, and the sight of a pack of the shaggy-haired animals, skulking in the tall grass at the edge of the settlement, was enough to excite fear in even the bravest men. All the settlers on the prairie kept their distance from the wolves—all, that is, except Agoston, who seemed to delight in defying them. One account (not his own) tells of his boldly entering a wolf's den in an attempt to steal a cub and being surprised as he left by the outraged mother. He was unarmed, and the ensuing struggle was furious. But he met the wolf's attack head on and strangled it with his bare hands. Like many another account, the story of this audacious encounter between a she-wolf and a Hungarian nobleman was to assume the status of a legend on Sauk Prairie.[16] Agoston seemed to exult in the hunt, and pioneers enjoyed sharing stories of his hunting exploits and the careless abandon with which he crashed through underbrush and over rocks, often clad in a green silk hunting shirt and flaming red sash, seemingly disdainful of the wear and tear on his expensive dress.[17]

The two Hungarians were shortly joined by their shipboard acquaintance Adolph Rendtorff, who had gone to Illinois. They wrote him there, telling him about Sauk Prairie, and invited him and his brother to join them, according to their shipboard compact. The Rendtorffs were apparently quite willing to come. Adolph's brother Edmond later recalled that they arrived at Sauk Prairie in the fall of 1840. "The day of our arrival I shall never forget," he wrote. "The weather was splendid. We stepped ashore and looked around, but stood still for a good while. The scenery—the beauty of nature made a great impression on me—on us I dare say. Oh yes, if possible, said we—if possible yes! yes, let us settle here." The German brothers were soon greeted by Agoston, Fischer, and a handful of Germans who were working for them. The Hungarians' welcome was so warm that the Rendtorffs felt as if they had been "friends 'long time ago.'"[18] An article in the *Madison Express* that September reported on a bustle of activities on the prairie. There were about forty settlers in all, and emigrants with large families were soon expected to arrive. The *Express* also noted that some "Hungarian noblemen have pitched their tent here, considering it one of Nature's chosen spots, and after some two months' residence, express themselves highly delighted with their situation."[19]

Agoston had a talent for attracting publicity, and it is likely that he was the source of the *Express*'s story. He had already made plans to build a "city" at Sauk, and the "emigrants" who would soon be coming there with "large families" may well have been his projection, for attracting immigrants was a key component of his building plan for the prairie. But another important component was attracting capital. He admitted from the start that he lacked the resources to build a "city" on his own, and on his trips to Madison and Milwaukee he kept his eyes open for a partner who might be willing to finance the project. That fall he found a man in Milwaukee who fitted the bill. He was a newly arrived Englishman named Robert Bryant, married, with a wife and three children. Beyond that not much is known about him, except that he was both willing and able to invest substantial sums of money in Agoston's projects.[20] Agoston's account of their meeting is interesting—though, as usual, not wholly accurate:

In Milwaukee I made the acquaintance of a Mr. Bryant, an English immigrant who had arrived only a fortnight before with his wife and three children. He had already bought some houses and land, but was disappointed with his acquisitions.

I took a liking to the gentleman and wished to know him better; we soon became inseparable. In glowing colors I described my newly acquired land, which I had bought with the expectation of reselling it soon at a great profit—for I was convinced that within a year its value would increase tenfold. My new friend became curious to see the place, and so soon we were in a carriage bound for Madison, which is only twenty miles from my property. Three days later we were in Sauk Prairie. The Englishman was most surprised; he had never seen such a beautiful place anywhere in the Union. "This is where I want to live, nowhere else," he exclaimed. We spent several days there, exploring the land in every direction, and then proceeded to the government land office at Mineral Point. My new friend immediately bought and paid for ten thousand acres of land, and had it recorded in both our names. At first I opposed this, arguing that I was not in a position to pay my share. (Although I had made considerable profit on the merchandise I had brought west with me, paying half the price of the land would not have left me enough to live on or to return home with.) My new friend resisted all my protestations. "My friend, let us be partners," he said. "I have enough money to get us started. We will share the profits equally. Let us proceed to found a city, building a mill and everything else we need. In time you can repay the capital from your share of the profits; and I won't accept any interest." This was a truly generous offer; after brief consideration I accepted it, and immediately returned to Sauk Prairie to make the necessary plans.[21]

Despite its charm, there are discrepancies enough in this story of the beginning of a frontier partnership to raise serious doubts about how Agoston and Bryant decided to join forces. Agoston says he told Bryant that he had bought his land at Sauk with the expectation of quick resale, though he had told the first settlers there that he planned to stay long enough to build a "city." He says that Bryant offered him a full partnership in the enterprise, but also expected his capital to be repaid, thus suggesting that the details of their financial arrangement were never carefully worked out. He also says that he and Bryant recorded their land purchase at the Land

Office in Mineral Point. But government land on Sauk Prairie was not made available for purchase until October 23, 1843, and there are no records of any land purchases north or west of the Wisconsin River before that date.[22] Agoston Haraszthy, Bryant, and others did purchase land from the government after the 1843 opening date, but there is no record of any purchase even remotely approaching in size the princely domain of ten thousand acres. The conclusion is inescapable that Agoston simply manufactured details of his early land purchases to impress his Hungarian readers. It was Agoston Haraszthy the land promoter, not Agoston Haraszthy the careful reporter, who was speaking in this passage.

Agoston's real negotiations with Bryant may have taken place in the winter of 1840–41 in Milwaukee. One writer has suggested that he spent that winter in the lakeside city;[23] since winters in central Wisconsin are typically severe and his cabin on the prairie cannot have been as comfortable as the new houses in Milwaukee, the suggestion is credible. The Great Lakes moderate weather along their shores, easing the cold of winter and the heat of summer. On the Wisconsin River, however, snow falls long and hard from about November through March, and in the coldest part of the winter all navigation is halted. The first settlers had to retire to their cabins to wait out the winter, venturing forth at intervals only to traverse the snowy trails in horse-drawn sleighs or tramp across the icy surface of the river in oiled boots.[24]

However he may have spent the winter, Agoston was back on the prairie in the spring of 1841, planning his incipient "city." The site for the new development was a choice parcel of land on the west bank of the Wisconsin, roughly opposite the point from which Agoston had first looked over the prairie. In their recollections, pioneers later remembered that the site had originally been claimed by a man named Berry Haney.[25] Haney was a stage driver on the Military Road before he began acquiring land in the southwest corner of Wisconsin in the late 1830's. He came to Sauk Prairie in 1838, broke out the first parcel of land, and established a ferry to carry travelers across the river. Before Haney, the land had been claimed by the Sauk Indians, who built their principal village on the site.[26] A Massachusetts-born cartographer named Jonathan Carver had passed by the Indian village in 1766 and proclaimed it "the Great Town of the Saukies," the "largest and best built Indian town I ever saw."[27] The village had regular and spacious streets, about ninety large houses built of hewn planks, and well-tended gardens. Agoston acquired Haney's claim and ferry and, with Bryant, made plans to develop the site.

The developers' first task was to hire a surveyor to lay out streets and subdivide lots. This job was given to Charles O. Baxter, a native Virginian who had lived on the prairie since 1839. Though Baxter's original 1841 plat has been lost, a copy recorded in the office of the Register of Deeds of Sauk County on April 26, 1845, survives.[28] In the book he later published, Agoston says that he named the "city" *Széptáj*, Hungarian for "Beautiful Place." But the map recorded by the Register of Deeds clearly shows that the name was "Haraszthy," at least in 1845. Was *Széptáj* only a literary device, invented to please Agoston's Hungarian readers? Or did he in fact give his new settlement the picturesque Hungarian name, and later change it to Haraszthy? The available evidence provides no clear answer to this question, although it is clear that "Haraszthy" was the name by which the town would be known in official records, on maps, and in the conversation of the settlers for most of the next ten years.

If the town was destined to bear a foreign-sounding name, the streets clearly reflected the American influence. The main street of the town, which occupied the top of the riverbank and commanded a fine view, was Water Street. Back of Water Street, the streets bore the names of the first five presidents of the United States: George Washington, John Adams, Thomas Jefferson, James Madison, and James Monroe. These north-south arteries were crossed by east-west streets bearing the names of John Quincy Adams, Andrew Jackson, Martin Van Buren, and William Henry Harrison.[29] The principal east-west thoroughfare was named Bryant, for Agoston's cofounder; another was named Baxter, for the surveyor; and a third was christened Carolina, possibly in honor of Caroline Bryant, the cofounder's wife.

Agoston says that the first house built in the town was occupied by Bryant and his family. In a letter written twenty years later, Edmond Rendtorff said the first frame house was Agoston's and that it was built by an English carpenter named Morgan.[30] It is likely that the Bryant and Haraszthy houses were built at about the same time, and probably by the same builder. The first real property record bearing the Haraszthy name in Wisconsin is a mortgage recorded in Madison at the end of October 1842. The mortgage was for $1,000 and was signed on October 25, 1842, by "Robert Bryant of Sauk Prairie in the Territory of Wisconsin" in favor of "Alfred Morgan, of the same place." The security was described as: "One two horse buggy waggon[.] One span of horses. Seventeen cows[.] [A] quantity of brick[,] being all of the brick in the brick yard of Harasty [*sic*] and Bryant[.] One peanna[.] One sofa[.] One lumber waggon. Two yoke of cattle[.]"[31] The brickyard was one of the earliest enterprises established by the firm of Haraszthy and Bryant in the new town. The mortgage was probably given to Morgan to pay for work he had done in Haraszthy Town, including the construction of the Bryant and Haraszthy houses. It was signed by Bryant but not by Agoston, probably because Agoston was traveling at the time the mortgage was given.

The house that Alfred Morgan built for Robert Bryant was a commodious structure in the Classical Revival style then popular throughout the United States. Rising two and a half stories above the northwest corner of Water and Bryant streets, it had a central hall, a front porch supported by four pillars, and two banks of shuttered windows that faced east across the Wisconsin. Agoston's house was two blocks north of Bryant's, at the southwest corner of Water and Van Buren.[32] A photograph taken of this house in later years shows it to have been a modest structure of one and one-half stories with a covered porch across the front. Its walls were neatly finished in clapboards, and its roof was covered with wood shingles.[33] It was neither grand nor imposing, but it had a certain refinement and cannot have failed to draw admiring glances from pioneers who were used to seeing log cabins on the prairie.

Their houses put up, Agoston and his partner now launched into other building projects, including the construction of a schoolhouse on Madison Street midway between Jackson and Van Buren and an inn on Water Street near the corner of Bryant. The inn, a three-story structure called the United States Hotel, was the showplace of the little town and a popular gathering place for settlers as well as visitors. Twenty years after it was built, William H. Canfield was to remember that it was "a palace of a building for so new a country."[34]

Agoston believed strongly that the town should have a mill, and he and Bryant scouted out a proper site for the facility. Since the Wisconsin was too turbulent to be harnessed to a wooden wheel, they chose a site on Honey Creek, one of the river's tributaries, about four miles from the town. They built a low dam across the creek to form a pond and a spillway and erected the mill at one end of the dam. It is not clear whether the mill was initially equipped with stones for grinding grain or saws for cutting lumber, although Agoston intended it to answer both purposes. It was called Honey Creek Mill.[35]

Another important link in Agoston's plans for the prairie was a steamboat. When he visited the lead-mining district around Mineral Point, he noticed that the ore was transported overland from the mines to Galena, Illinois, on the Fever River, where it was loaded on ships for eventual transport over the Mississippi and Ohio rivers to distant parts of the United States. Mineral Point was closer to the Wisconsin than it was to the Mississippi, and Agoston wondered why shipments could not be made to a point on the Wisconsin and, from there, transported to their ultimate destination. The only obstacle he saw to such a plan was the absence of steam power on the Wisconsin.[36] A Hungarian whose ideas of progress were molded by Count István Széchenyi could not fail to appreciate the importance of steamboats on a major river. Agoston believed that a steamboat stationed at his "city" on Sauk Prairie would not only be a boon to the surrounding country but would do much to promote the city itself. In his book he recalled that he approached Bryant with the suggestion that they commission the construction of a vessel. Bryant readily agreed to the proposal, and Agoston made plans to travel to Pittsburgh to make the necessary arrangements.

But before he could leave he discovered that a ship that could meet his needs had recently been completed in the village of Aztalan, about thirty miles east of Madison. It was built by a Milwaukee-based promoter named N. P. Hawks and launched on the Crawfish River, a tributary of the larger Rock River. Newspapers reported that the boat was a stern-wheeler, one hundred feet long and eighteen feet wide, and specially engineered to draw no more than twelve inches of water when fully loaded.[37] Hawks had built it to carry passengers and freight along the Rock to ports on the Mississippi, and local residents had supported his efforts by subscribing to shares in the vessel.[38]

The boat was launched at Aztalan on April 19, 1841, under the

name *N. P. Hawks*, in the presence of a crowd of enthusiastic supporters.[39] A newspaper story published in July said that the boat was
engaged in a lively passenger service between the Illinois cities of
Rockford and Dixon, and that on some trips it carried as many as
three hundred passengers.[40] On at least one trip, the boat went all
the way down the river to its confluence with the Mississippi, then
followed the Mississippi to St. Louis.

But the Rock River proved to be unnavigable in spots, apparently
because of rocks that, in the summertime, partially blocked the channel.[41] So Hawks put it up for sale. Hearing the news, Agoston made
haste to inspect the steamboat (whether on the Rock River itself, or
at some port along the Mississippi, is not clear) and make an offer
for its purchase. After negotiations, he agreed to pay $16,000 for a
half interest in the vessel (the other half being retained by Hawks
and the other investors) on the condition that it operate on the Wisconsin and Mississippi rivers.[42] He renamed the boat the *Rock River*.[43]

It is not hard to imagine the excitement on Sauk Prairie as the
steamboat made its first voyage up the Wisconsin, ringing its bells
and blowing clouds of steam into the sky. If the first settlers on the
prairie had any doubts about the intentions of the impetuous Hungarian who had recently plunged into their midst, the arrival of the
Rock River must have done much to reassure them, for under Agoston's energetic management the steamboat was soon engaged in a
busy trade on the Wisconsin and Mississippi rivers.[44]

About the time that Agoston was negotiating the purchase of
the steamboat, the firm of Haraszthy and Bryant became involved
in two other ventures. One was a store in Haraszthy Town. Agoston
later recalled that he traveled widely to purchase merchandise for
the store, on one occasion even going as far away as Cincinnati.[45]
It is likely, however, that the bulk of his goods were gathered from
sources closer at hand, including Madison, Milwaukee, and perhaps
Galena, which was easily reached by river connections. The second
venture was the brickyard mentioned in the Bryant-Morgan mortgage agreement. It was built near the river in Haraszthy Town, where
the bricks could easily be loaded onto the *Rock River* for delivery to
outlying points.[46]

Just when Agoston first started to till the land on Sauk Prairie is
difficult to determine, though it may well have been in the spring of

1841. He had made some friends at Fort Winnebago on his first visit there in 1840, and when he learned that the fort needed good supplies of wood and corn he promptly offered to furnish it with both commodities. To obtain the wood, he established a kind of headquarters on an island north of the fort. The adjacent country was generously supplied with timber from which firewood could be conveniently cut and transported to the fort. The corn was grown on prairie land west of Haraszthy Town.[47]

Although Sauk Prairie enjoyed a reputation among the pioneers as a fertile land, preparing previously unbroken land for tilling was no easy task. The ground was customarily broken with ox-drawn plows. As many as twelve of the draft animals could be linked to a single blade, while a plowman trudged alongside, barking orders through clouds of dust. Since the land had never before been disturbed, the plow uncovered some unexpected creatures in the deep grass: moles, field mice, and a profusion of snakes. The snakes were reluctant to cross plowed land, and as the plow and oxen circled round and round the field, they retreated into the grassy ground in the center, which soon resembled a kind of herpetarium, crowded with bull snakes, milk snakes, copperheads, and rattlesnakes. When, from time to time, the plow turned up a whole nest of writhing serpents, the plowman had to dance carefully through the grass, armed with rocks and big sticks, whacking defensively at snakes that seemed too menacing.[48]

After his corn was planted, Agoston apparently busied himself with other pursuits and did not notice that the crop was ready for harvest until the agreed time for delivery had nearly passed. Then, in a rush, he summoned all his hands to the fields and ordered them to pick the corn, throw it into boxes, load the boxes onto wagons, and load them onto a flatboat that was waiting at the riverbank. As the boat moved slowly up the Wisconsin, Agoston's hands fell to the job of husking. They apparently made it to Winnebago on time, but only barely. The incident impressed witnesses with a facet of Agoston Haraszthy's character that they would remember for years after: He may have had too many irons in the fire, and at times he could be almost shockingly neglectful of his obligations, but when it came time to get a job done, he was capable of extraordinary bursts of energy.[49]

Growing corn was not Agoston's first or even principal agricultural pursuit in Wisconsin. He grew wheat, raised hogs, and invested considerable time and effort in raising sheep. He also kept cattle and, of course, horses. William Canfield, a Sauk Prairie pioneer who knew Agoston in his earliest days in Wisconsin, recalled that he was especially fond of horses and delighted in showing them to visitors. He kept a fine saddle mare for which he had particular affection. One day he took Canfield to inspect his horses, informing him that a workhorse had gotten loose the night before and kicked the mare, inflicting a nasty wound. As Agoston approached the workhorse, he gave him a cut with his walking stick, saying: "You damned cad, you no gentleman: to kick a lady!" He repeated the rebuke several times, each time giving the offender another lick with his stick to underscore his displeasure.[50]

When Agoston first grew grapevines in Wisconsin is a matter of speculation. There is no evidence in the book he later wrote that he planted vines, or even thought about doing so, in his first two years on Sauk Prairie. But the fact that he did not discuss the subject in his book does not prove that it was not in his mind. In his comments on the infant wine industry in Ohio, he had made it clear that he considered European vine stocks the key to a successful American wine industry. If he was true to his word, his first efforts toward producing wine would have been to seek out European cuttings, if not in Europe itself, then from an American source. There is no evidence that he was able to do this in 1840 or 1841, or that he even made the attempt; but the lack of evidence does not foreclose the possibility. Establishing a vineyard is a time-consuming task, even in a country where suitable stocks are available for planting. When the only suitable cuttings are hundreds or even thousands of miles away, the task is much more difficult.

Contemporary accounts describe Sauk Prairie as a bustling place in 1841, thanks largely to Agoston's influence. An itinerant Methodist preacher named T. M. Fullerton crossed the river on June 23 of that year and found 270 inhabitants and a "flourishing little village" on the west bank. Fullerton met both Haraszthy and Bryant and was surprised to find that both men had grown long beards, which he thought made them look like "savages." "They are the great men of the place," Fullerton wrote in his journal, "and others adopt their customs, and make themselves as ridiculous as possible." Thirty years later, Fullerton was to remember this journal entry with a touch of embarrassment, for by that time he had adopted the style of the "savages" and himself wore a beard.[51] Another note in Fullerton's journal indicates that Agoston had by this time assumed the Old World title that was to alternately distinguish and embarrass him for the rest of his life. Fullerton described him as "a Hungarian Count—so he calls himself—who claims to have large quantities of money, and is expending it liberally in improvements." Bryant, he said, was an "Englishman . . . who claims to have been a Lord in the old country. He is in partnership with the Count."[52] Fullerton's journal entry is the earliest extant reference to "Count" Haraszthy. It indicates that Agoston had assumed the title on the prairie, though it does little to explain why.

Since Agoston had assumed the role of a land promoter at Sauk Prairie, the explanation may simply be that he thought his promotion would be more successful if the residents of Sauk Prairie believed that he was, not just a nobleman, but a titled nobleman. Fullerton's journal entry is interesting on three accounts. First, it helps indicate when and where Agoston Haraszthy became "Count" Haraszthy. Earlier records of Agoston in America (including the passenger list of the packet boat *Samson*) include no reference to a title, or any claim of a title. On June 23 of 1841, on Sauk Prairie, Agoston Haraszthy was clearly holding himself out as "Count" Haraszthy. Second, Fullerton's entry indicates that the claimed title was not altogether convincing. A "Count—so he calls himself" is not the same thing as a "Count." The traveling evangelist may not have been an expert on European aristocracy, but he could detect a pose when he saw one, and Agoston's "countship" (and Bryant's English "lordship") were clearly poses. Were these self-assumed titles the result of a common plot to deceive a community of unsophisticated frontiersmen and thus further their mutual enterprise? Did the idea to assume loftier stations than the circumstances of their birth would justify originate with Bryant, with Agoston, or with both? Since Agoston seems to have been the inspiration for most of the partners' activities on Sauk Prairie, it is probably only fair to assume that the "titles"—like the mill, the store, the brickyard, the steamboat, and even Haraszthy

Town itself—were his idea. If Agoston deserves credit for his many brilliant innovations, he also deserves blame for his deceptions.

Agoston's self-assumed title was alternately to puzzle and fascinate historians for generations. One Hungarian historian described it as a "courtesy title" of the sort that was "customary in America," and suggested that Agoston's "commanding presence, suave manners, and great executive ability" lent it an air of authenticity.[53] Verne Seth Pease, a Wisconsin historian who traced Agoston's story in the first years of the twentieth century, reached a similar conclusion. He asked pioneers who remembered Agoston if they knew anything about his "title." They said they had never heard the title "questioned"—and knew only that he was "Count Haraszthy."[54] Pease concluded that "there was about the man a certain bearing, natural and unstudied, that gave to the title of count an air of fitness and plausibility."[55]

Plausible or not, there is little doubt that Agoston wore his "title" comfortably—that in appearance and manner he seemed every inch the "Count." He was, after all, a nobleman, and the Haraszthys were an old Hungarian family. They were not magnates, and he had no right to claim that they were; but if the posture he assumed on the prairie was a pose, the pose was more an exaggeration than a fabrication. His noble lineage, along with his personal appearance and manner, may explain not only why he claimed to be "Count" Haraszthy but why he was almost universally accepted as such. And so in Haraszthy Town on Sauk Prairie in the territory of Wisconsin in the pioneer year of 1841, a twenty-eight-year-old Hungarian nobleman named Agoston Haraszthy became "Count Haraszthy." More than 150 years later, he would still be remembered by many as "the Count."

Károly Fischer, too, underwent a transformation on the frontier by adopting the name Charles Halasz. Charles is, of course, the English equivalent of the Hungarian Károly, and it was only natural that his American neighbors would prefer to address him by the English name, but the choice of Halasz is curious. *Halász* is the Hungarian word for a "fisher" or "fisherman," and thus a perfect translation for the German *Fischer*, but why a pioneer on the American frontier would prefer a Hungarian to a German surname is something of a mystery. Perhaps he, like his cousin, wanted to tell the world that he was a Hungarian and proud of his Magyar heritage. Whatever the explanation, the name change would stick, for Károly Fischer would be known as Charles Halasz for the rest of his life.[56]

And so, shortly after they arrived on the Wisconsin frontier, Agoston Haraszthy and Károly Fischer (alias Charles Halasz) had thrown off at least a part of their European pasts and assumed new identities. It was not perhaps so surprising, for the United States was a land in which men could be what they chose to be, not what centuries of tradition and the accidents of birth decreed that they must be. Neither man may have known it, but both were already well along the road to becoming Americans.

5

A Traveler's Tale

Agoston had been on Sauk Prairie less than two years, building a city, planting corn, working, but he had already decided to write a book about his American experiences, and to round out the narrative he was determined to see the "Indian country" and to make a tour through the Southern states.

If Agoston had arrived at Sauk three years before he did, he would already have been in Indian country, for up until 1837 the land north and west of the Wisconsin River, including all of Sauk Prairie, was claimed and occupied by the Winnebago Indians. In that year, in a parley with representatives of President Andrew Jackson in Washington, D.C., the Winnebago had abandoned their claims to the land and agreed to move west of the Mississippi. The bulk of the tribe did withdraw, though stragglers remained for several years afterward. In 1840, a band of Winnebago was found and removed from the Baraboo Valley north of Sauk Prairie, and for a dozen or more years small groups could be seen wandering through the hills in the summer, and when the weather turned bad, approaching cabins on the prairie to beg for food.

Agoston may well have scraped an acquaintance with Winnebago stragglers in and around Sauk Prairie, but to learn more about the

life of the American Indians he would have had to go farther west—
to the tribes' new "hunting grounds" beyond the Mississippi. He de-
votes three full chapters of his book to an account of his experiences
in the Indian country. These chapters rank among the most interesting in the book, although they are every bit as maddening as they
are interesting.[1]

Agoston says that the German "Doctor Roges" joined him at
Sauk Prairie in February 1841. "Roges" had, according to Agoston,
left him and Charles Halasz (then Károly Fischer) sometime after
they arrived at the prairie in the summer of 1840, returned to Milwaukee, and from there planned to make a trip through the South.
But "Roges" had agreed to join Agoston at Sauk in the spring. When
the German doctor reappeared, he was accompanied by an English
traveler whom Agoston identifies only as "Lord Malgred." "I had
never met Lord Malgred before," Agoston writes; "the doctor had
met him in his travels, and recounted our plan to visit the Indians.
Lord Malgred had shown great enthusiasm for the idea, and Doctor
Roges had invited him to join us." A search of standard references
for the British peerage reveals no name even remotely resembling
"Malgred," nor does the name "Lord Malgred" appear in the territorial records of Wisconsin. "Malgred" is as fictional as "Roges,"
and almost as fictional as the three Indian chapters in the book that
Agoston eventually published.

Agoston says that he, "Roges," and "Malgred" left Haraszthy
Town in the spring of 1841. Charles Halasz stayed behind to look
after his cousin's business affairs. They headed down the Wisconsin River to Fort Crawford, where they bought supplies and hired a
scout, the half-breed son of a French father and an Indian mother.
They crossed the Mississippi on a ferry, then struck out on horseback into the Indian country, accompanied by a hunting dog that
the commander at Fort Crawford had presented to Agoston.

Agoston and his party traveled through the Indian country for
more than three months. Although it is impossible to follow their
route with any precision, it is possible to determine the general direction in which they proceeded. From Fort Crawford (roughly opposite
the present-day town of Marquette, Iowa), they apparently traveled
toward the south, crossed the "Otter River," spent the night in a cave,

and then turned toward the west. The trail, Agoston says, lay "under the forty-second parallel," which would have placed them more than seventy-five miles south of Crawford. They shot pheasants and wild hens, then came upon a swift river "about six hundred feet wide" and, beyond it, a lake so large they could not see the other shore.

In the neighborhood of the lake (called "Tankora") the travelers met their first Indians, a large band of Winnebago. The Indians showed Agoston and his companions every courtesy. They ate in the Winnebago "wigwams," hunted with Winnebago braves, and smoked the "peace pipe" with the Winnebago chief. At several points in his narrative, Agoston notes the apparent nonchalance with which the Winnebago (and later the Sauk and Fox) offered their women—including wives and sisters—to the visitors. (Whether he or any of his companions accepted these generous "offers" he declines to say.) From the Winnebago country, the travelers continued (apparently still in a westerly direction) to territory occupied by the Sauk and Fox. These two tribes, once independent, had joined in an alliance in the early years of the nineteenth century and were now generally regarded as a single group. The travelers were hospitably greeted by the Sauk and Fox, who invited them to share their meals, watch their ceremonial dances, and even join their hunts.

Much of the written account of Agoston's tour among the Indians is devoted to thrilling tales of the hunt. There are encounters with wounded elk, slinking "panthers," angry bears, stampeding deer, and hulking buffalo. Agoston's own prowess as a hunter may well have inspired many of these tales, yet he is never reluctant to show how the Indian hunters' experience, skill, and instincts put his own to shame: He shoots an elk and foolishly attempts to approach the wounded animal with his knife, but the animal rears up, throws him aside, and, after a struggle, escapes into the brush with the knife still buried in its neck. His half-breed scout laughs at his inexperience, explaining that after wounding such an animal an Indian would always wait until the animal had been weakened by loss of blood before attempting to finish it off. "Don't you know the hunter's rule," the guide asks "—never run after an animal that has been shot, but reload your weapon and wait?"

One long passage describes the skill shown by a Winnebago chief in killing a huge bear. The chief spots the bear prowling in a nearby hollow, and after ordering Agoston and his companions to flatten themselves on the ground, tosses a stone into the hollow to provoke the bear:

In a minute or so we saw a large bear emerge raging with fury and start after the chief, who climbed a nearby oak with catlike swiftness. The bear followed, and when it reached the tree the Indian moved out to the end of the lowest branch. The bear pursued him onto the branch, but with great care. The chief shook the branch with his foot a few times, which scared the bear and made it stop to hold on. After doing this several times the Indian reached the end of the branch. Seeing the branch start to bend, the bear stopped and looked angrily at the Indian; who teased it to increase its fury. Finally the chief grasped the end of the branch, and jumped off just about the time it reached the ground. When the bear saw its enemy on the ground, it carefully turned around. The chief, his tomahawk raised, waited for it at the base of the tree; and as soon as he could reach it swung the tomahawk with great force into the shoulder of the bear. With a terrifying roar the animal jumped off the branch; the chief nimbly jumped to its other side, and while the bear reached out after him with its paw, he sank his tomahawk into the other shoulder. The bear collapsed, and the chief with a quick leap split its skull.

Agoston also describes the Winnebago's skill in hunting buffalo. They come upon a herd of the huge animals, and the chief, mounted on a swift pony, heads straight toward one of them, approaching to within two hundred feet. The buffalo raises its head from time to time to contemplate the approaching rider, but continues to graze. When the chief is only a hundred feet away, he prods his pony into a fast gallop, and, when he is only fifteen feet away, takes aim with his rifle and wounds the animal. The buffalo turns on its pursuer, but the Indian chief calmly reloads his rifle and spurs on his pony. The buffalo gains on them, and just at the right moment the chief digs his knee into the pony's flank. The horse quickly stops and turns, and the buffalo, unable to check its momentum, hurtles by. The chief, in a dazzling display of marksmanship, fires and brings the great animal down.

Agoston describes two scenes in which he and his companions are invited by Indian chiefs to smoke what he calls the "friendship pipe" and Americans generally know as the "peace pipe" (or "calumet"). The first scene occurs early in the Indian journey, around the fire in the "wigwam" of a Winnebago chief. The chief begins the ceremony by taking a deep draft from the pipe and blowing the smoke into Agoston's face. Agoston starts to cough and tears fill his eyes. He is about to get up when one of the guards orders him to take the pipe and blow the smoke at the person sitting next to him. Earlier, the chief had welcomed the visitors with hearty promises of hospitality and an equally hearty warning that if they did not behave according to the local customs, he would engage them in "mortal combat" and take their scalps. Remembering the chief's warning, Agoston and his companions dutifully accept the pipe as it passes round the circle, alternately drawing the smoke into their lungs and blowing it in the faces of their companions. When the pipe again returns to Agoston, he is obliged to repeat the ritual a second time, but he has become dizzy and cold sweat is running down his face. The wigwam is whirling, and he sees Doctor Roges slump down, apparently overcome by the smoke. Now willing to risk his scalp, Agoston jumps up, tries without success to revive the doctor, and staggers outside, where he rushes to a lake near by and throws himself into the water. After a few minutes, he is sufficiently revived to go back inside for another round of smoke. Agoston reports that the Indians smoked kinikkinik, "which was made from the bark of a certain root." "The bark of the sapling is peeled off," Agoston explains, "dried in the sun, crushed into powder, and smoked. It has the strength of hot paprika and a similar color." Agoston describes a similar experience with the Sauk and Fox, though by this time he has become used to the strong Indian tobacco and does not react so violently to the pipe.

After leaving the Sauk and the Fox, Agoston and his companions find their way along the shore of "Lake Nissisene," and thence to the Arkansas River, which takes them through country occupied by Winnebago, Chippewa, Menominee, and "Rade-Yakate" Indians to Fort Smith, an Army post on the Arkansas River.

Near the end of the account of his Indian journey, Agoston offers his Hungarian readers some general comments on the Indians and their society. Though he had not approved of everything he saw and heard in Indian country, he clearly admired the native Americans:

I am no longer as surprised as I was at first that the French were able to take Indian wives and spend their whole lives among the Indians. These people are not as terrifying and cruel as so many describe them; one can sleep more safely among them than he can at home in a shepherd's camp—he need not fear being killed or deprived of what the Indians consider the white man's most treasured possession, his gun. . . . One must give the Indians credit for being generous and kind to those who win their trust. It is easy to gain their affection and respect by showing them a few stratagems and tricks of war.

Agoston's story of his Indian journey is in its way quite winning— the tale of a young man who is fond of the out-of-doors, who revels in dangerous adventures, and who places a high premium on physical strength and courage. But very little of it—if anything at all—is true. The place names do not appear on any maps: there is no Otter River in Iowa; no Lake Tankora or Lake Nissisene in Iowa or any of the surrounding states. And it would be impossible to miss lakes as grand as he describes: "Tankora" is forty miles long and thirty miles wide, and has "mountains" alongside it; "Nissisene" is even grander, measuring forty miles across and seventy miles from end to end. Agoston says that it took him and his companions fully two days to ride from one side of "Nissisene" to the other. Lakes of such grand proportions cannot be concealed on maps, even the primitive maps of the trans-Mississippi West that were available in 1841; and there is no body of water even remotely approaching in size either of these fictional lakes under the latitude of forty-two degrees. Agoston correctly places the Winnebago and the Sauk and Fox on the plains in 1840, though his description of their hunting grounds more closely resembles the mixed woods and prairies of Wisconsin than the broad and treeless plains of Iowa and Kansas. There are no "mountains" on the plains, or even hills that could be likened to mountains.

Agoston's Indians are an appealing lot, and some of his descriptions of Indian camps are compelling. His story of the smoking of the "peace pipe," although perhaps overdramatized, rings true; and the Indians did smoke a substance called kinikkinik (or more properly "kinnikinnick") in their pipes. *Kinnikinnick* is an Algonquian word for "mixture" and was commonly used by tribes throughout the north-central states to describe a powder of red osier bark, mixed with sumac or small green leaves and smoked in pipes. But the word was familiar in Wisconsin in 1840 and 1841 and Agoston could well have learned it there.[2] However, his use of the word "wigwam" to describe the Indians' houses is probably incorrect. It is true that the Winnebago were recent arrivals from the woodlands of Wisconsin, and also true that some of their dwellings (oven-shaped houses covered with earth) resembled the wigwams of the Northeastern Indians. But the portable "tepee" (or "tipi") covered with buffalo skins was the most common style of Indian dwelling on the Plains when Agoston visited there, and that word would probably have been more descriptive of the dwelling in which he smoked kinikkinik.

These details aside, however, Agoston's Indians have the look and feel of stage characters. In camp, they deliver ponderous speeches, and on the trail they are almost unbelievably observant. The influence of James Fenimore Cooper is obvious in these passages. Cooper was the most popular American novelist of the period, and Agoston—like countless Americans and well-educated Europeans—had read and enjoyed his stories of Indians on the trail, mostly in New York and Canada but also on the Great Plains.[3] Cooper's Indians were notable for their powers of observation. A crushed tuft of grass, a broken twig, a limb with an unnatural crook in it—each of these things was, to Cooper's Indians, the clue to a whole panoply of observations—who had passed by that day (or two weeks earlier), whether white man or red, friendly or hostile, small or large.

In one scene Agoston invests his half-breed scout with the powers of one of Cooper's Indians. The travelers have been traversing the shores of "Lake Tankora" when the scout announces matter-of-factly, "There are Winnebago nearby, and within the hour we will see some of them." Agoston and his companions ask the scout to share the source of his remarkable information. "Can't you see the signs?" he asks, pointing to the ground. The white men carefully examine the grass and leaves beneath their feet, but they see nothing out of the ordinary. "Look," the scout continues, "an Indian went by here, a man, and I would even add that he was young and in a hurry." A little later he says: "Oho! Two women passed here with a child about nine years old. Soon we shall reach their camp. They were fishing, and I can see that they did not return empty-handed." Half an hour later, as the travelers emerge from the brush into a sparse forest of oak, the scout proclaims, "There they are, as I told you." The white men look up and see a party of four Indians, a man, two women, and a nine- or ten-year-old child, just returning from a fishing trip. Pressed by the white travelers, the scout explains the "secret" of his amazing perception:

I could tell that a man went by, for I saw his tracks on the leaves. I noticed that the leaves were crushed, which focused my attention on them. I observed that they were crushed one step apart, and therefore not by a falling tree or rolling stone. Furthermore I saw that they were crushed only by the heel and tip of a foot. An older man walking more slowly would have planted his entire foot and left it longer on the ground, and not exerted pressure only with his heel and toes. That the young man was after something in a hurry and not looking at the ground I deduced from the visible track on the side of a fallen tree and the torn moss, which indicated clearly enough that he stumbled and fell over the tree. The presence of the three others was easy to discern, for there were two sets of large footprints and one set of small ones. The outward turn of the large prints showed that they were made by women, for a man's prints always turn inward, or at least straight. That they were not empty-handed I could see from the crushed twigs here and there, and fish scales next to the tracks showed that they were carrying fish. That they passed here not long ago I suspected from the presence of crushed particles of leaves, which yesterday's wind would surely have blown away. And, finally, while you were laughing at me in the brush, I was watching the tops of the bushes closely and saw them moving. I could tell from the motion that at least three persons were causing it. This is my entire secret, and I do not consider it an accomplishment at all. Had you paid closer attention to everything, you would have known as much as I did.

Agoston ascribes the scout's acuteness to his Indian blood: "We were not a little surprised at this simple explanation, but of one thing we were certain: no white man could have drawn the same conclusions. Instinct and experience were required."

The scene is almost pure Cooper. Agoston's Hungarian biographer, Zoltán Sztáray, was the first to comment on the similarities between Agoston's Indian tale and Fenimore Cooper's novels: "There is almost nothing left out; there are rattlesnakes, deer-hunting, caves, harnessing of wild horses, calumets and the offering of Indian wives and girls for the grown-ups; and there is bear-hunting as well."[4]

Sztáray discovered an even more curious source for another of

Agoston's stories.[5] Daniel Defoe's *Adventures of Robinson Crusoe* contains an exciting account of a bear hunt conducted in the foothills of the French Pyrenees sometime in the middle of the seventeenth century. In Defoe's story, the bear is provoked when Crusoe's Man Friday throws a stone at him. The bear responds by chasing Friday up an oak tree and out onto a limb. Friday advances to the end of the branch, which bends toward the ground and permits him to jump to safety. The bear, now furious, retreats to the center of the tree and begins to inch its way down the trunk. As the bear is almost at the ground, Friday is waiting with his flintlock; he claps the muzzle into the bear's ear and shoots him "dead as a stone."[6] Replace the American plains for the Pyrenees, a sturdy Iowa or Kansas oak for a French oak, a Winnebago chief for a canny South Sea Islander, and a tomahawk for a flintlock, and Daniel Defoe's bear hunt becomes Agoston Haraszthy's bear hunt. The resemblance is too close to admit of any conclusion but that Agoston got his story from Defoe.[7]

Nor do Agoston's descriptions of the country ring true. A party of raw Europeans traversing the Great Plains in 1841 would not have seen mountains and huge lakes, but they would have seen rolling prairie, and they would have been quite aware of the scarcity of timber and water, at least during the hot months of summer. As Agoston himself was later to discover on his trek to California, travelers had to keep to the streams and rivers so that their animals would have water and grazing grass every night. Moreover, in this wide and empty country, far removed from the nearest outposts of civilization, Indians would have been regarded, not just as a curiosity but as a threat; massacres of whites traversing the Great Plains were far from unknown in the 1840's. Yet Agoston displays not the slightest concern for his safety or that of his companions. If he traveled as far and as long as he claims he did in 1841, he would have crossed much of what later became the states of Iowa and Kansas, perhaps a part of Missouri, and even a corner of Oklahoma. A Hungarian nobleman, a German doctor, and a British peer would have needed more than a half-breed scout to bring them through such a journey unscathed.

Finally, Agoston's own dates are enough to prove that he did not make the journey he claimed. He says he was in Haraszthy Town in

February when "Roges" and "Malgred" joined him. He says that when they arrived at Fort Smith they learned of the death of President William Henry Harrison (this occurred on April 4, 1841). Agoston further says that, from Fort Smith, he traveled on to New Orleans and across the South, thence to New York, where he embarked for his return to Hungary, without first returning to Wisconsin. Yet the Reverend T. M. Fullerton noted in his journal that Agoston was with his partner Robert Bryant on Sauk Prairie on June 23, 1841. The dates are simply irreconcilable. Agoston could not have been traveling among the Winnebago and Sauk south of the forty-second parallel when President Harrison died and still have been at Haraszthy Town in June of 1841.

Agoston may well have visited the Indians in 1841, even smoked a "friendship pipe" with a Winnebago chief, but if he did so he certainly did not venture as far from his home base in Wisconsin Territory as he wanted his Hungarian readers to believe. It is more likely that he spent some time in Indian villages in Wisconsin, or perhaps just beyond the Mississippi River; and, when it came time to leave Wisconsin for his tour of the South, traveled from Haraszthy Town to New Orleans by river boat, perhaps on his own steamer, the *Rock River*. It is known that that boat made several trips to the Louisiana city, though it is uncertain whether the trips began as early as 1841.

If Agoston's account of his journey in "Indian Country" in 1841 tells us next to nothing about the native American inhabitants of the Great Plains, it tells us a great deal about the young Hungarian who was its author. He clearly preferred an exciting story to a dull recitation of facts; he was a man who was not afraid to cut corners when corners could be cut (it was much easier to manufacture the details of Plains Indian life in the early 1840's than to painstakingly gather and record those details); and he was not a man who was overly careful about telling the truth. He was neither the first nor the last writer who was to foist off a "tall tale" on unwitting readers (Daniel Defoe was himself the author of one of the most celebrated literary hoaxes of all times, for when *Robinson Crusoe* first appeared in print it was held out—and widely accepted—as the genuine autobiography of a shipwrecked sailor). He was, however, unique in that he chose to lard an otherwise factual account of life in the United States with an interlude of sheerest fiction.

His tour through the "Indian Country" completed, Agoston's narrative turns to the more prosaic story of his journey through the American South. He says that he stayed in New Orleans only long enough to gather the "necessary data" for his book. "Doctor Roges" and "Lord Malgred" stayed with him for a time, and then left for their own destinations. The traveling companions toasted each other in champagne on the night of their parting. "We were so used to each other," Agoston says, "it was as if we had spent a lifetime together; this proves how a long and hazardous journey can cause even total strangers to become close. Before we said good-bye we promised each other to write whenever we had the chance; it was late at night when we parted." An emotional parting with two make-believe Europeans in an exotic American metropolis on the edge of a tropical sea—yet another example of Agoston's powers of imagination!

Agoston found the cultural diversity of New Orleans fascinating—half black, half white, with the whites divided into French, American, English, and German colonies. He noted the "splendid houses, built in good taste," but he did not find the city attractive: the streets were "narrow, untidy, and muddy," and many were "unpaved." Life in the French Quarter, he wrote, was "quite different from the American": "The French here are forever looking for amusement and spend little time working, while the industrious Americans are always busy." He found "any number of luxuriously furnished bordellos" and cocottes "as bold as their counterparts in Paris and London." Gambling and nightlong carousing were common, and morals were looser than in any other American city, even New York. The lax morals of the French were, he concluded rather smugly, "the natural consequence of idleness."

Agoston's American journey continued across the south to Florida. He went east by train to Lake Pontchartrain, where he boarded a steamer for a daylong voyage to Mobile, Alabama. After a brief tour, he took another steamer up the Mobile River to Montgomery, and then went on by train to Fort Gaines, on the line that divides Alabama and Georgia. He spent some time with the officers at Gaines, who accompanied him on a trip to nearby Fort Scott, then took a stagecoach to Jacksonville, on the St. Johns River, less than twenty-five miles from Florida's Atlantic Coast.

Before Agoston and his cousin Charles Halasz read Captain Marryat's travel diary about Wisconsin, they had intended to visit Florida, so Agoston was curious to learn as much as he could about the state that might have been his home. He was disappointed, particularly by the weather: "Florida is described by most travelers as a paradise with a healthy climate of perpetual spring. I did not find it so. During my entire stay I suffered day and night from the cruel and unbearable heat." He thought the swampy land under much of Florida explained why the United States Army had been so unsuccessful in its efforts to oust the Seminole Indians from the territory. For nearly nine years, soldiers had fought a kind of guerrilla war with the Seminoles, who always seemed to elude their pursuers: "This war has so far cost the Union thirty-five million dollars and numerous casualties; most of the latter fell victim, not to the Indians, but to the climate."

He spent some time in Jacksonville, then headed north through the coastal city of St. Augustine to Savannah, Georgia, and on by train to Charleston, South Carolina, where he spent an enjoyable week. He liked Charleston's tree-lined streets, well-tended gardens, and fine private homes, "luxurious and built in good taste," and the letters of introduction he had obtained in New York and Saratoga gave him ready entrance into the city's busy social life: "I believe Charleston is the most hospitable city in the Union. In its many social gatherings I met many highly educated and intelligent individuals. Social contact is characterized by a lack of excessive formality, which makes it all the more warm and friendly."

From Charleston he went by ocean steamer to Wilmington, North Carolina, where he boarded a train for a long trip through Virginia to George Washington's home at Mount Vernon, on the south shore of the Potomac River. He toured the grounds of the estate and paused to gaze at the modest marble slab that marked Washington's grave. He noted that the inscription on the slab read simply, "I am the resurrection and the life," but added: "Washington's memory is engraved with indelible letters of love and gratitude in the hearts of all Americans." From Mount Vernon, it was a short trip to Alexandria, where he visited a museum dedicated to Washington, and another short trip across the Potomac to Washington, capital of the "North American Free States."

In his book Agoston gives an elaborate description of the Capitol and a shorter description of the "president's national residence" at the other end of Pennsylvania Avenue. He comments on the layout of the city, with avenues radiating out from the Capitol and opening up splendid vistas to the north, south, east, and west; but the total effect of all the buildings, monuments, and streets seemed to him curiously empty—a city waiting to be peopled: "Anyone who expects Washington, the capital of the Union, to be a large and beautiful city will be disappointed, for he will find mostly empty streets, with two or three houses built next to each other, followed by vacant lots. The area of Washington is vast and could easily contain as many as 600,000 people, yet in 1840 the population was 23,364." He attributed the city's small population to lack of commerce: "Americans will not live where they cannot profitably invest their money."

Agoston sat in on some lively debates in Congress, had an audience with Secretary of State Daniel Webster, and may also have met with the Grand Old Man of the United States Senate, Henry Clay.[8] He also called on President John Tyler, the courtly Virginian who had succeeded to the chief executive's office on the death of William Henry Harrison. He was wearing his Hungarian noble uniform when he presented himself to Tyler. The President and his associates were impressed by the uniform, but they wondered why a man would wear two coats at the same time, and were puzzled by the unusual belt. All agreed, however, that there was no more "splendid and glamorous uniform than the Hungarian." A few days after his introduction to the president, Agoston was invited to a presidential soiree. Friends informed him that Tyler would like him to wear his Hungarian uniform, since many ladies would be present and they would be curious to see it. Agoston complied, but he was uncomfortably aware the whole evening that all eyes were "riveted" on him.

Agoston had planned to go from Washington to Baltimore, but while he was in the capital he received a letter from Robert Bryant advising him that he and his wife were in New York and asking Agoston to join them there. Soon after his arrival in New York, Agoston fell ill—of cholera, he later explained, induced by eating "spoiled lobster." Bryant purchased some goods to take back to Haraszthy Town and he and his wife left New York for Wisconsin. Agoston retired to Hamilton Jackson's Long Island estate to convalesce. When he had regained his strength, he set out to complete his tour of the "Free States": Philadelphia, the country around Wilmington, Delaware, and Baltimore.

Agoston's experiences in Baltimore deepened his favorable impressions of American industry. The Maryland city was relatively young, but it was already an important commercial center, and it was sophisticated: "The theaters are always full. Sparkling masked balls and other entertainments are common, and on summer evenings I noticed more strollers on the promenades than I had in any other large city." Philadelphia, home of Benjamin Franklin, the Declaration of Independence, and the Constitution, impressed him not only with its cultural roots and progressive public institutions but also with its well-ordered plan: "The streets run parallel from river to river, intersecting at right angles with those running north to south. This gives the city a pleasing form, and one can easily find any place in any part of it." He was amazed by the public water system, which took water from the Schuylkill River, pumped it uphill to a massive reservoir and, through a maze of lead pipes, delivered it to public buildings and private houses all over the city. "In every building," he noted, "even in churches and towers, and in almost every room in private houses, pipes are installed so that all one has to do to get ice-cold water is turn on the faucet."

His return to New York gave him another opportunity to marvel at the wonders of America's largest city. He climbed a flight of stairs to the roof of Castle Garden in the Battery, where tables and benches were set out for the convenience of visitors, and contemplated the magnificent vista that spread all around him. He described the spacious bay and harbor, the quarantine station for immigrants, Governor's Island with its powerful fort designed to protect the city from naval attack, and, beyond it, rocky Bedloe's Island; to the west, on the Hudson's opposite shore, was Jersey City, and to the south Brooklyn rose on heights from the banks of the East River, much as Buda rose from the banks of the Danube opposite Pest.

It was now late autumn. The tour concluded and a few business affairs attended to, Agoston was impatient to see his family and home again and determined to book passage on a ship without delay. As he prepared for his return to Hungary, he began to reflect on the impulses that had brought him to the United States. In his book he was to state them quite simply:

Originally I had come to America for one reason only—namely, to see this blessed country for myself. The thought of acquiring property and settling here had never entered my mind. I do not deny that I had entertained hopes of establishing commercial relations between my homeland and North America. My experiences here convinced me that there was a real possibility for these hopes to materialize, as a number of the products of my country are needed in the United States—our hemp, heavy linens, flour sacks, heavy blankets, wine, and so on. I overlooked no opportunity to inform interested parties or to organize a company for this purpose. My efforts were successful inasmuch as three wholesale houses accepted my proposals, and promised that one of their representatives would travel to the capital of my country next year and look me up. Should he find that the prices of the above articles are competitive, an annual trade of more than a million dollars could result.

This passage is interesting not only for what it says but for what it does not say. There is no hint here of political oppression; no suggestion of a desire to escape an oppressive government, or of a longing to trade a life without freedom for a new life in a land of liberty. Nor is there any mention of diplomatic intercession to enable him to return home.

After Agoston's death, his son Arpad would perpetuate a multitude of myths about his father and the Haraszthy family. In the manuscript he wrote for Hubert Howe Bancroft in 1886, Arpad stated that his father was able to return to Hungary only because he had in his possession "valuable state papers" that the Austrian government wished to have returned. Arpad said that General Lewis Cass, longtime governor of the Michigan Territory (which at one time included Wisconsin) and, in 1841, American minister to France, had interceded in Agoston's behalf with the Austrian authorities. They granted him permission to return to Hungary for one year, with Cass holding the "state papers" to guarantee his safe return to the United States.[9]

There is no indication in any of the published biographies of Lewis Cass that he engaged in negotiations with the Hapsburg government in 1841. Furthermore, since he was then in Paris,[10] it is unlikely that he would have had anything to do with the return home of a Hungarian who had bought property in Wisconsin. Cass had served as Secretary of War under Andrew Jackson, was to receive the Democratic nomination for President of the United States in 1848, and was to serve as Secretary of State under James Buchanan in the late 1850's. He was a real man of affairs, and if he helped Agoston negotiate his return to Hungary in 1841, that detail would not necessarily have been recorded by his biographers, and the absence of any reference to the negotiations in published sources should not be taken as proof that there were none.

A better indication that Arpad's tale of the "state papers" was false is Agoston's own account of his return to Hungary, which contains not the slightest hint that there were political complications. It would, of course, be unreasonable to expect explicit statements of this kind in a book designed to be published under the noses of the Hapsburgs. But if Agoston had been a political fugitive, as he later claimed — if his return to his homeland had been the result of diplomatic maneuvers, as Arpad later stated — there should be some hint of the fact in the book. There is none. On the contrary, Agoston's own account of his return is wholly inconsistent with the stories that he and his son later told. He was anxious to see his home and his family after an absence of nearly two years. He booked passage on a ship in New York, and set sail. All the evidence indicates that it was as simple as Agoston himself declared it to be in his book.

His friends had advised him against attempting to cross the ocean so late in the year, for the winter often brought dangerous storms to the north Atlantic. But he reveled in the thought of courting danger and eagerly booked passage on the packet boat *Ontario*, set to leave New York for Plymouth on December 4, 1841.[11] Some of the friends were on hand as the packet pushed away from the dock and was towed fourteen miles out to sea by the steamer *Hercules*. Then it hoisted its sails and, in a full wind, moved vigorously toward the north and east. Agoston, as usual, was on deck, scanning the horizon. As the wind grew stronger, the sails puffed up like clouds and the coastline of New York gradually disappeared from view.

Agoston's second Atlantic voyage might have seemed like something of an anticlimax if the *Ontario* had not been stricken by a severe storm about halfway across. He later described the tempest in almost melodramatic terms, regaling his readers with a thrilling tale of raging winds and crashing waves. At one point, the storm became so severe that a torrent of water broke through the ceiling of the dining hall, splintering wood, glass, and everything else in its way. For a while it seemed as if all the passengers and crew would be "washed overboard," but after thirty-six hours the storm broke. The *Ontario* arrived at Portsmouth harbor on December 26. Agoston went up to London, where he spent four days, and on January 1, 1842, he departed again for Ostend. A week of travel across Germany and Austria brought him to Vienna, where he spent another four days attending to his "affairs," and then set out for Pest. He spent a few days in the Hungarian city, and then hurried south to the Bácska and "the welcoming arms" of his loved ones.

Agoston left no personal account of the circumstances of his return to his family, except that he had notified them from London of his "pending arrival" and that they were "overjoyed at my homecoming." Eleonora and his parents must have been very happy to see him again after an absence of almost two years, yet there must also have been some tense moments; a lot can happen in two years. On June 28, 1840, only four months after his departure, Eleonora had given birth to his third son. In his absence she had gone down to Futtak from Kútas to stay with the Dedinszkys, and it was in Futtak that the baby was born and christened. His baptismal names were, in Latin, Franciscus Xaverius Arpadus Petrus Paulus and, in Hungarian, Ferencz Xavér Árpád Péter Pál. His godfather was his maternal grandfather, Ferencz Xaverius Dedinszky, the superintendent of the Futtak estate.[12] This boy would be known in his family as Arpad. If the baby felt any sense of deprivation because his father was absent during most of the first two years of his life, Agoston must have done much to compensate for that deprivation in the months and years to follow, for he and Arpad were to forge a close bond—nearly as close at the bond that tied Agoston and Károly; and years after his death Arpad was to declare that he held his father's memory "sacred."[13]

Agoston surely had returned to Hungary from his trip to the

United States with a clear course of action mapped out. First, he had committed himself to write a book about his American adventures. In Pest, he sounded out interest in the project, and found a publisher named Gusztáv Heckenast who was interested in taking it on. Heckenast was one of Pest's best-known publishers, with a popular lending library, a well-stocked bookstore, and a busy printing press all located on Váczi Street in one of the city's principal business districts.[14] Whether Agoston had completed any part of the manuscript by the time he arrived back in the Bácska is not known, but he must have had a mountain of notes, tables, and other data, because the book that he eventually produced was full of statistics about political, religious, social, and, above all, economic institutions in the United States.

It is also apparent that he had decided that his return to Hungary would only be a short trip, for he had firmly committed himself to a permanent life in the United States. He had probably informed Eleonora and his parents of his plans even before he came back. They may or may not have agreed before his return that they would pull up stakes and join him in America, but they did so soon after. Property had to be sold, travel arrangements made, good-byes said. But these things were all accomplished in good order, and barely six months after Agoston's return to the Bácska, his wife, his children, his mother, and his father were ready to join him on a return trip to the "Free States."

In the manuscript he wrote for Hubert Howe Bancroft, Arpad Haraszthy claimed that the Haraszthy estates in Hungary "were all confiscated." This claim was consistent with a return to Hungary under the diplomatic protection of General Lewis Cass, but not at all consistent with Agoston's own account of his return home, or of his arrangements to have his book published by Gusztáv Heckenast in Pest. If the Hapsburgs had agreed to let this "fugitive" from royal justice return to his country for a limited purpose, how was he able to contract openly for the publication of a book in Pest? Arpad noted that his father was able to salvage "the sum of about $200,000" which he had "settled" upon Eleonora at the time of their marriage, and also able to salvage "a large portion of the family plate and paintings."[15]

This, too, is puzzling. Certainly Agoston was able to bring treasured family belongings with him when he left Hungary, but there
was never any such sum of money as Arpad suggested. In 1842,
the sum of $200,000 would have been truly stupendous, enough to
qualify its possessor as one of the richest men in the United States.
The circumstances under which Agoston and Robert Bryant laid the
foundations for Haraszthy Town, and the subsequent life that the
Haraszthys led on Sauk Prairie, do not suggest any such fortune. But
Arpad was only two years old when the events took place, so the account he left years later could have been a family tale, told by his
father and perhaps embellished in the retelling. The conclusion is
nearly inescapable that this tale of the $200,000, like the tale of the
"valuable state papers," the tale of Lewis Cass's diplomatic "intercession" with the Hapsburgs, and the daring raid that Agoston made
on the prison at Peter Wardein, was apocryphal, another link in the
long chain of misrepresentations that would eventually form the Haraszthy Legend.

What is consistent is Agoston's enthusiasm and confidence. These
are evident in the book he submitted to Gusztáv Heckenast for publication, and there is little reason to wonder that his family was so
easily persuaded to turn their backs on their centuries-old Hungarian heritage. In the book, *Utazás Éjszakamerikában*, or *Travels in
North America*, Agoston is effusive in his praise for the institutions
and values of this "magical land" that never ceased to amaze European visitors. He thought that Hungarian travelers, who approached
all other countries with a certain smugness, were destined to have
their eyes opened as they moved through the "Free States." Nothing
seemed impossible to Americans, he said, and they pursued their
goals with a determination and energy that merited the admiration
and envy of the whole world.

Like Sándor Bölöni Farkas ten years earlier, Agoston thought
that Hungarians could learn a great deal from Americans. Farkas was
concerned largely with American political institutions and values,
while Agoston focused almost exclusively on economic life.[16] He was,
of course, a great admirer of American freedom, but he saw the real
flowering of that freedom in the economic vitality of the American
people:

Nowhere else will the traveler find so few idlers. . . . From early youth, everybody is engaged in commerce, agriculture, or some craft, and pursues it with passionate fervor. This vast country with all its freedoms is open to all, and all can freely choose to engage in any undertaking. The American does not have to ask permission to build railroads, canals, steamboats, machinery, factories, and the like. He is not hindered by two or three monopolies which try to suppress everybody who attempts to compete, to the great disadvantage of society.

Competition was the foundation stone of American enterprise. Whereas Europeans were inclined to regard competition as destructive, Americans saw it as a propelling and even purifying force. Competition resulted in lower freight rates on railroads and steamboats and made it possible for many people who could not otherwise afford to travel by these means to make full use of them.

He noted sharp contrasts between American cities and towns and their European counterparts. In American cities, unlike those of Hungary, it was not common to see fine carriages running up and down the streets for the apparent purpose of making a show. American cities were crowded, "but mostly with people diligently going about their business."[17] He thought that most Americans lived in modest but comfortable circumstances. There were wealthy families, of course, many of whom lived outside the larger cities in "handsome houses built in good taste, usually located on river banks and surrounded by beautiful gardens." But even America's wealthiest citizens did not lead the idle lives of European aristocrats but continued to be active and productive long after they acquired their fortunes.

He defended his adopted country against the charge that it was ruled by a "money aristocracy":

I really do not know how to answer this charge, or even what is meant by it. Is it meant that there are rich people here who wear fine clothes and live better than the poor, who travel in fine coaches instead of on foot, who have beautiful homes and keep lovely horses? I pose this question to these writers: What do the wealthy have to do to be the equal of the poor? Should they distribute their hard-earned money among those who have none? Should they live in the same kind of houses, keep the same poor table, drink water instead of wine, wear the same coarse clothes? Why did they work, why did they struggle, if not to enjoy the fruits of their labor?

He also rejected out of hand the common European notion that America's "money aristocracy" enjoyed legal and political privileges that their poorer fellow citizens did not. In every legal sense, he declared, the poor were "completely the equal of the richest man," indeed, "more than equal, for it is common knowledge that many of the rich do not bother to vote, whereas the poor are proud of the franchise and do not easily forgo its exercise (just as the minor nobility at home would not miss the election of officials). The difference is that here a vote cannot be bought for a drink or money, for the American, thanks to his upbringing, is far too proud to sell his right."

He noted, too, that wealthy Americans did not seem to be ashamed of their "poor relations":

Why should they be? All have equal rights and social standing. . . . Everybody here is equal, and all equally concentrate on a single goal: wealth (which is pursued not so much for social distinction as for the comfort and contentment money can provide its possessor and his loved ones). Everybody works ceaselessly, day and night, to reach this goal, which can only be achieved through individual efforts and not through influence of family connections. . . . Beyond the ocean millions pay tribute to a select few; but here a man pays tribute only to himself.

Obviously, some of Agoston's high praise for America and its people was prompted by a desire to promote his and Bryant's fledgling "city" on the Wisconsin frontier. He extolled the prairie—and scorned the South, whose summer heat and humidity made it generally unsuitable for European settlement. He also dismissed available agricultural land in the South as too low and marshy to be profitably cultivated, since all the best farming land had already been claimed.

He touted Wisconsin as the ideal site for European settlement in the United States. The ready availability of fertile land, the abundance of woods and navigable rivers, and the low prices set by the government for land purchases were all good reasons to favor the northwestern territory over other parts of the country. But he warned his readers that there was no paradise anywhere in America, and that any European who contemplated pulling up stakes and crossing the Atlantic should do so only after a careful appraisal of the opportunities and the problems of life in the new country:

There are so many impatient people who, when a rose does not bloom quickly enough, think that it never will. Their restlessness drives them from one place to another, and ultimately they end up discontented and cursing their fate. Although I am convinced that any sober-minded person could establish his future happiness and even affluence in the United States without too great an effort . . . I would not recommend the attempt to anyone who is without determination and a stout heart.

Agoston's *Travels in North America* was not published for more than two years after his return to Hungary. This delay suggests that the job of assembling the notes, tables, and other information he had gathered in the United States was not easy. No doubt he had to acquire some of the data necessary to complete the book by mail, perhaps through the publisher. But the book that Gusztáv Heckenast issued in Pest in the final days of 1844 was impressive. It ran to more than 550 pages and was published in a set of two volumes, each containing a frontispiece steel-engraving (the City of Albany in volume one and the Capitol in Washington in volume two). The book was offered in three different bindings — softcover, hardcover, and a hardcover that combined the two volumes in one book.[18]

On January 16, 1845, citizens of Pest were advised of the publication of the book by the *Pesti Hirlap* (Pest Gazette), a widely read newspaper established by Lajos Kossuth as the voice of progressivism in Hungary.[19] The *Hirlap* noted that it was only the second book about the United States published in Hungarian and expressed the opinion that Hungarian readers would look far to find a "more entertaining or instructive" volume. After summarizing Agoston's travels through the country (including his sojourn in "Indian country"), the newspaper pointed out some of the book's amazing statistics. The *Hirlap* was impressed by the rapid growth of the American population, particularly in the western states and territories, and noted that there was not one country in Europe in which the population was growing at a similar rate. A second article in the same newspaper three days later summarized some of Agoston's views on the American economy.[20] It thought that the trade the United States carried on with foreign countries was "fantastic," and although it attributed at least part of that trade to the country's favorable geographical situation, it conceded Agoston's argument that the "energy" of the American people was in large part responsible for the country's prosperity. It agreed that the freedom of Americans to move about the country was really "a great liberty," but it also noted that the country, though young, had already established a thriving educational system, with more than 1,000 colleges, 3,000 high schools, and 42,000 elementary schools. It was a truly remarkable achievement, and one that older countries like Hungary could only envy.[21]

We have no contemporary accounts of the popular reaction to *Travels in North America*, though later comments by Hungarian writers indicated that it was enthusiastic. They said that the book had a "sparkling effect" on the Hungarian people (at least those Hungarians who were inclined to read a book about the United States) and that "a free spirit imbued its every line."[22] One Hungarian writer has recently estimated that the book sold some 2,000 copies, a substantial enough number in a country in which the literate population was small.[23] Gusztáv Heckenast must have been satisfied with these sales, for in 1850 he issued the book in a second printing called a "popular edition," which was offered at a lower price than the original and attracted a whole new class of readers.

Some of these new readers were the young, who, like Defoe's and Cooper's readers, found fiction more exciting than facts. Proving, perhaps, the power of the tale told, the factual portions of Agoston's book were quickly overtaken by the tide of events, and the statistical portions soon became outdated, but his story of the Indians seemed to have a timeless quality. The three chapters about the Indian country were eventually reprinted as a separate volume for young readers,[24] and a generation of Hungarian boys grew up reading of the American Indians in the pages of a book written years earlier by an adventurous Hungarian nobleman from the Bácska. As late as the 1980's, portions of the Indian story were still in print in Hungary, and still amusing (if not delighting) Hungarian readers.[25]

6

A Home
on the
Prairie

The enthusiasm that Agoston expressed for the United States, both in his book and in his private conversations with his family, must have impressed his father. Károly, after all, had traveled widely in Europe, and he was open to progressive ideas. Agoston had gone to America to "see for himself," and he had returned a true believer in the American dream. Károly cannot have failed to feel a sense of pride and excitement as Agoston explained how he had founded a "city" on the Wisconsin prairie, how he had built a mill in the wilderness and purchased a steamboat to carry goods and passengers on the Wisconsin River. Károly was willing, perhaps even eager, to join his son in America. For Eleonora, the move to America would have been far less easy: it could well mean that she would never again see her parents, or her sisters and brothers. Anna Mária Haraszthy, Agoston's mother, a middle-aged woman who had been brought up in Hungarian traditions and customs, was so fearful that she consulted a gypsy fortune-teller. The fortune-teller told her that she would join her family in their epic migration, but would die in the new country.[1]

Despite the gypsy's forebodings, the Haraszthys made all the arrangements necessary to complete their emigration to the United States. They left the Bácska for the last time in the late spring or early

summer of 1842 and, probably following the same route that Agoston and his cousin had taken in 1840, went through Vienna, crossed
Bohemia and northern Germany, and arrived in London sometime
in July. On July 31 they left the English capital on the ship *Philadelphia,* bound for New York. There were eight in their party: Agoston,
Eleonora, Károly, Anna Mária, the three children—eight-year-old
Géza, seven-year-old Attila, and Arpad, who had just turned two—
and a servant.[2] After a crossing of almost two months, the *Philadelphia* arrived at New York on September 28. The Haraszthys were at
the top of the list of distinguished passengers noted in the *New York
Herald*'s report of the voyage.[3]

No records have been found of the family's route from New York
to Wisconsin. Because it was late in the year and winter was already
descending on the upper Middle West, they may well have avoided
the Great Lakes route that Agoston followed to Wisconsin in 1840,
choosing instead a more southerly route through Pennsylvania to the
Ohio River, thence by boat to the southwestern corner of Wisconsin.
Whatever route they selected, they would have arrived on the Sauk
Prairie late in 1842 or in the early part of 1843.

It was not the best time of the year for the family to be introduced to their new home. The winter of 1842–43 was one of the most
severe the upper Middle West had experienced in several years. Beginning about the middle of November, heavy snow fell along the
Wisconsin River, in the streets of Haraszthy Town, and on Agoston's
fields at the edge of Sauk Prairie, at some places reaching a depth
of four feet. The white blanket that covered the land was undisturbed until New Year's Day, when thunderclouds moved over the
prairie, discharging torrents of rain, melting the snow, and sending
floodwaters through the town. The water had scarcely run off before
another heavy snowstorm came, and the prairie was buried under
a second blanket of white until May. A young Swiss named Oswald
Ragatz, who had recently settled with his family on the western edge
of Sauk Prairie, remembered the rigors of the winter of 1842–43 for
years afterward: "Merciless cold pressed down upon a hapless world.
I have never known the like of it since. . . . Animals in town died in
large numbers. Several trees near us split open. Although our cabin
was heated by a fireplace at one end and a cook stove at the other,

and both were kept going full blast, the water bucket, standing on the table between them, was usually frozen over. . . . We most surely would have perished had it not been for the heavy featherbeds which we had brought along and in which we now spent most of our time, fully clothed." [4]

It is not hard to imagine the reaction of Eleonora, Anna Mária, and Károly Haraszthy when they first entered Haraszthy Town and approached Agoston's house facing the Wisconsin River. Although settlers on the prairie may have seen some beauty in the structure, it must have appeared quite different to cultured Europeans who were used to stone houses on the Danube. A Tyrolean priest, Father Maximilian Gärtner, who saw the house for the first time almost four years later, was decidedly unimpressed: he likened it to an "ordinary summerhouse in a German garden." [5] But then Gärtner was even less impressed by the log cabins the first settlers had built on the prairie, comparing them to "common hayricks in Tyrol." [6]

The whole family settled in to the same house. They cannot have been comfortable, particularly when it came time for Eleonora to give birth to another baby. She managed to be absent from the prairie in the fall of 1843, for in October of that year, somewhere in central Illinois, she gave birth to her fourth child and first daughter, a baby who was named Ida Helena. [7] The reason for Eleonora's absence from the prairie at the time of Ida's birth has never been explained: perhaps the family was traveling when Eleonora's time arrived and she had no choice but to stop and give birth; more likely, the absence of a resident doctor on Sauk Prairie prompted her to seek some more civilized place where she could give birth to her child with professional supervision. If contemporary records of the new baby's birth were kept, they have since been lost. [8] When she grew to adulthood, Ida Haraszthy would recall that she was born on October 5, 1843, at a place called "Imperial," Illinois; her brother Arpad remembered that her birth took place in Peoria. [9]

As they went about their business on Sauk Prairie, Agoston and Károly seemed inseparable. William H. Clark, a New York–born lawyer who had settled on the prairie during Agoston's absence in Hungary, became a friend and admirer of both Haraszthys and in later years left a tender recollection of the relationship between them. "In the structure of their minds," Clark wrote, "in their habits, tastes and dispositions, they were the very antipodes of each other, as unlike as ever could be. Nevertheless their attachment for each other was unbounded. Naught but death would separate them; where went the son, there accompanied or followed the father. In sunshine and in storm, through good and evil report alike, he cherished '*Mein son Augusta,*' as he called him."[10]

Although Károly Haraszthy was scarcely past fifty when he arrived in Wisconsin, he seems to have been regarded by most of the settlers as an old man. They called him "the old Count" or, in deference to his military experience, "the General" or "old General."[11] But references to his age may be taken more as evidence that the frontier was a young man's world than that Károly was decrepit. He took an active interest in his son's business affairs, and invested his own money in Haraszthy enterprises. Allowing for differences in his and his son's personalities, Károly was vigorous enough, and his intelligence and good education made an impression among the settlers. William Clark was struck by his command of languages. He thought that Károly had mastered the sciences through the medium of Latin, which he spoke even before he learned Hungarian, and remembered that he applied himself to the study of English soon after his arrival in Wisconsin. "After he had mastered it sufficiently to communicate his ideas intelligibly," Clark said, "a more entertaining and agreeable companion could not be found."[12]

Because many of the first settlers on Sauk Prairie were of German birth or, like the Haraszthys, came from countries in which German was commonly spoken, much of the early business and social life was carried on in that language. Soon after his arrival on the prairie, Károly Haraszthy became "Karl" to the Germans and "Charles" to the Americans. The first recorded documents in which his name appears identify him as "Charles Haraszthy," the anglicized name he was to use for most of the rest of his life.[13] (His grandson Géza was also to anglicize his name to "Gaza." Agoston, in contrast, appears never to have anglicized his given name, despite the persistent efforts of Germans to call him "Augustin" and Americans to transform him into "Augustine," "Augustus," or "Agostin.")

Eleonora Haraszthy may have had more difficulty adjusting to the frontier than her father-in-law. An American woman named Eliza Bull talked with Eleonora a few years after she arrived at Sauk Prairie and suggested that she did not take quickly or easily to life in Wisconsin. She refused to receive visitors for months after her arrival, Mrs. Bull said, and, at twilight, often sat at her parlor window, gazing silently into the wilderness outside. From that window she could see the river, and the wolves that sometimes came down to the riverbank for water. Mrs. Bull related that the family was once startled in the night by piercing cries and found a poor woman with a child at their door. The woman had been terrified by what she took as signs of "an impending Indian attack," and, since her husband was absent, had run several miles through the snow to seek protection at the Haraszthy house. The woman's alarm proved groundless, but her fright was real.[14]

Father Gärtner, who came to know the Haraszthys quite well after he arrived on Sauk Prairie in 1846, had a decidedly different view of Eleonora's frontier experience. He said she encountered many challenges in her early days on the prairie but met them all with courage and endurance. She "acted as a diligent German housewife," Gärtner wrote, "not as a prim American lady who only rocks herself in an easy chair and is pleased only to read newspapers and novels while her husband is chopping wood outdoors, milking the cows or driving the ox-cart to the field to fetch home his crop."[15] Eleonora impressed the priest not only with her beauty and elegant manners but also with her resourcefulness in the face of the rigors of the frontier.

Anna Mária Haraszthy remains a shadowy figure, even in Wisconsin. She was only fifty-one years old when she arrived on Sauk Prairie and could well have made an important contribution to the family's new life on the prairie. Her name appears in some of the first deeds recorded in the Haraszthy name, evidencing the fact that she was considered a co-owner of property in which her husband had an interest.[16] But after November 1, 1843, her name disappears from the real property records. The explanation is, of course, that she died. The exact date and place of her death have not been discovered. In later years her grandson Arpad could recall only that she died in 1844 or 1845, probably in Grand Gulf, Mississippi, a thriving port on the Mississippi River about twenty-five miles south of Vicksburg and

seventy-five miles north of Natchez.[17] Father Gärtner, whose recollections of the Haraszthy family's earliest years in Wisconsin were based
mainly on information received from Eleonora, stated that Agoston's
mother had contracted yellow fever in New Orleans and, while fleeing north along the Mississippi, died in St. Louis.[18] Whether Anna
Mária Haraszthy died in Grand Gulf or St. Louis, it seems likely that
she was traveling on her son's steamboat at the time she fell ill, and
that she was buried somewhere along the river, in a grave thousands
of miles from her homeland and hundreds of miles from her family's
new home in Wisconsin. The gypsy fortune-teller's prediction, delivered before she left Hungary in 1842, had sadly come true.

The Haraszthys seem to have blended well into the community
of settlers on Sauk Prairie. Agoston was always "the Count" or "the
young Count," Charles "the old Count" or "General," Eleonora "the
Countess," and Gaza, Attila, and Arpad the "young Counts."[19] But
there is no sense that the other settlers resented the family or entertained any feelings toward them other than genuine respect and affection. Gaza, Attila, and Arpad attended classes in the public school,
fished and swam in the river, and hiked in the summer across the
prairie and into the surrounding hills. For a while, they spent nearly
all their time with the Swiss boy, Oswald Ragatz, whose family lived
on a farm a few miles west of Haraszthy Town, but who came into
the village every day to attend school. Ragatz remembered that thirteen different nationalities were represented in the one-room school
where Gaza, Attila, and Arpad became his inseparable companions.[20]
It is likely that the boys spoke German, if not in their classes, at least
during recesses, and when they were playing in the streets of the
town. But Agoston knew the value of teaching English to his children
and made special efforts to see that they were properly instructed
in the prevailing language of the country. One winter, he sent his
youngest son, Arpad, to live with the American settler William Canfield and his family for the expressed purpose of learning English.[21]

Agoston resumed his business activities. With Bryant, he began
to build a brick building—the first such structure on Sauk Prairie—
to house his store. Constructed with bricks from the Haraszthy and
Bryant brickyard, it was a two-story structure with a gabled roof and

glazed windows that looked out over Water Street and the Wisconsin River. Charles Haraszthy became a regular fixture in the store, where he worked as a kind of clerk and apothecary, dispensing powders and potions to soothe the aches and pains of the townspeople.[22]

Agoston took a personal interest in his steamboat and its operations, often acting as its captain.[23] In later years, historians of Mississippi riverboats remembered that the *Rock River* was the first steamboat to carry passengers and freight on the upper Mississippi on a regular basis. Claimed "firsts" are always suspect, yet there is reason to believe that the Haraszthy steamboat was a pioneer in freight and passenger service on the great river. Lafayette H. Bunnell, a frequent traveler on the Mississippi, who himself made a trip on the *Rock River* in 1842, claimed that the Haraszthy boat was "the first steamer to venture into the unchartered trade"—that is, the first to make regularly scheduled trips on the upper river.[24] Edmond Rendtorff, who was employed for a time as clerk of the vessel, made three trips from Galena up the river as far as Fort Snelling (later Minneapolis), and another from Fort Crawford, at the mouth of the Wisconsin, to Fort Winnebago. The trip to Fort Winnebago was made to carry a contingent of U.S. Army troops who were returning from duty in the Seminole War in Florida.[25] Agoston personally commanded the boat on many of these trips and frequently brought his sons along for the ride.[26]

Though Agoston's Wisconsin River ferry was less glamorous than the steamboat, it was an important part of the transportation system on the frontier. Travelers who approached Haraszthy Town from the east all crossed the river on the ferry, and the tolls constituted a significant part of Agoston's income. The ferry that he bought from Berry Haney in 1840 was a small flatboat propelled by poles and anchored to the banks by ropes.[27] In the summer of 1843 he built a small house on the east bank and stationed a ferryman in it.[28] It was the ferryman's duty to greet travelers from Madison and beyond, load their goods and animals onto the boat, and then move the vessel slowly across the river to Haraszthy Town. The pole-driven ferry worked well enough, but it was hardly in keeping with the progressive spirit that Agoston wanted to impart to Haraszthy Town, and so he decided to replace it with a steam-powered side-wheeler. Years later, the son of one of Agoston's ferrymen recalled that the new ferry was powered by a "one-horse tread power on each side."[29] John Hawley, a teenaged boy who worked on the boat, recalled that there were two wheels, one on each side of the boat, each wheel being powered by a one-horsepower engine; Agoston got the engines from St. Louis. The boat was large enough to carry three teams of horses at a time. Agoston leased the ferry to a man named Robert Richards for a term of fourteen years but still maintained a close interest in its operations and, when problems arose with the boat, was always ready to give them his personal attention.

Hawley left a record of three incidents that happened on the ferry during the time he worked for Richards. One, which took place before the ferry was motorized, was precipitated by Gaza. Hawley had just completed a river crossing and had chained the boat to a post on the riverbank below Water Street when Agoston's oldest son walked down the bank and announced that he wanted to take the boat over to the island in the middle of the river. Hawley told Gaza that the boat was locked and he could not have it.

"It's my father's boat," Gaza reminded Hawley.

"You can't have it," Hawley said defiantly, "nor your father either."

With that, Gaza gave the Hawley boy a quick push and forced him flat on his back. Hawley later recalled that he lay still for a moment, and then pushed Gaza over on his back and "boxed his ears till he cried 'That's enough!'" Then Hawley let Gaza up and, as he started to walk away, gave him a swift kick.

As Gaza headed toward the Haraszthy house, Hawley sat down on the boat and began to think. He had kicked Count Haraszthy's son and was surely in trouble. As he looked up, he saw Agoston coming down the bank, his walking stick in hand. Agoston walked straight up to Hawley and asked him if he was the ferry boy.

"Yes, sir," Hawley answered.

"Do you know my boys?"

"Yes, sir."

"Was one of them here?"

"Yes, sir."

"Did you whip one of them?"

"Yes, sir."

"What did you do it for?"

Hawley explained that Gaza wanted to take the ferry boat to the island in the river, but Hawley refused to let him and gave him what Hawley called "a good whipping."

"You are a good boy," Agoston said, patting Hawley on the back and turning to go back to his house. As Hawley watched Agoston climb back up the bank to Water Street, he could not help thinking that Gaza probably got another "whipping" with Agoston's walking stick.

Hawley recalled another incident that occurred after Agoston had replaced the pole-driven ferry with the steam-powered sidewheeler. Hawley was on board the boat one day when one of the side-wheels disengaged from its engine and the boat started drifting downstream. Robert Richards was unprepared for the emergency.

"What shall we do?" he asked young Hawley.

"Run her on a sandbar," the boy answered smartly.

"All right," the ferryman said, quickly steering the boat toward the nearest bar.

As soon as the boat stopped, Hawley could see Agoston coming down the bank.

"What's the matter?" he shouted to Richards.

"A wheel came off," the ferryman answered.

"Go to the brickyard and get all the help you can to push the boat," Agoston countered.

Soon Agoston and five or six workmen were in a rowboat and heading out to the stranded ferry. Richards and Hawley managed to reengage the wheel and engine and, after the workmen from the brickyard pushed mightily, the ferry was back in the current. Agoston and his workmen returned to shore in the rowboat. Hawley remembers that Agoston was with his men during the whole ordeal and, as soon as the boat was securely tied to its mooring, he said, "Well, men, you got pretty wet."

"Yes," they answered.

"Now we need something to wet the inside. Go up to the store and get a quart of brandy!"

The men complied with Agoston's order, returned to the bank with the bottle, and, sharing the brandy with their employer, quickly polished it off.

"Go and get another bottle," Agoston said. And the second bottle was finished off as quickly as the first.

A third ferry incident occurred one day when Agoston's second son, Attila, was on board the boat. The ferry crew had just transported a team of horses from Haraszthy Town to the Dane County side of the river and secured it to the ferry post. While the ferrymen went up to the ferry house, Attila stayed with John Hawley and two other boys on the boat. One of the boys proposed that they take a swim in the river, and the others quickly agreed. Attila jumped from the edge of the boat, but misjudged his distance and struck his head on the edge of the vessel as he came down. He was immediately rendered unconscious. Hawley was quick to sense the peril.

"Get him out, or he'll drown," he shouted to the others.

"We can't see in the water," one of the other boys protested.

"I will fetch him out," Hawley continued, "if you will take him away from me when I come up."

The other boys quickly agreed that they would, and Hawley dived deep into the murky water. He later calculated that the river was nine feet deep at that point and that when he reached Attila on the bottom, he was rolling in the current. Hawley grabbed Attila by the hair and swam back to the surface. The other boys helped him take the still-unconscious boy to the bank, where they started rubbing his hands. Hawley started toward the boat, intending to go to town to ask for help, when the other boys announced that Attila was coming to. He began to throw up water and, after a while, announced that he was better and wanted to go back to the town.

"I'll take you in the rowboat," Hawley offered.

"No," Attila answered, "I'll take the big boat."

Years later, Hawley commented on the vastly different character of his contacts with the two Haraszthy boys. "I whipped one," he said, "and saved the life of the other," adding, "That is all I know of the Count." [30]

When Agoston was not navigating his steamboat on the Wisconsin or the Mississippi, or greeting customers in his store on Water

Street, or supervising the workmen in his brickyard or mill, or helping to free his ferry boat from sandbars, he was looking after the real
estate that he and other members of his family had acquired in and
about Haraszthy Town.

The first public record of land held by Agoston Haraszthy in Wisconsin appears in the office of the Register of Deeds of Dane County
in Madison. Then as now, the Wisconsin River marked the boundary between Dane and Sauk counties. Although Agoston eventually
acquired extensive property interests in both counties, his name appears in Dane County earlier than in Sauk because Dane was organized before Sauk and began to keep real property records at an
earlier date. On January 4, 1843, the clerk of the Board of Commissioners of the Territory of Wisconsin gave Anna Mária Haraszthy,
Eleonora Haraszthy, and Agoston Haraszthy deeds to three parcels
of land in Dane County across the Wisconsin River from Haraszthy
Town. These deeds, which covered 647 acres, were issued pursuant
to certificates of sale for unpaid taxes held by Berry Haney and assigned by him to the Haraszthys.[31]

On October 26, 1843, Charles Haraszthy and the transplanted
Virginian, Charles Baxter, appeared at the United States Land Office
in Mineral Point to purchase two tracts of land near the site of Haraszthy Town, one for 320 acres that was entered in the names of
Charles Haraszthy and Charles Baxter, and another for 387 acres
that was entered in the name of Charles Haraszthy alone.[32] About
two years later, Agoston appeared in Mineral Point to purchase 160
acres north of the town site in his own name.[33] All these purchases
were made at the official government price of $1.25 per acre. The Ha-
raszthys continued to acquire land on both sides of the river. Some
of the parcels were issued in Agoston's name, some in the name of
Charles, and others in the names of other family members. Since
the Haraszthys did not acquire government title to land on which
Haraszthy Town was laid out until the end of 1843, their earlier title
must have rested on claims acquired from Berry Haney (and perhaps
others) and been subject to eventual perfection through purchase
from the United States.

The town plat recorded on April 26, 1845, shows that several
men had interests in the town site: the "proprietors" are listed as
"Charles Haraszthy," "Robert Bryant, by C. Haraszthy, agent," and

"Stephen Bates, by A. Haraszthy, agent."[34] The map does not reveal
that Agoston himself had any title to the land on which the town
stood, though no one could have doubted that he was its founder and
the "Haraszthy" for whom the town was named. Bryant, of course,
was a partner in the town, as he was in other Haraszthy enterprises
on the prairie. Bates appears to have been an investor. Past seventy
years old when Haraszthy Town was platted he had been a judge before coming to Sauk Prairie. He was to survive the recording of the
official survey by only a few months, dying in September 1845 at
the age of seventy-two or seventy-three.[35] Though little is known of
the part that Stephen Bates played in the foundation of Haraszthy
Town, there is no doubt that he was one of the town fathers. More
than a century and a half after his death, his name was still memo-
rialized in Bates Street, an east-west avenue that runs from Water
Street on the east to the town limits on the west. His advanced age
(and the fact that he died less than five months after the plat was recorded) may indicate that he was not in good health when the plat
was recorded, and explain why Agoston signed as his agent. Charles
Haraszthy's signature in behalf of Robert Bryant must be explained
on different grounds—as will be noted later.

The plat of Haraszthy Town reveals that Agoston had already
adopted the characteristic business style that was to typify his financial activities for the rest of his life: to draw a number of investors
into a venture and distribute shares among them according to their
financial contributions, while personally retaining only a small financial interest but a commanding voice in the project's management.
He appears at all times to have been the dominant force in Haraszthy Town, although on paper he owned little or none of the land on
which the town was built.

Agoston and Charles Haraszthy were in the next few years, however, to acquire substantial property interests in and around Haraszthy Town. At one time or another, they owned one parcel of 480
acres north and west of the town, and another of 2,000 acres on the
east shore of the Wisconsin River in Dane County. But some of their
titles were a bit shaky, for they were acquired from the Territory of
Wisconsin which had, in turn, acquired them from defaulting tax-
payers. The Haraszthys received tax deeds from the Territory, subject

to later redemption by the original owners. The land the Haraszthys acquired in Sauk County was flat and fertile, while their land in Dane County was hilly, rising in places to densely wooded hilltops. Agoston kept some pigs on the Sauk County side of the river and grazed cattle and sheep on the prairie and on the lower slopes of his Dane County hills. He planted a variety of crops on both sides of the river, including a large plantation of almond trees.[36]

There is no direct evidence to indicate when or where Agoston planted his first vines, but it is almost certain that they were set out on the slopes of his Dane County hillsides. The southwestern slopes of these hillsides are among the sunniest in all Wisconsin. The soil is rich in limestone, supplied with enough summer rainfall to sustain vigorous growth, and well drained throughout the year. The winters are severe, but less so than in the surrounding country, for the hillsides shelter the southern and western slopes from the north winds, and the river has a moderating influence on temperatures.[37] If Agoston examined all the surrounding country, he could not have found a more inviting site for vineyards than these hillsides above the Wisconsin River.

A manuscript written in the 1880's for the California historian Hubert Howe Bancroft contains an intriguing note to the effect that Agoston "began work on flowers, and the planting of grape vines" on his Wisconsin property on May 7, 1848. This note was apparently based on an examination of Agoston's own account book, which has since disappeared.[38] But the note is ambiguous. It may be taken as evidence that Agoston did not begin to plant vines in Wisconsin before 1848, or merely that he did not begin his flower and vine planting for the year 1848 before May 7 of that year. As noted earlier, he was convinced from the beginning that good wine could be made in the United States only from European vine stocks. Although his efforts to obtain European cuttings would have taken time—perhaps even years—he could well have obtained them before 1848.

No record has survived of any wine produced by Agoston Haraszthy in Wisconsin. As late as 1846, Austrian priests who had come to Haraszthy Town found some wine in Agoston's store, but it was a poor sort of stuff that the priests considered unsuitable for sacramental use. One of the priests referred to it as a "so-called claret" and, after his return home, expressed the opinion that it was "not manufactured with genuine grapes as is customary in this country [i.e., Austria]."[39] If the wine was from Ohio, it was almost certainly made from an American grape of the *Vitis labrusca* species, or a hybrid of *labrusca* and *vinifera*—the red Alexander, perhaps, or the blue Isabella, both of which were popular wine grapes in Ohio in the 1840's. To sophisticated European palates, wines made from native American vines (or even hybrids of American and European vines) often taste horrible. If the priest assumed that wines of this kind were not made from "genuine grapes," he would have been neither the first nor the last to make that mistake.

Agoston could not himself have produced any drinkable wine in Wisconsin as early as 1846, even assuming that he had obtained suitable cuttings in his first two or three years on the prairie. From first planting to first vintage requires an interval of at least four years. After Agoston left Wisconsin for California in 1849, however, the Dane County hillsides that he owned in the 1840's were acclaimed as a viticultural wonderland. An observer who saw them in the 1870's noted that they were liberally covered with vineyards and that more grapes were grown there than in all the rest of Wisconsin.[40] The most important grape growers in the district after Agoston left Wisconsin were Christian Hurley and Peter Kehl.[41] Hurley was a native of Württemberg who had migrated to Illinois in 1840 and arrived in Haraszthy Town four years later.[42] On February 9, 1849, Agoston sold Hurley forty acres of land on the hillsides opposite Haraszthy Town.[43] Kehl was a German-Swiss brickmaker who had settled in Haraszthy Town in the 1840's. On January 5, 1848, he bought two town lots from Agoston.[44] He built a house for himself and his family on one of the lots and, sometime in the 1850's, acquired Hurley's hillside land, together with some adjoining acres. Kehl built a stone house and a large stone winery on the hillside property, but he also maintained an earlier structure—a tunnel that had been dug into the limestone slope a short distance above the house and winery. The tunnel, which had an arched entrance, rough stone walls, and a low vaulted ceiling, extended into the hillside for a distance of more than forty feet.[45]

The tunnel that Peter Kehl found on his property in the 1850's— and that still exists—bears a remarkable resemblance to the tunnels

that Agoston later dug into the side of the Mayacamas Mountains
in Sonoma, California. There is no direct evidence that Agoston
dug the tunnel on the Hurley-Kehl hillside, but the circumstantial
evidence that he did so is compelling: the Wisconsin and the California tunnels were all dug into limestone hillsides; all had arched
entrances, stone walls, and low, vaulted ceilings; all were dug on
properties that Agoston once owned and that later hosted flourishing vineyards. Assuming that the Wisconsin tunnel was dug before
1849 and that the California tunnels were dug between 1858 and
1864, they were separated in time by perhaps nine (or, at the most,
not more than fifteen) years. It is true that large cellar houses were
built in front of the tunnels in Sonoma, while the Wisconsin tunnel
had no such structure, but the tunnels in Sonoma were dug before
the cellar houses were built in front of them, and their arched entrances, like the entrance to the Wisconsin tunnel, were initially exposed to the weather.[46] If Agoston dug the tunnel in Wisconsin, as
he dug the tunnels in California, there is every reason to believe that
he intended to follow the same pattern of construction there—first
to dig the tunnel (perhaps even more than one tunnel) and later to
supply it with a proper structure for crushing, pressing, fermenting,
and aging the wine. He could well have planned such a structure but
left the project uncompleted when he decided to leave Wisconsin
for California. Of course, this conclusion is based on some speculation. The oral tradition in Wisconsin is that the tunnel was on Agoston's hillside when Kehl acquired the property in the 1850's.[47] But
if Kehl did not dig it, Christian Hurley might have done so after he
acquired the land from Agoston. Weighing all of the evidence, however—considering all of the similarities between the Wisconsin and
California structures and their locations—the most likely conclusion
is that Agoston dug the Wisconsin tunnel, leaving it behind when he
left for California as a tangible monument to his pioneering efforts
to make wine in Wisconsin.

Agoston spent much of his time in the 1840's promoting Haraszthy Town and attempting to entice settlers to move there. *Travels in
North America* was at least in part a promotional tract, designed to
attract immigrants, first, to the United States, second, to Wisconsin,
and finally to Haraszthy Town. It is hard to judge how successful the

book was in accomplishing this goal. Although the greatest number
of immigrants to Haraszthy Town were settlers who spoke German,
they came from various countries—a few, perhaps, from Hungary,
others from Austria and Switzerland, yet others from Bavaria, the
Rhineland, and Saxony. But *Travels in North America* was not Agoston's only promotional effort. He traveled widely through most of
the 1840's, and wherever he went he preached the gospel of Wisconsin and his infant "city" on the edge of Sauk Prairie.

Agoston's business activities often brought him to Madison, and
he soon became nearly as familiar a figure on the streets of the capital city as he was on the streets of Haraszthy Town. Since Madison
was only twenty-five miles east of Sauk Prairie, it was possible to
make the trip in a day, and to return on the following day. Madison
could not yet call itself a city (its population was only 628 in 1846),
but it was growing, and when the territorial legislature was in session
a sense of excitement pervaded the town. A sandstone capitol had
been built in 1837 on a hilltop on the narrow peninsula that divides
Lakes Mendota and Monona. From a distance, the yellow walls of the
capitol gleamed through the forest of native oaks, and the copper-
sheathed dome shone brightly above the treetops.

Agoston strode the streets of the town in his stovepipe hat, carrying a walking stick,[48] but when he attended sessions of the legislature
he wore his Hungarian noble uniform—two coats, long boots, and
Turkish scimitar, looking every inch the "count" he claimed to be.[49]
He made friends in Madison, and forged some business alliances
that were later to stand him in good stead.[50] In Madison, too, he
joined the Order of Freemasons. Although Catholics in Europe had
for more than a century been prohibited from becoming Masons,
those prohibitions were not always enforced in the United States,
and many prominent American Catholics openly affiliated with the
Order. Agoston petitioned for membership in Madison Lodge, No. 5,
on September 11, 1845, and was elected and initiated on December 15 of the same year. He remained active in the lodge as long as
he lived in Wisconsin.

Haraszthy Town seems to have been a successful promotion, at
least in its early years, but it soon had to contend with a rival on its
doorstep. Scarcely a mile north of the town that Agoston laid out in

1840 and 1841 was another pioneer settlement called Prairie du Sac. Although the village bore a French version of the name Sauk Prairie, it was settled mostly by English-speaking Americans. Prairie du Sac was about the same size as Agoston's settlement and in general plan and appearance bore a close resemblance to its southern neighbor. Local residents soon began to think of the towns as sister cities. In popular parlance, Haraszthy Town was dubbed the "Lower Village" or "Lower Sauk," while Prairie du Sac was the "Upper Village" or "Upper Sac."

Not surprisingly, a spirited rivalry soon sprang up between the neighboring towns. But what began as the good-natured efforts of each town to lure business away from the other took on a political dimension after 1844, when the Wisconsin Territorial Legislature decided to provide Sauk County with a local government and set up procedures to select a county seat. The legislature appointed three commissioners to designate the county seat. Both Haraszthy Town and Prairie du Sac were anxious to win the honor and tempted the commissioners with inducements. The Upper Village started by offering to give the new county several vacant lots on which the courthouse could be built; the Lower Village countered with an offer to donate Agoston's brick storehouse for use as the courthouse.[51] Before a decision could be made, one of the commissioners died, and the two remaining commissioners gave the nod to Prairie du Sac.[52] Hearing this, the people of Haraszthy Town called a public meeting and demanded that the legislature submit the issue to the voters.[53] The lawmakers obliged and called a special election to be held the first Tuesday in April 1846 for the purpose of finally settling the question of the county seat.[54]

In the meantime, the people of Haraszthy Town had despaired of winning the county seat for themselves and resolved instead to deny it to Prairie du Sac. Since both towns sat on the eastern edge of Sauk County, the Haraszthyans got the idea that a location closer to the geographic center of the county would better serve the general interests of the people. There was a delightful little valley about fifteen miles north of Haraszthy Town. Measuring about twenty miles from its eastern to western ends, and varying in width from a mile or two up to about five, the valley straddled the shores of the Baraboo

River, a pretty stream that joined the Wisconsin about twenty-five miles north of Haraszthy Town. Although only a handful of settlers lived in the Baraboo Valley, many believed that an important town would one day be built there. The valley was closer to the geographical center of Sauk County than either Haraszthy Town or Prairie du Sac and a logical site for the county seat. The people of Prairie du Sac thought the idea was ridiculous. The Baraboo Valley was separated from Sauk Prairie by a steep ridge of bluffs and nearly impenetrable woods, and it was not only remote but also quite unsuited for cultivation, and everybody knew that a town could not thrive without farms in its neighborhood.

The more the people of Prairie du Sac protested, the more confident the people of Haraszthy Town were that the Baraboo Valley was the best site for the county seat. To prove their point, they sent a committee of five local citizens—Agoston among them—to explore the interior of the county and report back on their findings. The little party of explorers set out from Sauk Prairie on November 10, 1845, and for nearly a week trudged through dense woods, climbing hills, fording streams, and at last returning to Haraszthy Town with their report, which they presented at a public meeting.[55] The interior of Sauk County was a superb country, Agoston and his fellow explorers told the meeting. The Baraboo was a fine stream, and the land that surrounded it was fertile and well suited to agriculture. The Baraboo Valley would support a substantial population and would make a fine site for the county seat. At the election held on April 7, 1846, the people of Sauk County accepted Agoston's recommendations and voted to locate the county seat in the Baraboo area.[56]

Agoston showed his faith in the new town site by purchasing 320 acres of land on the river.[57] On the south bank of the stream, he erected a frame building, which William Canfield later identified as the first frame structure erected in the Baraboo Valley. He opened a store in the building and installed Edmond Rendtorff and Rendtorff's brother-in-law, J. C. Grapel, as clerks.[58] At about the same time he also began a timber-cutting operation on the upper Baraboo River. His workmen felled towering pines and floated them down the Baraboo toward the Wisconsin. He sold the logs in Haraszthy Town or Madison, typically for a dollar each.[59]

Agoston's new activity in the Baraboo region did not evidence a lack of interest in Haraszthy Town. On the contrary, during all the time that he was attending to his new business interests in the Baraboo Valley, he continued to make plans for development of his infant "city" on Sauk Prairie. He was without a partner, now, however, and all his projects would have to be carried out alone, for Robert Bryant had decided to return to Milwaukee and sell his interest in the town.

The date Bryant left for Milwaukee can be established with some precision from the records of land transactions in the office of the Sauk County Register of Deeds. On October 14, 1844, Bryant conveyed all of his right, title, and interest in the ferry over the Wisconsin River to Agoston Haraszthy. In the deed of conveyance, Bryant was described as a resident of "Sauk County[,] Wisconsin Territory." [60] The very next day, Bryant and his wife sold two house lots in Haraszthy Town to Agoston Haraszthy for one hundred dollars. The deed for these lots described them as "Robert Bryant of Milwaukie [*sic*] W. T. and Caroline his wife." [61] On the basis of this evidence, it can be established that the Bryants returned to Milwaukee on October 15, 1844. Why they returned, abandoning their almost four-year-old interest in Haraszthy Town, is a mystery. Perhaps Bryant had grown impatient with the rate of progress in the town. Agoston very likely had promised more than he could deliver, and when Bryant realized that the little town on the Wisconsin would never become a metropolis, he may have decided to salvage what he could from the enterprise and get on with other efforts. Bryant continued his systematic liquidation of his property interests on Sauk Prairie through the summer of 1845. In addition to selling his interest in the river ferry, he also sold some lots in Haraszthy Town to Agoston, and in May 1845 he sold all the land he held in Dane County, except for a few lots in Madison, to Lucas Miller of Montpelier, Vermont.[62] In July of the same year he sold all his interest in the land on which Haraszthy Town was built to a transplanted New Englander named Marcus Warren.[63]

Bryant's departure marked a change in the pattern of life on Sauk Prairie, but there had been other changes, too. At the ripe old age of thirty-eight, Charles Halasz had given up his life as a bachelor and taken a bride. His wife was the twenty-seven-year-old Emma

Rendtorff, sister of Adolf and Edmond. Charles and Emma were married by Justice of the Peace Alvin Crane on June 20, 1843.[64] Two years later, Charles Haraszthy, a widower since the death of Anna María, also married. His wife was Frances Richardson, the widowed mother-in-law of attorney William Clark. Charles Haraszthy was fifty-five years old and Frances Richardson forty-four when they appeared before Justice of the Peace George Cargill on July 23, 1845, and took their vows.[65] Agoston was not entirely pleased with his father's re-marriage. A priest who later became a good friend of the Haraszthys said that Agoston was "fairly vexed" by the match.[66] Two days before the wedding, Charles conveyed all his interest in Haraszthy Town and the land on which it stood to Agoston for a consideration of one dollar.[67] It may be that Agoston was less troubled by the thought that a woman other than his mother would share his father's affections than by the prospect of admitting a middle-aged American woman with a lawyer for a son-in-law to co-ownership in Haraszthy Town.

But if the marriage of Charles Haraszthy and Frances Richardson caused any estrangement between Agoston and Charles, it was not long-lived. The bonds that bound the father and son were too strong to be so easily broken. After Charles set up a separate house with his new wife, he and Agoston remained as close as ever before. And Agoston seems to have remained on an entirely friendly basis with the new Mrs. Haraszthy, and with her son-in-law, William Clark.[68]

7

An
American
Cincinnatus

Agoston had been concerned even before Robert Bryant withdrew from Sauk Prairie about the lack of a Catholic church in Haraszthy Town. The Protestants in Prairie du Sac had had regular visits from traveling preachers since 1841, but the nearest Catholic priests were in Milwaukee, a place so distant from Haraszthy Town that most of the Catholic children born in the town were not baptized and had never been present at a celebration of the mass. The lack of a church was particularly rankling to the new German residents, most of whom were Catholics and regarded a parish as essential to life in a civilized community.

To remedy the situation, Agoston made a public offer of one hundred acres of land to any priest who would come to the prairie and build a parish.[1] News of his offer traveled widely through the upper Middle West, and as early as January 1844 the Rev. Martin Kundig informed readers of the *Catholic Western Register* of Detroit of "the interesting colony at Sac Prairie, where two Hungarian counts have purchased entire townships and settled with numerous families, and expect a hundred more families in the spring."[2] Kundig was intrigued by Wisconsin's pastoral fields but was too far away to explore them. But two other priests, the newly consecrated Bishop of

Milwaukee and a Norbertine missionary from the Tyrol, were closer at hand and in a better position to act on Agoston's offer.

The bishop was a forty-one-year-old Swiss named John Martin Henni who had come to the United States in the early 1830's and had spent most of his priestly life in Ohio. In March 1844, Henni took up his duties as first bishop of the Diocese of Milwaukee, a vast, diverse, and still largely untamed wilderness that extended from Lake Michigan on the east to the Mississippi River on the west, from Illinois on the south almost to the Canadian border on the north.[3] The missionary was a forty-six-year-old Tyrolean named Adalbert Inama who, after arriving in the United States in 1842, had embarked on missionary duties among German-speaking Catholics in upper New York State. Inama was a member of the Innsbruck-based Norbertine order and was anxious to bring the Catholic sacraments to pioneers of the upper Middle West. In 1844, he obtained permission from the Bishop of New York to make a tour of the Great Lakes, Illinois, Ohio, Missouri, and parts of Iowa, and survey the church's needs in that vast territory. The highlight of his journey was the visit he made to Haraszthy Town in September 1844.

The priest had stopped in Milwaukee to pay his respects to Bishop Henni, then pressed on to the Wisconsin River in a horse-drawn coach. All along the road, he heard people talking of the "Hungarian count who had settled at Sac Prairie." He was surprised, therefore, when, on the road between Madison and Haraszthy Town, "who should come speeding along but the much spoken of Hungarian count!" Inama hastened to introduce himself and explain the purpose of his visit. "I am pleased to meet a priest and a Tyrolean," Agoston replied affably. "You are my guest, and you will, I assure you, be a comforter to my family. I will give you a few lines to my father, the general; business hurries me to Madison, but I shall return by tomorrow." Disarmed by Agoston's friendly greeting, Inama hurried west. As he passed over the ring of hills that guard the east bank of the Wisconsin River, he was dazzled by the view that spread out before him—the majestic river in front, the wide Sauk Prairie beyond it, the circle of wooded hills in the distance, and the Upper and Lower villages—"incipient cities," he called them—

huddled together on the riverbank.[4] He crossed the river on Agoston's ferry and soon found himself in the parlor of the Haraszthy house on Water Street.

The priest met Charles Haraszthy, whom he later described as "an exceedingly cultured general of the Austrian army," and Eleonora, "a young matron with four flourishing children." Inama was charmed by the Haraszthy family and intrigued by the prospects of their frontier settlement. "Had I not been bound by previously accepted obligations," he later wrote to the superior of his Tyrolean monastery, "I should have stayed on permanently to assume the office of instructor to the three young counts and to take charge of the missionary affairs both of the few Catholic families here and of those in the surrounding country."[5] But he had promised the Bishop of New York that he would return to his missions around Syracuse and Utica and he was determined to keep his word.

Agoston was encouraged by Inama's interest in Haraszthy Town and, after the priest's return to New York, continued his efforts to lure him west. In the summer of 1845, the priest wrote him a letter asking for details of the land that he proposed to donate to the church. Agoston replied by affirming his intention of donating one hundred acres "entirely free from any payment whatsoever, except this, that you provide free instruction for the poor children of the environment."[6] Impressed with Agoston's sincerity, and encouraged by Bishop Henni, Inama agreed to leave his post in New York and move to Sauk Prairie, where he arrived on November 25, 1845.[7]

During his first few weeks in the town, the priest lived with the Haraszthys and, with Agoston, tramped over the surrounding fields and hillsides to select a proper location for his religious establishment. The men agreed that there should be two Catholic institutions in the community, a parish church in Haraszthy Town and a mission house in the hills of Dane County across the Wisconsin River. The parish was to bear the name of St. Aloysius, while the mission was to be named for the founder of the priest's order, St. Norbert. Father Inama himself bought eighty acres of land in Dane County,[8] and on January 12, 1846, Agoston and Eleonora Haraszthy gave him a deed for one hundred acres nearby, roughly opposite their house in Haraszthy Town. On February 17, they gave Bishop Henni a deed for two lots in Haraszthy Town, adjoining the public schoolhouse at the northwest corner of Jackson and Madison streets.[9]

While the deeds for all these land transfers were being prepared, Agoston went to Milwaukee to call on the bishop. Henni soon wrote the Archbishop of Vienna that "Count von Haraszthy of Hungary . . . has just made his first personal call on me to confer about matters pertaining to the welfare of the church. He has signed over to me and to my successors two lots in his settlement; and a foundation of 100 acres lying on this side of the Wisconsin River to Reverend Inama for the use of his order."[10]

Together, Agoston and Inama planned the future of their lands on the east side of the Wisconsin. The priest envisioned his mission house as a Norbertine priory and college that would eventually occupy grand buildings on a prominent hillside, visible for miles in every direction. The bulk of the land would be used for agricultural purposes, to support the religious institutions. Inama later admitted that his grandiose plan would be rejected in "traditional, conservative Europe," but in America it seemed plausible.[11] Caught up in Inama's enthusiasm, Agoston talked of combining a residence for himself and his family with the priory and college. He thought the combined pile could be an "Escorial in miniature," a grand combination of private residence, public offices, and church buildings, resembling, in inspiration if not in execution, the multipurpose palace that King Philip II of Spain had erected on a mountainside near Madrid in the sixteenth century.[12] But the priory and college, the "Escorial in miniature," were all dreams, as Agoston and Father Inama both realized. For now, the priest and the founder of Haraszthy Town would have to deal with the sober realities of life on the Wisconsin frontier. Inama's first St. Norbert House would not be a stone palace on the side of a hill but a crude log structure in a secluded valley east of Haraszthy Town, and St. Aloysius Church would not rival the Norbertine sanctuaries of the Tyrol but would rise from the grassy corner of Madison and Jackson streets as a simple frame building on log supports. Agoston sent some of his workmen onto Inama's property with a team of oxen to bring down towering oaks which were cut into logs and used to form the crude walls and rafters of St. Norbert

House.[13] The people of Haraszthy Town contributed funds for the construction of St. Aloysius Church, and those who were handy with hammers and saws volunteered to work on the building. Inama was impressed by the generosity of the local Protestants, who graciously helped their Catholic neighbors finish up the building.[14]

While St. Norbert House and St. Aloysius Church were under construction, Father Inama offered mass in the Haraszthy home. The first mass was offered on November 25, 1845, in Agoston's parlor on Water Street. It was an event of some importance, for it was not only the first mass ever said in the town—it was the first mass ever celebrated in Sauk County.[15] Subsequent services attracted Protestants as well as Catholics.

Inama was also busy tending to the sick of the neighborhood and administering the sacrament of baptism. The first baptism entered in the register of St. Aloysius parish was dated January 26, 1846. The child was Carolina Halbleib, daughter of Franz and Amalia Halbleib. "Eleonora Countess Haraszthy" was the godmother. The second was a child identified only as "Mary Ann," born December 22, 1842. The third was a baby boy born to Eleonora Haraszthy on March 31, 1846, and baptized by Father Inama on April 9—probably in the parlor of the Haraszthy home. This baby was named Ágoston Béla, in honor of his father and one of the great hero-kings of ancient Hungary. The baby, destined to be known in the family as Bela, was Agoston's and Eleonora's fourth son and fifth child. Edmond Rendtorff was the godfather.[16]

St. Norbert Mission was ready for occupancy by early July, and St. Aloysius was finished and ready for use in August. The church was a simple rectangle about thirty feet long, twenty feet wide, and twelve feet high, with a clapboard exterior and interior walls of rough boards. There had been no money in the townspeople's budget for furnishings, so the interior of the church was bare except for a simple wooden altar, an iron stove, and a hard wooden armchair designed to be used by the priest, or a visiting cleric, if there was one.

On October 8, Father Maximilian Gärtner arrived from the Tyrol to assume the duties of assistant to Father Inama.[17] He was a man of forty-five, a native of Heiterwang in the Tyrol, and he had been in the Norbertine order at Innsbruck since the 1820's, primarily teaching theology. After Father Inama wrote home requesting that he be given help in his missionary duties, Gärtner started his long journey to America, traveling with three lay brothers who longed for a taste of life on the American frontier. Three days after the little party arrived in Haraszthy Town, Gärtner joined Inama at the new St. Aloysius Church.[18] Inama celebrated a high mass, Gärtner a low mass. A handful of worshipers—about ten men and six women—was there to greet the priests when they arrived. The men stood in the rear and the women knelt on the bare wooden floor; the armchair was reserved for the "lovely Countess." After Gärtner preached his sermon, "the old Count" came forward to shake his hand and, in his courtly, Old World manner, congratulate the priest. "Such a glowing sermon," Charles Haraszthy told Gärtner, "must enkindle all hearts."[19]

Humble though it was, St. Aloysius instilled a sense of hope and pride in the people of Haraszthy Town. But hope and pride were soon dashed, for on Sunday, October 25, barely a month after Bishop Henni dedicated the church, it burned to the ground. Gärtner had just finished his twelve o'clock mass and had gone to visit a sick man in a nearby cabin. Inama remained behind to talk to some of the parishioners. Suddenly a woman outside the structure cried, "Fire! All get out. For God's sake!" Inama looked toward the door. He could see flames licking at the threshold and hear the wooden floor crackling beneath his feet. He hastily gathered up the altar linens and vestments, while two men hoisted the iron stove and carried it out the door. Father Gärtner was a short distance away when he heard a frightened boy shout, "Over there a house is burning!"[20] He ran back to the church, but it was hopeless; in less than ten minutes, the structure was totally consumed by the flames.

The cause of the fire was never determined. Gärtner and Inama saw wood shavings lying on the ground alongside the outside walls and supposed that one of the parishioners had carelessly tossed a match into them. A man named Adolf Fassbender, who had been seen smoking a pipe, was suspected, but he stoutly denied his guilt.[21] The little congregation was devastated. Agoston was elected chairman of a committee to determine means of rebuilding the church. He held some meetings, but the townspeople made it clear that they had contributed as much as they could to the original construction project.[22] Reconstruction would have to be put off. In the meantime, Gärtner and Inama held masses in the schoolhouse next door.

Inama and Gärtner were welcomed to Haraszthy Town not solely because of their spiritual ministrations but also because of the cultural dimension they added to the frontier community. The clerics were frequent visitors in the Haraszthy home, where they talked with Agoston about books and shared memories of European cities they had all visited. Agoston sometimes accompanied Inama on his missions to neighboring communities, traveling by horseback in the summer and in the winter by horse-drawn sleigh, a sleek conveyance with jingling bells that glided effortlessly over the frozen surface of the river. Eleonora in particular enjoyed the company of Father Gärtner, who was a writer and artist as well as a faithful spiritual adviser. At his invitation, she visited St. Norbert House with her children on Easter Sunday and gave him and Inama two large white curtains for use as an altar canopy.[23] Gärtner thought Eleonora both "lovely" and "noble." In his diary, he praised the courage with which she faced the rigors of life on the western frontier.

For his part, Agoston was pleased to learn that Gärtner had talents as an architect and landscape gardener. He had decided to build a new house on 160 acres of riverfront land he used as a farm between Haraszthy Town and Prairie du Sac. He wanted it to be a large structure, and one befitting his status as the founder of Haraszthy Town, and considered the possibility of building in stone. Charles Halasz had recently begun work on a stone house in Haraszthy Town, but the construction was painfully slow and expensive. Gärtner had traveled in Italy in 1841 and there learned another way to build a large and permanent house. He called it the "gravel method." Wooden forms were built and reinforced with tenons, then filled with gravel and slaked lime and moistened with water. When dry, the gravel, lime, and water formed a solid mass, much like stone. Gärtner told Agoston that the advantages of the "gravel method" were speed and economy. Always willing to experiment with new ideas, Agoston ordered his workmen to begin construction using the new method.[24]

Although Gärtner wrote that Agoston's new house was inspired by the villas he had seen in Italy, a girl whose father later acquired the property on which the house was built thought it was modeled in the style of Hungarian manor houses.²⁵ Perhaps it was a combination of both: the foundation, built of solid stone, was topped with "gravel method" walls pierced by small but high-arched windows. The center of the house, which rose two stories above the prairie and river, was marked by four columns. Gärtner's design for the grounds was certainly in the Italian style, with a semicircular driveway and tree-lined paths that spread out from a central point on the riverbank like the spokes of a wheel.²⁶

Agoston's manor house was designed on a grand scale—too grand, perhaps, for his purse. Although he was involved in a host of businesses in and around Haraszthy Town, none of his ventures had made much money. He held title to more than two thousand acres of land, but the properties were heavily mortgaged, some to local settlers, others to bankers in Madison and Milwaukee (and some as far away as New York) who showed little sympathy for "grand schemes" and expected, and demanded, that debts be paid as and when due. The mill at Honey Creek, launched with great promise in 1842, had never done a really good business. The ferry boat over the Wisconsin River earned a steady income, but much of it went to its hardworking operator, Robert Richards. Agoston's store had been a center of business activity in Haraszthy Town from the day it was opened, but he had extended credit with a liberal hand and found that many of his customers could not—or would not—make good on their debts. After Marcus Warren opened a competing store in the town, Agoston decided to close his Water Street emporium, and also his store in the Baraboo Valley.²⁷

Agoston's greatest business disappointment may well have been the steamboat *Rock River*. It had earned a place in the transportation history of the United States with its pioneering trips on the upper Mississippi, but it was beset by a host of problems. It was a slow boat; some said it was underpowered;²⁸ and it never carried enough passengers and freight to turn a healthy profit. When and under what circumstances Agoston relinquished his interest in the vessel is a mystery. Edmond Rendtorff said that the boat became stuck in the ice at Prairie du Chien one winter and could not be extricated.²⁹ Father Gärtner suggested that the vessel had been "sequestered" by creditors while it was docked at St. Louis.³⁰ It may well have been that the investors who sold Agoston and Bryant shares in the vessel had become impatient with Agoston's failure to pay dividends and decided to reclaim it. Whatever the reason, the *Rock River* disappeared from the Wisconsin and Haraszthy Town. It was most likely sold, whether by Agoston himself or by his creditors, taken to a new river, given a new name, and launched again in river traffic.[31]

According to Gärtner, after Agoston closed his stores in Haraszthy Town and on the Baraboo River, he decided to apply himself with greater vigor to his agricultural pursuits. There is no doubt that he enjoyed his work on the land more than any other. When asked to state his occupation, he usually replied that he was a "farmer," a title that he regarded as denoting special virtue. After his stores were closed, he took to the fields with his own plow, in Gärtner's words, "as if he had once gone to school in old Rome at the time of Cincinnatus."[32] He kept pigs on the opposite side of the river, horses and cattle near his house, and sheep both on the prairie and in the hills opposite Haraszthy Town. He was an earthy kind of farmer, no gentleman dabbler in the agrarian arts. He was willing to guide a plow through the fields and feed his hungry animals personally, and when the time came to slaughter a pig or a cow he would take up the knife and perform the "dirty deed" with his own hands. Two young men who lived and worked with the Haraszthy family in 1848 left recollections of the gusto with which Agoston slaughtered pigs. He pursued them with a menacing knife, even plunging headlong into a haystack to capture a recalcitrant porker and, when he had it securely in hand, sinking the blade deep in the animal's throat.[33]

In 1848 Agoston began a large new sheep-raising venture—one that he hoped would replenish his strained coffers with a steady stream of cash. In September of that year he acquired a flock of a thousand ewes and twenty bucks from a man named Calvin Williams. He agreed to deliver 1,500 pounds of "merchantable wool" to Williams at Milwaukee each year for five years and, at the end of that time, to return the original thousand sheep and twenty bucks (or their equivalents). The arrangement was, in effect, a kind of lease. Agoston would have the use of the sheep and bucks for five years, while Williams would receive annual shipments of wool. Agoston would keep any wool in excess of 1,500 pounds, and any increase in the flock. He was so confident of the soundness of the arrangement that he gave Williams a mortgage to secure his promises.[34]

Not long after Agoston acquired the sheep, a young man appeared at the door of the Haraszthy house on Water Street. His name was Edmund Jussen and he was a German who, less than a year earlier, had left his home in the Rhineland to join an uncle who had moved to America. He had found his uncle in Wisconsin and, with him, had explored much of the central part of the territory. But the uncle had decided to move west, and Edmund wanted to stay behind. He came to Haraszthy Town by chance, alone and hungry, and looking for work. Agoston recognized a special quality in the young man. They talked together about political conditions in Europe, and exchanged views on music and literature. The youth was intelligent and curious, but his English was rudimentary. Agoston thought he might profit from reading some of the English-language books in his library, but could not think of any work he could do. Then, pausing to reconsider, he announced that it might be possible for Jussen to tend his sheep while reading his books. It would be a good opportunity to increase his English-language skills while performing a useful service on the Haraszthy farm.[35]

Jussen was delighted with the proposal. For several weeks in the fall of 1848, he left the Haraszthy house each morning, a book in one hand and a specially prepared lunch in the other, and headed for the sheep pastures west of town. He read many books in those weeks, but his favorites were the plays of Shakespeare. While he read, he smoked a corncob pipe. One morning, he settled down in the grass, lit his pipe, tossed the match over his shoulder, and, as he later remembered, "was soon absorbed in Hamlet's soliloquy."[36] After a few minutes, he was startled to hear the sound of shouting voices. Turning to see what the commotion was about, he discovered that the long prairie grass was on fire and a dozen or more men were running toward him waving tree branches. The men intended to use the branches to fight the fire, but in the excitement of the moment Jussen thought they were chasing him, and he panicked and began to run away. The flames kindled by Jussen's match spread rapidly, roared through the dry grass, and advanced toward Agoston's sheep. Confused by the fire and by the men who were trying to fight it, the animals began running toward the flames. In few short minutes, almost all of them were horribly charred. After the fire was put out, the stench of burning flesh hung heavy over Haraszthy Town.

The frightened Edmund Jussen spent the night in the woods. The next morning, he summoned the courage to return to town and confront Agoston. His confidence was not reassured when he approached the Haraszthy house and found a hundred or more carcasses, pitifully burned, hanging on a fence. But he pressed on and found Agoston talking with a group of his workmen. To Jussen's surprise, all the men were glad to see him, and Agoston himself showed not a trace of anger. He placed his hand on the young man's shoulder and remarked that knowing something about the danger of prairie fires in the dry months of autumn was quite as important as Hamlet's speculations on the immortality of the soul.[37]

Jussen stayed on with the Haraszthys. A few days after the fire, Agoston announced at breakfast one morning that the time had arrived to slaughter the pigs and prepare smoked meats and sausage for the coming winter. He turned to the young German, who was enjoying a savory piece of bacon, and asked if he was willing to try his skill at "pig-sticking." Jussen had little taste for such an exercise but did not want to disappoint his host, so he followed Agoston and some of his men into an enclosure, where a dozen or more pigs were running about. He was given a large knife and told to catch one of the animals, grasp it securely about the middle with his left arm, and with his right hand thrust the blade into the animal's neck. He obediently set off in pursuit of one pig, but was chagrined when the animal slipped from his grasp. He lunged forward and tried to cut the animal's throat, but missed and buried his knife in the victim's shoulder. In the process, he lost his balance, and tumbled into the middle of the enclosure. Jussen decided then and there that farming was not his calling. Agoston laughingly agreed, but praised him for the pluck he had shown in attempting the unpleasant task.[38]

Not long after his romp with Agoston's pigs, Edmund Jussen left the Haraszthy house, moved to a neighboring town, and began to study law. He was admitted to the bar at Madison, and then elected to the Wisconsin Assembly. On the outbreak of the Civil War, he enlisted in the Twenty-third Wisconsin Infantry and rose to the rank of colonel. After the war, he moved to Chicago and became one of the best-known attorneys in that city. He served for a time as Collector of Internal Revenue in Illinois, and in 1885, by appointment of President Grover Cleveland, he became the United States consul-general in Vienna. Years after he left Haraszthy Town, the German boy-turned-American attorney and diplomat fondly remembered his experiences in the house of a generous and forgiving Hungarian nobleman on the frontier of Wisconsin, and the unusual opportunity the nobleman had given him to read Shakespeare while tending sheep.[39]

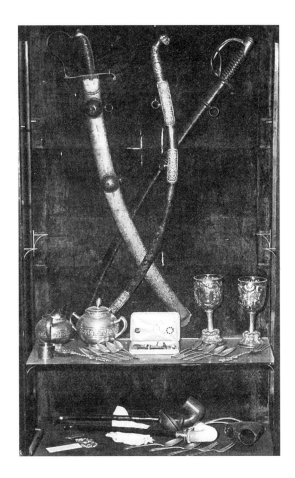

Hungarian swords and other family memorabilia belonging to the Haraszthy and Hancock families. The curved swords that Agoston Haraszthy brought with him to the United States are shown crossed in this photograph. Behind them is an American Army sword that once belonged to Haraszthy's son-in-law, Henry Hancock. Allan Hancock Collection.

Charles (originally Károly) Haraszthy, Agoston Haraszthy's father. Born at Szeged, Hungary, in 1789, he died at sea somewhere between Corinto, Nicaragua, and San Francisco, California, in July 1869. Wine Institute.

Coat of arms of the Mokcsai Haraszthy family. Agoston Haraszthy was a member of this Hungarian noble family, whose two names signified that it had at one time or another owned property both at Mokcsa and Haraszth. Siebmacher's grosses Wappenbuch Band 33.

Terézváros Church, Budapest. Agoston Haraszthy was baptized in this church, in what was then the Hungarian city of Pest (now part of Budapest), on August 30, 1812. Brian McGinty Collection.

Agoston Haraszthy. Full-length portrait by Charles D. Fredricks, New York City. This photograph was sent back to Hungary, where a relative named Tamás Haraszthy still had a copy in 1947. Wine Institute.

Haraszthy house in Haraszthy Town (later Sauk City), Wisconsin. The family's first home in the United States, this frame house commanded a view of the Wisconsin River. State Historical Society of Wisconsin, neg. # WHi (x3) 29720.

Probable site of Agoston Haraszthy's Wisconsin vineyards. These vine-covered hill-sides, now on the grounds of the Wollersheim vineyards overlooking Sauk Prairie, were owned by Haraszthy in the 1840's. Photograph by Brian McGinty.

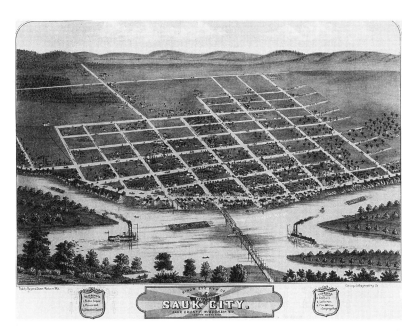

Lithograph of Sauk City (originally Haraszthy Town), a few years after Haraszthy left it. The Wisconsin River is in the foreground, Sauk Prairie in the background. State Historical Society of Wisconsin, neg. # WHi (x3) 34155.

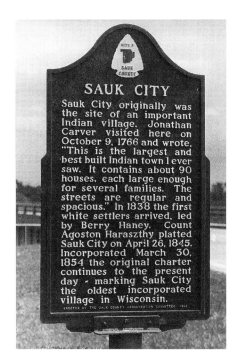

Historical marker at entrance to Sauk City, Wisconsin. It commemorates the settlement as "the oldest incorporated village in Wisconsin." Photograph by Brian McGinty.

Eleonora Dedinszky, wife of Agoston Haraszthy, as shown in a miniature portrait. Allan Hancock Collection.

Agoston Haraszthy in a thoughtful mood. Detail of portrait by William Shew, San Francisco. Frank H. Bartholomew Foundation.

Gaza (originally Géza) Haraszthy, oldest son of Agoston Haraszthy and his wife, Eleonora Dedinszky. Born in December 1833 on his father's estate in Bács County, Hungary, he died in Nicaragua in December 1879. Frank H. Bartholomew Foundation.

Attila Haraszthy, second son of Agoston Haraszthy and Eleonora Dedinszky. Born in April 1835 on his father's estate in Bács County, Hungary, he died in Sonoma, California, in 1888. Brian McGinty Collection.

Arpad Haraszthy, third son of Agoston Haraszthy and Eleonora Dedinszky. Born in June 1840 at Futtak, Hungary, he died in San Francisco in November 1900. Trained as a Champagne-maker in France, he manufactured Eclipse champagne in San Francisco after his father's death in 1869. He was the longtime president of the State Board of Viticultural Commissioners and, as such, the titular leader of the California wine industry. Wine Institute.

Ida Haraszthy Hancock. Fourth child and first daughter of Agoston Haraszthy and his wife, Eleonora, Ida was born in Illinois in 1843 and died in Los Angeles in 1913. Allan Hancock Collection.

Bela Haraszthy. Fifth child and fourth son of Agoston Haraszthy and his wife, Eleonora, he was born in 1846 in Haraszthy Town (later Sauk City), Wisconsin, and died in Los Angeles in 1912. Brian McGinty Collection.

First City Jail, San Diego. After Sheriff Haraszthy built this cobblestone structure in 1850–51, it became the center of a lively controversy in the seaside town. San Diego Historical Society, Ticor Collection.

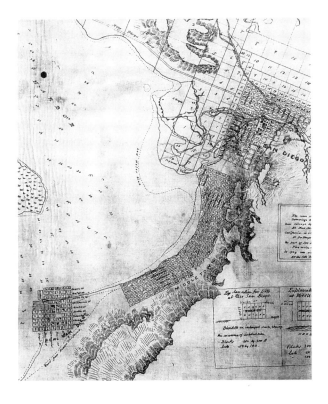

Map of Middletown, also known as "Haraszthyville," San Diego. In 1850, Agoston Haraszthy led a syndicate in the development of this portion of the San Diego Bay shore. San Diego Historical Society, Photograph Collection.

Running the gold into ingots in the San Francisco Mint. A woodcut from *Hutchings' California Magazine*, October 1856.

Haraszthy, Uznay & Co's Gold and Silver Refinery, San Francisco. In this large building at the corner of Brannan and Harris Streets, Agoston Haraszthy conducted business as a private assayer and refiner. The Bancroft Library, University of California, Berkeley.

8

News
from
Far Away

If there is one image of Agoston Haraszthy that pervades his Wisconsin years it is that of a vigorous and active man. The wide array of enterprises in which he involved himself, his frequent travels, and his passion for hunting—all point to a man with immense vitality. Yet he was not always brimming over with energy. He had suffered from a "fever" (which may have been malaria) at Lake Koshkonong and contracted cholera in New York City, and his son Arpad later claimed that he suffered from asthma while in Wisconsin.[1] Cholera can be a fatal illness, and the effects of malaria can sometimes linger on for years. Although there is no reason to suspect that Agoston was subject to chronic illnesses, he was sick from time to time, on occasion quite seriously so. The illness he suffered in the summer of 1847 may have been his most harrowing. On August 22 of that year Father Gärtner noted in his diary that the founder of Haraszthy Town "lay ill." The priest wrote that he seemed to recover for a while, but then suffered a relapse. On Saturday, August 28, Gärtner said mass in Haraszthy Town and led public prayers for Agoston's recovery, for his condition was now "critical." Two English doctors had recently settled on Sauk Prairie, and Charles Haraszthy summoned them to his son's bedside. According to Gärtner, the doctors prescribed twelve grains of calomel (a compound of mercury used as a purge). "The remedy really worked and saved the sick man," the priest noted on August 29. Although Agoston remained weak for a while, he seems to have fully recovered his strength by the beginning of 1848.[2]

While Agoston was recovering from his near-fatal illness in early 1848, events that were to affect the course of life in Haraszthy Town were unfolding halfway around the world.

The winds of rebellion were blowing across Europe in 1848, spurring demonstrations in Paris, Rome, Berlin, and Vienna, sending crowds into the streets to clamor for democratic reforms in countries in which freedom and opportunity had long been regarded as forbidden dreams. The unrest started in Sicily in January 1848, when mobs took to the streets to demand a constitution and civil liberties. At the end of February, demonstrations engulfed Paris, forcing the Orleanist King Louis Philippe to abdicate in favor of a republican government. Soon, the wine of revolution was being drunk in Sardinia, the Papal States, Luxembourg, Bavaria, Prussia, Bohemia, Moravia, Dalmatia, and Poland.

Hungary was not immune to the popular fervor. Lajos Kossuth, as the leader of the Hungarian opposition, was one of the first prominent Europeans to fan the flames of revolution, rising in the Diet in March 1848 to demand that the Hapsburg Emperor Ferdinand V abolish serfdom and grant the Hungarians free elections and a government chosen by the Hungarians themselves. When news of Kossuth's address reached Vienna, the streets erupted in pandemonium. The Austrians, too, wanted political reforms and an end to the repressive policies of Ferdinand's chancellor, Prince Klemens von Metternich. Alternately frightened and bewildered, von Metternich was forced out of power in the middle of March, and soon fled the capital. The Austrians quickly granted Kossuth's demands, permitting the appointment of Count Lajos Batthyány as the first Hungarian prime minister. Hungarians, so long dominated by their Austrian neighbors, now held their heads high, cheering Kossuth as he rode through the streets on his way to the Diet. But the Hapsburgs were already having second thoughts. They regrouped, and toward the end of the summer dispatched a powerful army to crush the Hungarian government. Kossuth responded by calling for 200,000 volunteers to defend the country.

News of the tumultuous events in Europe spread slowly across the Atlantic. In May, residents of Haraszthy Town received news of the riots in Rome. In June, they learned that Louis Philippe had surrendered his throne, that rebellions had erupted in Sicily and Sardinia, and that an almost unthinkable revolution had swept Hungary. Agoston received the news from his homeland with excitement and apprehension.[3] It was thrilling to learn that brave Hungarians had defied the Hapsburgs and taken charge of their own government—frightening to think of the probable consequences of the military struggle that was now beginning.

Most of the news from Europe came from newspaper stories printed in Milwaukee and Madison. But there were firsthand accounts, too, brought to Wisconsin by refugees who were fleeing their revolution-torn homelands for the comparative tranquillity of the American frontier. In July 1848, a large party of refugees reached Sauk Prairie. Among them were a twenty-four-year-old Bavarian named Karl (later Charles) Naffz, Naffz's brother-in-law, Karl (later Charles) Duerr, two of Naffz's sisters, and two young Hungarians, thirty-three-year-old Joseph Reiner and twenty-seven-year-old George Totto.[4] Naffz took up residence with his sisters, while Reiner and Totto lived with the Haraszthys. Agoston listened intently as Naffz described political conditions in Europe, then questioned him closely for news of events in Hungary. The young Bavarian was musically inclined, a fact that delighted Eleonora. At her request, he played the zither and sang German songs.[5] Another Hungarian arrived in Haraszthy Town not long after Reiner and Totto. He was Karl Hellinger, a young man whom Father Gärtner described as a "beardless youth."[6] Hellinger was warmly welcomed at the Haraszthy house, as Reiner, Totto, Naffz, and Duerr had been before him.

Years later, Naffz remembered the colorful mixture of languages that was spoken in the Haraszthy house. There was a shepherd who spoke French, a housemaid who spoke German and French, and a cook who spoke a dialect from Cologne. Agoston and Eleonora spoke German and Hungarian almost interchangeably, as did Reiner and Totto. Naffz and Jussen spoke German exclusively, while the Haraszthy boys all spoke Hungarian. Not surprisingly, Naffz likened the household to the Tower of Babel.[7]

In the fall of 1848 the Haraszthys entertained a large gathering of European refugees in their home. Toasts were drunk, speeches were delivered, and a sumptuous meal was served. Agoston was the principal speaker. Excited by the news from his native land, he launched into an impassioned defense of Kossuth and his reforms, speaking first in German but switching to Hungarian as he grew more excited.[8] The Hungarians proposed that they draft a proclamation expressing their support for Kossuth, forward it to Madison with a request that the governor of Wisconsin sign, and then send the document to Hungary in the care of a special courier. They contributed money to a special fund to pay the courier's travel expenses.[9] Agoston, as expected, was the principal contributor to the travel fund, and probably also the principal drafter of the proclamation. When all the signatures had been affixed to the document, Karl Hellinger was chosen to act as the courier.

Hellinger left Haraszthy Town with the money and the proclamation and headed for Madison, where he persuaded Governor Nelson Dewey to add his signature to the document. But the young Hungarian's courage was beginning to flag. What dangers would he fall prey to if he returned to Hungary? Could he make it through the opposing armies to deliver the proclamation to Kossuth? The more Hellinger thought about his mission, the more apprehensive he became—and he finally decided not to go at all. Gärtner was shocked to find Hellinger still in Madison in the first week of December. He had the proclamation in hand but coolly announced that he had decided to use the travel money, not to return to Hungary, but to tour the United States. When the priest told Agoston of Hellinger's decision, the founder of Haraszthy Town stamped on the floor and uttered an oath. Later, however, he laughed, at both himself and his friends. Perhaps it was presumptuous of them to believe that they could influence the course of events in Hungary, and it was surely foolish to entrust a callow youth with such an important mission. He could understand why Hellinger might place a higher value on his own skin than on a hazardous journey to a land torn by war. If he were in the boy's place, he might very well have done the same thing.[10]

Agoston could laugh about the loss of the money he had entrusted to Karl Hellinger—as he laughed about the loss of his sheep in the prairie fire of 1848—but both losses had done their bit to weaken his financial condition. He had bills now that he could not pay, and some of his creditors were growing insistent. Since Wisconsin had been admitted to the Union in May 1848, he had begun to think about augmenting his income by seeking a position in the new state government recently organized in Madison.[11] He had taken out his citizenship papers in the District Court at Galena, Illinois, on July 18, 1843,[12] and was eligible to hold public office from that date; but there is no record that he sought any official position until the fall of 1848, when he was elected to the board of school commissioners of Sauk County.[13] It was not a high office, and it is unlikely he sought it for glory or gain; but it was a sign that he was beginning to think once again like a politician.

He had a good reputation as a stump speaker, particularly in German, which was widely spoken in and around Sauk Prairie,[14] and he had always had strong political instincts. A staunch Democrat since his early years in Wisconsin (in *Travels in North America* he praised the party of Jefferson and Jackson as a "stout bastion of true republican ideals" and condemned the rival Whigs for their close ties to the banking interests),[15] he was pleased that Nelson Dewey, a Democrat, was governor and that Democrats controlled both houses of the legislature. But to assess his political opportunities at close hand he believed that he would have to move (at least temporarily) from Haraszthy Town to the capital.

Many years later, Charles Naffz remembered that he and Charles Duerr drove the Haraszthys from Sauk Prairie to Madison in a horse-drawn sleigh on Christmas Eve, 1848. But this was apparently not a final move,[16] for they returned to Sauk Prairie after that date, and as late as March 1849 Agoston and Eleonora were still affirming in legal documents that they were residents of Sauk County.[17] But they maintained a presence of sorts in the capital before that date, for on October 25, 1848, Eleonora gave birth to a baby girl in Madison. It was Eleonora's sixth child and second daughter. Father Gärtner came to Madison from Haraszthy Town to officiate at the infant's baptism, which took place in Madison's United States Hotel on November 4. Agoston's best friend in Madison, a young attorney named Thomas W. Sutherland, was present at the baptism, as was Sutherland's wife, Johanna. The baby was baptized as Johanna Eleonora

Ottilia—Johanna in honor of Mrs. Sutherland, Eleonora in honor of her mother, and Ottilia in honor of her mother's sister—but she was destined to be known in the family as Ottilia or (in an anglicized version) Otelia. At a little party given after the baptism, Eleonora served what Gärtner called "a cup of genuine Johannisberger."[18]

Sutherland was originally from Philadelphia. He had come to Wisconsin around 1835 and served first as United States District Attorney for the Territory, and later as first president of the Madison Village Council (the equivalent of mayor). In 1848, Governor Dewey appointed him a member of the first board of regents of the University of Wisconsin, and in the same year he was a founding vice president of the State Historical Society of Wisconsin. Agoston was a vice president of the society for Sauk County and, with Sutherland, attended the inaugural meeting in the Senate chamber at Madison on Monday evening, January 30, 1849.[19] Toward the end of 1848, Sutherland advanced Agoston some money on logs that Agoston had cut on the upper Baraboo River, and Agoston gave him a mortgage to secure repayment.[20] Although still in his early thirties, Sutherland had connections with influential men in Milwaukee, among them the Scottish-born insurance executive, Alexander Mitchell. Mitchell was the manager of the Wisconsin Marine and Fire Insurance Company, the most powerful business organization in Wisconsin, and a power to be reckoned with in the state's business affairs.

On December 16, 1848, the following notice appeared in the *Wisconsin Democrat*, published in Madison:

NOTICE,

Is hereby given that application will be made at the next session of the Legislature of the State of Wisconsin, for a charter to build a bridge across the Wisconsin river, between the towns of Prairie du Sac and Haraszthy, in the county of Sauk, and on land belonging to the subscriber in Dane County.

AGOSTON HARASZTHY,
For himself and associates.

Dec. 9th, 1848.[21]

The notice must have created a stir on Sauk Prairie, where settlers had for years talked about building a bridge over the Wisconsin without any firm sense of how such an ambitious project could actually be realized. In the four-hundred-mile length of the river, there was not a single bridge that linked the opposite shores. The place where Agoston proposed to erect his span was a logical enough location, if the volume of traffic that could be expected to pass over the bridge was the only criterion. The Upper and Lower Villages, though still small, were among the most important population centers on the river, and they were separated from Madison by twenty-five miles of well-traveled road. But the river was broad at Haraszthy Town, and it would be an engineering feat of no small dimensions to span it.

With Sutherland, Agoston had formed a company to plan, finance, construct, and then operate the bridge. The company was originally named the Haraszthy Bridge Company and consisted of Agoston, Charles, and Sutherland as incorporators. But when the legislature was asked in January 1849 to incorporate the company and authorize the construction of the bridge, the lawmakers insisted on two changes: the company's name would be changed to the Wisconsin Bridge Company, and Alexander Mitchell of Milwaukee would be added to the list of incorporators.[22] Whether Mitchell used his influence in Madison to be admitted to the company, or Sutherland and Haraszthy had asked him to join the effort, is not known. In either case, Mitchell's financial strength and fiscal know-how would make it easier to raise the capital needed to finance the structure.

As passed by the legislature, the law authorizing the construction of the bridge called for a structure at least twenty feet wide and thirty feet high, rising at least fifty feet above the main shipping channel, with two lanes for wagons, a single lane for foot passengers, and secure railings on both sides. Agoston Haraszthy, Charles Haraszthy, Thomas Sutherland, and Alexander Mitchell were appointed as commissioners to receive subscriptions of capital stock in the bridge company, with a book of subscription to be maintained in Agoston's house in Haraszthy Town. The capital stock was set at $20,000 and the company was authorized to charge tolls for a period of thirty years. The legislation was signed into law by Governor Dewey on March 2, 1849.[23]

But Agoston was never to build that great bridge, for an event that had occurred more than a year earlier and more than two thousand miles away, in a valley and on a river that he can never have heard of—indeed, that no one in Wisconsin can be expected to have heard of—was to change the course of his life forever. This event was the discovery of gold on January 24, 1848, at a place called Sutter's Mill on the South Fork of the American River in the Sacramento Valley in far-off California. On that date a carpenter named James Marshall found a few lumps of gold in the sandy bed of a tailrace. News of Marshall's discovery did not reach San Francisco until the middle of March, and it was not known in the California capital at Monterey until June. Reports of the discovery appeared in newspapers in Missouri in early August, but official dispatches did not arrive in Washington until late November. President James K. Polk received the dispatches with more than casual interest, for they were accompanied by heavy boxes containing more than two hundred ounces of shiny yellow metal. Polk had the metal assayed and, on December 5, told an astonished Congress and nation that it was almost unbelievably rich.

Polk's announcement was sensational. In Wisconsin, as elsewhere in the Union, men who for years had plodded behind plows suddenly entertained dreams of becoming rich by gathering gold nuggets from stream beds. Clerks in stores, fishermen on lakes and rivers, brick masons, carpenters, lumberjacks, lawyers—all were infected with the California gold fever. Newspapers printed the latest news from California, most of them dispatches sent by ship from Panama (where travelers from California customarily crossed by land from the Pacific to the Atlantic) and thence forwarded through New Orleans and up the Mississippi River to be spread to every town and hamlet in the nation.

"The accounts of gold found in California are most astonishing," the *Wisconsin Democrat* announced on December 30, 1848, "and has set the whole country in a fever for emigrating where gold is picked up like chips."[24] "The excitement seems to grow by what it feeds on," the *Wisconsin Argus* reported on January 2, 1849, "and there is no prospect of any abatement."[25] There were reports that Wisconsinites were already banding together to form "mining companies," and that the companies were making plans to leave for California in the spring.

Agoston got the fever. Years later, his son Arpad and his daughter

Ida both claimed that his decision to join the Gold Rush to California was motivated by poor health.[26] Arpad said that his father "was suffering from asthma and his physicians advised him either to go to Florida or to California."[27] If this is true, his decision to choose California over Florida would not be difficult to understand, for he had already concluded that Florida was not a fit place to live in. But there is little evidence that he suffered from any permanently debilitating illnesses while he was in Wisconsin. On the contrary, the very vigorous manner in which he deported himself during the nine grueling months he was on the trail to California would tend to indicate that, if he had any ailments, they were minor and easily overcome.

It has been suggested that his debts may have become oppressive and prompted him to seek protection from creditors in the westernmost reaches of the country.[28] There is no doubt that his creditors were pressing him harder, and some had even threatened him with lawsuits, but his debts were not so large that he could not have paid them off over a period of a few years. If his bridge project succeeded, his financial condition would have improved dramatically, and his properties in and around Haraszthy Town could have been expected to appreciate in value. If he obtained a salaried position with the state, as he had set out to do at the end of 1848, his income would have risen, giving him cash with which to satisfy his creditors and finance other projects on and around Sauk Prairie. Neither poor health nor large debts in themselves seem adequate to explain the suddenness and irrevocability of the decision Agoston made in the spring of 1849.

Shortly after he arrived in California, Agoston told another emigrant that he came there "to settle, not for the gold"—and that he intended to plant a vineyard near San Diego.[29] He had undoubtedly heard stories of California's warm climate and concluded that it was a more suitable environment for a would-be winemaker than Wisconsin. Of course, a trip across the great American plains would also be an adventure, a supreme test of his courage and resourcefulness; and if California's climate proved to be healthier than Wisconsin's, and if the move put some miles between him and his creditors, all the better. Given the excitement that was sweeping the country in the spring of 1849, the chance for brave and ambitious men to discover new worlds of opportunity and achievement in a sunny land by the Pacific, Agoston's decision to leave Wisconsin and move to California is hardly surprising. The real question is not why he would set out for California in 1849, but why in the world he would not.

Many of the men who made plans to go to California in the spring of 1849 were going alone, leaving their families behind them with the intention of staying only long enough to make their fortunes and then returning to resume their quiet lives in Wisconsin (or Illinois, or Ohio, or New York, or whatever state they called home). Agoston's decision to take his entire family with him marks him apart from most of the other emigrants of 1849. He never seems to have seriously entertained the thought of going alone, or of coming back to his home on Sauk Prairie. Once made, the decision to pull up stakes and head for California was total and unequivocal.

It was a quick decision, but it cannot have been easy. Agoston was leaving a community that he had built almost from nothing. The settlement he launched with such enthusiasm in 1841 had not become a "city," as he once hoped; but it was a substantial community, the kind of community that hardworking men and women would choose to live their whole lives in. The census of 1850 showed that, of the little more than two hundred residents in the town, there were thirteen laborers, six farmers, six carpenters, six blacksmiths, three cabinetmakers, three stonemasons, three tailors, two physicians, two merchants, two clerks, two brickmakers, one attorney, one butcher, one brewer, one chairmaker, one gardener, one harnessmaker, one land agent, one landlord, one plasterer, one shoemaker, and one wagonmaker. Ethnically, the town was less diverse. A little more than one hundred of the residents hailed from "Germany" (i.e., from German-speaking states in Central Europe). Twenty-seven had been born in Wisconsin (most of these were children) and fifty were from other states. Sixteen came from England, five from Ireland, one from Switzerland, and three from other countries. Except for the decidedly German bent to the population, the town in 1850 was a representative community of the upper Middle West, in its way a fair cross section of the state in which it stood and the nation to which it belonged.

Agoston's manor house on the Wisconsin River was only half built when he decided to leave for California, and the bridge over the Wisconsin River was still in the planning stages. The manor house was destined never to be completed, for, in the end, the experiment of building a house by the "gravel method" proved to be a failure. The walls developed cracks even before Agoston left Haraszthy Town, and the new owner of the property decided to raze the half-finished walls and replace them with more conventional bricks and mortar.[30] The bridge would not be built promptly either. Agoston's departure may have dampened investors' enthusiasm for this substantial project; it would not be until 1856 that the first bridge would be built over the Wisconsin at Sauk Prairie, and this would have its anchorage in Prairie du Sac rather than Haraszthy Town. A bridge would not be built where Agoston planned it until 1860.[31]

Agoston's departure from Sauk Prairie also brought about a change in the name of Haraszthy Town. On March 17, 1849, Governor Dewey signed a bill changing the name Haraszthy to Westfield.[32] It is not hard to imagine why the residents of the village would hanker for a new name. Haraszthy was a mouthful, even for the German residents, and the Americans must have thought it hopeless.[33] Westfield was a homely American name, as easy to spell as it was to pronounce.[34] But Westfield was destined to be an even less durable name than Haraszthy, for in the spring of 1852 the legislature again changed the name of Agoston's village, this time to Sauk City.[35] Sauk City made more sense than either Haraszthy or Westfield, for the place had been called Sauk since Indian times and the name was used in common parlance to refer to both the Upper and Lower villages. So the village that was conceived as Széptáj, came to life as Haraszthy Town, and briefly called itself Westfield, entered its maturity as Sauk City. The last name was to stick. More than a hundred years later it would still be Sauk City.

Before all these changes could take place, however, the founder of the town had to make his exit. For Agoston, the first order of business was to liquidate his property interests in and around Sauk Prairie.[36] Next he had to make arrangements for actually getting to California. The sea route might include a voyage of four to six months' duration around South America, or a shorter but somewhat more hazardous voyage by steamer to the Atlantic coast of Central America (at either Panama or Nicaragua), a river and land trip by canoe and mule across the isthmus to the Pacific Ocean, and another ocean voyage up the west coast of Mexico and California to San Francisco. The sea routes were less taxing, and certainly less dangerous, than the land routes, and emigrants who chose to travel by sea could leave at once. Emigrants who opted to cross the plains had to wait for the winter snow to thaw, for ice in the rivers to break up, and for mud in the roads to dry. The land journey could be expected to take as long as either sea voyage, but it was less expensive, and for Americans who lived in the western states, much more direct. Most of those who went to California by sea in 1849 came from the Atlantic Coast; most of those who traveled by land were from the western states.

On March 10, 1849, a meeting was held in Madison for the purpose of organizing a California Emigrant Association, to be composed of California-bound residents of Madison and the surrounding country. Sutherland was elected chairman and Daniel Holt secretary. Agoston, Sutherland, W. M. Rasdall, and Thomas Walker were members of a committee that drafted a resolution stating the purposes of the association:

Resolved, That the Madison Emigrant Society will leave Madison for California on Monday the 26th March inst.

Resolved, That the members of this company pledge themselves each to the other, to protect one another at all hazards and under every circumstance.

Resolved, That an invitation be extended to the citizens of Wisconsin desirous of emigrating to California, with ox teams to join us on or before the 26th inst.

Resolved, That a committee, consisting of Messrs. Haraszthy, Claghorn and Williams, be appointed a committee of inspection to examine the wagons and teams of the different emigrants, and that no person be permitted to join this association unless their wagons, &c. are approved by said committee.

Resolved, That the editors of the English and German papers in the eastern portion of the state, be requested to publish the above resolutions.[37]

Charles Haraszthy did not take part in the organization of the Wisconsin Emigrant Association. He was still in Haraszthy Town with his wife Frances, agonizing over the impending separation between himself and his son.

It was in March, too, that the Wisconsin legislature invited Agoston to a public dinner. He was one of the state's most notable pioneers, and they wanted to bid him a proper farewell. And so the legislators feted him with toasts and speeches. He was to remember the celebration with fondness for years afterward.[38]

The departure of the Madison Emigrant Society was delayed a few days beyond the appointed date of March 26. Father Gärtner happened to be in Madison on March 30, giving a mission, and stopped to visit the Haraszthy family. The priest said that there were five big "luggage vans" (wagons) in their train and that they were drawn by fifteen teams of oxen. Agoston's was the only wagon that was drawn by horses. He told Gärtner that he would exchange the horses for a team of four oxen when he reached the other side of the Mississippi. The priest noted that the Haraszthy wagon was equipped with hammocks and even a cookstove.

Gärtner made a farewell gift to the Haraszthys—an illuminated image of the Virgin Mary bearing the inscription: "Towards the land of blessing near the Peace Ocean." (In his diary, the priest noted that the "Peace Ocean" was called the "Pacific Ocean" in English.) Eleonora returned the priest's favor with a wooden capsule containing a delicate ivory crucifix and a tiny garnet rosary which she had received in her convent days. Agoston, in what Gärtner called "a gay humor," promised to send the priest some handfuls of gold from California for the erection of a new church in Haraszthy Town.[39]

Around April 1, the brave little train of California-bound emigrants headed out of Madison toward the West. They went to Sauk Prairie first. Robert Richards, Jr., son of the man who operated Agoston's ferry, remembered that Agoston stopped at their house on the morning he left for California. "I shall never forget how he was dressed," Richards wrote. "His clothes were black and he wore bright red stockings on the outside of his pants which reached half way from knee to hip."[40]

The next leg of the journey lay to the southwest, along a road that roughly paralleled the Wisconsin River. If Agoston looked back after his last visit to Haraszthy Town, there is no evidence of it in any of the records. The future lay to the west, and his eyes were firmly fixed on the road ahead.

9

Across

the

Plains

There were five big wagons and fifteen teams of oxen in the train that Agoston led out of Madison in the first week of April 1849.[1] Agoston, Eleonora, and five of their six children were in one. (Their oldest son, fifteen-year-old Gaza, was in school somewhere in the East, preparing for entrance into the United States Naval Academy at Annapolis).[2] Joseph Reiner who, at the last minute, had decided to join the trek to California, may have traveled in the same wagon with the Haraszthys. It was common for emigrants to form partnerships for the journey to California—the partners would pool their resources, share their expenses, and pledge each other their mutual assistance—and Reiner was proud to tell the other emigrants that he was Agoston Haraszthy's partner.[3]

Whether Charles Haraszthy was in the same wagon as Agoston, Eleonora, and the children is not certain. Charles had been torn by divided loyalties when Agoston announced his decision to go to California. He longed to join his son on the westward trek, yet felt bound to remain in Haraszthy Town with his second wife, Frances. Frances, in turn, may have been torn by a desire to remain with her daughter, Matilda Clark, and her wifely duty to follow Charles. Unable to resolve their differences, she and Charles decided to separate

and divide their property, with Charles following Agoston to California and Frances remaining in Wisconsin with Matilda. (Frances
would eventually follow her husband to California, but only after a
long—and, for Charles, quite lonely—separation of several years.) It
is not clear, however, whether Frances and Charles made their decision to separate in time for Charles to join Agoston on the first leg
of the westward journey, or whether he had to catch up with him
some time later.[4]

There was only a trace of snow on the ground when the wagons
pulled out of Haraszthy Town in the first week of April, but the roads
were thick with mud, and the big wagons plodded through deep
ruts. Vehicles that were drawn by oxen were better able to cope with
the mud than Agoston's horse-drawn van. He was aware, of course,
of the advantages of oxen—they were stronger than horses, and
able to exist on sparser feed—but he thought the fleet-footed horses
would enable him to make better time as he moved toward the final
jumping-off point on the Missouri.

On Tuesday, April 4, the travelers stopped in Mineral Point, one
of the last places where they could find such amenities of civilization
as stores and taverns. From Mineral Point, they headed south toward
Galena, where it was possible to obtain passage on steamboats bound
for St. Louis and, beyond it, Independence and St. Joseph on the
Missouri River. A good wagon road led westward from Galena to the
Mississippi opposite Dubuque, Iowa, where a ferry waited to carry
wagons and passengers across the great river. In the neighborhood
of Galena, Agoston and his traveling companions decided that they
would make better time and put less strain on their animals if they
transferred some of their equipment and supplies from their wagons to riverboats. The goods and supplies could be floated through
St. Louis and up the Missouri to St. Joseph, then reloaded in the
wagons. But some of the men would have to leave the wagons and
accompany the goods and supplies by water. The Haraszthys decided
that Charles would take on this responsibility, while Agoston continued to lead the wagons across Iowa and Missouri.

Wagons from all over southwestern Wisconsin and northwestern
Illinois converged on the Dubuque ferry. The Mississippi was nearly
a mile wide at this point, and many trips were necessary to get all

the wagons and animals across. During one of the crossings Joseph Reiner and the ferryman "had words," and the words were followed by blows. The ferryman hit Reiner on the head with a stone and "very nearly killed him," but Reiner was lucky enough to come away with no more than a very bad bruise.[5]

The Iowa countryside was very similar to the southwestern corner of Wisconsin. Low hills rolled up from the banks of the Mississippi to dense stands of timber, divided here and there by narrow valleys and broad prairies.[6] Although it is little more than three hundred miles from Dubuque to St. Joseph in a straight line, the wagon roads traced a sometimes circuitous route so the distance that Agoston and his companions actually had to cover was closer to five hundred miles. The journey was slow and arduous. For the first few days, the travelers kept close to the Mississippi, passing through the frontier town of Maquoketa. On April 11 they arrived at a place called Lyn Grove (probably within the present city limits of Davenport).[7] There they met another train of wagons from Wisconsin. This train, called the Walworth County Mutual Mining Company, had left Delavan, Wisconsin (seat of Walworth County), on March 26 and had traveled southwesterly to the Mississippi River at Dubuque, where they crossed their wagons on April 1. They had proceeded slowly through eastern Iowa before meeting the Haraszthys on April 11, still only a few miles from the Mississippi.

The Walworth train consisted of twelve unmarried men and perhaps half a dozen wagons. They were acquainted with Agoston, if not personally, at least by reputation, and greeted him as "Count." One of the Walworth emigrants, a man named David Brainard, kept a journal of the trip. At Lyn Grove, Brainard noted in his journal that "the Count informed us that he thought it best to go to St. Joseph, as the feed to the Bluffs was very scarce." The "Bluffs" (Council Bluffs, on the east bank of the Missouri River) was one of the most popular outfitting points for emigrants on the California and Oregon trails. Travelers bound for these northern trails could still rendezvous at St. Joseph before proceeding across the plains. It would make little sense, however, for travelers who wished to follow the more southerly Santa Fe Trail to California to pass through Council Bluffs, for the villages of Independence and Weston, Missouri, more than a hundred miles south, were the gateways to the Santa Fe Trail. If the Walworth Company proceeded to "the Bluffs," they would be committing themselves to the California or Oregon trail. If they accompanied the Haraszthys to St. Joseph, they could defer a decision on their ultimate route. They were impressed by Agoston's warnings about the scarcity of feed on the way to the Bluffs and decided to join the Haraszthy train. From Lyn Grove westward, it is possible to follow Agoston's journey in the pages of David Brainard's journal.[8]

Brainard had little to say about the journey from Lyn Grove to St. Joseph, noting only that it took about four weeks and led the emigrants "through some very pretty villages, and over any quantity of mud." They arrived on the outskirts of St. Joseph in the afternoon of May 15. Close to two thousand gold-seekers were waiting in and around the town when the Wisconsin parties arrived, though it was estimated that more than ten thousand had previously passed through and were already on the prairie.

St. Joseph was crowded with taverns, boardinghouses, and stores, and the streets seemed to be in constant commotion. Here it was possible for emigrants who came up the river on steamboats to acquire all the equipment and supplies needed for the trip to California. Great lumbering oxen and mules could also be bought here at reasonable prices, or traded for horses. Agoston probably took advantage of the supply of draft animals in St. Joseph to trade some of his horses for a team of oxen. St. Joseph was also a great center of information for those who were about to set out for California. News traveled up and down the Missouri on the riverboats, and travelers came into town from the plains every day with reports on the condition of the roads, the length of the grass on the prairies, movements of the Indian tribes, and the prevalence of diseases. Cholera, a truly terrifying malady, remained a worry throughout the spring. It typically announced its arrival by sending sharp and painful cramps through the bowels. A violent, almost constant diarrhea and vomiting soon followed, quickly dehydrating the body and rendering the victim unable to stand or even sit unaided. In many cases, death followed within a matter of hours. Cholera caused twenty-six deaths in St. Louis during a single week in April, and a thousand lives were lost to it in the month of June. Every emigrant who approached the Missouri River in the late spring of 1849 lived in constant fear of the disease.

Many guidebooks were available, and every wagon train carried at least one. Army Lieutenant John C. Frémont's *Report of an Exploration of the Country Lying Between the Missouri River and the Rocky Mountains* was the best-known and most detailed report of the northern Great Plains. A famous book from the moment the U.S. Senate ordered it published in 1843, it contained valuable maps not only of the Great Plains but also of the Rocky Mountains as far as eastern Wyoming. Edwin Bryant's *What I Saw in California*, published in 1846, was another valuable account of travel over the northern plains, following the California Trail all the way to the Pacific Coast. The Santa Fe Trail was described in Josiah Gregg's *The Commerce of the Prairies*, published in 1844, and in William H. Emory's *Notes of a Military Reconnaissance from Ft. Leavenworth in Missouri to San Diego in California*, published in 1848. Emory was a lieutenant in the U.S. Army's Topographical Engineers who had traveled with General Stephen Watts Kearny's Army of the West through New Mexico to California in 1846 and 1847. After Kearny reached California, Emory published a detailed description of the country traversed.

All the guidebooks had pocket maps. Those in Emory's book were based in part on the author's own journey, in part on another army expedition conducted in 1846–47 by Lieutenant Colonel Philip St. George Cooke, a dragoon who was ordered by General Kearny to take command of the all-volunteer Mormon Battalion formed in 1846 to help the United States complete the military occupation of California. Since Kearny himself could not take the time to find a wagon route through the mountains west of Santa Fe, he proceeded on pack mules and ordered Cooke, following behind, to find such a route. "Cooke's Wagon Road," as the pioneer route was called, was the only known route by which wagons could travel in a direct line from New Mexico to California. Emory's guidebook contained meticulous descriptions of the countryside on the southern route to California. One intriguing note concerned the California coast between Los Angeles and San Diego:

Of the many fruits capable of being produced with success, by culture and irrigation, the grape is perhaps that which is brought nearest to perfection. Men experienced in growing it, and Europeans, pronounce the soil and climate of this portion of California unequalled for the quality of wine produced from it.[9]

It was necessary at this point to decide which trail to follow and which wagon trains to join (or quit). At this point, too, some travelers gave up the journey. Any number of would-be gold-seekers found when they arrived on the Missouri frontier that their lust for California gold was not as keen as they had thought. Some were discouraged by the threat of cholera, others by the rigors of travel in wagons that lumbered clumsily over almost nonexistent roads, others by stories of treacherous Indians who were waiting to greet them on the plains. Some were just plain homesick. But there were always more to take the place of those who left. One of these was Gaza, who turned up suddenly toward the end of May. He had left school to join his family on the trek west. Agoston was not pleased, for he put a high store on education, but he could understand the desire, and so Gaza found a place in the Haraszthy wagon. With Gaza's arrival, the family was complete.[10]

Some members of the Madison Company who had arrived in St. Joseph ahead of the Haraszthys had already struck off north to Council Bluffs. They had asked Thomas Sutherland, one of the early arrivals, to join them, but Sutherland preferred to wait for Agoston.[11] After Agoston and the Walworth County company pulled into town on May 15, Sutherland huddled with Agoston and Charles and decided that they would form a train bound for San Diego via the Santa Fe Trail.

The Santa Fe Trail was one of the great roads of the American West. Pioneered in the 1820's by Americans who wished to open trade with Mexico's northern frontier, it had been blazed through the wilderness by hunters and trappers and then regularized by more than twenty-five years of pack trains. As far as the New Mexican capital at Santa Fe, it was plotted on maps and marked, after a fashion, by wagon ruts in the prairies. But beyond Santa Fe, the so-called Gila Trail to California was little known. The whole length of the

Santa Fe route (as extended westward by the Gila route) was more than 2,500 miles. The trip could be expected to take as much as three months longer than the trip over the more northern California Trail. What's more, the Santa Fe route would lead the travelers, not to Sacramento, the commercial and transportation center of the California gold country, but to the coastal settlements of southern California. But the Santa Fe route was generally thought to be safer than the California Trail, and Agoston for one had no desire to reach the gold fields. His destination lay farther to the south, in a sunny, southwestern clime suitable for planting vineyards.

It is not known precisely how many wagons were in the train Agoston, Sutherland, and the Walworth Company formed at St. Joseph in May. Many years later, Agoston's daughter Ida recalled that there were twenty,[12] but Ida was only six years old at the time of the trek and her memory of the event is subject to question. When the train reached the Gila River in mid-October, David Brainard indicated that there were a total of ten "teams," by which he presumably meant ten wagons, each pulled by two or three teams. If Ida's recollection is correct, we may surmise that some wagons dropped out between St. Joseph and the Gila, because of damage in travel or because the oxen that pulled them had perished. After Agoston arrived in California, he recalled only that there were ninety men, women, and children in the caravan.[13]

On Friday afternoon, May 18, Agoston and his companions headed south from St. Joseph along the east bank of the Missouri. On Saturday evening, they camped by a small creek and turned their cattle into a pasture. Then all the men of the train met around a campfire to appoint four of their number—Sutherland, Agoston, Charles, and a man named William A. Phoenix—to draft bylaws for the journey. In his diary entry for this day, Brainard identified Charles as "Gen'l Haraszthy" and Agoston as "Col. Haraszthy." Agoston had apparently given up the title of "Count" for good, and it would not again appear in Brainard's journal. The committee members agreed to report a set of bylaws at their next camp.

Sunday, May 20, was windy along the Missouri. The wagons left camp about seven in the morning and in the afternoon passed through the village of Weston, on a bank above the river. Bright and early the following morning, the emigrants loaded their wagons and teams on the ferry and began to cross the Missouri. The job was long and laborious and was not finished until Tuesday about noon. When it was done, the emigrants had a feeling of satisfaction. "Now we are ready for a start, sure," Brainard wrote in his journal. "We have crossed the great dividing line of the white man and the Indian."

From the ferry landing opposite Weston the trail led south along the west bank of the Missouri to Fort Leavenworth, a U.S. Army post established in 1828 to protect traders on the trail between Missouri and Santa Fe, New Mexico, from the Indians. Agoston and his companions camped about a mile from the fort and, at nine o'clock, heard the soldiers beat out the evening tattoo. From Fort Leavenworth, the trail led in a southwesterly direction toward the Kansas River, which joined the Missouri near the town of Westport (later to be renamed Kansas City).

On the evening of May 23, the first day out of Leavenworth, the Wisconsin wagons made camp. The committee appointed to draw up bylaws reported the results of its work, and officers were elected. Agoston was chosen to head up the train with the title of captain. S. A. Phoenix was his first lieutenant and N. P. Phillips his second lieutenant. William A. Phoenix was named wagon master, and Sutherland judge.[14] The rules of the train required every able-bodied man to take his turn at guard duty. Though the wagons had not yet entered Indian country, they were aware that they could meet Indians at any time and were determined to be prepared. Men were called to guard duty in alphabetical order and were required to serve eight-hour shifts throughout the night.

The wagons crossed the Kansas River on Saturday, May 26, and camped in the evening on the "high prairie." On Thursday, May 31, they crossed a beautiful stream lined with trees. It was called 110 Mile Creek because it lay exactly one hundred and ten miles from old Fort Osage on the Missouri River east of Westport.[15] The following day they passed the graves of two emigrants who had died of cholera, and later in the same day they had their first encounter with Indians. They were members of the Kansas tribe, and they wanted to swap moccasins for meal and powder. Their heads were shaved, except for a tuft of hair that was braided, and their faces were painted red. As sunset approached, the chief made his appearance, attended by his interpreter. "He was very gaudy with feathers and skins and little bells," Brainard noted. "He said he was friendly with the whites and liked them. After giving them their supper, they left us, and a good riddance."

On Saturday, June 2, the train passed the grave of a white man who, Brainard noted, had been murdered by the Osage Indians. Just past the grave, the wagons came to a stop. They were about two miles from Council Grove, one of the most famous landmarks on the Santa Fe Trail. Here a forest of trees, nearly half a mile wide in places, rose up from the grassy prairie alongside the Neosho River. Council Grove received its name in 1825, when George C. Sibley, surveying the Santa Fe Trail at the behest of the United States Congress, met under the trees to negotiate a peace treaty with the Osage Indians.[16] The abundance of good wood and water made Council Grove a mandatory stopping place for all the trains on the trail. The Haraszthy train remained in camp for two days. On Sunday, June 5, some Kansas Indians passed by on their way to their buffalo-hunting grounds. Agoston and his companions made some trades with the Indians, in the course of which they acquired what Brainard called "robes" (probably buffalo hides).

Leaving Council Grove, the wagons headed west toward Diamond Springs. They were on a barren plain now, without any streams nearby. They saw antelope running on the distant prairie, but could not come close enough to shoot any, and camped in the evening at a place called Lost Springs. About ten o'clock in the morning on Friday, June 8, they caught their first sight of buffalo. The animals were far off from the train, and several horsemen—Agoston undoubtedly among them—immediately set out on a chase. "Buffalo! Buffalo!" they all shouted. "Hurrah for buffalo."

Soon the hunters disappeared from sight. About an hour later, they reappeared, chasing a big, furry buffalo. As the animal came within ten rods of the wagons, the whole company met it with their rifles, and the buffalo was quickly brought down. "This was the first one that most of us had ever seen," Brainard wrote, "and such an excitement I never saw. If we had found a gold mine there could not have been a greater commotion. Some with an ax, others with knives and hatchets commenced a general slaughter, all anxious to get the best piece."[17] The hunters estimated the animal's weight at twelve hundred pounds.

On Monday, June 11, the train arrived at the Arkansas River. The Arkansas was an important and historic stream, long recognized as the international boundary between the United States and Mexico. They stopped at a place called Camp Osage, fed their cattle, and then pushed on to Walnut Creek, a tributary of the Arkansas. The following day, thousands of buffalo appeared on either side of the trail, and the hunters killed a large bull near the side of the road. They killed another buffalo four days later, then camped at noon on the Pawnee Forks, a narrow tributary of the Arkansas. They kept close to the Arkansas for the next two days, pleased by the good supply of water but more than a little worried by the absence of wood. On the morning of June 16, they saw two Indians approaching, the first they had seen since they left the Kansas tribe in Council Grove. They were Arapaho and professed to be friendly, but the men were concerned when a large number of the Indians, mounted on fine horses, followed them at a distance.

The wagons camped in the evening and soon found that they were in Comanche territory. A party of braves came down to the train to talk with Agoston and his fellow officers. Brainard thought there were between three and four hundred Indians, and about fifteen hundred horses. "Although the chiefs and braves came to us and professed great friendship," Brainard noted in his journal, "we could not banish from our minds their treacherous dispositions. We made twenty miles today. We expected an attack this evening and every man was armed to the teeth but we were happily disappointed."

The following day, more Indians came in to the camp. It may have been on this day that one of the chiefs, according to a story later handed down in the Haraszthy family, made an offer to buy Agoston's six-year-old daughter Ida. The price started out modestly enough, but soon escalated to four squaws and twelve ponies. Years later, Ida laughingly recalled that the offer must have tempted her father.[18] Certainly the Comanches did come into Agoston's camp, and he did speak with them, but whether the topic of conversation was little Ida —or conditions on the trail, or the availability of game in the vicinity, or any of a dozen other topics that might plausibly be discussed by Indians and the captain of a wagon train in the pioneer year of 1849 —must be left to speculation. David Brainard recorded only that the travelers gave the Indians "something to eat and they left us."

The train soon passed Fort Mann, a collection of log cabins built in 1847 to repair wagons and abandoned a year later. Here the travelers found the fragments of hundreds of wagons lying scattered over the ground. They were out of Comanche territory now and in the hunting grounds of the neighboring Arapaho. On June 17, Brainard noted that the Arapaho "have followed our wagons in great numbers. This evening camped as usual on the bank of the river. Some Indians camped near us. This day made 20 miles."

In the four weeks since Agoston and his fellow emigrants had left Fort Leavenworth they had covered nearly four hundred miles. They were now approaching one of the great forks in the Santa Fe Trail, the point at which they had to decide whether they would follow the northern, or "Mountain," branch of the trail into what would later become the southeastern corner of Colorado, or cross the Arkansas and head in a southwesterly direction toward the Cimarron River on what was variously known as the Cimarron Cutoff, the Desert Route, or the Dry Route. The Mountain Branch was a hundred miles longer than the Cimarron Cutoff, but it followed the Arkansas all the way to Bent's Fort, in the foothills of the Rockies, and it was better supplied with wood and water. The Cutoff traversed flatter country and was more accessible to wagons than the Mountain Branch, but it was much drier than the northern route, and it crossed hostile Indian country.

The Cimarron Cutoff was known to be the most desolate and forbidding stretch of the entire Santa Fe Trail. From the place where the trail left the Arkansas to the Cimarron River, about sixty miles distant, there was not a single river, stream, or creek on the map. Mexicans called the Cutoff a *jornada*, or desert "journey." When they saw human bones lying bleached in the sand by the side of the road, the Mexicans expanded the phrase to *jornada del muerto*—"journey of the dead." Besides the lack of water, there was also constant danger of Indian attack. The Comanche and the Apache were the most dangerous Indians on the plains, and the *jornada* cut straight through their hunting grounds. In 1831, while the celebrated mountain man Jedediah Smith was on the Cutoff, a band of Comanche caught him at a water hole and ran him through with their lances. As late as October 1849, a group of Apache ambushed an American merchant named James White and six or seven companions on the Cutoff near a place called Point of Rocks. White was killed on the spot, and his wife and young daughter were carried away and brutally slaughtered. The famous scout Kit Carson was one of those who tried, without success, to apprehend White's murderers.[19]

However difficult the decision, Agoston and his lieutenants did not take long to make it. On Monday, June 18, they forded the Arkansas and camped on the opposite shore. They filled every container on the train with precious water from the Arkansas. This would protect the humans from thirst, though it would do nothing for the animals. Oxen needed daily and copious drafts of fresh water to keep up their strength. Grass, which was ordinarily found only along streams, was also necessary to the animals' health. The travelers remained in the camp for three days, preparing for the inevitable, then on June 21 headed boldly to the southwest.

The ground here was sandy, and almost totally barren. In the evening, they passed the scene of a battle fought by the Mexicans and Texans in 1843 and found the ground still littered with human bones. The following day, they were able to shoot a buffalo and feast on the meat, and to make camp at a place called Sand Creek. They pushed doggedly on, their supplies of water growing lower with each mile, until the morning of June 23, when they reached the Cimarron River. The stream was no match for the Arkansas, but it had a trickle of water in its sandy bed and the thirsty oxen nearly trampled themselves in a mad dash to the stream.

The trail now led along the north bank of the Cimarron. On June 24 the train passed a grave. The bones had been disturbed—by a human being or a wild animal, they could not be sure. On June 28, the train reached Cold Springs, the first good water they had seen in more than 150 miles of travel. They were now in the northwestern corner of what would later become the panhandle of Oklahoma. On July 1 they passed McNees Creek, named for a pioneer who had been slaughtered by the Indians a few years before,[20] and remem-

bered that they were still in Indian territory. They had now crossed
into the northeastern corner of what would later become the state of
New Mexico—a vast expanse of mountain and desert inhabited by
Mexicans and Indians and ruled over by the stern eye of the occupying American army.

On July 2 they passed two rocky peaks rising up from the flat
plain (the mountains called Rabbit Ears), and on July 3 they saw the
famous Round Mound, a solitary cone of rock that rose more than a
thousand feet above the level plain. The train stopped at the base of
Round Mound, while some of the men climbed to its summit. When
they reached the top, they marveled at the splendid vista. Far away
to the northwest, they could see the snowcapped tops of the Sangre
de Cristo Mountains rising in splendor to the clouds.

Coming down from the summit, Agoston and some of his companions visited with Captain Croghan Ker of the Second Dragoons,
who were patrolling in the vicinity. Gaza Haraszthy was much taken
with these mounted warriors of the plains, with their handsome
horses, smart blue uniforms, and gleaming sabers, and asked his
father if he could leave the train and join them. Gaza was hardly
more than a boy, and Agoston cannot have relished the prospect of
sending him forth into the world of men—at least not in the midst of
a frontier desert teeming with Indians. But Gaza was determined to
have a military career and would not take no for an answer. Precisely
when and where Agoston agreed to his son's request is not known,
though Gaza did not actually enlist until the wagons reached Albuquerque at the end of July.[21]

The trail was growing more mountainous now. On Sunday, July 8,
the wagons passed another great monument of the Santa Fe Trail,
a brooding monolith of rock carved by nature into what the emigrants thought was the image of a covered wagon. They all called
it the Wagon Mound. It was reassuring at last to be done with the
flat prairie and see real mountains along the trail. A few miles more
and the wagons came to the Mora River, where they found three
Mexican huts, the first "village" they had encountered since entering New Mexico. Another day of travel brought the travelers to the
town of Las Vegas and, beyond it, a formidable pass in the mountains. They were at an altitude of more than six thousand feet now.

On July 16, they passed Old Pecos, where the ruins of a large Indian pueblo stood alongside the crumbling remains of a Spanish church, built in the eighteenth century and finally abandoned in 1838. Beyond Pecos, the trail climbed ever higher into the Glorieta Pass. One of the wagons broke in a rocky section of the trail and had to be left behind until the next day. With their other wagons creaking in the mountain air, they lumbered into the village of Galisteo on July 17.

Galisteo was a little collection of huts huddled at the edge of a meandering stream, and it was a good place for the travelers to stop and take stock of their position. Santa Fe, the capital of New Mexico, was only about twenty-five miles to the north, but it was on higher ground than Galisteo, and the next stretch of the trail lay on lower ground to the south. Taking the wagons into Santa Fe would not be easy, and they would only have to be brought out again to get back on the trail. Considering their position, Agoston and his lieutenants decided to leave their wagons in Galisteo while individual parties set out on horseback to visit the capital.

Santa Fe was then a town of 6,000 people. It was situated in a broad valley at the foot of the Sangre de Cristo Mountains, about fourteen miles east of the Rio Grande del Norte, New Mexico's longest and most important river. "The inhabitants are principally Mexicans," Brainard wrote; "only one thousand Americans, including the soldiers who are stationed there. The houses are built of adobe and one story high." He thought it all looked like a "dilapidated brick-kiln."

The Haraszthy wagons had now been on the road three and a half months. They had traveled about eight hundred miles since leaving Fort Leavenworth, perhaps fourteen hundred miles since leaving Madison. And they were still a world away from their ultimate destination. To the west of Santa Fe were range after range of towering mountains. The map of Cooke's Wagon Road showed the trail to California leading south from Santa Fe through the valley of the Rio Grande, then across the mountains that straddled the international boundary between New Mexico and Old Sonora to the Gila River in what would later become the Arizona territory, then down the Gila to its confluence with the Colorado, and finally across the desert of southern California to San Diego. According to Cooke's estimate, the total distance from Santa Fe to San Diego was 775 miles. The map indicated only a few landmarks, and great stretches of territory were totally blank. If the travelers thought that by reaching Santa Fe they had accomplished something, they were right. If they thought they had accomplished half of what they had set out to accomplish, they were gravely mistaken.

10

And On
to the
Promised
Land

The Haraszthy wagons remained in Galisteo for six days. On Thursday, July 26, they headed south through a steep mountain pass, where the trail in some places was so narrow that the wagons could barely pass.[1] After a few hours, the road widened to reveal the valley of the Rio Grande spread out before them.

Their first stop was on July 29, at a camp near the village of Albuquerque. Here Agoston went with Gaza to the headquarters of the Second Dragoons and watched as Captain Ker took the boy's enlistment in Company K.[2] The high-spirited teenager, who had given up a hoped-for naval career to join his family on the road to California, had now embarked on a career in the United States Army. Agoston cannot have failed to be proud.

As the wagons resumed their march down the valley, Agoston watched the local farmers (mostly Indians) at work in their fields. He saw corn and wheat, orchards planted to apples, peaches and apricots, and luxuriant vineyards that grew along the riverbed. Above the orchards and the vineyards, he could see herds of mules and goats, and sheep grazing on the mountainsides.

Two incidents conspired to disturb the tranquillity of the travelers' journey down the Rio Grande Valley. The first occurred when one of the oxen stumbled on an uneven section of road and the wagon it was pulling turned over and spilled its contents on the road. Fortunately, no serious damage was done, and the vehicle was righted and refilled after a short delay. The second occurred on the morning of August 13, when the men and women of the train awoke to discover that they had been visited during the night by thieves who had made off with a variety of personal property—boots, shoes, hats, shirts, and even keys and snuffboxes. This was the first theft of any consequence that the travelers had suffered, and they were angered by the boldness of the crime. Agoston made a search for the missing articles in the village but could not find them. Then he went to see the *alcalde* (chief magistrate) of the village, but could not find him at home. So he left a message and, to guarantee that the alcalde would answer it, took two of the villagers' horses. The next day the alcalde appeared in the camp to say that if the stolen goods were not returned within three days he would make the villagers pay for them. The wagons remained in camp for two days, waiting for news from the village, but they heard nothing. Finally, Agoston announced that the wagons would have to push on while he went back and forced a settlement.

The wagons lumbered south as Agoston and his lieutenants headed north. The wagon road was good that day, and the train made seventeen miles before stopping by the river for the night. The following morning, Agoston rode into camp and announced that he had recovered a part of the stolen property, and what Brainard called "mules enough for the balance." The travelers seemed mollified by the captain's decisive action.

The next village on the wagon road was Socorro, a pretty little town of adobes clustered around a plaza. It was Tuesday, August 21, the feast of the Martyrdom of St. Augustine, and the townspeople were celebrating the day. There was a mass in the morning and a feast during the day. In the evening a carved and painted image of the saint was carried through the streets as the crowd sang to the accompaniment of a fiddle and triangle. South of Socorro the road grew increasingly rough and dry, almost treeless, with only scrubby grass for the oxen. On September 3, while the travelers were descending a rocky slope, the axletree of one of the wagons suddenly shattered. Every man joined in the job of moving the contents of the crippled vehicle to another wagon, and then towing the broken wagon into camp. The men searched along the river for a suitable tree with which to fashion a new axle, and considered themselves lucky when they found one.

On September 9, the train passed a fresh grave—a simple board inscribed with a name that Brainard recognized as that of a young Missourian who was traveling with a train that had earlier passed them on the trail. The man was about twenty-five years old and had seemed to be in good health. Brainard confided to his diary that he was shaken by the sight of the humble grave. The next day the train turned sharply to the west, away from the Rio Grande and toward the mountains. They were in a strange and inhospitable land now, almost totally devoid of recognizable landmarks, and forced to rely more than ever before on the map prepared by Philip St. George Cooke in 1847.

For the first day or so, their trail led across a level plain carpeted by wildflowers. The second day they entered a canyon in hopes of finding water, but without luck. They stopped in the canyon about noon and soon saw a party of four Apache approaching on horseback. The Indians claimed to be friendly, but Agoston and his lieutenants were wary. That night, double guards were posted around the wagons. Leaving the canyon, the wagons crossed the Mimbres River, camped at a spring called Ojo de Vaca, then headed into a broad expanse of desert. Agoston set out on horseback to examine the ground that lay ahead. He had to report that the wagons were about to enter "the forty miles where Cooke found no water." The travelers received the news soberly, then proceeded to fill every barrel and cask in the train with precious water in preparation for the *jornada* that lay ahead.

Two days into the dry march, the train came on another canyon. Agoston spotted some Indians on the trail ahead—two mounted horsemen and, behind them, fourteen more, with lances set—and quickly gave orders to every man and woman to take up their arms. Soon shotguns, rifles, and pistols were pointed in the direction of the Indians. Agoston rode ahead, motioning to the Indians to stand back while the train proceeded. If the Indians did not keep their distance, he announced, he would fire. But the Indians were determined and refused to move. So the wagons stopped and waited, while the Indians went into a kind of council. After a while, the Indians looked over their shoulders at the wagons, then prodded their horses and disappeared into the hills.[3]

On September 27, the train reached a place called San Bernardino, where they found the ruins of a Mexican settlement on a bluff overlooking a rich valley. They were in the Mexican state of Sonora now, beyond the protection of the U.S. Army. Agoston and a few of the other men decided to hunt some of the local cattle. They set off with great hopes of replenishing the train's meager store of food, but were disappointed when they bagged only one animal, a fat bull that weighed about eight hundred pounds.

When the hunters returned to the train, they discovered that Agoston and a doctor named W. R. Kerr were both missing. As darkness descended, signal guns were fired in hopes of attracting the missing men's attention, and several men volunteered to climb a steep mountain with signal torches. But this too proved to be in vain. Not long after the climbers arrived back at the train, they were relieved to see Agoston ride in from the darkness. He had not been lost, he explained, but merely pursuing a wild bull. He had strayed farther from the wagons than he intended and had not meant to cause any alarm. But he had seen nothing of the missing Dr. Kerr.

A search party was organized for Kerr the following day, again to no avail. Then, sometime after dark, Kerr rode back into the camp. He had lost his way while hunting the bulls and mistook another wagon camp about six miles up the trail for the Haraszthy train. Arriving there in the moonlight, he had decided to spend the night and wait for his own wagons to catch up. But when they did not appear, he decided to ride back.

On October 3, the train crossed the headwaters of the San Pedro River. The river had appeared to be a substantial stream on Cooke's map, but it proved to be only a creek that meandered through a spongy marsh. They followed the San Pedro until October 7, then left the stream and headed west toward the Mexican village of Santa Cruz, where they struck the bed of the Santa Cruz River, a good stream that led them north into a long and spacious valley. The wag-

ons were approaching the Spanish village of Tucson now, in territory
that would later be known as Arizona.

On Saturday, October 13, the train approached a large church
built of adobe and stone, but standing strangely empty. They paused
long enough to walk into the sanctuary, examine the columns and
domes, and stroll through the gardens that surrounded the building.
Brainard left an admiring description of the church in his journal.
"The front was after the Gothic style," he wrote, "and displayed considerable taste and skill. The belfry was built of large burnt brick,
four-square. In each side was an aperture for the bells, three of
which were still hanging. One had fallen down." Brainard guessed
that the church had been built by Jesuit missionaries. In fact, it had
been erected in the early years of the nineteenth century by Spanish
Franciscans, and abandoned as recently as December of 1848, when
local Apache went on the warpath and drove every Spanish and
Mexican resident into the safety of the fort at Tucson. The church
was the headquarters of the Mission of San José de Tumacacori.

From Tucson the train proceeded north toward the Gila River.
Cooke's map showed that there were friendly Indian villages along
the Gila, and water for thirsty animals, but they first had to cross
the hot, dry bed of the Santa Cruz Valley. The oxen plodded heavily,
breathing billows of dust. On October 15 the train traveled only four
miles before stopping by the edge of a muddy pool of water. Five
days later they found a few more pools of water by the roadside,
but the water was clogged with mud, and there was nowhere near
enough for the stock. "Some of the oxen were nearly given out,"
Brainard noted in his journal. "From this place it was 36 miles to the
Gila, and no water."

The following day, Agoston, Sutherland, and Dr. Kerr made a
painful decision. Their animals were too weak to go on. They would
hold back a few days, hoping the oxen could regain some strength,
while the other wagons continued on to the Gila. Reluctantly, the
other wagons moved forward. The first of them reached the river on
October 24, and on October 30, at about three o'clock in the afternoon, Agoston, Sutherland, and Kerr came up from the rear. Their
animals had sensed that the water was near and were running now.
When they reached the river they rushed over the bank and plunged

headlong into the swift current. The river was a welcome sight for the thirsty travelers too. It was about fifty yards wide, with hard banks on which cottonwoods swayed in the breeze.

Five to ten thousand Pima Indians lived in a series of villages scattered along the Gila River. They were a peaceful tribe, and diligent farmers, and as the wagons approached the river, the Indians came out to meet them with corn, beans, melons, and pumpkins. If the emigrants expected the Indians to make donations of these items, however, they were mistaken, for the Pima had seen enough of wagon trains to know they could strike a good bargain. They demanded that they be paid for their produce in coin or, if coin was not available, double the value in clothing.

Proceeding west, the travelers found another fresh grave by the roadside and beside it the coffin of a child, inscribed with the victim's name and date of burial—October 16. The Indians had unearthed the box and scattered its contents on the road. They stopped to put the coffin back in the ground and cover it with earth. A few miles farther on they came upon a lone man, near death by the side of the road. He had been traveling with pack mules, but in a moment of inattention the Indians had approached, seized his animals, and left him alone in the desert. Some men carried him into one of their wagons.

All along the road, the travelers found ominous evidence of the hardships that previous trains had suffered—abandoned wagons and yokes, chains, barrels, boxes, bridles, and bits, all tossed into the sand. On November 5, Brainard noted in his diary that the oxen had been traveling for nearly a week with little or no grass. Far away to the west, they could see the tops of high mountains. They supposed that they were approaching California now, the "golden land of California." The goal was so near, and yet still so unattainable.

Agoston's oxen were now pitifully weak; even the best of them were hobbling. Another train from Missouri happened by, and a doctor who was in one of the wagons looked at Agoston's teams with horror. Augustus M. Heslep pushed on toward California, but the awful spectacle of Agoston's nearly crippled animals haunted him. When he reached California, he posted a letter to a St. Louis newspaper in which he noted that the animals were in such an extreme condition that he thought it was impossible for them to reach the Colorado. "It is madness to attempt the passage of this route with ox teams," he wrote ominously.[4] Heslep noted that some of the travelers had hit on the expedient of building small flatboats or rafts, loading their goods and equipment on the vessels, and then floating them down the Gila to the Colorado. The lighter loads made it easier for the oxen to march and permitted some trains that otherwise would have perished to make it down the river. Heslep could not have known that Agoston had already considered the idea and adopted it.

The men in the Haraszthy train began building their rafts on November 11. The plan was to build two boats, each measuring nine by sixteen feet, and then couple them together. They would use timbers from abandoned wagons as their lumber, and load their cargos on the makeshift vessels. The train now broke up into two groups— one to stay with the wagons, following the bed of the Gila to its confluence with the Colorado at Yuma, more than a hundred miles distant, and another, smaller, group of five men who would sail the rafts down the river. As captain, Agoston was in charge of the river company.

The Gila River was shallow and full of sandbars, but the current was rapid, and when a raft got stuck it was easy to push it off with poles and get it back in the current. Besides poles and oars, the rafts were equipped with large stones attached to ropes, which served the purpose of anchors when it was necessary to stop the boats for an extended time. After he got to California, Agoston would speak with relish of his voyage down the Gila, boasting that it caused him no more trouble than a trip down the Wisconsin River.[5]

The wagons reached Yuma ahead of the rafts on November 24. They waited anxiously for the boats to appear, asking each wagon train that pulled into the little settlement if they had seen or heard of the boats. Yes, they had seen them, the other emigrants reported. They were still on the river, and seemed to be progressing satisfactorily. Then, about noon on Thursday, November 29, the rafts appeared. A cheer rose up throughout the camp, as the boats tied up to the bank and Agoston and his companions came ashore. They had been on the river for twelve days. The water had been rough in places, they said, and their loads had been thoroughly soaked, but they had all survived—all, that is, except a man named Smith, who had died on the nineteenth and been laid to rest in a dusty grave by the side of the river.

The confluence of the Gila and the Colorado rivers was a busy place in November of 1849. The Indians who made their homes in the surrounding desert were a farming people, traditionally friendly to the whites, though not at all pleased with the sudden arrival of emigrant wagons and a company of U.S. dragoons. The dragoons had been posted at the confluence to protect the United States Boundary Commission and provide aid and comfort to the wagon trains that were struggling over the desert. The commander was Lt. Cave Johnson Couts, a Tennessee-born West Pointer who had been in California with the dragoons since 1846. Acting under orders of his captain, Couts had established an army post on the California side of the Colorado, and a rope-drawn ferry that moved wagons and passengers across the river. Agoston and his train met Couts on the east bank of the Colorado, then boarded his ferry and crossed the river.

The immigrants were now in California—but they had little reason to rejoice, for two hundred miles of daunting desert and mountains still separated them from San Diego. The first part of the trail to San Diego lay along the Mexican border, through the heart of a dry and windswept desert. About twenty miles after they left Yuma, they came to an immense drift of shifting sand that was almost totally devoid of water and vegetation. It was marked on the map of Cooke's Wagon Road as the "Sand Hill." After a few miles of torturous progress through the sand, the wagons left the dunes and emerged on firmer ground. Another thirty miles or so and the oxen caught the scent of water. In a little while they were plunging over the banks of a strange stream of water in the middle of the desert. It was called the New River, though it was not a river at all but a series of freshwater ponds created when the Colorado River overflowed its banks and turned back into the desert. The river had done this many times in the past and would do so again many times in the future, but the ponds that appeared so miraculously would always disappear after a few months, or years. Agoston Haraszthy and his weary band of emigrants could only thank God that the Colorado had chosen to perform its miracle in the sand yet another time in this month of November in the year of Our Lord 1849.

The Haraszthy train had been losing oxen steadily along this stretch of the trail. After Agoston reached San Diego, he would remember that he lost twelve animals in all. Some, he thought, died from eating poison herbs.[6] When an animal could not go on, it was turned loose to fend for itself in the desert. A wagon left without animals had to be abandoned—sometimes with its load if there was no room for it in other wagons. Ida Haraszthy remembered that her father had to abandon one wagon on the desert east of San Diego. He buried its load in the sand in the middle of the trail, and the whole party tramped on the "grave" to conceal it from the Indians, or from emigrants who would later pass by.

As the weary remnants of the train continued on, the trail snaked through a sandy waste, then up a long and rocky slope, turning slightly to the northwest as it entered the mountains east of San Diego. The mountains here were too steep to permit direct transit to the coast. Instead, the trail followed a chain of high passes to a place called Warner's Ranch in the San José Valley. A little over three thousand feet above sea level and hemmed in on all sides by high mountains, the valley was the center of a rancho of more than 25,000 acres that the Mexican authorities had granted in 1844 to a Connecticut-born fur trapper named Jonathan Trumbull Warner. Warner ruled over his mountain domain like a feudal lord—barking orders in Spanish and two or three Indian dialects to crews of laborers who tended the grain fields, orchards, and vineyards that surrounded his house. Not far from the house was a store, in which travelers could obtain much-needed supplies, and a hot sulphur spring (called Agua Caliente by the Spanish and Mexicans) in which they could bathe and wash the trail dust from their clothes.

Warner's Ranch stood at a strategic fork of the emigrant trail. To the right, the trail continued north toward Los Angeles, about one hundred fifty miles distant. To the left, it turned southwestward toward the coastal town of San Diego, about seventy-five miles away. Warner's Ranch was the first white settlement the travelers had seen west of the Colorado River, and they welcomed the chance to stop, refresh themselves and their animals, and share news with the friendly proprietor. Here—if not earlier—Agoston decided that he and his family would head toward San Diego rather than Los Angeles.

A few miles beyond the point where the emigrant trail left Warner's Ranch and pointed toward San Diego was an old Spanish church called Santa Ysabel. There was a small community of Indians nearby, some grain fields, a little vineyard, and a comfortable ranch house occupied by a Mexican. Charles, Eleonora, and the youngest children were exhausted by the long overland journey and badly in need of rest. Agoston had no idea what housing he might find for his family in San Diego, for he had heard that the town was small and its accommodations sparse, and he decided it would be best if his family remained at Santa Ysabel while he pushed on to the coast and made arrangements for them to come on.[7]

Agoston, accompanied by Dr. Kerr and perhaps a few other men from the wagon train, hurried down the mountain road from Santa Ysabel, through a succession of canyons and valleys, and across some low hills, toward San Diego. Their first sight of the blue Pacific Ocean shimmering in the sun was from a mountain slope a few miles north of the town. They descended to the coastal plain and crossed a shallow river into San Diego. Nine months and more than 2,500 miles after he left Madison, Wisconsin, Agoston's long journey was done.

11

A Genial
Climate

San Diego was the oldest European settlement in California, but it offered little to please the eyes of visitors. The plaza in the center of the town was a dusty square adorned with a single flagpole and some cactus plants; there were no trees, and hardly a blade of grass relieved the brownness of the landscape. The adobe houses that clustered around the plaza were constructed, in Spanish colonial style, of adobe bricks covered over with a thin skin of plaster, but they seemed dark and gloomy, and some had obviously seen better days.

San Diego's population cannot have been much more than six hundred when Agoston first saw it,[1] and a good portion of those were American soldiers, the remnants of General Kearny's occupying army. The population was divided between two principal locations, the little town that centered on the plaza and an even smaller village called La Playa, about four miles to the west. Perched on a rocky coast near the mouth of San Diego Bay, a narrow, hook-shaped inlet of the Pacific that ran southward for about fifteen miles, La Playa had developed in the 1820's as a place where ships dropped anchor and cargos of cattle hides and tallow—California's principal exports in the 1830's and 1840's—were taken aboard for transport to distant parts of the world.

San Diego had originally been the home of the first Spanish mission in California, founded in 1769 by the legendary Franciscan missionary Padre Junipero Serra, but in the 1770's the mission was moved about ten miles to the east. There, in a narrow cleft in the coastal mountains called San Diego Valley, the padres built a substantial church and surrounded it with trees, flowers, and vines. But the Mexican authorities evicted them from the place in the 1830's, and in the 1840's the mission compound rapidly took on the appearance of a ruin.

Despite its dreary visage, San Diego was hardly a backwater in 1849. Its strategic location at the far southwestern corner of the American republic guaranteed it an important military presence; and its port—astride the shipping lanes that connected the gold fields of northern California with Central and South America—assured that the town would have plenty of visitors. All Americans who set out for California by sea, whether they made the arduous crossing through Central America or took the longer route around the tip of South America, passed by San Diego on their way to the northern cities of San Francisco and Sacramento. Steamers and sailing ships alike made regular stops at La Playa, and when a ship was in, the plaza could take on a lively appearance as innkeepers sought to make room for the overflow of guests.

Agoston was hospitably welcomed in San Diego. The people of the little town gave him food to eat, a bed in which to sleep, and friendly conversation. He learned quickly about events that had occurred during his months on the overland trail. California was still a United States territory, he was informed, but during the summer the people had elected delegates to a constitutional convention, and the convention had called for the immediate formation of a state government. At an election in November, the voters had approved the state constitution and elected a governor, lieutenant governor, and legislature.

Agoston, too, had important news to transmit to his San Diego hosts. He told them of his trip across the plains and the Southwestern desert, and of the grim conditions that he encountered, particularly along the Gila River and on the last leg of the journey from the Colorado River to Warner's Ranch. Many more California-bound

emigrants were on the trail behind him, he said. They were all suffering from thirst and hunger, and it was imperative that something
be done to help them.

He took his urgent message to William H. Emory, now a major in
the Topographical Engineers and assigned to the staff of the United
States Boundary Commission, the agency charged by Congress with
the duty of surveying and marking the international boundary between the United States and Mexico. Agoston knew that Emory had
army rations at his disposal and offered to take them into the desert
if Emory would release them to him. The major agreed to the request
and gave him four hundred army rations of flour and pork, with
written instructions to distribute them among "distressed" emigrants
between Warner's Ranch and Camp Salvation, near New River.[2] The
San Diego town council supported Agoston's mission by appropriat-
ing a dollar a day for two men to accompany him into the desert.
Dr. Kerr agreed to be one of those men. The other was a younger
man, probably Agoston's fourteen-year-old son Attila.

One of the emigrants who benefited from Agoston's mission was
a thirty-four-year-old lawyer from Missouri named Benjamin Hayes.
In a few years, Hayes would become a prominent judge in southern
California and amass an important collection of historical records of
the region. For now, however, his only goal was to make it through
the desert without starving. Agoston came on Hayes and his weary
party on January 12 at a camp in the mountains beyond Warner's
Ranch. He gave them their allotted rations and invited them to join
him around his campfire for a supper of fried pork and California
beef. He told Hayes about the newly organized state government,
and shared the latest news from Hungary. The Kossuth government
had been overthrown, he said, and its leaders forced to flee the
country, but he still had hopes that they could regroup and reassert
Hungary's independence.

In what was probably his most interesting revelation to Hayes,
Agoston allowed that he was a "practical agriculturalist" and had
come to California, not to look for gold but to make his home. "He
will settle near San Diego," Hayes noted in his diary, "and plant his
vineyard in its genial climate, which he compares to that of Athens."
Hayes was disarmed by Agoston's friendly manner. "Time passes

rapidly while around his hospitable campfire," the Missourian wrote. "The Col. recounts his various adventures; on retiring late at night, the Col. insists on our breakfasting with him to-morrow. He calls himself an old settler."[3]

Agoston was joking, of course, about being an "old settler," although in a country as new as California—one that had grown more rapidly than any section of the United States had ever grown in so short a time—a man who had been in the country for more than a week or two was rightly accorded a measure of deference. It is significant, too, that Agoston told Hayes he was a "settler," for most of the men who came to California in the Gold Rush did so with no intent of staying any longer than was necessary to "strike it rich." Agoston had obviously come for a different purpose.

The sincerity of Agoston's argicultural intentions was underscored in the middle of March when a traveling artist named H. M. T. Powell encountered him in the gardens of the Mission San Luis Rey, on a hillside above the ocean about forty miles north of San Diego. In the days of the mission fathers, San Luis Rey had been the largest and one of the richest of the California missions, and though the missionaries had left it in the 1840's it was still a grand place, with lush gardens, orchards, and even a small vineyard. "A Hungarian Colonel has taken up residence here," Powell noted in his diary on March 12. "Means to settle here, I believe."[4]

Years later, Arpad Haraszthy recalled that he, his brother Attila, and two Americans worked with his father at San Luis Rey, taking up young trees which they later planted at San Diego.[5] Arpad recalled that his father remained at San Luis Rey for several months,[6] enough time for him to return to Santa Ysabel and bring Eleonora, Charles, and the youngest children down to the coast. No evidence has survived showing how Eleonora reacted to the family's new home by the Pacific. She must have been horrified by her first view of San Diego and its dusty plaza, but cheered when she saw the gardens and orchards of San Luis Rey. The fresh breezes that wafted in from the ocean provided welcome relief from the desert heat, and the bright sunshine gave the mission a cheerful aspect. Agoston, however, wanted to find a home in San Diego. The available sites there were not very good, but after some inquiry he was able to find an adobe on Calhoun Street, three doors north of the plaza, that seemed to fit the family's needs. It was one of several houses owned by a wealthy widow named Josefa Fitch. Agoston agreed to rent the property from Mrs. Fitch, and moved his family in sometime in the spring or summer.[7]

He lost no time in scouting out the business and agricultural possibilities of San Diego. Most of the land around the town itself was dry and forbidding, but the bed of the nearby Mission Valley was well-watered. The valley was about a mile wide and nearly ten miles long and threaded throughout its length by the San Diego River. In the days of the padres, the western end had been given over to pasturage for the mission's cattle and horses. Some fields had been fenced off near the mission and used for the cultivation of San Diego's first crops of wheat and barley. Mission Valley was also the site of one of the earliest vineyards ever planted in California.

The grapes that the padres planted were vigorous vines with medium-sized berries that varied in color from reddish-purple to black. They had been brought to Alta California by the Franciscans, presumably from the Jesuit missions of Baja California. In California, they came to be known as the Mission, or sometimes the California, grape. After other varieties of grapes were brought to California from Europe, the Mission grape was sometimes called the "native" grape, but this was a misnomer, since the grape was not indigenous to California but a member of the great *vinifera* family of Old World grapes. The Mission grape has never been precisely traced to any European vines, though it closely resembles a grape grown in Mexico and South America under the name Criolla di vino (the "Creole vine").

The soil in Mission Valley was easily tilled. Although the river went dry in the summer, there was enough well water to irrigate the crops when there was no rain. Perhaps the most outstanding attribute of Mission Valley for agriculturalists was its climate. Agoston had told Benjamin Hayes that San Diego had a "genial climate," and nowhere was this "geniality" more evident than in Mission Valley. There are no extremes of hot or cold in the valley, and the growing season is long. There is a fair amount of fog, particularly during the summer, but it usually clears before noon, and during most of the year the valley basks in sunshine.

The eastern end of the valley formed a part of the San Diego Mission lands and was closed to private development, but the western end was municipal land and had been divided into parcels by the first city surveyors. Though the parcels were called "lots," some were in fact 160-acre farm plots. Agoston acquired several of these plots in the spring of 1850, and on at least one of them—a quarter-section of land that hugged the banks of the San Diego River a short distance north of the San Diego plaza—began to plant an orchard and vineyard.[8]

The date of Agoston's first vine plantings in San Diego has been set down as March 4, 1850.[9] They were undoubtedly of Mission vines, since these were readily available in San Diego and at San Luis Rey and had always flourished in San Diego's warm climate. But Agoston soon made efforts to obtain other stocks. He probably received his first shipment of European cuttings in the fall of 1850 or the early months of 1851.[10] No contemporaneous record of this shipment has survived, though it is reasonable to assume that it came by sea and that it originated in a commercial hothouse in Massachusetts or on Long Island. Notes taken from Agoston's old account books indicate that some of his first vine importations came from New York.[11] Selections of *vinifera* grapes were offered through catalog listings by hothouse growers in Massachusetts and on Long Island in 1850–51. There is no reason to believe that any of the vines that Agoston imported to San Diego were of the Zinfandel, the mysterious (possibly Hungarian) grape that was later to become an inextricable (and elusive) component of the Haraszthy Legend.[12]

No contemporary descriptions of Agoston's San Diego vineyards have been found, but a good description of at least one of his plantations was set down in writing by Benjamin Hayes just four years after Agoston left San Diego for northern California. Hayes, following his pleasant encounter with Agoston in the mountains beyond Warner's Ranch, had gone on to Los Angeles, where he opened a law office and was elected judge of the District Court. His judicial duties required him to ride circuit through Los Angeles and San Diego

counties, and on one of his visits to San Diego in 1856 he stopped to
visit Joseph Reiner. Reiner had taken over Agoston's business properties in San Diego, including the vineyard he had planted on the
banks of the San Diego River not far from the San Diego plaza.[13] In
his diary for September 18, 1856, Hayes described the property as
consisting of two and a third acres of cultivated land irrigated by six
shallow wells and enclosed by a fence of sapling sycamores. Reiner
had put an Indian in charge of the property, and the Indian greeted
the judge and showed him over the plot.

Hayes said there were about four hundred vines, and they were
all "doing well." There were also young fruit trees, and flourishing patches of watermelons, sweet potatoes, and tomatoes. Hayes
thought that the grapes had been planted a year and a half earlier
from cuttings, but they were already bearing fruit and must have
been older. "From one we pulled a large bunch of grapes," Hayes
wrote in his diary, "not very sweet, probably because they were the
first, quite small, with rather a rough taste."[14]

The comparatively small plot of land that Agoston planted in
Mission Valley indicates that his agricultural efforts in San Diego
were never conducted on a very large scale. This fact should give no
surprise when the amazing extent of his other activities in the southern town is considered. For in the two years he lived in San Diego he
not only planted a vineyard, he also operated a stable and omnibus
line, participated in the operation of a butcher shop, took at least
two mineral-prospecting trips, took the lead in subdividing a major
stretch of the San Diego bay shore, built the first San Diego city jail,
held two important public offices and waged a successful campaign
for a third, and played a leading role in a short but bloody "Indian
War" that sent waves of fear through settled communities throughout southern California.

Agoston's first business enterprise in San Diego was apparently a
livery stable and omnibus line that he operated in partnership with
a Spanish-Californian named Juan Bandini. Although the fifty-year-
old Bandini was not of pure Spanish blood (he was born in Peru to
an Italian father and a Spanish mother), he had come to California
while still a young man, married into a prominent local family, and
eventually become the leading member of the town's Hispanic com-

munity. Bandini owned large stretches of cattle land south and east of San Diego, but he was not content to rest on his laurels, and when Agoston approached him with an offer for a partnership, he was only too willing to accept.

The omnibus line operated by the firm of Haraszthy and Bandini ran horse-drawn coaches between the plaza and La Playa.[15] When ships dropped anchor at the port and discharged their passengers onto the wooden wharf, the coaches were waiting to carry them to the plaza. According to Arpad, Attila was employed for a time as one of the drivers on the Haraszthy-Bandini stage line.[16] Another business that Agoston operated in partnership with Bandini was a butcher shop near the plaza.[17] Bandini's cattle ranches undoubtedly supplied the shop with beef, although Agoston may have supplemented the supply with animals raised on his own land. A few years later, Reiner recalled that Agoston had a large herd of cattle while he was in San Diego, and an impressive number of horses.[18] His horses were used both for personal transport and to draw the Haraszthy and Bandini coaches between La Playa and the plaza; the cattle were fattened and slaughtered to supply the butcher shop.

Although Agoston had made it clear from his earliest days in San Diego that he had not come to California for gold, he was not entirely immune to the lure of precious metals. There is no evidence that he ever left San Diego for the northern mining country, but he did make two interesting trips to investigate mining prospects nearer at hand. The first trip was reported in the *San Diego Herald* on August 21, 1851. This trip was made into Lower California in the company of a man named James R. Robinson. Robinson was one of the most interesting men who settled in San Diego during Agoston's time.[19] Born in Ohio in 1800, he had migrated first to Kentucky, then to Arkansas, and finally to Texas, where he became a prominent lawyer and judge. For a short time before Texas obtained its independence from Mexico, he served as governor. During one of the many skirmishes between the Mexican General Antonio Lopez de Santa Anna and leaders of the Texas independence movement, he was captured by the Mexicans and taken south of the Rio Grande. He eventually obtained his release, returned to his law practice in Texas, and in 1849 joined a wagon train to California. In San Diego, Robin-

son became one of the town's most sought after lawyers, and in 1852
he was elected to the post of district attorney.[20] Before that election,
however, he joined his friend Agoston Haraszthy on a curious journey into the sun-bleached deserts of the Baja California peninsula.

Why Agoston and Robinson decided to travel south is not entirely clear. They may have been motivated in part by the desire for
a good old-fashioned outing in the wilderness—the kind of outing
that had given Agoston so much pleasure in Wisconsin. It is likely
that the men brought their hunting rifles, and pots and pans for
cooking. Knowing Agoston, however, it is almost certain that he also
had a commercial purpose in mind, and the *Herald* article leaves
little doubt that this was the case. According to the newspaper, the
results of the trip were "sufficiently encouraging to make the necessary investments for realizing the rich stores of earth so near us, and
preparations therefore are said to be in progress." Specimens of the
ore recovered by Agoston and his partner were put on display at a
local store and in Robinson's law office.[21] The *Herald* did not disclose
whether the ore contained gold or silver.

A little more than a month after the trip with Robinson, Agoston
embarked on another prospecting trip, this time in the company of
a Massachusetts-born steamship agent named Charles R. Johnson.
The men traveled into what the *Herald* called "the mining district in
Southern California." Whether this "district" was in the mountains
or the desert, or somewhere along the seacoast, the *Herald* did not
reveal; but it made it clear that the explorers were looking for silver:
the district through which they traveled contained "new silver mines
which are now about being opened," and the mines "are likely to
yield as great, if not a greater profit than any of the silver mines now
being worked in Mexico." Johnson told the *Herald* that he and Agoston had also traveled to "the newly discovered copper mines of San
Antonia [*sic*]." From one of those mines they had taken eight ounces
of pure copper by the simple expedient of burning and hammering
it to break out the rock.[22]

Some time after he returned to San Diego, Agoston made a trip
by ship to San Francisco. While in the northern city, he displayed a
hulking chunk of silver that weighed nearly two pounds. He said he
had personally seen it extracted from ore. The only description of

the silver known to have survived—a letter written by one of Agoston's San Diego acquaintances who was visiting San Francisco at the same time—says simply that it came "from below," which could have meant either southern California or the Baja Peninsula.[23] Perhaps the silver came from "the copper mines of San Antonia" described by Charles Johnson. Silver commonly occurs in proximity to copper, and the name San Antonio is common in all countries where the Spanish have settled. But if there was a San Antonio mining district in southern California in 1851, its location was not revealed in the pages of the *San Diego Herald*.[24] Nor, surprisingly, was there any further mention of Agoston's mineral explorations in the newspaper.

Perhaps the ore was not as rich as first reported; or perhaps the difficulties of organizing an investment company discouraged Agoston from following up on the discovery. More likely, he simply did not have time to pursue the matter, for by September of 1851 his life was becoming even busier than it had been before, and the silver mines of southern California were quietly shunted aside for other and more pressing pursuits.

12

Pillars
of the
Community

Agoston had seriously considered embarking on a political career during the last year he lived in Wisconsin, but his sudden decision to leave for California had changed all his plans. The speed with which he entered the political life of San Diego in the spring of 1850 suggests that political opportunities may have presented themselves to him almost uninvited.

California was still governed by Mexican laws when Agoston first saw it, and local officials still bore Mexican titles. Thomas Sutherland had plunged into the political life of San Diego in the early months of 1850, securing a position as one of the *regidores* (or councilmen) of the town and later serving as alcalde, the equivalent of mayor. But the new state legislature quickly changed the political structure of the state, carving it into distinctly American districts called counties and calling for the election of mayors, councilmen, district attorneys, and sheriffs. On April 1, 1850, the voters of San Diego County trooped to the polls in the first election held under the new American system and elected John Hays of Texas as county judge, William Ferrell of North Carolina as district attorney, Thomas Sutherland of Wisconsin as county attorney; and Agoston Haraszthy, native of Hungary and late resident of Haraszthy Town in the state of Wisconsin, as sheriff.[1]

Under the legislature's new plan for California's government, San Diego was not only the most southerly county in the state, it was also the largest. The county boundaries embraced a vast tract of land, running from the Pacific Ocean to the Colorado River, from the Mexican border to the southern peaks of the Sierra Nevada. It included 37,400 square miles of mountains and valleys and deserts and was larger than eleven of the thirty United States, more than half as large as Wisconsin, and nearly as extensive as the old kingdom of Hungary itself. And in all of that area, Sheriff Agoston Haraszthy was solely responsible for enforcement of the law.

The vote for sheriff was a landslide of sorts; Agoston's opponent, the Irish-born Philip Crosthwaite, received only 47 votes to Agoston's 107.[2] Agoston must have been pleased by the confidence his fellow citizens showed in him, and even more pleased when, on June 16, ten weeks after he was elected sheriff, the voters elected him to serve as city marshal and chose his father, Charles Haraszthy, to serve as one of the five members of the common council of the newly incorporated City of San Diego.[3] At or about the same time that he was elected to the council, Charles Haraszthy was also elected to the post of justice of the peace.[4] A little more than six months after the Haraszthys arrived in San Diego, they were pillars of the community— men of honor and influence on the far western frontier of America.

As sheriff of San Diego County, Agoston was charged with the duty of keeping the peace, executing writs and warrants, collecting county taxes, and attending all sessions of courts of record held in the county. He was also the keeper of the county jail and, as such, responsible for the detention of all legally incarcerated persons. His duties as city marshal were similar, requiring him to arrest all those who violated city laws, preside over the city jail, collect city taxes, and attend all meetings of the common council. To help him carry out the duties of both offices he named Joseph Reiner to serve as his deputy.[5]

Though San Diego was not one of the largest towns in California, it was one of the liveliest, and Agoston's duties as sheriff and marshal kept him busy. Clustered around the plaza was an odd assortment of hotels, taverns, and gambling parlors, in all of which liquor was sold freely. These establishments catered particularly to the needs of the travelers who were passing through the town, but some had a local clientele as well, for there were a fair number of unmarried men in the town who had nothing better to do in the evenings or on weekends than meet their friends in a local bar to play monte or billiards and, when the spirit moved them, repair to the plaza for some impromptu pistol shooting. If we may judge from contemporary accounts, Agoston kept a tight rein on activities in and around the plaza, and the old adobe jail built by the Mexicans was never empty for long.

The common council's first meeting was held on June 17, 1850, in a little adobe on the San Diego plaza that the town fathers had grandly designated the City Hall. County Judge John Hays was on hand to administer the oath of office to the newly elected mayor, Joshua Bean, and to councilmen Charles Haraszthy, Charles Noell, Atkins Wright, Charles Johnson, and William Leamy. Sutherland was the city attorney, responsible for giving the mayor and council legal advice and drafting all resolutions and ordinances. The council's regular weekly meetings quickly became one of the highlights of life in the town. After some spirited debate, the lawmakers adopted a comprehensive license ordinance designed to bring local business under municipal control and raise revenues for the city coffers. They also passed ordinances punishing those who made "riotous or disorderly noise by firing guns, pistols, or otherwise," prohibiting the sale of liquor to Indians, forbidding the slaughter of cattle, goats, or swine on the public streets, and creating a Board of Health to consult on the "best means to prevent the introduction and spreading of diseases."[6] Charles Haraszthy was one of four members appointed to the Board of Health.[7]

San Diego was far from a rich town, but the Mexican government had provided it with a rich endowment of land, the so-called pueblo (or city) lands that stretched north and south of the plaza for a distance of ten miles or so. With an almost steady stream of new settlers coming into California, the council believed that the pueblo lands would provide a good source of income for the city; and, not surprisingly, much of its time in the first years was devoted to land sales. Charles Haraszthy was designated by his colleagues as Commissioner of City Lands, with authority to superintend sales, execute deeds, and remit the sales proceeds to the city treasurer.

Even before the council was organized, the city had sold land to local citizens. One of the earliest sales was made on March 18, 1850, when Alcalde Sutherland gave a group of developers a deed for 160 acres of land on the shore of San Diego Bay, about four miles south of the plaza. The developers were headed up by William Heath Davis, a Hawaii-born shipmaster who had made a fortune transporting goods between Honolulu and California and wanted to put some of his money to work in San Diego. Believing that a substantial city could be built at the new site, he and four partners paid $2,304 for the land and immediately began to build a wharf and lay out streets and public squares. They called their development New San Diego, or New Town.

Impressed by Davis's new project, Agoston conceived an idea for a similar development to be located on the bayshore between New Town and the area around the plaza, now called Old Town. He took the idea to some of his friends in San Diego, and nine of them joined him to form a kind of syndicate. Four of the syndicate members were county and city officials: District Judge Oliver Witherby, city councilmen Charles Noell and Atkins Wright, and city surveyor Henry Clayton. Two—Juan Bandini and José María Estudillo—were prominent members of the Spanish community, while the local military establishment was represented by Major Emory and Lt. Cave Couts, who had operated the ferry over the Colorado River when Agoston and his fellow travelers crossed there the previous fall. Sutherland was a member of the syndicate and acted as its attorney.

Joshua Bean was alcalde when Agoston and his new partners applied for a grant of city land on May 20, 1850.[8] They offered to pay five dollars an acre for a tract of 627 acres, assuring Bean that the price was fair and that the public would derive more benefit from selling the land than leaving it vacant. Bean responded by giving Agoston and his partners a deed in consideration of their payment into the city treasury of the sum of $3,135 and their promise to have the land surveyed and mapped.[9] Henry Clayton promptly plotted the boundaries of the tract and drew up a map showing streets and public squares. Because the new development stood between Old Town on the north and Davis's New Town on the south, Agoston and his partners called it Middletown, or Middle San Diego. Many residents of the town, however, insisted on calling it Haraszthyville.[10]

Although Clayton's original map is no longer in existence, it is possible to form some idea of the layout of Middletown by examining maps drawn up a few years later. The tract began at the edge of Old Town, followed the bayshore south to a point 125 feet north of the northern boundary of New Town, and ran back 1,980 feet from the low water line. It was divided into 182 blocks and five public squares, with a main street, called California Avenue, that began at the edge of Old Town, intersected an open area called The Triangle, and angled southwest toward New Town.[11]

Agoston and his partners appointed Sutherland as their attorney-in-fact for the purpose of selling lots in Middletown and handling the day-to-day business of the syndicate.[12] This left Agoston free to devise ways to give Middletown a competitive edge over Davis's New Town. By June 18, he had settled on a plan, and on that date he and his partners presented a written memorial to the council offering to donate an entire block of land facing one of Middletown's most attractive squares if the city would agree to construct "buildings suited for the transaction of the public business" (i.e., a civic center).[13] The developers promised to make a similar offer to the county if it would put up county buildings at the same site. The proposal may have stirred some interest on the council, but it was never formally acted on, for the City of San Diego simply did not have the means to undertake so ambitious a project, even one on such an inviting plot of land as that offered by the developers of Haraszthyville.

It is not known what improvements were actually made in Middletown in 1850. New Town had got off to a fast start in the spring of that year, but it soon became apparent that San Diego was not ready for a "city" on the southern bayshore, and the men who gathered around the plaza in Old Town to drink and gamble were already referring to the project as "Davis's Folly." At least one house was built in Middletown in its first year. It was a wooden structure put up by Agoston himself near the line where Middletown joined Old Town.[14] Years later, notes from Agoston's old account book revealed that he planted a garden and orchard around the new house, and that the garden included grapevines as well as peach and cherry trees imported from New York.[15]

The eagerness with which investors were snapping up the city lands persuaded the council that the city had the means to embark on a series of projects designed to improve the quality of life in the town. At the outset they directed their attention to the glaring need for some institution of public education: there was no functioning school of any kind when the new city government was launched in June. But before a school could be established the council had to find a qualified teacher and locate a building or room that was suitable for classroom use. There was a flurry of excitement in City Hall in November when Mayor Bean reported that a lady had arrived in town who had a reputation as a good teacher and wanted to open a school. Her name was Miss Dillon and Bean proposed that the front room of the City Hall be set aside for her use. But Miss Dillon pronounced the room unsuitable and asked the council to find other space.[16]

The lawmakers referred the matter to the city marshal, instructing Agoston to procure a suitable room somewhere in the town and furnish it at city expense. He reported back on December 26 that he had been unable to find any suitable rooms for the school but was willing to rent the city two of the rooms in his own house for that purpose, and the council accepted his offer.[17] In the meantime, a second teacher had appeared in San Diego. His name was Adolph Waite, and he informed the council that he was willing to accept employment as a teacher in what he called the San Diego Free School. Sensing that it was making progress on the school issue, the council voted on December 12 to offer the teacher a salary not to exceed $1,200 a year and to appoint three of their members to a Board of Education to supervise the fledgling institution.[18] By February 20 of the following year, the council was informed that a teacher had been employed (whether Miss Dillon, Adolph Waite, or some other person is not known) and that Agoston had rented two rooms for school use for the period of six months. And so in the late winter of 1851, the first public school in the city of San Diego was launched in the house of Agoston Haraszthy.[19]

While the council was attempting to establish a school for the children of the town, it was also making efforts to establish a regular church in Old Town. Most of the people of the town were Catholics, but the nearest Catholic church was the old mission in Mission Valley. Early in 1850, the Catholics organized a congregation and

secured a priest to serve as pastor, and on August 24 Charles Haraszthy proposed that the council give the new congregation a lot near
the plaza on condition that they build a church on it.[20]

Despite his involvement in the town affairs of San Diego, Agoston
had not lost interest in affairs in far-off Hungary. Though he was now
more than seven thousand miles away from his native land, he still
eagerly perused the newspapers for Hungarian news. After the fall
of the free Hungarian government, Kossuth had been forced to flee
into Turkey. But the United States government had taken an interest
in Hungarian affairs, and proclaimed its special friendship for the
Hungarian leader. At the instance of Congress, President Millard Fillmore sent an American warship to Turkey to bring Kossuth and his
followers to the United States. On December 5, 1851, the Hungarian
leader arrived in New York, where he was greeted by public officials
and a cheering crowd of more than 200,000 supporters. From New
York, he traveled to Philadelphia, Baltimore, and Washington, and
then set out down the Ohio and Mississippi to New Orleans.

Anxious to support the cause of Hungarian independence, the
San Diego common council voted on December 30, 1850, to set
aside 5,000 acres of city land for a period of one year for the exclusive use of Hungarian refugees. At the end of the year, the land
would be sold to the Hungarians on the same terms that city lands
were sold to other persons. The action was prompted by a "petition
signed by several citizens." Although the "citizens" were not identified in the council's minutes, it is reasonable to assume that Agoston
was one of them. Thomas Sutherland and Charles Haraszthy were
given authority to locate the land.[21]

Another problem that concerned the council in 1850–51 was the
annual flooding of the San Diego River. Like many of southern California's coastal streams, the river was dry most of the year, but when
heavy rains fell in the winter it could turn almost overnight into a
raging torrent. Before 1840, the river had emptied into the ocean at
a place called False Bay, but a series of heavy storms that year forced
it to change its course and seek its mouth farther south in San Diego
Bay. The new river channel came perilously close to the Old Town
plaza and threatened to destroy some of the houses there, and the
mud and sand that the stream emptied into the bay raised concerns

that the shipping lanes there might be blocked. The council decided
to attack the problem on two levels. First, it investigated the feasibility of building a dam to block the river's opening into the bay and
force it back into its old channel. Second, it called on Congress in
faraway Washington to help it tame the river.

On September 23, 1850, the council appointed a committee of
three members to examine the riverbed and report back on the
expediency of diverting the channel. Charles joined Councilman
Leamy and Council President Wright on the committee; three days
later, the council petitioned Congress for an appropriation of funds
to finance the diversion project.[22] Realizing that any Congressional
help would not come in time for the approaching winter, they also
appointed a committee of three persons to negotiate a contract for
the construction of a pile dam to divert the river, at a total cost not
to exceed $4,000.[23] In October, however, the committee reported
that it had been unable to find anyone who was willing to take on
the construction project, and the council temporarily suspended the
diversion efforts.[24] Rains fell that winter with their usual force. The
river flooded, its channel inched closer to the plaza, and the mud
and sand in the bay grew thicker.

Another problem that vexed the council was the city jail. They
had inherited an old adobe "calaboose" from the Mexican regime,
but it was small, cramped, and ill-fitted to its purpose. On June 29,
1850, the council voted to instruct Agoston as city marshal to find a
"good and secure room" somewhere in the town that could be rented
and fitted up as a jail.[25] No suitable room having been found, the
council ordered Agoston on July 13 to repair the existing jail. But
this, too, seemed an impossible task, and on July 29 Charles Haraszthy proposed that the city build a new jail. He recommended that it
have at least three rooms and be built on a plot of city-owned land.
The lawmakers were intrigued by Charles's proposal and appointed
three councilmen (Charles Haraszthy, Charles Noell, and William
Leamy) to look into it. On August 5 they reported their conclusions.
A new jail should be built, but it should have four rooms, and the
cost should be determined by the construction material: if brick,
the committee thought the total cost would run to about $9,813; if
cement, $5,074; if adobe, about $3,055.[26] The lawmakers decided to

build with cement and chose a site on city-owned land about four blocks south of the old plaza.[27]

Notices were ordered to be printed in English and Spanish and posted in three of the most public places in the city, asking for sealed bids for the construction work. The successful bidder would be required to give a bond of $5,000 for the faithful performance of the contract, with two or more sureties to be approved by the council. The mayor would inspect the work and keep the council advised on its progress.[28]

When the council met on August 21 to consider bids for the jail, it was reported that the lowest bid had been made by none other than the city marshal and sheriff, Agoston Haraszthy.[29] The amount of his bid was $4,995. If anyone in San Diego was surprised that a prominent public official should undertake to execute a private contract for the very agency he was employed to serve, there is nothing in the council minutes to indicate the fact. Conflicts of interest were hardly unknown in San Diego in the early 1850's. No law prohibited city officials from engaging in private business with the city; and no effort was made to conceal Agoston's identity as the prospective jail contractor—nor would any such effort have been successful, for in a town as small as San Diego it was inevitable that everybody knew everybody else's business. And so on August 21, 1850, a contract was duly entered into between the City of San Diego and Agoston Haraszthy for the construction of a jail.

The contract specified that the jail was to be thirty-four feet long and twenty-four feet wide. The walls were to be ten feet high and one and a half feet thick. The interior was to be divided by a hall six feet wide, with two rooms of equal size on either side of the hall. The walls and floor were to be of cement and the windows covered with iron bars. The jail was to be "durable and secure" and built in "good and workmanlike manner." The contract price was to be paid in five installments: $1,000 when the work was begun; another $1,000 when the walls were five feet high; another $1,000 when the walls were ten feet high; $995 when the roof was finished; and the final $1,000 when the jail was completed. The contract was signed by Agoston as contractor, Joshua Bean as mayor, Atkins Wright as president of the common council, and William Leamy and Charles Haraszthy as councilmen. Sutherland and a man named John Conger signed as witnesses.[30]

Years after Agoston left San Diego, the contract for the building of the San Diego city jail was to be the subject of recriminations and fulminations. One of the local citizens, a blacksmith and saloon-keeper named Robert Israel, was to claim that he had submitted a lower bid for the project but that Agoston's influence on the council unfairly enabled him to sew the project up. The author of one of the best-known histories of early San Diego, a journalist named William Smythe, was to charge that Agoston owed the jail contract to his father, Charles Haraszthy, and that the contract was "possibly the first instance of graft in California."[31]

Smythe accepted Israel's claims about the jail bid without question, and buttressed them with a very unflattering story that Israel told about Charles Haraszthy's performance as a justice of the peace. According to Israel, a Mexican named Morales had filed a suit to recover some money that he claimed was owed him by Lt. Cave Couts's brother, Blount Couts. Israel had agreed to help Morales present his case before Judge Haraszthy in return for fifteen dollars to be paid out of the recovery. But when the case came on for trial, Morales admitted that Couts had already paid him and that, in fact, he owed Couts twenty-five cents. Smythe later recorded a colloquy that is supposed to have taken place between Charles and Israel, told in Israel's words:

"Vell," says Haraszthy to me, "vat ve goin' to do now?" "Well enter judgment against this Mexican for twenty-five cents." "Vell, but dis man, he got no moneys. Ve must gif de shudgment to de man vat gifts us de pizness."

But Couts was angry and refused to pay. He stormed out, forcing Charles to bow to the evidence and law and enter judgment against Morales.

Israel had been keeping a fine horse, saddle, and bridle in his corral that belonged to Morales, and he was pretty sure that Couts would now attempt to attach them. He advised Morales that he could avoid attachment by selling the items, and offered to pay the Mexican sixty-five dollars on condition that he be allowed a credit for the fifteen dollars he had expected to earn in the courtroom.

Morales agreed, and Israel gave him fifty dollars. But no sooner had the money changed hands than Sheriff Agoston Haraszthy appeared, brandishing a writ of attachment issued in favor of Couts, and asking Israel if Morales didn't have a horse, saddle, and bridle.

"No," Israel answered coolly.

"Well, he did have," Agoston countered.

"Yes," Israel continued, "but he has none now; he has just sold them." And Israel showed Agoston the bill of sale. But Agoston threw it down and angrily swore that it was one of Israel's "damned Yankee tricks!"[32]

The available evidence is inadequate to either confirm or refute Israel's description of Charles's peculiar sense of justice. But there are some obvious problems with the blacksmith's story. First, Israel claimed he was "city marshal" at the time—but the public records clearly show that Agoston was marshal. Further, he apparently told different versions of his story to different people. The version related above was told to Smythe some time before 1908. But, in 1900, a San Diego pioneer named Ephraim Morse (apparently repeating information given him by Israel) told the San Diego Chamber of Commerce that *Israel* was the defendant in the suit and that Charles Haraszthy had entered judgment in Israel's favor but ordered him to pay the costs, explaining: "The plaintiff has nothing, therefore the defendant must pay, for the court must be supported."[33] There was obviously bad blood between Israel and the Haraszthys, though it is impossible to determine whether it originated in Charles Haraszthy's courtroom or outside Robert Israel's corral when Agoston tried to execute the writ against Morales.

The fact that Israel enjoyed making fun of Charles's thick eastern European accent, and that William Smythe was willing to share the "fun" with his readers, does not speak well either for the blacksmith or for the historian. Israel was born in Pennsylvania and Smythe in Massachusetts, and both presumably spoke a more acceptable brand of standard American English than Agoston's father. But it may also be presumed that neither was as adept in German or Latin or French —and certainly not in Magyar—as the scholarly old Hungarian.

A further point is worth noting: Robert Israel's claim that he submitted a bid of $3,000 for the project—almost $2,000 less than

Agoston's bid of $4,995 [34] — is not supported in the voluminous minutes kept by the council during the time the jail project was under consideration. The minutes clearly reveal that, before bids were invited, the council had estimated that a cement jail would cost $5,074. Why would Israel offer to build a cement jail for 40 percent less than the cost estimated by the council? Agoston's bid was just $79 less than the estimated cost.

Agoston began his work on the jail sometime in September of 1850. He rounded up a crew of local workmen and began to gather the necessary materials to mix the cement and form it into stout walls. But the work did not go well, and on November 7 he appeared before the council with the bad news that, under the beating of heavy rains, the structure had "fallen down." He blamed the collapse on the poor quality of the lime used in mixing the cement (though it was the best that could be found in the area). He asked the council to look into the matter and, if it was convinced that it was impossible to construct the jail according to the plans, to release him from his contract.[35] But the council refused. Agoston then protested that he had sustained heavy losses in the work and could not go forward under the existing plan; if the council would not release him from his obligations, it should permit him to build the jail with stone rather than cement, and pay him an additional $2,000 for the more expensive material. On motion of Councilman Leamy, the council agreed to this second request and increased the total amount of the contract from $4,995 to $6,995.[36] Though this new price was a substantial increase, it was still almost $3,000 less than the council's original estimate of the cost of building a brick jail.

Agoston's workmen now began to collect cobblestones for the structure. The work proceeded at a good pace during November, but by the early part of December Agoston found himself in a financial pinch. He had been advancing construction funds out of his own pocket and found that he needed money from the council to complete the project. On December 19 he asked the council to pay him a part of the contract price. When the council replied that it had no money for the purpose, he offered to accept some state bonds held by the city at a discount of seventy cents on the dollar. The council accepted the offer and ordered the treasurer to give him all the bonds necessary to satisfy his claim, except those that the city needed to pay its tax obligations to the state.[37]

On January 21, 1851, Agoston appeared before the council to inform them that he was about to put a roof on the jail and to ask if they wanted him to use cement, shingles, or some other material. A committee of three members examined the building and gave him the necessary instructions.[38] On January 31, Agoston informed the council that the jail was finished. Another committee was appointed to inspect the building, determine if it had been built in accordance with the contract, and either accept or reject it.[39]

Charles Haraszthy was not a member of the inspection committee, for the voters had on January 3 elected a new slate of city officials. Daniel Kurtz had succeeded Joshua Bean as mayor, and George Tebbets, John Brown, Enos Wall, Anthony Blackburn, and a man identified only as J. Jordan were the new council members. The inspection committee consisted of Mayor Kurtz, Councilmen Wall and Brown, and two citizens, identified in the council minutes only as "Mr. Campbell" and "Dr. Tremain."[40] The committee visited the structure and, on March 25, 1851, reported to the council that they had accepted it.[41]

Years later, it was claimed by various writers that the first prisoner housed in the new San Diego jail was a younger brother of the outgoing Mayor Joshua Bean, a callow Kentuckian named Roy Bean. Bean was later to earn a kind of immortality in literature (and motion pictures) as the pistol-toting saloon-keeper and justice of the peace known as "The Law West of the Pecos." Long before he became a motion picture hero, Bean was the subject of an entertaining story put down in print by a pioneer journalist named Horace Bell.[42] Since the story involves Agoston's jail and the use to which it was put, it is worth retelling.

According to Bell, Roy Bean was a good-looking young man who liked to ride around town on horseback, impressing the señoritas with his fancy trappings and equestrian skills. But the young men of the town seethed at his penchant for showing off. One of them, a hotheaded young Frenchman who prided himself on his ability to shoot from the saddle with a revolver, met Bean at the plaza and challenged him to a duel. Dueling had been outlawed by the new state constitution, but the prohibition was widely ignored, and challenges were still issued—and accepted—with some regularity. The challenge that the Frenchman issued to Bean was unusual, however, in that it called for a duel on horseback. As Bell tells the story, when Agoston got word of the impending encounter, he made no effort to prevent it but simply informed the principals that they should arrange their firing so that no innocent bystanders would be in the way. But he warned that if either of the combatants shot an onlooker, he would step in with a penalty.

Bean and his French challenger maneuvered their horses, each jockeying for a position that would enable him to fire at his opponent without incurring the wrath of Sheriff Haraszthy. Bean's gallery of admiring señoritas watched anxiously as the horses went round and round. Finally, Roy Bean saw an opportunity and fired his gun. As the Frenchman reeled in his saddle, Bean fired another round at his horse. Down went the horse and rider in a pile in the middle of the street. The Frenchman was wounded but not fatally. Agoston now decided that the time had come to intervene, and he entered the fray with an announcement that the law had been broken and that he was taking Roy Bean to his newly finished cobblestone jail.

Bean's señoritas were distraught. They visited him in the jail and showered him with gifts—baskets of tamales and bouquets of flowers. Let Horace Bell continue the story:

Concealed among the fragrant petals of the bouquets, or maybe imbedded in the succulent hearts of tamales, were tools of escape. Roy cut his way through that miraculous concrete in less than no time. True gallant that he was he afterward denied that the ladies supplied him with contraband and claimed that no tools were needed to burrow through that public contract job. However, some one had seen to it that his horse stood all caparisoned behind the jail, with holsters and pistol swung at the pommel, and the young gentleman cut stick for Los Angeles.[43]

It did not take long for the story of Roy Bean's escape from the San Diego city jail to assume the status of a legend. The story was passed by word of mouth, embellished, embroidered, and finally so twisted that it bore little resemblance to the facts as they actually occurred. In San Diego, it became popular to say that Roy Bean had escaped from the jail in "an hour"; that not only was he the first prisoner to escape from Agoston Haraszthy's jail, he was the *only* prisoner ever confined within its walls. Years after Agoston had left for the north, residents of San Diego liked to take visitors to see the old jail and watch the expression on their faces as they explained that it was "the first jail in California" and "the very first prisoner incarcerated there dug his way out of it with his pocket knife." Historians who should have known better repeated the misinformation time and time again, and popular writers followed suit.[44]

The truth of the San Diego city jail is much more prosaic than the legend. In fact, the structure was used without incident for more than a year after it was completed. The minutes of the common council contain numerous references to the men who were employed there as jailers and to the compensation they received for their services.[45] The city fathers apparently thought enough of the jail to suggest that it be used not only to confine city prisoners, but also to incarcerate the county prisoners, and in March 1851 the council rented half of the building to Sheriff Haraszthy for use as a county jail.[46] And the people of the town were very glad to have the jail when, in December 1851, Agoston captured the leaders of an Indian uprising that had struck terror into the hearts of the townspeople. He promptly clapped the rebels into the jail, where they remained until their fate—hanging from a gallows erected at the edge of the town—was decided.[47]

But there *were* problems with the jail. On February 7, 1852 (a year after it was put in service), the *Herald* reported that a couple of Indians, incarcerated in the jail "for drunkenness, or some such disorderly behavior, effected their escape through the medium of a broken window." Two weeks later the council was informed that the jail was in need of repairs.[48] Apparently the repairs were not made, for on March 6 the *Herald* reported that a horse thief had been marched off to the jail but had escaped less than two hours later.[49]

In February, Roy Bean's difficulties with the law were reported in the *Herald.* According to the newspaper's account, Bean had been arrested "for shooting a man whose name we did not learn. . . . Private difficulty the cause." On April 17, the *Herald* reported that Bean's victim was a Scot (not a Frenchman as Bell claimed) named John Collins; the Kentuckian's offense was assault with intent to commit murder and "accepting a challenge." His escape was due not to any weakness of the prison walls but to the by-now familiar lack of jail guards.[50]

Agoston was not faulted for failing to guard Bean more closely. Contrary to Bell's story, he had not been anywhere near San Diego when the future "Law West of the Pecos" took his leave from the jail. In fact, he was then in Sacramento, representing the people of San Diego County in the California State Assembly. It is amusing to assume that he took the nonchalant attitude toward dueling that Bell described, but the facts of history are often less amusing than the myth. Perhaps George Hooper, who was Agoston's successor as sheriff of San Diego, was the man who gave orders that the duelers were not to shoot in the direction of the spectators—but it was surely not Agoston.

After Agoston left San Diego for the legislature, the jail was to become the center of a swirling local controversy. When the construction was completed, the city was financially embarrassed and the council lacked the funds necessary to pay the full contract price, so in lieu of cash the council offered to pay the balance in scrip certificates (the equivalent of bonds). The scrip was issued in denominations of one hundred dollars each and carried interest at the then-current rate of 8 percent per month.[51] But even this scrip was not paid. Agoston was able to negotiate some of his scrip in San Diego and thereby recover a part of the balance due him; but he received only pennies on the dollar, and the money came nowhere near satisfying the full contract price.

Mayor Daniel Kurtz was one of the men who bought some of Agoston's scrip. Toward the end of 1853, Kurtz made an attempt to collect on it. By that time, the common council had been disbanded and replaced with a board of trustees. The trustees refused Kurtz's demand that they pay the full interest of 8 percent per month, and Kurtz filed a lawsuit to collect. In an effort to avoid the obligation, the trustees claimed that the scrip was not legally issued, that the jail contract required the expenditure of more than the city's annual income and therefore violated the city charter, and that the project was not completed in a "workmanlike manner." (Significantly, the trustees did not claim that Robert Israel—or any other person—had entered a lower bid than Agoston.) After some preliminary legal skirmishing, the suit was finally compromised, with the city agreeing to pay the principal amount of the scrip and interest at the rate of 4 percent per month.[52]

In 1859 Agoston himself tried to collect on some of the scrip. Again the trustees refused to honor the obligation, claiming, as before, that the jail contract violated the city charter and that the jail itself was not properly constructed. When Agoston filed suit, the trustees claimed that the court lacked jurisdiction and that Agoston's complaint failed to "state facts sufficient to constitute a cause of action." (Again, no claim was made of irregularities in the bidding procedures.) The court sustained the trustees' claim and summarily dismissed the suit.[53] In one of the ironies with which history abounds, the order of dismissal was signed by District Judge Benjamin Hayes, the onetime overland immigrant who, exactly ten years before, had been befriended by Agoston in the desert east of Warner's Ranch.

The charges of "graft" and conflict of interests that later swirled around the first San Diego jail appear to have been without any real basis in fact. The minutes of the San Diego council make it clear that the jail was inspected and accepted before Agoston received the scrip, yet when efforts were made to collect on the scrip the city trustees claimed that the jail had not been built in a "workmanlike manner." Smythe later claimed that the cobblestones were set "in ordinary mortar, without cement," and thus were easily removed with a knife.[54] But if this is the case, the defect was not apparent when the inspection committee examined the structure in 1851 and it did not prevent the jail from being put to good use in 1851 and 1852.

Since claims of "unworkmanlike" construction did not surface until after efforts were made to collect the city scrip, it seems quite clear that the claims were defensive. San Diego in the late 1850's was in a miserable financial condition, and it would have been nearly impossible for the city to honor the principal amount of the scrip, much less the enormous interest that had accrued. In 1871, a man who held one of the hundred-dollar certificates estimated that, if it were collectible, it would then be worth $2,020.[55] Multiply that sum by the total number of scrip certificates then outstanding, and the awesome dimensions of the debt that the little city could have faced can be fully appreciated.

If San Diego had grown as the pioneers of 1850 and 1851 expected it would, the city would have had no problem paying Agoston for the jail, and it is unlikely that the project would later have become the center of controversy. As it was, however, the city was unable even to keep the jail in repair.[56] When windows broke, they were not repaired, and when shingles blew off the roof, they were not replaced. By the late 1880's, the roof was completely gone, and a tree was growing from the floor of one of the cells, although the walls were still firm.[57] By that time, however, a new jail had been built in San Diego, and the old jail had already passed into legend.

13

Drawing
a Line

Agoston's service as sheriff of San Diego County and marshal of the City of San Diego had thrust him into the center of local politics. If he did not always like his experiences as a city and county official, he handled them with equanimity, and as he went about his public duties he honed both his skills and his ambitions. By the middle of 1851 he was beginning to raise his political sights from the local to the state level. If the people of San Diego trusted him to enforce the law in a county the size of a European kingdom, why wouldn't they trust him to represent their interests in the state capital? Although it is not known when he first seriously entertained the idea of running for a state office, his name was mentioned in print as a possible candidate for the California Assembly as early as August 1851.[1]

He had shown that his political interests transcended local concerns more than a year earlier, when he took sides on an issue that was looming larger and larger in the eyes of many southern Californians. This was the division of California along geographical lines. When the constitutional convention met at Monterey in 1849, the delegates had rejected proposals that different forms of government be established in the northern and southern parts of the state. The large population centers of California were in the gold-rich north, which enthusiastically favored a state government, while the south, where cattle-raising was the principal industry, feared that the new state would ignore its best interests and unfairly tax the southerners to support the government. The southerners argued that southern California should be set aside as a territory until its population justified the creation of a separate state, while northern California should be permitted to form a state government. But the convention was controlled by the north, and the constitution it adopted called for a state government throughout California.

The southern delegates returned home nursing a resentment. If the delegates in Monterey would not listen to their concerns, perhaps Congress would. It was not until September of 1850 that Congress finally decided to admit all of California to the Union. News of the decision reached California a month later, but until that time, many southern Californians harbored the hope that they could escape the new state and maintain their independence as a United States territory.

California historian Hubert Howe Bancroft thought that efforts to separate the southern and northern parts of California were part of a clandestine "plot" to install slavery on the Pacific Coast. He charged that Senator William M. Gwin, a onetime Mississippian who had taken a lead in the formation of the new state, secretly harbored the hope that, if California were divided, the south could be opened to slavery.[2] Gwin was the leader of one of the two principal factions of the Democratic Party in California, the Southern or so-called Chivalry wing that supported the interests of large landholders and adopted a friendly attitude toward the slaveholding states of the Old South. Gwin and his Chivalry Democrats were opposed by a faction of Democrats who looked to an Irish-American from New York named David C. Broderick as its leader. Broderick had cut his political teeth in the rough-and-tumble of New York City's Tammany Hall, and after his arrival in California in 1849 he lost no time in creating a political organization modeled on its eastern counterpart. In state affairs, Broderick championed the cause of working men and miners, while on national issues he criticized the Democratic Party's pro-Southern policies. Because so many of Broderick's supporters were working men, Chivalry Democrats spoke of them disparagingly as "Shovelry" Democrats. It was an epithet that the politically ambitious Broderick and his followers took almost as a badge of honor.

After he went to the legislature in 1852, Agoston allied himself with Gwin and the Chivalry Democrats, consistently supporting their candidates for statewide offices and supporting Gwin proposals in the legislature. In San Diego, he took an early and enthusiastic part in the campaign to keep southern California out of the new state of California and, after the state was admitted to the Union, to separate the northern and southern halves. Whether he was motivated in this effort by his support of Gwin, or whether his efforts were in any way linked to Gwin's "plot" to install slavery on the Pacific Coast, is an intriguing question, but not one that can easily be answered on the basis of the available record.

Agoston's attitudes toward slavery, like those of millions of other Americans, were not always consistent. In *Travels in North America*, he noted the Catholic church's traditional opposition to slavery and branded the institution as "cruel and unjust." Slavery, he said, was "a sin," and not just for Roman Catholics but for "all mankind."[3] But in the same book he repeated the popular canard that blacks were the only persons capable of doing hard agricultural work in the South, and offered the opinion that any European who contemplated taking up a farm in the southern part of the United States would have to be rich enough to "acquire slaves to cultivate it."[4] Beyond this, he was curiously silent about slavery. He had nothing to say about the slave auctions that were openly conducted in the largest cities of the South (even in the shadow of the capitol at Washington) or about the advertisements offering rewards for the capture and return of runaway slaves that appeared with frightening regularity in newspapers in both the North and South. Other European travelers in America (including Alexis de Tocqueville and Sándor Bölöni Farkas) had expressed revulsion with American slavery, an oppressive and demeaning social institution that bore little resemblance to anything seen in Europe at the time (at its worst, European serfdom was never as demeaning as the American institution of chattel slavery). But Agoston appears to have accepted the view, common among many

Americans at the time, that however offensive slavery was, it was not so offensive that Northerners should risk the wrath of the South by attempting to abolish it.

Gwin was himself a slaveholder and a longtime apologist for the "peculiar institution."[5] In the Monterey convention, he had readily agreed to a constitutional provision banning slavery from California, but when he reached his Senate seat in Washington he took pro-slavery positions on a whole host of issues.[6] Neither Bancroft nor Smythe cited any very convincing evidence of Gwin's "plot" to bring slavery to southern California, and Gwin's own biographer denies that he harbored any such intention.[7] But the denial is not entirely convincing. Gwin was an ambitious man who was quite capable of devious machinations, and it would have suited his grand geopolitical view quite well to have extended slavery from the Atlantic to the Pacific through the means of a new State of Southern California.

Assuming that Gwin did indeed aspire to bring slavery to southern California through a north-south division of the state, it is another question entirely whether Agoston took any part in the "plot." He too was an ambitious man and not above sacrificing principle for personal gain. He knew that slavery was a moral offense, but he also knew that many Catholics not only defended slavery but actually owned slaves. When asked to explain his political views, he said that he was guided by "genuine Jeffersonian principles" and that he believed those principles were "broad enough for the whole human family."[8] But he also knew that Thomas Jefferson had owned slaves, and that many of the Southerners who now threatened secession if the North tried to interfere with slavery claimed to be Jefferson's spiritual descendants. If Agoston sacrificed moral principle on the anvil of political expediency, he would have not been the first (or the last) man to do so—in California or elsewhere.

Agoston's statements about slavery indicate an insensitivity to the true horrors of the institution, but there is no good evidence that he ever enlisted in a plot to transport those horrors from the Old South to southern California. Notwithstanding his later association with the Chivalry Democrats, his efforts to pursue the separate interests of southern California in the early 1850's seem to have been a sincere attempt to rescue a sparsely populated agricultural region from

the control of a newly urbanized mining region and not a decision
to join in a transcontinental "slaveholders' plot." This conclusion is
buttressed by evidence that a good majority of the Americans who
lived in San Diego (from the North as well as the South) supported
his efforts, and that the Spanish and Mexican landowners of southern California also seemed to be enthusiastic about them. It is true
that Hispanic Californians had long oppressed the California Indians, subjecting them to a system of forced labor and discipline that
was often indistinguishable from slavery.[9] But they had never bought
and sold Indians, as Southerners did black slaves,[10] and they had no
real interest in introducing a system that would permit them to treat
human beings as chattels. They were alarmed by the sudden influx
of Americans in their midst and fearful that the newly organized
American state would accelerate the destruction of their old way of
life. Holding off the ultimate day of statehood could, in their minds,
give them a few more years to enjoy the kind of life they had come
to know and love.[11]

Agoston had been in California for less than five months when
he raised his voice in defense of the interests of southern Californians. In early April 1850 he wrote a letter to Henry S. Foote, United
States Senator from Mississippi, informing him that a public meeting had been held in San Diego to consider the formation of a territorial government in the southern part of California. Those who
attended the meeting had strong feelings against the extension of
state government to the south, Agoston said, and he wanted members of Congress to be aware of their feelings. The letter had to go by
steamboat from La Playa to Central America, where mailbags were
transported across the isthmus to the Atlantic side and loaded onto
another ship for the long sea voyage to Washington. When Foote
opened the letter, he thought it important enough to read into the
journal of the Senate.[12] The Senator also received communications
from Los Angeles expressing similar views. At a public meeting in
Los Angeles, a memorial had been drawn up petitioning Congress to
establish a territorial government in southern California. This meeting had been attended by Spanish Californians and some longtime
American residents of the town. But sentiment on the subject was by
no means undivided. Foote reported that residents of Santa Barbara

and San Luis Obispo had expressed opposition to the Los Angeles memorial, and an attempt to organize a mass meeting in San Diego had failed when only six landowners attended.[13]

The Congressional debate on California's request for admission to the Union continued through most of the spring and summer of 1850, Northerners arguing against Southerners. Many in Washington, including the slaveholding President Zachary Taylor, were glad to welcome California into the Union as a free state, but the Southerners were vehemently opposed. Senator Jefferson Davis of Mississippi insisted that a line should be drawn across the United States into the new western territories and that all territory south of the line should be open to slaveholders. The dying Senator John C. Calhoun of South Carolina predicted ominously that the admission of California as a free state would destroy the equilibrium between North and South and eventually lead to civil war. But Henry Clay of Kentucky proposed a compromise that would ensure California's admission as a free state while placating Southerners and avoiding civil war. This proposal, called the Compromise of 1850, won the day, and the guns remained silent—at least for another ten years.

As 1850 led into 1851, however, southern Californians began to grumble about their state government. They had feared that they would be treated unfairly by the northern-dominated state legislature, and with every passing day their fears were heightened. Taxation was the principal bone of contention. The first legislature had imposed two taxes, a capitation (or "poll" tax) and a property tax. The poll tax required every male between the ages of twenty-one and fifty to pay a specified annual sum (originally five dollars) for the support of the government. Indians as well as whites were subject to the tax, although there was a special exemption for "wild and unchristianized Indians."[14] The property tax was based on the assessed value of land and personal property and required officials in each county to collect fifty cents for each hundred dollars' worth of property in the county and remit it to the state treasurer at the end of every year.[15]

On paper, the tax system seemed to comport with the state constitution's mandate that taxation be "equal and uniform throughout the State."[16] In practice, however, the tax burden did not fall equally on all parts of the state. In the years 1850–51, the six southern counties of the state, with a population of a little over 6,000, paid more than $41,000 in property taxes, while the twelve northern counties, with nearly 120,000 inhabitants, paid just $21,000. There were many miners in the north, and some were making fortunes by extracting gold from land they did not own but in which they claimed the mineral rights, but because the claims were mostly on federally owned land, they were not subject to taxation. Theoretically, the poll tax ought to have raised more money in the populous north than in the underpopulated south, but the truth was just the opposite, for the northern mining population was constantly on the move, and many of the miners were able to avoid the tax entirely. Taken together, all the taxes collected in northern California during 1851 amounted to only $120,000, while the same taxes in southern California came to more than $246,000—this despite the fact that two-thirds of the state senators and assemblymen represented the north, and only one-third were from the south.[17]

It is hardly surprising that southern Californians were dissatisfied with the state government and anxious to do something about it. After Congress rejected their original request to limit the state government to the northern counties, they hoped that the legislature would amend the tax laws to lessen their burden on the south. But no legislative relief was forthcoming, and in the summer of 1851 prominent southern Californians began to talk about going to Congress once again—petitioning the national legislature either to divide California into two states or to set aside the southern counties as a territory. Meetings were held in towns and on ranches from San Diego to Monterey to plan a common strategy.

The cause of those who sought to divide California was strengthened in the late spring of 1851 when a weekly newspaper, the *Herald,* was launched in San Diego. The *San Diego Herald* was the first regular newspaper in the town and only the second in southern California (the *Los Angeles Star* made its debut just twelve days earlier). The *Herald*'s publisher, John Judson Ames, believed that southern California had been unfairly treated by the new state government and that something should be done to right the wrong. Though Ames was born in Maine, he had spent some time in Tennessee and Louisiana before joining the Gold Rush to California. In 1851, he hauled an old printing press that he had once used in New Orleans across Panama and up to San Diego, where he published the first issue of the *Herald* on May 29, 1851.[18] It did not take Agoston long to strike up a friendship with Ames, and less than two months after the *Herald* was born the sheriff of San Diego took to its pages with a long letter detailing the grievances of southern California. The letter was printed in the issue of July 24.

Agoston complained that, at the last session of the legislature, nearly every law that was passed had different provisions for the northern and southern parts of the state. There were differences in the laws prescribing fees to be charged by public officers, in the laws setting judges' salaries, and even in the laws relating to stray animals. These differences were not really surprising in view of the plain fact, Agoston asserted, that "the southern interest is utterly different from the northern one." It was unfair for the state to impose equal tax rates on the different sections of the state, since the south was an agricultural and grazing community and had none of the commercial advantages of the north. Also, the enormous distances that separated most of the people of southern California from the state government (the capital was more than six hundred miles from the population centers of the south) put a burden on the south. Since the legislature had turned a deaf ear to southern grievances, Agoston argued that the only course open to southerners was to call a convention to petition Congress for a territorial government.[19]

In an editorial published in the following week's issue, editor Ames agreed that southern California had been "neglected and abused by the more prosperous and monopolising portions of the north," but he thought it was still possible for southern Californians to work through the legislature to remedy the existing evils, and he urged the people to elect "men of industry, intelligence, and inflexible integrity" to represent them in the state elections set for the first week in September.[20]

The question was clearly controversial. Many took Agoston's view, and in late August, the newspapers in both San Diego and Los Angeles published a manifesto signed by prominent citizens of San Diego, Los Angeles, Santa Barbara, and Monterey urging that a convention assemble at Santa Barbara at the end of September. The list of San Diego signatories was almost a Who's Who of the prominent citizens of the town, and included William Heath Davis, Juan Bandini, José Antonio Estudillo, Charles Noell, Judson Ames, Cave Couts, John Hays, James Robinson, and Joaquin Ortega. Agoston's signature appeared at the head of the San Diego list.[21] A public meeting was held in San Diego on Saturday evening, August 30, to discuss plans for the convention. With Robinson presiding, Agoston was chosen to head up a committee to contact representatives of the other counties and agree on a date and place for the convention.

Thirty-one delegates attended the convention that opened in Santa Barbara on October 20, 1851. Sutherland, who had recently moved to San Francisco, came down on a coastal steamer to join his San Diego friends and nominate Agoston for president. But, in a close vote, the prominent Los Angeleno José Antonio Carrillo was given the nod, and Agoston was chosen to head up the rules committee.

Although the delegates were unanimous in their view that the state should be divided, they differed on whether the convention should draw a firm dividing line or leave that task to the legislature after Congress decreed the division. One group of delegates wanted to draw a line that would commence on the coast in the vicinity of Santa Cruz County, run eastward to the Coast Range Mountains, thence south to the southern end of the San Joaquin Valley, and from there eastward to the state boundary. Agoston took to the floor to argue against any firm boundary. The only effect of drawing a line at this stage, he said, would be to allow opponents of state division to quarrel with its specifics. Where to fix the line was a proper question for the legislature to decide. "Let the South gain all the votes and sympathies it can," he said, "but let it not act as if it wantonly insulted the Legislature." Agoston's faction won the first vote on the boundary question. But, after he and Sutherland withdrew (thinking the question had been settled), the other side tried again to force the issue. Their persistence angered the remaining delegates and, on the fifth day of the meeting, eleven of them—including all but one of the remaining San Diego delegates—stormed out.

In the meantime, however, Agoston had gained a different forum in which to press the boundary issue. On September 6, 1851, he had been elected to represent San Diego County in the State Assembly for the third session of the California legislature, set to convene in January 1852; the question of state division had been the central plank in his campaign platform. Though in the future his eyes would be turned northward, for the time being at least his sympathies were still with the south.

Before he could leave for the state capital, however, he had some important business to finish in San Diego.

14

An Indian
"War"

In addition to the other duties of his office, the sheriff of San Diego was the ex officio tax collector of the county.[1] He was required by law to set up offices at Old Town and La Playa in the fall and wait for residents to come in with their property declarations and the money necessary to discharge their tax obligations to the county and state governments. If a taxpayer failed to comply with the law, the county treasurer would file liens, and the tax collector would collect on the liens. The rural nature of San Diego County meant that Agoston had to make long trips into the countryside to confront recalcitrant taxpayers, inform them of their legal obligations, and post legal notices in Spanish and English advising property owners that their property was subject to sale.

His trips into the countryside brought him into contact with the many Indians who lived around the old mission compounds, or in villages (called *rancherías*) farther up in the canyons and hills. The Indians had never reconciled themselves to the white men in their midst. In the more than eighty years since Junipero Serra planted the first seeds of Christianity in California, many Indians had been baptized in the missions and accepted at least the outward trappings of Catholicism, but others remained essentially untouched by the

European invasion. Most of the christianized Indians had lived in and around the missions, held there by the padres' stern (and often unforgiving) discipline. After the Mexican government "secularized" the institutions in the 1830's and stripped the padres of their civil authority, turning the buildings and lands over to the government, many Indians returned to their rancherías to resume their old ways and customs.

At the height of the Spanish and Mexican settlement of California, there were not many more than 7,500 whites in all California; within five years of the American conquest the number of whites in the state was more than fifteen times that number. The Indians looked upon the new invaders of the country as even more menacing than the Spanish, threatening not only their way of life but perhaps their very existence. They resented the settlers who were moving in from the thin line of Spanish and Mexican settlement along the coast, building ranch houses, digging wells, occupying land that the Indians had traditionally claimed as their own. And, in the fall of 1851, they resented the sheriff of San Diego, who rode boldly into their midst, demanding that they pay taxes to a government more than six hundred miles away that they had had no share in choosing and for whose welfare they had not the slightest concern.

The California Constitution had made it clear that Indians were not eligible to vote, but when the legislature enacted the revenue act of 1850 it specifically subjected "christianized" Indians to the same taxes as the white residents.[2] It is true that many Indians maintained ranches of sorts, on which they grazed cattle and sheep, tended patches of beans and other vegetables, and even cultivated a few, small vineyards. But the Indians kept largely to themselves. Their stock and crops were mostly consumed at home, and they rarely had any money—certainly not enough to pay taxes to the State of California.

One of the main centers of Indian settlement in southern California was the area around Warner's Ranch in the mountains east of San Diego. Jonathan Warner had been elected to represent San Diego in the state Senate in 1850, but when he was not attending the legislature he returned to his mountain domain to oversee his herds of cattle, flocks of sheep, and fields of grain, and stand watch over the hot sulphur spring that bubbled up out of the ground about two miles from his ranch house. There was a substantial population of Indians at Agua Caliente; they derived their name—Cupeño—from the native name for the springs, which was *Cupa* (or *Kupa*). There were about five hundred Cupeños, led by a christianized Indian named Antonio Garra. Garra had been baptized at San Luis Rey, but after the padres left he returned to the Cupeño country around Warner's Ranch and assumed the position of *naat*, or chief, of his *ranchería*. White men who knew Garra found him to be energetic, determined, and unpredictable.

The tax collector had visited the Indian villages in 1850 and collected the taxes they owed. But when Agoston went out to make his collections in 1851, he encountered an entirely different mood. Joshua Bean, after his term as mayor of San Diego expired, had moved to Los Angeles County and become a major general of the state militia. Apparently on his own authority, Bean decided that it was not fair to ask Indians to pay taxes to the white man's government and issued an order "forbidding" the natives to comply with the 1851 assessments. To Agoston himself, Bean issued a curious challenge. If he wanted to collect taxes from the Indians, Bean said, he would have to sue Bean first.[3] Agoston later recalled his response to Bean:

My answer was that "the tax is a judgment against the property, and does not require suit, and I am not over anxious to collect taxes from the Indians, but I am charged by the county Auditor with the sum, and I cannot, therefore, release them; but to settle the matter I will write to the Attorney General, and ask his advice, and I will stop collecting taxes until his answer arrives."[4]

Replying to Agoston's query, the attorney general reaffirmed that the taxes had to be collected from the Indians.[5] Agoston turned the state official's letter over to the *Herald* and then wrote the Indian chiefs informing them that the government had not released them from their obligations. But the Indians still refused to pay, explaining that the "general" had ordered them not to pay. Agoston later wrote:

At first I intended to take a posse to enforce the law, but on reflection I found that it would cost the Indians a great deal, and therefore I went among them, attended only by a servant, very much against the advice of my friends, disregarding the danger I was actually running. On my arrival I told them they would have to pay, and in case they did not, it was my duty to come out again and seize their stock and sell the same for taxes.

After a short consultation among themselves, they told me that they would pay, but those who possessed a large number of cattle would like to pay with cattle.

I told them to drive the cattle to San Diego and sell them there to somebody, as I had no authority to receive anything but money.[6]

Faced by the sheriff's determination, several of the chiefs now decided to comply with the law. Representatives of the villages of Pala, Portrera, La Joya, and Pauma sent cattle, horses, and sheep to San Diego, where they were sold and the proceeds turned over to the sheriff. But the money was not enough to cover all the taxes due. Some later charged that Agoston tried to collect the deficiencies by visiting the villages and seizing horses, cows, and mules.[7] He denied that he did any such thing, and assured the editor of the *Los Angeles Star* that "no levy or seizure was made on any Indian property for taxes, either by myself or by any of my deputies."[8]

The tax collections seemed to have gone well enough until the night of Saturday, November 22, when an exhausted courier rode into San Diego from the junction of the Gila and Colorado rivers with news that some Indians there had attacked a party of Americans driving sheep into California from Mexico. While losing a few of their men in the ensuing battle, the Indians had succeeded in killing four or five of the Americans and making off with all their sheep. A few hours later, a second courier arrived in San Diego with even more alarming news: Cupeño Indians had just attacked Warner's Ranch and wreaked deadly destruction on the white people there. Resentment over the year's tax collections was reported to be the cause of the Indians' wrath.

County Judge John Hays had been absent from San Diego for several months when the news from Warner's arrived, and Agoston was the highest official in the town. As such, he had the responsibility of dealing with the crisis. He conferred with Captain Samuel P. Heintzelman, a U.S. Army officer stationed in San Diego, and asked the town's lawyers for his legal options, then announced that he would hold a town meeting to discuss the matter. But before the meeting convened, Senator Warner's wife arrived in town with her

children and some Indian servants. She said that her husband had
been warned that the Indians were planning to attack his ranch and
that he had ordered his family to go to San Diego. She had not seen
him since and had no idea what might have happened to him when
the Indians arrived.

Three hours later, Warner himself rode into the plaza. He said
that the Indians had awakened him about sunrise with a terrible
"war-whoop," and when he opened the door of his house he was met
by a rain of arrows. But he had a gun in hand and was able to defend
himself. He shot one of the attackers dead and, while holding off the
others, managed to get to his horse and beat a hasty retreat. He went
to a nearby village, where he found some of his vaqueros and stock.
Mounting a fresh horse, he rode back to his house and surveyed the
scene. The building had been looted and burned. An Indian who
was lurking nearby fired at him but missed. In all, he estimated that
there were more than a hundred Indians in the original attack party.

Virtually every adult male in San Diego was present at the town
meeting that evening. Senator Warner said he thought that the Indians had joined forces in a general rebellion against white authority
in southern California. The attacks on the Colorado and at his ranch
were not isolated events, he said, but part of a conspiracy. The district attorney told Agoston that he had legal authority to raise a
force of men to suppress the rebellion and bring the perpetrators to
justice. Cave Couts said there were plenty of men in San Diego to
give the sheriff the force he needed, and he himself would be willing
to serve in any capacity. Heintzelman offered to lend the sheriff fifty
muskets if he needed them; Major Edward H. Fitzgerald said that he
expected eighty stands of arms to arrive in San Diego the next day
and that the sheriff could use them all if Mayor Kurtz would personally guarantee their return.

Agoston was then asked to form a company of volunteer soldiers. An enrollment list was quickly drawn up, and Fitzgerald was
invited to assume command. He promptly appointed West Pointer
Couts his captain and Agoston his first lieutenant. Joshua Bean had
also come to the meeting and, apparently forgetting his differences
with Agoston over the Indian taxes, expressed his approval of the
citizens' action. On motion of Couts, the meeting voted to send a

copy of its minutes to Governor John McDougal with the request
that "Fitzgerald's Volunteers" (as the company was dubbed) be enrolled in the state militia.[9]

Martial law was now proclaimed in San Diego. Sentinels were
posted at every approach to the town, and no Indian was permitted
to pass without explaining his business.[10] When news of the attacks
on the Colorado and at Warner's Ranch reached Los Angeles, residents hastily began to assemble arms and make plans for a defense
of the town. The talk in Los Angeles was that all the Indians from
the Colorado River in the south to the Merced River in the north
were planning to join in a simultaneous attack on San Diego, Los
Angeles, and Santa Barbara counties.[11]

The day after the town meeting, there was more disturbing news:
a messenger reported that four white men who had been suffering
from illnesses and had gone to Agua Caliente to recoup their health
had been brutally murdered by the same band of Cupeños who attacked Warner. On Tuesday, November 25, a curious letter arrived in
San Diego from the Cupeño chief, Antonio Garra. It was addressed
to Agoston's friend, the respected Spanish-Californian José Antonio
Estudillo. Translated from Spanish into English, it said "now the blow
is struck" and "all the Indians are invited in all parts." The letter was
cryptic, and its meaning not entirely clear. Some thought it indicated
that Estudillo was in league with the Indians, but Agoston scoffed at
the suggestion. He said that the letter was Antonio Garra's "declaration of war" and had to be treated as such. He estimated that Garra
had four or five hundred men in his force, but the number could be
increased to three thousand within a few days; and he believed that
the white citizens of San Diego needed immediate reinforcements
from the state. Accordingly, he set pen to paper to advise Governor
McDougal that the whites in San Diego were under siege and would
need "prompt aid and assistance" to help them hold off the Indians.[12]

Meanwhile, San Diego was filling up with refugees from the
countryside. Agoston sent Joseph Reiner into the mountains as a
scout. Reiner returned with the report that Garra had set up a kind
of headquarters at Agua Caliente and was in command of a "strong
force."[13]

The Fitzgerald Volunteers were ready to move on November 27.

There were about forty mounted men in the company, with Major Fitzgerald in command and Couts and Agoston as his chief assistants. The company reached Warner's Ranch on December 1. There they found one dead Indian, apparently the Indian that Warner had shot, and the ashes of the ranch house. All but a few of the senator's livestock had been driven off. At Agua Caliente, they found the bloodied bodies of the four murdered Americans, all with their hands tied. They buried the corpses and, not finding any Indians in the vicinity, set fire to the Indian huts, then headed back to San Diego.[14]

Not long after the volunteers returned to town, Agoston received a bit of good news. Antonio Garra had been captured in the mountains—not by a white man, but by a Cahuilla chief named Juan Antonio. Four of the men who conspired with Garra in the attack on Warner's had also been spotted at Santa Ysabel. Fitzgerald sent Agoston out to round up the four. He found them at the old mission where he had left his family in December 1849, arrested them without incident, marched them back to San Diego, and clapped them into his cobblestone jail.[15]

The prisoners were an odd assortment of men. One was an American named William Marshall, a onetime sailor who had deserted his ship to San Diego in 1844, fled into the mountains, and married a Cupeño. A second was Marshall's father-in-law, an old Cupeño named José Noca. A third was a Sonoran named Juan Verdugo, who was also sometimes known as Juan Berro. The fourth was an Indian boy named Santos who had been in Warner's house at the time of the Cupeño attack but, when the senator asked him to go outside and "parley" with the attackers, had promptly disappeared. All four of the prisoners were believed to have had prior knowledge of the attack on Warner's and to have taken an actual hand in the murder of the four Americans at Agua Caliente.

Fitzgerald promptly ordered that the prisoners in Agoston's jail be held to a court-martial. He appointed James Robinson to present the case for the prosecution and Army Major Justus McKinstry to represent the defendants. As presiding judge, he called on Agoston.

The trial got under way on Wednesday, December 10. At first, Marshall and Noca stoutly denied that they had had anything to do with the attack on Warner's. When confronted with evidence that they had been seen with Garra and his Cupeños after the attack, they protested that they had been forced to go with Garra and did not do so willingly. Verdugo (alias Berro) contradicted Marshall's claim that he had been forced to go with the attackers. He said that, some time after Warner's Ranch was burned, he had seen Marshall with a party of forty warriors in a canyon east of the ranch and that Marshall had threatened to kill him if he did not join the uprising. Verdugo also said he had heard Marshall order the murder of one of the Americans at Agua Caliente. Marshall had a lot of influence among the Cupeños, Verdugo said, and many of them regarded him as a kind of chief. The Indian boy Santos at first confirmed Marshall's and Noca's protestations of innocence. But when he was cross-examined, he admitted that he had been lying—that the truth was that both Marshall and Verdugo had joined Garra in his raid, and that they did so willingly.

The trial concluded on Friday, December 12, at which time the court announced its decision: Noca would be released with a stern reprimand and the strong suggestion that he use his influence among the Cupeños to see that the attackers who were still at large were captured and brought to justice. Santos was acquitted of all the charges brought against him, but sentenced to forty lashes for having given false testimony. Marshall and Verdugo were found guilty of murder and sentenced to be hanged by their necks until they were dead.

The condemned men were allowed to see a priest before they were led to the gallows. Marshall continued to protest that he was innocent of murder, although he asked his enemies to forgive him his "many transgressions." Verdugo, speaking in Spanish, admitted his guilt and acknowledged the justice of his sentence.[16] At two o'clock in the afternoon, the men were taken to the cemetery outside town where they were made to stand in the bed of a wagon while nooses were slipped over their heads. Marshall struggled violently when the wagon was pulled out from under him, but Verdugo twisted only slightly. Both bodies were left dangling for more than an hour before they were cut down.[17]

Antonio Garra was brought into San Diego early in January 1852, and a second court-martial was convened to try him. Joshua Bean was the presiding judge, Cave Couts was the judge advocate, and

Major McKinstry was again the defense counsel. After the testimony was heard, Garra was condemned to be shot. He met his fate defiantly, laughing at his accusers while kneeling over a freshly dug grave in the San Diego city cemetery. Then a ten-man firing squad let fly with a volley of bullets, and the Indian chief tumbled into his grave.

The execution of Antonio Garra marked a bloody end to a bloody episode in the history of frontier San Diego. But Agoston had taken no part in the denouement of the tragedy, for he had left San Diego more than a week earlier for the new state capital in the San Francisco Bay city of Vallejo to assume his duties as San Diego County's newly elected assemblyman.

For a month or more after the San Diego executions, military units continued to patrol the hills of southern California, capturing Indians who were believed to have had a part in the "rebellion" and attempting to secure frontier outposts in the desert. And the United States government in far-off Washington sent agents to the Indian villages to attempt to negotiate peace treaties with the disaffected tribes.

Agoston's role in what came to be known to historians as the "Garra Uprising" is not easy to assess. He was one of the principal actors in the drama, and some residents of Los Angeles and San Diego thought he had precipitated the whole affair by his overzealous efforts to extract taxes from the Indians. Judson Ames in the *Herald* defended Agoston's role by reminding his readers that the sheriff was only acting in compliance with the law, and after first asking the advice of the attorney general.[18] But the *Los Angeles Star* took a different position, charging that if the law required that the Indians be taxed "the law should be changed, for certainly the Indians receive no protection from the government and there can be no good reason why they should be compelled to bear its burdens. . . . Rebellions have grown out of slighter causes than this."[19] The tax collectors in Los Angeles County "had sufficient discretion to avoid levying contributions from the Indians," the *Star* commented, while Agoston obviously lacked that "discretion."[20]

Agoston might have shown more tact, but Ames was right in saying that the law required him to collect the taxes; and, after he solicited the attorney general's advice, he had no choice but to go forward with the effort. But deciding whether he was sufficiently tactful in his contacts with the Indians may be missing the real issues that Garra's uprising presented. The author of a scholarly treatise on the events surrounding the uprising points out that the Indian's complaints about their treatment at the hands of the whites were many and of long standing.[21] The Indians had been mistreated by the Spanish, Mexicans, and Americans for decades, and there had been bad blood between Warner and the Cupeños long before Agoston attempted to collect taxes. The tax collections of 1851 may have been the fuse that ignited the Garra Uprising, but the explosive power was supplied by long-smoldering tensions between whites and Indians in southern California and, indeed, throughout the United States.

There seems little ground to fault Agoston for his vigorous response to the uprising once it had begun. Grievances, however legitimate, can never justify murder or arson, and a sheriff who responds to a "declaration of war" by raising a paramilitary force to defend white settlements against the threat of attack is doing no more than the people have a right to expect of their chief law enforcement officer. Cave Couts said as much in a letter he wrote to the *Alta California* in San Francisco just after the Fitzgerald Volunteers returned from Warner's Ranch:

Too much credit cannot be given Major Fitzgerald and our worthy citizen and representative, Col. Haraszthy, who was 1st Lieut. of the company, for the zeal and activity manifest upon all occasions during their excursion, and for the manner in which this scouting party was conducted. They have thus expeditiously brought to an end a war that promised to harass not only the whole of the rancherías in this and Los Angeles county, but the cities also.[22]

Agoston's request for military assistance from Governor McDougal had not produced much help. The executive had assembled a company of volunteers called the San Francisco Rangers, but disbanded them when news was received that the situation in San Diego County had become more stable. But some of the Rangers (mostly unemployed miners) still insisted on coming south. They arrived in San Diego by ship around Christmas and, because there was no place for them to sleep in the town, camped in Mission Valley. They were hard-drinking men, and while they were waiting for something useful to do they ranged through Old Town on drunken sprees; there were several angry arguments with residents of the town, and at least one shooting. Agoston could do nothing to restore law and order, for he had already left San Diego to take up his duties as state assemblyman, and so the anguished townspeople sent an urgent call to Army headquarters in La Playa, asking that troops be dispatched to restore order and hurry the Rangers back to San Francisco. One San Diegan wrote the *Alta California*: "Our Old Sheriff, Col. Agoston Haraszthy, was wished for by all the good citizens of the place; his presence as Sheriff would have relieved our town of sending these disgraceful transactions abroad." [23]

15

The
Legislature

When Agoston was first suggested as a candidate for the State Assembly in August of 1851,[1] Joshua Bean and John Cook were also thought to be likely candidates for the office. But Bean lost interest in the contest after he moved to Los Angeles and received an appointment as major general of the state militia. Cook had been elected as San Diego's representative to the Assembly in 1850, but he was a Whig in an overwhelmingly Democratic county and was given little chance of winning a second term.

Judson Ames, the editor of the *San Diego Herald*, was one of Agoston's strongest supporters. He backed him not only because he had been an energetic sheriff and marshal but also because the two men saw nearly eye-to-eye on the question of division of the state. "This great measure is dear to our heart," Ames wrote in one editorial, "as it should be to every man who is identified with, or has any interest in the southern portion of the State."[2] At the time of the Santa Barbara convention, Agoston had proposed that Congress be approached directly with a request that southern California be split off from the state of California and organized as a territory. Ames thought better results could be obtained if southern California's case was pleaded in the legislature, and he urged Agoston to become a candidate. Some

San Diegans criticized Ames for backing Agoston, arguing that, since the *Herald* claimed to be politically independent, it should take no stands in partisan contests. Ames scoffed at the criticism: "It will be a fine state of things, truly, when the publisher of an independent paper cannot go to the polls to vote, or will be threatened with a withdrawal of patronage because he happened to express, publicly, his preference for any particular candidate for public office." [3]

Agoston's election prospects were enhanced by the circle of friends and business associates he had formed during the year and a half he had lived in San Diego. Among other things, he had become an active member and officer of San Diego's first Masonic lodge, and many of San Diego's most prominent citizens had joined him in it. The lodge had been organized in June 1851, when Ames summoned all Masons in good standing to meet at San Diego's Exchange Hotel. At the meeting, a petition for a Masonic dispensation was drawn up and signed by charter members William C. Ferrell, Judson Ames, Daniel Barbee, R. E. Raymond, Agoston Haraszthy, William H. Moon, James Robinson, William Heath Davis, and John Cook. The petition was granted, and a charter was issued to "San Diego Lodge," the first Masonic lodge in southern California. Ferrell was elected as master and Agoston as secretary.[4] John Cook was not elected to any office, a fact that may have boded poorly for his chances in the coming election—for, when the votes for assemblyman from San Diego County were counted in the first week of September, Agoston defeated Cook by the decisive margin of 110 to 52.

Before he could leave for the legislature, Agoston had some public and some personal matters to attend to. He had to resign his positions as sheriff and city marshal, and settle his financial accounts with the county treasurer. He also had to make arrangements for his family while he was away. Attila was sixteen years old now and big and strong enough to accompany his father on his northern trip, but the four youngest children were another matter. Arpad was eleven, Ida nine, Bela five, and baby Otelia three, and they were all too young to travel north into the raw and often-dangerous mining country of the north. San Francisco was growing rapidly, it was true, but it was populated almost exclusively by a rough class of men who had left their wives and children behind them in the mad rush for gold. Eleonora apparently had no interest in going north with Agoston, probably even less interest in remaining behind in San Diego, which was still primitive and dusty and, after such a short time, cannot have felt like home. She had followed Agoston to Sauk Prairie, accompanied him on the long trek from Wisconsin to California, and endured two hard years in an adobe village at the edge of the Pacific Ocean. Now she wanted to pursue her own course, to take her children to New York, where she could enroll them in good schools and where she could lead a more comfortable life in a more civilized environment than she had known in either Wisconsin or California. Whatever other reasons, if any, brought her to the decision to leave California for the East we do not know. We know only that sometime toward the end of 1851 Agoston took his wife and youngest children to the wharf at La Playa where they boarded a steamer bound for New York via Cape Horn. Arriving on the east coast late in 1851 or early in 1852, they lived for a while in New York City. Eleanora was in New York when Lajos Kossuth was regaled there as a conquering hero and was among the women who helped welcome the Hungarian hero to the new land.[5] After a few months, she and the children settled in a little town in New Jersey, about twenty-five miles west of New York. Letters were exchanged, but Agoston would not see his wife or four youngest children again for more than five years.[6]

Agoston himself left San Diego some time around January 1, 1852, on the coastal steamer *Gold Hunter*, bound for San Francisco.[7] There he stopped to visit Thomas Sutherland and his family. Sutherland had started a newspaper in San Francisco called the *Pacific Star*, but he had sold it after a few weeks and gone back to the practice of law.[8] He had made some valuable political contacts in the city and in May 1851 had been elected a vice president of the first state convention of the Democratic Party, which met at Benicia.[9]

The legislature of 1852 was scheduled to meet on January 5 in the brand-new town of Vallejo, about twenty-five miles north of San Francisco. Vallejo dated only to the spring of 1850, when General Mariano Guadalupe Vallejo, a Spanish grandee of the region north of San Francisco Bay, proposed to build a city on a part of his huge Soscol Rancho in Solano County. Vallejo chose a hilly site overlooking Carquinez Strait, where the Napa River flows into San Pablo Bay, and suggested that the city be named Eureka. His friends in the legislature, however, insisted that it be called Vallejo. In a grand gesture, Vallejo offered to give the State of California 146 acres of land and provide funds for a state house, governor's mansion, university, common schools, hospitals, asylums, a botanical garden, and even a state penitentiary.[10] The voters approved the offer in a statewide referendum, and in the spring of 1851 the legislature decreed that it would hold its first session in Vallejo in January 1852. Until General Vallejo could complete the necessary buildings, however, state offices would remain in San Jose.

Agoston traveled from San Francisco to Vallejo on the steamer *Empire* with other members of the legislature, expecting good quarters. Instead, they found a solitary wooden structure that General Vallejo described as a "temporary state house." Food was scarce, and there were practically no hotels in the town. Most of the legislators slept at night aboard the *Empire,* and in the morning climbed a muddy hill to the "temporary state house" to attend the legislature's opening session.[11]

It took some time for all of the assemblymen and senators to make their way to Vallejo, and some members continued to straggle in for a week or so. Agoston was on hand for the first session of the Assembly on January 5 and was one of the first four members to take the oath of office.[12] Two days later he joined his colleagues in the Senate and Assembly to hear the farewell address of the outgoing governor, John McDougal. Originally elected as lieutenant governor in 1849, McDougal had assumed the governor's chair when Peter H. Burnett resigned in January 1851. An Ohio-born Democrat, McDougal was friendly to the southern Californians and devoted a substantial part of his address to their complaints that the state tax system treated them unfairly. He agreed that the interests of the north and south were in many ways inimical, but thought the constitutional provision requiring that taxation be "equal and uniform throughout the State" effectively prevented the legislature from changing the tax laws.[13] He thought the best solution under the circumstances was to call a convention to revise the constitution and thus provide the southerners some relief.[14]

The new governor, John Bigler, delivered his address on January 8. Bigler was a Pennsylvania-born lawyer who had come to California in 1849 and promptly been elected to the Assembly. His friendly, down-to-earth manner won him many friends in the mining country and, in September 1851, helped him win a close election for the state's top elective office. His inaugural address contained not a word about the complaints of the southern Californians and was devoted mostly to platitudes about the progress California had made in its first two years of statehood. He did take a strong stand in support of the Compromise of 1850, expressing the opinion that its provisions had saved the Union at a time when it was "seriously endangered" and pledging himself to strictly enforce its provisions.[15]

While McDougal and Bigler spoke, legislators continued to grumble about the lack of proper facilities in Vallejo. Though it was generally agreed that Vallejo should remain the state capital, it was also agreed that the government could not continue its work there until substantial improvements were made. Agoston joined his colleagues in the Assembly in voting for a series of resolutions affirming that Vallejo was the "constitutional and legal permanent seat of government of the State of California" but that temporary quarters for the government had to be found in another town. The resolutions were a blow to General Vallejo, but not altogether unexpected. A group of citizens in the Central Valley town of Sacramento had offered to make the new Sacramento County Courthouse available for use as a temporary capital, and the legislature determined to accept the offer. And so on Monday, January 12, the senators and assemblymen adjourned from Vallejo to Sacramento,[16] and the next afternoon they went up the Sacramento River on the steamer *Empire* to the new legislative venue. They were greeted in Sacramento with music, oratory, thundering cannons, and a grand ball at the Orleans Hotel. Legislative business resumed on Friday, January 16.[17]

Agoston had come to the legislature with an agenda, and he lost no time in addressing it. Even before the lawmakers pulled up stakes in Vallejo, he made two important points in the Assembly. On January 10, he presented his colleagues with a petition from the residents of San Diego asking that the legislature memorialize Congress for help in changing the course of the San Diego River. The petition was promptly referred to a special committee of five assemblymen, with Agoston as chairman.[18] On the same day, he asked the Assembly to appoint a special committee to look into southern California's tax complaints and Governor McDougal's suggestion that a constitutional convention be called to address them. In compliance with his request, a Select Committee on Revision of the Constitution was appointed to consider the issue. Thirteen members were named to the committee, with Agoston as chairman.[19]

Both the river-diversion and tax issues were of concern to Agoston's constituents, but a third issue was also on their minds. It seemed apparent to most San Diegans that the Common Council, inaugurated with such enthusiasm in 1850, had become an albatross around their necks. Business activity in San Diego had slowed to a snail's pace. The city lands were no longer salable, and tax revenues were alarmingly low. The council found itself unable to pay the costs of continuing city government, much less to retire the substantial debt it had run up in its first year and a half of operation. Agoston himself was still owed a substantial sum of money for construction of the city jail, and there was no prospect that the scrip the city had given him at the end of 1850 would ever be redeemed. In November, the council had even been forced to borrow the money it needed to pay its own tax obligations to the State of California. It had instructed Mayor Kurtz to find a lender who was willing to let the city have $286.37 at the lowest available interest rate. Agoston had submitted the lowest bid and advanced the city the funds it needed to pay its taxes, taking back a promissory note.[20] The note was supposed to be paid in three months, but nobody was sure if, or when, the city would be able to discharge the obligation.

San Diego was not the only community that was having trouble meeting its bills. After the flush times of 1849 and 1850, cities and counties throughout California were feeling the pinch of a sharp financial downturn. The counties of El Dorado, San Joaquin, Yuba, and Nevada were asking the legislature for help in funding their debts, and the cities of Stockton, Sonoma, Marysville, and Nevada City were all asking that their charters be repealed. The repeal of a city's charter ended the governmental authority of the common council, and a commissioner or board of trustees was then created to take charge of the city's property and pay its debts. The citizens

of San Diego had asked State Senator Jonathan Warner to introduce
a bill in the 1851 legislature to repeal the city charter, but Warner
had taken no action on the request.[21] One of Agoston's first actions
in the 1852 legislature (on January 19) was to introduce a bill to repeal the charter. The bill called for a three-member board of trustees
empowered to take charge of all the city's property and sell enough
of it to pay the city's debts.[22] It sailed through both houses and was
signed into law by Governor Bigler on February 3.

A more important matter was the election of a United States
Senator. The legislature had been in Sacramento only ten days when
it took up this business. When the new state was formed in 1849,
the legislature had selected two men to represent it in the Senate,
one the celebrated "Pathfinder," John C. Frémont, and the other the
lesser known, but veteran politician, William M. Gwin. One of the
available seats was to run for a full six years; the other was to expire
after two. Gwin and Frémont drew lots to see who would take the
longer term. Gwin came up the winner, and Frémont's term expired
when the Thirty-first Congress adjourned on March 4, 1851. Frémont had returned to California hoping to persuade the legislature
to reelect him, but there were too many candidates in the field by
then; and after 142 inconclusive ballots, the legislature threw up its
hands in frustration and left the selection to the legislature of 1852.
Until that legislature made a choice, one of California's two senatorial seats would remain vacant.

The political life of the state had by now taken on a distinctive cast. The two principal parties were the Whigs and the Democrats. The Democrats had a slight majority in state elections, but this
advantage was largely undermined by the growing rivalry between
the Chivalry and Shovelry factions. Senator William Gwin's Chivalry
Democrats had jumped to an early lead in the contest over control
of the party apparatus, but Gwin's rival, David Broderick, was rapidly
gaining ground. By 1852, Broderick was serving as state senator from
San Francisco and president of the State Senate in Sacramento, and
it was no secret that he had his eye on the vacant seat in the United
States Senate.

Agoston had probably cast his lot with the Chivalry even before
he arrived in Vallejo. It was not necessary to be a Southerner to

find points of agreement with Gwin and his supporters. Many of the large landowners of southern California were Chivalry Democrats, as were most of the prominent residents of San Diego, and Gwin men were much more sympathetic than the Shovelry Democrats to the southern Californians' tax complaints. When the two houses of the legislature met in convention on Wednesday, January 28, 1852, to receive nominations for United States senator, Agoston did not have to ponder his vote. The Tammany Democrats nominated Broderick, and the Chivalry put up John B. Weller. The Whigs nominated George Tingley, a state senator representing Santa Clara and Contra Costa counties.

Weller, a lawyer from Ohio, had served three terms in Congress and narrowly lost an election for governor of his native state before volunteering for service in the Mexican War. He led a regiment of Ohio volunteers in the Battle of Monterrey, and after the fighting was over came to California as a member of the United States Boundary Commission. Late in 1849, he settled in San Francisco, where he resumed the practice of law and once again became active in Democratic politics. After Sutherland moved to San Francisco in 1851, he and Weller formed a law partnership called Weller and Sutherland.[23] Weller was a competent man who enjoyed the confidence of Senator Gwin. In addition to Broderick and Weller and Tingley, three minor candidates were nominated.[24]

In the senatorial convention, each of the twenty-seven senators and sixty-two assemblymen was entitled to one vote, and all the votes counted equally. In the first ballot, taken on January 28, Weller received 23 votes, Tingley 16, and Broderick 15. The San Diego delegation was unanimous in its support for Weller, for Senator Jonathan Warner joined Assemblyman Agoston Haraszthy in backing the Chivalry candidate. None of the candidates having received a majority, however, the convention proceeded to a second ballot and then a third. Broderick's and Weller's support remained constant on these ballots, but Tingley's seemed to be melting away. Sensing victory, the Democrats met in a caucus on January 29 and decided on a single candidate to carry their banner. It was Weller, and Broderick promptly withdrew from the race. The Whigs mounted a last-ditch effort to stave off the inevitable by nominating a onetime miner

and businessman named Pierson B. Reading as their candidate, but
Reading was no match for the combined forces of the Chivalry and
Shovelry, and Weller won the final vote by a margin of 71 to 17. Agos-
ton had supported Weller on every ballot in the convention and the
Democratic caucus.

Agoston had already (January 22) offered a resolution requesting that Congress appropriate funds to divert the river from San
Diego Bay north of Point Loma. The resolution was referred to the
Committee on Commerce, which recommended its passage. When
the resolution came up for a final vote on February 3, Assemblyman E. F. W. Ellis of Nevada City questioned whether Congress had
constitutional authority to make internal improvements and moved
to recommit the resolution to committee. But Ellis's motion was defeated, and the resolution was passed.[25] The Senate concurred in the
resolution, and it was signed by Governor Bigler on February 14.[26]

Agoston advanced two other measures designed to meet his constituents' special needs. One was a bill calling for the erection of a
state hospital in San Diego. He introduced this bill on February 6; it
was referred to a special committee of five on State Hospitals, which
on February 18 recommended against it, citing the existence of state
hospitals in San Francisco, Stockton, and Sacramento, and the "embarrassed and depressed" condition of the state's finances. Agoston
moved to table his bill, and two days later he withdrew it.[27] But on
March 16 he was back with another proposal, this one a bill providing relief for the indigent sick of San Diego. Only three days after it
was introduced, this bill was considered by the Assembly acting as a
committee of the whole and passed by voice vote. The Senate passed
the bill on April 5, and it was signed by Governor Bigler on April 16.
The bill authorized the newly created San Diego Board of Trustees
to draw up to $2,000 each year from the state treasurer and apply
the money "towards the maintenance and relief of such indigent sick
persons as may arrive at the Port of San Diego, in such manner as
said Trustees may deem most beneficial to such persons."[28] When
word was received back in San Diego that Agoston had taken action
in behalf of the indigent sick, the *Herald* commended him. "This is
indeed an excellent move," the newspaper commented, "and reflects
the greatest credit on the head and heart of the originator of it."[29]

On February 11, Agoston presented the majority report of the Committee on the Revision of the Constitution. This long document (it occupied five pages of small type in the Assembly *Journal*) repeated the by-now familiar complaints of southern Californians that they were the victims of an unfair tax system and that the only way to right matters was to call a constitutional convention. The report asserted that, while tax laws of uniform operation were good provisions in states of moderate dimensions, they were quite the opposite in a state as large as California, which embraced widely different climates, soils, and resources. A minority report pointed out that the constitution contained provisions for its own amendment[30] and argued that it was unwise to call a convention until those provisions were exercised.[31]

The state's newspapers took sides on the issue. In San Francisco, the *Alta California* charged that the call for a convention had been started by propagandists who hoped to divide the state and introduce slavery into southern California; it thought that a new convention would only resurrect the debate over slavery and threaten the Union. But the *Los Angeles Star* said that the movement to revise the constitution had its beginnings in the Santa Barbara convention and that the views stated there correctly expressed the views of southern California. The people of the south, the *Star* said, resented the introduction of the slavery question into the discussion because it pushed the real issues into the background.[32]

The Assembly resolved itself into a committee of the whole to consider the convention proposal. The debate began on February 20 and continued (with interruptions) through March 2, when a final vote was taken. On that date, Agoston's position won the day, and the Assembly voted 51 to 7 to submit the convention proposal to the state's voters.[33] The proposal fared less well in the Senate, where, on April 28, it was indefinitely postponed. For the time being at least, southern Californians would have to wait for tax relief, and California would be spared the ordeal of a new constitutional convention.

The business of the legislature went smoothly enough in Sacramento. With a population of more than 11,000, Sacramento was the second largest city in California in 1852. It owed its commercial prosperity to its location at the confluence of two of the most important

rivers in the state, the Sacramento and the American, and to its proximity to the mining towns of the Sierra Nevada. The courthouse that
was put into service as a temporary state house was a commodious
structure, and much better suited to the legislature's needs than the
buildings in either Vallejo or San Jose. Sacramento was a lively town,
too, with a thriving business district, a good supply of hotels and res-
taurants, and a busy waterfront where ships from San Francisco Bay
met riverboats from the Central Valley. The legislature's decision to
move to Sacramento in January had prompted the two major political parties to hold their conventions in the city the following month.
The Whigs met on February 19 in a Sacramento church and elected
delegates to attend the party's national convention that summer.
The Democratic convention met on February 23, but the Gwin and
Broderick factions were so contentious that each designated its own
temporary chairman and attempted to wrest the rostrum away from
the other. Agoston represented San Diego County in company with
Senator Jonathan Warner. The convention was looking forward to the
national elections in the fall, and anxious to express its preference
for a presidential candidate. There was support for Stephen Douglas
of Illinois, Lewis Cass of Michigan, James Buchanan of Pennsylvania,
and Sam Houston of Texas. One resolution was offered declaring the
convention's support for Douglas, and another for "any union compromise candidate." But the delegates were too sharply divided to
agree on any candidate, and they adjourned without expressing any
preference.[34]

Much of the city of Sacramento was built on low ground adjoining the two rivers, and floods were frequent. After a devastating
flood in 1850, the townspeople had built earthen levees along the
riverbanks to prevent a recurrence, but in the first week of March
1852, rains fell long and hard, raising the prospect that the strength
of the levees would soon be put to a test. On March 6 the rivers
began pouring over the tops of the earthworks. Sometime in the
early morning hours of March 7, the levees gave way. By the next day
a good part of Sacramento was under water. The courthouse itself
was surrounded by water, and though legislative sessions continued,
members had to wade through the water to get to the building, or
venture a ride in any unsteady boat through the streets, in danger

every minute of capsizing. When a quorum was at last assembled, some members demanded that they adjourn to San Francisco, while others argued that they should move temporarily to Benicia, or even return to San Jose; but there was no clear consensus, so the government stayed where it was. A week later the waters receded, the work of cleaning up the city began, and the legislature settled back into its official routine.

One of the key elements of the Compromise of 1850—which both McDougal and Bigler supported—had been a renewed effort to return fugitive slaves to their masters, and there was strong support in the legislature for the adoption of a California fugitive slave law. Under the proposed statute, if any person "held to labor in another state or territory" (i.e., a slave) escaped into California, the "person to whom such labor or service may be due" (i.e., the master) had the right to arrest the fugitive and obtain a warrant for his return. The law prescribed penalties for anyone who knowingly and willingly obstructed the arrest of such a fugitive. Since blacks were forbidden by law to give testimony against whites,[35] the new law in effect gave free rein to anyone who came to California and claimed that a black was a fugitive. Since the "fugitive" could not deny the claim, the case was over even before it was begun.[36]

The fugitive slave law passed the Assembly on February 5, 1852, by a lopsided vote of 42 to 11. Agoston voted with the majority.[37] When the bill got to the Senate, Broderick expressed reservations and, after some hesitation, voted against it. But the Shovelry leader was outvoted by his colleagues, and the bill became law when Governor Bigler signed it on April 15.[38]

The overwhelmingly hostile attitude that was exhibited toward blacks in California was underscored by another incident that occurred on March 22, when Assemblyman Patrick Cannay of Placer County presented a petition from a group of free blacks in San Francisco requesting that the legislature change the law that prevented them from giving testimony against whites. The law was the source of no end of injustice, for it gave whites unlimited license to attack blacks and their families, steal their property, and, if there were no white witnesses to the crimes, completely escape punishment. It is not difficult to understand why free blacks would seek relief from the law, nor, given the racist attitudes that prevailed at the time, why the overwhelming majority of whites would refuse to grant it. The fact that a group of blacks had the "temerity" to petition the legislature was apparently a source of outrage to many members; and, immediately after the San Francisco petition was lodged, Speaker Richard Hammond of San Joaquin County offered a resolution refusing to consider "any petition upon such subject from such source." The Assembly passed the resolution by a vote of 47 to 1.[39] Agoston's support of this resolution does nothing to support his claim to be an "enthusiastic democrat." The most that can be said for his views on this issue is that they were no worse than those of forty-six of his colleagues. But that fact could have been of little solace to the free blacks in San Francisco, who continued to suffer under a barbaric law that condemned men and women to rank injustice simply because of the color of their skins.

Another racially charged issue that came before the legislature in 1852 was the matter of Chinese immigration to California. The number of Chinese immigrants who arrived in California in the first years of the Gold Rush was relatively small. They were treated for the most part with courtesy and consideration, and when San Francisco celebrated California's admission to the Union in October 1850 the Chinese took a prominent part in the festivities. Encouraged by their first reception, the Chinese began to come in greater numbers after 1850. They were good citizens—peaceable, thrifty, and exceedingly industrious. Most of them came to California under contract to associations known as "companies." The associations paid for immigrants' passages to California, in return for which the immigrants agreed to work for them for a period of years. There were eventually six associations in San Francisco, and they became known as the Chinese Six Companies. But as the Chinese moved into the mining towns of the Sierra Nevada, they encountered a wall of white hostility. Whites resented the fact that Chinese miners were willing to work long hours for relatively little pay; they resented the tendency of the Chinese to keep to themselves, shunning white society; and they resented the fact that the Chinese rarely spent their money with local merchants, but returned most of it to the Six Companies, whence it eventually made its way back to China. Most of all, perhaps, they resented the fact that these hardworking, patient miners were taking gold out of the hills and riverbeds—gold that the white miners would much rather have put into their own pockets.

Californians who resented the Chinese were now complaining to the legislature about the "hordes" of Chinese who were descending on the state. Responding to the complaints, Governor Bigler urged the legislature on April 23, 1852, to adopt measures to stem the tide of Chinese immigration. The naturalization laws, he said, extended only to free white persons and did not include the black classes of Africa, the "yellow" or "tawny" races of Asia, or the "copper-colored" races of America. As for the Chinese, the governor said, they had come to California out of "cupidity" and not to enjoy the blessings of a free government.[40] Other legislators, however, valued the Chinese and supported legislation that would make their labor contracts as enforceable in California as in China. Former Governor McDougal praised the Chinese as "one of the most worthy classes of our newly adopted citizens" and expressed the opinion that the "climate and character" of California were peculiarly suited to Chinese settlement.[41]

A variety of proposals had been made to deal with Chinese immigration. In 1850, the legislature had passed a law requiring all noncitizens who wished to mine in any part of the state to pay twenty dollars per month for a license to do so.[42] But the 1850 tax was so high that it amounted to a virtual ban on foreign mining, and it was repealed in 1851.[43] In 1852, a new law was proposed, requiring all "noncitizens" (except California Indians) to pay a monthly tax of three dollars for the privilege of mining gold. The county sheriffs would collect the tax, and the receipts would be divided equally between the state and county governments.[44]

Agoston took the lead against the proposed miner's tax. When the measure was considered by the Assembly as the committee of the whole, he presided over the debate and offered an amendment relieving foreigners who had declared their intentions of becoming citizens from the tax. In ensuing years, he was to become one of the leading defenders of Chinese labor in California and to speak out frequently in support of the Chinese contribution to California agriculture. But in 1852, his belief in the merits of Chinese labor was shared by only a minority of his colleagues, and his amendment lost by a vote of 35 to 6. On the final vote, the tax law was approved by forty ayes to four nays. Agoston was one of the four nays.[45]

Judged on the basis of all its work, the legislature of 1852 was a reasonably productive body. In addition to the election of a United States senator, the adoption of laws respecting fugitive slaves and foreign laborers, and the special matters of concern to Agoston's constituents in San Diego County, the legislature passed laws funding a California State Library, calling for a statewide census in the fall of 1852, creating three new counties, establishing the framework for a statewide system of common schools, taking the first steps toward the erection of a state prison in the San Francisco Bay area, and consenting to the federal government's purchase of California land for a transcontinental railroad. It also passed resolutions approving the Compromise of 1850, calling on Congress to finance the transcontinental railroad with tax revenues, and asking the national legislature to establish a branch of the United States Mint in California "at the earliest possible moment." The need for a mint in gold-rich California was a matter on which all parties and factions agreed, and the resolution requesting Congress to provide one sailed through both houses without opposition.

Agoston enjoyed a reasonably good record on the matters that were of special concern to his constituents. His efforts to call a new constitutional convention failed, but the legislature supported his efforts to repeal the San Diego city charter and replace the Common Council with a board of trustees, to provide relief for indigents in San Diego, and to change the course of the San Diego River.

The important business of the legislature was all concluded by the last week of April, and on Monday, May 4, the Assembly met for the last time to hear final words from Speaker Hammond and then to adjourn sine die.[46]

Agoston's supporters in San Diego had reason to be pleased by his efforts as their assemblyman. Judson Ames, in particular, must have congratulated himself for having supported his candidacy. But when Ames touted Agoston as a candidate for the Assembly in the fall of 1851, he had said that Agoston had "an interest at stake amongst us, and will not be 'pulling up stakes' and putting out as soon as his term of office expires."[47] Ames, no doubt, was alluding to other public officials (among them San Diego County Judge John Hays) who had mysteriously left San Diego for parts north, there to pursue their careers in the mines or the commercial emporiums of San Francisco or Sacramento. By the middle of 1852, San Diego was taking on the appearance of a backwater. Its population had not only stopped growing—it was actually shrinking. The "tide of empire" in California had definitely swung to the north, and even elected public officials were heeding its pull.

Agoston did not seek reelection to the legislature for the term beginning in January 1853; nor did he return to San Diego to live after the final adjournment in Sacramento—thus failing to fulfill Judson Ames's prediction that he would not "pull up stakes" and move on. What neither Ames nor Agoston had anticipated, apparently, was the spell of San Francisco, a city unlike any that Agoston had ever seen in his life. And so, even before the legislature's final adjournment, he had purchased property in the northern city and was making plans to move his home there from San Diego.

16

Las Flores
and Crystal
Springs

Though its population was not much above 35,000 and its steep, narrow streets were alternately clogged with mud and clouded with dust, San Francisco in the spring of 1852 was a thriving city, the only real city in the American West. The town's first settlers had built their stores and houses at the northeastern corner of the San Francisco Peninsula, facing an inlet called Yerba Buena Cove. They selected the inlet because it was a good place for landing boats and goods, and it soon became the center of the fledgling city. Later settlers continued to build around the cove because no better site could be found to anchor ships and build wharves and warehouses.

Agoston had visited San Francisco several times while he still lived in San Diego. Coastal steamers on the Panama–San Francisco route made biweekly stops at La Playa to pick up northbound passengers from San Diego. Some of his trips were made on personal business, though his official duties also required him to travel north from time to time. In April 1851, for example, the San Diego Common Council had given him official permission to visit San Francisco for twelve to fifteen days, presumably on personal business. But at the same time the council entrusted him with important public business, instructing him to call on San Francisco banks and sell some bonds that belonged to the city.[1]

Agoston never gave any reasons in print for his move from San Diego to San Francisco, but there is some hint of his motivations in his attitude toward dividing the state into northern and southern portions. When he called for a convention on that question, he described the north as a rich and prosperous region that supported a thriving commerce, while the south and its people were "entirely dependent upon agriculture, and the grazing of cattle, and without a sufficient market amongst themselves for their products."[2] Though he had failed in his efforts to divide California north from south and thereby alleviate the burdens of the south, as a man of energy and ambition he certainly was ready to change his own fortunes, at least, by leaving the south and seeking his fortune in the north.

The first property that he acquired in the north was about two miles south of the San Francisco city limits, in the shadow of a Spanish mission founded by the Franciscans in 1776. The mission was still a functioning church in 1852, though its Indian population was gone and its outbuildings and storehouses had been taken over by shopkeepers and lodgers. A plank road called Mission Street led across creeks and sandhills from the city limits to the mission. Agoston did not waste any time. He bought his first land in San Francisco on March 25, 1852, while he was on a leave of absence from the legislature in Sacramento. He paid $2,000 for a tract of fifty acres near Mission Dolores. On the deed, his residence is given as "the County of San Diego";[3] but two days later, when he paid another $2,000 for an adjoining tract of 160 acres, he was described as "late of the County of San Diego."[4] Thus, barely three months after he left San Diego, he was the owner of more than two hundred acres of land on the San Francisco Peninsula and had officially declared his intentions of making his home in the north.

Notes left after his death indicate that his Mission Dolores property was originally known as Park Valley,[5] but he later changed the name to Las Flores. Las Flores ("The Flowers") is the kind of romantic name Agoston liked to give his properties, and it apparently stuck. As might be expected, he lost no time in developing the land.

On the date of his first purchase, March 25, 1852, he began to build a house on the property.[6] Outbuildings, fences, and other structures soon followed.

His purpose in acquiring acreage near San Francisco was to raise fruits, vegetables, flowers, and possibly even grain that could be taken to market in the city. During the early years of the Gold Rush, immigrants to northern California had largely neglected the needs of the growing population for food, particularly fresh fruit and vegetables, and supplies had to be brought in by ship from up and down the Pacific Coast. Notes taken from one of Agoston's account books show that, in 1852, he planted 320 acres to wheat, corn, potatoes, and oats.[7] The figures evidently include crops grown on land he still owned in San Diego, now entrusted to Joseph Reiner. Reiner frequently consulted with Agoston about its management,[8] and Agoston himself returned to San Diego at least once to look after his properties there. Grain (and other crops) grown on the San Diego land could easily have been loaded on ships at La Playa, transported north, and there combined with the produce of Las Flores to supply the markets of San Francisco.

There was a demand for fresh table grapes in San Francisco, and the nearest dependable supply of this commodity was also in southern California. Sensing that good money could be made by bringing grapes up the coast from Los Angeles, Agoston bought up whole crops from small producers in Los Angeles, had them shipped to San Francisco, and offered them there for sale.[9] Arpad later remembered that the price for grapes in Los Angeles was six cents a pound in 1852 and 1853, while the same grapes could be sold in San Francisco for fifty cents to a dollar a pound—"a handsome profit, even in those flush times."[10]

Agoston also grew flowers on his San Francisco property. Notes taken from his account books indicate that he sold rosebushes from Las Flores in 1853.[11] He may also have sold cut roses, for the infant city, surrounded by sandhills and shrouded during most of the summer by fog, needed flowers almost as much as it needed fresh fruits and vegetables. Bowls of freshly cut flowers were just the thing to brighten dreary hotel lobbies and gloomy offices on grey summer days.

Arpad remembered that his father developed a nursery and a horticultural garden at Las Flores.[12] A horticultural garden was the kind of place where, in European cities, seeds, cuttings, and rooted plants were collected, tested, and disseminated to the community. A few years later, Agoston established an ambitious horticultural garden in Sonoma. The plans for his San Francisco garden may have been equally ambitious, though there is little evidence to show how far they were carried out. Arpad said only that his father gathered seeds and plants that were "procurable both at home and abroad."[13] Notes from his account books indicate that he sold a variety of trees and shrubs from the property.[14]

If grain was produced at Las Flores, it surely found a good market in San Francisco. Attila had joined his father in the city. Though only seventeen years old in 1852, he was ready to assume his responsibilities as an adult and soon opened a store on Kearny Street in which grain and hay, and presumably other crops grown on the Haraszthy acres (and possibly on other properties too) were offered to the hungry city.[15]

The plants gathered at Las Flores included a large number of foreign (that is, European) grapevines. Whether the Zinfandel was among them is a matter of speculation, although there is some evidence that it was. The story of the Zinfandel, however, is a large one and must wait until later pages to be told.

Las Flores was an ambitious undertaking, and there is reason to believe that it was profitable, at least in its early years. As Agoston was eventually to realize, however, it was not a suitable place in which to grow wine grapes. In fact, Mission Dolores was one of only four of the California missions in which the Franciscans had been unsuccessful in their efforts to grow grapes. The padres had made wine there, but the grapes came from the missions at San Jose and Santa Clara, at the warmer southern end of the bay.[16] The upper San Francisco peninsula was too cold in the summer to bring grapes to maturity. If Agoston had investigated the climate of San Francisco before buying his property there, he might have saved valuable time and money. It did not take him long, however, to conclude, as the padres had before him, that he would have to look beyond Mission Dolores if he wanted to have a thriving vineyard.

He began the process of finding another location in July 1853 by selling half his acreage at Las Flores to Colonel Jonathan D. Stevenson.[17] Stevenson had come to California from New York in 1847 as leader of a regiment of citizen-soldiers who had volunteered to help the American cause in the war with Mexico. Called Stevenson's Regiment, the force was a motley crew of farmers, clerks, mechanics, and ward-heeling politicians who intended to settle in California after the war was over. Stevenson remained in San Francisco, where he was active as an investor and widely respected as one of the state's pioneers. He agreed to pay Agoston $6,000 for half of Las Flores. The transaction netted Agoston a good profit for his year-old investment and gave him cash with which he could purchase other land.

Agoston remained friendly with the Sutherlands after his move to San Francisco. Thomas had opened a law office on Montgomery Street, and he continued to represent Agoston in many of his business transactions.[18] Both men were still interested in Democratic politics and attended meetings and rallies together. But San Francisco in 1852 offered Agoston many opportunities to make new friends. Immigrants from all over the world had flocked to the streets of the little city. It was natural that he should become friendly with the local community of German-speakers, for most of the residents of Haraszthy Town had been German, and German was his second language. In San Francisco, he became a member of a German-language social club called the San Francisco Verein. The Verein was a fine place for a man to spend his leisure hours—especially a man like Agoston whose wife and young children were a continent away. The society's club rooms on Kearny Street were fitted out with a library of 3,000 books and more than thirty different newspapers, and interesting men were always on hand to discuss the events of the day. Agoston made many friends in the Verein, and the members responded by electing him in 1856 as their president.[19]

In short order, too, he became friendly with a little circle of men who had fled Hungary during the revolution of 1848–49 and ultimately determined to seek their fortunes in California. The unofficial leader of the local Hungarian community was Sámuel C. Wass. Like Agoston, Wass was a man of energy and ability who had a yearning to see the world beyond the Danube. Unlike Agoston, he was a real count in his native land. Born in Budapest in 1814, Count Wass had entered the Hungarian civil service in the 1830's and eventually rose to become *fõispán* of Doboka County. He was serving in the Hungarian National Assembly when the Austrians and their Russian allies invaded Hungary in late 1848. Dedicated to the cause of Hungarian independence, he left the country hoping to secure arms with which Kossuth and his supporters could fend off the invaders. His travels took him first to Constantinople, then to Paris and London, and finally to New York.[20] But, by the time he arrived in the United States, he learned that his compatriots had lost their war with the Austrians and Russians, and he decided to push on to San Francisco, where he arrived on September 7, 1850.[21]

Traveling with Wass on the ship from Panama was another Hungarian named Charles (originally Károly) Uznay.[22] As Wass was habitually addressed as "Count," Uznay was called "Captain," suggesting that he had seen some service in the Hungarian army. Not long after their arrival in San Francisco, Wass and Uznay found work as gold assayers in the San Francisco office of Adams & Co., a large express and banking firm with headquarters on Montgomery Street and branch offices throughout the California mining districts. Adams received large deposits of gold dust from miners, transported them to San Francisco by stagecoach, and there put them on ships bound for the United States Mint in Philadelphia. Even after Wells, Fargo & Co. opened a rival office in San Francisco in July 1852, Adams & Co. retained its position as the premier express and banking firm of the American West.

Business was very good for private assayers in San Francisco. Although much of the gold that poured into the city was shipped to Philadelphia, a good part of it remained behind to oil the wheels of local commerce. But before the gold could be used in trade its purity had to be tested and it had to be melted and formed into ingots and coins. The business community in California had repeatedly asked Congress to establish a branch mint in San Francisco where this work could be done promptly, but the national legislature dragged its heels on the issue and the local business community felt compelled to improvise. As early as 1849, private firms began to assay gold dust, melt it into bars, and stamp it into coins that could be used for local trade. The private coins were not legal tender in the same way that gold minted in Philadelphia or New Orleans was legal, but they were not illegal, either, and they were eagerly accepted by bankers and merchants.[23]

Wass and Uznay performed assays for Adams for a few months, but the demand for assayers was so brisk that by November 1851, they opened their own office on Montgomery Street, where they offered their services as assayers, mining examiners, and agents.[24] They claimed in their advertisements that they were graduates of "the celebrated German School of Mines" and had worked many years in the gold mines of Hungary.[25] There is little doubt that they were skilled metallurgists, for their firm quickly established a reputation as one of the most efficient private refining offices in the city and they soon began to issue private coins bearing their firm name and imprint. After a few months a third Hungarian joined them in their office. He was Agoston Molitor, like Uznay a veteran of the Hungarian army and, like Wass, a refugee of the abortive Hungarian war for independence. Their firm was called Wass, Molitor & Co.[26]

Wass, Uznay, and Molitor were all gentlemen, and all regarded themselves as Hungarian patriots, so it was only natural that they should become friendly with Agoston. It is not known precisely when he first became acquainted with the Hungarian assayers, but they were on intimate terms by the latter part of 1853, when Agoston and Uznay formed a business partnership to buy some land on the peninsula south of San Francisco.

By a law passed in 1841, Congress had agreed to give each state half a million acres of public land for the support of public education. When Agoston was in the Assembly the legislature had passed a bill permitting private citizens to purchase so-called "school warrants" and use them to claim federal land at the price of two dollars per acre.[27] Holders of warrants could locate claims on any vacant and unappropriated federal land in the state. If the claims were in order, patents would be issued by the governor. If a claim was made on land that proved to be part of a Spanish or Mexican ranch, the claimant could relocate his claim to another tract of federal land.[28] The school warrant law encouraged private individuals to support public education and provided a mechanism for public distribution of the rich legacy of federal land given to California by the United States government.

In the summer of 1853 Agoston, Molitor, Uznay, and Sutherland all decided to take advantage of the law by purchasing warrants and locating claims on the hilly peninsula south of San Francisco. The land there was chiefly accessible by a wagon road that twisted from the town of San Mateo on the western edge of San Francisco Bay up through a narrow canyon to a chain of valleys that formed the spine of the peninsula, about twenty miles south of the city. The Spanish and Mexicans had called the most northerly of these valleys San Andreas and the most southerly the Cañada de Raymundo. When Agoston first saw them they were within the limits of San Francisco County. In July of 1856, however, the legislature divided the county into two new jurisdictions, one called the City and County of San Francisco and the other San Mateo County, and after the division the valleys lay in the northern third of the new San Mateo County.

San Andreas Valley and the Cañada de Raymundo ranged in altitude from about two hundred to more than four hundred feet above sea level. They were bordered on the east by a ridge of low hills covered with grass and oak and on the west by steep mountains, densely wooded with oak, madrone, and California redwood. The eastern hills were known locally as the Pulgas Hills, for a large Mexican ranch that ran down from their summit to the marshy bayshore. The western mountains, called the Santa Cruz Mountains, extended in an unbroken chain for more than fifty miles to the south. Past the summits of the mountains, the ground sloped gradually to the edge of the Pacific Ocean, about ten miles to the west.

The valleys were watered by two creeks, the San Andreas in the north and the San Mateo in the south. The creeks fed two small lakes or lagoons, one called the San Andreas Lake and the other the Laguna, or Laguna Grande. The creeks met in the canyon through which the wagon road led and, through that canyon, flowed down to the bay. A stream of pure water bubbled out of a spring in the hills near the confluence of the creeks. It was called Crystal Springs by the first American residents of the area. In 1851, a country inn, called the Crystal Springs Hotel, was erected near the springs and quickly became a favorite stopping place for travelers.

Agoston of course did not know that the San Andreas Valley and

Cañada de Raymundo lay precisely on top of a great fault in the crust of the earth, a fault that in 1906 would rupture and give rise to the most famous earthquake of modern times; the San Andreas fault (so named from the upper valley and creek) was not identified by scientists until 1893. Beginning in the 1870's and continuing on until 1890, these same valleys would be walled off by a series of dams to create a chain of three reservoirs or lakes—called San Andreas, Lower Crystal Springs, and Upper Crystal Springs—that would form the backbone of the municipal water system for San Francisco. Agoston can only have known that, in 1853, the valleys presented an inviting spot for a farm and vineyard amid an unspoiled California landscape.

On September 3, 1853, he joined Molitor, Uznay, and Sutherland, and two assayers employed by Wass and Uznay, James Condon and Charles F. Riehn, to locate a series of claims to 2,240 acres of land where the San Andreas and Raymundo valleys met.[29] Under the school warrant law, one person could claim as many as 640 acres, but Agoston chose to claim only 320, while twenty-year-old Gaza, recently discharged from the dragoons, claimed another 320.[30] Molitor also claimed 320 acres, while his son Stephen claimed another 320. Uznay and Sutherland each claimed 320 acres; Condon and Riehn shared a single 320-acre claim between them. Each of the claims extended a quarter of a mile from north to south and a full mile from east to west. The eastern boundaries of the tracts coincided roughly with the Pulgas hills; the western limits were on the summit of the Santa Cruz Mountains.[31]

Agoston's claim covered a varied terrain. Part of it lay on the floor of the Cañada de Raymundo, where a little stream meandered toward the east, while the rest was on higher ground. A ridge of hills at the southern edge of the claim led into Gaza's claim, which was even more uneven than his father's. It is not known what name Agoston gave to his land when he first claimed it, though in later years it was variously called "Crystal Springs," for the nearby springs and hotel, "Pulgas," for the adjoining ranch and hills, and "Redwoods," for the soaring trees that hugged the slopes of the Santa Cruz Mountains. Crystal Springs is the name by which historians have remembered it.[32]

According to Reiner, Agoston and Uznay agreed to contribute

their Crystal Springs lands, and some other properties, to a partnership. Agoston put up all of his Crystal Springs land, his Las Flores property, 320 acres of land he still owned in San Diego, and forty or fifty lots he retained in San Diego's Middletown. Reiner was asked to appraise Agoston's properties, and he valued them together at $30,000. Uznay thereupon contributed the same amount in cash.[33]

Agoston built a barn at Crystal Springs and a neighboring house in which he could stay when he was not in San Francisco. When the place was done, he brought his friends down from San Francisco to inspect it. He liked to show off his properties, and on at least one occasion he threw a large party to which he invited not only his San Francisco friends but also some of the men who worked for him in the city. He called the event, in good American slang, a "big blowout."[34]

He made some good friends among other farmers who lived in the vicinity of Crystal Springs. Besides Molitor, Uznay, and Sutherland, his neighbors included a young Prussian named Charles (originally Karl) Krug, a San Francisco lawyer named Julius K. Rose, and a wealthy San Francisco merchant named Frederick W. Macondray.

Born in Prussia in 1825, Krug had come to the United States for the first time in the late 1840's, settling in Philadelphia. He returned to his native country in time to participate in the uprisings of 1848 and then came back to America in 1852. This time he made his way to San Francisco, where he published a German-language newspaper called the *Freie Presse* and, with a partner named N. O. Nolting, operated a brewery on First Street near Mission.[35] Krug may have acquired his San Mateo property to grow grain and hops for his brewery, and possibly to experiment with grapes, in which he also had an interest.

Rose was a lawyer by profession who had acquired interests in properties widely scattered through northern California. His interest in agriculture was revealed when, in 1854, he became one of the founders of the California State Agricultural Society.[36] A few years later Rose was to play a key role in persuading Agoston to move to Sonoma, for among Rose's portfolio of investment properties was a tract of land east of the town of Sonoma on which Agoston was to develop the Buena Vista Vineyard beginning in 1857.

The Massachusetts-born Macondray was one of San Francisco's

wealthiest merchants. He had visited California in 1822 as a young sailor on a trading vessel; but he did not stay long, preferring to pursue an adventurous life at sea and then to return to Massachusetts, where, in the 1840's, he became a member of the Massachusetts Horticultural Society. Macondray's decision to return to California in 1849 was prompted in part by concerns over his chronically weak health, in part by a desire to establish a trading firm in San Francisco. In the early 1850's, he built Macondray & Co. into one of the Gold Rush city's most profitable businesses. He also dabbled in agriculture, establishing a nursery for grapes (called a "grapery") in a greenhouse adjoining his San Francisco house. In 1854, at a San Francisco meeting presided over by Julius Rose, he was elected first president of the California Agricultural Society.[37] But Macondray was still in poor health, and sometime in the mid-1850's he retired to a country home on the peninsula south of San Francisco. His property there, called Baywood, was two or three miles east of Agoston's Crystal Springs property.

With 640 acres of land at Crystal Springs now under his management, Agoston began to set his mind seriously to agricultural pursuits. Arpad later recalled that his father began his work at Crystal Springs by planting a "considerable patch" of strawberries and a large orchard. Arpad said that the trees were grown "for nursery purposes" and that they yielded a good profit when they were later resold.[38]

Agoston also began to plant grapevines at Crystal Springs. He probably brought some of the vines north from San Diego, purchased others in San Francisco, and sent away for yet others that could be obtained only outside the state. Some of the vines were undoubtedly native (that is, Mission) vines; Agoston, like other California winemakers, still held out hopes that good wine could be made from the padres' old grapes. But others were European grapes, for he had recently acquired a new and dependable source of *vinifera* vines.

After Eleonora sailed to the eastern United States late in 1851, she had settled with her four youngest children in the town of Plainfield, New Jersey, about twenty-five miles west of New York City. She was still living in Plainfield in 1853 when a Hungarian exile named Lázár Mészáros took up residence on a farm just a few minutes away. A career soldier, Mészáros had worked his way up through the ranks of the Hungarian military, serving first as a Hussar officer, then as a regimental commander in northern Italy, and, after Kossuth and his supporters formed the first truly Hungarian government in 1848, receiving a promotion to brigadier general and an appointment as Hungarian Minister of War. When fighting erupted between the Hungarians and the Austrians, Mészáros took personal command of a part of the Hungarian army and led it in a siege of the Bács County town of Szenttamás, where a pro-Austrian army of Serbs had dug themselves in. After the czar's army helped the Austrians crush the fledgling Hungarian government, Mészáros fled with Kossuth toward Turkey. He eventually made his way to England, then to the Isle of Jersey, and finally to New Jersey, where he arrived late in 1853.[39]

There is no direct evidence that Mészáros and Agoston were personally acquainted in Hungary, but indirect evidence suggests quite strongly that they were. Although Mészáros was sixteen years Agoston's senior, he was born in the Bács County town of Baja, and his family owned estates in Pacsér, where the Haraszthys also had property. All his life, the soldier had been keenly interested in scientific and natural subjects, including biology and botany, and his expertise in the field had won him an appointment to the prestigious Hungarian Academy of Sciences. If Agoston's own interest in agriculture, sericulture, and viticulture did not bring him into contact with Mészáros in Bács County, the men would at least have scraped an acquaintance in the General Assemblies of Bács County nobles. And Mészáros, if he was not personally acquainted with Agoston, at least knew him by reputation, for a letter he wrote on the Isle of Jersey late in 1852 (preserved in his published correspondence) refers to Agoston as "the founder of Harasztopolis" (i.e., Haraszthy Town in Wisconsin).[40] It is fair to assume that he had read Agoston's *Travels in North America*, and he may well have exchanged letters (and possibly even parcels) with him before crossing the ocean. After he came to New Jersey, the exiled Minister of War bought a farm at a place called Scotch Plains, where he assembled a nursery of fruit trees, shrubs, and grapevines with which he hoped to support himself. By the spring of 1854 he informed a friend back in Hungary that he had more than 150 different kinds of trees, more than 2,000 saplings, and 500 rooted vine cuttings.[41]

Mészáros's farm at Scotch Plains was only two miles north of Eleonora's Plainfield house, and she and the lifelong bachelor soon became close friends. In letters back home to Hungary, Mészáros referred to Eleonora as a "Dedinszky girl" from the Bácska and to Agoston as "Guszti" Haraszthy.[42] Eleonora was the first to console him when, in March 1854, a fire destroyed his Scotch Plains house and he lost plants that had been stored in his basement and dug into the nearby ground.[43] He rebuilt the nursery, planted fruit trees, and set out American grapevines at the base of some arbors; by April of the same year he noted in a letter that he had six varieties of pears, forty of apples, twelve of peaches, and twenty-four different varieties of grapes.[44] On July 4, 1854, Eleonora was one of the guests when Mészáros gave a party for his sister, who was returning to Europe after a short visit in New Jersey.[45]

Agoston and Mészáros exchanged letters, and probably vine shipments as well. Agoston at one time invited Mészáros to join him in California, but the general could not afford to make the long trip on his own resources and Agoston was unable to pay his way.[46] And so the two Hungarians, separated by a continent but united by a common interest in grapevines, had to content themselves for the time with a friendship maintained only by mail.

Years later, Arpad recalled that Mészáros sent foreign vines to his father in California.[47] It is quite possible that some of these vines were obtained by Mészáros from horticultural gardens in Europe, possibly even from gardens in Hungary. Others he probably obtained from sources nearer at hand, including nurseries around New York. In 1854, the largest nursery in New York (possibly in the United States) was located at Flushing on Long Island, about ten miles northeast of Manhattan. It was the celebrated Linnaean Botanic Garden of William Robert Prince. The Prince family had maintained a nursery at Flushing since 1771, and their nursery there had grown over the years to more than one hundred acres. William Robert Prince and his father, William Prince, had a special interest in European grapevines. In 1830, they had collaborated to produce a pioneering study of grapevines throughout the world. Called *A Treatise on the Vine,* the book was widely circulated throughout the United States. Over the years, the Princes imported grapevines from France, Germany, Italy, and other places in Europe, and, by 1830, their collections included more than two hundred varieties that were identical to those grown in the Luxembourg Gardens in Paris. Steadily from 1830 up until the eve of the Civil War, Prince published catalogs of grapevines that he sent to virtually every nurseryman in the United States.[48] From the 1850's on, Prince's catalogs listed a curious vine first noted in *A Treatise on the Vine.* It was originally described as the "Black Zinfardel [*sic*], of Hungary," although later editions of the catalog noted that it was also called "Zinfindal."[49] Given the fact that both Agoston and Mészáros were interested in grapevines, that both hailed from the Bácska and were keeping up a lively transcontinental correspondence, and that both were then in the process of assembling collections of grapevines, it seems almost inevitable that Mészáros would have sent Agoston grapevine cuttings, as Arpad later claimed. And it seems equally probable that the cuttings would have included Prince's "Black Zinfardel" or "Zinfindal."

Was Prince's "Zinfardel/Zinfindal" the same as the Zinfandel that later achieved so much renown in the vineyards of California? Arpad believed that it was. He repeatedly stated that his father received the Zinfandel in the early 1850's, though he was a little unclear about when and from whom the first vine was received. In 1877, Arpad told a reporter for the *San Francisco Bulletin* that his father received his first Zinfandel vines as early as 1852; he did not state the source.[50] Sometime between 1877 and 1882, Arpad further stated that his father first received the Zinfandel in shipments of foreign vines "from the East and from Europe" made through General Mészáros.[51] If this was true (and if Mészáros forwarded the vines from New Jersey, and not from Europe), then Agoston could not have received them before 1854. In 1885, Arpad repeated his claim that his father obtained his first Zinfandel in 1852 and that it came from Hungary, but again without mentioning Mészáros.[52]

Arpad's inconsistent statements on this subject led some to suspect the reliability of his recollections. While it is legitimate to question the details of Arpad's recollections, his recollection that Mészáros sent his father some Zinfandels from New Jersey is entirely credible. Arpad was, after all, in New Jersey during most of the time that Mészáros lived there, and as an intelligent teenager with a growing interest in viticulture, he was in a good position to know what the general-turned-farmer was sending his father in far-off California.[53] Whether those Zinfandels were the first Zinfandel cuttings that Agoston received is another question entirely. If he received Zinfandels from Mészáros in 1854 or later, that fact would not preclude the possibility that he received earlier shipments of the same vine directly from Europe, perhaps also from Mészáros.

It is possible, of course, that Prince's "Zinfardel/Zinfandal" was not the "Zinfandel" that later became famous in California. Since no description of Prince's grape has been found, and since it is impossible now to see it growing in a vineyard, it cannot be stated categorically that the two grapes were the same. But it seems very likely that they were.[54] If Agoston received a "Black Zinfardel" (or "Zinfindal") claimed by Prince to have originated in Hungary, he would certainly have given it special attention in his nursery, planted it in his vineyard at Crystal Springs, nurtured it, pruned it, and harvested its grapes—all the while carefully watching its progress and noting its characteristics. And, when the grape showed promise of becoming one of California's best wine grapes, he would have had no hesitation in trumpeting its virtues to the world.

But even with these lingering questions about how and when Agoston first received the Zinfandel, there is no doubt that he planted large numbers of grapevines at Crystal Springs. When Joseph Reiner came up from San Diego to appraise Agoston's new vineyards and orchards, he saw "about 20,000 fruit trees and a large number of grape vines" on the property;[55] and a special agent for the Treasury Department who examined Crystal Springs in 1857 counted 20,000 grapevines worth about $10,000 and 25,000 grafted fruit trees worth about $75,000.[56] More than thirty years later, Arpad recalled that his father's Crystal Springs vineyards covered nearly thirty acres.[57] Arpad did not estimate how many of his father's vines were foreign, but other evidence shows that the number was substantial, for when Agoston decided to move his vineyard from Crystal Springs to Sonoma in 1857 he had a large collection of foreign vines—many that had good roots and were ready to start bearing soon after they were set in the ground.[58]

Agoston invested a lot of time and money in Crystal Springs. But planting orchards, laying out vineyards, and building a house and barn on land claimed under school warrants was a risky proposition in the early 1850's, for there was a real possibility that the land would later be claimed by a Spanish or Mexican ranchero. If the claim was valid, all the improvements could be lost. The Spanish and Mexican ranchos were sources of controversy and no little dispute in California. Although the treaty that settled the war between Mexico and the United States provided that the property rights of former citizens of Mexico were to be "inviolably respected," many of the Spanish and Mexican titles were poorly documented, and the boundaries of some of the ranchos were hopelessly vague. A typical Mexican rancho was used for cattle grazing and often had little in the way of improvements; so, to a traveler viewing the land from the back of a horse or the cab of a coach in the early 1850's, it might not be apparent that it was privately owned and that a Spanish or Mexican title lay behind it.

The United States government had on the one hand guaranteed Spanish and Mexican land titles and on the other encouraged American citizens to settle on land that might form part of Spanish and Mexican ranchos. Congress had attempted to deal with the resulting dilemma by creating the United States Land Commission in 1851. It was the duty of the commission to receive claims to Spanish and Mexican ranchos, hear evidence about them, and, if convinced that the grants were made in accordance with the Spanish or Mexican law, confirm the titles. If a decision went against the claimant, an appeal could be prosecuted in the federal courts.

There is no reason to believe that Agoston and his friends from San Francisco had any suspicion that their land at Crystal Springs was part of a Mexican rancho when they located their claims there in 1853. But a year or so earlier, on February 17, 1852, a man named Domingo Feliz had filed papers with the Land Commission in San Francisco, claiming that he was the owner of a square league (or 4,438 acres) of land running from the San Andreas Valley down into the Cañada de Raymundo. Feliz had since sold his interest in the claim, but the buyers were still pursuing his title in the Land Commission. Thus, while Agoston was busy putting up a house and barns at Crystal Springs, planting trees and vines, and otherwise transforming the land into a working farm and vineyard, lawyers in the Land Commission's office in San Francisco were examining the evidence that supported Feliz's claim. On June 27, 1854, the Commission announced a decision confirming Feliz's claim and, ipso facto, invalidating the later claims of Agoston, Molitor, Uznay, Sutherland, Condon, and Riehn.[59]

In due course, Agoston managed to work out a solution to his lost property—though he had gone on to a new venture and had many affairs to attend to. He was successful in striking a bargain with the investors who had bought Feliz's rights to the land, and on February 6, 1855, he took a new title to 385 acres of the Feliz grant.[60] The sellers were Soledad Ortega de Argüello, José Ramón Argüello, Simon M. Mezes, Samuel R. Throckmorton, and Julius K. Rose.[61] At the end of October 1856, he bought an adjoining tract of 645 acres from the same persons,[62] and on July 22, 1856, he joined with John A. Szabo, a Hungarian who worked for Wass and Molitor, and an American named Michael Hayes to buy an undivided one-tenth interest in the Rancho Buri Buri, on the bayshore north of San Mateo.[63] The loss of his original Crystal Springs school warrant claim had, of course, entitled him to claim an equal area of federal land elsewhere in the state, and he chose to make his claim to 640 acres of land south of Crystal Springs and west of the new town of Redwood City. This land, which became known as the Anglo Tract,[64] was steep and wooded.

Agoston's friendship with Wass, Molitor, and Uznay gave him an opportunity to participate in the very lucrative gold refining business in California. It is not clear what background, if any, he had in metallurgy before his arrival in San Francisco, though he no doubt had some knowledge of chemistry, if not through formal study at least through his long association with his father, whose skills as a chemist had been demonstrated in Haraszthy Town. However, nobody who had met Agoston ever had any doubt about his ability to learn quickly, and if he had never seen a melter's crucible or mixed refining acids before he arrived in San Francisco it would certainly have presented no obstacles to his taking a place in the assaying and refining rooms of Wass, Molitor & Co. In time, Wass, Molitor, and Uznay were to show their confidence in his metallurgical skills by admitting him to a partnership in their assaying and refining business, and the United States government was to give him another vote of confidence by choosing him to fill two very responsible positions at the Branch Mint in San Francisco, which, after what seemed to many San Franciscans an interminable delay, opened for business on April 3, 1854.

17

A House
of Gold

The resolution that the legislature passed in 1852 supporting a
San Francisco mint was only one of many steps that were required
to get the mint approved. Senator Gwin gave the cause a powerful
boost when, in 1851, he introduced a bill calling for prompt construction and outfitting of a branch mint in San Francisco. The bill
passed the Senate on December 15, 1851, but the House of Representatives did not assent until June 19, 1852. The bill became law on
July 3, 1852, when it was signed by President Millard Fillmore.

Congress appropriated $300,000 for the purpose of construct-
ing a mint building and putting it into operation. It also forbade the
purchase of any existing building for mint use. But after President
Franklin Pierce took office in March 1853, the Treasury Department
embarked on a different course. Pierce's Secretary of the Treasury,
Thomas Corwin, opened negotiations with a San Francisco assaying
firm that owned a small building on Commercial Street just above
Montgomery. The firm was Curtis, Ward, and Perry, and it apparently
had some influence in Washington, for Corwin soon announced a
decision to purchase the assay office and remodel it into a branch
mint. It was an ambitious project: when all the work was done, the

government reported that it had invested $350,000 in the structure and its equipment.¹

The finished building was sixty feet square and three stories tall. Its brick walls were covered with cement, and its long doors and windows were fitted with iron shutters. An ornamental American eagle peered vigilantly over the main entrance, ready to guard the golden treasure that was to be housed below. Behind the eagle was a small forest of smoke stacks, connected through chimneys and flues to furnaces in the basement. Despite all the money that had been lavished on it, the onetime assay office seemed small and cramped, and many San Franciscans wondered if it could do all that the people of the West demanded—and believed they had a right to expect—of a United States mint.²

As the date for the formal opening of the mint approached, San Franciscans waited with interest for news of the men President Pierce would appoint as officers of the institution. Pierce was a Democrat, and since choice federal positions were traditionally awarded to members of the president's own party, it was a foregone conclusion that the officers would be Democrats. But Senator Gwin had, by skillful political maneuvering, managed to acquire control over the federal patronage in California, and the appointees would also have to be acceptable to him and his Chivalry wing of the Democratic Party.

As superintendent, Pierce named Lewis A. Birdsall, a medical doctor from New York who had arrived in California in 1849. Birdsall had prominent friends in Washington, chief among them his son-in-law, Democratic Congressman Milton S. Latham. Pierce chose John Hewston, Jr., as the melter and refiner. Hewston had worked in the Philadelphia mint before coming to San Francisco in 1853 to supervise the organization of the melting and refining department in the new branch mint. Jacob Rink Snyder, selected as treasurer of the mint, was a Pennsylvania native who had crossed the plains to California in 1845, served as major in a battalion of volunteers during the Mexican War, and then won election to represent San Francisco in the California constitutional convention of 1849. He and Agoston had become acquainted in 1852, when Snyder was a state senator from San Francisco and Agoston was the assemblyman from San Diego.[3] John Eckfeldt, son of George Eckfeldt, one of the officials of the Philadelphia mint, was named as first coiner at San Francisco.

President Pierce named Agoston to the post of assayer, while Charles Haraszthy landed an appointment as assistant melter and refiner under Hewston. Charles had joined Agoston in San Francisco not long after he left San Diego and had taken up residence in a house on Jessie Street. As assistant assayer, Agoston obtained the services of an experienced metallurgist named Emmanuel Justh.

Nobody had any doubt that politics played a role in the selection of the mint officers. Birdsall and Snyder were both politicians, and both were totally lacking in any metallurgical experience, though Snyder had been a banker in San Francisco and therefore had some experience in handling large amounts of money. But Hewston and Eckfeldt were seasoned professionals, and though Agoston's appointment was in some ways political, he had at least some background as an assayer and refiner in Wass, Molitor, and Uznay's offices. Hewston was somewhat unsure of the extent of Agoston's assaying experience, but he did not think he was unfit for the job. "I am perfectly satisfied," Hewston wrote shortly after the mint opened, "that when he began he knew nothing about the minutiae which I would not have attempted to perform myself previously. The assistant assayer is a tolerable assayer (I think) and as Haraszthy & his assistant make separate assays of the same piece and do not report unless they agree exactly I think they will do well after having such a time."[4]

On Saturday, April 2, 1854, members of the San Francisco press toured the new mint, meeting its officers, examining its equipment, and then adjourning to a reception room, where they were feted with French champagne and Sparkling Catawba from Ohio.[5] The following Monday morning, the mint went into operation.

From its first day, the mint was a very busy place. The pavement in front of the building was piled with boxes containing bottles of acid for the refining process. Express couriers bounded up the steps with tightly wrapped packages of gold from the mines, and miners in plain clothes were constantly arriving with gold in carpetbags. The treasurer, the melter and refiner, and the coiner operated their individual departments with a large degree of independence. Each was charged by law with responsibility for the security of the precious metals when they were in his department. When a depositor brought gold to the mint, it was the duty of the treasurer to give him a receipt and immediately deliver the metal to the melter and refiner. The melter and refiner put the gold into a lead crucible and then melted it into a bar. A chip, weighing about one-tenth of an ounce, was taken from each end of the bar and delivered to the assayer in the assaying room. It was the duty of the assayer to analyze the chip by chemical process and accurately report to the treasurer on the gold, silver, and other metals it contained. When the treasurer received the assayer's report, he gave the depositor a certificate reflecting the contents of his deposit and giving the depositor the right to receive a specified sum in gold and silver coin.[6] The melter and refiner then subjected the bar to a refining process, after which he delivered the refined metal—and any silver found in it—to the coiner, who stamped it into legal coins.

Agoston's official title was Assayer of the United States Branch Mint, but unofficially he was known as the United States Assayer. In a city where gold was king, the title carried some prestige, and Agoston was proud of it.[7] But he was determined not to be an assayer in name only, and he entered on his duties with characteristic energy and enthusiasm. He spent long hours in the mint, arriving early in the morning and staying until well past midnight.[8] He sometimes left the mint on Saturday afternoons for a quick trip to Crystal Springs, but he was always back in his office on Monday morning.[9] He relished the practical work and eagerly took his place alongside the common workers, weighing deposits and mixing chemicals. To be closer to his work, he moved into a house on Harrison Street between Second and Third on Rincon Hill. Wass and Molitor also lived on Harrison Street, so the Hungarians were neighbors. Agoston's house was about a dozen blocks from the mint, and he could make the trip by carriage in just a few minutes.[10]

But all was not happiness at the mint. Agoston knew that the mining and mercantile communities depended on the mint's production of gold and silver coin and constantly strove to work faster, and when his fellow officers did not share his sense of urgency, he openly expressed his displeasure. He was particularly disturbed by

John Hewston's work as melter and refiner. The melting and refining department under Hewston worked so slowly that depositors had to wait up to forty days to be paid for their deposits. But when Agoston suggested changes in his procedures, Hewston and the other "professionals" from Philadelphia reminded him that his suggested changes were not "the Philadelphia way." He heard the objections so often that he grew exasperated. "Damn their way," he finally said of the Philadelphians. "They don't know how to do anything except to be slow."[11]

Everybody agreed that the facilities were inadequate. The rooms were small and crowded, and the vault provided for Agoston's use was so tiny that he had to borrow space in his fellow officers' vaults, which were also overcrowded.[12] For lack of room in the main building, Superintendent Birdsall had to have his office in an adjoining structure, where Agoston often went to request supplies and confer about deposits. When he took gold to the superintendent's office, he carried it in a metal box.[13]

Late in 1854, Agoston announced a plan to ease the crowded conditions of the mint and help alleviate the city's needs for coin. With Superintendent Birdsall, Adams & Co., and a San Francisco banker named James King of William as his partners, he proposed to establish a private refinery that would take over some of the mint's refining work. Miners would deposit their gold with the refinery, and after it was converted into ingots and bars it would be taken to the mint for coining. The private refinery would complement the mint by relieving the government facility of some of the drudgery of the melting and refining. Agoston and his partners would be paid for their efforts, and depositors would get their returns more quickly.

In a city filled with odd and unusual characters, Agoston's newest partner, James King of William, was one of the oddest. Born James King in the District of Columbia in 1822, he added his father's given name (William) to his own to mark himself apart from other James Kings. After coming to California in 1848, he worked for a while as a miner, then as a clerk in Sacramento, and finally opened a bank in San Francisco, with Jacob R. Snyder as his partner. The Bank of James King of William was one of the city's most profitable until a dishonest employee raided its vault and forced King into bankruptcy.

A small, nervous man with a thick mop of hair, King was rebounding from the loss of his bank when he agreed to form a partnership with Agoston, Birdsall, and Adams.

The partnership agreement was signed on October 9, 1854. By its terms, King, Adams, and Birdsall each received a one-fifth interest in the new refinery, while Agoston received two-fifths. Birdsall agreed to promote the refinery's business, King to attend to its books, and Adams to supply the necessary capital. Agoston agreed to superintend the assaying and refining and permit the partnership to use a new process that he had developed for assaying, parting, and refining gold. He had applied for a patent for the process and was characteristically enthusiastic about its use.[14]

The new partnership took up quarters in the Montgomery Block on Montgomery Street, a magnificent, block-long building that had opened two days before Christmas in 1853.[15] The edifice was the pride of San Francisco—a four-story pile of bricks and iron that was, by common agreement, the finest building west of the Mississippi. Certainly the new quarters were an advantage over the cramped and crowded mint;[16] but Agoston was to remain in the building for only a few months. He had asked the director of the mint in Philadelphia to approve his affiliation with the private business, and the director had flatly denied the request, citing the rather obvious conflict of interest between a private businessman who prepared gold for deposit with the mint and a public assayer who was called on to assay the same gold. The director stated flatly that one man could not properly act in both capacities.[17]

Agoston would have been hesitant to withdraw from the private refinery (indeed, he might even have preferred to give up his position at the mint), if conditions entirely outside his control had not forced him to do abandon it; for in February 1855, Adams & Co. was the subject of one of the fiercest "runs" ever suffered by a San Francisco bank and was quickly forced out of business. The trouble began on February 17, when a ship arrived in San Francisco with news that the St. Louis office of the powerful banking firm of Page, Bacon & Co., had been forced to close its doors. Page, Bacon's San Francisco branch tried for a week to satisfy its depositors' demands for gold coin, but eventually had to give up. Adams's handsome San Francisco headquarters was next door to Page, Bacon on Montgomery Street, and many San Franciscans believed that there was a business connection between the two firms. Soon depositors were also clamoring for cash in Adams's lobby. Adams tried valiantly to satisfy the demands, but on Friday, February 22, it had to follow Page, Bacon's example and close its doors. The day went down in history as "Black Friday" on Montgomery Street.[18] Overnight, Agoston's contract with Adams became worthless. Adams bowed out, not only of the banking business, but also of the lucrative express business, leaving the upstart Wells, Fargo & Co., as the principal player in that field. Wells, Fargo took over Adams's Montgomery Street office, and James King of William was once again looking for employment.

Agoston decided to remain at the mint. King decided to start a newspaper. His journal, inaugurated in October 1855, was called the *Daily Evening Bulletin*, and in it he assumed the role of a crusader against all manner of evils, public and private. He railed against what he called "crime and corruption among prominent and wealthy (but not respectable) men" in San Francisco, and promised to "leave nothing undone that can be done, to rid our city and State of the pests that infest them."[19] It was a stirring ambition, and the *Bulletin* quickly attracted a large subscription list. But readers soon noticed a bullying tone in the paper. King's editorials took on an almost hysterical quality, with marked anti-Irish and anti-Catholic overtones. He lashed out at public figures (many of whom were Irish Catholics) and made some bitter enemies.

One of the objects of King's vitriol proved to be his undoing. He was an Irish Catholic member of the San Francisco County Board of Supervisors named James P. Casey, a man who had come out from the East and was now editor of a small newspaper called the *Sunday Times*. Casey and King began quarreling in print, and on May 14, 1856, King charged in the *Bulletin* that Casey had served time in Sing Sing prison in New York. When Casey read the accusation, he at once demanded that King withdraw it. King refused to do so. About an hour later, as King was on his way home, Casey shot him dead in the street.[20] The leading businessmen of San Francisco gathered to form a Vigilance Committee. It was San Francisco's second effort at vigilante justice (the first vigilance committee had been formed and disbanded in 1851). The vigilantes took Casey and another criminal named Charles Cora to their "headquarters" on the waterfront and, before a hushed crowd of several thousand spectators, hanged them until they were dead. After a funeral procession in which thousands of San Franciscans marched, King was buried in a grave on the western edge of the city.

Agoston's opinions of his erstwhile partner's character and sensational newspaper campaigns have not been recorded. Many San Franciscans revered James King of William as a martyr to the cause of public virtue; others thought he was a provocateur. But with King dead and Adams & Co. consigned to history, Agoston had little choice but to continue his work at the mint. The roster of mint officers was juggled several times in 1855–56. In May 1855, Hewston relinquished his post as melter and refiner to join a private refining firm, and Charles Haraszthy was named to succeed him. Emmanuel Justh also left to form a private assaying firm in partnership with a man named S. Hillen Hunter; to ease his transition into private business, he earned a warm encomium from Agoston and Superintendent Birdsall, which he used in his advertisements.[21]

Charles was certainly qualified to carry out the duties of melter and refiner, but the job was strenuous and he was now almost seventy years old, so in August 1855, he relinquished the position in favor of his son. Agoston's succession to the post of melter and refiner opened up the assayer's position to a man named Conrad Wiegand. In November 1855, Birdsall resigned as superintendent and was succeeded by Peter Lott, a lawyer who had been the chief clerk for the U.S. Land Commission.[22] Lott was a popular man both inside and outside the mint, and he and Agoston soon became good friends.

Immediately after he became melter and refiner, Agoston made changes in the melting and refining rooms. He added four furnaces to the three already in use and increased the working hours of his men. Soon, more than $1,500,000 worth of gold was being processed each month, and returns to depositors were more current than ever before.[23] But he was still not satisfied that the mint had reached optimum efficiency. Toward the end of 1856, he approached Lott with a proposal that he believed could significantly reduce the cost of the mint's refining work. He had devised an apparatus that would refine gold with sulfuric acid instead of the commonly used nitric acid. He told Lott that sulfuric acid was used for refining in Europe but that the melters and refiners in Philadelphia had all rejected it. He wanted to conduct some experiments to prove the Philadelphians wrong and asked the superintendent for permission to install his apparatus on the roof of the mint building. Lott initially gave him permission, but after he discovered that the apparatus included a heavy tank that threatened the structural integrity of the building, he ordered that it be taken down. Agoston grumbled at the superintendent's decision, saying that if he had been able to keep it up a week or two longer his experiments would have been finished.[24]

In spite of the many difficulties, Agoston increased the capacity of the melting and refining department, significantly reducing the time depositors had to wait for payment and increasing the amount of gold coin in circulation in San Francisco. In the year or so that Hewston had been melter and refiner, the mint had melted and refined slightly more than 800,000 ounces of gold.[25] During the three months that Charles Haraszthy was melter and refiner, a little over 500,000 ounces were melted and refined. In the twenty months that followed, Agoston was able to melt and refine two and a half million ounces—more than three times the amount processed under Hewston.[26]

But this record had been achieved at a price. Lott insisted that the melting and refining rooms be worked day and night, and although Agoston had never objected to long hours in rooms where the heat was at times unbearable, he was apprehensive that extensive night work would result in the loss of a large amount of gold. It was inevitable that some gold should be lost in the melting and refining processes—the government recognized this by allowing a certain percentage of the total deposits for wastage—but the official allowance for wastage assumed that the mint operated under normal conditions and during normal working hours.[27] In a letter dated October 20, 1856, Agoston warned Lott that extending the night work would increase the wastage; but he concluded, "if you consider the public interest benefitted more by speedy returns than the large waste, in consequence of the work at night, would amount to, I am willing to continue as I have done before."[28]

By agreeing to Lott's entreaties, Agoston had let his eagerness to achieve overcome his better judgment. Some months earlier, Hewston had refused point-blank to work the melting and refining department at night. When he heard that Agoston had agreed to do so, the Philadelphia-trained professional predicted that he would surely meet with "some accident."[29] Events would soon prove Hewston's prediction prophetic.

In the middle of 1854, a special agent of the Treasury Department arrived in San Francisco to investigate a broad spectrum of government affairs. His name was J. Ross Browne, and he was an urbane traveler and writer with an impressive background as a journalist, humorist, and government official. Born near Dublin in 1821, Browne had come to the United States while still a boy. When California's first constitutional convention assembled at Monterey in 1849, Browne was employed as its official reporter, and he produced the standard journal of the official deliberations.[30] He came to San Francisco in 1854 under special orders of Secretary of the Treasury James Guthrie to investigate operations at key federal installations in California, including the Custom House, the U.S. Appraiser's Office and Marine Hospital, and the Branch Mint on Commercial Street.

By the end of 1854, Browne had finished his examination of other federal installations in San Francisco and was ready to move on to the mint. His early investigations there revealed that there were frequent shortages of the acids needed for refining which necessitated closures while new supplies were obtained. The facilities for refining were clearly inadequate and the staff was overworked. Browne believed that the officers of the mint were doing all they could to make the best of their crowded quarters, but he also believed that some had been indiscreet in their private activities. In September 1855, Browne reported to Guthrie that he considered the partnership formed a year earlier by Agoston, Birdsall, King, and Adams to be improper.[31] But he told the secretary that Agoston was "a very capable and efficient officer, and if he has erred at all in this matter, it has been with the full knowledge and sanction of the Superintendent. It would be very difficult to fill his place, and I feel assured that a letter of warning would prevent a recurrence of the impropriety."[32]

In the months that followed, however, Browne became increasingly concerned about Agoston's private business activities. He was particularly uneasy about his continued association with Wass, Uznay, and Molitor, who still operated their private refinery on Merchant Street. In the process of melting and refining gold, small particles of the precious metal were volatilized and deposited in the cracks and crevices of the furnaces, chimneys, and flues. The wandering gold could be recovered only by sweeping the apparatus and fluxing the metal from the deposits of soot and grime. The Hungarian trio, like other private assayers and refiners, had offered to purchase the mint's sweeps. The offer would ordinarily have attracted no attention, but Browne raised his eyebrows because of Agoston's personal connection with the Hungarian refinery. Could it be, Browne wondered, that there was hidden treasure in the drifts of soot and grime—and that Agoston and his Hungarian compatriots were trying to get their hands on it?

In October 1856 Browne wrote Secretary Guthrie that Agoston had made no secret of his association with Wass and Uznay, and added: "He is a very efficient officer, but of late has been engaged a great deal in his private affairs. When he came here it was supposed that he was very poor; it is now generally believed that he is worth some thirty or forty thousand dollars, owns a large house, etc. From these and other reports which have reached me, as well as from his attempt to obtain the mint sweeps, I consider him an unsafe man and would recommend his removal."[33]

Browne's suspicions appear to have been fed by a misconception of Agoston's financial condition. Although the special agent "supposed" that Agoston was poor when he arrived in San Francisco, his financial condition had actually been quite healthy when he left the legislature in 1852. Joseph Reiner, who knew his assets as well as any man, thought that he was worth between fifty and sixty thousand dollars at that time.[34] Although Reiner's estimate may have been exaggerated, Agoston clearly came to San Francisco with a substantial pocketbook—enough to buy land, build a house, and launch himself in business—all while still holding on to his San Diego property. Although the value of San Diego real estate was depressed, Agoston was able to sell some of his San Diego holdings at good prices: in

June 1854, for example, he sold a large chunk of his San Diego real estate (including the vineyard property he had developed at the entrance to Mission Valley) to Wass and Uznay for $10,000 in cash.[35] The Hungarian assayers had prospered in San Francisco and apparently were willing to share some of their good fortune with their enterprising friend. The price they paid for Agoston's San Diego land was very good, even by the standards of Gold Rush San Francisco. Ross Browne, apparently, was unaware of the transaction—a fact that was soon to cost Agoston dearly.

Browne was also concerned by persistent reports that large amounts of gold were mysteriously disappearing from the mint. To determine the amount of gold deposited in the sweeps, it was necessary to completely dismantle the furnaces, chimneys, and flues, separate their parts, and carefully glean them for particles of gold. When the equipment was dismantled, the mint's operations ground to a halt and impatient depositors fumed. Accounts were frequently balanced in the mint's other departments, but the melter and refiner's settlements came only once a year—oftener only if there was a change of officers.

Agoston, too, was concerned about the losses. At the end of 1856 he informed Superintendent Lott and Treasurer Snyder that he feared that large quantities of gold were being lost in the refining process.[36] He had personally scraped gold dust from the roofs of buildings in the neighborhood and concluded that losses of the precious metal had been aggravated by the furious pace of the night work and the inadequate facilities of the refinery. He pointed out that the chimney over the toughened bar furnace, though only eight inches wide, extended upward a distance of forty-eight feet.[37] The chimney would not draw without artificial drafts, and when blowers were used to fan the fires, the volume of air-borne gold increased rapidly. In an effort to trap the escaping gold, he removed the blowers and stoked the fires with stone coal, then installed horizontal, zigzag, and zinc-lined flues.[38] But the precious metal was elusive. Gold was found on the roofs of buildings three hundred feet from the mint. "How much more must have been lost in the streets," Agoston wrote Lott, "is impossible to calculate."[39]

Lott and Snyder confirmed Agoston's discoveries by personally climbing to the top of a building opposite the mint and scraping gold from its roof. In November, Browne reported to Guthrie that gold had been found "on the roofs of all neighboring buildings, as also in the gutters of the adjoining lots"; but Browne wondered if waste through the chimneys would account for all the losses. Was it possible that gold was also being stolen? The fact that metal was discovered on neighboring rooftops, he suggested, might be "a very easy mode of explaining a greater wastage than perhaps actually exists."[40]

While Browne worried over the chimneys and flues, Agoston struggled to find the cause of the losses. He suspended night work and remodeled his furnaces. He examined his deposits and asked Lott to send some of them to Philadelphia for analysis. Perhaps Conrad Wiegand, the new assayer, was assaying the gold inaccurately and therefore charging him with more gold than he was actually receiving. After the deposits were returned from Philadelphia, Lott showed Agoston a letter from Secretary Guthrie confirming that there were errors in Wiegand's reports.[41]

Wiegand's conduct had been a source of distress to Agoston as well as to other mint officers. Shortly after he assumed his position, Wiegand discharged the most competent men in his department and replaced them with inexperienced workers. As a result, assays were often late and completed in haste, and in some cases "estimates" of value were substituted for formal reports. In October 1856, Browne reported to Secretary Guthrie that Wiegand had been acting irrationally. "Mr. Wiegand appears to me from his conversation and acts to be laboring under partial mental derangement," the special agent wrote, "brought on by certain extraordinary religious and political connections." Browne added that Wiegand's "continuance in office on that ground, apart from any other, would be detrimental to the public interests."[42]

As the year 1856 drew to a close, Agoston began to think about leaving the mint. His work there had become more and more frustrating, and his private interests were growing. With Wass and Uznay, he was building a large gold and silver refinery on the outskirts of the city, and he had already made plans to develop a large vineyard north of San Francisco. Sometime before the middle of January 1857, he submitted his resignation to the Treasury Department.[43]

The mails were slow, however, and he would have to wait several weeks for word that his resignation was accepted. Browne wrote Secretary Guthrie: "As nothing to the discredit of Mr. Haraszthy has transpired beyond his connection with the establishment of Messers. Wass, Uznay & Co., which he justifies as totally disconnected with Mint operations, I recommend that his resignation be accepted and his successor appointed. . . . New furnaces, chimneys, etc. have just been erected at great expense, and should there be another settlement at this time, these works would all have to be torn down, and the gold extracted from them. I would suggest that the new officer be required to receipt for the gold in the melter & refiner's department, whether it be more or less. When the next annual settlement takes place, the exact amount can be determined. In the meantime the gold will be as safe in the chimneys and furnaces as if stored away in the form of sweeps."[44]

The refinery that Agoston was building with Wass and Uznay was a very substantial operation, one whose scale and plan would have suited the operations of the United States mint much better than the crowded building on Commercial Street. It was called the Eureka Gold and Silver Refinery and it was rising at the northwest corner of Harris and Brannan streets in San Francisco.[45] The Hungarians had built a large metallurgical works on Harris near Brannan some months before ground was broken for the Eureka Gold and Silver Refinery. Called the California Metallurgical Works, it consisted of a series of wooden buildings equipped with grinding mills, stone furnaces, and soaring brick chimneys.[46] Whether Agoston participated with Wass, Molitor, and Uznay in the construction of the metallurgical works is not clear, but he was one of the owners of the operation, at least by the spring of 1857.[47]

The Eureka Gold and Silver Refinery was something of a showplace. It occupied a low hill at the northwest corner of Harris and Brannan in front of the Metallurgical Works. It was built of brick and measured sixty feet in width and one hundred thirty in length.[48] Though it was a one-story building, its hilltop site gave it a commanding appearance from the street. The front wall was pierced by ten windows, each fitted with shutters. Brick chimneys rose from either

end, and a low masonry wall topped by a picket fence marked the
boundary between the street and the refinery grounds, which were
landscaped with shrubs and flowers.[49] The refinery was designed to
assay minerals, refine gold and silver, and produce fine bars and
ingots. The metallurgical works processed gold-bearing quartz and
other sources of raw metal.[50] Although the facilities were separate,
they were designed to work together to provide complete metallurgical services to California's mining community.

The Eureka Gold and Silver Refinery was ready for business in
March 1857.[51] A Hungarian traveler named John (originally János)
Xántus visited the facility early in May. He reported that the building was "so elegant, in the true sense of the word, that any Hungarian magnate could use it for his palace."[52] On entering the main
doors, visitors found themselves in a room equipped with tables and
four large banker's scales. The east and west sides of the room were
enclosed in glass, so supervisors could watch the workers scattered
throughout the building. On one side of the weighing room was the
main vault, which was burglar proof and fireproof and equipped with
a large metal safe. Behind the vault was Wass's office, which Xántus
called "a small sanctum furnished with excellent taste." "I say sanctum advisedly," Xántus added, "for the walls are lined with gold-
framed pictures of great Hungarian writers and publicists, who I am
sure collectively have never seen as much treasure at home as they
see sharing the room with Wass."[53] The refining room occupied the
western part of the building. It was furnished with a steam engine
and a large collection of tubs, vats, and furnaces. "One would think
that the intense fire and the great variety of chemicals would make
the room extremely hot," Xántus wrote, "but the astonished visitor
finds that just the opposite is true; for the entire room is ventilated
by twelve to twenty-five foot-high windows, through which the city's
westerly winds circulate freely."[54]

Xántus was familiar with Agoston's writings about the United
States and described him as "a famous globe-trotting compatriot."[55]
He thought the Eureka Gold and Silver Refinery was one of the
monuments of San Francisco and enthusiastically wrote home to
Hungary, "This enterprise is the most remarkable one on the Pacific

Coast, and we Hungarians can be justly proud of Count Wass and his partners, who represent our homeland with so much distinction in one of the greatest nations of the world."[56]

Some time earlier, before the Eureka opened for business, Agoston and his partners had applied to the Treasury Department for a contract to refine gold for the mint. Browne was suspicious of the proposal, calling it a "speculation" and charging that it would "sooner or later result in immense frauds and great loss to the Government." In a letter he addressed to Secretary Guthrie just as the Eureka was opening, Browne wrote: "It is true that ample security is offered; but permit me to suggest that the Government has never yet derived much benefit from its securities in California—especially in San Francisco. Where the melting and refining would soon average from three to five millions per month, although returns are promised daily, what security could there be for the safe and prompt return of such large amounts of treasure in private hands?"[57]

Though Wass played a large role in building the Eureka Gold and Silver Refinery, his name is absent from a letterhead depiction of the building issued by the pioneer lithography firm of Kuchel & Dresel. That lithograph, which offers a fine view of the refinery and the streets in front, is captioned "Haraszthy, Uznay & Co's. Gold and Silver Refinery."[58] Wass had apparently left the city for a time, leaving Agoston and Captain Uznay in charge of the refinery.[59] But the firm of Haraszthy, Uznay & Co. was to be short-lived, for, on May 29, Agoston and Uznay agreed to dissolve their partnership, and Uznay promptly formed a new partnership with Justh and Hunter.[60] At about the same time, Uznay formed another partnership with Wass and a metallurgist from New York named John Warwick.[61]

The reason for the dissolution of the Haraszthy-Uznay partnership was a sudden and ugly turn in affairs at the mint that forced Agoston to quickly liquidate his interests in the Eureka Refinery and the adjoining California Metallurgical Works and attempt to sort out his other property interests both inside and outside San Francisco. At the end of May, he sold his interest in the Metallurgical Works to Warwick for $15,000 and his interest in the Eureka Refinery to Justh for $20,000.[62]

In the first week of June, Agoston became the subject of a series of sensational newspaper stories that heralded the opening of a public scandal and the beginning of a long and tortuous judicial process. Before the scandal and the judicial process were finally concluded, they were to sap his strength and his purse and come very close to shattering his personal reputation.

18

Called

to

Account

The burgeoning scandal had its roots in J. Ross Browne's investigation of affairs in the melting and refining department at the mint. "I have felt very uneasy and solicitous of late about the Branch Mint here," Browne had written the Secretary of the Treasury in March 1857. "Returns to depositors have not been promptly made. In some instances there have been delays of eight or nine days. Upon due inquiry as to the causes of these delays, the Superintendent and Melter and Refiner have explained the matter very fully, but the explanation has not altogether removed my doubts." [1]

Suspension of night work had slowed the refinery, and some of the machinery had failed at critical moments. Still suspicious, Browne wondered if the mint's sluggishness might be designed to divert business to the Eureka Gold and Silver Refinery. Since Agoston's departure from the mint was growing closer, Browne advised Guthrie that he no longer favored a postponement of Agoston's settlement but believed there should be "a most thorough and rigid examination and settlement." [2] Agoston's resignation was finally accepted at the end of April, and the work of dismantling the chimneys, furnaces, and flues began at once.

As gold was retrieved from the crevices and cracks it became increasingly apparent that waste since the last settlement had been substantial. In the seven months since the accounts were last balanced, more than $16,000,000 worth of gold had passed through the mint's refinery.[3] Workmen fluxed gold from the chimneys, and Agoston climbed roofs in search of the precious metal, as clerks in their crowded offices wrestled with debits and credits, struggling to balance the accounts. By the beginning of June, the work of the settlement was still going on, and Browne wrote the new Secretary of the Treasury, Howell Cobb, that he feared the final figures would show a large deficiency. "The actual loss cannot be accurately determined until all the precious metals now in process of reduction are assayed," Browne said; "but it is more than probable that it will amount to 7,000 ozs., or about $135,000."[4] By the middle of the summer, the accounts were finally finished. In the seven months ending in April, the mint had shown a loss of $201,642.63. Of this amount, $51,091.93 was allowed by the law as wastage, but there was no explanation for the disappearance of the remainder. In the melter and refiner's accounts, bookkeepers entered the sum of $150,550.70 opposite the words "balance unaccounted for."[5]

Even before the final figures were tallied, Browne became concerned. His powers as special agent were broad, but so were his responsibilities. The mint had operated under his nose for more than a year and a half, and he had failed to detect the losses in time to prevent them from growing alarmingly large. Would Secretary Cobb be satisfied that he had been duly vigilant? Perhaps wisely, Browne believed that he must do something to restore confidence in himself. He still did not suspect Agoston's honesty, and wrote Cobb that "it would be unjust in the present stage of the investigation to hazard an opinion as to his guilt. The deficit may have occurred from natural causes, or from malfeasance on the part of his subordinates." Notwithstanding this, he demanded that Agoston turn over to the government enough property to cover any losses for which he might be held responsible, and threatened him with arrest if he refused.

The special agent met with Agoston at the beginning of June and delivered his ultimatum. Agoston's attorney had advised him to submit to arrest and trial, Browne told Secretary Cobb; "but he preferred turning over his property, and accordingly placed in my hands deeds and mortgages, amounting at his own estimate to \$215,000 — the actual value being probably \$150,000. Most of the property is well known to me, and I consider it amply sufficient to secure the Government against any loss resulting from the deficiency."[6]

Under a long deed of trust prepared by the United States District Attorney, William R. Blanding, Agoston transferred property in San Francisco and San Mateo counties to Jacob R. Snyder as trustee for the United States. By terms of the deed, if judgment was recovered against Agoston for the mint deficiency, the government could sell the property at private auction and apply the proceeds to satisfy the judgment. If Agoston was finally absolved of liability, full title to the property would be returned to him. The transfer included all the land he owned at Las Flores and Crystal Springs, an undivided one-third interest in two acres of the Las Pulgas ranch, his house on Harrison Street, fractional interests in some lots on the San Francisco waterfront, the Anglo Tract near Redwood City, and two mortgages received from Justh and Warwick upon sale of his interest in the Eureka refinery. Excluded from the conveyance were his remaining properties in Wisconsin and San Diego and the vineyard property that he had recently acquired north of San Francisco. The deed of trust was completed and signed on June 10.[7]

In a letter to Cobb, Browne attempted to explain the causes of the mint's losses. He thought that the hurried night work, the defective chimneys and flues, and the crowded conditions of the refinery had all contributed to the wastage. Much of the bullion had been inadequately safeguarded against theft, he said, and Agoston's reckonings of wastage had not been frequent enough to detect the losses at an early stage. The mint's assays had been woefully inadequate — in fact, some of the deposits had never been analyzed — and the losses could have commenced with the opening of the mint in 1854 and continued progressively until the time of Agoston's resignation. Browne instructed Agoston's successor as melter and refiner, Louis A. Garnett, to take extra precautions to guard against loss, and defensively reminded Cobb: "The Government having been secured against loss by conveyance of property, and due precautions taken to prevent a recurrence of the difficulties referred to, I hope the Department will find no ground for dissatisfaction so far as regards my action in the premises."[8]

Even before Agoston conveyed his property to the government, however, newspapers were reporting developments at the mint. The city's premier daily, the *Alta California*, was sympathetic to Agoston's situation, pointing out that losses had been aggravated by the mint's crowded conditions and its defective chimneys and flues. "The sweepings from the roof of Davidson's Building," the *Alta* reported on June 5, "amounted to three hundred ounces. Eleven hundred and eighty ounces were collected from the chimneys after two and a half months work."[9] The *Bulletin* (now edited by James King of William's brother, Thomas King) reported on June 2:

At Armory Hall, which is at least two hundred yards distant from the Mint, one hundred and eighty dollars was collected. Other neighboring buildings produced a like proportion of loss. Major Snyder, the Treasurer of the Mint, than whom we believe there is not a more honorable man in the State, and who is extremely cautious in any statement he may make, informs us, that to satisfy himself, he went on a frame building nearby, and personally collected a considerable amount. The employees and officers of the Mint, with whom we have conversed, look upon the deficiency, whatever it may prove to be, as caused by natural means, for which no officer of the establishment could be responsible.[10]

On June 7, however, the *Herald* pointed an accusatory finger at Agoston, charging that "it will require a very extensive knowledge of science to reconcile the fact that during the coining of the first $15,000,000 no auriferous smoke issued from the chimneys of the Mint, whilst during Col. Haraszthy's term of office they belched it forth continually. The dilemma is that the deficiency has been caused either by malfeasance in office on the part of Col. Haraszthy, or from gross ignorance of the duties of Melter and Refiner. From the facts no other conclusions are possible."[11]

On the morning of June 4, posters were found attached to buildings surrounding the mint, announcing that claims had been staked in the "Famous Haraszthy Diggings" and that "interlopers" were forbidden to intrude. One of the posters, tacked to the wall of a bank, proclaimed:

Know ye, whom it may concern, that we, undersigners, do claim for min-ing purposes, the ground situated between the corner of Montgomery and Commercial streets, running in an easterly direction, 600 feet. This claim is to be worked as soon as some swindlers will do us the favor to clear out.

J. Hugary,
S. Yankee.

This 3d of June of 1857.
Commercial Street.

The poster was reprinted in the *Bulletin*, the editor explaining: "The names of Hugary and Yankee are supposed to represent those of Haraszthy and Uznay, and the swindlers are supposed to be those incredulous persons who will not believe that gold will fly up a chim-ney."[12]

Public interest in the mint controversy was heightened in Sep-tember when two new stories broke. The first involved John Szabo, one of Agoston's partners in a share of the Buri Buri Rancho in San Mateo County and a former employee of Wass, Molitor and Co. After leaving Wass and Molitor's employ, Szabo had taken a job at the mint. He was apparently in the habit of depositing small amounts of gold for coining from time to time. He said he obtained the gold from the mines but thought it unseemly for a mint employee to bring his own gold to the mint, and so he two asked two storekeepers on Montgomery Street to make the deposits for him. When news of the deficiency in Agoston's accounts broke in the newspapers, the store-keepers thought that Szabo was ripe for blackmail and threatened to report him for "stealing" gold from the mint unless he paid them a large sum of money. Szabo responded by going to the police and charging the storekeepers with extortion. The fact that Szabo was a Hungarian, a mint employee, and one of Agoston's business associ-ates, seemed suspicious to many; and rumors immediately began to circulate that Szabo was stealing gold with Agoston's knowledge — or perhaps even *for* Agoston. But Szabo was not under Agoston's super-vision at the mint, and there was no evidence suggesting that Agos-ton knew anything at all about his dealings with the storekeepers. Still, some of the newspapers pointed to Szabo as evidence of a "smoking gun" and urged that the authorities take prompt action to bring Agoston to "justice."[13]

The second story broke on September 15, when the *Morning Call* published a long article headed "Criminality of Major Snyder," charging, first, that Agoston was guilty of "fraud" in his handling of the mint's melting and refining department and, second, that Snyder had "connived" in the fraud. According to the *Call,* Snyder had permitted Agoston to repeatedly claim credit for the same bars of gold and thereby cover up the fact that other bars had been stolen; and, after Agoston resigned his position, Snyder had further attempted to cover up his and Agoston's misconduct by recommending that Szabo be appointed as his successor.[14]

Snyder was outraged by the allegations and immediately demanded that the grand jury investigate the *Call* for criminal libel.[15] The jury obliged, and the publishers soon found themselves on trial in the Court of Sessions. Edward Dickinson Baker, one of the lights of the San Francisco bar, took charge of the prosecution. Baker had come to San Francisco from Illinois, where he was an intimate friend of a prairie lawyer named Abraham Lincoln (Lincoln's second son was named Edward Baker Lincoln in his honor). In San Francisco, he won a reputation as a powerful courtroom advocate and orator. It took a little more than two days for Baker to demonstrate that Agoston had never claimed credit for the same bars more than once; and, if he had been guilty of any misconduct, Snyder certainly had no knowledge of it. His closing argument lasted four hours, but the jury was unable to agree on whether the *Call*'s libel was criminal, and they had to be discharged without reaching a verdict.[16]

Early in August, a group of Agoston's friends and former employees gathered at his home to present him with a silver service and pledge him their support. The service was engraved with the following inscription: "Presented to Col. A. Haraszthy, late Melter and Refiner of the U. S. B. Mint, by his friends and assistants, as a token of their regard and esteem upon the occasion of his resignation. San Francisco, 31st July, 1857."[17]

All through the summer of 1857, the federal grand jury investigated the mint deficiency. The U.S. District Attorney apparently had no appetite for the investigation, and the grand jurors had to proceed without him, calling witnesses (some quite unwilling) and poring over the mint's account books. They were unanimous in their opinion that the mint building was unfit for the purposes for which it was being used, and strongly urged the government to build a new and more suitable structure. They faulted the mint's officers for the lax security that prevailed in the building, noting that the vaults were too small to hold the vast treasure consigned to them and that there were many opportunities for theft. Some small thefts had already been detected, and the grand jury suspected that others had gone totally undiscovered.

The grand jury's chief concern, quite naturally, was the large deficiency in Agoston's accounts. After what they called "an investigation as thorough as we could institute," they confessed that they were unable to arrive at "any satisfactory explanation for the deficiency." They noted that the settlements made by John Hewston in 1855 and by Agoston in 1855 and 1856 all reported relatively modest losses, but that Agoston's final settlement had reported a very large loss. "This increase of loss is said to be caused by the great increase of business in the Branch Mint," the grand jury said, "causing the Melter and Refiner to work his department day and night, which prevented the same care being observed to avoid loss. This possibly may have been the case, as the Mint was worked to three or four times its capacity, owing to the great demand for coin at that time." Of course, if the loss could be explained by overwork, by the thefts of minor mint employees, or even by careless management, Agoston would be guilty of no offense greater than negligence. But the grand jury was not willing to let him off so easily; and on Saturday, September 19, 1857, they gathered in the courtroom of Circuit Judge Matthew Hall McAllister to formally charge Agoston with the crime of embezzlement. The amount he was charged with embezzling was 8,092 ounces of gold bullion valued at $150,550, and a single gold bar valued at $1,000 — for a total value of $151,550.[18]

Immediately after the charge was filed with the court, a bench warrant was issued for Agoston's arrest. He was taken into custody by the U.S. Marshal and brought before Judge McAllister for arraignment about five o'clock in the evening. The new United States District Attorney, Pablo Della Torre, was on hand to represent the government. He pointed out that the crime with which Agoston was charged was very serious, with a maximum penalty of $10,000 in fines and five to ten years in prison, and urged that he be required to post reasonable bail before he was released. Agoston's attorney, Edward Stanly, reminded the court that Agoston had an unblemished reputation in the community and that he had already transferred to the government enough property to indemnify it against any losses for which he might be held responsible. McAllister then ordered that Agoston be released as soon as he posted bonds signed by personal sureties in the amount of $10,000, and an additional bond signed by himself in the amount of $20,000. Agoston's sureties were Dr. Carl Precht, a German-born physician who, like Agoston, was a member of the San Francisco Verein, and Thomas Hayes, one of the leaders of the Irish community in San Francisco. Precht and Hayes quickly signed the required bonds, and Agoston was released from custody.[19]

Edward Stanly was a partner in Hoge and Stanly, one of San Francisco's most respected law firms. Joseph P. Hoge, the senior partner, was a former congressman from Illinois and a member of the California Democratic State Central Committee; Stanly was a former congressman from North Carolina and the fledgling Republican Party's 1857 candidate for governor of California. The gubernatorial election had been held just two weeks earlier, and though Stanly had lost to the Democratic candidate, John Weller, he ran a respectable race, actually outpolling Weller in San Francisco.[20] In addition to their years of courtroom experience, Hoge and Stanly offered the advantages of political bipartisanship, a quality that Agoston may well have thought important in the politically charged atmosphere that surrounded the mint controversy.

The trial was originally scheduled to begin in November, but before the date set for impaneling the jury Hoge and Stanly moved for a continuance. In support of their motion they submitted an affidavit signed by Agoston detailing the facts that he expected to prove at the trial and declaring that his attorneys had not had sufficient time to prepare for the complicated issues in the case. The press had prejudiced public opinion against him, he said, and some witnesses in the case were now out of the state and would have to be brought back to testify. "This case is one of vast importance to the defendant," he declared, "involving his reputation and his liberty."[21] Judge McAllister agreed, ordering the case continued until the next

term of the court, scheduled for February 1858.[22] But in February
yet another continuance was ordered; and, by March, the attorneys
and judge had agreed to refer the entire controversy to a commission of special investigators for the purpose of taking testimony.

The commission was warmly supported by Treasury officials in
Washington, who thought a thorough investigation was needed to
get to the bottom of the mystery of the missing gold. Two distinguished commissioners were appointed in Washington to serve on
the body: Murray Whallon, a veteran attorney from Pennsylvania,
and Hugh J. Anderson, the former governor of Maine. Cutler McAllister, Judge McAllister's son and the clerk of the Circuit Court in
San Francisco, was named to preside over the hearings.[23]

For more than two months, the commissioners examined witnesses in a building on Commercial Street opposite the mint. Stanly
appeared in behalf of Agoston and Della Torre in behalf of the government. One by one, all the principal officers of the mint, and many
of the workmen, were called to explain the processes of melting and
refining and offer insights into Agoston's conduct in office. The newspapers followed the case closely, offering regular transcripts of the
testimony to their readers.

Lewis Garnett, Agoston's successor as melter and refiner, took
the stand to explain how the melting and refining department was
organized. Since Agoston left the mint, Garnett said, substantial
changes had been made in the department. More than twenty feet
of pipe had been added to the flue above the gold furnace, and the
zigzag flue that Agoston first installed had been extended another
twenty-five feet. When Agoston was in charge of the department,
the flues and chimneys had been much smaller and more likely to
cause gold particles to volatilize. After Agoston submitted his resignation, three ounces of gold were found in a stone pot on the roof of
the mint, and another eighteen ounces in an old filter. Yet another
store of gold was found in a warehouse where mint equipment and
supplies were kept. When Agoston was melter and refiner, Garnett
said, there were many opportunities for mint employees to steal. The
thefts could have been made at almost any stage of the melting and
refining process, and in almost any amounts. Asked if, at his first
settlement, Agoston had not turned over to the government four

thousand ounces of silver for which he was not charged on the mint's books, Garnett agreed that he had. He thought he had done so because the assays of gold had been too high during that period—that is, some of the metal charged on the books to gold had in fact been silver. When Agoston discovered the error, he voluntarily surrendered the excess silver to the mint's treasurer.[24]

Lott took the stand to testify that, during the year and a half he served as the mint's superintendent, he had often asked Agoston to work at night to meet the increasing demands of the mint's depositors. He said that Agoston was a tireless worker and often remained at the mint until the early hours of the morning to finish his duties. On occasion, he had taken gold bars from the mint, but only for the purpose of showing them to the superintendent in his office in an adjoining building. Assayer Wiegand had been a source of constant concern to Agoston, Lott declared, because his assays were slow and inaccurate.

When Lott first heard of the losses charged to Agoston, he thought there must be some mistake in the books. Then Agoston came to him and Treasurer Snyder with bricks taken from the top of one of the chimneys. They were coated with flakes from the furnace, and granules of gold were interspersed among the flakes. Agoston revealed that he had been up on the roof and found gold dust scattered about. Snyder and Lott were concerned about Agoston's discoveries, and determined to look into the matter for themselves. Snyder owned a building adjoining the mint, and he and Lott decided together to go up to its roof and see what they could find. They gathered the dirt and dust they found in the gutters and took it back to their offices, where they put it in a leaden dish and washed it in water. At the bottom of the pan, they found a fine deposit of gold dust—so fine that it was hard to separate it from the other deposits. They summoned Agoston, gave him the pan, and told him he had better go back and get "the rest of the dirt in those gutters." The discovery of gold on the roof of Major Snyder's building convinced Lott that Agoston's losses must have been caused by defective chimneys and flues, and by all the work he had done at night. But he thought that some of the losses might also have been due to thefts committed by mint employees, for security in the overcrowded building was lax and there were many opportunities for dishonest employees to make off with precious metal. "I have known a great deal of Col. Haraszthy's reputation and character since my coming to California," Lott declared, "and had known him before; and from my personal knowledge of the man and his standing in the community, I have always esteemed his character morally, and as a businessman above reproach."[25]

Major Snyder was called next to testify about the mint's accounts. During the time that Hewston was melter and refiner, Snyder said, the mint had received 836,172 ounces of gold in deposits and returned 810,064 in refined gold, for a net loss of 3.012 percent. During Charles Haraszthy's term, the mint had received 522,000 ounces and returned 504,921, for a net loss of 5.09 percent. During Agoston's term, the mint received 2,538,582 ounces and returned 2,455,517, for a net loss of 3.12 percent. Snyder confirmed that he and Judge Lott had found gold on top of his own building neighboring the mint. Asked what he knew of Agoston's background and character, Snyder replied: "I first knew Col. Haraszthy in 1852, as a member of the Legislature of this State. I have known him since as Assayer and as Melter and Refiner in the U.S. Branch Mint, during which time I was acting as Treasurer of the Mint. As far as I know his conduct has always been correct, and his character good officially and otherwise."[26]

Eyebrows were raised when John Felix, an employee in the melting and refining department, testified that he had often seen Agoston carrying his metal box in and out of the mint building. "I have even seen it go out in the evening under a big cloak," Felix said, "and brought back in the morning, but what he put in it I cannot say." Felix said that Agoston had often sent chips of gold to private assayers because he suspected the accuracy of Conrad Wiegand's assays. Agoston had entertained Felix and other mint employees at his Crystal Springs ranch. Felix denied that he had ill feelings towards Agoston and said, "No man under Col. Haraszthy, during his term of office, was ill-treated by him." But Felix clearly harbored resentments against his onetime employer. He said that he had an invention for granulating gold that he wished to sell to the government. Agoston had expressed some interest in acquiring the invention for private use, but he had only been willing to pay a monthly license fee, and Felix wanted to sell it outright. Agoston never gave Felix a definite answer as to whether he was interested in the invention. "I regard Col. Haraszthy as belonging to a class who wish to be above their fellow citizens," Felix commented. Yet, when pressed about the probable cause of the gold losses in Agoston's department, Felix admitted that he had gone up to the mint's roof to see for himself whether gold could have fallen there. "Incredible as it may appear to many," Felix said, "in order to convince myself that gold was actually found on the roof of the building, I myself scraped some together where the roof has been cleaned before, and in a space of about 12 feet by 14 feet, I took all the sweep and fluxed it." After the fluxing, the sweep was found to contain "near four ounces of gold mixed with base metal."[27]

Joseph Harmstead, a machinist in the mint, testified that he had once seen Agoston carry a gold bar worth $1,000 out of the mint. But this was explained by the fact that the superintendent's office was outside the building and it was often necessary for Agoston to bring gold to the superintendent for him to examine. Harmstead admitted that Agoston "always treated the men employed in the Mint in a gentlemanly manner, and was as attentive to his duties as could be expected of him."[28]

There were tense moments when James Condon, a former employee of the Eureka Gold and Silver Refinery (and one of the men who had joined Agoston in claiming land at Crystal Springs in 1853), took the stand to testify. Condon had been accused of stealing gold from the refinery and had been arrested with a quantity of gold on his person. At his request, he had been taken from jail to Agoston's house to confer with him. On May 20, 1857, he signed a confession that was witnessed by John Short, a jailer. When Condon's case was called in court, Agoston declined to prosecute. Before the federal commissioners, Condon claimed that he signed the confession while drunk and under threats from Agoston and advice from Police Chief James Curtis. Condon further claimed that Agoston had told him that if he refused to sign the confession he would be convicted, whether or not he was guilty. Agoston was supposed to have said, "God forbid, Condon, that I would have you arrested, even if I knew you were guilty, but I must protect myself." Condon also said that he had seen Captain Uznay at the Eureka refinery with some bars of government gold that he thought belonged to the mint, and he charged that Agoston's motive in procuring his arrest was to silence him.[29]

Curtis, Uznay, and Short flatly controverted Condon's testimony. They insisted that Condon was not drunk when he signed the confession, and that before he met with Agoston, he gave conflicting stories to explain the gold found in his possession. Uznay denied that he had ever had possession of gold from the mint, and stated that Agoston had declined to prosecute Condon out of consideration for the man's wife and family.[30] Henry Johnson, a special police officer, testified that Condon had confessed to the theft at the jail, before he met with Agoston, and that he had told Johnson that Agoston was a "good, kind-hearted man"; if he could only get to see him, he was sure he could convince him not to prosecute. Johnson said that Condon was sober but noticeably elated when he returned from his meeting with Agoston.[31]

If San Franciscans hoped for a speedy decision in Agoston's case, they were destined to be disappointed. The U.S. District Attorney's appetite for the criminal prosecution was clearly blunted by the testimony taken before the federal commissioners. The statements of Felix and Condon might have helped the government's case if they had not been effectively rebutted. Whatever the cause of the mint's losses, it was clear that Agoston had a host of defenders. An agreement was reached to drop the indictment from the trial calendar, subject to being reset at the request of either side, and in March 1858 the U.S. District Attorney filed a civil complaint against Agoston, alleging that he was indebted to the government in the amount of $152,227.03.[32] The burden of proof was, as the prosecution knew, less onerous in a civil than in a criminal case, and the government's chances for prevailing greater. In May of the same year, the government also brought a civil suit against Agoston, Wass, and Uznay for $10,000. Wass and Uznay had signed faithful performances bonds for Agoston when he assumed his duties as melter and refiner; if he was found to have breached his duties to the government, they were liable as his sureties, up to the $10,000 limits of their bonds.[33]

On November 27, 1860, the new U.S. District Attorney, Calhoun

Benham, appeared before Judge McAllister to ask that the three-year-old criminal indictment be dropped. The judge acquiesced, and an order was entered dismissing the indictment.[34] The *Alta California* reported the dismissal with approval:

It was high time that it should be either tried or dismissed, for it has laid in the Court about three years. That there was a defalcation of $152,000, and that it happened in Col. Haraszthy's department of the Mint, are undenied facts; but the government officers admit by their course that they cannot prove any criminal responsibility for this defalcation upon him. . . . That much of the missing gold was carried off through the chimney, was considered to be conclusively proved by the amounts found in the sweepings of the roofs of adjacent buildings. The policy of running the Mint night and day, as was done during Haraszthy's term, is considered dangerous, because the furnaces may get overheated, and the Melter and Refiner has not that opportunity of keeping an account of the metal received and transferred, which he should keep, for the safety of himself and the Mint.

We understand that the returns from the sweepings of the Mint, sent to Philadelphia and there assayed, show a large amount to the credit of Haraszthy; much beyond that of ordinary sweepings, but we do not know how far the defalcation is reduced.[35]

The attorneys had meanwhile agreed that trial would proceed in the civil action against Agoston, Wass, and Uznay and that, if judgment went for the defendants there, it would be binding in the larger suit against Agoston alone. Murray Whallon, one of the commissioners who took oral testimony in Agoston's case, was named special counsel to assist the United States district attorney in the prosecution of the government's case.

Trial began on February 26, 1861. Much of the testimony taken before the commissioners was read into the record. Evidence was offered of the erratic behavior of the assayer, Conrad Wiegand, and of Agoston's continued but unsuccessful efforts to obtain accurate assays of the gold in his department. Charles Haraszthy was also present to testify. Now more than seventy years old, he confirmed that Wiegand's assays were unreliable and that, on more than one occasion, it had been found that the assayer overvalued the gold charged to Agoston.[36] Edward Stanly showed the jury a brick taken from the top of the chimney at the mint. It was covered with a glittering deposit of gold that was clearly visible to the jurors.

When the evidence was concluded, Judge McAllister gave the jury his instructions. The melter and refiner at the mint was, he said, absolutely accountable under the law for the conduct of his department. It was no defense to assert that gold had been stolen, or that the melter and refiner had been diligent and careful in the discharge of his duties. But the judge added forcefully, "There is no evidence in this case to prove the slightest fraud in the defendant."[37]

The jurors retired to deliberate at three o'clock in the afternoon. To the surprise of many in the courtroom, they returned to the box after only five minutes and announced that they had reached a verdict. The trial had lasted five days, but that time seemed trivial compared with the four long years that had passed since the mint controversy first exploded in the newspapers. The judge and the attorneys listened closely as the foreman rose to announce the jury's decision.

The verdict was for the defendants.[38] Agoston did not owe the government a dollar or a dime or a penny. Count Wass and Captain Uznay were also exonerated.

The mint litigation had been long and costly. Agoston's legal bills were enormous (before the jury's verdict was handed down, he paid Edward Stanly alone $6,000),[39] but other costs had been even more substantial. His reputation had suffered in ways he could never accurately assess. While the litigation dragged on, he had been the object of derision in the newspapers and suspicion among a large segment of the public. Judge McAllister's ruling that there was no evidence of any fraud, and the jury's verdict that there was no other basis for holding him responsible for the mint's losses, did much to restore his reputation, but these decisive rulings could never completely heal the wounds he had suffered. For years after, suspicions lingered among some Californians that he had unjustly escaped responsibility for his misconduct—that the judge's ruling and the jury's verdict resulted from clever lawyering, or fuzzy-headed reasoning, or merely incredible good luck.

Since Major Snyder held title to Agoston's Crystal Springs land as trustee for the government, many would-be settlers claimed that it was government land and therefore open to public settlement. On June 7, 1861, Snyder reconveyed all the property Agoston had transferred to him as security for the government,[40] but before the reconveyance some settlers had entered on parts of the property, claiming it as their own.[41] These men (whom Agoston condemned as squatters) had to be dealt with in some way. They could be sued for ejectment, but lawsuits (as Agoston knew only too painfully) were expensive propositions, and the results could not always be predicted. Given the confused state of land titles in California in the 1850's and 1860's, it was often more prudent for a landowner to strike bargains with squatters than to ask the courts to force them off the land. And so Agoston began selling off parts of his Crystal Springs property, some to men who were already on it, others to newcomers.[42]

The money that Agoston received from these sales was put to good use. A part was applied to the payment of debts he had accumulated during the mint litigation; another part was used to defer the current living expenses of himself and his family; and a third part was used to provide working capital for a new venture he was embarking on north of San Francisco. This venture, which began to occupy his attention during his last year at the mint, was in the end to be the most ambitious, and the most satisfying, of his entire career.

19

In the
Vineyards

The town of Sonoma lies a little more than thirty miles north of San Francisco. In 1856, as now, it was the principal population center of the Sonoma Valley, a narrow trough in the Coast Range Mountains that begins at the edge of San Pablo Bay (the northern arm of San Francisco Bay) and stretches in a northwesterly direction for about thirty miles until it opens onto the plain of Santa Rosa. On the east, the valley is walled off from the Napa Valley by the Mayacamas Mountains, and on the west it is separated from the Petaluma Valley by the Sonoma Mountains. Though the valley narrows as it nears Santa Rosa, it measures about eight miles across at Sonoma, where the Mayacamas change their generally north-south course to march three or four miles to the east before continuing south to lose themselves in the marshy shore of the bay. The town of Sonoma sits comfortably at the base of the Mayacamas, facing south toward the bay and San Francisco.

Sonoma traces its roots to the Sonoma Mission, founded by the Franciscan padres in 1823 as the last and most northerly of the twenty-one California missions. The town itself was laid out in 1834, when Mexican governor José Figueroa ordered Mariano Guadalupe Vallejo, the twenty-seven-year-old commandant of the Presidio of

San Francisco, to secure California's northern frontier against the threat posed by the Russian settlement at Fort Ross, on the seacoast about fifty miles to the northwest. Vallejo laid out a large plaza adjacent to the mission and began to fortify the place against possible attacks by the Russians and nearby Indian tribes. The Russians abandoned Fort Ross in 1839, but Sonoma continued and thrived. In 1836, a revolution against Mexican authority was started in Monterey, and Vallejo's nephew, Juan Bautista Alvarado, proclaimed himself governor and Vallejo *comandante general* of all of Alta California. For six years, Alvarado occupied the governor's chair in Monterey, but everybody recognized that the real power was exercised by his uncle the *comandante*. Vallejo—now habitually addressed as general—built a garrison at Sonoma and acquired title to vast stretches of the surrounding countryside. His large family—brothers and sisters and nephews and nieces, with their wives and husbands and sons and daughters—settled on ranchos in all the surrounding territory, making Sonoma a kind of provincial capital of the frontier area north of San Francisco Bay. By 1846, the town was important enough that, when a group of American settlers banded together to declare California an independent republic, they made their declaration at Sonoma, where they took General Vallejo into custody, fashioned a flag adorned with the crude image of a bear and the words "California Republic," and, with the sanction of American Captain John Charles Frémont, presided over the short-lived Bear Flag Republic. The Bear Flag came down and the Stars and Stripes went up in July 1846, when American naval forces occupied Monterey and San Francisco and proclaimed all of California a part of the United States.

Sonoma was the headquarters of the Pacific Division of the United States Army from 1849 to 1852, but after that the tide of history seemed to pass it by. It was a little town of a few hundred inhabitants huddled around General Vallejo's plaza when Agoston first saw it. Vallejo's own home, popularly called the "palace" because of its great size and the three-story tower that crowned its western end, was the most notable building in the town. But Vallejo now used the "palace" as an office, for he had recently erected a new home at the base of a hill about half a mile to the northwest. Built in the Gothic Revival style then popular in the northeastern United States, the general's new home was called Lachryma Montis (Latin for Tears of the Mountain) for a spring that bubbled out of the hillside above the house. Vallejo lived at Lachryma Montis in a kind of pastoral splendor, surrounded by his extended family, a living and generally beloved link with a historical era that was fast fading in the memories of the oldest pioneers.

For Agoston, the attractions of Sonoma had little to do with its historic past—though they bore a direct relation to that past. His interest lay in the promise of the grapevines, which the padres themselves had planted there, probably soon after they built the mission church in the early 1820's. Like those planted elsewhere in California, the vines were of the familiar Mission variety, but in the Sonoma climate and soil they produced a distinct wine. In the more southerly missions, the wine produced from Mission grapes tended to be sweet and lacking in acid. In Los Angeles, the most celebrated product was a sweet, golden dessert wine with a high alcoholic content called Angelica. Angelica was produced from the juice of Mission grapes to which brandy was added before (or sometimes during) fermentation. Angelica was praised by some who drank it, although others dismissed it as a cordial unworthy to be called a real wine.[1] If anything like Angelica was produced in Sonoma, it never assumed the importance of the Los Angeles product. Rather, the Sonoma wines tended to have little residual sugar and only moderate levels of alcohol. They were, in other words, traditional table wines.

Though the Franciscans were no longer at the Sonoma Mission when Agoston first came there, the vines they planted were still flourishing. The small mission vineyard had been supplemented by a few other vineyards planted over the intervening years by the people of the town. General Vallejo himself had two of the most important vineyards, one that lay just north of the palace and bore the picturesque name of Quiquiriqui (Cock-a-doodle-doo), and another that adjoined his new home and, like it, was called Lachryma Montis. Altogether, General Vallejo's vineyards occupied about sixteen acres.[2]

There was a third vineyard of note in the Sonoma area when Agoston first came there. It had been planted in the early 1830's by a Christianized Indian who wished to establish a home for himself and his family under the laws of Mexico.[3] He may have been attracted to the site because it had once been the location of an Indian village called Lac and was littered with remnants of the old occupation — scattered arrowheads, bones, and bits of broken pottery. But he may also have been attracted by the creek that flowed nearby. Though the Spanish called the creek Arroyo Seco (Dry Stream), its flow was steady during most of the year, and it promised a dependable supply of water for the vines.

The nameless Indian did not hold onto the vineyard for long. By the early 1840's it was owned by General Vallejo's younger brother, Salvador Vallejo,[4] who in about 1842 transferred the property to a Mexican soldier named Damaso Antonio Rodriguez. Two years later Rodriguez applied to Governor Manuel Micheltorena for a formal title to the land. Unlike most of the California land grants, which were measured in square leagues (a California league was equal to about six thousand American acres), the tract that Micheltorena gave Rodriguez in 1844 was measured in *varas* (a unit of Spanish measurement equal to thirty-three inches).[5] Called Rancho Lac in the formal papers, it was a perfect square of land that measured one thousand varas on each side and included slightly more than 176 acres. The vineyard that the Indian had planted in the 1830's stood in the very center of the property.

In 1846 Rodriguez transferred Lac to an American named Jacob P. Leese (a brother-in-law of General Vallejo).[6] Three years later, Leese sold Lac to an American frontiersman named Benjamin Kelsey, who in 1852 sold a half-interest in the property to another American, one Joseph Wardlow.[7] In 1853, Kelsey and Wardlow joined to convey the whole property to Julius K. Rose.[8] Rose, an investor and lawyer who owned property all over northern California, was one of the men who sold Agoston the land on which his Crystal Springs vineyards were laid out. When Agoston first saw the Sonoma vineyard, it was variously called Salvador Vallejo's Vineyard, Leese's Vineyard, Ben Kelsey's Vineyard, or just The Vineyard. Rose called it the Vineyard Farm.[9]

Years later, Arpad Haraszthy remembered that his father had tasted some of the wine produced on the Vineyard Farm in 1855 and thought it had promise.[10] There is no evidence that Rose took any personal hand in producing the wine,[11] which was probably made by other men "on shares" (General Vallejo's wines were also produced in this way.).[12] During the three years that Rose owned the Vineyard Farm, he did improve the property, however, putting up a few buildings and increasing the size of the vineyards from four acres to just under twenty-three.[13] But the property was not profitable, and in 1853, the year he acquired the land, he sold part of his interest, and in 1855 and 1856 he took out mortgages. Both mortgages went into default in 1856.

In 1858, Rose testified in Agoston's behalf before the U.S. Commissioners who were investigating the disappearance of gold at the mint in San Francisco. He told the commissioners that he sold the Vineyard Farm to Agoston in the early part of 1857 for $11,500. But there is good reason to believe that the sale was made pursuant to an agreement reached the previous year that permitted Agoston to take possession of the property before the title was finally transferred. In later years, both Agoston and Arpad recalled that Agoston first came to Sonoma in 1856.[14] Rose said he sold half of the property in his own right and the other half as agent for a man named W. R. McReady, who lived in New York.[15] The public records confirm that Agoston acquired McReady's half of the property under a deed signed by Rose, but they also show that he acquired the other half by foreclosing on a mortgage that Rose had given on the property and that Agoston had acquired from the mortgage holder. The foreclosure seems to have been friendly, for Rose admitted service of process when the suit was filed and even agreed that judgment could be taken against him (the foreclosure suit was actually begun in the name of Attila Haraszthy, but Attila was undoubtedly acting as his father's agent). Rose gave Agoston the deed for McReady's half of the vineyard property in January 1857, but the sheriff did not deliver a deed for Rose's half until December 19, 1857. When the sheriff's deed was finally delivered, it was made out to Agoston.[16]

Rose had acquired some adjoining land after his original purchase, so the property that Agoston acquired from him and McReady totaled more than seven hundred acres. In addition to the 176-acre Lac Rancho, it included two smaller parcels in the mountains east of Lac and an irregularly shaped tract of 496 acres lying to the southeast. The property was wedged between two flanks of the mountains, where the floor of the valley runs up the banks of the Arroyo Seco into a ravine. The creek was fringed with willows, sycamores, and cottonwoods that outlined a graceful path as it meandered out of the ravine and down the valley toward the larger Sonoma Creek, which led to the bay. Several springs bubbled out of the hillsides, forming little streams that tumbled over rocks and into gullies until they made their way to the Arroyo Seco. There were sulphur and soda springs on the property, too, richly charged with minerals and naturally heated by hot rocks buried deep beneath the surface of the ground.

Agoston put Attila in charge of his new Sonoma property.[17] Years later, Attila remembered that he moved to Sonoma in December 1856,[18] but it is likely that he made trips there before that date. Agoston called the Sonoma property Buena Vista Ranch. The name was suggested by the broad views of Sonoma Valley and San Pablo Bay that could be had from some parts of the property, and recalled the picturesque name he had first given his town on the Sauk Prairie. (Széptáj is Hungarian for "Beautiful Place"; Buena Vista is "Beautiful View" in Spanish). Attila was probably on the Sonoma property during the harvest and crush of 1856, since a note in the *California Farmer* for November of that year indicated that wine was being made in Sonoma by the "Buena Vista Vineyard."[19]

Agoston himself did not move to Sonoma until 1857, probably late in the summer.[20] He and Eleonora, who had recently returned to California from New Jersey, took up residence in a house that Leese had built around 1845 or 1846 in the very center of the old vineyard. It was not a large house, but it occupied an impressive site on the brow of a low knoll, and from its front porch there was a fine view over the valley and bay. Perhaps it was the promise of a house in a vineyard with a view over San Francisco Bay that lured Eleonora back to California in 1857. Or perhaps she and Agoston had grown tired of their long separation. California had taken on a more civilized appearance in the five years since she and the children left San Diego in 1851, and there were better schools for the children now. Whatever the reason for Eleonora's return from New Jersey, fifteen-year-old Ida, eleven-year-old Bela, and nine-year-old

Otelia must have relished the reunion with their father and their oldest brothers, Gaza and Attila. And they all must have been overjoyed when seventeen-year-old Arpad joined them late in the spring. Arpad was to remain with the family until midsummer when, anxious to resume his studies, he again headed back to New York.[21] Bela accompanied Arpad on his return trip, for he too had decided to resume his studies in the East.

One of the first missions of the Haraszthy family in Sonoma was to make the acquaintance of their neighbors. General Vallejo's Lachryma Montis was two miles to the west, and the Haraszthys lost no time in calling on the Vallejos and laying the foundations of what was to become a firm friendship between the two families. Both Agoston and General Vallejo were gentlemen with extensive business and agricultural interests, and Agoston was anxious to learn as much as he could from the general about winemaking techniques and traditions in Sonoma. The home of William McPherson Hill, about nine miles northwest of the Sonoma plaza, was another important stop for the Haraszthys. Hill was a graduate of the University of Pennsylvania who had come to California in 1849, made a fortune as a commission merchant in San Francisco, and started to plant fruit trees and grapevines in the Sonoma Valley in 1852. In 1856, Hill had about five acres of vines on his property, the oldest of which were three years old.[22]

The Haraszthys also became friendly with Lilburn W. Boggs and his family. Born in Kentucky in 1792, Boggs had been governor of Missouri from 1836 to 1840, then, in 1846, set out across the plains to California. When he and his party reached Sonoma in the fall of 1846, they were warmly welcomed by General Vallejo, who put them up in the huge adobe house on his Petaluma Rancho, just over the ridge of mountains west of Sonoma. Boggs had come to California in the hope that the conquering American government would tap him to serve as governor. But opposition among Mormon settlers, who remembered that he had forcibly driven the Mormons out of Missouri when he was governor, was too great, and he had to satisfy himself with an appointment as alcalde of Sonoma. In about 1847 Governor Boggs and his son William bought property between the Sonoma plaza and the Lac Rancho and began to lay out a farm for themselves. When the Haraszthys moved in to the old Leese house on the Vineyard Farm, the Boggses were their closest neighbors. William Boggs lived in a cabin down the hill from Agoston's house, and he and his new Hungarian neighbor often hiked together over the countryside, locating landmarks, fixing survey lines, and otherwise attempting to determine the proper boundaries of the Buena Vista Ranch.[23]

On his trips around Sonoma, Agoston learned that winemaking in the area was still in its infancy. Vallejo's and Hill's vineyards were the most extensive plantations besides his own, and in all the rest of the Sonoma Valley there were not more than fifteen acres of vines. The grapes were mostly Mission grapes, intended for table use, but there was a handful of other varieties: Hill, for example, had acquired a few cuttings of the Rose of Peru, the Italia, the Black Hamburg, and the Chasselas (also called the Chasselas Doré) at auctions in San Francisco, and some other farmers in the valley had begun to experiment with native American vines imported from the eastern United States. But none of these other varieties had shown much promise, and the prevailing belief was that the Mission was the only grape that had any real commercial use in California.[24] Two or three of the Sonoma Valley growers were making wine from their grapes in 1857—Vallejo, for example, had contracted with a French doctor named Victor Fauré to produce wine in the old Mexican barracks on the Sonoma plaza on shares—but most of the other growers sent their grapes to San Francisco where they were sold for table use.

Arpad's return to California in the spring of 1857 enabled him to inspect his father's Crystal Springs vineyards and help his brothers prepare the Sonoma property for the upcoming season. Although Agoston had not yet decided to give up Crystal Springs, his enthusiasm for that location had diminished, and he had decided to transfer the vines from there to Sonoma. As Arpad later explained, when the Crystal Springs vines reached bearing age, Agoston found that the grapes did not ripen on account of the "fog, winds and extreme cold,"[25] and he instructed his sons to begin moving the vines across the bay to Sonoma.

The move was probably made by boat from San Mateo County (possibly from the port in Redwood City) to the embarcadero at Sonoma, situated at the head of navigation on the Sonoma Creek, about four miles from the plaza. Part of the trip could also have been made by wagon from Crystal Springs to San Francisco, where boats suitable for moving large quantities of plants could have been more easily chartered. It is impossible to determine the total number of vines that were transported, although some idea of the number can be gained from the planting figures given for Buena Vista in 1857 and 1858.

In a report he made to the State Agricultural Society in October 1858, Agoston reported that 16,850 vines were planted in February 1857. Since these vines were all planted eight feet apart, they covered just under twenty-five acres, more than all the vines that had been planted on the property in the previous twenty-five years. But the vines in the vineyards only hinted at the total number on the property. There were 450,000 rooted "native" (i.e., Mission) vines and 26,000 "foreign" (i.e., European) vines, and Agoston had already begun a nursery in which 300,000 rooted native vines were offered for sale, along with 2,000 rooted foreign vines and 30,000 foreign cuttings.[26] In January 1858 an additional 40,000 rooted vines, covering nearly sixty acres, were planted at Buena Vista. "A large portion of these will soon bear considerably," Agoston told the State Agricultural Society, "inasmuch as they made immense growth for their age."[27]

Years after his father left Buena Vista, Arpad remembered that the vines that his father moved from Crystal Springs to Sonoma in 1857 and 1858 included the celebrated Zinfandel.[28] When Arpad made these statements, he was the generally acknowledged leader of the California wine industry—proprietor of the Eclipse champagne cellars in San Francisco, owner of the Orleans Hill vineyards in Yolo County, and president of the California State Board of Viticultural Commissioners—and his statements were widely accepted. But in 1885, a dissenting voice was raised by a Sonoma county newspaper editor and onetime Sonoma county clerk named Robert A. Thompson. Thompson was then researching a history of the California wine industry and had contacted Agoston's old Sonoma neighbor, William Boggs, then living in the Napa Valley, for his recollections of how the Zinfandel had first come to Sonoma. Boggs insisted that the vine had not come into the Sonoma Valley until 1859, when he and Agoston visited the Napa Valley farm of a man named J. W. Osborn and brought back two wagon loads of grape cuttings. Boggs recalled that the wagon loads included a number of foreign vines, among them the Zinfandel. He said he had been told that Osborn obtained the Zinfandels from Frederick W. Macondray, Agoston's old Crystal Springs neighbor.

Surprised by Boggs's assertion, Thompson did some research into the records of the Massachusetts Horticultural Society. He discovered that a table grape called the "Zinfandal" had been regularly exhibited at functions of the Massachusetts society in the middle 1840's, and that Frederick Macondray had been an active member of the society in those years. Thompson reasoned that Macondray must have been acquainted with the "Zinfandal" in Massachusetts; and since Osborn said that he had received the vine from Macondray, Macondray must have grown it in his "grapery" in San Francisco. Thompson and Boggs both published letters in San Francisco newspapers in which they advanced the theory that Macondray was the first man to bring the Zinfandel to California and that the vine did not reach Sonoma until Osborn's cuttings were brought there in 1859.[29]

Thompson's research about the Massachusetts Horticultural Society was quite accurate, and his conclusion that Macondray probably knew the "Zinfandal" in his native state was entirely valid; but his conclusion that Macondray was the first to bring the Zinfandel to California, and that he grew the vine in his San Francisco greenhouse, was almost wholly speculative. Beyond Boggs's hearsay recollections that Osborn had obtained the Zinfandel from Macondray, there was no direct evidence that Macondray ever had the Zinfandel in California. Further, there was a key problem with Boggs's account: he not only claimed that Agoston obtained the Zinfandel from Osborn in Napa, he also insisted that Agoston brought no foreign vines of any kind to Sonoma when he moved his vineyard there from Crystal Springs. Moreover, Boggs emphatically asserted that there were no foreign vines in Sonoma County before 1859, except a few white Sweetwaters, a table grape called the Black Hamburg, and a vine called the "Black St. Peter's" that Victor Fauré had planted for General Vallejo. "I am thus particular in detail," Boggs wrote somewhat petulantly, "as I wish to convince Mr. Arpad Haraszthy that I know whereof I write."[30]

Boggs also challenged Arpad's assertion that the Zinfandel was a Hungarian grape, and said that Dr. Fauré had told him it was French (there has never been any credible evidence that the Zinfandel was a French grape). According to Boggs, Agoston himself was unimpressed by the Zinfandels he obtained from Osborn, saying that the best grapes in Hungary were sweet and that no grape grown in Hungary was "so sour" as the Zinfandel ("sour" is a word that wine novices sometimes use to mean "dry," or lacking in sweetness, though experienced winemakers rarely make this mistake). Agoston speculated, so Boggs said, that the grape had probably come from France or Germany.[31]

Boggs's assertions—like many of Arpad's—reveal the frailties of human memory. There is no reason to believe that Boggs had any ill feelings toward Agoston—to the contrary, he insisted that he did not wish to detract "one jot or tittle" from the honor due him as a pioneer winegrower. And yet, nearly thirty years after the events he was trying to recall, Boggs insisted that Agoston had no foreign vines before 1859. Contemporary printed evidence from 1856, 1857 and 1858 clearly proves that Boggs was wrong.

Agoston's own description of his Buena Vista property, published in the State Agricultural Society's annual report for 1858, reveals that he had 14,000 foreign vines in bearing that year and another 12,000 rooted in the nursery, and that these vines represented no fewer than 165 different varieties.[32] A visiting committee of the State Agricultural Society inspected the vines and noted in the same report: "The Committee have seen the foreign varieties, being one and one-half years old. They were planted in February, one thousand eight hundred and fifty-seven—bearing splendid grapes from one pound up to thirty pounds to a single vine."[33] To have been fully bearing in 1858, these vines must have been rooted when they were brought from Crystal Springs. Further, advertisements that Agoston placed in agricultural journals at the end of 1858 reveal not only that he had a large number of foreign vines in Sonoma before 1859, but that he was offering them for sale to other wine growers. These advertisements listed 30,000 cuttings (representing the same 165 foreign varieties noted in his report) and 2,000 rooted vines (representing fifteen foreign varieties). The vines could be purchased either in Sonoma or by applying to a man named G. W. Kinzer, who operated a sawmill at the corner of Market and Beale streets in San Francisco and had apparently agreed to act as Agoston's agent in selling the vines.[34]

By the 1880's William Boggs's memory may well have been confused by the recollection that Agoston had gone to Europe in 1861 and the following year brought back the most famous single importation of grapevines in the history of California.[35] If Boggs and Agoston had indeed visited Osborn's Napa Valley farm in 1859, Boggs, like many another old pioneer, could have mistakenly thought that Agoston's celebrated 1862 importation was his only importation.[36] Thompson himself was confused on this point.[37] Arpad was not. He stated emphatically that "the importation of 1862 was my father's very *last* effort in that direction. His first importations went back into the early fifties."[38] And, to counter the contention that Macondray had imported the Zinfandel before his father, Arpad told a convention of winegrowers that the gardener who had charge of Macondray's San Francisco greenhouse in the early 1850's himself asserted that the Zinfandel was "never grown in that grapery."[39]

Boggs did recall that there were some native American vines on the Buena Vista property when Agoston arrived there in 1857. They were Catawbas, a grape variety that had attained some popularity in Ohio and that Rose had planted on the property in 1855. But Agoston had tasted wines made from native American grapes before he came to California and wanted no part of them.[40] He dug the Catawbas out of the ground, ignoring Boggs's pleas that they be saved.[41]

From the outset, Agoston had ambitious plans for Buena Vista. Boggs recalled that he was determined to add to his original property there, vowing that he would pay a thousand dollars an acre if necessary.[42] But that was not necessary. Before the foreclosure proceedings against Rose were concluded, Agoston was able to purchase a one hundred–acre tract lying southwest of the original Lac Rancho from a man named Jonas Woods for $5,500.[43] And, in the spring of

1858, he entered into an agreement with Thomas O. Larkin of San Francisco to acquire a large, irregularly shaped portion of Larkin's Huichica Rancho, which bordered Lac on the east. He struck quite a favorable bargain with Larkin, agreeing to exchange the house he had recently vacated on Rincon Hill in San Francisco for the Huichica land. He agreed to give Larkin a good title to the Rincon Hill property within eighteen months; but, mindful that the house was part of the property that Jacob Snyder was holding in trust for the United States government until the mint litigation was concluded, he agreed that, if he could not convey a good title in that time, he would pay Larkin $3,000 in cash.[44] Larkin died in late 1858, before the mint litigation was concluded, and at the end of 1859 Agoston paid Larkin's estate the agreed price and in return received a deed for the Huichica tract.[45]

The land that Agoston acquired from Larkin was mostly mountainous terrain: it ran from the northeastern corner of Lac up through the Mayacamas Mountains, rising in spots to nearly eight hundred feet above sea level; but it also included a grassy depression in the hills measuring about a quarter of a mile in width and a mile in length that pioneers called the Lovall Valley. The tract, which lay partly in Sonoma and partly in Napa County, included close to four thousand acres. With this purchase, Agoston increased his holdings in Sonoma to about five thousand acres.[46] His total cost for this property was just under $20,000.

Planting at Buena Vista proceeded apace in 1857 and 1858. In February and March of the first year, Agoston planted 16,850 vines on the property, and in January of the second year he added another 40,000, making eighty-three acres of new vineyards in the two years. Added to the vineyards that were already in place, his new plantings brought the total vineyards at Buena Vista up to one hundred acres—a truly surprising total for a California vineyard. But he was not satisfied with this progress and announced his intention of ultimately planting one thousand acres of Buena Vista to vines.[47]

Since Agoston was still under the cloud of the mint litigation, he found it necessary to squeeze every penny he could out of his Sonoma property. He ran cattle on the some of the higher hillsides, sold off fruit from the orchards he had acquired from Rose, and planted 350 acres of the flatlands to wheat. Most of the grapes he harvested in the first two years were sent to the fresh fruit markets in San Francisco. The prices there for fresh grapes—nine to ten cents a pound—were too good to be ignored, although he would have preferred to turn the whole crop into wine. But he was able to make a respectable amount of the precious liquid. In 1857 he made 6,500 gallons of wine. At prevailing prices of a dollar and a half to two dollars a gallon, this was a good start for his winemaking business. He also made 120 gallons of brandy, which his neighbors thought to be quite good, and 60 gallons of the Hungarian specialty, tokay, for which he was quickly offered eight dollars a gallon; he declined the offer, explaining that the wine was still young and, if he sold it prematurely, its reputation would be damaged.[48]

The labor at Buena Vista was performed by crews of Chinese workmen that Agoston contracted for in San Francisco. He—and others like him who championed the cause of Chinese labor—was roundly criticized for doing so. The most vocal opposition to Chinese workers came from members of the Shovelry wing of Agoston's own Democratic party. Whenever a Chinese laborer was given work, so the Shovelry Democrats argued, a white man was unfairly denied a job. There was only so much work to go around, and by working at wages white men would never accept the Chinese were unfairly competing for the limited stock of jobs. Racial feelings, already high when Agoston was in the legislature in 1852, had grown even higher by 1857, and politicians were railing against the "Chinese menace" with greater and greater vehemence. When Agoston refused to accede to demands that he give up his Chinese workers for whites, a demonstration was mounted in Sonoma. Threats were made against him and his family, and to protect himself he took to carrying a gun whenever he went out in the fields.[49]

He realized, of course, that he could save money by employing Chinese at Buena Vista. The average white laborer would not work for less than thirty dollars a month (much more than the same worker would receive in the eastern states); a Chinese laborer would do the same work for eight dollars a month, plus room. Agoston felt keenly that the higher costs of labor in California put local manufacturers and farmers at a disadvantage with their eastern competitors. By seeking to exclude Chinese from the labor force, the Shovelry Democrats were not only inflating the costs of labor, they were also excluding an important segment of the population from real participation in the economic life of the state.[50]

The Chinese may have worked on some of the building projects that Agoston initiated at Buena Vista, probably not as craftsmen but as helpers. Agoston's first major construction project in Sonoma, in 1857–58, was a pair of cellars and an adjoining press house. The cellars were dug into the side of a steep hill near the eastern edge of the original Lac tract; the press house was constructed at the entrance to the cellars. The first cellar, which was completed in 1857, was described by a newspaper reporter as measuring twenty feet wide, seven feet high, and a hundred feet deep.[51] Agoston himself described the second, which he began to dig in the fall of 1850, as twenty feet wide, ten feet high, and thirty-five feet long.[52] The entrances to the cellars formed two arches that stood just a few feet apart.

These cellars were substantial achievements. They were the first hillside cellars dug in the Sonoma Valley—perhaps the first in California—and they were capable of holding large quantities of wine at a uniform, year-round temperature of fifty-five to sixty-five degrees Fahrenheit. Agoston calculated that when the second cellar was completed it would accommodate two rows of hogsheads, each holding five hundred gallons of wine, and still leave room enough for a walk of seven feet down the middle. In all, this cellar would provide storage for about forty thousand gallons of wine.[53] The first press house, which was completed by the fall of 1858, was a temporary building, probably of wood construction and just large enough to cover the arched entrances to the two cellars.[54] Although it was not a large building, it was large enough to accommodate a crusher, fermenting tubs, and all the empty barrels and other equipment needed to manufacture wine.[55]

Agoston was eager to experiment with new ways to press, ferment, and age his wine. Providing proper barrels was a serious problem, for when wine was stored in barrels made of California oak, it seemed to acquire a bitter, tannic taste. Nobody seriously entertained the idea of using European oak, or white oak grown in the eastern United States, because those woods had to be brought to California by sea and were prohibitively expensive. Some winemakers had toyed with the idea of using redwood for their barrels, but they rejected the idea when they discovered that redwood was saturated with resins that leached into the wine and ruined its flavor and aroma. Agoston recognized that green redwood was unsuitable for barrels, but he thought the wood could be used if the resins were removed from it before it was put in contact with the wine.

To test his idea, he had some small redwood barrels constructed, then connected a rubber hose to his brandy still and, with the escaping steam, scalded the barrels inside and out. The water that ran out of the barrels was at first black as ink; but as the steaming continued, the stream became clearer and clearer until, after about an hour, it ran as clear and pure as spring water. To test whether the barrels could now safely hold wine, he filled them up, and at the same time filled some barrels made of California oak with the same liquid. In the months ahead, he periodically sampled the contents of both sets of barrels to determine how the wine was aging. To his delight, he found that the wine in the redwood barrels was free of any contamination from the redwood resins. He promptly instructed his workmen to start making more redwood barrels, and began to inform his neighbors that he had discovered the perfect wood for cooperage — a native of California that could be procured in the nearby woods for a fraction of the cost of fine European or eastern American oak.[56]

First things first, of course, but after the press house and cellars were finished, Agoston directed his attention to the old farmhouse in which he and Eleonora had been living since they arrived in Sonoma. Probably sometime in 1859, he leveled the house and in its place began the construction of a handsome new residence.[57] It was built in the style of a Roman villa (a "Pompeiian villa," its admirers were later to say), with a classical facade consisting of a central grouping of four tall columns flanked on each side by two separate groupings of four columns each. A broad porch, which ran across the full width of the house, was lined with glass-paneled doors that opened on the rooms inside. In front of the house, Agoston installed a cast-iron fountain and pool surrounded by a wrought-iron fence and wide flower beds. Although it was designed primarily as a personal residence, the house also served the function of an office and ranch headquarters. It was built of wood and painted white but so skillfully conceived that, from a distance, it seemed to have been fashioned out of sandstone, or even marble.

Agoston had every reason to be satisfied with his first two years in Sonoma. He had assembled the largest estate in California devoted primarily to vine cultivation and winemaking, and he had planted more vineyards in that time than any one man had planted in the ninety years since Europeans first came into California. He had dug two hillside cellars, built a press house, and erected a handsome mansion on a knoll, and his vineyard now ranked as one of the two or three largest vineyards in the state (if not the very largest).

But he was not an easy man to satisfy. He had come to Sonoma not just to found a great vineyard and make fine wine but to build an industry. He believed that planting vineyards and making wines were the kinds of activities that men could profitably engage in throughout California, and that his own efforts at Sonoma could serve as an example to others. And so in the fall of 1858 he agreed to a request from the directors of the California State Agricultural Society that he write a practical treatise on viticulture and winemaking that would help farmers throughout the state plant vineyards, erect wine cellars, and make wine. He realized, of course, that such a treatise would not only disseminate valuable information; it would also help to spread his reputation, and that of Buena Vista, throughout the state.

His "Report on Grapes and Wine of California,"[58] which he began to write in February 1858, ran to only nineteen pages in the Agricultural Society's *Transactions* of 1858, but it was packed with information. It began with a history of early vine-growing efforts in California and a complete tabulation of the number of grapevines growing in California in the years 1856, 1857, and 1858. The greater part of the text was practical advice: brief discussions of the three essentials of a good vineyard—climate, locality, and soil—and instructions on laying out a vineyard; planting, cultivating, and pruning the vines; harvesting, making, and aging the wine; and designing and building cellars. It also contained short descriptions of the traditional methods by which special styles of European wines are made—including champagne, port, and Hungary's treasure, tokay—

as well as a discussion of the manufacture of brandy, and a detailed estimate of the costs of planting a typical vineyard. Throughout the report he spoke in concrete terms, using simple words that farmers would be sure to understand. But his words conveyed an unmistakable enthusiasm. Making wine was a noble undertaking, he seemed to be saying—but one that was within reach of every farmer in California, however modest or humble.

His enthusiasm was evident in the closing paragraph of the "Report," in which he sounded a note that he would stress again and again in the years to come: the need for the government to foster the production of fine wine in the United States by gathering and disseminating vines. He urged the federal government to instruct its consuls throughout the world to collect cuttings from the widest possible varieties of vines and send them to the U.S. Patent Office. The Commissioner of Patents could plant the cuttings in a suitable place and then distribute them to those sections of the country in which the climate and soil were most suitable for vinegrowing. He added:

The expenditure to the Government would be a trifle in comparison with the immense benefit our citizens would derive from it, and it would save, in a few years, millions of dollars that are now sent to foreign countries for wine, brandy, and raisins. California, with such aid, would not only produce as noble a wine as any country on the face of the globe, but it would export more dollars' worth of wine, brandy, and raisins, than it now does of gold.[59]

The "Report" was widely praised. In an official statement to the board of managers of the State Agricultural Society, Wilson Flint of Sacramento, owner of one of California's most important nurseries, said that Agoston was an "intelligent and practical vintner" and that the value of his report could "never be too highly estimated." Flint thought that, if large editions of the report were circulated throughout the state, they would "materially aid" the development of California winemaking.[60] Heeding the suggestion, the society's directors ordered the treatise printed in its annual reports for 1859 and, when that report was sold out, ordered extra copies printed for distribution in the principal agricultural areas of the state.[61] In years to come, the "Report" was to be recognized as a California classic: the first treatise on winemaking written and published in California, and the "first American explication of traditional European winemaking practices."[62]

In October of the same year (1858), Agoston submitted a second report to the State Agricultural Society on the work he had done at Buena Vista. This report described the vineyards he had planted and the press house and hillside cellars he had built, and it again urged farmers throughout California to join him in the effort to plant vines and make fine wines. He closed this second report by repeating his call for proper varieties of foreign grapes. He was now more sure than ever before that what California's vineyards needed most was fine European varieties of grapes:

No man can fully comprehend yet what fine wines we will be able to make, when we have once the proper assortments of the different qualities of foreign grapes. Then, if we make such good wines already from one quality of our native grapes, how much better wines will we make when we have differently flavored varieties of grapes for it, in a certain proportion mixed together? To illustrate it to persons not acquainted with wine-making, I will say that carrots will make a vegetable soup, but it will be a poor one; but take carrots, turnips, celery, parsley, cabbage, potatoes, onions, etc., and you will have a superior vegetable soup. So with grapes: take the proper variety of them and you will make a splendid wine.[63]

Agoston had always been a driven man, but his activity in Sonoma seemed more intense than ever before. He set an almost frenetic pace as he strode through the vineyards in his long coat and stovepipe hat, swinging a walking stick, giving orders to the crews of Chinese workmen who were always busy on the place, then climbing into the saddle of his favorite riding horse and galloping into the hills to survey the site for a new vineyard planting. When he was not busy in Sonoma, he was in San Francisco, buying supplies for the vineyards and press house, seeking buyers for his new wines, and conferring with his lawyers, who were still busy picking up the pieces of the mint imbroglio.

It was almost as if he knew he had to make up for lost time. He had told Benjamin Hayes in January of 1850 that he had come to California to plant a vineyard, and in the seven years that followed he had planted three of them—in San Diego, in San Francisco, and at Crystal Springs. But those vineyards were not really what he had envisioned. They produced little, if any, wine, and did nothing to prove his theory that California could one day make great wine. And, while he was busy fighting Indians in San Diego County, making laws in Sacramento, refining gold and silver in San Francisco, other pioneers were quietly going about the business of planting vineyards and making wine. They were on the same trail that he was, and though they were more modest in their approaches to vinegrowing and winemaking, they had by 1857 made important contributions to achieving the goal of transforming California into a wine land.

The center of California's burgeoning wine production in 1857 was Los Angeles. It was natural that winemaking should be important in the City of the Angels, for the first vineyards outside the missions had been planted there in the 1820's and 1830's, and the warm, sunny climate of southern California was conducive to luxuriant crops of grapes. A French cooper from Bordeaux named Jean Louis Vignes had pioneered the Los Angeles wine trade in the 1830's. Vignes soon brought two of his nephews, Pierre and Jean Louis Sainsevain, over from France, and they helped him build his pioneering business (called Sainsevain Brothers after 1855) into a small but respectable firm.[64] Their vineyards were still not very extensive in 1857—something under forty acres—but they were making enough wine to send regular shipments to San Francisco. A handful of other producers had congregated around the old Vignes vineyard in Los Angeles by 1857, and there were a total of six hundred acres of vineyards in the county, though not all were bearing, and not all that were bearing were used to make wine.

The most important competitors of the Sainsevains were two German musicians named Charles Kohler and John Frohling, who arrived in San Francisco in 1853 and shortly thereafter began shipping wines to the city from a twelve-acre vineyard that they bought in Los Angeles. By 1856, Kohler and Frohling had a cellar on Merchant Street in which they stored their casks. Their Los Angeles wines were mostly sweet—Angelica, and a kind of port—though they also produced two dry wines, a red that some thought resembled French claret and a white that was modeled after the dry white wines of the

Rhine Valley and was meant to appeal to the tastes of the many German residents of San Francisco.[66]

Another competitor of the Sainsevains was a onetime Tennessee trapper and frontiersman named Benjamin D. Wilson. Wilson, whom the Spanish Californians affectionately called "Don Benito," had come to southern California in the early 1840's, married into the prominent Yorba family and, through their influence, acquired thousands of acres of rich grazing land in and around Los Angeles. On one of his ranchos, the 14,000-acre San Pascual Rancho at the base of the San Gabriel Mountains, he began in the early 1850's to plant what he called the Lake Vineyard. Wilson's vineyard was not large — about seventeen acres in 1857 — but its wines were gaining some reputation, and he was already making plans to expand his plantings.

There were also some vineyards in the Santa Clara Valley at the southern end of San Francisco Bay, where a colony of Frenchmen had settled in the early years of the Gold Rush and begun to set out grapevines. Antoine Delmas, who bought land in San Jose in 1852, was one of the earliest pioneers in the Santa Clara Valley. As early as 1855, he assembled a good collection of European grapes, which he exhibited at the California State Fair. Although Delmas was primarily a nurseryman, he may have made a little wine along the way. The first important winemaker in the Santa Clara Valley was Etienne Thée, who planted his first vines along the banks of the Guadalupe Creek south of San Jose, probably in 1852. By the time Agoston came to Sonoma, Thée and his son-in-law, Charles Lefranc, had upwards of twenty acres of vineyards in the neighboring Almaden Valley, and they were beginning to produce some wine.

The vineyards in Los Angeles and Santa Clara in 1857 hardly amounted to a "wine industry," but they did show that enterprising nurserymen and vineyardists were busy in both the southern and northern parts of the state. When Agoston came to Sonoma in 1857 he was not the only pioneer who was determined to prove that good wine could be made in California—nor even the first. But he was soon to prove that he was a different kind of winemaker from all the rest.

20

Bacchus
Loves
the Hills

The Indian who planted the first vines at Buena Vista in the 1830's had chosen the site in part because of the steady flow of water in the Arroyo Seco, and all the subsequent owners had used the creek to irrigate the vines.[1] Agoston, however, did not believe that irrigation was necessary to grow good grapes in Sonoma. The valley was blessed with a good supply of rainfall—about twenty-five inches in a typical year—and he believed this was enough to sustain any vines he might plant. More water would only promote faster growth, diminish the intensity of the grapes, and produce a weak, flavorless wine. If good vines had to struggle for moisture, they would produce fewer grapes, but the grapes would be richer and more intense.

An anonymous Roman vintner was credited with first enunciating the axiom, *Bacchus colles amat*—"Bacchus loves the hills"; but the axiom attained a special meaning in Hungary where, for centuries, vineyards had been tucked up against the foothills of the Carpathians, carved into terraces on the Mecsek hills, or, in the neighborhood of Futtak in the Bácska, spread over the mountain slopes of Szerémség.[2] Irrigation was all but impossible on a hillside, where vines had to extract every bit of moisture they needed to survive from the soil. But hillsides offered many advantages for wine vineyards.

Land on hillsides was often more protected from frosts than land on the valley bottoms. This was particularly true in California's coastal valleys, where the winters were never severe but cold snaps in the early spring could severely damage the budding vines. Killing frosts often struck the bottomlands, but the hillsides were only rarely affected, perhaps because the hillside air circulated more freely about the vines. Hillsides also made it possible to vary the exposure of the vines to the sun and the wind. If the winter was ordinarily cold, a southern or southeastern exposure would maximize the warming effects of the sunshine; if the summers were hot, a north or northwestern exposure would help to ameliorate the heat; and, if the winds were persistent, an exposure could be selected to protect the vines from their prevailing direction. In areas where there is fog in the summer (as along much of the California coast), hillsides can raise the vines above the fog line and extend the time during which they are exposed to the sun.

Hillside land was also less apt to be clayey than lands in the valley bottoms. Agoston's experience had taught him that light soil containing a mixture of clay, magnesia, and lime was the best for grapevines, because it did not crack in the summer heat and it permitted the roots of the vines to move freely beneath the surface. He favored gentle slopes with western exposures, but thought that vines could also be planted on mountaintops if the proper soil could be found to feed the roots and nourish the grapes.[3] To prove his point, he planted some of his new vines on steep hillsides surrounding the old Lac Rancho tract. He said he would "irrigate with the plow,"[4] arguing that by stirring the ground regularly he would encourage the soil to absorb moisture from the air. Old-timers in the valley shook their heads disapprovingly as he sent his Chinese laborers up the hillsides with plows (or, where the ground was too steep to accommodate plows, hand hoes). In California, they told him, vineyards had always been planted where their roots could be kept moist in the summer.[5] But he was determined; and, when the heat of July and August turned the hills around Sonoma from green to gold, the hills above Lac fairly sparkled with the green leaves of long rows of grapevines. Bacchus, indeed, was smiling on the vineyards of Buena Vista.

In the winter of 1858–59, Agoston added a little more than fifty acres to the vineyards at Buena Vista, and in the winter of 1859–60 another thirty acres. His vineyards were fast approaching two hundred acres, a very large plantation for California. Although many of the vines were still under bearing age, Buena Vista was already producing a bumper crop of grapes. In 1857, for example, the vineyards produced enough grapes to make 5,000 gallons of wine.[6] In 1858 this number was increased to 12,000 gallons of wine and 400 gallons of brandy, while still leaving 65 tons of grapes for the fresh table grape market in San Francisco.[7]

In 1860 Agoston entered into a contract with the San Francisco firm of Groezinger and Co. to sell them 150 tons of grapes. He would have preferred to turn the grapes into wine, but wine did not produce an immediate return and Groezinger was willing to pay seven dollars a ton for Buena Vista's grapes, delivered at the Sonoma embarcadero;[8] and so, when the grapes were ripe for picking in the late summer, they were piled onto wagons, taken to the embarcadero, and loaded into boats for the twenty-five-mile trip across the bay to San Francisco.

But Agoston was able to turn a part of his crop into wine, and with good results. His cellars, always scrupulously clean, were fitted with the best equipment he could find. His first press was a cider press that could accommodate only a small quantity of must at a time, but it did its job. His fermenting tanks and storage barrels were probably obtained in San Francisco, where there was a good supply of local cooperage. But he was not satisfied with the barrels and insisted on carefully preparing them before they were used. Before he put any wine into a new barrel, he took out the head and filled the tank with combustible material—usually a sprinkling of wood shavings or straw. Then he ignited the material, burning it until the inside of the barrel was charred to a depth of about one-eighth of an inch. After the charred wood had cooled, he washed the barrel several times with water.[9] When the barrel was filled with wine, it was free of any substance that would contaminate its taste or aroma.

When a barrel was emptied, he also took precautions to keep it clean and free of sour or musty odors. To do this, he inserted a sulphur-coated strip of linen halfway into the bunghole, ignited it, then pushed the burning linen into the barrel with a piece of wire and sealed up the hole with a clean cloth. As the linen burned, it filled the barrel with sulphur fumes. When all the oxygen in the barrel was exhausted and the fire went out, he removed the wire, sealed up the bunghole, and stored the barrel in a sheltered place for future use.[10]

In his first two years at Sonoma, Agoston made no attempt to enter his wines in the annual competitions of the California State Fair. The wines that Dr. Fauré had been making for General Vallejo had been winning a host of awards at those competitions, and Agoston knew that his wines were not yet equal to those of his Sonoma neighbor. But his vineyard was a different matter. Although Lachryma Montis and Quiquiriqui were handsome places, he believed that the new and transformed Buena Vista outshone them both, and when the State Agricultural Society held its 1858 fair in Marysville he entered Buena Vista in the competition for the best vineyard, and won the first prize. Sainsevain Brothers and William Wolfskill of Los Angeles won the second and third prizes, while John Sutter won the fourth prize for his vineyard on the Feather River above Sacramento.[11]

By 1859, Agoston felt confident enough of his wines and brandy to enter them in the State Fair, held that year in Sacramento. His confidence was not misplaced, for when the awards for 1859 were announced in September he won no less than six: special diplomas for red wine, white wine, and brandy; silver cups for best year-old white wine and second-best year-old red wine; and, as, a kind of grand prize, a silver cup for the best first-class wine among all those entered in the fair. Of the ten other wine exhibitors that year, Kohler & Frohling won a silver cup for the best two-year-old white wine, Sainsevain Brothers won a diploma for white sparkling wine, and General Vallejo won four awards: first prizes for two-year-old red wine, two-year-old white wine, and three-year-old white wine, and a second prize for red wine of the first class.[12]

In August 1860 Agoston entered his wines in the Sonoma County Fair held in the town of Petaluma. This time he won first-place awards for the best white wine and the best brandy, while Vallejo won for red wine and the best vineyard.[13] At the 1860 State Fair, he entered thirty-three bottles of wine and brandy, representing the vintages of 1857, 1858, and 1859. Eight of the bottles were of red wine, six of white, four of port, three of tokay, two of muscat, and four of champagne. There were six bottles of brandy.[14] No other exhibitor displayed such a wide variety of wine that year. When the awards for 1860 were announced, Agoston won six first-place prizes and one second-place. His vineyard was judged to be the best vineyard of the first class among all those entered, and his one- and two-year-old white wines and his one- and three-year-old red wines received the highest awards. He won a second-place prize for his champagne (called "white sparkling wine") and special prizes for his tokay, muscat, and brandy. In the overall categories of wines, judged according to the number and variety entered, he won first place.[15]

It would be interesting to know more about the characteristics of the wine that Agoston produced in his first years in Sonoma, but beyond the simple descriptions printed in the records of the state fair—and the directions for making a few types of wine that he gave in his 1858 "Report on Grapes and Wine of California"—there is little evidence to establish their style or character. The tokay was, no doubt, modeled on the great Tokay of Hungary, a sweet wine, golden in color, with an alcohol content probably not much above 13 percent. In the "Report," Agoston described his method for making "California Tokay." He selected the "best and ripest" grapes in the vineyard, spread them on straw mats or cloths, and let them rest in a shady place for four or five weeks, or until they were "well shriveled." He then picked out all the spoiled berries and put about a hundred pounds of those that remained in a common coffee bag, which he hung over a tub or barrel. Thus suspended, the grapes slowly dripped their juice into the vessel below. When the grapes were finished dripping, he emptied the bag into the crusher, crushed the grapes, and pressed out the juice. Both the pressed juice and the dripped liquid were then fermented. The latter produced what he called "first quality" tokay, and the former "second quality." This formula for producing tokay closely resembled the traditional Hungarian methods of producing *tokaji esszencia* (the "first quality" wine, made from the "essence" of the grapes) and *tokaji aszú* (the "second quality" wine, made from old, or "dried," tokay grapes).[16] Although these wines have long been ranked among the most celebrated wines in all Europe, Agoston's claims for his product were modest. He said only that his formula would produce "an excellent Tokay-like wine," which would be ready for market after three or four years of aging.[17]

If the "Report" is a reliable guide, the port wine that Agoston made at Sonoma was also made with shriveled grapes, although these were spread out in the sun and left there long enough to turn almost into raisins. When the grapes reached the desired dryness, they were separated from their stems and poured into a fermenting vat. If the juice was not sweet enough, it was sweetened with New Orleans (i.e., cane) sugar, finished red wine, or even some brandy. When the fermentation was done, the wine was drawn off into barrels, which were filled two-thirds full. The remaining liquid was then placed in a boiler and raised to the boiling point, then used to fill the barrels to within six inches of their tops. The bungholes were covered with leaves or clean rags while the wine went through a second fermentation. In the month of May, the wine was drawn off into a clean barrel and set aside for aging. After a couple of years of aging, Agoston said, this wine would produce an "elegant" port.[18]

In his "Report," Agoston gave an interesting description of the methods by which he made champagne in Sonoma. The description included the selection of grapes (he favored "over-ripe" berries, "sticking to the fingers"), the time for picking (the berries should be gathered "on a frosty or very cold morning, early—if possible, before the sun rises"), pressing (the best juice was pressed from grapes collected in a strong linen sack), and directions for the primary and secondary fermentations. The secondary fermentation was carried on in the individual bottles, according to the standards of the traditional *méthode champenoise*. Aside from the fact that this champagne was considered inferior to the sparkling wine produced for General Vallejo by Dr. Fauré, it is difficult to judge how successful it may have been. Other California winemakers had attempted to make sparkling wine before Agoston and Fauré, and all had been more or less unsuccessful. The most notable attempt was made by the Sainsevain Brothers in 1857–58. They employed an experienced French champagne maker and invested a large sum of money in a champagne "manufactory" in San Francisco. Although their product received some compliments, their venture ended in severe losses, indicating that the wine did not find favor with consumers.[19] As Agoston was later to learn (quite painfully), making sparkling wine from California grapes was a difficult proposition at best, and there is no record that he renewed the attempt until the end of 1862, when Arpad—newly returned from France with valuable training gained in the Champagne district— mounted a second effort to make champagne at Buena Vista.

Even more interesting perhaps than the style and character of the wines that Agoston made in his first years at Sonoma are the varieties of grapes from which the wines were made. There is little doubt that Mission grapes were the major constituents of all the wines produced at Buena Vista in the early years. Although Agoston had a substantial number of foreign vines at Sonoma from the first year, they would not have been enough to produce any great amount of red or white table wine. The practice of designating table wines for the varieties of grapes from which they were produced (called "varietal labeling") was almost unknown in California in the 1850's; indeed, it was practically unknown in the great wine-producing regions of Europe, where the practice was to label wines with place or proprietary names. Agoston's own comments on wines indicate that he believed in the virtues of blending. To the extent that he used foreign grapes, he may well have blended them with Mission grapes.

Researchers interested in discovering when Agoston produced his first wines from Zinfandel grapes are doomed to frustration. The first Zinfandels to be crushed at Buena Vista may well have found their way into a blend, or, if left unblended, been marketed under a simple generic designation. Other wine producers in California in the 1850's (and continuing on up into the early years of the twentieth century) continued to produce red and white table wines that were identified on their labels only by the name of the producer, the color of the wine, and the district in which the grapes were grown. Thus, a wine would find its way to market as "Sonoma Red" or "Los Angeles White." And many of the wines were sold directly from casks rather than in bottles, for it was the practice in many salesrooms for purchasers to bring in their own jugs and bottles and have them filled and corked on the premises. Of course, this method of dispensing wine (also common until well into the twentieth century) entirely avoided the necessity of labeling.

It was quite natural that winemakers should produce brandy, for brandy is distilled wine. But brandy offered additional financial incentives to winemakers because it commanded a higher price and required less storage space than wine, and could be kept for a number of years. If a winemaker did not think that he could turn all his grapes into readily marketable wine, and if the market for fresh grapes was unfavorable, he could convert a portion of his crop into brandy, store it, and wait until the time was ripe to release it to the market. Further, acceptable—if not particularly pleasing—brandy could be made not just from wine but also from the pomace of the grapes (the skins, seeds, and pulp left after the first pressing).

By September of 1860 Agoston was able to advertise in the San Francisco newspapers that he had established a "depot" at 110 Montgomery Street, where his wine and brandy were offered for sale. His agent was Agoston Molitor's son, Stephen, who was doing business under the name S. Molitor and Co. "Persons furnishing their own casks or bottles," his advertisement concluded, "will not be charged for filling or corking."[20]

Now, when wine-conscious visitors came to Sonoma, they were not content just to inspect the sprawling vineyards of Buena Vista— they also made it a point to gather in the press house on the banks of the Arroyo Seco and taste the wines of the estate. And they were, by all accounts, pleased with what they tasted. After a visit to Sonoma in the fall of 1860, the editor of the *California Farmer* informed his readers that "Col. Haraszthy's Wine is now becoming a favorite with those who formerly used the best French Wine."[21] It was a compliment Agoston was pleased to accept.

But, compliments aside, Agoston was still unsatisfied with his efforts at Buena Vista. He thought Sonoma could be not just the seat of California's greatest vineyard, but a community of vineyards—a place where farmers could come together to till the land, share information, and, by their mutual efforts, improve the economy of the county and state. And, as always, he was full of ideas as to how this goal could be achieved.

One of his first ideas was to establish a horticultural (or botanic) garden at Sonoma. He had made an effort in this direction at Las Flores, where he gathered seeds and plants into a single nursery and offered them for sale to the public. But a true horticultural garden should be maintained by a society, a community of like-minded men who banded together to achieve a common purpose. In Europe, it was the practice of governments—national and local—to maintain public gardens in which seeds and plants from all over the world were gathered in one place, cataloged, tested, propagated, and made available to botanists, horticulturists, and farmers.[22] It was too much for a single individual to accomplish such a lofty goal. And so, in April of 1859, Agoston announced a plan for a joint stock association to be called the Sonoma and Napa Horticultural Society. It would be incorporated with five hundred shares of stock valued at ten dollars each. Of the $5,000 that this initial stock offering would raise, $3,000 would be used to purchase plants, trees, and vines and $2,000 to acquire suitable land for a garden. He published his plan in the newspapers and invited all interested persons to attend a public meeting in Sonoma to iron out the details and draft the charter.[23]

The meeting came off as planned on May 14. After Agoston addressed the audience, J. W. Osborn of Napa rose to express his approval of the plan, and a resolution was promptly passed adopting all of Agoston's major suggestions. Not surprisingly, Agoston was elected president; General Vallejo and Dr. J. L. Hill were chosen as vice presidents. Fred Leidig was treasurer and George L. Wratten secretary. These officers, with the addition of D. S. Bryant and Agoston's neighbor, William M. Boggs, formed the board of directors. Editorial comments on the society were all enthusiastic. The *California Culturist* thought it would prove a great benefit to horticulture; while the *California Farmer* hoped that other counties would follow the example of Sonoma and Napa and form similar societies.[24]

The proceeds of the stock sale were enough to purchase ten acres of good land on the banks of the Sonoma Creek about a mile west of the Sonoma plaza, buy plants, and start improving the place. Agoston was superintendent of the garden as well as president of the society, and his hand was soon evident in the layout and organization of the garden. The property was circled with a neat fence and a broad walk lined with almond trees. A small building at the main gate was fitted up to serve as the office.[25] One part of the land was planted to corn, another to almonds, a third to walnuts, and a fourth to peach seedlings. A large plot was reserved exclusively for European grapevines.

The garden properly laid out and furnished, Agoston lost no time in gathering botanical specimens—seeds, cuttings, shrubs, trees, and roots—from wherever he could find them. The vine cuttings that William Boggs later recalled he obtained from J. W. Osborn (the cuttings that Boggs insisted included the first Zinfandels introduced into the Sonoma Valley) were in fact purchased for the Sonoma and Napa Horticultural Society and promptly planted in the garden in Sonoma. When the *California Farmer* reporter visited Sonoma late in the summer of 1860, he paused to walk through the garden, admiring the trees, shrubs, and vines. Then he wrote his editor back in San Francisco that "the plan, location, and all appertaining to it, are creditable to the gentlemen that have started it. In coming years it will be indeed a source of pride to all concerned." [26]

The Horticultural Society marked a significant advance in Agoston's efforts to create an agricultural community in Sonoma. But in September of 1859 he announced another plan to attract vineyardists to the land around Buena Vista. The announcement took the form of a large advertisement in the *Daily Alta California*, in which he offered to sell off portions of the Buena Vista Ranch, plant them with grapevines, and cultivate the vineyards until they were of bearing age (that is, three years old). For this package he offered attractive terms. A vineyard of 6,800 vines, for example, could be planted on ten acres, with two additional acres reserved for a building site and vegetable garden, and all purchased for $2,140. A vineyard of 13,000 vines covering twenty acres with two and a half acres for a house and garden could be had for $4,180. A plantation of forty acres was priced at $8,160, while a one hundred–acre vineyard with five additional acres for domestic use could be had for $20,400. He offered installment plans for each of these purchase plans. Payments could be made for thirty months, ranging from just over $71 per month for the smallest plot to $680 per month for the largest.

Agoston argued that his offer put it within the reach of almost every man to acquire a tract of land that would provide him with a comfortable home and, after the lapse of three years, a secure income. Sonoma Valley was, after all, a place of great natural beauty with a wonderful climate, and close enough to San Francisco to lure purchasers from the city. He pointed out that it was possible for a businessman who lived in Sonoma to take a seat on the San Francisco steamer, which left the Sonoma embarcadero at eight o'clock in the morning, go to San Francisco, spend three hours tending to his business, and return to Sonoma in the afternoon in time to enjoy his evening dinner—and, all the while, his vineyard would be producing bounteous crops of grapes. Agoston was confident that his land would practically sell itself, and so he invited all interested parties to come up to Sonoma and inspect the property for themselves.[27]

John S. Hittell, the principal writer for the *Alta California*, lost no time in endorsing Agoston's offer. Hittell was not only one of Gold Rush California's most prolific writers (he had written for the newspaper continuously since 1853, and was also a frequent contributor to literary journals), he was also intimately acquainted with winegrowing efforts in California. In the summer of 1857, he had been one of a group of fifty Germans who came together in San Francisco to form the so-called Los Angeles Vineyard Society to acquire a thousand acres on the Santa Ana River in rural Los Angeles County and form a settlement called "Anaheim."[28] Although Hittell was German by descent and not by birth (he was born in Pennsylvania in 1825), he was welcomed to Anaheim when the first colonists began to plant their vineyards there in 1858. Anaheim was laid out in fifty lots of twenty acres each, with a central area for a park, school, and businesses.[29] Hittell recognized Agoston's Sonoma proposal as a potential rival to Anaheim, but he was still favorably impressed by it and warmly endorsed it in an editorial printed in the *Alta* on October 3, 1859.[30]

There was not exactly a rush to respond to the offer. Although Agoston's terms for payment were attractive, it still required a substantial chunk of money to buy one of his vineyard plots, and purchasers could not expect any profit from the land for at least three years. Anybody who wanted to become a vineyardist in Sonoma would have to be a man of some substance—and patience. But there were men of that kind in San Francisco, and in due time they made their way to Sonoma to confer with the proprietor of Buena Vista.

The first man who accepted his proposal was Charles H. S. Williams, one of San Francisco's best-known attorneys. A native of New Hampshire, Williams had moved to New York while still a young man and there rose to become attorney general of the state (ever afterward, he was habitually addressed as "General"). In San Francisco, he won a reputation as a lion in the courtroom and a fearsome drinker outside. But he represented some of the most important businessmen in the city, had a good income, and longed for a "country place" where he could entertain his friends. On December 1, 1859, Williams bought 138 acres of the Buena Vista estate for $11,000—apparently in cash, for the records show that he did not accept Agoston's offer to make monthly payments. The parcel lay along the Arroyo Seco southeast of the old Lac Rancho.[31]

Agoston made two other sales in December of 1859. The first was to a young schoolteacher from San Francisco named John Swett. Like Williams, Swett was a native of New Hampshire. Unlike the lawyer, however, he had dedicated his life to the ideals of public education. In a little more than two years, Swett was to become California's State Superintendent of Public Instruction and enunciate the progressive educational policies that ultimately won him the title "Horace Mann of the Pacific Coast." But in 1859 he was interested in a country place where he could retire from the city on weekends and quietly till the land. On December 20, 1859, Agoston and Swett entered into an agreement for the sale of forty acres southeast of Williams's property for $7,500, payable in thirty monthly installments of $251 each. The land included an existing house, and Agoston agreed to plant thirty-seven acres to vines.[32]

Agoston's third sale, on December 31, was, like the sale to Williams, an outright transfer. The land was thirty-five acres lying southeast of the Lac Rancho, and the purchaser was Agoston's old friend and neighbor from Crystal Springs and San Francisco, Charles Krug. Krug paid only a thousand dollars for his land, indicating that he was content to plant and cultivate it himself;[33] but he lost no time in setting the property out to vines, for by the summer of the following year the *California Farmer* was able to report that he had planted twenty-five acres of vineyards and conferred a pretty name—Monte

Bello—on his new property.³⁴ While he was planting his land and building his house, Krug lived with Agoston and Eleonora in the big house at Buena Vista.³⁵

The sales to Williams, Swett, and Krug did not mean that Agoston was attempting to reduce his landholdings at Buena Vista. On the contrary, he was still on the lookout for good buys in the neighborhood. About the time that he announced his proposal to plant vineyards for others, he found a good opportunity on his very doorstep, when Governor Boggs announced his intention of moving from Sonoma to Napa and Agoston was able to buy more than one hundred acres of his Sonoma property for $7,200.³⁶ This parcel was quickly supplemented with an adjoining parcel of ten acres that he acquired from the City of Sonoma and three smaller parcels of two acres each that he acquired from a man named William Attenbury.³⁷

In the fall of 1860, Agoston welcomed two more vineyardists into his Sonoma fold. The first was his old friend at the San Francisco Mint, Major Jacob R. Snyder, who had been looking for a country place where he could build a house, cultivate vineyards, and perhaps make some wine. On November 5, 1860, Agoston sold Snyder a choice tract of seventy-four acres lying between Buena Vista and General Vallejo's Lachryma Montis estate for $4,000. On the same date, Joseph H. Snyder (a friend but not a relative of Major Snyder) purchased fifteen and a half acres of adjoining land for $1,500. Neither of the Snyders knew anything about the business of cultivating vineyards or making wine, but Major Snyder at least was determined to learn. He began to build a house on a little hill in the midst of his new Sonoma estate and to construct a wine cellar nearby. His property, which he called El Cerrito (Little Hill), was eventually to become one of the showplaces of the Sonoma Valley.

Less than two weeks after the sales to the Snyders, Agoston embarked on an ambitious plan to develop the Lovall Valley. Up to that time, he had used that part of the old Huichica grant for grazing cattle, but he had decided to give up the cattle and develop the land for vineyards.³⁸ The valley, which straddled the line that separated Sonoma and Napa counties, was a large and still mostly inaccessible tract. Agoston decided that, if he built a road from the Buena Vista headquarters and divided the valley into small tracts, he could find investors who would be willing to buy parts of it, pay him to plant vines, and eventually make it into a vast expanse of vineyards. In the fall of 1860 he asked the Napa County surveyor to survey and map the valley. The surveyor's map, which divided the valley into twenty-three lots of ten acres each, was completed and signed on November 27, 1860.[39]

The sale of these ten-acre lots started briskly. On December 10, 1860, Agoston signed contracts to sell lots to three San Franciscans for $2,400 each and to plant and care for 5,100 Mission and 1,700 foreign vines on each tract, and the following February he sold two lots and another tract of more than eight hundred acres to his old friend Agoston Molitor for something over $12,000.[40] Soon after the first Lovall Valley sales were made, Agoston sent Attila up into the valley to begin clearing brush from the hillsides. Attila worked with crews of Chinese laborers—sometimes as many as thirty men to a gang—clearing the land, digging holes, planting vines, cultivating, and feeding the new plants.[41]

The community of agriculturists that Agoston had envisioned in 1859 was fast becoming a reality. But he could not really be satisfied with the community until members of his own family had joined it. He was pleased when Charles came up from San Francisco in October of 1860 to purchase his own plot of Sonoma land. Charles was living with his wife, Frances, who had left Wisconsin to join him in California. Frances's daughter, Matilda, was in San Francisco, too, for she had divorced her Wisconsin husband, Major William Clark, and followed her mother and stepfather to California. Matilda lived with Charles and Frances for a while before she met a San Francisco businessman named A. S. Edwards, who asked her to marry him, and their wedding took place in Charles's Jessie Street home on May 5, 1859.[42] Charles, of course, was a frequent visitor at Buena Vista, but he wanted to have a place of his own in Sonoma; and so, the year after Matilda's marriage, he acquired thirty-one acres about a mile and a half southeast of the plaza.[43]

Gaza and Attila had worked at Buena Vista almost from the start, though they took some time off in 1858, the year after the transfer of the vines from Crystal Springs to Sonoma, to try their hand at prospecting.[44] They were not successful in that effort (by 1859, the real money in California's gold fields was being made by big companies with powerful earth-moving equipment), and it was not long before they were back in Sonoma. In 1861, Agoston decided to give the boys a chance to take charge of their own vineyards. On February 20 of that year, he transferred thirty-three acres of the Huichica Rancho to Attila, then twenty-six years old, and an adjoining tract of thirty-two acres to Gaza, then twenty-seven. These transfers were not gifts; Agoston expected his sons to carry their own loads in Sonoma. And so each agreed to pay their father $3,000 for his land.[45]

Arpad and Bela were still absent from the family. After leaving for the East in 1857, Arpad had taken his younger brother to New York and then set off on his own across the Atlantic to Paris, where he enrolled in the École Centrale, Civile Polytechnique, specializing in civil engineering. But as Arpad kept up a steady correspondence with his family in Sonoma, his thoughts turned more and more to the vines his father and brothers were planting in far-off California. Agoston was more confident than ever before that California would one day be a great wine-producing country, and he and Gaza and Attila were doing their part to help it realize its destiny. It all seemed like a great adventure, particularly for a young man just about to embark on a career. And so in the latter part of 1860 Arpad left Paris for the French Champagne country to take instruction in the best methods of French winemaking. He arranged to be taught in the Champagne house of Venoge at Épernay.[46] There, in cellars buried deep beneath the streets of the medieval city, he listened and watched and took careful notes as masters of the *méthode champenoise* explained the secrets of their craft. He worked with other French vintners as they blended *cuvées*, bottled the blends with small doses of sugar and yeast, waited apprehensively as the mixture underwent the first "violent," and the second "quiet," fermentation, then racked, disgorged, dosed, wired, and aged the wine. While Arpad was hard at his studies in Paris and Épernay, Bela was attending classes at St. Timothy's School in Maryland; and, back in California, Ida and Otelia were receiving proper educations at a school for "young ladies" in San Jose.

Impressive though it was, the list of men who purchased land directly from Agoston constituted only a part of the growing community of winegrowers and winemakers in Sonoma. It was natural that other landowners in Sonoma should take advantage of the increased demand for vineyard land by putting some of their own property on the market, and there were plenty of purchasers. Further, some of the old settlers were so impressed by the new vineyards burgeoning around Buena Vista that they decided to plant their own farms to vineyards. There was a good supply of vines now, close at hand. If a budding vineyardist could not find exactly what he wanted in the Sonoma Horticultural Garden, he could ride up the road to Buena Vista and wander through the nursery there. Agoston always kept some foreign vines on hand; and, if one of his neighbors needed help in laying out a vineyard, he was more than willing to lend assistance.

In October 1860, he prepared a list of the men who were then cultivating vineyards in the Sonoma Valley. Published in the *California Farmer*, the list—which ran to more than forty names—included a good mixture of recent arrivals along with old Sonoma pioneers: Mariano Guadalupe Vallejo, Nicholas Carriger, William Hood, William Boggs, Granville P. Swift, Franklin Sears, Louis Adler, Charles H. S. Williams, H. L. Kamp, A. M. Hay, O. W. Craig, Charles Justi, Emil Dresel, Jacob Gundlach, Charles Krug, C. C. Kuchel, John Luttgens, John Swett, Gaza Haraszthy, and Attila Haraszthy. The table showed that the rate of planting had increased dramatically every year since Agoston arrived in Sonoma. In the winter of 1857–58, for example, a little more than 150 acres had been planted in the valley; the following year, more than 300 acres had been added; and, in the winter of 1859–60, the new plantings had approached 600 acres. Agoston calculated that there were 789,500 vines in the valley in the summer of 1860, which translated into 1,161 acres. His own plantings, of course, led all the others, with 151,600 vines covering about 223 acres.[47]

As if these numbers were not impressive enough, the planters of the Sonoma Valley increased their vineyards yet more in the winter of 1860–61. In March of the latter year, the *California Farmer* reported that farmers all over the state were planting millions of new vines. "Many persons are planting ten, twenty, forty, fifty, and even one hundred acres each," the *Farmer* noted; "and what is gratifying, a large proportion is the Foreign Vines."[48] Nowhere in California, however, were the vineyards spreading as rapidly as in Sonoma. In August 1860, the *Farmer* proclaimed Sonoma the "Banner" County, reporting that it had planted more than 1,200 acres of vineyards. "What other County has done so much?" the journal asked. "Beside all this, Sonoma has increased in every kind of business. Stock, Grainfields, Orchards, and Vineyards, are rapidly being brought to perfection."[49]

Agoston's own vineyards, which were now approaching 250 acres, led the field in Sonoma. The corresponding secretary of the State Agricultural Society, who visited Sonoma in the late summer of 1860, reported that Buena Vista was "the most extensive vineyard enterprise yet undertaken by one individual in the state." Agoston's vines were growing on hillside slopes all about the old Lac Rancho tract, and some were even raising their green leaves from the tops of hills. "The greater portion of his vines are of the California variety," the secretary reported, "but he is rapidly increasing the foreign sorts, which seem to do best as they ripen earlier and make a richer wine."[50]

But, before Agoston could begin to plant foreign vines on a large scale, he had to determine which of the foreign varieties in his nursery were best suited to produce wine in Sonoma. This question was far more complicated than it might have seemed to later planters, who had the benefits of years (and sometimes decades) of earlier experimentation to help them arrive at an answer. Agoston had a good supply of foreign varieties, to be sure, but none of them had been tested in a systematic way. Which of these varieties would grow most vigorously on the floor of the Sonoma Valley? Which would adapt themselves best to the hillsides? Which were best suited to the dry California summers? To find answers to these and other questions, he set out in the winter of 1860–61 to plant one vineyard at Buena Vista exclusively to foreign wine grapes. The grapes were planted on a hillside and carefully cultivated, pruned, and observed. This was an experimental vineyard only, intended to put foreign grapes to trial and thus determine which should later be planted on a large scale.[51]

The *California Farmer* visited Sonoma again in the spring of 1861 and found it in a swirl of activity. After reporting on the spring planting, the *Farmer* paused to commend Agoston's efforts in behalf of the community, "his zeal in Vine-growing, and his general good feeling for his own County and the State." "We but attest to the truth," the *Farmer* continued, "when we say that he has done more than any other citizen of our State who is a planter of the Vine, to advance this great Interest."[52]

Agoston also received recognition closer to home. He had joined with some other Sonoma residents in 1859 to form the Sonoma County Agricultural and Mechanics' Society, and at the first organizational meeting he was elected one of the society's directors.[53] In 1860, at the society's annual fair in Petaluma, he was invited to be the featured speaker—a distinct honor, and also an opportunity for him to express his views on the future of agriculture in Sonoma County and the whole state.

He began his address by extolling the special virtues of Sonoma for aspiring farmers and vineyardists. "What traveler can pass through our valleys without being moved to exclamations of wonder by the scenery around him?" he asked. "What Emperor can boast of a domain so eminent in natural advantages?" He predicted that Sonoma—in fact, all California—was about to embark on a great agricultural future, and he had some ideas as to how that future could be enhanced. He strongly recommended that the state and the various counties establish an agricultural school where young men could receive sound, practical educations in all matters relating to agriculture: "The really ambitious and scientific farmer must experiment," he told his listeners; and what better place could there be for experimentation than a publicly financed school, where agricultural experts from all over the state would come together to make their collective knowledge and experience available to young farmers? "Such an institution," he said, "located in a favorable place, with sufficient land—320 or 640 acres—and with competent, practical, and theoretical farmers as teachers, would be of incalculable benefit to the whole of California."

He stressed the importance that viticulture and winemaking would have in California's agricultural future. "It is generally admitted," he said, "that vine-growing in this State will, before long, exceed in value the amount of gold exported." Although Europe had been producing wines for countless centuries, its production had declined in recent years, thus opening up a world of opportunities for

California's wine-producers. To further these opportunities, he said, the state agricultural school should have its own vineyard, planted and maintained by competent professors. He urged his listeners to organize a committee to devise a plan by which such an institution could be established. "Do not stop until you have accomplished this," he said, "and you will leave a rich inheritance to posterity. I need not tell you that knowledge is of more worth than wealth. Wealth may be swept away by the winds of adversity, but knowledge remains and is always an equivalent."

The *Alta California* reported that the "dense crowd" that listened to Agoston's speech received it "with flattering demonstrations of applause." And the crowd included more than just country farmers, for some influential state leaders (including former U.S. Senator and California Governor John Weller) were among the listeners. The *Alta* thought enough of the speech to print the full text on its front page.[54]

Agoston's principal interest in Sonoma was, of course, the vineyards that he and other men were planting in the hills about Buena Vista. But his mind was too restless not to wander now and again, and his family knew that it would only be a matter of time before he would again be dipping his toes in other waters.

One of the first enterprises he embarked on that was not strictly confined to the vineyards was a project to drain a part of the sprawling marshes that lay along the shore of San Pablo Bay. Wetlands along California's interior waterways had traditionally been known as "tule lands," for the dense reeds (or "tules") that grew there. From time immemorial the Indians had used the reeds to build boats, and they (and the early Chinese immigrants) had used the roots of the reeds for food; the Spanish, in turn, had used the tules as thatch on their adobe houses. But Gold Rush settlers had quickly developed an aversion to the reeds because they impeded the progress of their boats, and the marshlands seemed to enterprising Yankees to be a terrible waste of good land. Acting on these complaints, the legislature passed laws encouraging citizens to clear the tules and drain the marshlands so that they could become productive farmland. Draining a marsh was a costly, labor-intensive undertaking, since the prevailing wages for laborers around San Francisco were high. Agoston decided that he could employ Chinese laborers on the project, save substantial sums in labor costs, and get a jump on his competitors.

In the summer of 1860, he formed a corporation called the Sonoma Tule Land Company, with himself as president, a man named Judson Haycock as secretary, and Agoston Molitor's son, Stephen, as treasurer. The company filed a claim to 8,000 acres of marshland bordering San Pablo Bay and set about the task of draining the land and building what Agoston promised would be ten miles of earthen dikes. The work was well under way when a reporter for the *California Farmer* visited Sonoma that fall. More than eight miles of dikes had already been completed, and Agoston told the reporter that when the land was all drained the company would bring in steam-powered plows and cultivate the land for a variety of cash crops, including rice, tobacco, hemp, flax, cranberries, asparagus, and cabbages.[55]

A second project not directly related to the vineyards was the construction of a steamship dedicated to San Francisco–Sonoma traffic. There was a steamship that made trips between San Francisco and the Sonoma embarcadero, but it was not locally owned and its service was unreliable. Important business could not always wait for the whims of the steamship captain, and so some Sonomans got in the habit of crossing over the hills to the Petaluma Valley where, at a little town called Lakeville on the Petaluma River, a more reliable steamship could be boarded for the trip to the city. Agoston believed that regular steamship service to Sonoma was essential if the valley was to maintain its ties with San Francisco, and in the spring of 1861 he sounded out some of his neighbors on the possibility of organizing a group of Sonomans to build their own ship. He was, he reminded them, an old steamboat captain himself, and though the Wisconsin River was quite different from San Francisco Bay, there were similarities enough between the two waterways to convince him to try his hand once again at running a regular steamer. In characteristic fashion, he called on local men he thought might be willing to join him in such an enterprise, and quickly found one in a young and very rich man named Granville P. Swift.

Born in Kentucky about 1821, Swift had migrated, first to Missouri, then to Oregon, and finally to California, where he arrived about 1844. A strapping six-footer with a legendary skill as a rifleman, he had joined the short-lived Bear Flag uprising at Sonoma in 1846, and when war broke out between Mexico and the United States, he served as a captain in the California Battalion. After gold was discovered in the Sierra Nevada, he headed for the mountains, where he amassed a fortune in gold, then returned to Sonoma to build Temelec Hall, a stone mansion that ranked as Sonoma's most expensive private residence when it was completed in 1858. When Agoston called on Swift and suggested that the two men join forces to build a steamer, Swift agreed to put up $5,000 if Agoston could raise the rest from the citizens of the valley.

In characteristic fashion, Agoston issued a call for a public meeting to be held in Sonoma. He announced that he would match Swift's investment if citizens of the valley would make up the balance of the cost. A regular steamer, he said, was "important and necessary" to Sonoma's economic welfare. Property values had risen all over the valley since vineyards had blossomed on the hills above Buena Vista, but unless a steamer was built, those values could plummet just as rapidly as they had risen. If the valley's residents joined together to build their own vessel, the whole valley would have an interest in its success.[56]

The meeting was held according to Agoston's call on June 8, 1861. The *California Farmer* reported that the meeting was "well attended."[57] Agoston, however, was not present. He was in San Francisco all that week, making last-minute preparations for a new venture—a bold enterprise that was to be one of the most innovative, and at the same time one of the most controversial, of his entire career.

Mariano Guadalupe Vallejo. The most prominent Spanish-Californian of his day, Vallejo was also a Sonoma Valley grape grower and winemaker. Two of his daughters married two of Haraszthy's sons in 1863. The Bancroft Library, University of California, Berkeley.

GRAPE VINES & FRUIT TREES
FOR SALE AT LOW PRICES.

300,000 Native Vines
30,000 CUTTINGS,
(165 Foreign Varieties.)
2,000 ROOTED VINES,
(Embracing 15 Foreign Varieties,) which will bear the second year.

Also, a fine assortment of Grafted and Budded

FRUIT TREES,

Comprising the Choicest Varieties.
Apply to A. HARASZTHY, Sonoma,
Or to G. W. KINZER,

Chace's Saw Mill, cor. of Market and Beale Sts.,
San Francisco.

November 15.   1m.

One of Haraszthy's advertisements for "foreign" (i.e., European) grape vines. He offered a wide array of vines and fruit trees for sale in Sonoma and San Francisco. *California Culturist*, November 15, 1858.

Buena Vista, October 21, 1864. This pen, pencil, and wash drawing of Haraszthy's Sonoma vineyards and home was done by English artist Frederick Whymper. Haraszthy's stone cellars, with tunnels dug into the mountainside, are at the right. Chinese laborers are picking grapes in the foreground. Frank H. Bartholomew Foundation.

"Works of the Buena Vista Vinicultural Association." This woodcut shows
the stone cellars at Buena Vista as they appeared in late 1863 or early 1864.
The two-story structure was probably completed in 1862. The three arched
entrances to the left represent the openings of the second cellar, which
eventually rose to three stories. Storage tunnels were dug into the limestone
mountain behind each of these cellars. *Harper's Monthly*, June 1864.

"Buena Vista Ranch, Sonoma County, California." This engraving of
Haraszthy's Sonoma home was the frontispiece of his 1862 book,
Grape Culture, Wines, and Wine-Making. Brian McGinty Collection.

Bronze bell at Buena Vista. Cast in Boston in 1857 and installed at Buena Vista some time before 1864, the bell was used by Haraszthy to call his Chinese workers in from the vineyards. It still stands at Buena Vista today. Wine Institute.

Wine tunnel at Buena Vista. Both of Haraszthy's wine cellars were equipped with tunnels that pierced the adjoining mountain and provided cool, temperature-constant storage for his wines. This photograph shows one of the cellars as it appeared in the 1950's. Brian McGinty Collection.

Ho Po, a San Francisco labor contractor who supplied Chinese laborers for Haraszthy's vineyards at Buena Vista. Haraszthy was an articulate and consistent defender of Chinese labor in a time of growing anti-Chinese agitation. Wine Institute.

Haraszthy's first stone cellar at Buena Vista. Completed about 1862, this building was badly damaged in the San Francisco earthquake of 1906. This photograph shows the structure after its restoration by Frank H. Bartholomew in the 1940's. Wine Institute.

Wine cellars at Buena Vista. Famed photographer Eadweard Muybridge took this photograph of Haraszthy's cellars in the early 1870's. The two-story building in the foreground was completed about 1862. The three-story structure in the background was begun in 1863 and completed around 1867. Wine Institute.

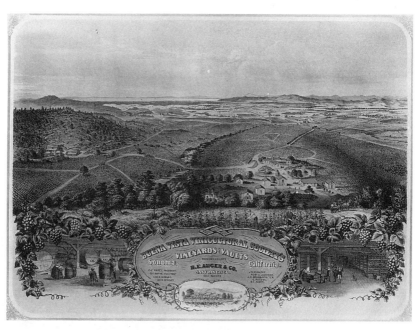

"Buena Vista Vinicultural Society's Vineyards & Vaults, Sonoma, California." This lithograph shows the vineyards and buildings of the BVVS as they appeared in the 1870's. San Pablo Bay, the northern arm of San Francisco Bay, appears in the background. Wine Institute.

Labels of the
Buena Vista
Vinicultural
Society. Wine
Institute.

Bronze monument honoring Agoston Haraszthy. The work of a Hungarian sculptor, this monument was erected opposite Haraszthy's wine cellars at Buena Vista in 1957. A copy was installed in San Diego's Balboa Park in the 1970's. Brian McGinty Collection.

Bronze tablet honoring Haraszthy as "Father of California Viticulture." Mounted on a boulder from the nearby mountains, it was dedicated in the plaza in Sonoma, California, in 1946. Brian McGinty Collection.

21

A Bold
Proposal

When the California State Agricultural Society convened in Sacramento at the end of January 1861, for its eighth annual meeting, its first order of business was to elect a new president for the coming year. Agoston's name was put in nomination for the office, along with those of some prominent politicians. But he declined to be considered as a candidate, and after the ballots were counted, the office went to Jerome C. Davis of Yolo County.[1]

Agoston had a good reason for declining the society's presidential nomination, for when he arrived in Sacramento he had the draft of a resolution in his pocket, a resolution that, if adopted, would make it impossible for him to discharge the duties of president in 1861. The resolution proposed that the society use its influence with the state legislature to urge the appointment of a commissioner to travel to Europe during the coming summer to, in Agoston's words, "investigate the different processes of manufacture, and to purchase and collect, for the benefit of the State, specimens of each variety of the grape-vine." It urged that the commissioner be "competent and responsible," that he be required to give a bond for the faithful execution of his duties, and that he present "a full report of the result of his observations" to the legislature of 1862. The resolution also called for a legislative appropriation to defray the commissioner's expenses and the costs of purchasing the grapevines and shipping them back to California.[2]

In addition to its immediate object, Agoston's proposed resolution had a secondary, and ultimately much more important, goal— to enlist the participation of the state government in a program of fostering and encouraging viticulture and winemaking in California. The resolution noted that European nations traditionally fostered the winemaking arts with generous appropriations of money and urged that California follow the Old World example.[3] The long-range objective of the resolution was entirely consistent with the call Agoston had made at the Sonoma County Fair in 1860 for the establishment of a state-supported school of agriculture, complete with a vineyard planted and maintained by competent professors.[4] The establishment of a state-supported vineyard would, of course, be of immense benefit to winegrowers throughout the state; but sending a state commissioner to Europe to gather vines for that vineyard would also benefit the state's infant wine industry by supplying an important part of the vine stocks with which the state vineyard would one day be planted.

If Agoston's proposal received any discussion in the State Agricultural Society's meeting, the annual report does not record the fact. It must have been generally assumed that the "competent and responsible" commissioner called for by the resolution would be none other than Agoston himself. He was, after all, the most prominent winemaker in California. What's more, he was a Californian of impeccable European credentials, and thus well suited to the task of traveling through Europe and reporting on European winemaking and vinegrowing practices.

Agoston was also known to have good political connections with Governor John G. Downey, and if the legislature authorized a commissioner the governor would undoubtedly be called on to name him. In the statewide election held in the fall of 1859, Agoston had enthusiastically supported the candidacy of Milton S. Latham for governor and Downey for lieutenant governor. Agoston knew Latham quite well. He was the son-in-law of Agoston's old colleague at the San Francisco Mint, Superintendent Lewis Birdsall. Latham had been a leading light of the Chivalry Democrats during most of the 1850's and in that capacity had often conferred with Agoston on political matters. In 1859, he had assumed leadership of the so-called "Lecompton" wing of the California Democratic Party (so named because it supported the pro-slavery state constitution drawn up at Lecompton, Kansas, in 1857). The Lecompton Democrats were pro-Southern in their national sympathies and pro-agriculture in their California policies.

The Irish-born Downey was a large landowner in southern California and sympathetic to the Lecompton position. Agoston supported Latham's gubernatorial bid, not only with words but also with money,[5] and he was pleased when Latham and Downey were both elected by wide margins. But Latham's tenure as governor was to be very short; for U.S. Senator David Broderick, leader of the Shovelry Democrats in California, was killed in a scandalous duel with California's Chivalry Chief Justice David Terry only days after the election, and when the legislature met in January 1860 to choose a successor to Broderick, Latham was quickly settled on for the post. Latham resigned as governor after having served only five days in office, and Lieutenant Governor Downey became governor.[6]

Besides the political support that Agoston's proposal was likely to receive from the governor, the proposal also had good support among the state's newspapers. Both the *California Farmer* and the *Alta* warmly endorsed it. "True," the *Alta* noted in an editorial published on February 15, "we have many varieties of European grapes now, but we should try them all." The *Alta* thought that as much good could be done by gathering information in Europe as by gathering plants. "A competent Commissioner," the *Alta* wrote, "a man familiar with horticulture and agriculture in California, knowing our soil and climate well, familiar with the different capabilities of the prominent agricultural districts, and able to conversely freely in their native tongues with the farmers and fruit-growers of the principal countries of continental Europe, might make very useful observations which, published, here, would be of great service."[7] Although there is no mention in the records of the State Agricultural Society of any particular discussion of Agoston's proposal, the records are clear that his resolution passed quickly and unanimously.[8]

The legislature lost no time in taking up the new proposal. In the first week of February, the Assembly created a special committee on the "Culture and Improvement of the Grape-Vine" to study the proposal and render a report. Completed in less than two weeks, the report took a very positive view of the prospects for viticulture in California. The climate and soil of the state were, in the committee's view, particularly well suited to the development of a great winemaking industry; and the committee believed that if a successful wine industry was developed, the state would benefit enormously. There was such a great potential for wine production in California that California might reasonably be expected to supply all the domestic American demand for wine, and even to export wines to Europe. And as California's vineyards expanded, the state's tax base would grow, to the great benefit of the state government and all the people it served.

The committee noted that European governments had traditionally fostered their wine industries by creating and maintaining botanic gardens in which vines of all varieties could be collected, nurtured, tested, and distributed. The committee believed that it was time for the government of California to emulate its Old World counterparts and begin measures to foster the budding wine industry in the state. "The vital considerations of health, wealth, and happiness of the people of California," the committee told the Assembly, "press upon us the necessity of taking some steps toward this great end."

As "a first step," the committee proposed that the legislature authorize the governor to appoint three commissioners—not merely one, as Agoston had proposed—and instruct them to "collect together all the useful and valuable Grape-vines, cuttings, and seeds for distribution among our people," and report back to the legislature of 1862 "upon the means best adapted to promote the improvement and growth of the Vine in California." The report was unanimously approved by the seven committee members.[9]

On March 2, Assemblyman Murray Morrison of Los Angeles, one of the committee members, introduced a resolution to implement the committee's recommendations. However, Morrison modified the committee's proposal in two significant ways: first, he omitted any language concerning the collection of grapevines, either in

Europe or elsewhere; second, he included language prohibiting the commissioners from receiving any pay for their services. As finally adopted by the Assembly, the resolution provided as follows:

Resolved, by the Assembly, the Senate concurring, that the Governor of the State be, and he is hereby, authorized and requested to appoint three Commissioners to report to the next Legislature upon the ways and means best adapted to promote the improvement and growth of the grape-vine in California; *provided*, such Commissioners who may accept the office shall not ask, or receive, any pay, or other compensation, for the performance of the duties of their offices.[10]

A month later, on April 1, the Senate concurred in the Assembly resolution.[11]

Agoston cannot have objected to the legislature's decision to expand his proposed commission from one member to three. By calling for three commissioners, the legislature had broadened the commission's scope, possibly broadened public support for its work, and certainly lessened the burden that would otherwise have fallen on his shoulders alone. The omission of language regarding the collection of vines did not particularly concern him. He later explained that he assumed that the legislature's purpose was "to promote the Vine-growing and Fruit interest of the State" and that, by refraining from specifying particular duties, the lawmakers signaled their willingness to leave it to the judgment of the commissioners as to how they should accomplish this purpose.[12] The language prohibiting the commissioners from receiving "pay" for their work should have raised a red (or at least a yellow) flag in Agoston's mind, but he may well have dismissed it as not inconsistent with his own proposal. After all, he had never suggested that the legislature "pay" the commissioner (or commissioners); he had merely proposed that it appropriate money "to defray the reasonable expenses" of the commission. Was it unreasonable to assume that legislators, being intelligent men of affairs, could readily distinguish between "pay" and "expenses"?

When Governor Downey received the legislature's resolution, he promptly named three men to the commission: Agoston Haraszthy, Agoston's old friend from San Diego days, Jonathan Warner, and a little-known Spanish Californian named José M. Ramirez.[13] Warner was an altogether good choice. By 1861, the onetime proprietor of

Warner's Ranch had moved to Los Angeles, where he published a weekly newspaper called *The Southern Vineyard.* It was not exclusively a viticultural journal, though, as a Los Angeles newspaper, it naturally devoted a good deal of its space to reporting on vineyards and winemaking, both in Los Angeles and in other parts of the state. Little is known of José M. Ramirez, except that he received Downey's appointment at Marysville and, on May 17, 1861, addressed a letter to Secretary of State Johnson Price declining to accept it. Ramirez acknowledged that the appointment was an honor, but pleaded that "business of importance will necessitate my leaving the state for Chile probably in a few weeks."[14]

It was a foregone conclusion that Agoston would assume the principal work of the commission, and that his major effort would consist of the vine- and information-gathering tour of Europe he had first proposed to the State Agricultural Society. As the *Alta* editorialized:

There is, probably, no one in the State better qualified than Col. Haraszthy for the position of Commissioner. He is, undoubtedly, entitled to be considered the first grape grower of California. He has the largest and most valuable vineyard in the State; has the largest number of foreign vines; has been the largest importer of foreign vines, and has done more than any other person to encourage the cultivation of the grape, particularly of the foreign varieties. He commenced to cultivate the vine extensively four years ago, when little attention had been given to the business, and immediately began to set out great numbers of cuttings, and to import largely of the best foreign varieties, and thus he gave such an impulse to the industry of the State, and particularly to that of his own neighborhood in Sonoma Valley, that he has been a public benefactor. For himself and others he has planted more than 400,000 vines. He attends in person to all the labors of the vineyard and winemaking, directs the laborers in his orchard, and knows, by his own experience, how fruits and vines are treated. He writes fluently, clearly, and to the point; and has published a comprehensive essay on the cultivation of the grape in California, printed in the annual report of the State Agricultural Society for 1858. We therefore think there is good reason to hope that his trip to Europe will be of service to the State.[15]

Agoston later reported that, upon receipt of Downey's appointment, he contacted the governor, advising him that he believed that the objects of the legislature's resolution "would be best secured by an examination of the different varieties of grapes, and the various modes of making wine, in the wine-growing countries of Europe." He offered his services to the governor "to proceed to Europe, if he should think it desirable." Downey's response to this suggestion was quick and favorable.[16]

If Agoston had not already made preparations for a European trip, he now began in earnest to do all the things that had to be done to embark on such an ambitious adventure. He and Warner exchanged some letters, but, given the time constraints under which Agoston was working (he wanted to visit Europe in the summer and it was already the middle of April), there was insufficient time to work out an allocation of their respective responsibilities. So each commissioner was left to decide for himself how best to carry out the legislature's mandate.[17] Warner decided to remain in California and report back to the legislature on the condition of vinegrowing and winemaking in the state, while Agoston made arrangements to leave for Europe as quickly as possible.

The first and most important arrangement that had to be made was, of course, to put his California affairs in good hands. Gaza and Attila would be in charge of all his businesses in Sonoma—the vineyards and cellars at Buena Vista, the Sonoma Tule Land Company, and the burgeoning Sonoma steamship line[18]—while Charles's stepson-in-law, A. S. Edwards, would manage the wine "depot" in San Francisco. Fifteen-year-old Bela and twelve-year-old Otelia would remain behind with Gaza and Attila while Eleonora and Ida, now eighteen, would accompany Agoston.

Second in importance, perhaps, were financial arrangements for the European trip. Since the legislature had made no appropriation for expenses, Agoston would have to dig into his own pockets, not only to pay his and his family's traveling expenses, but also to purchase all the vines and trees that he proposed to bring back from Europe. Until such time as the legislature could be persuaded to encourage California's winegrowing potential with money as well as with words, Agoston had an idea for bridging the financial gap. He would offer, in advance, to sell specimens of the European vines and trees that he would bring back to California. The specimens would be offered in four packages priced at $25, $50, $100, and $500 each and include varying selections of almonds, oranges, olives, figs, Italian chestnuts, and pomegranates as well as grapevines. All subscribers would receive bound copies of the report that Agoston proposed to write. Subscribers to the $500 package would receive "two cuttings of every variety of Grape now in cultivation in the civilized world (eleven hundred are known now), also two trees of every variety of Olive, Orange, Lemon, Pomegranate, Almond, Fig, etc., with a bound volume of the report." Agoston placed large advertisements in the *California Farmer* detailing the terms of his offer and urging farmers and nurserymen to form clubs to raise the $500 necessary to acquire the largest and most complete packages.[19]

This language—and the earlier language promising cuttings of "every variety of Grape now in cultivation in the civilized world"— was very broad, but there is no reason to believe that it was insincere.[20] Agoston could reasonably assume that, if he purchased vines and trees in the principal botanical gardens of the great winegrowing countries of Europe, he would ipso facto acquire "every variety of Grape now in cultivation in the civilized world," for the European gardens had for decades been searching the world for new and better vines for their collections. And, if he missed a few vines here and there, who could object? For the vines that he promised to bring into California would far exceed in number and variety anything already in the state.

The early months of 1861 must have been more than usually hectic in Sonoma. In addition to the normal planting and cultivation of the vineyards, the planning of the new Sonoma steamship company, and making arrangements for the European trip, Agoston had to concern himself with the loose ends of the mint litigation. It may have been considered something of a formality by then, but the government's nearly four-year-old lawsuit still remained to be resolved when the legislature first took up his suggestion for a viticultural commission. In fact, the trial did not conclude until March 2, 1861,[21] and Major Snyder did not return all the property he had been holding as trustee for the government until June 7 of that year.[22] It is quite amazing how sharply events had telescoped in Agoston's life. All the time he was building his great vineyard in Sonoma, persuading investors to come north from San Francisco to add to the vineyard acreage in the Sonoma Valley, spreading his views on viticultural techniques and methods through writings and public addresses, and proposing that the State of California send him to Europe as a commissioner to gather vines from all over the world, he was still subject to a potentially crippling lawsuit. That he was able to get on with his life in the face of such a threat—and to do so with such obvious aplomb—is a tribute both to his courage and to his resilience.

Agoston also made preparations to take some things with him to Europe that would make his work there easier. He wanted to have some of the printed reports of the California State Agricultural Society to present to European vineyardists, to show them that California was not an agricultural backwater but a progressive community of forward-looking farmers,[23] and he thought he might exchange these reports for European publications, thereby increasing his wine library. He also decided to bring some of his own wine along with him, to show sophisticated European connoisseurs what kind of wine California was capable of producing, and to determine how a long sea voyage would affect the quality of the wine.[24]

Agoston's plan for the European trip was to leave San Francisco early in June by steamship, go first to New York, then to Washington to confer with Secretary of State William Seward, and then cross the Atlantic to England and France. From France he planned to visit Spain, Portugal, Germany, Hungary, Italy, Greece, Smyrna, and Egypt, purchasing vines and trees in each country.[25]

He made arrangements with the *Alta California* to write some letters from various points along his itinerary. The letters would keep California readers apprised of his progress and make sure they did not forget his work. He also made arrangements with the *California Farmer* for it to publish some letters written by Arpad from France. In his studies at Épernay, Arpad was developing into a knowledgeable winemaker, and he had evidenced a natural literary flair—a talent for writing clearly, and even elegantly, on otherwise dry and technical subjects. Agoston believed that it would help his mission if Arpad kept the Haraszthy name before the public in the *Farmer* while he did his bit to accomplish the same purpose in the *Alta*. His *Alta* letters would help him when it came time to write his "report" for the legislature, and they might well be incorporated into the book that he expected to write about his European tour.

22

Mission
to
Europe

Agoston, Eleonora, and Ida were on board the steamship *Golden Age* as it pulled out of the harbor in San Francisco on June 11, 1861, headed out to sea through the Golden Gate, turned south, and followed the coast of California, Mexico, and Central America to Panama. They crossed over the isthmus on the Panama railroad and, on the Caribbean side, boarded another steamship for the second half of the voyage to New York, where they arrived on July 4.

Agoston quickly went down to Washington, D.C., which he found filled with soldiers in blue. The Civil War was barely two months old, but there was already a sense of tragedy in the federal city. His purpose was to call on Senator Latham and his California colleague, Senator James McDougall, and seek their aid in securing a passport. No law required American citizens traveling abroad to obtain passports, and many left the country without them; but travelers who cared to take the trouble often obtained passports to ease their contacts with foreign customs officials. Since Agoston intended to conduct important business in Europe, he believed that credentials issued by the State Department would be useful. Latham and McDougall agreed to accompany him to the office of Secretary of

State William H. Seward, where he promptly obtained both a passport and a circular letter of introduction:

To the Diplomatic Agents and Consuls of the United States in Foreign Countries.
Department of State, Washington, 6th July, 1861.

GENTLEMEN,—Mr. A. Haraszthy, the bearer of this communication,
has been appointed by the government of the State of California to proceed abroad for the purpose of collecting information in regard to wine-
producing countries, and reporting the results of his observations and in-
quiries to that government.

I will consequently thank you to extend to him any facilities which may
be necessary for so important an object.

I am your obedient servant,

WILLIAM H. SEWARD.

Passport firmly in hand, Agoston returned to New York, where he
had booked passage for Southampton on the Hamburg steamer *Ham-
monia*, scheduled to depart on July 13. He then called at the publishing house of Harper & Brothers and signed a contract for the book
he planned to write.

The sea voyage took thirteen days. Agoston's first order of business after the ship docked at Southampton was to telegraph Arpad,
who was waiting in France for the family's arrival. They were scheduled to leave for Le Havre that same evening, and Agoston used the
interim hours to hire a carriage for a little tour of the surrounding
countryside. The French steamer from Southampton arrived at Le
Havre the next morning at eleven. At five o'clock that afternoon, the
Haraszthys went on to Paris, a train journey of six or seven hours.[1]

They arrived in the French capital a little before midnight, took
lodgings in the Hotel du Louvre and, the following morning, met
Arpad. Arpad was now acquainted with French winemaking methods
and eager to help his father complete arrangements for his tour of
the Continent, so it was decided that he would travel with the family,
acting as Agoston's secretary and handling his correspondence with
local officials and scientific societies, and also copying his father's
journal entries each day. When Arpad's other duties left him no time
for copying, Ida would act as his assistant.

Agoston and Arpad had hoped that the American minister in

Paris would provide them with introductions to French agricultural and horticultural societies, but the minister's secretary informed them that it would be several days before he could meet them, so they decided to write directly to the societies. While they were composing their letters, Agoston tended to some of the other business he had in Paris. Not surprisingly, he had come to Paris with plenty of irons to be thrust into the fire. Before leaving California, he had addressed an open letter to the residents of Sonoma Valley pledging to use every opportunity to promote California's business and agricultural interests in Europe.[2] And he had also made arrangements to recruit European investors for a large corporation that proposed to plant vines, olives, almonds, and mulberries in southern California.[3]

In Paris, he called on Bertalan Szemere, prime minister of Hungary in the Kossuth government, who had been living as an exile in Paris. Besides being a seasoned politician, Szemere was an experienced botanist with a special interest in grapes and winemaking. He had become acquainted with Arpad while he was a student in Paris (the introduction had been provided by General Mészáros), and he had exchanged some letters with Agoston. Szemere's recorded opinions of Arpad are worth noting. He thought that Arpad was a "nice character" when he first came to Paris, but he had "degenerated" in the interim, and he was shocked by the young man's racist opinions. Arpad was a "fiery spokesman of slavery," Szemere said, and had once declared in very definite terms that he would not stay in the same room with a mulatto. Szemere ascribed some of Arpad's views to his youth (he was only twenty years old), but he obviously thought there was more to them than that. Szemere was also acquainted with Agoston's old San Francisco friend and metallurgical associate, Emmanuel Justh, and Justh had forewarned him that Agoston was a very unusual man. Justh told Szemere that Agoston "recklessly launches one enterprise after the other and risks everything every time."[4] Agoston told Szemere that he proposed to gather grapevines throughout Europe and "sell them at a large profit in America." "Moreover, he is empowered to sell a huge Californian estate; a portion can be kept by the owners." (Was this perhaps one of General Vallejo's ranchos, or the unspecified southern California property that Agoston hoped to sell to a large corporation?) If he was successful in finding a buyer for the land, Agoston told Szemere, he stood to earn a very large commission. He offered the ex-prime minister one half of the commission if he could find investors. But Szemere was uninterested—not just in Agoston's proposition, but in the whole idea of investing in California: "It is just like a fairy tale," he wrote in his diary, "and it is not really anything else. California in France means a Utopia. A French capitalist does not give a farthing to a California enterprise, even if someone offered 1,000 in return for one. It is even ridiculous to mention it here." Szemere did, however, describe Agoston, in German, as "a Geschäftsmacher [business maker]—a brave entrepreneur, a real American." Nonetheless, the wary exile resolved to keep his distance from the "reckless" Californian.[5]

It was now the beginning of August, and temperatures were rising in the valley of the Seine. Everybody who could do so was leaving the capital for *vacances.* The presidents of the societies whom Agoston had hoped to see had fled Paris, some for the Burgundy region. Agoston was carrying a letter from the editor of a French-language newspaper in San Francisco introducing him to Professor Claude Ladrey, one of Dijon's leading viticultural experts, so he decided to proceed there at once. The Haraszthys left Paris by train on August 6. That evening at the Hotel de la Cloche in Dijon, they washed off "the dust that almost buried us" and enjoyed what Agoston called "the finest dinner that I have eaten since the beginning of my tour."

Ladrey was president of the Dijon wine district, editor of a monthly magazine, and author of some well-respected works on wine. He greeted the wine pilgrims from far-off California with courtesy and warmth, conducted them through the botanical garden of Dijon, and later acted as their guide on a tour of vineyards and wine cellars surrounding the city. Agoston was delighted to learn that the garden in Dijon contained no less than six hundred different varieties of grapevines. After leaving Dijon, the travelers visited the villages of Gevrey and Chambertin, and the nearby city of Beaune, legendary "Wine Capital of Burgundy." Everywhere they went, Agoston carefully observed the landscape, the soil, the vineyards, and took detailed notes. In the Côte d'Or, the "backbone" of Burgundy, he noted that the soil was red and gravelly and contained a good deal of limestone, somewhat like the soil in Sonoma. Vines climbed high up over the slopes of the hills, almost to the very top: "The reason why they do not extend to the very crest," he noted, "is that no soil exists on the rocks toward the very top."

In the Clos de Vougeot in the Côte d'Or, one of France's most celebrated vineyards, he admired a stone abbey built by Cistercian monks in the twelfth century, inspected the underground cellars, and paused to examine the long rows of "Pineau" (Pinot) vines in the vineyards. He noted the distances between the vines, the varieties of grapes that were planted in the vineyards, and the prevailing methods of pruning. In Burgundy, he observed, the vineyards were usually small plots (a "clos" was a vineyard that was originally enclosed by a stone wall). The Clos de Vougeot, of about one hundred eighty acres, was large by Burgundian standards; many of the other vineyards were as small as two or three acres. At Clos de Vougeot he observed the process of "layering" a vineyard, that is, increasing the number of vines in cultivation by burying one branch in a ditch and thus encouraging two vines to grow where there had originally been only one.

On August 13, the Haraszthys took leave of Dijon and returned to Paris for three days of rest and relaxation, then left for Koblenz, at the confluence of two of Germany's fabled wine rivers, the Moselle and the Rhine. From Koblenz, they traveled by carriage to the nearby resort town of Bad Ems, on a tributary of the Rhine. Ems was the property of the Duke of Nassau, who maintained an elegant casino, a stylish palace, and well-appointed mineral baths in the town. There was a happy reunion in Bad Ems with one of Agoston's old friends from the San Francisco Verein, Dr. Carl Precht, now the U.S. consul in Cologne, who had come to Ems specifically to greet the Haraszthys. To celebrate the occasion, they all had dinner, "accompanied by a few bottles of the best wine the cellar of the Duke could furnish."[6]

From Ems, the Haraszthys returned to Koblenz, then doubled back to Frankfurt, where Agoston obtained introductions to German vineyard proprietors and called at the U.S. consul's office to inquire about J. Ross Browne, his old nemesis from the mint affair in San Francisco, who had been living in Frankfurt with his family. He and Browne had long since bridged over their differences, and Agoston had hoped to meet him. But the consul informed him that Browne was traveling in Norway, probably gathering material for one of his books, and so Agoston headed south to Hochheim.

With his innkeeper as a guide, he visited several of the wine cellars in Hochheim, savored wine made from the Riesling grape, and was introduced to Herman Dresel, the director of a large champagne-making firm—and, as it turned out, a brother of Emil Dresel, one of Agoston's neighbors in Sonoma. Agoston spent four hours in Dresel's cellars and was impressed enough to write: "I spoke to him of coming to California to put up for me a similar establishment, if not so great in extent, at least producing as good wines."

From Hochheim the Haraszthys proceeded to the city of Wiesbaden, where they met Dr. Carl Thomä, the director of an agricultural institute. With Thomä acting as their guide, they visited the vineyards and cellars at Steinberg, Erbach, and the legendary Schloss Johannisberg. Johannisberg, perched on an eminence overlooking the Rhine, had been a proprietary estate of Prince Klemens von Metternich since the Congress of Vienna. The longtime Austrian chancellor had died in 1859, but the property was maintained by his successor. If Agoston harbored any ill feelings toward the onetime "Despot of Vienna," they did not color the pages of his journal: "The Prince may boast of the view from his palace," he wrote in a happy mood, "as I can from my ranch in Sonoma; or, rather, I may boast of having scenery equal to that of the Prince Metternich. It is true that I have no River Rhine, but in its place there lies the St. Pablo Bay." All the wine grapes in the vineyards of Johannisberg were Rieslings, although a few other varieties were grown for table use. Agoston tasted many wines, and noted in his journal that the wines of Johannisberg "*must* be tasted to know their magnificence, for it is beyond the power of description."

On the train south from Wiesbaden to Mainz, there was an amusing encounter with a Russian woman who was traveling with a mountain of luggage and a young woman servant. Agoston helped her to explain her circumstances to the baffled conductor, who thought she must belong to an "opera troupe traveling to some interior town." The Russian woman was astonished to learn that the Haraszthys were from California—and still alive! "I became the lion of the time," Agoston wrote. "My fair neighbor asked me many questions about the gold; how long I had lived in California, and so on. I told her eleven years. 'Why,' she said, 'and you have not been killed! How have you escaped so many years without having been murdered? But, maybe you had a strong guard around you.'" Agoston, like many a traveler after him, described the methods of the American press: "I explained to her that whenever a murder is committed the local paper will chronicle it, and neighboring papers in the towns and cities repeat it, so that it appears to the foreigner that each announcement refers to a different murder. I remarked, too, that we had no more murders than other nations, but that with us every murder, suicide, or railroad accident is published far and wide, whereas in European countries no such thing is done."

After Mainz, the travelers went to Mannheim and to Heidelberg, where Agoston visited a nursery, toured the ruins of the old Heidelberg castle, and inspected the Great Tun of Heidelberg, a massive wine cask built in the middle of the eighteenth century.

At about this point in the tour, the party of four divided into two duos, with Eleanor and Ida traveling on their own and Agoston and Arpad, with business in mind, going on to inspect the wine country farther south. The family would eventually reunite in Paris.

Agoston and Arpad left Heidelberg on September 1, proceeded down to the Rhine, and then followed the river into the Black Forest. The river led them into the Swiss city of Basel, from which they traveled by train along Lake Neuchâtel to Geneva. They paused briefly in Geneva to tour the city, call on the U.S. consul, and meet with Samuel Brannan, a pioneer of the California Gold Rush who was visiting his estranged wife and children in their handsome villa nearby. Brannan, a renegade Mormon who came to California in the 1840's, had amassed a great fortune in the Golden State, not by mining but by making canny investments in a host of businesses (one of his most recent ventures was a spa called Calistoga at the upper end of the Napa Valley). Agoston and Arpad called at the Brannan place, overlooking Lake Geneva, and Samuel cordially invited them to stay a few days; but Agoston begged off: time was growing short and they still had many wine districts to visit. But he did have time to accompany Brannan to another house in Geneva, where he met a beautiful young woman from San Francisco named Lillie Hitchcock. Just seventeen years old, the beauteous Lillie had been banished to Europe by her physician father for the duration of the Civil War. "With this young woman's graceful reception and accomplished manners," Agoston wrote in his journal, "we were very much struck." And understandably so, for when she returned to San Francisco in a few years young Lillie Hitchcock Coit (the last name was acquired from a short but financially rewarding marriage) was to become one of the legends of the city by the Golden Gate—a civic leader, patron of the city's many volunteer fire companies, and a generous benefactress as well (Coit Tower on Telegraph Hill was erected after Lillie's death with money she left to San Francisco).

From Geneva, Agoston and Arpad traveled south along the River Rhône, then, by carriage, through an Alpine pass and onto the Italian frontier, where they boarded a railroad car for a short trip through the Italian Piedmont into Turin. Although a united Kingdom of Italy had been proclaimed only that spring, the head of the Italian state, King Victor Emmanuel, still lived in his palace in Turin (Pope Pius IX reigned in Rome, the capital of the Papal States), and the city was a busy governmental as well as commercial center. Agoston visited the American minister and the papal ambassador, then drove out of the city to survey the local vineyards. It was a hot summer afternoon when he reached the town of Asti in the Monferrato Hills, home of some of northern Italy's most famous still and sparkling wines. He chose a bottle of the still wine for quick refreshment and emptied it "almost at one draught." From Asti, the road led across a vineyard-filled plain into the port city of Genoa. Agoston and Arpad made several trips out of Genoa into the vineyards and spent a whole day inspecting a silk-making factory. Harking back to his old silk-growing days in the Bácska, Agoston made serious efforts to learn how the worms were grown, how the silk was spun, and what machinery the Italians had devised to aid the work, and was disappointed to learn that the Italian methods were no better than those he had known thirty years earlier in Hungary. In the town of Nova he shared a bottle of Asti *spumante* with Arpad. It was "very sweet," he noted in his journal, "sparkling like Champagne. It had a fine bouquet, but was made without care or system."

Aboard the train for the return trip to Genoa, Agoston was suddenly seized with an agonizing pain; as the pain increased, he grew

weak and nearly fainted. The consul general of Holland happened
to be on the train and offered his help. What had Agoston eaten,
the consul asked? "As soon as I told him I had taken some Asti, he
said that was the cause of my illness, and that it had the same effect
upon all strangers, as it is badly fermented, and frequently the peasants put honey in to make it sweet. Therefore I warn all my readers
never to drink Asti wine, and then journey in the cars."

Agoston and Arpad had intended to take an ocean steamer to
Rome and Naples, but when they discovered that they would have
to wait at least five days for passage—perhaps longer—they changed
their plans. It was already the middle of September, and Agoston
still had to visit the vineyards in the south of France and Spain,
and return to California in time to meet the legislature in January.
That meant forgoing the Italian journey as well as visits to Hungary, Greece, Smyrna, and Egypt. He would write to the countries
he missed for the trees and vines he needed.

From Genoa, Agoston and Arpad sailed for Marseilles on a
steamer. From the port city they traveled west by train, crossed the
Rhône at Arles, traced the Mediterranean coast to Narbonne, and
then followed the Garonne River to Bordeaux.

Agoston thought Bordeaux "a very fine city" and was impressed
by its large shady walks, promenades, and squares, and by its botanical garden, complete with ponds "in which hundreds of gold-fish
swim, and upon which swans extend their white and graceful forms."
He was impressed, too, by the crowded harbor, which formed part of
the Garonne, and by the ships from all over the world that crowded
the busy wharves. In his journal, he reminded his American readers
that, although he was born a European, he was stirred by the sight
of ships from his adopted country proudly flying "the beautiful *Star-
spangled Banner.*" "In beholding the flag of my country," he wrote, "I
felt rush into my heart a thrill of pleasure and pride. Even without
the flag, it was easy to recognize at once our American ships. Their
high masts, towering far above the forest around them, their sharp-
cut bows, their finely-molded lines, pronounced them American."

Soon after their arrival, Agoston and Arpad made their way to
one of Bordeaux's important wine firms, the House of Alfred de
Luze. In addition to supervising his wine business, De Luze served
as the Bordeaux consul of Frankfurt and the Grand Duchy of Hesse.

Guided by Alfred de Luze's son, Francis, the visitors inspected the
de Luze wine vaults. Entering through dark passageways and doors,
they found themselves in a succession of increasingly larger and
larger rooms, all filled with stacks of barrels, some six tiers high.
Francis de Luze gave them samples of all their principal wines. "I
need hardly say that they were delicious," Agoston wrote. "Never before had I tasted such Bordeaux or Sauterne, though of each I had
previously known excellent brands." Francis de Luze and one of his
nephews then took the visitors on a tour of the principal nurseries,
vineyards, and wine cellars around Bordeaux. At the largest nursery in the district, Agoston made a large purchase of vines. Eighteen miles out of the city, they visited the Château Margaux, one of
the most celebrated wine producers of the Médoc district. Agoston
noted that the soil there was gravelly and mixed with "a great quantity of pebbles. It is of a gray color, some clay, but more sand." The
vines were planted only three feet apart in each direction, and many
were weak and withered, but he did not think the short distance between the vines had anything to do with their weakened condition;
rather he thought the damage was inflicted by frost, or possibly by
some sickness that might have infected them. "I was really astonished," he noted in his journal, "how they could make any wine at
all, the vines were so much affected by disease." (Was this perhaps an
early sign of the great and frightening blight—the microscopic root
louse called *Phylloxera vastatrix*—that would in a few years devastate
both the French and the California vineyards?)

Leaving Bordeaux, the travelers headed south on the train to
Bayonne, near the Spanish frontier. Beyond that point, rails were not
available, and they were informed that they would have to make the
two-and-a-half-day journey through the Pyrenees and into Madrid
in a horse-drawn diligence. "When I speak of a diligence," Agoston
noted in his journal, "let not my readers imagine an American stage;
it differs in every respect." It was a heavy, lumbering vehicle, with
four passenger compartments designed to accommodate twenty travelers and to be drawn by six large horses. The compartments—*Ber-
line, Interior, Rotonde, Coupé*—were priced according to their position
in the vehicle and the comparative degree of comfort. Agoston and
Arpad took places in the Coupé, the rearmost of the compartments

and therefore the cheapest. The Coupé had four seats only—one for the conductor, three for passengers. "At the end of our journey," Agoston wrote, "far from repenting of our choice, we found that it was a most happy one; for, while the other passengers were half suffocated from dust and the want of air, we suffered from neither."

Agoston was hardly fazed by the news that the journey into Madrid would be long and exhausting—with stops only for food and a change of horses—but he was a little disturbed by the warning printed on his ticket, which said: "*The Company is not responsible for any effects taken by armed force.*" Believing "discretion the better part of valor," he sought out a gunsmith to load his Colt revolver. "With an eight-inch 'Colt,'" he noted in the journal, "I thought I might meet on pretty equal terms quite a considerable 'armed force.'" Thus armed, the Californians traveled all night through country "as wild as the Rocky Mountains." At Burgos, the diligence—baggage and all —was hoisted onto a railroad car, and the passengers were given seats in the train. Six hours later, the diligence was taken off again, hitched up to fourteen mules, and sent off in the direction of Madrid.

Agoston was not much impressed by Madrid—perhaps because they arrived there at one o'clock in the morning (September 22) and at their hotel had to make do with a bottle of wine and two little cakes, "called *ladies' fingers*, from their size, no doubt." "There are many provincial cities in Europe which are much handsomer," he noted. The country outside Madrid reminded him of the barren plains of New Mexico, "except that on the Plains we sometimes pass a cottonwood-tree; here not a bush could be seen."

Traveling again by diligence, Agoston and Arpad headed south to Granada, the city of the Alhambra; Agoston liked the Alhambra, though not the beggars. From Granada, they traveled (again by diligence) to the important winemaking and raisin-producing center of Málaga, on the Mediterranean Sea. Here Agoston hired horses and set out to visit a local vineyard. He observed the local techniques for drying raisins and making Málaga wine, which he described as "very heavy, and extremely sweet."

The travelers had hoped to continue on to Portugal, to see Oporto, but that plan, too, had to be scuttled, because of a five-day quarantine requirement that would have lengthened their journey overlong. Instead, they booked passage on an ocean steamer for Alicante, on the coast of Valencia, where they arrived at the very end of September. Agoston spent two days buying vines and trees. They then headed back, at last, to Paris, by way of steamers to Barcelona and Marseilles, and train to Paris. They arrived in Paris on October 4.

Agoston found some letters awaiting him that, he noted, "demanded my immediate return home." He needed no prodding. He had been away from California for four months; there was still a long journey ahead; and he wanted to be on hand when the legislature convened in Sacramento in January.

Eleanora and Ida were to stay in Paris a bit longer, partly to avoid a possibly very rough Atlantic crossing—but also, surely, to enjoy Paris. Arpad, too, would remain in France, to continue his champagne studies at Épernay. Agoston therefore made the trip alone, starting from Le Havre, where he had arranged to have his vines shipped direct to New York and on to San Francisco. He went by way of London to Liverpool and sailed to Boston on the English steamer *Europe*. It was a stormy crossing of fifteen days.

In the months that Agoston had been in Europe, the war between the North and the South had escalated sharply, and casualties on both sides were mounting rapidly. While he was crossing the Atlantic, the North had suffered one of its most painful losses when President Lincoln's old friend from Springfield, Illinois, Edward D. Baker, was killed leading a brigade of Union troops across the Potomac River. Baker had represented Major Snyder in his libel suit against the *Morning Call* for allegations arising out of Agoston's mint deficiencies. In 1860, when Congress admitted Oregon to the Union, Baker had abdicated his position at the head of the San Francisco bar to go north and win election as United States senator from the new state. After the outbreak of war, he volunteered to serve Lincoln as a field commander. Agoston and Baker were not politically congenial: Agoston was a Chivalry (and later a Lecompton) Democrat, whereas Baker was, first a Whig, and then a Republican. But Agoston was saddened to learn that Baker had been killed, and he readily accepted the honor that was now offered to him: to serve on a committee of three men delegated with the responsibility of accompanying the fallen hero's remains to San Francisco, where they would be interred.[7]

Before the ship with Baker's remains left, Agoston took care of some personal business—probably meeting with Harper & Brothers to discuss his projected book, and also visiting the recently opened New York cellars of Kohler & Frohling, the Los Angeles-based wine-making firm that had been the first to establish important salesrooms in San Francisco. Kohler & Frohling were pioneers in the ocean trade to New York, and Agoston wanted to sample their wines to determine how they had withstood the voyage from California. He found that, far from damaging the wines, the voyage seemed to have improved them. Kohler & Frohling were California's largest wine firm (and thus his most formidable competitors), but he praised their efforts: their wines were, he said, "very good"; he included this compliment in the manuscript of the book that he gave to Harper & Brothers for publication.

Agoston joined San Francisco banker Abel Guy and C. W. Drew of Oregon on November 11 to stand beside Baker's coffin as it was raised onto the deck of the steamer *Northern Light* bound for Panama. The coffin and the committee members crossed over to the Pacific side on the Panama Railroad, then boarded the *Golden Gate* for the last leg of their journey back to San Francisco. In the early morning hours of December 5, the *Golden Gate* sailed silently into San Francisco Bay. A little after four o'clock, it tied up to a wharf at the harbor's edge and began to discharge its unusual cargo: the coffin of a fallen United States senator and Civil War hero and a viticultural commissioner just returned from an exciting, and historically momentous, tour of Europe. Baker's funeral services were held before a great throng of mourners in San Francisco's Platt's Hall on December 11; Agoston's attorney, Edward Stanly, delivered the eulogy.

Agoston's vines did not reach San Francisco until January 23, 1862. It took a while for all the crates to be opened and all the vines to be taken up to Sonoma to be sorted and numbered and planted in Agoston's nursery. They were all in good condition. All told, Agoston had at least 100,000 cuttings. There were not 1,400 varieties, as he first estimated[8]—only 350—but that was still an impressive number.[9]

23

An Official
Rebuff

In the six months that Agoston had been gone from California, many changes had taken place. The vineyards at Buena Vista had added another year's growth and produced another harvest of grapes, many of which had been made into wine by Attila and Gaza. The green hills that he left at the end of spring had turned gold during the summer and, with the return of the year-end rains, once again sprouted a carpet of green grass.

But the rains that fell in the fall of 1861 were more than the usual light, refreshing showers of the season. Hard rains began in November and continued until the rainfall for that month exceeded four inches. In December, ten more inches of rain fell, and in January more than twenty-four. All the streams in the northern part of the state were flooded, and it became nearly impossible to cross over the creeks that separated Sonoma from the neighboring towns of Petaluma, Santa Rosa, and Napa. Snow fell hard on the Sierra Nevada and even dusted the hills around Sonoma with a mantle of white.[1] The Central Valley bore the brunt of the deluge; the rivers that flow down from the Sierra into the bed of the valley became uncontrollable torrents, and Sacramento became the center of a great inland sea. The legislature convened there on January 6, 1862, but immediately began preparations to move to a higher and drier location. On January 22, the lawmakers made the final break, voting to move the capital from Sacramento to San Francisco for the remainder of the 1862 session.[2]

As the weather changed, so did the state's political complexion. News from the battlefields of the Civil War was becoming increasingly grim, and Californians were showing more and more support for the Union. The pro-Southern wing of the California Democratic Party—once called the Chivalry, later the Lecomptonites, and now the Breckinridge faction (for their 1860 presidential candidate, Kentucky's John C. Breckinridge)—was swept aside in the September elections of 1861 by a new coalition of Republicans and Union Democrats. Republican Leland Stanford was elected governor, and an alliance of Republicans and Union Democrats took control of the legislature. If Agoston expected any favors from the state government in 1862, his long association with the Chivalry-Lecompton-Breckinridge wing of the Democratic Party would certainly not help him gain them.

When Agoston's European vines arrived at Sonoma, he laid out open-air beds to accommodate the great bulk of them and built a temporary hothouse to protect the more exotic varieties from the weather. He reckoned that if he handled the vines properly and no extraordinary event intervened, he would have 300,000 rooted vines ready for distribution in the fall of 1862.[3]

While he was still waiting for his vines to arrive in San Francisco, he received good news from Sacramento. Governor Downey had on January 8 delivered his farewell address to the legislature, in the course of which he recommended that the legislature appropriate money to pay the expenses of Agoston's trip to Europe. He reminded the legislators that the trip was made as a California state commissioner and argued that his efforts should be "rewarded in a manner becoming the subject and the dignity of the State."[4] Two days later, Downey turned the governor's office over to Stanford.

While Downey was addressing the legislature and Stanford was getting his new office in order, Agoston and Jonathan Warner were busy composing the reports that they were obligated to render to the lawmakers. Since the legislature provided that the commissioners would receive no pay for their work, Warner had decided to limit his investigations to resources readily at hand, and he concentrated his report on the southern California grapes and vineyards he was familiar with. In his report he reminded the legislators that planting a vineyard "is not for a season or year, or decade of years, but for generations," and that the selection of proper sites for grape plantings was critically important. He regretted that there was no "storehouse of facts, treasured up from the contribution of past generations," from which California winemakers could draw in planning new vineyards, and he strongly urged the state to take some action to supply this want. "There are numberless ways in which the Legislature might encourage 'the improvement and growth of the grape in California,'" he said.[5]

Agoston's views on the need for state encouragement of the California wine industry coincided with Warner's, but, while Warner was reluctant to suggest particular ways in which the state might encourage the industry, Agoston was only too eager to do so. In the report he prepared for the legislature in January, he suggested that the state authorize agents to travel through Europe (much as he had just done) to gather further information about European viticultural production and, in turn, spread the word about the viticultural progress being made in California. "These agents would come in contact with all classes of persons," he wrote, "questions would be eagerly asked, and opportunities be thus afforded to publish the advantages California possesses." He urged the legislature to continue its annual appropriations to cover printing and distribution of the State Agricultural Society's annual reports, but argued that these reports should be sent not just to other agricultural societies but also to prominent newspaper editors, who would publicize them widely. He noted that many members of the public distrusted the purity of wines offered for sale by merchants; and, to remedy this problem, he urged the legislature to pass a law appointing a "General Agent for Wines," with headquarters in San Francisco and authority to receive wines from private producers, certify their purity, and offer them for sale to the public. This officer would charge each producer a small commission to cover the cost of his services and make all the wine submitted to him equally available for sale. Agoston argued that the law creating the "General Agent" should also impose heavy penalties for any adulterated wines that were sent to the agent.[6]

Agoston's report included a general summary of his European trip. He noted that he had made careful observations of vine-growing and winemaking practices all along his route, and appended a "condensed statement" showing the contents of the book that he was preparing for publication. Each member of the legislature would, he promised, receive a copy of the book as soon as it was published.[7]

The vines that Agoston had brought back from Europe were, of course, uppermost in his mind. He advised the legislators that he had made all his purchases through United States consuls, so as to guarantee that the vines would be properly delivered and paid for. He had employed a gardener to attend to their proper packing and shipping, and had made arrangements with Wells, Fargo & Co. for their transportation by ship from New York to San Francisco. He did not yet know the total amount he had paid for the vines and the shipping, but he promised to give the legislature the figure as soon as it was available to him.[8]

By early February he had a more precise idea of the amount of money involved. In a letter to Governor Stanford dated February 8, he asked for directions on how the vines should be distributed. He noted that the Patent Office in Washington distributed some of its plants through members of the United States House of Representatives, and suggested that in California the vines could be distributed through members of the legislature. He assured the legislators that there was not a single county in California that did not have lands that were suited to viticulture, then added:

Permit me to draw here your attention to the necessity of having, as soon as possible, an appropriation passed to defray the expenses already incurred for the purchase of the vines and trees, the travelling expenses, for procuring the same, and collecting all the information necessary to make our State also a prosperous vine-growing district. The above named expenditures, including freight on railroads and steamers in Europe, on the vines, trees, etc., I have paid out of my own means, expecting the same to be refunded to me by an appropriation to be passed by the present Legislature. I ask no remuneration for my personal services as Commissioner; on the contrary, I feel proud of the honor, and I will be richly remunerated if I have done any service to my adopted country.[9]

He was still unable to give the legislators an exact total of the amount he had laid out (many of the consuls had not yet reported back to him), but he estimated it at $12,000—a very substantial sum in 1862, as he no doubt realized, for he added: "The sum thus expended will be a trifle to the real value of said vines . . . but to the people of this State it will in time be worth as many millions."[10]

Agoston's request that the legislature reimburse him for the expenses he incurred in gathering his vines in Europe has been condemned by one wine historian as "an astonishing piece of effrontery."[11] This historian points out that the legislature's resolution authorizing the governor to appoint three commissioners had not included any authorization for the purchase of vines and had made it clear that the commissioners were not to be paid for their services.[12] Moreover, Agoston had already tried to sell the vines on his own account, and had even placed advertisements in newspapers in an effort to find purchasers.

But Governor Downey had authorized Agoston to gather vines in Europe, and he had urged that Agoston be reimbursed for his expenses in doing so. Of course, "pay" is not the same thing as "expenses," even though both may involve an appropriation of money. Further, no legislature has the power to tie the hands of another legislature (except perhaps when one party has acquired enforceable rights under a contract). If the legislature of 1861 thought the commissioners not only should work for nothing but also should not ask reimbursement for a penny of any money they laid out in the course of their work, the legislature of 1862 was not bound by that determination. If the later legislature thought that, under all the circumstances, it should reimburse Agoston for all—or even a part—of the money he had advanced in Europe, there was no legal obstacle to its doing so.

Was it "effrontery" for Agoston to suggest a sum of money by which his admittedly extraordinary efforts to advance the interests of vine-growing and winemaking in California could be appropriately "rewarded"? Certainly the newspapers that reported on the state's agricultural affairs in 1861 and 1862 did not think so. Both the *Alta* in San Francisco and the *Union* in Sacramento were favorably disposed to Agoston's request for reimbursement, as well as to the plan that he suggested for distributing his vines throughout the state. The *Alta* thought the expense to the state "would be as nothing" compared to the benefits that the people of the state would derive from his vines.[13] The *California Farmer* pronounced Agoston's report to the legislature "a good one" and urged that his plan for distributing the vines be "carried out to the letter and spirit."[14] The *Farmer* wrote on February 14:

If the whole labors of Col. Haraszthy, and the collections of vines and trees, as well as the important information, shall revert to the State, as is intimated in that Report, then we trust a truly liberal compensation may be made the Commissioner for what he has done for California; for it is so very seldom we can record such public spirit or enterprise made *pro bono publico*, that when they do appear they look like the rainbow in the clouds bright and beautiful, wonderfully contrasting with the general darkness that surrounds the selfish treasure grabbing of our office-holders generally.[15]

On February 14 the State Assembly proposed that a committee of three members from each house visit Buena Vista and personally inspect the vines Agoston brought back from Europe.[16] The Senate promptly agreed to the proposal and named three of its members to join the committee.[17] These were John Hill, a Union Democrat from the Sonoma Valley, Richard Irwin, a Union Democrat who represented Butte and Plumas counties, and C. H. Chamberlain, a Republican from San Joaquin County. Chamberlain was alternately indifferent and hostile to the whole idea of supporting California winemaking, and a week after he was named to the committee he confessed that he "knew but little about wines" and, since he supposed there would be "a good deal of tasting" when the committee reached Buena Vista, he asked to be excused. Senator Richard Perkins, a Republican from San Francisco, was named to take his place.[18]

The joint committee made its inspection in March. Agoston conducted them through his vineyard and temporary hothouse and showed them his hillside cellars, where, as Senator Chamberlain had feared, there was "a good deal of tasting." On April 3, a report signed by Senators Hill, Perkins, and Irwin, and Assemblymen Brown, Watson, Evey, Teegarden, Dow, and Saul was filed with the two houses. It stated that the committee had seen Agoston's vines and found them "in such good condition that ninety-five percent of them will grow." The committee recommended that the state reimburse him $8,457 for the money he spent in purchasing the vines and fruit trees and pay Wells, Fargo an additional $1,542 for freight; it also recommended that Governor Stanford appoint a suitable person to take charge of the vines and distribute them to the members of the legislature. The legislators in turn would distribute the vines among Californians who were engaged in viticulture or who intended to engage in it. The committee also reported the following interesting news:

A letter was received by your Committee from Col. Haraszthy, in which he stated his willingness to teach vine growers practically the manufacture of wine and brandy, as soon as he commences manufacturing his own next fall, in the following manner: Each county shall be entitled to send three persons. If the county has an agricultural society, the board shall elect them, and the President furnish each of the elected with a certificate; if there be no agricultural society, the County Supervisors shall elect and certify. These individuals will receive the practical knowledge of the art of making wine and brandy free.

This liberal offer, at a time when so little is known of the process by our beginners, is most welcome. The knowledge is thus placed within the reach of all, the poor as well as the rich.[19]

In the Senate, the joint committee report was referred to the Committee on Agriculture, "with instructions to report by bill or otherwise."[20] While the Senate committee was busy composing its report, the Assembly's Committee on the Culture of the Vine was preparing its own report—not only on the question of what to do with Agoston's vines but on the broader question of the policy the state should adopt toward California's infant wine industry.[21] The Assembly report, which was filed on April 9, was filled with interesting statistics about wine production and equally interesting quotations from philosophers and economists about the benefits of wine consumption. The committee strongly believed that wine drinking would promote temperance among the people of California, and that it would also do much to stimulate the state's economy. The committee recommended that the legislature adopt Agoston's suggestion for a "General Agent for Wines," and accept his offer to teach winemaking to aspiring winemakers. It was convinced that "a great benefit would be conferred upon the people of California" if the legislature

took over Agoston's vines and judiciously distributed them throughout the state.

The committee was apparently undecided about reimbursing
Agoston for the expenses he had incurred, but it noted, without precisely mentioning Agoston, that the legislature was proposing to appropriate $10,000 to found a "Home for Inebriates" in San Francisco
and suggested that the same sum might much better be spent to *prevent* drunkenness, rather than on trying to *cure* it. It then proposed
a resolution thanking Agoston "for the able and efficient manner in
which he has performed his duties as Commissioner on the Growth,
Culture, and Improvement of the Grape-Vine in California." [22] This
resolution was quickly adopted and entered into the statute books
of the state. [23]

On April 7, the Senate Agriculture Committee filed its report—
or, to be precise, its *reports,* for there were two, with dramatically
opposing views. Although San Joaquin County's Senator Chamberlain had declined to go to Buena Vista because he knew "but little
about wines," he was not hesitant about presenting the majority report, which strongly recommended that the legislature do nothing
to distribute Agoston's vines. In a minority report, Senators James R.
Vineyard of Los Angeles County and William Holden of Mendocino,
Lake, and Napa counties (both Breckinridge Democrats), urged that
the legislature reimburse Agoston for his expenditures and take
charge of the vines. Because the majority report was the basis for
much of the debate that followed—and because the majority report
itself became the subject of some controversy—it is worthwhile to
set it forth verbatim:

The majority of the Committee on Agriculture, to whom was referred the
report of the Special Committee appointed to visit the "plantation" of Col.
Haraszthy, and to inspect and report on the vines imported by him, have
had the same under consideration; and being instructed to report by bill or
otherwise, beg leave to report *otherwise.*

Your Committee do not doubt that the vines are a valuable acquisition
to the vine-growing interests of our State; that the cuttings are planted in
rich soil, just four inches apart, and in rows two feet apart (and here your
Committee beg leave to suggest that four inches and a quarter would not be
too much in the one case, and that twenty-two and one half inches would

have been amply sufficient in the other); that the rooted vines are planted three feet apart; that their buds are bursting and prepared *to leave*—in fact, that some of them have already *put out*; nor do we doubt, if the State should go into the wholesale or retail vine business as proposed, future Californians sitting beneath their own vine, "with none to molest or make them afraid," in the rich native wines of our own State would drink to the memory of the Legislature of Sixty-Two; that the names of its members would be preserved in California champagne, and float down the tide of time like letters from a foundered ship on a literal ocean, in a bottle, or "in a horn;" nevertheless, considering that the State has done nothing that, even by implication, could make her responsible for these vines; considering that there are already, exclusive of these, about one million foreign grape vines in the State, of the choicest varieties; considering the complicated machinery that would be necessary for their distribution in case the State should purchase and assume control over these vines, and the danger in that case that favoritism would apportion to the few what was intended for the benefit of the many; considering, that if we should thus show our willingness to worship Bacchus, our constituents might not *back us*, but accuse us of playing *roots* on them; considering that these vines are already sufficiently advertised by the action of the Legislature in regard to them, so that private enterprise—if there really is any scarcity of or demand for choice vines—will secure their distribution; and considering the condition of the State Treasury, your Committee decline reporting by bill, and recommend that no action be taken on the matter.[24]

Senator Vineyard presented the minority report, and an accompanying bill titled "An act to purchase certain grape vines, and to provide for the distribution of the same." The bill was designed to implement the earlier recommendations of the joint committee and provided that, upon Agoston's delivery of the vines to duly appointed state agents, he be paid $8,457 and Wells, Fargo receive the additional sum of $1,549 for freight.[25]

The brief debate following the presentation of the two reports only strengthened the two opposing positions. Sonoma's Senator Hill expressed "surprise" that the majority should present such a sarcastic report. He reviewed the circumstances under which Agoston was authorized to go to Europe and argued that the vines belonged to the State. Chamberlain read the original resolution under which Downey appointed the three commissioners and noted that there was nothing in it making the state responsible for the expense of importing any vines. The only question, Chamberlain said, was whether the state could afford to enter into such expense at the present time, and it was clear that it could not.[26]

Newspaper opinion on the committee reports, like newspaper opinion on the underlying question of reimbursement, was decidedly in Agoston's favor. The *Alta* deplored the majority's attempt to "ridicule" the idea of buying the vines.[27] The *Union* found the majority's "attempts at wit" "excruciating": "such trifling upon a subject of real interest to the people of the State is so entirely out of character that we are surprised at seeing the names of three Senators appended to the report."[28]

The majority and minority reports came up for debate in the Senate on April 16. George Porter, a Republican representing Santa Cruz and Monterey counties, moved that the bill be postponed indefinitely. Senator Hill, opposing the motion, advised "the author of the witty report against this bill to bottle up a portion of his wit, which was probably in danger of bursting him, and cast it into the gutter for the benefit of some school boy."[29] Hill argued at some length in support of the bill. He said he supported it because of the "incalculable advantages" it would bring to the state—because its passage "would enure to the benefit, not of the Commissioner [Agoston], but of the people of the whole State."[30]

Porter revealed an appalling ignorance of the whole question of vineyard cultivation and winemaking in California when he baldly asserted that "it was well known that the vine does not flourish in this state."[31] Senator R. Burnell, a Union Democrat of Amador County, in support of the bill, expressed the opinion that "good grapes in the mountains" were "a source of great revenue." Senator Walter Van Dyke, a Union Democrat representing Humboldt, Klamath, and Del Norte counties, thought the state's finances did not justify the proposed appropriation and that "private enterprise would regulate the matter of vine culture in the state."[32]

When the motion to indefinitely postpone came to a final vote, twenty senators voted for it and nine against.[33] The motion was passed, and the bill was killed. The vote not only assured that Agoston would receive no reimbursement for his expenses—it also meant that he would have to pay Wells, Fargo's claim for unpaid freight out of his own pocket. The Senate did not even express a vote of thanks for his efforts (or, for that matter, for the efforts of Jonathan Warner) in behalf of the state commission.

It has frequently been suggested that the vote against Agoston was prompted by political rivalries in the legislature of 1862—that, because of his Southern sympathies, the pro-Union forces united to deny him any money for the vines.[34] The suggestion, like so many other components of the Haraszthy Legend, had its roots in recollections left many years later by Arpad Haraszthy. In the manuscript he prepared for Hubert Howe Bancroft in 1886, Arpad charged that the legislature "was strongly Republican and Col. Haraszthy was Chairman of the State Democratic Committee and was falsely accused of being a Secessionist. The war was proceeding at that time and party feeling ran high."[35] We can forgive Arpad for his erroneous assertion that his father was chairman of the State Democratic Committee (he was active in the Breckinridge wing of the Democratic Party, but he never held the office of chairman). It would be foolish to assert that political in-fighting played no part in the decision—politicians, after all, are political animals; and it is true that Agoston's mission to Europe was originally supported by Governor Downey and other Breckinridge Democrats, who certainly were no friends of the Union Democrats and Republicans who controlled the legislature of 1862. But these interparty rivalries were not determinative of the question. An analysis of the final vote on the question of reimbursing Agoston for his expense shows that he was supported by four Union Democrats, two Republicans, and three Breckinridge Democrats, and opposed by thirteen Republicans, six Union Democrats, and one Breckinridge man. The Breckinridge Democrats were in the minority on both sides of the question; but this is not surprising, for they constituted a small minority of the total membership of the 1862 legislature.

The real reason for the legislature's decision can be found in comments made during the Assembly's early debate on the proposal to send a joint committee to Buena Vista to inspect Agoston's vines. In that debate, Assemblyman Caleb Fay, a Republican from San Francisco, had charged that all those who favored the proposed committee were from counties in which agriculture was the principal economic activity, while those who opposed it were all from mining counties. Assemblyman Shannon, from the mining county of Plumas, had conceded Fay's point. Shannon admitted that the mining representatives were opposed to measures designed to encourage viticulture and winemaking—but he thought their opposition was justified. If California's infant wine industry was really as important as the farming county representatives claimed, it needed no special governmental support. "The culture of the grape," Shannon said, "will work out its own solution." [36]

Analyzed on the basis of farming vs. mining representatives, the final vote on the question of reimbursing Agoston for his vines makes more sense. The vote in favor of reimbursement was opposed by the mining county representatives by a margin of more than two to one; it was favored by a bare majority (five to four) of the farming counties. Of course, this split was as unfavorable to the reimbursement bill as the division between unionists and Breckinridge supporters, for in 1862 the mining counties had the overwhelming population of California, and their representatives firmly controlled the legislature.

Rebuffed by the legislature, Agoston was left to his own devices to distribute the vines he had gathered in Europe. It was a difficult task, not only because of the great number of the vines but also because of the considerable expense he had incurred in gathering and caring for them during their first year in California. He had at first estimated that his imported vines represented nearly 1,400 different varieties.[37] The catalog that he prepared after the legislature refused to take over the vines listed 492 varieties by name,[38] but a study revealed that many of the varieties were listed by more than one name, so that by 1864 he estimated there were in fact only 350 different varieties.[39] What were they? Not surprisingly, the greatest proportion of them came from France, Germany, and Hungary— three of the most important winemaking countries in Europe. Of the 492 listed names, 171 were from France, 160 from Hungary, and 109 from Germany (meaning all the German-speaking states of Central Europe except Switzerland, which was listed separately). Another nineteen were from Italy, ten from Spain, six from Corinthia, three from Switzerland, and two each from Portugal, the Tyrol, Illyria, and Corsica. European countries represented by one vine each were the Crimea and Bohemia. A handful of vines came from non-European countries surrounding the Mediterranean: three from Smyrna province, two each from Morocco, Turkey, and Palestine, and one from Algiers. One vine was listed as being from Persia.

The stated countries of origin represented only the countries from which Agoston directly obtained the vines. The original sources in other countries or regions can sometimes be speculated at on the basis of the names provided. For example, vine no. 265, which Agoston obtained from France, is identified as the "Malvoisé d'Aragon"; no. 364 (also from France) is identified as the "blue Portugisi (or Oporto)." Similarly, no. 221, obtained from Hungary, is the "Kalabresea, Calabria"; no. 375 (also from Hungary) is the "Recine Marocco"; and no. 342 is described as "Persiai, white, very large, imported from Persia to Germany." These names are quite understandable when it is remembered that there had been a vigorous trade in grapevines among the countries of Europe and the Mediterranean for centuries before Agoston's tour of 1861.

Many of the names listed in the catalog are difficult (if not impossible) to identify today. Others, however, are grape names that later became quite familiar to California vineyardists and wine consumers. At least three of the four grapes commonly described as the "Noble Wine Grapes" (the Cabernet Sauvignon of Bordeaux, the Pinot Noir of Burgundy, and the Riesling of the Rhineland) were represented in the catalog; the fourth, the Chardonnay, was not identified by that name, although it may well have been the grape identified as the "Champagne" grape of France, or perhaps the "white Bourgunder" of Germany (Chardonnay is the principal white grape of the Champagne district, but it is also widely used in Burgundy). The Black Hamburg, the Carignane ("Crignane" in the catalog), the Grignolino ("Grignoli"), the Gewürtztraminer, the Mataro, the Merlot ("Merlau"), the Muscat de Frontignan (also known as the Muscat Canelli), the Pedro Ximenes ("Pedro Ximen"), the Sauvignon Blanc, the Sauvignon Vert ("Verdure Sauvignon"), the Sémillon ("Semilon"), the Sylvaner (also known as the Franken Riesling), and the Traminer were also listed; and, to varying degrees, these grapes all became important California wine grapes in later years. Other grapes that were grown with some success in the last years of the nineteenth century but thereafter passed into neglect include the Chasselas Doré (also known as the Gutedel), the Rousanne (called "Grosse de roussanne" in the catalog), the Blaue Elba, the Pinot Blanc, the Pinot Gris, the Orleans, the Meunier, the Malbeck ("Malbec"), and the Teinturier. The catalog included several examples of the celebrated Furmint grape (principal grape of the Tokay district of Hungary) and several examples of Muscats. Some important raisin grapes were also represented in the catalog (the Muscat of Alexandria and the Muscatel Gordo Blanco, among others), as were some important table grapes (several kinds of Chasselas and the Magdalene).

It has often been noted that the name "Zinfandel" appeared nowhere in Agoston's catalog.[40] This absence has been seized upon by those who seek to prove that Agoston was not the first to import the Zinfandel into California, perhaps even as proof that he never brought any Zinfandel vines into the state.[41] But the elusive grape may well be there, masquerading under a different name. It has already been noted that the name Zinfandel may derive from Sylvaner, and that it probably shares the same root as the German Zierfandler.[42] Zinfandel is, of course, a red grape, so neither no. 417 in the catalog (the "green Szilvânyi," from Hungary) nor no. 414 (the "green Silvaner" from Germany) can be considered. However, no. 418 (the "red Szilvânyi" from Hungary), no. 414 (the "black Silvaner" from Germany), or no. 416 (the "red Silvaner" from Germany), might qualify for the honor. No. 485 (the "red Zierfandler" from Germany) is another possible candidate. It must be remembered, however, that the Zinfandel was in California years before the 1862 importation, and any claim that Agoston was the first to bring it into California must rest on earlier importations. Notwithstanding this, it is interesting to speculate on the possibility that the vine was brought into California, not just in the 1850's, but also in 1862, as part of the large importation that Agoston made in that year.

Since the legislature would have none of the vines, Agoston made diligent attempts to sell them. He had to propagate the vines, of course, so there would be adequate stocks to supply the expected demand, and for this purpose he selected varieties that were "famous for generous wines" for cutting and rooting, and soon built up a stock of twenty to thirty thousand vines of each of these varieties. In the introduction to his catalog, he asked prospective buyers to mail their orders to Sonoma and indicate whether they intended to raise grapes for fresh fruit or for winemaking. If they wished to make wine, he said he could "suggest the best qualities for wine making": "Wine growers must bear in mind that generous wines, with the desired bouquet, can only be made from proper foreign vines, and it costs no more to plant and cultivate one acre of foreign vines than of native, and the wine made from the former will sell for quadruple the price."[43]

Upon the receipt of an order, Agoston replied with a statement of the cost and a request that the requisite amount be forwarded to him. When the payment was received, he wrapped the vines and delivered them to the Wells, Fargo express office in Sonoma, whence they could be delivered by stage to any place in California.

From an early date, an important element of the Haraszthy Legend has been the notion that the grapes that Agoston brought back from Europe in 1862 formed the basic vine stock of the state's wine industry in later years. This notion cannot be laid at the feet of Arpad Haraszthy, for he took quite a different view of the importation. Arpad thought that the vines his father imported in 1862 resulted in the first "general and large plantation of foreign vines in every direction," but he believed that, on account of the legislature's refusal to take over the vines, the importation had not fulfilled its promise. The vines became "scattered through the country," and many of them wound up in the hands of vineyardists and farmers who "lacked the necessary knowledge and soon grew tired of experimenting with them."[44]

Agoston's critics, who generally take issue with Arpad's conclusions, have been eager to embrace his negative view of the 1862 importation. They have dismissed it as an unimportant footnote in the history of California wine, asserting that there is "no evidence that the Haraszthy collection ever had any important effect on the material development of the California wine industry"[45] and that "few, if any, of the varieties . . . have any importance now."[46]

It is interesting to compare these judgments with the views of some nineteenth-century Californians, particularly those who were personally acquainted with the California wine industry during its earliest years. In 1869, John S. Hittell, a vineyardist as well as a veteran wine journalist, reported that Agoston's 1862 vines had had a "wide circulation" and that they had furnished cuttings from which "extensive vineyards" were being cultivated "everywhere."[47] In 1872, the Prussian-born Charles Nordhoff, one of the first journalists of national reputation to report on the California wine industry, expressed a similar view when he noted that many of the foreign grapes that Agoston brought to California were "thriving," and that the state's new vineyards were planted "almost entirely with these" vines.[48] In 1879, in his pioneering *History of Sonoma County*, J. P. Munro-Fraser, a Sonoma County journalist and sometime county official, echoed Hittell's and Nordhoff's views, writing that Agoston's 1862 vines had been "planted quite extensively in most of the vineyards of the State," and that "the most valuable wines we now produce" were made from them.[49]

In 1877, the *San Francisco Bulletin* printed an unsigned article assessing the progress made up to that date in the California wine industry. This long and thoughtful article pointed out that many of the vines Agoston brought back from Europe in 1862 were still growing in California's vineyards in 1877, although a substantial number of them had been "destroyed" by Agoston's successor at the Buena Vista vineyards. Agoston had planted many of his 1862 vines between the rows of other, more familiar vines, and the vineyardist who took over responsibility for Buena Vista after Agoston's departure did not believe that vines should be planted so closely, so he plowed up whole rows of the plants, in the process totally destroying "many varieties which had been so carefully collected and imported." "What varieties were thus destroyed has not yet been ascertained," the article added: "It may possibly never be revealed."[50]

The truth was that Agoston's 1862 importation was a very important event in the history of California wine, although it could have been, and should have been, even more important. The number and variety of the vines that Agoston brought to California in that year were in themselves significant. It is true, of course, that many of the varieties had been introduced into California before 1862 (some by Agoston himself); it is also true that there were a large number of foreign vines in the state before Agoston's 1861 tour—perhaps even as many as the one million the majority of the Senate committee estimated. But many of the vines that he gathered on his tour were wholly new to the state, and those vines had tremendous potential for improving the quality of the state's wine production.

Charles Wetmore, one of the state's first scholarly students of wine and winemaking history, assessed the importance of Agoston's 1861 tour in the early 1880's. In Wetmore's opinion, if the state government had "realized the importance of the work undertaken, and provided for popular instruction in viticulture, especially as to the relative merits and uses of the different varieties introduced, we should have been far more advanced in the quality of our products than we are today." [51]

The importance of Agoston's 1862 importation was not solely (or even primarily) in the vines that he brought in. Far more important were the ideas that he attempted to communicate through the medium of the importation, first to the state government, and secondarily to the grape growers and winemakers of California. He was saying that winemaking was a noble and economically important industry that deserved state support, and that good wine could be made in California only if the best varieties of European grapes were obtained, identified, tested, propagated, and cultivated. But such an effort was beyond the resources of any one individual, and had to be fostered by the state. If the vines that Agoston brought back from Europe in 1862 had been taken over by the state, as he wished, they would have formed the basis for an official "state collection" of vines—a "botanical" or "horticultural" garden, like those maintained by governmental authorities throughout Europe. The vines would have been grown in a central location, carefully identified, systematically tested and propagated, and made freely available to vineyardists and would-be vineyardists. If the legislature had accepted his offer to provide free instruction in wine and brandy production, the state would have taken the first step toward providing a program of state-sponsored viticultural instruction.

But the legislature of 1862 could not see very far into the future. It refused to accept Agoston's vines, refused his offer to provide instruction in viticulture and winemaking, refused to lend the state's support to a program of fostering the state's wine industry. The 1862 vote was taken by many as an indication that, contrary to what Agoston said, the varieties of grapes from which wines were made were not really very important.[52] Any grape would suffice to produce a decent enough wine—even the old Mission grapes of the padres, which, after all, were the cheapest vines that a would-be winemaker could find. And so many California vineyardists continued to plant Mission grapes far into the 1870's and 1880's.

But the legislature's obduracy would not continue forever. Eighteen years after the legislature of 1862 passed into history, the legislature of 1880 passed "An Act for the promotion of the viticultural industries of the State,"[53] creating a Board of State Viticultural Commissioners and ordering the University of California to undertake a broad program of viticultural research. Pursuant to this act, Professor Eugene Hilgard was authorized to establish an experimental vineyard on the university's campus in Berkeley. From that day forward, the University of California was an important force in fostering and encouraging the development of the California wine industry. The Berkeley vineyard, important in its own right, was even more important as the germ from which the vineyards of the University of California at Davis were later developed—experimental and teaching vineyards that, in the twentieth century, were to contribute in uncounted ways to the viticultural and enological resources of California.

Agoston had envisioned the beginnings of such a state program in 1862, but the men who held the votes in the legislature did not share his vision. He went to his reward before the Board of State Viticultural Commissioners was created, before the university vineyard was planted, and he could not see the fruits of these two institutions. But he would, no doubt, have been pleased to know that Arpad, his faithful traveling companion on the 1861 tour of Europe, was chosen as the first president of the Board, an office that gave him official recognition as the leader of the state's wine industry and responsibility for overseeing its program of fostering and encouraging the growth and improvement of grapevines and wine in California. The recognition took a long time coming, but when it came it was still in the family.

24

Taking
Stock

On April 23, 1862, just a week after the State Senate voted not to reimburse Agoston for the expenses he incurred in bringing his vines into California, the California State Agricultural Society convened for its annual meeting in Sacramento. If the society shared any of the misgivings about Agoston's vines that were voiced in the legislature, there was no hint of it in the meeting in Sacramento, for on the first day of the meeting the society passed a resolution noting Agoston's tour and thanking the Europeans who helped him gather his vines; and, on the same day, it conferred on him the highest honor in its power to award by electing him as president for the coming year.[1]

As president of the State Agricultural Society, Agoston was the titular leader of the state's farmers and vineyardists and in a good position to command audiences for his views on California agriculture. He took full advantage of the opportunity, particularly at the society's principal event of the year, the State Fair, which opened in Sacramento on September 30. On the evening of the opening day, a large crowd assembled in the Hall of the Pavilion at the fairgrounds to hear him deliver the President's opening address.

Agoston began his speech by recalling the destructive floods that swept through the state the previous winter and congratulating the state's farmers for the cooperation and generosity they displayed in responding to the crisis. "For energy and determination," he said, "the Californians are unequalled by any people in the world." He also congratulated the farmers and mechanics on the progress they had made in developing the state's infant agricultural resources. "The unparalleled success of our State is an instance of good fortune seldom encountered," he said, adding:

A few years ago it was a wilderness, without roads, stages, steamboats or any other public conveyance, but in the short space of twelve years the unbounded energy of our people has overcome all these obstacles, and now an easy and cheap communication is established between all parts of the State. . . . If the traveler makes a tour through our young State, if he passes through our cities, towns, magnificent farms, orchards and vineyards—when he sees our aqueducts leading over mountains, through ravines, gulches, over hundreds of miles—when he sees all this, and glances into our census, and finds that, all told, we have no more than five hundred thousand souls, he cannot help exclaiming—What a country! What a people!

But he cautioned his listeners not to rest on their laurels, for there were still many challenges to be met. He was concerned by the continuing efforts of prominent politicians in the State to exclude Chinese immigrants; as he had said many times before, the Chinese who worked in the vineyards of Sonoma—and on farms all over the state—not only were good for California's agriculture, they were essential to its continuing prosperity. By performing work that white laborers would not perform (or would not perform so efficiently), the Chinese were helping to develop the state's resources and contributing to the prosperity of the entire population. The Chinese were also consumers of the state's agricultural products and manufactured goods. A member of the State Senate had recently calculated that Chinese workers spent nearly a million and a half dollars in California each year. This was a very substantial sum, Agoston pointed out, and it contributed in important ways to the economic activity of the state. "Why, then," he asked, "does an unfriendly Legislature drive these people out of our country?"

He was encouraged by some good news he had recently received from Senator Latham in Washington. The Senate had just passed an important bill designed to benefit the cause of agriculture in the states that remained loyal to the Union by making large grants of federal land to endow state agricultural colleges. Agoston reminded

his listeners that he had pleaded for the establishment of agricultural schools in California in his address to the Sonoma County Fair
in 1860, and he expressed the hope that the House of Representatives would quickly approve the Senate measure. (He did not know
that Congress had already approved this proposal, thus laying the
groundwork for the opening in 1869 of the University of California,
destined in time to become one of the greatest agricultural schools
in the United States and an important force in the gathering and
dissemination of winemaking and viticultural knowledge.) [2]

Agoston concluded his address (which lasted a little more than
an hour) by noting that Congress had vigorously supported the construction of the long-wished-for Atlantic-Pacific railroad, and the day
when that road would open California up to the Atlantic states was
drawing ever nearer. He hoped that Congress would also encourage
the opening of steamship lines to Japan, China, and the Sandwich
Islands, for, if it did so, California would become a "half way house"
on the road to Asia, linking the eastern states and Europe to the
important commercial emporiums of the Far East and helping to ensure the state a rich and rewarding future.[3]

While Agoston was expounding on his views at the State Fair,
copies of the book that he had written for Harper & Brothers were
on their way from New York to San Francisco. *Grape Culture, Wines,
and Wine-Making, With Notes upon Agriculture and Horticulture* was a
handsomely printed volume of slightly more than 400 pages. These
included 140 pages of Agoston's European journal; the remainder of
the volume consisted of an updated version of his 1858 "Report on
Grapes and Wine of California," written for the State Agricultural
Society, and English translations of technical essays on winemaking,
viticulture, and related agricultural subjects by European authorities. The book also included the text of Agoston's official report to
the state legislature, delivered to Governor Stanford in February.

The journal of Agoston's European tour revealed all the qualities
of Agoston's writing that were most attractive to readers. His style
was direct, informal, sometimes even chatty, and his sense of humor
was never far below the surface. The journal was a good combination
of narrative and discourse—a chronological account interlaced with
careful descriptions of the vineyards and wine cellars and numerous

comparisons of European and California methods and conditions. The book was a landmark publication—the first book by a California winemaker to be given circulation throughout the United States[4]— and it attracted considerable interest in the American, and particularly the California, press.

The *New York Times* review of the book noted that it included a host of "scientific articles, most from German sources," but warned that it should not be dismissed as a mere technical treatise, since it contained much that would interest "the general reader, and indeed all persons of *taste*."[5] *Harper's New Monthly Magazine*, in its "Literary Notices" column in the December 1862 issue, recommended the book enthusiastically. "Few more readable books of travel have been produced than that portion of the book," the reviewer said: the author "always keeps in view the special object of his journey, describing fully and clearly all the processes employed in the culture of the vine, the gathering of the grapes, and the fabrication of wines; noting also all other subjects which could relate to the agricultural interests of his adopted State." The wealth of wine statistics was impressive: "Making the largest possible deductions from the results of the statistics of Mr. Haraszthy, there can be no doubt that the vine-culture is destined to become a most important element in the productions of California; and the sum expended in gathering the immense mass of information embodied in this volume can not fail to have been well bestowed."[6]

It was perhaps to be expected that the reception to the book on Agoston's home ground would be a tad more critical. The *Alta California's* review (probably written by John S. Hittell) was mixed. "So far as the notes of travel are concerned," the review said, "they do not differ in any remarkable degree from other books of travel, unless here and there a little turn in the language reminds us that English is not the author's mother tongue." But the *Alta* still thought that the book was "substantial," and "full of the most valuable information upon all the branches of wine-growing." "As California is the greatest of Anglo Saxon wine countries," the *Alta* continued, "so it is proper and natural that we should produce the most comprehensive book upon this branch of industry. . . . It should not simply be read and thrown into a corner, but studied over and over again; and if there be any man in California who can make himself complete master of its contents in a month, we do not know where to find him, nor is there a Californian wine-grower who cannot learn much in regard to his occupation from its pages."[7]

Agoston's colleagues in the wine industry recognized the value of the book and made it a premium for displays of wine, grapes, and other fruits at agricultural fairs throughout the state. At the combined Napa and Sonoma County Fair held in Sonoma in October of 1862, for example, copies of the book were awarded in competitions for the best orchard, best red wines, and best white wines.[8] The book was also awarded as premiums at the State Fair in Sacramento the following summer.[9] In 1863 also, the newly organized California Wine-Growers Association praised the book as "the most comprehensive and instructive book in the English language" on the subject of wine,[10] while as far away as New York City the book was recommended to the prestigious Farmers' Club of the American Institute as a "valuable work" uniquely adapted to the needs of American grape growers.[11]

The 1862 county fair in Sonoma was a particularly happy convocation for the author of *Grape Culture, Wines, and Wine-Making*. For the better part of a week, the streets surrounding the plaza were crowded with wagons and carriages, as farmers and their families came in from all the surrounding valleys to display their products and stock, race their horses, and show off their wives and daughters at the "grand ball" held in the fair pavilion. On the next to last night of the fair, as a late-summer moon hovered over Sonoma, a band of local musicians determined to march from the pavilion to the homes of some of the valley's most prominent residents. They visited both Lachryma Montis and Buena Vista, playing "serenades" at both places. At Buena Vista, the musicians encountered a group of Agoston's friends, who had gathered to enjoy the warm evening and the proprietor's hospitality, and regaled them with polkas, schottisches, and mazurkas.[12]

The California Wine-Growers Association that praised Agoston's book in 1863 was formed in San Francisco in late 1862 for the purpose of bringing all the state's viticulturists and winemakers together to promote their common interests. It was, in effect, a trade association of winegrowers, the first ever formed in California. Not surprisingly, the spark behind this organization came from Agoston. He issued the first call for members and was chairman of the first meeting. Though he held no office in the organization, he took an active interest in its affairs in the months and years that followed. The idea of such an organization was prompted by the tax that Congress had imposed on wine in the middle of 1862. Agoston had long argued that government should promote and foster the wine interest, and he was chagrined when the legislature of 1862 scoffed at the argument. When he urged the lawmakers to help the infant wine industry, he probably did not suspect that they could do just as much to injure it. By taxing wine at the rate of five cents per gallon per year, Congress had imposed a heavy (some thought unbearable) burden on California's winegrowers.[13]

The impact of the tax could be understood when measured against the current market price of a gallon of wine, which was not much more than thirty cents, or a little more than six times the amount of the tax. When measured by the acreage required to produce a given quantity of wine, the tax assumed even more oppressive proportions. In California a vineyard in full bearing typically produced six hundred gallons of wine per acre—in some places as much as a thousand. If each of those gallons was charged with a tax of five cents, the total tax for the acre would range from thirty to fifty dollars, as much as (in some cases more than) the value of the land itself.[14] The wine producers were particularly vexed by the tax because no similar levy was laid on other agricultural products. Corn, wheat, barley, potatoes, apples, pears—the mainstays of American agriculture—were all exempt from taxation, while wine was singled out for an onerous burden.[15]

Congress did impose a tax of twenty cents per gallon on distilled liquors, which, of course, included brandy;[16] and this, too, was a heavy burden for winegrowers to bear, since winemakers typically transformed a substantial part of their annual wine production into brandy. Although modest tariffs were imposed on imported wines and liquors, California winegrowers thought the tariffs too puny to discourage the importation of wines into the United States.[17]

In accordance with a call published in the *Alta*, the state's winegrowers met on November 19 in the Union Hotel in San Francisco. Agoston presided over the meeting, with Hittell as secretary.[18] Nearly all the winegrowers who attended were from northern California, a fact that concerned some observers, for Los Angeles remained an important winegrowing area, and it was represented only by Charles Kohler, who, though he owned vineyards in Los Angeles, had his offices in San Francisco and hardly represented the typical southern California producer.

The upshot of the November meeting was a decision to call a convention of the state's winegrowers to assemble in San Francisco in the second week of December.[19] That convention, held at Minerva Hall on December 9–10, was presided over by Wilson Flint of Sacramento, with Hittell again serving as secretary. This time, Kohler came armed with the proxies of thirty winegrowers in the Los Angeles area; Agoston headed up the Sonoma delegation, the largest from any one county. After two days of spirited discussions, the delegates made two important decisions. First, they prepared a memorial addressed to Congress arguing that the tax on wine was "unjust, oppressive, and impolitic" and asking that it be reduced to a level proportionate to that paid by other manufactured products. Second, they adopted a constitution for the "California Wine-Growers' Association," pledged "to encourage grape and wine producing in the State, and to discourage and expose all attempts at the adulteration of California wines or brandies."[20]

Membership in the association was open to all grape and wine producers upon payment of dues in the amount of three dollars a year. The constitution made it clear, however, that any member who was found to have adulterated any wines or brandies would be subject to immediate expulsion. Meetings were to be held in San Francisco in June and December of each year. Wilson Flint was elected president; Hugo Schenk of Anaheim, George West of Stockton, and Louis Csomortanyi of Sonoma were the vice presidents. Agoston agreed to serve on two committees, one whose purpose was to seek out the cooperation of winegrowers in the Atlantic states and another to investigate the possibility of importing oak staves from the Atlantic states for use in California wine barrels.[21]

Agoston's leadership in the formation of the California Wine-Growers' Association, coupled with his presidency of the State Agricultural Society, not only gave him a high profile among the state's agriculturists in 1862 — it also made him an attractive target for criticism, on personal and even political grounds. Politics was, of course, the subject of heated opinions in that second year of the Civil War, and controversies within California's Democratic party, still sharply divided over the questions of secession and loyalty to the Union, were bitter and stormy. In the summer, the regular State Democratic Party (unofficially the Breckinridge faction) and the newly organized Union Democratic Party held separate conventions. Agoston, still loyal to the Breckinridge faction, attended their meeting in Sacramento. Not surprisingly, the war that raged in the East was a major subject of the convention debates. A number of resolutions were advanced that touched on the war and the best means of bringing it to a conclusion, all more or less agreeing that the Union's war on the South was unjust and that, however much the Union ought to be preserved, it could not be preserved by means of the sword.[22] Agoston was one of five vice presidents of the convention, and though he was not a leader in the debate over the war he was quite naturally associated with the resolutions that were passed. Within days after the convention adjourned, questions were asked about whether he was "loyal to the Union" and, if not, whether he was qualified to hold the office of president of the State Agricultural Society.

On August 15 the *California Farmer* published an open letter written by a longtime member of the Agricultural Society (who was also a member of the legislature) reviewing the financial support that the state provided to the society and expressing the view that all its officers "should be loyal men, friendly to the State and National Government." "Is the President of the State Agricultural Society sound on the Union question?" the writer asked. "Is he and the Board, each and all, with our Union, for the Union, and for sustaining the Federal Government, and of course our State, as a branch of the same, in her present effort to crush out treason, and save the Union?" The letter was signed, "A Union Man, and for many members of the S.A.S."[23] The *California Farmer*, normally supportive of Agoston in all agricultural matters, lost no time in publishing the provocative letter, along with a comment that it had heard the "same question" raised by other members of the Agricultural Society. "We hope for a speedy reply," the *Farmer* added.[24]

Realizing the seriousness of the challenge, Agoston lost no time in composing a long response to the question, which was published in the *Farmer* on August 29. "My rule has been to refrain from all newspaper controversies," he noted at the outset, "but [in] this instance I will make an exception, and as information is desired, I will reply for the promotion of the interest of the State Agricultural Society, of which I have the honor to be President."

To the question of whether he was "sound on the Union question," Agoston wrote:

If the interrogator considers as a Union man, one who wishes, and desires the whole Union, and nothing less than the Union, then I am sound on the Union question. I ardently long to see all the States united. If a citizen who pays his taxes—Federal and State—and is ready and willing to vote for more money to sustain the Federal Government in terminating this war *honorably*, according to, and in the spirit of the Constitution, then I am sound on the Union question, as I am disposed to do all this. If disapproving rebellion in our once (and I hope again) glorious Republic, signifies to be sound on the Union question, then I am *sound*, as I disapprove of Rebellion as well as I do of Abolitionism.

Mr. "Union Man," so much am I for the Union, and nothing but the Union, and Constitution of old, that should it now fail, with a broken heart I would leave California and emigrate to some remote portion of the American continent—as neither part of the Republic, North or South, would in my humble judgment be safe for property or enterprise.

I approve and admire President Lincoln's honest endeavors to prevent Abolitionists from forever severing North and South; and if endorsement of the President's conservative measures constitute supporting the Government, then I do uphold it.

But if, in the opinion of the questioner, the man sound on the Union question must be an Abolitionist, a Republican or a fanatic; if a man must have no opinion with regard to the carrying on of the war, expending the money; must not disapprove of the acts of some of the officers, and Republican party, both in this State and in Washington; if to be a Union man it is necessary to underrate the enemy's ability to fight; if I must speak—howl—roar—that the Rebels have no arms, no ammunition, no clothing; that they are a parcel of unorganized vagabonds, and all that is wanted is to make a rush at them with a will and they will be overrun, crushed, dispersed, or strung up at pleasure; if, as I said before, all this is necessary to be a Union man, then I am no Union man; for I have always heard that the rule universally adopted by the greatest military heroes, both of past ages and the present century, was and is: "Never to underrate your foe."

I disapprove of some movements, some orders, proclamations, laws passed by Congress; not on account of the enemy, but from my very love of the Republic, for in my humble judgment, I think those laws, etc., etc., will injure Union men as well as Rebels in the rebellious States. If the above opinion of mine constitutes an anti-Union man, then the ultras will consider me as such. I claim the right to express my opinion concerning public measures—public men. This privilege the Constitution and the laws of the country give me; this right I must and will have; I am entitled to it as one of the tax-payers—one who labors for the prosperity of the State with the little energy and ability with which nature endowed me. It has been my endeavor to improve the land and country; to impart to others the knowledge which they did not possess; to write and labor for the common benefit. All this I have done, and still will do cheerfully, without asking persons what is their politics or creed.

He pointed out that, in his position as president of the State Agricultural Society, he had "nothing to do with parties or factions." When called on to appoint persons to responsible offices, he had always made his choices on the basis of merit and not on political opinions or affiliations. He had, for example, chosen a prominent Republican to be the grand marshal of the State Fair, and another Republican to deliver the annual address. He assumed that questions about his loyalty had been prompted by his participation in the Breckinridge convention. About that he was prepared to offer an explanation, and a statement of his political creed:

If it be a crime to have accepted the position of delegate from my county, then I confess I have sinned; though I assure my interrogator that I meant well. I went there with the vain hope to do good, and go hand-in-hand with the conservative men; but to my sorrow I find that the majority are as ultra and hot-headed as are the Abolitionists on the other side.

I am a Democrat in the strictest sense of the word. Not one, however, who goes for men and measures, but who cherishes naught but genuine Jeffersonian principles. They are broad enough for the whole human family, and when the leaders of those principles, for selfish motives, deviate from those divine doctrines, through which true Democracy gives security to life and property, which holds the old time-honored Constitution sacred, then

I will stand aside. Never shall I be guilty of helping to destroy the glorious Temple of Liberty erected with suffering, soil and blood, by the immortal Washington, supported by Jefferson and other noble patriots.

Agoston closed his letter with a challenge: "Now, 'Mr. Union Man and many others of the State Agricultural Society,' you wished a full, clear statement of my sentiments. I have given them as well as I could. Whether that statement is satisfactory, you have to judge."[25]

Many members of the society were placated by Agoston's letter. Others—both those who believed fervently in the cause of the Confederacy and those who considered the slightest criticism of the Union's war measures treasonable—were not. The heavy current of suspicion and innuendos must have gnawed at him, however defiantly he denied it, and they were also troubling to his family. Twenty-eight-year-old Gaza, who had fought bravely with the United States dragoons in the Southwest, surely felt the sting of the gossip that his father was not loyal to the Union.

Years later, Arpad Haraszthy told an interesting story of his older brother's efforts to obtain a commission in the Union Army through the influence of Senator Latham. According to Arpad, Gaza wrote to Latham not long after the outbreak of the war, detailing his four years of honorable military service in the dragoons and asking for his help in obtaining a commission. When Latham took no action, Agoston put in a good word for his son, but still the senator turned a deaf ear—this despite the fact that Agoston had been an enthusiastic supporter in Latham's last statewide election campaign. The senator's indifference rankled the young Haraszthy, and when, on one of his visits back to California in early 1863, Latham stopped at Buena Vista to visit with Agoston, Gaza pointedly asked the senator if he had "my commission." When Latham answered with apologies and excuses, Gaza answered: "Everybody is getting a commission and I have served my country. Now, since you cannot procure me a commission, I shall go and get one without you."[26]

Whether events transpired in just the way Arpad remembered is open to question. Surely not "everybody" was getting a commission in 1861 and 1862, and it may even be questioned whether Gaza was quite so zealous a champion of the Union in the early years of the war as his brother later asserted he was. His father, after all, had doubts about the way the war was being prosecuted, and neither Agoston nor Arpad shared the Abolitionists' goal of bringing about an immediate end to slavery. But there is no reason to doubt that Gaza was a brave young man, or that he sincerely believed in the cause of the Union, at least by the spring of 1863. For the records are clear that, in April of that year, he sold his vineyard in Sonoma to his brother Attila,[27] and, with the proceeds, made preparations to go east and join the Union army.

He went to New York, probably in late June, where he thought the prospects for mustering a company of men were most propitious. There he enlisted in the 18th Regiment of the New York Cavalry, with a commission as captain. By the beginning of July, he had succeeded in organizing and outfitting a company, which was denominated Company B. When mobs armed with pitchforks took to the streets of New York to protest the federal government's National Conscription Act, Gaza's company helped restore order to the city, and in September the company joined the New York State Rendezvous on Staten Island. From Staten Island, they went south to Washington, D.C., where they participated in scouting missions along the Potomac; and in February 1864 they were sent by ocean steamer to New Orleans, which was then occupied by Union troops.[28] Agoston followed the news of his son's progress from New York to the South's biggest city with concern. Whatever his critics might say about his own positions on the war and the Confederacy, Gaza was certainly no secessionist.

Eleonora, accompanied by Arpad, had returned to Sonoma in the fall of 1862, Arpad having at long last completed his training in Épernay. Ida remained in Paris, pursuing her French studies and enjoying the cultural atmosphere of the sophisticated metropolis.

Arpad was eager to put some of his knowledge of winemaking to work at Buena Vista. He made several lots of wine, using grapes harvested from his father's vineyards. Years later he was to recall that among the wines he made in 1862 were two "claret casks" of Zinfandel.[29] He also began to make champagne. The making of champagne is an exacting process that requires both skill and patience, beginning with a carefully blended cuvée (or batch) of still wine. In the fall of 1862 Arpad blended a cuvée of white wines from the Buena Vista vintage of 1861, and with it began the long process of transforming it into "Sparkling Buena Vista Champagne."

Visitors were coming up to Sonoma more and more frequently now, for the steamship that Agoston proposed in the spring of 1861 was running on a regular basis from San Francisco to the Sonoma embarcadero. Although not enough money had been raised by subscriptions among the residents of Sonoma Valley to build a new ship, it was enough to lease a boat and dedicate it to the San Francisco–Sonoma run. The ship was christened the *Princess*, and the company organized to operate it was called the Sonoma Steam Navigation Company. Agoston was both an incorporator of the company and a joint guarantor with Granville P. Swift of the lease. The trip from San Francisco to Sonoma took about three hours, pleasantly short for travelers used to the old route through Petaluma and Lakeville. As the *Princess* made its way up the Sonoma Creek to the landing, stagecoaches waited to whisk passengers up to the plaza. From the plaza, it was a short carriage ride to Buena Vista.[30]

Agoston had embarked on an ambitious program to expand and improve his winemaking plant, and visitors to Buena Vista in the summer and fall of 1862 found construction workers busy at the entrances to the two hillside tunnels. He had begun to dig a third tunnel into the hillside sometime before he left for Europe and determined now to complete it.[31] The third tunnel, just west of the first two, was initially sixteen feet wide and seven and a half feet high. It was designed to run into the mountain to a depth of four hundred feet, but Agoston stopped work on it when it reached 140 to 150 feet. Even so, it was an impressive cellar, longer and deeper than anything seen in California up to that time.[32]

With three tunnels now standing side by side, Agoston decided to replace the old press house he built in 1858 with a new structure.[33] The rock that was taken from the tunnel was a good-quality limestone, and he decided to use it in the new project.[34] Plans for the new building called for a two-story structure measuring 54 by 64 feet.[35] The main entrance, which was formed by an arch and two heavy doors, faced north toward the Arroyo Seco. The south wall, which adjoined the hillside, was pierced by three arches that marked the entrances to the three hillside tunnels. The second story was supported by heavy redwood timbers; the roof was covered with wooden shingles. The walls were of solid stone and varied from a foot and a half to more than two feet thick. Although they were stouter than strictly required for a building of this size, they would help to ensure a constant temperature inside the building and further insulate the adjoining tunnels from the extremes of heat and cold outside.

Large doors opened at either end of the second floor onto a narrow road that had been cut into the hillside above the tunnels. The road made it possible for wagons to come in from the vineyards and discharge grapes onto tables set up on the upper floor. From the tables, the grapes were loaded into a crusher equipped with rollers.[36] After the fruit was crushed, the must was collected in tubs and then emptied through trapdoors in the floor into vats that waited below. The press house thus operated on the principle of gravity flow, permitting the wine to move from one part of the building to another without any pumping. The vats that stood on the first floor were built of redwood. They were the first redwood vats in the Sonoma Valley, possibly the first in California. They were used to store white must before pressing, and to ferment both white and red must. These vats, like Agoston's redwood barrels, were thoroughly steamed before use in order to remove the unpalatable resins from the wood.[37]

The new press house was equipped with the most modern winemaking equipment available. The crusher was powered by a steam engine capable of crushing 50,000 pounds of grapes a day. The wine press, situated on the first floor opposite the fermenting vats, was a large, wooden structure, measuring eleven feet by ten feet on the floor. It was equipped with an iron screw four inches in diameter and two eleven-foot levers. Fully tightened, the screw and levers were capable of applying a pressure of 200,000 pounds.[38]

When a reporter for the *California Wine, Wool, and Stock Journal* visited the press house early in 1863, he found all the machinery in good working order, and the three cellars well stocked with wines, champagne, and brandy. Greeted by Agoston, the reporter inspected the crusher, fermenting vats, and wine press. He found that redwood casks were being used for aging wines, as well as for fermenting. He and Agoston entered the hillside tunnels by the light of handheld candles. The reporter noted that the main tunnel was thirteen feet wide, eight feet high, and seven feet long; it had originally been forty feet long, he explained, but when the workmen were boring the shaft they struck a spring and were forced to wall it up. In this cellar, Agoston had stowed his old wines and brandies. The reporter found the white wine of 1857 "a splendid wine, somewhat resembling a three year old Chablis Wine." The white wine of 1860 had a "fine bouquet" and was considered the best in the cellars. There was also some five-year-old brandy in the main cellar; it had "an excellent Cognac odor and a beautiful bouquet like a basket of fruit." [39]

To the left of the main tunnel was another cellar twenty-five feet wide and thirty-five feet long, which Agoston had filled with bottled wine. On the right was the third and newest tunnel, which the reporter for the *Wine, Wool, and Stock Journal* found to be "a model, owing to its temperature and dryness over head and under feet. The floor was dry and hard, while the temperature, I am told, is constantly between 56½ and 58½ Fahrenheit at all seasons of the year: such a temperature, and so constant, is the real making of the wine." This third tunnel was filled with casks containing Agoston's latest vintage, of 1862. "We tasted the White and Red Wines of 1862," the reporter wrote, "—the White possessing a trifle Sautern[e] bouquet—also some California brandies. Other samples of White and Red Wines of 1862, which require only age to give them the proper degree of perfection." [40]

All the Haraszthy boys (with the exception of the absent soldier Gaza) were busily employed at Buena Vista now. Arpad proudly wore his new title of cellar master, while Attila held forth as foreman of the vineyards. Even Bela, now sixteen years old, found work to keep him busy in the vineyards and the cellars.

But Arpad and Attila were not so busy that they could not find time to make frequent visits to nearby Lachryma Montis. Attila had, for a long time now, been fascinated by General Vallejo's daughter Natalia. Now twenty-five years of age, Natalia was skilled in all the domestic arts—sewing and drawing and poetry—and she also played the piano well. Before Attila began to pay attention to her, she had been the object of the affections of some prominent men in the

Sonoma Valley, among them State Senator Martin E. Cooke and the wealthy frontiersman, Granville P. Swift. In 1861, she had received a formal invitation to attend President Abraham Lincoln's inaugural ball in Washington, and had happily accepted. According to family tradition, while at the ball she actually shared a dance with the one-time rail-splitter from Illinois (Natalia and Lincoln shared the same birthday, February 12). When, back in California, General Vallejo suggested that Granville Swift might make a suitable husband for her, Natalia wrote her father quite defiantly, pointing out that, though Swift was both rich and handsome, he was hopelessly "awkward," and "so speechless as not to let a single word escape from his lips while he calls on the young ladies." "No, Papa," Natalia insisted, "I am General Vallejo's daughter and I think I will have a better choice than that."[41]

The "better choice" that Natalia Vallejo had in mind was none other than the vineyard foreman at Buena Vista, the twenty-eight-year-old Attila Haraszthy. Natalia had a younger sister named Jovita, who was smitten with the cellar master at Buena Vista, Attila's twenty-two-year-old brother Arpad. And so plans were made in the spring of 1863 for a double wedding of the two Vallejo girls and the two Haraszthy boys, to take place at Lachryma Montis. There was no resident priest in Sonoma at the time, so the Belgian "padre on horseback" Father Peter Deyaert rode his horse over hills from Napa to hear the wedding vows, which were given on June 1 in the parlor at Lachryma Montis.[42] A reception followed in the same house. After the wedding Attila and Natalia took up residence in a little house on Attila's vineyard property near Buena Vista, a house that Natalia christened "Champagne." Arpad and Jovita set up housekeeping in a "shanty" that Arpad built in a ravine above Buena Vista.[43]

Both Agoston and General Vallejo must have been pleased by the Vallejo-Haraszthy nuptials, which united two of Sonoma Valley's most prominent families and did much to ensure that the tradition of fine winemaking both men had done so much to establish and perpetuate would be kept alive in the Sonoma Valley. But then, as he looked around the Sonoma Valley in the spring of 1863, Agoston must have been pleased by almost everything he saw. At Buena Vista, there were nearly two hundred fifty acres of vineyards. Beyond Buena Vista, green rows of vines spread out in every direction—more than two thousand acres of them.[44] The list of the men who were cultivating vineyards near his own had now grown to more than fifty, and included such names as Louis Adler, A. J. Butler, Nicholas Carriger, O. W. Craig, Louis Csomortanyi, Emil Dresel, Jacob Gundlach, Attila Haraszthy, William Hayes, William McPherson Hill, William Hood, Charles Justi, Alfred Lamotte, Charles Lutgens, Agoston Molitor, William O'Brien, Mortimer Ryan, Franklin Sears, William Shaw, Jacob R. Snyder, C. V. Stuart, John Swett, William Thompson, Louis Tichener, M. G. Vallejo, J. B. Warfield, George Watriss, C. H. S. Williams, Murray Whallon, and George L. Wratten.[45]

Charles Krug was not one of Agoston's Sonoma neighbors in 1863. His old friend from Crystal Springs days had sold the Sonoma vineyard he purchased from Agoston and moved in the fall of 1860 to the northern reaches of the Napa Valley, near the newly founded town of St. Helena.[46] There he planted vines on property owned by a young woman named Caroline Bale. Miss Bale, who was a grand-niece of General Vallejo and one of the heirs to a large Mexican land grant, became Mrs. Charles Krug in 1860;[47] but, the year before, Krug had made wine for some of Miss Bale's Napa Valley neighbors. There were a handful of small vineyards in the Napa Valley when Charles Krug came there—probably not more than a dozen in all— and most had been planted for table grapes rather than for wine.[48] Krug, however, was determined to make his mark on the valley as a winemaker. Since there was no wine press in the valley when he first arrived (Napa Valley wine was still made in the old Mexican way by trampling the grapes by foot and fermenting the must in rawhide bags), he borrowed Agoston's old cider press from Buena Vista; and, with it, made the first important lot of commercial wine produced in the Napa Valley.[49]

Agoston could take pride in the knowledge that he had helped many of his neighbors start their winemaking businesses; that he had planted—or helped to plant—many of the vineyards in and around Sonoma; and that, of those he did not have an actual hand in planting, nearly all had been inspired by his example and by his almost constant exhortations to other planters.[50] His stone press house, and the three long tunnels that he dug into the limestone hill back of the press house—tunnels that were to inspire similar tunnels in both

Sonoma and Napa—were well stocked with wine now: white wine and red wine, sweet wine and dry wine, still wine and sparkling wine, all carefully stowed in casks and barrels and pipes that lined the dark recesses of the tunnels.

But there were still problems that remained to be solved. He had borrowed heavily to make Buena Vista the grandest wine estate in California, and it was not easy for him to meet his payments in a timely way. After he returned from Europe, he had taken out three large mortgages that had to be paid within five years.[51] But the debts and the mortgages did not really worry him; for he had a plan to deal with them and, in the process, make Buena Vista into an institution that would dazzle his neighbors and attract the attention of wine lovers all over the world.

25

The Largest Vineyard in the World

When Agoston was in Paris in 1861, his Hungarian compatriot Bertalan Szemere had dismissed his efforts to find French investors for his California projects as a "fairy tale."[1] But there were apparently some European investors who were willing to listen to "fairy tales" told by a Hungarian from California. In May 1862, about six months after he returned to Buena Vista, Agoston obtained a loan of 4,700 pounds sterling from a man named Charles G. Zaehnsdorf, who resided in the Paris suburb of St.-Cloud. This loan (roughly equivalent to $23,000) enabled him to pay off the expenses he had incurred in gathering his European vines and left some capital for improving Buena Vista (the new stone press house that he put up in 1862 was almost certainly financed with the money provided by Zaehnsdorf). But the French investor demanded stiff terms: a mortgage on the Buena Vista property that called for repayment of the entire principal sum in five years, plus interest at the rate of 12 percent per year. Although interest payments were to be made to Zaehnsdorf's bankers in San Francisco, they were to be made in British pounds, with Agoston absorbing any premiums on the currency exchange.[2]

Whether Agoston made his first contacts with Zaehnsdorf while he was in Paris, or was introduced to him afterward through some of the French businessmen who had settled in San Francisco, is not known. It is known, however, that in the spring of 1863 he made further arrangements with French investors in San Francisco to transfer ownership of the Buena Vista property to a newly formed corporation in which he and a half-dozen prominent French Californians would be the principal shareholders.

Since the state government was organized in 1849, California's lawmakers had evidenced a deep distrust of corporations. The state constitution had forbidden the legislature to charter banking corporations, and the first state laws had severely limited the use of corporations in business enterprises.[3] It was not until 1858 that California law authorized the formation of corporations for agricultural purposes, and even then the law limited the land that an agricultural corporation could own to 1,440 acres.[4] In 1863 Agoston's Buena Vista property extended to approximately 6,000 acres, and it could not be transferred to a corporation unless the law was changed. But the legislature, which had proved so uncooperative with Agoston's plans in 1862, proved to be much more tractable in 1863 and readily passed a special law authorizing the new corporation to "own, possess, occupy, and cultivate any number of acres of land, not exceeding, in the aggregate, six thousand." The provision was approved by Governor Stanford and became law on April 17, 1863.[5]

According to the Haraszthy Legend, the Buena Vista Vinicultural Society (BVVS) was formed with money supplied by William Chapman Ralston, the powerful banker and entrepreneur who was responsible for much of the commercial development of San Francisco in the first two decades after the Gold Rush.[6] The Ohio-born Ralston was a controversial character in his own right, alternately praised as "The Man Who Built San Francisco" and reviled as the leader of a "ring" of unprincipled money men who plundered the Comstock Lode in Nevada to create scandalously profitable business enterprises in California. Ralston's two most enduring monuments were the Bank of California, which he organized in 1864, and the fabulous Palace Hotel (once the largest hotel in the United States, if not the world), which he built in San Francisco in 1875.

Although Ralston became an investor in the BVVS after 1865, there is no good evidence that he was one of its original promoters.

The articles of incorporation were drafted by Agoston's own attorneys, Stanly and Hayes of San Francisco, and signed on March 27, 1863, by Agoston, Eugene Cazalis, B. Eugene Auger, Herman Michels, Adolphus Wapler, Isidor Landsberger, J. Ernest René, Gustave Dussol, and Louis G. Bruguiere.[7] Of these men, only Michels was associated with other Ralston enterprises (he was a director of the Bank of California in 1864–65); Cazalis, Auger, Wapler, René, Dussol, and Bruguiere were prominent members of the French business community in San Francisco.

The extent to which the BVVS was, at its outset, a French enterprise is evidenced by two interesting publications issued upon incorporation of the society in 1863. One is an English-language pamphlet entitled *By-Laws and Prospectus of the Buena Vista Vinicultural Society: Incorporated March 27th, 1863*, the other a French-language pamphlet entitled *Buena Vista Vinicultural Society, Prospectus: Incorporée le 27 Mars 1863*. Both list the names of the first officers and directors of the society and include a statement of the society's aims, assets, and prospects for business success. Since no records of the first stockholders of the Buena Vista Vinicultural Society have been discovered, it cannot be determined who supplied the original capital, or in what amounts. It is possible, of course, that Michels may have been acting in Ralston's behalf when he signed the articles of incorporation. Perhaps Ralston had agreed to invest some money in the enterprise but chose not to lend it his name (although he would later have no hesitancy in publicizing his connection with Buena Vista). It is more likely, however, that the Frenchmen who signed the articles of incorporation were the source of the first funds, and that those funds were either their own money or came from other French investors for whom they were acting as agents.

Though most of the incorporators of the BVVS were French, the society owed much of its inspiration to the German champagne company whose cellars Agoston had visited at Hochheim in 1861. He had been impressed by this large establishment, presided over by Herman Dresel, and by its extensive complement of modern wine- and champagne-making equipment. When in Hochheim, he asked Dresel's superintendent if he might come to California and help him create "a similar establishment."[8] There is no record that the superintendent ever accepted Agoston's invitation, but it is clear that the society that Agoston organized in the spring of 1863 was modeled on the Hochheim firm and that, in fitting up his new press house and distillery, he was trying, with the resources then available to him, to fashion a comparable California operation.

The BVVS was incorporated with a capital stock of $600,000, which was divided into 6,000 shares of $100 each. In return for his transfer to the corporation of the Buena Vista estate, its buildings, equipment, and inventory, Agoston received 2,600 shares of the stock, or 43.33 percent of the total. Michels was president, Cazalis vice president, and Auger treasurer. The secretary was Bernhard Gattel, agent for the Germania Life Insurance Co. in San Francisco. Agoston occupied the position of superintendent. The administrative officers of the corporation acted on instructions from a board of nine trustees that, besides Agoston, Michels, Cazalis, and Auger, included Wapler, Landsberger, René, Dussol, and Bruguiere.[9] As superintendent at Buena Vista, Agoston had responsibility for the actual management of the society's property, including planting and cultivating the vineyards, harvesting the grapes, and producing the wine and brandy. Michels, Cazalis, Auger, and Gattel operated out of the society's San Francisco offices.

On April 23, 1863, Agoston and Eleonora executed a long deed conveying approximately 6,000 acres at Buena Vista to the new corporation.[10] The conveyance was subject to three mortgages: the first for £4,700 that Agoston gave Zaehnsdorf in May 1862; the second for 2,086 1/10 ounces of gold given to William Blanding of San Francisco just two weeks before the BVVS was formed; and the third another mortgage for £5,300 given to Zaehnsdorf on April 20, 1863.[11] Taken together, the three obligations totaled just over $93,000.

It is interesting that both Zaehnsdorf and Blanding were willing to advance such large sums of money on the strength of the Buena Vista property. Blanding had been the United States District Attorney in San Francisco when Agoston was indicted for embezzling gold from the mint, and he had prepared the deed of trust under which Agoston transferred property in San Francisco and San Mateo counties to Major Snyder as trustee for the government. It is remarkable that a man who once sought to put Agoston behind bars should, only a few years later, invest a very substantial sum of money in his business. Blanding was now engaged in the private practice of law in San Francisco and, at the same time, tending to a large portfolio of investments. If he had genuinely believed that Agoston was an embezzler, as he argued in 1857, it is unlikely that he would have been willing to lend him so much money in 1863.

The prospectus issued by the BVVS described the Buena Vista property and its facilities in expectedly rosy terms. "The richness and variety of the soil of this property," the prospectus said, "admits of the cultivation of every kind of grape grown for the manufacture of red and white wines and brandy; while the mild and equable climate, marked by a total absence of frost and hail, those scourges of European wine-producers, gives an entire certainty of full yearly crops." There were 10,000 fruit trees and 187,000 vines on the property, "most of them foreign vines lately imported at a heavy expense." [12]

The incorporation of the Buena Vista Vinicultural Society in 1863 was an event of some historical importance. It was, so far as has been determined, the first incorporation of a producing vineyard ever accomplished in California. It was easily the largest agricultural enterprise yet undertaken by any corporation in the state, and possibly in the nation. And it marked an important experiment in co-ownership of a wine-producing estate. The Los Angeles Vineyard Society at Anaheim had been a cooperative enterprise, with each grower owning his own plot of vines but agreeing to share common facilities. Buena Vista, in contrast, was a full-blown, modern corporation, in which no individual held title to any part of the property, but all the land, improvements, equipment, and goodwill were owned by the corporate shareholders and held under the management of a board of trustees.

It was a risky venture, too. For Agoston, it marked the end of his sole proprietorship of the Buena Vista estate and an agreement to manage the property and the corporation's business under the scrutiny of outside investors. For the investors, it represented a very substantial allocation of capital in the hope that a large wine-making venture could prove to be, not only profitable, but as profitable as competing investments. If a gold mine in the Sierra Nevada, or a silver lode in the Nevada desert, could produce a given return on a dollar of investment, the incorporators of the BVVS had every reason to expect that vineyards and wine cellars in the Sonoma Valley would produce an equal, or even greater, return.

Of course, Agoston's motive in incorporating Buena Vista was to gain the support of new investors. He had always preferred to enlist investors for his business ventures, and the nearly seven years during which he operated Buena Vista as an individual represented an anomaly in his business career. On his own, he had built Buena Vista into the largest wine-producing property in California. But it had become too big for one man. With the new corporation he returned to his old pattern of working with others in business, although on a more ambitious scale than ever before.

Although the articles of incorporation authorized 6,000 shares, only 5,689 shares were actually issued. Of that number, Agoston received 2,600; 1,175 were sold at the par value of $80, producing $104,575 in cash; an additional 914 were sold on installment terms, and 1,000 shares were issued to designated agents in New York and Paris, to be sold by them for the society's benefit.

The capital raised through the sale of stock enabled Agoston to embark on an ambitious plan for improving and expanding the vineyards and winemaking plant at Buena Vista. In the spring of 1864, he was able to enlarge the vineyards by something over one hundred acres, at least eighty-five of which were planted to new varieties of European grapes.[13] He built a new stable, with room for fifty horses; put a new roof on the main house (which still served as both family residence and ranch headquarters); made an addition to the granary; built a short railway to haul grapes from the vineyards up to the second floor of the press house; and laid down nearly three-quarters of a mile of three-inch pipe to bring water to the cellars, distillery, stables, and other buildings. In the press house, he improved the steam engine with the addition of pulleys, and added pumps that facilitated the rapid transfer of wine from one cellar to another. Nineteen new tanks, with a capacity of four thousand gallons each, were built and set up, and two others were planned; and a new distilling apparatus was erected, with a capacity of distilling from five hundred to a thousand gallons of wine every twenty-four hours.[14]

The most noteworthy building projects undertaken in the society's first year were the addition of a large machine shop at one end of the press house, the excavation of three new hillside tunnels a short distance east of the machine shop, and the commencement of a new stone building immediately in front of the new tunnels. Each of the new tunnels was designed to be sixteen and a half feet wide, twelve and a half feet high, and 170 feet deep. The new stone building, which measured 90 by 48 feet on the ground, was to be used for making champagne and fermenting wines. Although the new structure (informally called the "champagne house") was designed eventually to rise three stories above the ground, it reached a height of only one story in the first year.[15]

Even before the new champagne house was finished, Agoston made a serious commitment to the production of champagne at Buena Vista. When Arpad returned from Paris in 1862, he almost immediately began to blend a cuvée of white wine suitable for the first run of sparkling wine. The wine was made from Mission grapes, not because they were the most suitable for sparkling wine but because they were still the most abundant grapes in Sonoma. The champagne produced at the end of 1862 consisted of what Arpad called "a few experimental dozens, perhaps a hundred bottles." He remembered years later that these first bottles "gave a very satisfactory result," and that a second trial run was also successful. Thereupon Agoston decided to proceed with champagne manufacture "on a large scale."[16]

The first cuvées of 1863 included nine or ten thousand bottles. This lot was probably bottled, corked, and racked early in the year, for Arpad later recalled that it was cold in Sonoma when he put the bottles up and that, for three months, he took his blankets and slept in the fermenting room, stoking fires during the night to keep up the temperature. But, for all his efforts, the wine was a failure. The bottles did not sparkle, and when the wire closures were removed, the corks refused to pop. It was only with great effort, and with the use of dozens of corkscrews, that they were able to extract all the wine from the bottles. Some of the wine was converted into vinegar; the rest was taken to the distillery and transformed into brandy.[17] Obviously embarrassed, Agoston reimbursed the BVVS to the tune of between five and six thousand dollars for his abortive attempt to enter the California champagne market.[18] It was a bitter, and very costly, pill.

Arpad renewed his experiments, and soon announced that he had "discovered the faults of the previous bottling." Agoston had invested years of money and emotional energy in his son's European training and was willing to give him another chance to succeed. But the directors of the BVVS were not so forgiving. They thought a more experienced champagne producer should be brought in and asked Arpad to tender his resignation. They then called on Pierre Debanne, the Frenchman who produced the Sainsevain Brothers' Los Angeles champagne back in 1857, to come up to Sonoma and take charge of the champagne works.

As Debanne took up his new duties at Buena Vista, Arpad retired to his "shanty" in the hills. He continued to write articles on wine for agricultural journals published in San Francisco and, in 1864, formed a partnership with an Italian-Swiss named Pietro Giovanari to make wine for various Sonoma Valley grape growers. Giovanari had gained valuable experience as superintendent of General Vallejo's vineyards and was only too glad to join forces with Vallejo's talented young son-in-law.

In the spring of 1864, Arpad also presented Agoston and Eleonora with a new addition to the Haraszthy family, their first grandchild. Named Agostine Benicia (for her paternal grandfather and her maternal grandmother, Francisca Benicia Vallejo), the baby girl was born to Arpad's wife, Jovita, on April 11, 1864.[19] Four months later, on August 2, 1864, Attila's wife, Natalia, gave birth to her first child, a son named (for his father and paternal grandfather) Attila de Agosto. But the happiness that Agoston felt on the birth of his first grandson soon gave way to grief, for little Attila de Agosto quickly died.[20]

Gaza, meanwhile, was having quite different experiences in war-torn Louisiana. After his New York company arrived in New Orleans in February 1864, it joined a large Union force in an advance on the Confederate stronghold at Shreveport. On March 7 the unit left New Orleans under the command of Major General Nathaniel Banks and moved west toward the swampy shore of the Gulf of Mexico. At the town of Franklin, they were assigned to the Fifth Cavalry Brigade, then ordered to proceed north toward the Mississippi. They marched through the towns of Alexandria and Natchitoches without incident, but at Campti on April 4 engaged in what they later called a "skirmish" with Confederate troops, in the course of which six of their horses were killed and twelve men were wounded. From Campti, they marched through Pleasant Hill and Grand Ecore to Alexandria, where they arrived on April 25. By this time they were deep in Confederate territory and meeting almost daily opposition. They participated in several small battles before finding themselves on May 17 at a place called Yellow Bayou, where, in the course of a two-day encounter, Gaza's Company B was captured by Confederate troops under the command of Major General John Bankhead Magruder and taken away to prison in Tyler, Texas.[21]

The news of Gaza's capture did not reach California until almost two months later. Animosities engendered by the war were still running high when the Sacramento *Star* published the news, together with a charge that Gaza was a "Copperhead" and that he had probably cooperated in his capture. Agoston was outraged by the *Star*'s suggestion and asked the *Alta* to publish a correct version of Gaza's capture. The *Alta* condemned the *Star*'s report and recalled that Gaza had gone east for the express purpose of raising a company of loyal soldiers, all at his own expense. He had served bravely during the New York City draft riots and had led his company in some fierce fighting in Louisiana. The *Alta* noted that Colonel Byrne of the Eighteenth Cavalry New York Volunteers (Gaza's regiment) had sent Agoston a letter announcing Gaza's capture and speaking of him in high terms.[22]

While his brother languished in a Texas prison, Arpad was working hard in his new wine business with Giovanari. In October 1864, the firm of Haraszthy and Giovanari exhibited twelve bottles of wine and three bottles of brandy at the Napa County Fair;[23] and, in the same month, they entered the largest single exhibit of wines at the annual Mechanics Institute Fair in San Francisco.[24] The following year, they advertised in the San Francisco newspapers that they had produced and were selling both red and white wine produced in Sonoma.[25] Their "Sonoma Burgundy" was, according to one of their advertisements, a superior red wine made from "General Vallejo's celebrated vineyards" in Sonoma.[26]

With Arpad now on his own and Gaza still in Confederate hands, Agoston came to rely more and more on the help of Attila and Bela in his management of the Buena Vista property. Attila was still the manager of the vineyards and overseer of the Chinese laborers who worked so tirelessly all over the sprawling estate, while Bela was busy in the press house and the new champagne cellars.

At the close of BVVS's first year of operation, the corporation's officers prepared formal reports for the shareholders. President Michels's report revealed that income for the year had been less than predicted at the time of incorporation. He thought this was due in large part to the drought that had afflicted California in 1863 and reduced the yield of the vineyards. But the drought had also raised the prices of wine and lowered the costs of the society's operations, so the balance sheet had not suffered unduly. "We consider our society no longer an experiment," Michels stated, "but an established and successful fact."[27] In his report, Agoston reviewed the planting activities of the year, paying special attention to the costs of labor (all performed by Chinese), and he described the physical improvements that he had made to the Buena Vista estate during the year, including the new equipment added in the press house and the champagne house that was under construction. "The expenses of the coming year for permanent improvements will be very little," he said, "and we shall have a very large margin in our favor in that item, as compared with the estimate of the prospectus for 1864."[28]

The reports of Michels and Agoston were submitted to the shareholders at the first annual meeting of the society, which was held in San Francisco on June 25, 1864. Pursuant to the by-laws, new officers and trustees were elected at that meeting. The results of the balloting hint at some changes in the shareholders' list. President Michels, vice president Cazalis, and trustees Dussol and Bruguiere were all out, replaced by Charles Baum as president, W. M. Rockwell as vice president, and W. R. Garrison and C. F. Mebius as trustees. Auger, however, was reelected treasurer, and Landsberger and Wapler retained their seats on the board.[29]

If William Chapman Ralston had begun to assert control over Buena Vista by the summer of 1864, the results of the 1864 election provide no evidence of the fact. Of the four new men who joined the list of officers and trustees at the first annual meeting, only one was prominently identified with Ralston's enterprises. That was William R. Garrison, son of the wealthy banker, steamship operator, and railroad magnate, "Commodore" Cornelius K. Garrison. The elder Garrison had come to San Francisco in 1853 to partake of its lucrative business opportunities, and had promptly been elected mayor; but in 1859 he had returned to his home state of New York, leaving his son in charge of his business interests in California, some of which were joint enterprises with Ralston. William R. Garrison may have represented Ralston on the board of the BVVS; but it is more likely that he represented his father, whose investment appetites were as varied as they were voracious.

Agoston had good reason to be satisfied with his first year as superintendent of the Buena Vista Vinicultural Society. The vineyards were fast approaching four hundred acres—a truly vast extent for any California plantation. He had refined and expanded the winemaking facilities, and the wines of the estate were beginning to build a national reputation, with sales representatives in New York as well as in San Francisco. Ida had recently returned from Paris to join the family. Gaza, though a Confederate prisoner, was presumably safe and would be released as soon as the Confederates bowed to the inevitable and laid down their arms.

Agoston had traveled east early in 1864—before Gaza embarked on his ill-fated Louisiana campaign, but probably chiefly for business purposes. Besides meeting the New York financiers who had invested in the BVVS, he undoubtedly planned to initiate contacts with agriculturists and journalists who might help him publicize the society. He was in New York by February 16, where he made an unannounced appearance before the Farmers' Club of the American Institute of the City of New York. A member of the Institute spotted him sitting in the audience at one of the club's formal sessions, recognized him as "the well-known vine-grower and wine-manufacturer" from California, and suggested that the chairman invite him to the rostrum. For an hour, the Hungarian from California entertained questions from the club members, touching on virtually every subject that might be of interest to aspiring winegrowers: the best modes of selecting and cultivating wines; the use of fertilizers in the vineyard; his successful efforts to grow vines without irrigation; the press house and winemaking machinery he had erected at Buena Vista. He discussed his latest ideas on vine-spacing and, responding to a question about "the best grapes for wine," stated quite sensibly that "it depends upon the kind of wine that you want to make." He noted that the "Épernay" (probably the Chardonnay) was good for champagne, while the Riesling should be used to make wine in the Johannisberg style. He also recommended the Pinot Noir for making red wine in the style of Burgundy. But he added that "the quality of the soil makes a vast difference in the quality of the wine." Asked if he was acquainted with the eastern American grapes, the Catawba, Delaware, Isabella, and Scuppernong, he replied that he was but that these grapes could not be compared to "the fine imported varieties."

It is worth noting that in the printed reports of this interesting question-and-answer session there is no hint that he said anything whatever about the Zinfandel. If he was as enthusiastic about this grape as Arpad later claimed he was, why would he fail to sing its praises to the attentive audience he encountered at the American Institute in New York? The printed reports of his appearance there (there were two) were not verbatim transcripts of his remarks, and they were full of obvious errors, omissions, and even inconsistencies,[30] so it is possible that he did mention the Zinfandel and the reporters failed to record his remarks, either because the word sounded so strange or because they simply could not spell it (they had great difficulty in rendering such comparatively simple words as "Riesling" and "Pinot Noir," variously recording them "Risling," "Kisling," "Noiree," "Pignon," "Noria," and "Pinio"). If he did not mention the Zinfandel, however, it is fair to conclude that, at least by February of 1864, the grape was not yet one of his favorites—and that, Arpad Haraszthy's protestations to the contrary notwithstanding, he was not its earliest and most vocal California champion.

Agoston made a second appearance before the American Institute's Farmers' Club on February 28, this time to provide information about the growth of the California wine industry. He brought an article published in the *San Francisco Mercantile Gazette* that was crammed with statistics showing a virtual explosion in California vineyard planting and wine production since 1856. Institute members still seemed fascinated by the voluble European from the Golden State, and, after a lengthy period on the rostrum he begged "to be excused from occupying all the time."[31]

It is likely that Agoston called on Cornelius K. Garrison while he was in New York City, for in May he received a very large loan (more than $40,000) from the railroad magnate.[32] It is also likely that he called on influential editors in New York, and perhaps also in Boston, for about the time he got back to California two prestigious national magazines ran important articles on the burgeoning California wine industry and Agoston's role in promoting it. In May, the Boston-based *Atlantic Monthly* published an article entitled "California as a Vineland," which included generous supplies of winegrowing statistics supplied by Agoston; and in June, the New York–based *Harper's Monthly* ran an article titled "Wine-Making in California," which included interesting descriptions of Buena Vista.[33]

The *Atlantic* article was unsigned, but the *Harper's* piece was credited to "A. Haraszthy," a fact that has led some wine historians to conclude that Agoston wrote it. However, the *Harper's* article contains numerous third-person references to "Mr. Haraszthy," the founder and superintendent of the BVVS, which make no sense if Agoston was the author; and it seems much more likely that it was written by Arpad. Arpad had established a good reputation as a wine writer in California, and he was entirely capable of writing for a larger audience. If he was not an altogether objective judge when it came to reporting on his father's activities, he was as well informed about them as any man (save Agoston himself), and the article that he produced was crammed with interesting statistics, historical references, and projections for the future of the wine industry in California.

The *Atlantic* article noted the pioneering efforts of Kohler & Frohling in establishing the first important commercial wine business in California in 1854. "They have the satisfaction," the magazine added, "of to-day being the pioneers in what is soon to be one of the most important branches of industry in California." Kohler & Frohling's wine was, of course, a Los Angeles product, characteristically sweeter and heavier than the wines produced farther north, and generally "deficient in flavor and bouquet." In contrast, the magazine noted, Agoston produced the "lighter and tarter wine" that was characteristic of Sonoma.[34]

The *Harper's* article was illustrated with wood engravings that showed the vineyards and winemaking facilities at Buena Vista and illustrated practical techniques for propagating and pruning grapevines. The text was suffused with Haraszthyan enthusiasm. "We are assured on as good authority as that of Mr. Haraszthy," Arpad wrote, "that California has five millions of acres suited to grape-culture; that in a considerable part the vine flourishes better than in the most favored regions of Europe; so that when, in a generation or so, this shall be planted with vines, the wine product of that State will be worth, on the spot, at only twenty-five cents a gallon, more than five hundred million dollars. . . . Making all due allowances for the enthusiasm of a sanguine vine-grower, and guided only by what has actually been demonstrated, we may be certain that the production of wine is to become a leading branch of the industry of the Golden State. We therefore present an account of the processes of grape-culture and wine-making as now conducted in California, at the largest establishment of the kind in the world."[35]

The "largest establishment of the kind in the world"! Was this a factual statement, or a bald exercise in self-promotion?[36] Was Arpad engaging in hyperbole to inflate his father's accomplishments and promote his wine business, or was he accurately assessing the comparative size of the Buena Vista estate? In *Grape Culture, Wines, and Wine-Making* Agoston had noted that his Sonoma vineyard covered some four hundred acres and added, rather modestly, that it was "to the best of our belief . . . the largest in the United States."[37] In his tour of Europe in 1861 he had observed that the vineyards in France, Germany, Italy, and Spain were typically small, individually owned domains. It was rare to find a French vineyard that embraced twenty-five acres, even rarer to find one that topped fifty or a hundred. Of course, large expanses of the Burgundy region were given over to grapevines, but stone walls separated the growers' plots, and where there were no walls, boundary lines marked off one vineyardist's property from that of his neighbor. So Arpad's claim that

Buena Vista, with more than four hundred acres of vines under single ownership and management (and with room enough on the same property to plant several thousand acres more), was "the largest establishment of the kind in the world" was probably not so far from the truth. California reporters, at least, seemed to have no difficulty in accepting it, and they soon began to refer to Buena Vista in newspaper stories as "the largest vineyard in the world," "the largest wine-growing estate in the world," "the largest wine-growing enterprise of the world," or (in a peculiarly Californian phrase) "the largest grape ranch in the world."[38]

After the harvest of 1864 was completed, Agoston and Eleonora decided to invite their friends to the big house at Buena Vista to help them celebrate their good fortune with a festive ball. Eleonora and Ida wrote the invitations by hand and sealed the envelopes with hot wax into which the Haraszthy coat of arms was pressed with Agoston's gold signet ring. They called the event a "vintage masquerade" and asked all guests to wear masks.[39]

The invitations went out on October 9, and the guests arrived in the evening of Friday, October 28, many having come from San Francisco on the Sonoma steamer. The Vallejos were much in evidence—and naturally so, for General Vallejo's daughters Natalia and Jovita were now very much a part of the Haraszthy family. Many of the guests were officers, trustees, and shareholders of the Buena Vista Vinicultural Society, among them treasurer B. Eugene Auger and his wife. For years after, the carefully penned and sealed invitation that the Augers received would be saved by them, and later by their children. It was one of their most treasured possessions, a tangible record of a special event held in a special place and time— a glamorous vintage ball presided over in the autumn of 1864 by a dashing Hungarian nobleman and his handsome wife in the middle of the largest vineyard in the world.[40]

26

Restless
Again

It was in the spring of 1865 that the influence of William Chapman Ralston became publicly evident in the affairs of the Buena Vista Vinicultural Society. In an effort to complete the sale of the society's stock, the officers and trustees of the BVVS invited the San Francisco capitalist and a group of his business associates to Buena Vista to inspect the property and determine whether they could help persuade large investors to support its efforts.

Ralston came up to Sonoma from San Francisco with George H. Howard, G. W. Beaver, and Frederick Law Olmsted. Of this trio, the forty-three-year-old Olmsted was the most interesting. Born in Connecticut in 1822, he had earned a national reputation as a travel writer and landscape architect in the 1850's. His most notable accomplishment was the plan he devised for New York City's great Central Park in 1858, but he also gained renown during 1862–63 for serving as first chairman of the U.S. Sanitary Commission, the forerunner of the American Red Cross. Olmsted had come to California toward the end of 1863 to manage the sprawling Mariposa Rancho in the foothills of the Sierra Nevada. But after that property fell into insolvency, he went to San Francisco to look for new business opportunities and was only too glad to oblige when Ralston asked him to come up to Sonoma and help him look into the BVVS.[1]

Ralston, Olmsted, Howard, and Beaver arrived at Buena Vista on March 18, 1865.[2] They spent two days inspecting the property, then returned to San Francisco, where Olmsted drafted a report on what they had seen. His report was published as a pamphlet under the title, *The Production of Wine in California: Particularly Referring to the Establishment of the Buena Vista Vinicultural Society*. The report described the BVVS as "the first extensive joint-stock agricultural enterprise in the United States," with 645 acres of vineyards, a total of 1,128,120 vines in the ground, and about half that number of full bearing age.[3] It noted that the vines were managed "under a system of extreme simplicity," without either staking or training, and that "an extraordinary economy of labor" was attained in their cultivation. The buildings and machinery were "of substantial construction, and well adapted for the accomplishment of a large amount of work, with great economy of current expense."

Ralston, Olmsted, and the others did not make any precise estimates of the profits likely to be earned by the BVVS, both because the market for California wines was still new and because so much new wine of poor quality had recently been offered for sale that it was impossible to determine how consumers would react to really good wine. But they had been informed that some of Buena Vista's white wine had recently been sold in New York for a good price, enough to produce a net profit to the society of ninety-two cents per gallon. If these prices continued, Ralston's group speculated that the value of one year's production could be as much as $500,000.

The report reviewed the advantages for wine production of the California climate, which Olmsted and Ralston thought was "probably the best in the world for this purpose," but noted that, until recently, all the climatic advantages had been offset by the high price of labor in California. The employment of Chinese laborers, the use of labor-saving machinery, and the large-scale production contemplated by the society largely compensated for this disadvantage, "But even should the expense of labor be doubled," the report continued, "as far as can be judged at present, the business is one promising extraordinary profits." The report was signed by Ralston, Howard, Bea-

ver, and Olmsted, and also by Horace W. Carpentier, who, in a separate statement, noted that he had not personally visited Buena Vista
but that he concurred "in the main conclusions" of those who had.[4]

Ralston's endorsement of the BVVS had the expected result. At
the second annual meeting, held in San Francisco on June 24, 1865,
Walter M. Rockwell, president of the board of trustees, announced
that, with the aid of the San Francisco capitalist, a large number
of the unsold shares of the BVVS had been subscribed for. A subscription list was opened both in San Francisco and New York, and
prospects of selling all the stock appeared favorable.[5]

Along with the good news about the new stock subscriptions,
there were, however, some worrisome facts to be reported to the
shareholders at the 1865 meeting. Contrary to Agoston's early pre-
dictions that rainfall would be abundant in 1864,[6] that year had actually seen an extension of the statewide drought, and Buena Vista's
wine production was unexpectedly low.[7] Heavy expenses occasioned
by the development of the property, together with the difficulty
of realizing immediate profits on BVVS products, had caused what
President Rockwell described as "serious financial difficulties." Further, the society had had a confrontation with the local federal
revenue inspector, who claimed that Buena Vista's brandy was tax-
able not just at the rate of twenty-five cents a gallon as required by
the law passed in 1864, but at the confiscatory rate of two dollars a
gallon. The higher tax was claimed to be due because "some sweetening matter had been used in the process of distillation" and the
inspector had refused to classify the brandy as "grape brandy." Rockwell protested that the sweetening matter was used "to increase the
fermentation, and for no other purpose," and that this practice was
"universal all over the world." These setbacks made it impossible for
BVVS to declare current dividends on its stock, or even to predict
when dividends might be paid.[8]

Attila was acting superintendent of the BVVS when it came time
for the superintendent's annual report to be submitted on June 23.
Sounding an optimistic note, the young vineyardist reported that
the new plantings of 1865 were "coming exceedingly well," and that
the vines planted in the nursery for rooting (which included both
European and Mission grapes) were "also in a very prosperous con-

dition." In addition to the new champagne house, building projects for the year 1864–65 had included a large dwelling house for the Chinese laborers. Attila reported that about 40,000 bottles of champagne had been put up, and that the wines of 1864 were "quite clear and improving very rapidly."[9]

Around the time that Ralston and his associates invested in Buena Vista, Agoston began to make some important changes in the vineyards, incorporating ideas gleaned from his European tour. He had paid close attention to the distances between the vines in different vineyards: in the Médoc district of Bordeaux, the rows were only three feet apart, and the vines in each row were between one and two feet apart; in Burgundy, the vines were typically one foot apart. Since first arriving in Sonoma, Agoston had followed the old northern California practice of planting vines eight feet on center, on the assumption that the wide spacing suited the needs of California vineyards better than the close plantings typical of Europe. In the Imperial Gardens at Dijon, however, he had learned of a series of studies designed to determine the optimal spacing for good wine vineyards. The gardeners at Dijon had planted vines at various distances, ranging from one foot up to sixteen, cultivated them carefully (in some cases for as many as twenty years), and then compared the costs of cultivation and the quality of the resulting wines. They found that the best results were all obtained with the closest plantations.

Back in Sonoma, Agoston conducted some studies of his own, and by 1865 he had satisfied himself that significant economies could be achieved and better wine produced if the vines were planted four feet on center. Since his existing vines were all eight feet on center, he decided to cut that spacing in half by layering the vines. A vine is "layered" by digging a hole adjacent to a vine and bending a "cane" (or branch) down into the hole and covering it with soil, leaving two buds exposed to the air. The buried cane receives food and nutrition from the parent plant and quickly begins to produce roots, while the two buds left above ground produce new canes. The vine continues to grow, and toward the end of the year produces a crop of grapes. The connection to the parent vine remains until the new vine has developed firm roots and the link to the parent can safely be cut.[10] Vines had traditionally been layered to replace dead plants in existing vineyards (cuttings rarely survive when planted in the midst of mature vineyards, but layers have high rates of survival). Agoston's idea, however, was not to layer a vine here and there, but to layer all his existing vines, so that the spacing throughout the vineyard would be four feet on center.

As Agoston warmed to the idea of layering, he proposed a method whereby layers could be used not only to decrease the spacing in existing vineyards but also to plant entirely new vineyards. A vineyardist could begin by planting vines in rows four feet on center, but with forty feet separating each row. For three years, the new vines would be carefully cultivated. In the winter of the third year, two canes would be bent down from each of the existing vines to a ditch dug at a distance of four feet on either side of the existing rows. The ditch would be filled in, with the tips of the bent canes protruding above the soil line. Thus there would be three vines for each existing vine. In the fourth year, the vines would again be layered to a distance of four feet, but this time in only one direction. The same process would be repeated each year thereafter, until the whole vineyard was filled with vines planted four feet apart. In this way the entire vineyard could be planted in seven years. Each acre of vineyard planted in the new way would have 2,722 vines, as opposed to 680 per acre when planted in the old northern California style.[11]

Agoston's first serious efforts to layer the vineyards at Buena Vista began in the winter of 1864–65. In that year 260,000 vines were layered and 640,000 entirely new vines were planted.[12] The new vines, set out in rows four feet on center, were planted to some of the European vines Agoston had recently determined were best suited to wine production at Sonoma. The varieties varied from row to row, so that one row of Johannisberg Riesling might face another row of Chasselas, and one row of Zinfandel might face another of Merlot.[13] Grape varieties planted in alternate rows could be blended in the crushers and fermenting vats.

As Chinese laborers spread out over the sprawling vineyards, digging ditches between the existing rows of vines and bending long canes down into them, Agoston's neighbors looked on, puzzled. They had long since accepted the old northern California pattern of vine spacing and were suspicious of Agoston's innovations. They argued that it was necessary to leave eight feet between the vines so two-horse plows could comfortably pass between the rows, and they believed that closer spacing would force the vines to compete for food and moisture and result in smaller crops of fruit. But Agoston had already considered these objections and was ready to answer them.

Toward the end of 1865, he took his pen to paper to explain his new planting methods, producing an essay that appeared in the February 15, 1866, issue of the *California Rural Home Journal*, published in San Francisco. The essay was reprinted that same year in the State Agricultural Society's yearbook and the following year in *Hyatt's Hand-Book of Grape Culture*, the first book on wine published in California.[14] Titled "Best Modes of Cultivating the Grape in California," the essay reviewed the observations about vine spacing that Agoston made in Europe and alluded to his own experiments at Buena Vista. It recalled that, although he had originally thought the traditional spacing pattern suited California vineyards because land was cheap and plowing would be easier when the vines were well separated, the experiments he conducted after his return from Europe convinced him that wide planting encouraged the vines to bear too heavily and produced grapes with poor sugar and color. He recognized that overbearing could be controlled to a certain degree by pruning, but unnecessary pruning was costly, and, in any case, wide planting required the vineyardist to cultivate more land than was strictly necessary. Two-horse plows could still be used when vines were planted four feet apart, and there was much less land to be plowed. Closely planted vines produced less fruit, but the juice was richer and the flavors and aromas were more intense.

He thought that his method of starting a new vineyard with rows forty feet apart and gradually filling in the spaces between would be most advantageous to farmers of modest means who wanted to start vineyards on the proverbial "shoestring." If a poor farmer could not afford to plant all his vines at one time, he might never be able to start. But a farmer who planted a vineyard by the layering method could begin at a nominal cost and gradually complete the planting over a period of seven years.[15]

Agoston's new planting methods aroused immediate controversy among winegrowers. Many of his neighbors scoffed at his "experimentation," disputing his assertion that a vineyard with 2,722 vines per acre would produce any more salable wine than a vineyard with only 680 per acre, and repeating the argument about plowing. Most of this negative comment was prompted by traditional aversion to agricultural innovation: if vines had been planted eight feet apart for more than a generation, why change? But some of the comment was aimed personally at Agoston. As the founder and manager of the largest vineyard in California, he was well known for attracting attention and, in the process, ruffling some feathers. Some of his fellow winegrowers frankly envied him; others resented him; and there was hardly a farmer who did not consider him fair game for faultfinding. Many believed that his plan to layer the whole of Buena Vista was, if nothing else, wildly extravagant, a costly venture that would do little to improve the quality of California wines and even less to pay off the debts of the BVVS.

But Agoston had some important defenders. One was John S. Hittell of the *Alta California.* Hittell visited Sonoma early in 1865 and found the valley in an uproar over Agoston's plans for layering Buena Vista. He reviewed the arguments on both sides:

At present Colonel Haraszthy is in the minority; but it is not the first time. When he advised the planting of vineyards in Sonoma Valley, and when, afterwards, he urged planting on land which could not be irrigated, and when, still later, he urged the importation of foreign vines, he was met on every side by incredulous persons, who said it would pay better to grow wheat; though at a later day all admitted that he was right. They may, hereafter, do the same about this question of distance between vines.[16]

Thomas Hart Hyatt, editor of the *California Rural Home Journal,* thought that Agoston's proposals seemed "very feasible" and showed "a great saving in time and expense over the old methods." At the very least, Hyatt wrote, "they are well worthy of being tested by those entering upon the culture of the grape."[17]

Agoston was still experimenting with the foreign varieties he had imported in 1861, but he was beginning to zero in on a few varieties that seemed to produce particularly good wine in Sonoma. There is no good written evidence of when the first wine was pressed from Zinfandel at Buena Vista. This lack of a written record connecting the most prominent winemaker in the early years of the California wine industry with the most distinctively California vinifera grape would be the cause of consternation for years after. But the lack is not as surprising as some historians insist. Most California wines, including those produced at Buena Vista, were still blends of different varieties, and the recognition of particularly outstanding varieties took many years in coming. As late as 1863, Hittell noted that "it is not known yet what grape will make the best wine in California; and that knowledge cannot be obtained for some years to come."[18] By the middle of the 1860's, however, the virtues of the Zinfandel were beginning to be widely recognized. An occasional correspondent for the *Alta* who visited Sonoma in the spring of 1866 reported that the Zinfandel was being used for the production of "good claret":

It has long been established that California could produce a white wine equal to the best of, and much resembling, the Rhine wine; also, Los Angeles and some places more interior, upon this latitude, yield a fair quality of port; but since a good astringent and acid wine of the claret nature was not to be had, many refused to drink our home-made wines. A grape called the Zinfindal [*sic*] is decided to be the best for producing this claret, mixed with native; consequently there has been a very great demand for cuttings from such vines the present spring.[19]

This paragraph is interesting on several accounts: first, because the Zinfandel was still unknown to most winegrowers as late as the spring of 1866; second, because a standardized spelling for the name had not yet been settled on; and third, because the grape was still thought to be most useful when blended with the old and familiar Mission ("native" or "California") grape. When, just three years later, another writer for the *Alta* visited Buena Vista, he tasted some red wine produced from a blend of grapes grown "high up on a hill" behind the main vineyard. This writer found the blended wine to be "a perfect Burgundy in character" and "the most delicious red wine in the cellar."[20] Did this wine include the Zinfandel? There is no proof that it did, but the fact that Agoston had long argued in favor of blending, that the Mission and the Zinfandel had already been successfully blended in Sonoma, and that the "delicious red wine" was so obviously pleasing to the palate, all combine to suggest that the magical grape may well have been a part of the blend.

Agoston may not have devoted a great deal of his time to the day-to-day affairs of Buena Vista in 1865–66, for he was involved during those years in numerous other activities that required his frequent absences from Sonoma. Attila prepared the superintendent's annual report for 1865, for example, because his father was traveling in the eastern states when the report came due. Agoston's eastern trip had been authorized by the board of trustees of the BVVS, who had instructed him to visit Washington, D.C., and attempt to persuade Congress to reduce the federal taxes on wine and brandy. Agoston later explained that this trip was made "for the benefit of the wine-growers of California" and grumbled that other wine producers had shown no interest in supporting the efforts of the BVVS.[21] The trip to Washington was productive: after listening to his arguments, Congress agreed to modest reductions in the domestic wine and brandy taxes and corresponding increases in the tariffs on imported wine and brandy.[22] Although the net savings to winemakers were not large, Agoston was able to head off real mischief by arousing opposition to suggestions that the domestic wine and brandy taxes should not only be reduced, but raised. The *Alta* expressed the opinion that the domestic taxes "would have been larger but for the exertions of Col. Haraszthy at Washington."[23] By going to Washington and laying the arguments of California's winemakers directly before the national lawmakers, Agoston had acted as the legislative representative of the state's wine industry. He was the first person to undertake these responsibilities, thus becoming, in the words of one wine historian, "the precursor of the California wine lobby."[24]

Pleased as he was by his success in Washington, Agoston believed it was important to set up some system whereby the interests of California wine producers could be looked after on a regular basis. To accomplish this, he proposed that the winegrowers join forces to send a "competent person" to Washington to represent their interests there. While California's own representatives in Congress might be well informed about the needs of the state's growing wine industry, he argued, those representing other states would not always be. An industry representative (or "lobbyist") could keep current on conditions in the vineyards and wine markets and in that way foster and protect the infant industry. "This mode of procedure," he argued, "would not only be satisfactory to our representatives, and aid them in their efforts, but also most beneficial to the vine growers' interest."[25]

After his business was done in Washington, Agoston embarked on a tour of some of the eastern states, in the course of which he delivered lectures and wrote articles for newspapers.[26] Acting as a kind of ambassador-at-large for the California wine industry, he met with local scientific and horticultural societies, attempting to acquaint them with California's agricultural opportunities. He found that many easterners had a very limited understanding of the changes that had taken place in California since the discovery of gold. They still thought of the state as an almost totally undeveloped mining country. Agoston later reported that his audiences were "astonished and seemed incredulous" when he informed them that California had the potential of soon becoming the greatest agricultural producer in the United States, and one of the greatest in the world.

Predictably, he took advantage of his travels through the eastern states not only to expound the virtues of California agriculture but also to scout out business opportunities for himself. Soon after his first lecture in Philadelphia, the directors of a new corporation called the Philadelphia and California Petroleum Company called on him and explained that they owned a large tract of land in southern California and planned to plant part of it to a wine vineyard.[27] He enthusiastically answered their questions about vinegrowing conditions and market potentials for California wine. In New York, he was contacted by the directors of another corporation called the New York and California Petroleum Company, who confided that they had similar plans for another large tract of land they owned in southern California, but in addition to grapevines they planned to plant olive trees. Before he returned to San Francisco toward the middle of the summer, Agoston agreed to visit the southern California properties of these two eastern companies and report back to them on the feasibility of carrying out their plans.[28]

He was back in Sonoma in August, and on the twenty-sixth of that month boarded the steamer *Pacific* in San Francisco for a trip down the coast to Santa Barbara. In the picturesque coastal town, he called on Dr. James L. Ord, a Maryland-born surgeon who had married into a prominent Spanish family and become one of the leading citizens of the town. Ord had assembled a collection of wines produced in the valleys behind Santa Barbara and invited Agoston to taste them. Agoston was pleasantly surprised to discover that several of the bottles were labeled not just with the names of their producers but also with the names of the vineyards in which the grapes were grown, the years in which the wines were pressed, and the dates on which they were bottled. He tasted the wines and found several of excellent quality, even though they were still made in the old Mexican way by trampling the grapes by foot and fermenting the must in rawhide bags.[29]

The next morning, he and some companions set out in a four-horse stage for the town of Ojai, about thirty miles to the southeast. The road took them first to the coastal town of San Buenaventura (later called Ventura), then on to the headquarters of the New York and California Petroleum Company. Here they saw new frame buildings, built to house the company's officers and workmen, and a large steam engine that powered a drill. Greeted by the assistant superintendent, Agoston was shown some nearby springs, where a dark, slick liquid oozed out of the ground. The following morning, he and his companions set out on horseback to explore the company's sprawling property, which included about 60,000 acres. As he rode over the rolling hills, he found much of the land to be well watered and timbered. He estimated that at least 20,000 acres of this property were suitable for growing vines, olives, almonds, oranges, walnuts, and other trees, and that fully 1,000 acres could be planted to premium white wine grapes. He also inspected the 200,000-acre property of the Philadelphia and California Company, near San Buenaventura. He thought that this land was suitable for a wide variety of crops, ranging from hemp, tobacco, linseed, corn, and grains, to olives, tea, sugar cane, sorghum, and other vegetables. At least 80,000 acres could be planted to vines, and a thriving silk culture might be established if mulberry trees were planted and Chinese workers employed to perform the necessary labor.[30]

Agoston's enthusiastic report on his southern California trip, and his eastern tour, duly appeared in the *Alta California.* The Philadelphia and California Oil Company, he declared, was "determined" to put ten million vines on their southern California property.[31] No vineyard of this scope had ever been planted or even contemplated anywhere in California (it would take at least 9,000 acres, and pos-

sibly as many as 15,000, to accommodate that many vines), and
Agoston's obviously exaggerated prose may have been something of
an exercise in wishful thinking. At any rate, Levi Parsons, a San Francisco lawyer and one of the trustees of the Philadelphia company,
later claimed that Agoston himself had proposed that ten million
vines be set out on the company's property, and that the planting
be accomplished under his supervision. Parsons acknowledged that
Agoston had "more knowledge upon the vine question than anyone
in California," but the number of vines he suggested was simply too
great.[32] So far as is known, the Philadelphia and California Petroleum Company never planted any vines on its Ojai property.

While he was in southern California, Agoston had been on the
lookout for properties that might be purchased by eastern capitalists, and he had noted a particularly attractive tract of land that
adjoined the Philadelphia company's Ojai property. A few months
later he told Hyatt, of the *California Rural Home Journal,* that he had
purchased a large tract of land for a company of eastern capitalists.
According to Hyatt, the tract included something like one hundred
thousand acres and the buyers intended to plant a thousand acres to
vines.[33] Hyatt did not report where the land was located or identify
the capitalists who financed the purchase, and since Agoston left no
record of any transaction of that sort, we can only wonder.

Agoston's suggestion that the California wine industry send a
representative to Washington to represent their interests in the capital bore fruit in 1866. Shortly after his trip to the nation's capital in
September 1865, he had complained in a letter to the *Alta* that the
BVVS had borne the full expense of efforts to represent the California wine industry in Washington "and never received even a line of
thanks for its trouble and expenditures." He thought his efforts had
been of particular help to the winegrowers of Los Angeles, whose
expanding vineyards had benefited greatly from sharply rising prices
for California wine: "Some time or other," he wrote, "they will awake
to their interest, and contribute to the expense of having somebody
to represent their interests at the National Capitol."[34]

The Los Angeles vineyardists apparently took note, for in April
1866 they assembled a convention of local winegrowers, and one of

the most prominent of the delegates decided to underwrite the expense of sending a lobbyist to Washington. Benjamin D. Wilson was interested in selling his large Lake Vineyard north of Los Angeles and had already talked to J. Ross Browne about traveling East and attempting to find a buyer.[35] Wilson thought that, while Browne was in the East, he could also call on members of Congress and urge some action to relieve California winemakers of their federal tax burdens. There was no doubt that Browne was the kind of "competent person" Agoston had suggested should look after the wine industry's interests, and since he and Browne had been on friendly terms for several years, he endorsed Wilson's suggestion and saw to it that the BVVS contributed the substantial sum of $500 toward payment of Browne's expenses.[36]

Browne proceeded without delay to Washington, where he called on key lawmakers and took up his ever-ready pen in defense of the California wine industry. He wrote long and persuasive letters to Senator W. P. Fessenden, chairman of the Senate Committee on Finance, and sent some samples of California wine to Congressman (later President) James A. Garfield of Ohio.[37] Agoston was pleased when Browne returned from Washington with news that his legislative supplications had met with some success. Congress had not only declined to raise the tax on wine, it had abolished it altogether.[38] It had, however, quadrupled the tax on brandy from fifty cents to two dollars a gallon. Agoston was outraged by the measure. At a convention of winegrowers of Sonoma, Napa, and Yolo counties held in the city of Napa on September 20—Agoston was made president and Browne secretary—he explained the new law and the difficulties it presented to winegrowers. The tax of two dollars per gallon amounted to an "absolute prohibition" on the manufacture of brandy, he declared, since the market price was only $1.90 per gallon. The vintage of 1866 was nearly at hand, and winemakers had to decide without delay upon a course of action. Following discussion, the convention passed a resolution imploring the Secretary of the Treasury to give local collectors discretion to decide where brandy could be stored and urging winemakers throughout the state to elect delegates to a state convention to meet in San Francisco on November 1 "for the purposing of uniting in a memorial to Congress, and taking such other steps as may be necessary to procure a reduction or remission of this onerous provision of law."[39]

The state's winemakers convened at Knell's saloon in San Francisco on November 1. The Los Angeles delegation was headed up by Agoston's old friend from San Diego, Jonathan Warner, with Charles Kohler and Benjamin D. Wilson also in attendance. The Sonoma delegation included Agoston's neighbors General C. H. S. Williams, Charles V. Stuart, and George Wratten. Agoston was a delegate from Sonoma, and Arpad was one of the delegates from San Francisco, to which he had recently moved. Williams was elected president of the meeting, and Browne again acted as secretary. During three days of meetings, speaker after speaker described the havoc that the increased brandy tax was certain to wreak on the wine industry. Warner pointed out that in Los Angeles much of the 1865 grape crop had been made into brandy, but because the Los Angeles product did not taste like French brandy, it commanded poor prices. Arpad noted that Sonoma wine producers had obtained licenses to convert large quantities of wine into brandy, but the new law had frustrated all their plans.[40] Both Warner and H. D. Dunn of San Francisco presented memorials calling on Congress to abolish (or at least reduce) the brandy tax.[41]

But it was evident from the start that the winegrowers were looking beyond the immediate crisis to other difficulties they were sure to encounter in the years to come. The California Wine-Growers' Association formed in 1862 had become moribund, and there was an obvious need for a successor organization. To that end the delegates adopted a constitution for a "California State Wine-Growers' Association," which would be open to membership by any person in the state who was interested in winegrowing or winemaking.[42] The officers were Williams as president, Browne as secretary, and Kohler treasurer. Agoston, who had initiated the process that gave birth to the new organization, was not named either an officer or a trustee.

The organization of the State Wine-Growers' Association complete, the delegates launched into a discussion of methods whereby the market for California wines could be improved. It was obvious to all the delegates that California wine sales were lagging. The market had not kept pace with the great burst of vine-planting of the late

1850's and early 1860's and surpluses were accumulating all over the state. One delegate noted that he had recently spent several months in the East and was surprised to discover that California wine was still almost unknown in that part of the country. Browne suggested that a New York corporation be formed for the purpose of buying, storing, and selling California wines and brandy in the eastern states. After some discussion, Browne's proposal was agreed to, but without any strong conviction that it would solve the industry's marketing problems.[43]

There was also some discussion about the Universal Industrial Exhibition planned for Paris in 1867. Professor William P. Blake of the College of California had been designated as state commissioner to the exposition, and the delegates in San Francisco wanted to coordinate their plans for exhibiting California wines with the commissioner. It was decided to designate a committee of fourteen winemakers to confer with Blake and supply him with any information that might facilitate his work. Rodmon Gibbons was chairman of the committee; Agoston was the member from Sonoma County.[44]

Agoston's long absences from Sonoma in 1865 and 1866 may be taken as evidence that he was once again growing restless. The BVVS had not yet met the objectives set forth in its prospectus, and there was still much work to be done on the property, yet it seemed that he was already looking beyond Sonoma. Was he incapable of maintaining his focus for any appreciable length of time? Was he one of those men who are suited to launch businesses with great promise, but never to see them through to their greatness—a gifted, even brilliant, entrepreneur, but an erratic, undependable manager?

There is little doubt that his enthusiasm for Buena Vista was waning as 1866 gave way to 1867. But the reasons for that lack of enthusiasm were complex. It was not just a case of wandering eyes, for troubles were lurking not far below the surface of the great vineyard that he had conceived and built in the Sonoma Valley. Those troubles were building in scope and intensity and would soon demand drastic remedies.

27

Tangled
Vines

Buena Vista was the scene of a happy family gathering in early
1865. On February 26, in the big house in the center of the Buena
Vista vineyards, Agoston gave his daughter Ida in marriage to Major
Henry Hancock of Los Angeles.[1] There was a large age difference
between the bride and groom (Ida was twenty-two and her husband
was forty-three), but Hancock was a man of substance. Born in New
Hampshire in 1822, he had studied at the Harvard Law School,
worked as a surveyor, and earned a major's commission in the U.S.
Army before he and two younger brothers sailed around Cape Horn
for California in 1849.[2] Landing at San Francisco in September of
that year, he headed for the gold fields east of Sacramento to try his
hand at prospecting.[3] But his mining fervor soon cooled, and he returned to the coast, determined to make use of his legal training and
experience as a surveyor. He settled in southern California, where
he represented Los Angeles in the State Assembly in 1852, the same
year in which Agoston represented San Diego. He became Deputy
U.S. Surveyor in southern California and in 1857 completed one of
the first important land surveys of Los Angeles, producing a map
that was to form the basis of important land titles for more than a
century afterward.[4] Hancock continued to represent Los Angeles in

the Assembly during the late 1850's and often conferred with Agoston on issues of interest to the state's burgeoning wine industry. His interest in viticultural issues was sharpened when he acquired vineyard property of his own and joined the growing ranks of southern California grape growers.[5]

Hancock had a house in the old pueblo of Los Angeles, but he and Ida spent much of their time on the nearby Rancho La Brea, which Henry and his brother John had acquired from its Mexican owners around 1860. La Brea was not one of the largest ranchos in southern California (only 4,439 acres), but its location immediately to the north and west of Los Angeles and the pools of oil and tar that oozed out of the ground on the property marked it apart from its neighbors. The Hancocks sold the tar (called *brea* by the Spanish and Mexicans) to homeowners in Los Angeles, who used it to waterproof their roofs. The income Major Hancock derived from his sales of brea and grapes, combined with the healthy surveying and legal fees he charged his many clients, made him one of the most prosperous citizens of the southern city.

If Agoston and Eleonora suffered any pangs when Ida left Sonoma in 1865, they must have been relieved when, just seven months later, Attila's wife, Natalia, gave birth to a second son, a healthy boy, born on September 6, 1865. He was given the names Attila Mariano, in honor of his father and his maternal grandfather, General Vallejo.[6] Gaza returned to Sonoma toward the middle of 1866. He had been released from prison in May 1865 in a Union-Confederate prisoner exchange and had rejoined his regiment, first in western Mississippi and then in Texas. He was elevated to the rank of major on December 5, 1865, and finally mustered out of service with his company on May 31, 1866.[7] He then headed back to Sonoma.

Gaza had sold his Sonoma vineyard before he left for the war, but he was still interested in winemaking. Not long after he returned, a new wine firm called Haraszthy Brothers was formed in Sonoma.[8] Just which brothers were in the partnership is not known; it may well have been all four. Attila and Arpad were well-established winemakers, and Bela, though just twenty years old, was already experienced in the craft. Attila grew grapes and made wine on his Sonoma property. Arpad had recently joined Isidor Landsberger in forming a new wine firm in San Francisco. Landsberger, a San Francisco commission merchant, had been one of the original trustees of the BVVS, but he had severed his relations with the society about the time that Ralston and his investors took control.[9] Sometime in late 1865 or early 1866, Arpad and Landsberger organized the firm of I. Landsberger and Co., which operated out of a complex of brick buildings on Jackson Street.[10] Landsberger was the senior partner in the firm; Arpad was the principal wine and champagne maker. Although Arpad's duties in San Francisco were undoubtedly demanding, there is no reason why he could not have helped Gaza, Attila, and Bela supply grapes and wine to Landsberger's San Francisco "depot."

The growing business activities of Agoston's sons is evidence that, at least by the end of 1866, they had little if any involvement in the affairs of the BVVS. The reason for their withdrawal may be inferred from other events that occurred in Sonoma during 1865–66 and that indicated that Agoston himself was gradually distancing himself from Buena Vista. Sometime before the summer of 1866, the founder of the BVVS became the center of a storm of controversy in Sonoma. The controversy had its roots in criticism leveled against his management of the BVVS property. The attacks came from outside the BVVS, but the charges resonated deeply enough to reach the ears of the trustees and officers in San Francisco.

No record has been found of the specific allegations made against Agoston, except that he was charged with "extravagance and unfaithfulness in the performance of his duties."[11] It is not difficult, however, to speculate about the particulars. It was well known that he made long trips away from Sonoma, and that he had spent a good deal of his time, energy, and money investigating new vineyard prospects in southern California. His sons were promoting the firm of Haraszthy Brothers, and he may well have been helping them get their new business established (some of his neighbors may even have suspected that the firm was a "front" for his own business efforts, separate and apart from the BVVS). It was rather generally known, too, that Buena Vista was not yet reporting profits and that its debts seemed to be growing larger every day. Agoston was not directly responsible for the society's shaky financial condition—a good part of the current problem was attributable to the statewide decline of wine prices—but he was the easy and obvious person to blame, especially since he had begun what people regarded as a foolish "layering" of the Buena Vista vineyards.

The trustees sought at first to ignore the charges, in the hope that they would go away. But they did not go away, and at some point in the early part of 1866 they decided to investigate them. The only record that remains of their investigation is the written report submitted by the trustees at their annual meeting on June 23, 1866. That report, which was signed for the board by the new president, George C. Johnson, described the charges as "constant" and "malignant." It noted that the board had "taken pains to make a thorough investigation of these charges, and can state that we not only found none of them substantiated, but by comparing our accounts with those of other vine growers in the neighborhood it was satisfactorily proven to us that there is no vineyard in Sonoma Valley worked for less money or even as economically and with the same comparative result than our own." The report continued:

Perhaps the maxim is true that the real worth of a man is best reflected by the number of his enemies; we feel it, however, but justice to Col. Haraszthy to make known herewith our full confidence in his capacity and his integrity, and to state that we regard the success of our enterprise as wholly due to the intelligence, energy, and diligence he has shown as manager of our property.[12]

Reviewing the society's financial affairs, Johnson noted that BVVS had paid William Blanding $34,500 to retire the mortgage he held on the vineyard property, and the Pacific Insurance Company had received an additional $25,000, representing one half of the $50,000 mortgage it held on the property. But $25,000 was still unpaid on the Pacific Insurance mortgage, and the mortgage that Agoston gave Charles Zaehnsdorf in 1862 had grown from $23,000 to $50,000. In addition to the two unpaid mortgages, the financial statement for the year ended June 23, 1866, showed that the society had gone in debt to the additional sum of $41,000, most of which was for loans taken out with leading San Francisco banks. The cost of the labor performed by Chinese workers during the year was modest (the total bill came to just under $8,000); but the trip Agoston made to Washington, D.C., New York, and Philadelphia in 1865 had cost the society nearly $4,000, about half as much as all the Chinese labor for the year.[13]

George Johnson was a tough-minded businessman. Born in Norway in 1811, he went to sea while still a boy and eventually became the captain of a ship that took him all over the world. He came to California in 1849 and, within a few years, established a large iron factory. By the middle 1860's, he was one of the richest men in San Francisco, with an elegant home in the exclusive South Park neighborhood and a fortune estimated at nearly a million dollars. The government of his native land recognized his ability when it called on him to serve as consul general in San Francisco of the United Kingdom of Sweden and Norway, an office that he filled with distinction.[14]

By signing the annual report of the trustees of the BVVS in June 1866, Johnson assumed some personal responsibility for the matters it covered. He was mindful of the seriousness of the charges leveled against Agoston and sensitive to suggestions that the board of trustees was not doing all it should to make the BVVS profitable. The report he signed on June 23, 1866, dwelt at some length on this last allegation. He stated that the trustees did not accept their positions on the board for personal gain, but because they believed the BVVS was an enterprise of "national importance" which promised "vast benefit" to California and every branch of business in it. He acknowledged that economic conditions had not been favorable to the society's efforts—interest rates were "enormous," and the market prices for grapes, wines, and brandy were low. Nonetheless, the BVVS had gone a long way toward proving that planting vines, raising grapes, and manufacturing wine and brandy could be a successful—even lucrative—business in California.

But Johnson counseled the shareholders not to expect too much too soon: patience was important in any business, doubly so in the wine business, where nature's timetable is long. He drew an analogy between the Pacific railroad, then building eastward from Sacramento over the Sierra Nevada, and the BVVS: "No shareholder of the Pacific Railroad Company expects that a track completed one hundred miles should pay a dividend on the capital stock of the whole road besides build the balance of the road; but they calculate every dollar invested so much added to the value of their shares."[5] The society, in other words, was like a railroad that had yet to finish laying its tracks—a heroic enterprise that was then inching its way across a great range of mountains. Once the mountains were crossed, the going would be clear and free to the end of the road.

If the shareholders detected a defensive tone in the trustees' report for 1866, Agoston's report for the year was typically effusive. He began by stating that everything at Buena Vista was in "a thriving condition." Rain had fallen in Sonoma late in the spring, greatly benefiting the vines, particularly those most recently planted. Sonoma had suffered three nights of severe frost late in the spring—the first frost of consequence he had experienced since he arrived in the valley in 1856—but it had struck hardest on the valley floor and had not damaged the vines on the hills and mountainsides. He reminded the shareholders that he had been the first to recommend mountain plantings and the first to experiment with hillside plantations; sloping lands once considered worthless had since proved to be better for winegrowing than any lands in the valley. "The vines grow quicker," he added, "give more grapes to the vine, bear uniformly, and above all give better wine, without being subject to the night frosts." The BVVS had about 5,000 acres of this choice land, most of which was still undeveloped.

He also reported that BVVS had at last succeeded in producing a champagne of really first quality. A blind tasting of Buena Vista "Sparkling Sonoma" and imported French champagne by distinguished citizens had proved its merits: "Of about thirty gentlemen, bankers, general importers of foreign wines, and good consumers, but one distinguished the French from the Buena Vista, and even this gentleman acknowledged that having imported this brand for years aided him in distinguishing the same."[16]

Favorable though they were, however, the reports filed by the trustees and officers of the BVVS in June 1866 did not tell the full story. The financial condition of the society was in fact much more precarious than President Johnson or the trustees intimated, and the vines were not nearly so healthy as Agoston made them out to be. There had, in fact, been signs of trouble in the Buena Vista vineyards for several years. As far back as 1860, Agoston had noticed that some of his vines were growing weak and eventually dying. He pulled them up and replaced them with new vines, but in the course of disposing of the old plants he noticed that their roots were badly decayed. The decay seemed to be most prevalent in the old vineyards planted on flat ground; the newer plantations on the hillsides seemed to be immune to the problem. Agoston theorized that the difference was the alkali water lying under the flat ground. New plants would seem to do well for a time, but then grow weak and limp. Here and there, whole rows of vines were yellowing, and the canes were stunted and the grapes small and colorless.[17] Elsewhere, the vines seemed to be sensitive to other ailments such as leaf wilt and powdery mildew (or oidium), which had long afflicted the vineyards of France.[18] The vines seemed to lack the strength to throw off these complaints quickly, or, in some cases, to throw them off at all.

Agoston cannot have known that the afflicted vines he took up in his vineyards in the early and middle 1860's were victims of the dreaded root louse, or *Phylloxera vastatrix*, which in the 1870's and 1880's would ravage the finest wine vineyards of California and Europe and at one time threaten to destroy the wine industry all over the world. But descriptions that were given years after he left Sonoma leave little doubt that these early ailments were signs that the phylloxera was on the march in California. It is possible, even likely, that Buena Vista was the first vineyard in the state in which the dreaded pest took root.[19]

Because the phylloxera attacks only the roots of grapevines, and because it does not cause instant death but a kind of slow strangulation, it defied identification for years after its first appearance in California. Botanists were later to discover that the pest was a native of the United States east of the Rocky Mountains and that, for millennia, it had lived in an uneasy coexistence with grapevines native to the area. The vines were attacked by the insect, to be sure, but over the eons they developed a resistance to it, so that the attacks were usually no worse than an irritation. It was a different matter entirely when the phylloxera encountered the delicate European *Vitis vinifera*, for the Old World vines had little resistance to the pest and slowly but inevitably succumbed to its voracious sucking.[20]

It is now generally believed that the phylloxera was brought to Europe on American vines and transferred there to *vinifera*. It may have made its way to California when *vinifera* vines were imported from Europe, but it could also have come directly from the eastern states, with one of the early importations of eastern American grapes such as Catawba and Isabella.[21] If it came to California on *viniferas*, it may well have been brought there by Agoston in one of his many importations of European vines. If it came directly from the eastern United States, it probably predated Agoston's European importations, for he had no use for vines like the Catawba and Isabella and never brought any of them to California.[22]

Since the phylloxera is almost microscopically small (a typical root louse is only one twenty-fifth of an inch long), and since all its damage is inflicted beneath the ground, it is hardly surprising that it escaped detection for so long. It is a curious fact, too, that as soon as the insects have killed one vine, they leave it in search of another, so that when dead plants are dug up their roots reveal not a trace of the deadly predators (although the insects can be detected if an infected plant is dug up before it dies). When the effects of phylloxera infestations were first noticed, vineyardists looked to other causes to explain the yellowing leaves, the stunted canes, the small, dried fruit (Agoston himself thought that alkali water beneath his vineyards had caused the first damage in 1860). When the first vineyards planted by English colonists in Virginia began to turn yellow and wither early in the seventeenth century, the vineyardists charged with their care were angrily accused of "neglecting" them, although the symptoms were almost certainly the results of phylloxera; similarly, when phylloxera damage was first discovered in France in the 1860's, the problem was attributed to overpruning or just "bad growing."[23] In Sonoma in 1866–67, the phylloxera that was slowly spreading through the vineyards of the BVVS provoked heated attacks on the man who was responsible for their care. Agoston's critics charged that his vines were dying because they had been "weakened" by the layers he laced through the vineyards. This was a devastating charge and one that, given the paucity of scientific knowledge then available, was virtually impossible to disprove.

The spreading malaise in the vineyards came at a time when Agoston himself was under unusual stress. As he expanded the vineyards at Buena Vista, he had negotiated some personal loans. Even after the incorporation of the BVVS, he continued to borrow money from various investors in San Francisco and also New York. In September 1863, for example, he borrowed $10,000 in gold coin from the San Francisco banker Abel Guy.[24] As part of the loan arrangement, he gave Guy a security interest in more than 30,000 gallons of wine and brandy (some stored in San Francisco, some in Sonoma); the original trustees of the BVVS cosigned his note.[25] In May 1864, Agoston obtained a larger loan for $42,800, from Cornelius K. Garrison of New York City. Before making this loan, Garrison insisted that Agoston give him a security interest in one thousand shares of BVVS stock; the stock was valued on the society's books at $80 a share, so Garrison acquired stock worth $80,000 as security for the payment of a $42,800 obligation.[26]

The existing records do not reveal what Agoston did with the money he borrowed from Guy and Garrison. He may have used part of it to cover the expenses of his travels—at least those expenses that were not reimbursed by the BVVS. It is possible (even likely) that he invested some of the money in enterprises unrelated to the BVVS—enterprises for which no written record has survived and that were later forgotten, perhaps because they never came to fruition. And he may well have made short-term investments in stocks or other securities hoping that they might produce a quick profit and help him pay off his existing debts. He was by nature a gambler—a congenital, even compulsive, optimist who always minimized the risk and maximized the profit potential of investments—and investments of this kind would be wholly in character.[27]

He may also have used some of the money to help his children establish their own winemaking business in Sonoma. Although Attila had had his own vineyard property since the early 1860's, the grapes from that vineyard were initially sold to the BVVS. With the establishment of the firm of Haraszthy Brothers, it became necessary to fit up fermenting rooms and cellars. It seems likely that Attila, Bela, and Arpad—joined by Gaza after his return to California—began to build facilities of this kind in Sonoma toward the end of 1865.

Agoston initially had little doubt that he would be able to repay the large amounts he borrowed from Guy and Garrison. But as prices for wine declined, as the federal government continued to tax wine and brandy, and as the chorus of criticism directed against his layering of the Buena Vista vineyards increased, he found it more and more difficult to do so. The loan from Guy in September 1863 had been a short-term obligation (all the principal was due and payable in one month), but Guy had apparently been renewing it from month to month. When after several months Agoston still had not met his obligation, Guy demanded payment. Agoston stalled, Guy grew impatient, and in September 1864 he sold the wine and brandy that Agoston had pledged as security (some 30,000 gallons). Though it should have fetched enough to cover the note, it did not, and in November Guy filed suit for payment of the balance remaining: $3,433.75.[28] The suit was filed in the District Court in San Francisco. The attorney Agoston hired to represent him in the San Francisco action was Murray Whallon, a member of the federal commission appointed in 1858 to investigate Agoston's suspected embezzlement of gold from the San Francisco mint and later an assistant to the U.S. District Attorney in the prosecution against Agoston.[29] Another of the many men who had once been Agoston's adversaries but later came to work with him, Whallon had purchased vineyard property west of Buena Vista in the early 1860's and had eventually set up a law office in Santa Rosa. For his services in the Guy suit, Whallon charged Agoston more than a thousand dollars.[30] But his efforts cannot have been much more than a holding action, for there was no question that the Guy loan had been made and not repaid.

While Whallon was attempting to stave off Abel Guy, Agoston looked for other sources of credit. In August 1865, he was able to negotiate two loans, one from the San Francisco firm of Eggers and Co. for something under $1,000 and another from the San Francisco banker John Parrott for about $5,000. Both loans cost him more of his stock in the BVVS: Eggers and Co. received a pledge of ten shares as security for its loan and Parrott received another 136 shares. The Guy lawsuit was still pending in December, when Agoston borrowed $2,500 from the San Francisco firm of Dana Brothin and Co. and another $2,500 from Walter M. Rockwell, former president of the board of trustees of the BVVS. Then in January 1866 Agoston negotiated still another loan, this in the amount of $10,000, from George Johnson. Brothin, Rockwell, and Johnson all exacted more shares of

Agoston's stock as security for their loans—with 64 shares going to Brothin, 64 to Rockwell, and 370 to Johnson.[31]

The almost careless manner in which Agoston was borrowing money and pledging shares of stock in an enterprise he had devoted more than ten years of his life to creating and nurturing is frankly troubling. Did he really imagine that he could repay all these loans, with interest, as and when they came due? Did he really believe that he would be able to save his BVVS shares from the creditors' clutches? Or had he given up on Buena Vista, and decided merely to extract what money he could from the great vineyard and take it elsewhere?

The threat that Agoston's rapidly escalating debts posed to his financial well-being became apparent to his family at least by the end of 1865, for in December of that year Agoston, Attila, and Eleonora entered into a series of transactions designed to put at least some of his assets beyond the reach of creditors.

A good vineyard located just west of General Vallejo's property had recently come on the market, and Attila had looked into the possibility of buying it. It had been planted a few years earlier by Colonel A. J. Butler, but Butler had died, and his heirs, most of whom lived in Massachusetts, wanted to sell. The original Butler tract (known in Sonoma as the "Butler Place") occupied an irregularly shaped parcel of thirty-five acres just north of the wagon road from Sonoma to Santa Rosa; but the Butlers also owned three other parcels of vineyard land that lay between the first tract and West Spain Street in Sonoma. Taken together, the four parcels totaled just over 126 acres.[32] They were all apparently planted to vines, so that they constituted one of the largest vineyards (excluding, of course, Buena Vista) in the vicinity of Sonoma. When Attila contacted the Butler heirs, he learned that they wanted $21,000 for their Sonoma property. Since he was unable to raise this sum in cash, he gave them a mortgage in the amount of $20,000. The Butlers apparently asked for additional security, so Agoston cosigned the mortgage with his son.[33]

Whether Attila ever intended to occupy the Butler property is doubtful, for only six months after he purchased it he deeded the property to Eleonora. The transaction was a gift and intended to establish that, under California law, the property was not the common (or "community") property of Agoston and Eleonora, but her separate property. The deed recited that the only consideration for the transfer was the "love and affection" that Attila had for his mother. To underscore the separate property character of the transfer, the deed added that the rents, issues, and profits of the property were to be "the sole and separate property of the said Eleonora free from the debts[,] control or interference of her husband the said Agoston Haraszthy."[34]

At the same time that Attila purchased the Butler property, Agoston became indebted to his son "as trustee for Eleonora" in the amount of $20,000. This debt may be taken as an indication that Attila was acting as his father's agent in obtaining the property and that Agoston felt committed to repay him for the $20,000 obligation he had assumed on the Butler mortgage. Agoston may also have transferred some shares of the BVVS to his son as trustee for his mother, perhaps as security for the debt, or simply to put them beyond the reach of his creditors.

This series of transactions raises some questions that are not easy to answer. Why, for example, did Agoston feel obligated to Attila for $20,000 when he had cosigned a mortgage for that amount with his son? And if the Butler property was truly to be Eleonora's and not Agoston's, why did Agoston sign formal documents (documents that he knew would be recorded and thus open to the scrutiny of all of his creditors) showing that he actively aided his son in acquiring the property for her?

No records have been kept of the date on which the Haraszthys began to manage the Butler property. Haraszthy Brothers may have worked the property for the Butler heirs even before Attila acquired title in January 1866, since the heirs were all out of the state and the 1865 crop would have gone to waste if it had not been harvested and crushed. In the spring of 1866, however, Agoston's sons were almost certainly busy on the property, for the vines had to be tended in preparation for the coming year's crop.[35] Agoston may well have taken a personal hand in the management of the property, even though he was still superintendent of the BVVS. He was still at Buena Vista in June of 1866 when George Johnson and the board of trustees defended him in print from charges of "unfaithfulness and extravagance" (perhaps his involvement in the Butler property was partly responsible for the charges leveled against him).

And he was still on the property in December, for the *Alta* reported on December 11 of that year that he had been involved the previous day in a serious accident at Buena Vista. He had apparently been standing on the second floor of the distillery at about five o'clock in the evening when the head of one of the steam tanks suddenly blew out, filling the building with steam. To escape the scalding vapor, he jumped about twelve feet. He landed among some boxes and lumber, dislocating his ankle and receiving what the *Alta* described as "serious internal injuries." He was carried to his house in a fainting condition. The newspaper reported that he was a little better the following morning,[36] though it would obviously take him a long time to recover completely.

There is no record of the date on which Agoston left Buena Vista for the last time, but it was some time between his almost-fatal fall in December 1866 and June 1867, when for the first time since the BVVS was organized in 1863 the annual reports were issued without the Haraszthy name. During that interval, he either resigned as superintendent or was dismissed by the new board of trustees. It may be assumed that his creditors had continued to exert pressure on him during this time, and that they eventually stripped him of all of his BVVS stock. The annual reports for 1867 show the name of John Parrott, one of Agoston's creditors, on the board of trustees, and there are several other new names: Joseph A. Donohoe, John Bensley, Christian Christiansen, Charles Baum, and R. N. Van Brunt. William Ralston and B. Eugene Auger were the only old names. William Blanding, whose association with Agoston dated back to the mint prosecution, had also joined the board and been elected president.

The man selected to take Agoston's place as superintendent of the Buena Vista vineyards was Emil Dresel, the onetime Rhinelander who had operated a nearby vineyard since about 1858. The exact date on which Dresel took over his new duties is not clear, but when he filed his first superintendent's report in June 1867, he stated that it covered "the last eight months."[37] If this is correct, Dresel would have assumed the superintendent's duties in October 1866, or nearly two months before Agoston's distillery accident. Agoston may have remained at Buena Vista after Dresel began working there because he needed time to complete arrangements for his move, or simply because his help and experience were needed during the transition period.

Whether there were any personal differences between Agoston and Dresel, deep-seated professional differences certainly divided them. Dresel may have been one of the "outside parties" that president Johnson and the board of trustees referred to when, in June 1866, they answered the charges that Agoston was not true to his duties as superintendent. Dresel's own vineyard adjoined Buena Vista on the southeast, and he would have had ample opportunity to watch Agoston layer Buena Vista. He would also have seen the wilt that settled over the vineyard in the spring of 1866, the leaves that yellowed and curled as the weather turned warmer, the canes that shriveled, and the fruit that grew hard and dry.

Dresel had no more scientific understanding of the causes of these symptoms than Agoston himself. Yet he seemed convinced that the vineyard's problems lay in the close spacing that the founder had adopted and so vocally championed.[38] It was admittedly difficult to plow the vineyards, at least before the connections between the layers and the parent vines were severed; for, while those connections remained, the spaces between the vines were blocked, and the long canes formed a thick web of tangled vines.

But Dresel believed that the evils of layering transcended mere difficulties of cultivation. The layers crowded the roots of the vines, he thought, and weakened every part of the vineyard. One of Dresel's first tasks on assuming his duties as superintendent of the BVVS was to plow up the layers that Agoston had laid down in the previous two years; he also plowed under every other row that Agoston had planted in the new sections of the vineyard, and in the process destroyed thousands of vines that Agoston had planted in the previous three years. Since Agoston had planted choice *vinifera* varieties in alternating rows, whole varieties were thus ripped out of the ground and cast aside.[39]

Dresel immediately restored Buena Vista to the eight-foot spacing pattern that the old Californians had so long favored. But this change did little to restore the vineyard to health, for the problems that beset the vines were still hidden beneath the earth—biding their time until they could mount a systematic attack, not only on Agoston Haraszthy's vines but on those of every other *vinifera* vineyard in California.

28

A Very
Sad Place

Agoston Haraszthy, at the age of fifty-four, had left a magnificent estate of more than 5,000 acres for a modest vineyard of 125 acres— hardly large enough to occupy his attention, and certainly not large enough to give him the income he needed to pay off his debts. He and Eleonora were nearer to the Vallejos now than they had been at Buena Vista, but the once all-powerful grandee of northern California was himself in reduced circumstances and in no position to lend a helping hand. He still hung on to his house at Lachryma Montis and a few hundred acres surrounding it, but the vast tracts of land he once surveyed as a kind of feudal lord were all gone. Mrs. Vallejo sat down in January 1867 to write a letter to her daughter Jovita in San Francisco. She complained that her children—all except Natalia and Jovita—seemed to be avoiding her, in fear she might ask them for financial help. But the Haraszthy girls stood by her with constant reminders of their affection. "Sonoma is a very sad place," Mrs. Vallejo confided to Jovita, "especially Lachryma Montis and Buena Vista."[1]

Bad news seemed to be in the air. Early in January, the *Alta* reported that General C. H. S. Williams, president of the new California State Wine-Growers' Association and the owner of a Sonoma vineyard that he had bought from Agoston, had shot himself to death in his office in San Francisco. The newspaper described the incident as a terrible accident, but the circumstances were puzzling enough to suggest suicide. Three days after Williams's death, Charles V. Stuart of Sonoma was elected to succeed him at the head of the Wine-Growers' Association. The Williams' heirs asked Attila to take charge of Williams's vineyard and ready it for the coming year's harvest. All four Haraszthy sons seemed to be unusually busy as the spring of 1867 arrived in Sonoma. Attila was producing wine for the San Francisco champagne cellars run by Arpad and Isidor Landsberger, while continuing to produce wine for himself and several of his neighbors. Gaza and Bela worked with Attila in the firm of Haraszthy Brothers, and Arpad was busy in San Francisco, transforming his brothers' Sonoma wine into California champagne.

To the east, Pierre Debanne was still making champagne for the BVVS. Debanne was able to put up the respectable number of 90,000 bottles in the spring. Buena Vista had recently sent a shipment of its 1865 sparkling wine to the Paris International Exhibition, scheduled to open later in the year, and the trustees and officers of the society had hopes that the effervescence would help to convince Europeans that California wine was not the product of a wild and ragged frontier but a worthy competitor for the attention of consumers around the world. Agoston had a personal, if not a financial, interest in the success of this BVVS wine, for he had conceived it and nurtured it to fruition.

Agoston's creditors continued to bear down on him. On April 13, 1867, Able Guy recovered judgment against him in San Francisco for $4,679.47, plus interest at the rate of 2 percent per month; but Agoston could not possibly pay, at least not with his present income. The day before the Guy judgment was rendered, he sold a few acres he still owned on the east side of Sonoma to Attila for $400; Henry Hancock, up from Los Angeles for a Sonoma visit, was a witness to the deed.[2] But Agoston could not use any part of the $400 to apply to the Guy debt, for he had other more pressing needs.

Agoston must have been grateful for Attila's support in this troubling time. Attila had never been as facile or brilliant as Arpad, but he was solid and trustworthy—someone who could be depended on to help when help was needed. The fact that Attila was now thirty-two years old reminded Agoston of the swift passage of time. It was not so very long ago that this little boy, his second son, had played with pigs in a muddy sty beside the family house at Kútas. Now he was a respected Sonoma businessman and father. A month after Attila celebrated his birthday, another event reminded Agoston of how much time had passed since he arrived in the United States. Bela, born in Haraszthy Town on Sauk Prairie in the territory of Wisconsin, was now twenty-one years old and engaged to a Sonoma girl named Edna Smith. On May 18, Bela and Edna were married in the home of one of the Haraszthys' neighbors, an old valley resident named Charles W. Lubeck. Agoston would have liked the marriage to be held, like Ida's, in the big house at Buena Vista; that could not be, but he must have been pleased that the wedding was performed by a Catholic priest.[3] Two weeks after Bela's wedding, Agoston and Eleonora were gladdened by happy news from San Francisco. On June 2, Arpad's wife, Jovita, gave birth to a baby boy. It was Arpad's first son and second child (little Agostine was just three years old). This boy, Agoston and Eleonora's third grandchild, was named Carlos.[4]

As much as he loved Sonoma, Agoston was growing more and more anxious to escape the familiar valley and its circling chain of hills and mountains. Late in April, he wrote an article for the *Alta California* describing a plan he had devised for bringing new settlers to California. Everybody agreed that what California needed most was a good, dependable supply of labor to help unlock its vast resources, but the cost of transporting workers from the eastern states or Europe was so great that few made the long journey to the Golden State. Immigrants from Europe to the United States almost all settled along the eastern seaboard, or somewhere in the middle western heartland of the country, and few gave any serious thought to making the extra journey to the Pacific Coast. The problem, Agoston told the *Alta*'s readers, was that the costs of travel to California were just too great. But he had devised a plan that would "speedily populate large tracts of land, enable our enterprising manufacturers to compete with the most distant countries, and insure prosperity to our cities." He gave no details, but he offered to disclose his plan to the Chamber of Commerce if they were interested in hearing about it.[5] Whether the Chamber ever asked him to do so is not known. So many of his ideas of late had seemed like grand schemes with little of real substance to back them up.

Undaunted, Agoston turned his attention to the political events of the day. He had not sought elective office since he left San Diego more than fifteen years earlier, but he had maintained close contacts with public officials and candidates. During all those years he had been a faithful defender of the Democratic cause, even when, during the war, he was reviled for his loyalty by suggestions that he (or his son) had "Copperhead" leanings. A gubernatorial election was due to be held in the fall of 1867 to elect a successor to the outgoing executive, Republican Frederick F. Low. The Union Party, a coalition of loyalist Republicans and Union Democrats formed to lead California safely through the political minefields of the secessionist years, was still active in 1867, under the titular leadership of California's United States Senator John Conness. The Unionists met in Sacramento on June 12 for their gubernatorial nominating convention and selected a onetime newspaper editor and state superintendent of instruction named George C. Gorham as their candidate. The regular Republicans, who objected to Conness's influence in the Union Party, met about a month later and nominated a perennial office seeker named Caleb Fay as their candidate. In the meantime, the Democrats chose San Francisco attorney Henry H. Haight as their candidate.

One of the noisiest issues of the 1867 campaign was the old but still corrosive question of Chinese labor in California. This question had been hotly debated when Agoston was in the legislature in 1852, and despite all the terrible events of the intervening years it was still a seminal issue in California. The Democrats in 1867 were generally hostile to the Chinese, while some of the Republicans tried to evade the issue. Only the Union Party squarely addressed the question, with George C. Gorham taking a strongly pro-Chinese stand. Agoston could feel the strain of contending loyalties. Since he arrived in the United States in 1840 he had been faithful to the party of Jefferson and Jackson. But in California he had been one of the most consistently articulate defenders of the Chinese. He was confronted by a difficult choice, but the difficulty may not have troubled him much, for he was never one to agonize over decisions.

Sometime during the summer of 1867 he announced that he

had decided to leave the Democratic Party and join forces with the Gorham supporters. He was aware that this would set him up for some very sharp criticism, but he seemed not to be concerned. In San Francisco, the *Examiner* (a bellicose Democratic journal) received the news with a mixture of horror and glee. It announced that Agoston had "bid farewell" to the Democratic party "after enjoying its favor for many years." Revealing the racist motives of the anti-Chinese agitators, the newspaper accused him of selling out to the "Coolie" forces:

Col. H. (for whom we entertain great personal regard) is a man of considerable acuteness, and looks ahead to the distant future with an eye single to personal advantages, but often basing extravagant speculative views upon a one-sided theory, overlooking consequent effects upon other interests. He has attached himself for life to the business of grape growing, and has gone into it more extensively than any other citizen of our State. But he has experimented with the various kinds of labor, American, German, Irish, and Coolie, and has come to the conclusion that the latter class is best and most profitably adapted to his business. . . . He believes the grape interest of this State can best be developed and enhanced by Coolies, and he is therefore in favor of their importation and employment in this branch of industry, regardless of the detrimental effects upon other classes of laborers or industrial interests. It is not to be wondered at then, that he should ally himself with Gorham, who is the declared friend and fervent advocate of Chinese immigration. Col. Haraszthy anticipates some day employing a thousand Chinamen or more, and when he has them, and when Gorham's idea of enfranchising them is carried out, he will be shrewd enough to control the local politics of his County with their votes.[6]

Again sounding a racist note, the *Examiner* reminded its readers that Agoston was not a native American, but "an exile from his native land," and it snidely declared that it would not "even complain of his turning his back upon the party that favored him so much and suffered some contumely on his account specially, but we wish it simply to be known why he prefers the Coolie candidate Gorham to the white man's candidate Henry H. Haight." The *Examiner* was undoubtedly aware that Agoston no longer controlled a large vinicultural estate but lived on a small vineyard owned by his wife and had no realistic hopes of controlling the politics of Sonoma County through the employment of a thousand "Coolies." But it suited the news-

paper's purpose not to remind its readers of the fact. And the use of
the word "contumely" (a not-so-veiled reference to the decade-old
mint affair) was surely a low blow, for Agoston had long since been
absolved of any guilt in connection with that episode, and dozens of
men who knew the details of the mint affair much better than the
Examiner had long since put those old and discredited charges behind them.

On Friday evening, August 30, Agoston appeared at a Republican rally in Sonoma. The chief speaker of the evening was U.S.
Senator William M. Stewart of Nevada, who gave a long speech extolling the memory of Abraham Lincoln. The Republican candidate
for county judge spoke next, after which Agoston took to the rostrum. He acknowledged that he was not a native American, but an
"adopted child of California" who had voted the straight Democratic
ticket for twenty-three years. But he was, he said, a "progressive man"
and, as such, he must join forces with the "progressive party." He recalled a discussion he had recently had with a Sonoman who inquired
concerning his political views. After determining that he had indeed
deserted the anti-Chinese Democrats, the Sonoman sought out his
views on the newly freed population of black Americans. Scarcely
two months earlier, Congress had proposed the Fourteenth Amendment to the Constitution, defining citizenship to include Negroes
and forbidding the states to deny "equal protection of the laws."
The amendment had not yet been ratified by the states, and it did
not extend the right to vote to the former slaves, but there was talk
among some Republicans that the next amendment to the Constitution should do just that. The curious Sonoman asked Agoston if he
would go so far as to "give the nigger a vote," to which Agoston replied emphatically, "I would." With this statement, the Republicans
on the platform and in the audience erupted in cheers. The *Examiner*
reporter who was covering the event was aghast. He called the rally
"a mongrel gathering" and excoriated Agoston as a "cloven-hoofed"
Hungarian exile who had come to California and, for twenty-seven
years, "duped the people," finally joining in with a "partisan attempt
to elevate the Negro and depress the Anglo-Saxon."[7]

There is little doubt that Agoston's new political opinions were
sincere. He had so long championed the cause of the Chinese in

California that he could not in good faith support a Democratic Party that appealed to the basest racial instincts of the voters, and if he hoped to feather his own nest by joining the Republicans he would have little luck in doing that in Sonoma, for the county was still overwhelmingly Democratic. When, on September 4, the voters trooped to the polls, Henry Haight was easily elected governor with more than 50,000 votes to Gorham's 40,000 and Caleb Fay's 2,000. Out of a little more than 4,000 votes cast in Sonoma County, Haight polled over 3,000.[8] So much for Agoston's attempts to control the politics of Sonoma County through "Coolie" labor!

But dabbling in politics was not the way to get his financial house back in order. He might enjoy the attention that was focused on him during the gubernatorial election, but what he really needed was money, not publicity. Abel Guy was not the only creditor who was bearing down hard on him. He seemed to be besieged on all sides, like a caged animal with no route of escape.

There was one route of escape, at least from seemingly insurmountable financial troubles: bankruptcy. Despite the aversion that many businessmen held for bankruptcy, it had been available since the foundation of the republic.[9] The Founding Fathers (some of whom had themselves been forced to declare bankruptcy or, even worse, serve terms of confinement in debtor's prison) had considered bankruptcy a natural and necessary feature of a free society, and the wisdom of the constitutional provision granting Congress the power to establish uniform laws of bankruptcy had never been seriously challenged. Still, there was a stigma attached to bankruptcy. Like the priest in the confessional, who demanded a penance before absolving a sinner of his sins, the bankruptcy judge demanded a penalty before he would absolve a debtor of his debts. In the case of the priest, a few Hail Marys or a Rosary might suffice; in the case of the bankruptcy judge, an order that the debtor surrender all his nonexempt property to his creditors and publicly acknowledge his poverty was necessary. It was the equivalent of a declaration of financial failure—humbling, even humiliating, but unavoidable.

Agoston went back to Murray Whallon and, just thirteen days after the gubernatorial election was over, filed a petition in bankruptcy in the office of the Register in Bankruptcy in Santa Rosa.[10]

There were schedules to be filled out and declarations to sign (the bankruptcy law obviously made no effort to save paper or ink). But Agoston dutifully complied with all the legal requirements. The petition and accompanying schedules that he filed on September 17, 1867, do not present a pretty picture. In all, he listed debts of $116,741.97 and assets of $24,975.00.[11] But both of these figures were deceptive, for some of the "debts" were not really owing—they were undoubtedly listed out of a superabundance of caution and after listening to Murray Whallon's lawyerly advice that it is better to be over- rather than under-inclusive—and the assets were a ragtag collection of memories and broken hopes. The only real property Agoston still owned in Sonoma County was "an interest" in some 600 acres of marshland on the edge of San Francisco Bay. Even this was not fully paid for, since he had been buying on a contract with the State of California, and it probably had little value. He also claimed that he still owned some 568 acres of land in Dane County, Wisconsin, though he admitted that he had not seen the property since 1848 or 1849 and had no idea what it might be worth; and he claimed to own some lots in and around San Diego, and a one-tenth interest in the tract of land called Middletown (or "Haraszthyville"), also of unknown value, for he had not seen it since 1853.

Agoston's declarations revealed that he owned household goods and furniture, wearing apparel, and "personal ornaments" having a value of $500; books, prints, and pictures worth $300; one saddle and bridle worth $60; and one gun and one pistol valued at $75. He had no animals of any sort, not even a saddle horse. He listed the copyright to *Grape Culture, Wines and Wine-Making*, plus his interest in the contract with Harper & Brothers, and valued them together at $5,000, but the figure was surely exaggerated. The most curious entry in the bankruptcy schedules was the listing of a "claim" against the State of California for reimbursement for the expenses he had incurred on his tour of Europe in 1861. The issue of whether he was entitled to be reimbursed for those expenses had been argued in the legislature of 1862, and he had lost that argument. Whatever the basis of his "claim," it had always rested more on a moral than on a strictly legal foundation. His argument had been, not that the State of California was bound by law to repay him for the moneys he had advanced as Commissioner on the Vine, but that it was bound in good conscience to do so. Was he now descending from the high ground of morals and conscience to the low ground of legal technicalities? As prepared by Murray Whallon, Agoston's bankruptcy petition read: "The Petitioner claims to recover from the State of California, his expenses in going to Europe and returning therefrom as Commissioner of said State, also money paid for grape vines including freight and other charges upon the same—amounting in all as fairly due him $12,000."[12]

Perhaps the words "fairly due him" were enough to reaffirm the moral foundation of the claim, to reiterate that his argument with the legislature had not been about what the law *would compel it to do*, but what in good conscience it *should have done*. When the bankruptcy court offered this "claim" against the state for sale at public auction, the highest bid was only $20, sufficient proof that the legislature's obligation was not strictly legal. Good morals, after all, are worth little in dollars.

Agoston's final discharge in bankruptcy was not granted until January 5, 1869,[13] but it was a foregone conclusion from the day he filed his petition that it would be granted, and he wasted no time in worrying about it. After all his years in Wisconsin, in San Diego, in San Francisco, and finally in Sonoma, he had no more to show for his efforts than a court order absolving him of his debts.

29

The Final
Frontier

At fifty-five years of age, Agoston was no longer as vigorous as
he had been when he first arrived on Sauk Prairie, or even when he
came to Sonoma and began to build the great Buena Vista vineyard.
His black hair was streaked with gray and his lined face seemed to
have lost some of its energy. But he was still full of ambition. He was
not a young man, but he was not old either, and he was convinced
there were still opportunities waiting to be seized.

In the fall of 1867, he made some wine at the Butler Place. He
also produced ten thousand gallons of brandy that he sold to the
San Francisco firm of Tilman and Bendel.[1] Arpad was having some
success with the wine he was producing for Landsberger. His first
Landsberger champagne went on sale that same fall, and it promptly
won a premium at the State Fair in Sacramento. Landsberger was
so pleased with Arpad's first champagne that he sent cases of it to
England, New York, and even as far away as Japan. He had had
no reports from England or Japan, but his New York correspon-
dents reported that the wine had arrived there in "perfect order." It
was, Landsberger reported, "diamond-bright, and sparkled long and
continuously," and "its taste was perfect."[2] Agoston was pleased by
Arpad's success, and also by word from Paris that, at the Universal

Exposition of 1867, Buena Vista Sparkling Sonoma won an honorable mention. This was the highest prize awarded to any American wine in Paris.[3] After the wine was tested, the remaining bottles (along with other California wines entered in the competition) were given to Professor Louis Pasteur for use in his ongoing experiments on the effects of microbial action in wines.[4]

Agoston spent the latter part of 1867 and the early months of 1868 looking for new business opportunities. No record has survived of the men he talked to, or of the enterprises that he proposed, but there is little doubt that he was interested in a new winemaking enterprise somewhere in California, perhaps near the properties of the Philadelphia and California and New York and California Petroleum companies south of Santa Barbara. But he was not able to convince anybody that he should be given a second chance. Bankruptcy may not be a sin, but it is not a badge of merit either, and potential investors will think long and hard before entrusting their money to a man who has a record of not paying his debts. Agoston obviously had two strikes against him in his new entrepreneurial efforts, and it was difficult to convince anyone that he could get on base before the third strike was called. In January 1868, a wine cellar on the Butler property caught fire and burned. Agoston estimated the loss at $7,000[5]— a considerable sum for a man just emerging from bankruptcy—but he had seen worse, and he was still resourceful. If California investors were not interested in his proposals, perhaps he could convince capitalists in another country that he could still put a business plan together.

Late in February 1868 Agoston, accompanied by Gaza, boarded a ship in San Francisco. The exact date of their departure, and the ship on which they took passage, have not been discovered. But we know where they went, for on March 23 of that year, in the ancient city of León in the Central American Republic of Nicaragua, more than two thousand miles from Sonoma, Agoston put his pen to paper to write a letter. It is hard to imagine that he brought much money with him to Nicaragua, but he had not forgotten to bring along his wit, his good humor, and the knack for writing readable English that he had developed in Wisconsin and California. He was writing a letter, not to a relative or friend back in Sonoma, but to the readers of the *Alta California* in San Francisco. It was the first of a series of missives that he would send to the *Alta* from Central America. The newspaper identified him as its "special correspondent" and published his letters on the front page, under the boldface title, "Haraszthy's Letters from Nicaragua."

Agoston seemed to be in fine fettle as he described his arrival at the coastal town of San Juan del Sur, where he and Gaza presented themselves and their letters of introduction to the local *comandante*, who promptly and courteously gave them passage into the country. They proceeded at once to a hotel run by an American named Green. The friendly hotelier not only provided them with food but helped them obtain riding animals and a guide. And thus, less than two hours after their landing, they were on their way again, heading east from San Juan on a road that led up a gentle slope to a kind of plateau, scattered here and there with handsome trees.[6]

As they continued northward, they saw monkeys skipping along the road. "It is remarkable with what swiftness they travel," Agoston wrote, "never touch the ground, but swing themselves by the hands and tails from limb to limb and from tree to tree."[7] He noticed one monkey, more daring than the rest, that planted itself on a tall tree not far from the road and proceeded to make faces at the travelers. Always prepared for the hunt, he unslung his shotgun, took aim, and discharged a barrel full of goose shot at the insolent animal. But the blast did not kill the monkey. He lodged a second shot into the animal, but with no better effect. The monkey clung to the limb of his tree "with a death grasp, making horrible faces." Gaza then dismounted and brought the animal down with his revolver. But the monkey was still not dead. "The poor animal stretched himself on the ground," Agoston wrote, "moaning like a man, and from time to time gave a cry of pain and agony until he expired. It was more like a human being dying than anything we had seen in animals, and sorrow and great remorse we felt for this rash act. I resolved never to kill so innocent an animal without any use or necessity whatever."[8]

After four and a half hours, the travelers arrived in the town of Rivas, on the west shore of Lake Nicaragua, the largest body of fresh water in Central America. There they paid their guide, gave up their animals, and entered a large adobe building called the Hotel de Rivas. Agoston had trouble sleeping that night, for a room adjoining his own was filled with cocks that residents of the town used for cockfights.[9] He admired the straight streets of the town and the long, tile-roofed adobes that lined them, but he found the main plaza "the receptacle of all dirt and filth; not a tree or shrub ornaments it; dogs, pigs and donkeys are at home there, unmolested, and live in good harmony with one another."[10]

After a stroll through Rivas, Agoston and Gaza presented themselves to the prefect and informed him that they intended to travel north to the capital city of Managua, where the Nicaraguan Congress was in session. The helpful official offered to procure animals for the next leg of their journey, and in short order a set of mules was waiting at the hotel. The animals were rather "small" and "lean," and Agoston wondered whether they would be able to carry them all the way to the capital. But the prefect assured them that they were equal to the task, so they set out about two in the afternoon on the road leading northward.[11]

They proceeded through a country of cocoa and coffee plantations, then passed through a wonderland of tropical trees—oranges, mangos, papayas, cashews. Agoston was surprised to see the rare fruits and nuts, so costly in the North, lying ungathered on the ground. But they were so abundant here that there was nobody—not even hogs—to eat them. Around eight o'clock, after darkness had fallen, they arrived at a ranch, where they were advised to stop and wait until the moon rose. They unsaddled their mules and procured some corn for the animals to feed on, then laid their saddles and blankets on the ground and attempted to rest. But they were soon disturbed by snorting hogs that literally ran over them in their efforts to get to the corn. "The guide drove them away with some vehemence," Agoston wrote, "but they returned. The charge and repulse lasted for some time, when, at last, the guide fell asleep, and the hogs took undisturbed possession of the premises. This only relieved us from the hogs, but not from the fleas and the terrible screeching of night birds, which congregated on surrounding trees to settle some great dispute. Such shrieking and chattering we never heard before."[12]

They resumed their journey through timbered country. About daybreak, Agoston asked the guide how long it would be before they came to their next resting place. He was "somewhat nettled" when the guard told him that they had already passed it. When he inquired how much more distance they would have to cover before they stopped for breakfast, the guide said, "Four leagues from here will be breakfast." Agoston sensed that the guide intended to take him to a friend so the friend would have a little morning business. "I pulled up on my mule," Agoston continued, "rose indignantly in my saddle, and told the guide in plain Spanish, ornamenting the expressions with something like plain English, that we would not go a mile beyond the first house we met, and that he must take us at once to the nearest one."[13]

The guide took the travelers to a little settlement some distance off the road. There they approached an Indian hut and asked the occupants if they could have some breakfast. The welcome answer was, "Why not?" So they again removed the saddles from their animals, spread their blankets on the ground, and stretched out for some badly needed rest. Soon breakfast was announced, "with plenty of broiled chickens, fried eggs, beef, rice, fruits, etc."

The first large town they came to was Masaya, an old town of about 30,000 inhabitants, most of them Indians. Agoston found the Indians to be "the most industrious people of Nicaragua" and marveled at the handmade wares they offered for sale every evening in the plaza—colorful baskets, carved wooden dishes, finely woven matting, beautiful hammocks, halters for horses and mules, bed coverings. Always alert to commercial opportunities, he thought that the Indians' products would find a good market in San Francisco and New York, where inferior products from Japan brought good prices.[14]

In Masaya, he stopped at the first store he could find and asked where he could buy some wine. He wanted California wine, he told the clerk, and nothing else. The clerk offered him some ale (which he quaffed willingly), and then some wine from another country, but he insisted on wine from his "own state." He and his companions explained that they insisted on the California product because of its high quality and dependability. So the clerk relented and produced two bottles of California wine. Agoston and Gaza asked to inspect the bottles, the corking, and the boxes in which the bottles were packed, to assure themselves that this was a genuine California product. As Agoston later noted in his *Alta* letter: "The appearance of all was satisfactory to our judgment, and we started home to our supper, which was not bad—but, alas! for the wine! More miserable stuff, under the title of wine, none of your readers ever drank, or attempted to drink."[15]

From Masaya, they continued on to Managua, on the southern shore of Lake Managua. It was a large city, built in the Spanish colonial style around a spacious plaza, with a cathedral, a government palace, barracks, and a state prison. They went to the only hotel in the town and met some men who spoke English. One was a man named Henry Gottel, who edited a local newspaper called the *Porvenir*, another a man named Werthemann, who was sojourning in Nicaragua while he waited to learn if the Congress would grant him a bank charter. Agoston and Gaza were put up for the night in a single large room, crudely furnished with a table, two chairs, a washstand, some cots, and an earthen basin filled with water. Agoston admitted that the room was not very attractive, but confided to his *Alta* readers:

In justice we must say, we had splendid ventilation during our whole stay in Managua. We never suffered a moment, either day or night, from close or foul air; for, why should we? the walls of our room were sixteen feet high, without ceiling; the eaves were not closed; the tiles were semi-cylindrical, and let in all the breeze; the windows were tall, and five feet high, without glass, but secured by iron bars. The rooms are separated by board partitions, which do not rise to the roof; so with the open tiles, and the open windows, there is no danger of bad ventilation.[16]

From Managua, father and son continued thirty-five miles north to the city of León. For more than three centuries before Managua became Nicaragua's capital in 1858, León had been the capital and most important city of the country. It was a graceful city, with blocks of low, tile-roofed houses and a plaza adorned with the largest cathedral in Central America. The cathedral was said to have been built in error, when plans for a great church in the gold-rich city of Lima, Peru, were sent out from Spain on a ship that was also carrying plans for a more modest basilica in León. The plans were mixed up en route, and León got an edifice that would ever after be its glory. At León, Agoston introduced himself to local businessmen, and immediately began to explore the prospects for some new enterprise.

One of the men Agoston conferred with in Nicaragua was Dr. Theodore Wassmer, a German-born physician and surgeon who had migrated, first to San Francisco and then to Nicaragua. Dr. Wassmer's brother, Leopold, had also come to Nicaragua to live. Both brothers had married Nicaraguan women and started to raise families. It is not known if Agoston had known the Wassmers in San Francisco, or if he first became acquainted with them after he arrived in Nicaragua. In due time, however, the men became good friends.

Nicaragua when Agoston first saw it was an old country with a long and troubled history. The Spanish had arrived there in the 1520's, barely a generation after Columbus made his first landing in the New World. But the rugged hills that ringed Lake Nicaragua (some of them fire-spitting volcanos) had not yielded the gold and silver that the conquistadors coveted, and so they settled into a slow but comfortable coexistence with the native-American population. The country was governed from Madrid as part of the captaincy-general of Guatemala until the 1820's, when Latin America achieved its independence from Spain. A brief period under Mexican control was followed by a halfhearted attempt to unite the provinces of Central America into a confederation, but the attempt failed and the confederation fragmented into a string of small and contentious republics.

Nicaragua was the largest of the Central American states, with an area about equal to that of England or the state of Iowa, but its size and rich natural resources had not helped it achieve stability or prosperity. Revolutions and insurrections seemed to be the most predictable events in the country's political life, with the troops of the contending parties regularly massing in the plazas of the leading towns, firing guns and waving banners, bringing down one government and erecting another in its place with predictable regularity.

In the 1850's, a strange American who came from Tennessee by way of Gold Rush San Francisco had invaded Nicaragua, had himself elected president (in a rigged election), and then astonished the world by asking the Congress in Washington to admit the country to the Union as a slave state. William Walker, whom the American newspapers called "The Grey-Eyed Man of Destiny," was part charlatan, part visionary; but the Nicaraguans wanted nothing of him and, with the help of some U.S. Marines, managed to send him into exile in neighboring Honduras. The Hondurans stood him up before a firing squad in 1860, but the legacy of resentment he sowed among Nicaraguans endured. For years after Walker's ignominious death, it seemed that no problem could be solved in the country without help from the North; and, when the help was forthcoming, the Nicaraguans inevitably condemned it as "Yanqui" meddling.

The Nicaraguans had inaugurated a new president, Fernando Guzman, in March of 1867. Guzman had won the office in a fair election and seemed to enjoy the confidence of the people. He offered amnesty to political prisoners and informed the archbishop that he would work for harmonious relations between the country's civil and ecclesiastical authorities.[17] When Agoston arrived in the country, Nicaragua was enjoying a welcome period of domestic peace, which many in the country were confident would soon bloom into prosperity.

On July 16, 1868, the *Alta California* in San Francisco published a front-page story about Agoston's new career in Nicaragua. Under the heading, "Struck a Good Thing," the newspaper wrote:

The many friends of Col. Agostin [*sic*] Haraszthy in California will hear with pleasure that he has succeeded in bettering his condition and prospects in Nicaragua. It is stated, on what we deem good authority, that he has secured from the Government of that Republic the exclusive right, for twenty years, for the distillation of spirits from sugar cane and its products, for export, on such terms and with such facilities that he is certain of making a fortune out of it. The royalty to be paid the Government is light, and the material for making abundant. The necessary apparatus will be shipped from San Francisco this season.[18]

The available records do not tell much about the details of Agoston's business arrangement with the Nicaraguan government. Arpad later recalled that Gaza and Dr. Theodore Wassmer were his partners in the new venture and that the three men joined together to obtain control of a large sugar plantation near the seaside port of Corinto. Arpad may well have been exaggerating when he said the plantation embraced a hundred thousand acres and that it was the second largest in the country,[19] but all the reports seem to agree that it was large. The plantation was known as the Hacienda San Antonio. The partners began without delay to extend the plantable portions of the property by clearing the timber and plowing under the grass. Agoston apparently thought there would be a good market for both sugar and rum produced on the plantation. The property was also well supplied with timber, for which he also envisioned a ready market.

Arpad was not in Nicaragua with his father, but he maintained close contacts with him by mail. Some years later, he wrote that his father intended "to make the rich products of that country tributary to the wealth and material progress of California." This quaintly fustian burst of prose may be taken to mean that Agoston believed Nicaraguan goods could readily be sold in California, and that Californians were the logical people to develop the country. It was a colonialistic view, flattering neither to Nicaragua nor to the man who entertained it, but it comported with the prevailing American belief that all the vast territory to the south of the United States was a commercial wasteland waiting for enterprising Americans (be they native born or adopted) to inject it with life. As a Hungarian who had lived for years among Spanish-speaking Californians, and as a Roman Catholic in good standing with his church, Agoston would not inspire the animosity among Nicaraguans that Anglo-Saxon Protestants aroused, even though he held many of the same views.

The idea that the products of the Hacienda San Antonio could readily be sold in California was not as far-fetched as it might first appear. The population of the Golden State was growing rapidly, particularly in the region around San Francisco Bay, and the market for new products there seemed strong. It was a long way from Corinto to San Francisco, to be sure, but shipping lanes from Panama north to San Francisco were well established, and it did not cost much more to transport a ton of sugar from Corinto than from Honolulu, or a cargo of timber from the Hacienda San Antonio than from Portland in Oregon or Seattle on Puget Sound. The Hacienda San Antonio was close to the ocean, and a good-sized stream of fresh water led down from the forest to the coastline.

Eleonora had not accompanied Agoston to Nicaragua. Her decision to remain behind in California is understandable, for her children were comfortably situated in Sonoma and San Francisco; she herself was the owner of a vineyard in Sonoma; and she could hardly have relished the prospect of following her husband on yet another wild adventure to the far edge of civilization. But her decision was not, apparently, easy, for she was torn by divided loyalties—a desire to remain in California with her children and grandchildren, and the gnawing feeling that her place was beside her husband in Central America. Arpad later wrote that she had a "hard, hard struggle with her feelings."[20] Agoston had written her, of course, describing the hacienda and advising her that he had prepared a home for her there and that the Nicaragua climate pleased him.[21] Though his letters have not survived, we can imagine that he painted a very rosy picture of his prospects for success in his new venture. Eleonora had known him long enough to balance his congenital optimism with a stark measure of reality, but she also knew that he had an almost uncanny ability to make things happen in unlikely places. It took her only three months to resolve her dilemma, for at the end of May, accompanied by nineteen-year-old Otelia, she arrived in Nicaragua to take her place beside her husband.

Eleonora was pleased by her first impressions of Central America. The Hacienda San Antonio was, indeed, a promising venture, and she was as pleased as her husband by the warm Nicaraguan climate. As if to reassure her children back in California that she did not regret her decision to come south, she wrote them two long letters in which she expressed sanguine hopes for the family's future and described the country as an "earthly paradise."[22] But there was a bitter dimension to this tropical paradise, as Eleonora was soon to learn.

Despite its tropical beauty, Nicaragua was still a dangerous country, with bandits lurking on the highways, wild animals in the forests and brush, alligators in rivers near the coast, and nettlesome—and potentially lethal—mosquitoes swarming along the edges of the lakes and marshes. Agoston never went out on the roads without a rifle or pistol near at hand, and when he was on his horse he was always vigilant for suspicious rustlings in the trees. But vigilance cannot protect a man or his family in a country that is rife with disease, as Central

America—indeed the whole Caribbean area—was in the spring and summer of 1868; and it was disease that was to take its first toll on the Haraszthy family in their new tropical home.

Early in the month of July, only two months after she arrived at the Hacienda San Antonio, Eleonora was bitten by a mosquito—a tiny female member of the species *Aedes aegypti*. It was a little puncture, not unlike many others she and her family had already endured, and she may have been almost unaware of the attack. She did not know, of course, that the mosquito was the bearer of a microscopic virus, and that the virus was the cause of one of the world's most dreaded maladies, yellow fever. Scientists would not finally establish the connection between the fever and the virus, and the virus and the mosquito, for another half-century, and in the intervening years hundreds of thousands—perhaps millions—of men, women, and children would suffer the same bites, and fall victim to the same debilitating illness. Three to six days after the virus first entered Eleonora's blood she was beset by a sudden fever, chills, flushed features, perhaps a backache, and probably some nausea. Two or three days after the first onset of the illness, she experienced a welcome and hopeful remission. For most victims of yellow fever, this remission marked the end of the illness. For others, however, the remission was a false hope, for after a few days the worst symptoms of the disease began to appear: the skin turned a frightening yellow, the victim suffered fevered hallucinations, and massive internal bleeding was followed by a terrifying black vomit. With Eleonora, the vomit was the signal that the end was near.

At two o'clock in the morning on July 15, 1868, Eleonora succumbed to the final ravages of yellow fever.[23] She was fifty-three years old. Although Agoston was never one to dwell on the past, Eleonora's sudden death must have compelled him to reflect on the long journey that had brought him and his wife halfway round the world. It was thirty-five years, six months, and nine days since he had pledged Eleonora his love and protection in the parish church at Futtak. She had not always been with him as he wended his long and tortuous route through the New World, and they had spent seven of those thirty-five years apart. But she had crossed the ocean with him in 1842, willingly entered on her wifely duties on Sauk Prairie, and had traveled beside him in the covered wagon from Wisconsin to San Diego. After a long sojourn in New Jersey, she had returned to California, lived with him at Buena Vista, and accompanied him on at least part of his whirlwind tour of Europe in 1861. Perhaps most importantly, she had followed him to Nicaragua when she did not really have to do so.

It fell to Otelia to take the shocking news of her mother's death back to California. Sometime after July 31 Otelia boarded the North American Steamship Company's steamship *Oregonian* bound for San Francisco. She arrived in the city by the Golden Gate on August 13 [24] and promptly transmitted the news of her mother's fate to her family and to the San Francisco newspapers. The obligatory obituaries appeared in the papers the following day.[25]

Agoston and Gaza stayed on at the Hacienda San Antonio. They were planning to build a sawmill on the estate, and a large distillery for their rum production. There was plenty of labor in Nicaragua— Indians mostly, and they were sure and dependable workers—but Agoston knew he would have to obtain some machinery from California and began to make plans for a trip back to San Francisco and Sonoma.

He was back in Sonoma in November. Arpad and Attila brought him up to date on developments in the vineyards. Attila had been making wine for himself and the estate of General Williams. Arpad thought Attila's new red wine was "excellent." Dr. Fauré was still making wine for General Vallejo from the grapes harvested at Lachryma Montis, and Major Snyder's wine was developing a reputation as "the finest and cleanest tasting" in the valley. Isidor Landsberger and Gottlieb Groezinger had bought Sonoma grapes to make wine from them. Even Benjamin Wilson had come up to Sonoma from Los Angeles to buy grapes for use in making his wine. Arpad and Landsberger alone had made 50,000 gallons of wine, 25,000 of which Arpad would soon transform into champagne.[26] At Buena Vista, Emil Dresel had put a temporary wooden press house up on the roof of the new stone cellar that Agoston built in 1864; the press house was being used for the production of all the society's wine except the champagne. That was being made in the stone press house that Agoston finished in 1862. Dresel was planning to replace the temporary press house with two more stories of stone. When this addition was completed, the three-story cellar would be the largest building in the Sonoma Valley—perhaps in all California—exclusively devoted to the production of wine.[27]

Agoston could well feel a sense of pride in knowing that the wine business was thriving in Sonoma, for he more than any other man had been responsible for that business. As he looked across the valley, he could see an almost unbroken sea of vineyards, extending from the foothills of the Mayacamas in the east to the foothills of the Sonoma Mountains in the west.[28] It was a sight well calculated to gladden the eye of a wine lover.

He may have wished for a moment that he was still a participant in the wine business, as Attila and Arpad were—or even hoped that he could return one day to Sonoma and the vineyards in which he had invested so much of his life. Certainly he did not plan to spend the rest of his life making rum in the tropics. He promised his children that he would only stay in Nicaragua long enough to amass the means to live a comfortable life, and when he had achieved that goal—he did not think it would take him more than three or four years—he would come back to them.[29]

The family discussed the Butler place, which was held in the name of Attila as trustee for Eleonora. They decided that it would be best if the property were sold, all of Eleonora's heirs joined in signing a deed to the property. Charles Haraszthy's son-in-law, A. S. Edwards of San Francisco, had expressed an interest in buying the place, and the price he was willing to pay—$4,000 more than the mortgage held by the Butler heirs—seemed fair. The deed was signed by Agoston, Attila, Ida, Bela, and Otelia between December 19, 1868, and the first week of January 1869. Attila also signed as attorney-in-fact for Gaza, who was still in Nicaragua. Ida, who had come north to greet her father, signed with the rest of the family, but Henry Hancock's signature, thought to be necessary because of his possible community property interest in Ida's share of the property, had to be obtained in Los Angeles. Agoston personally appeared before a notary public in San Francisco on January 6 to affix his name to the document.[30]

Agoston's business in San Francisco was all finished by January 22, for on that date he boarded the Pacific Mail Steamship Company's side-wheeler *Constitution*, outward bound for Central America. With him as the ship steamed out of port were Otelia, Ida, Charles, and Charles's wife, Frances. Agoston's father, now seventy-nine years old, had been itching for months to go down to Nicaragua with his son. Arpad later recalled that Agoston tried to persuade Charles not to make the trip. It was a long journey to a hot and humid country, which had few of the comforts of California; Charles had been suffering from an accumulation of fluids in his lower extremities—a condition the doctors diagnosed as dropsy—and the tropical climate would not help his condition. Agoston may even have feared that Charles would fall prey to some tropical illness, as Eleonora had. But Charles was insistent. He consulted his doctors, who informed him that, since he wanted so badly to visit Agoston in Nicaragua, it would probably be best if he made the trip, for if he remained behind he might "grieve himself to death."[31] So Agoston relented, and Charles and Frances boarded the *Constitution* with the rest of the family.

Charles was overjoyed to be reunited with his son. But after he arrived in Nicaragua, he found that Agoston's warnings about the life in Nicaragua had some validity. The Central American climate did not suit his dropsy at all. He found the going there very rough and after only a few months announced that he was ready to go back to San Francisco. And so, at the end of May, Charles and Frances went up to Corinto and boarded a small sailing ship, the bark *Mary Belle Roberts*, and headed north.

Agoston continued his work at the hacienda. He was planning to build a new sawmill on the bank of a river that crossed the estate, and on July 6 he set out on muleback to confer with a man named Lewis about the project. As he approached the site, he found the construction workers, but not Mr. Lewis. He thought the mill would have been better on the other side of the river, and told the workmen. But since Mr. Lewis wasn't there, he decided to stop a while and rest. He spread his oilcloth coat on the ground, rolled up his other coat, and lay down on it for a time.

When he failed to return to the hacienda that evening, his family became concerned. They joined Dr. Wassmer in organizing a search. By the riverbank where he had lain down to rest, they found his two coats still lying on the ground. His mule was tied to a nearby tree, and his pistols were still holstered in the saddle.[32] But Agoston was nowhere to be seen.

Now fifty of his neighbors joined in the search, scouring the countryside. Rewards were offered for the recovery of his body or any of the clothes he was wearing when he disappeared, but to no avail—no trace of him or the clothes could be found.[33]

Had he wandered off into the forest somewhere? Was he the victim of foul play? Just twelve days earlier, a party of "Nicaraguan patriots" had attacked the army barracks in León and announced their intention of overthrowing Fernando Guzman. They had formed a "provisional government" and enlisted the support of a former president of the republic and many of the country's priests in their cause. President Guzman had responded by declaring martial law and sending his troops into the countryside to hunt out the rebels. Once again, Nicaragua was in the throes of a revolution.[34]

News of Agoston's disappearance was carried back to San Francisco by ship, where it caused an immediate stir. On August 5, the *California Farmer* advised its readers that he had disappeared and speculated that he might have been taken prisoner by the Nicaraguan rebels, or perhaps even been killed. The *Farmer* commiserated with the Haraszthy family and expressed the hope that, if Agoston could not be found, his disappearance could be ascribed to a capture and not murder.[35]

The following day, the *Alta* announced the "probable death of Colonel Haraszthy." It noted that his coats and guns, and even his watch, had been left behind after he disappeared, and these circumstances were hardly consistent with the theory of a voluntary disappearance.[36]

On August 26, the newspaper reported that the latest steamer from Central America had brought Arpad a letter from one of his sisters advising him that there was no longer any doubt that their father was dead.[37] The letter, dated at San Antonio on July 22, advised Arpad that Agoston's footsteps had been traced from the riverbank where he had apparently lain down for a nap to the base of a nearby tree. The letter noted that the tree was very large and that some of its limbs reached to the other side of the river. "About the middle of the stream," the letter continued, "a large limb was found to be broken, and at the same place, a few days before, an alligator had dragged a cow into the stream from the bank. We must conclude that father tried to cross the river by the tree and that losing his balance, he fell, grasping the limb, and then the alligator must have drawn him forever down." [38]

The original letter that Arpad received and forwarded to the *Alta California* has not been preserved. Nothing more is known about the letter than the text published in the newspaper. We do not even know the identity of its author (it could have been either Ida or Otelia, for both were in Nicaragua at the time of the disappearance). The theory (for such it truly was) that Agoston had met his death in the jaws of a hungry alligator was gruesome; but it had a strangely believable quality to it. The truth of Agoston's life had always been "stranger than fiction," and it seemed somehow appropriate that he should die, not in his bed from some natural cause, not even in the prime of his life "with his boots still on," but in a struggle to the death with a voracious reptile on a remote, tropical frontier. And so reporters, journalists and, later, historians accepted the theory presented by the letter dated July 6, 1869, at San Antonio in Nicaragua.

It is curious, however, to note that Arpad himself was apparently not wholly convinced by the theory. Ten years after his father's disappearance, he prepared a short manuscript titled "Colonel Agoston Haraszthy," in which he reviewed the basic facts of his father's life and the circumstances of his death. In that manuscript, Arpad stated that the letter of July 6, 1869, had removed "all doubt" as to the circumstances of his father's death, but then went on to note that, "from the letter in question and information since acquired," he had been able to formulate a somewhat different reconstruction of his father's final agony. According to this reconstruction, Agoston had gone to the riverbank for the purpose of meeting Mr. Lewis and, not finding him, had lain down on the ground for a nap. Two days later, his footsteps were traced to a large tree that, in rainy weather, was used as a natural bridge over the stream. A freshly broken limb was found about halfway across the bridge. An Indian boy reported that he had been passing by and saw Agoston approach the tree, but it was not an unusual occurrence and he paid no further attention to it. Arpad continued: "And that was the last that was ever seen of him. His body was not recovered, nor was there ever found any trace of it or of his clothing, but as the stream emptied itself but a few miles below into the ocean, it may have been swept out and devoured by the man eating shark, so abundant in those waters."[39]

Arpad's 1879 manuscript is interesting for its substitution of a shark for an alligator, and the additional information provided by the Indian boy. But a manuscript that Arpad wrote a few years later for Hubert Howe Bancroft provides yet another theory as to how Agoston died. In this manuscript, prepared in 1886, Arpad again quoted from the letter of July 6, 1869, but he edited the letter by deleting any references to the alligator. In its 1886, edited version, the critical last sentence of the letter reads as follows: "About the middle of the stream, a large limb was found to be broken, from which we must conclude that father tried to cross the river by the tree and that losing his balance, he fell, grasping the limb and was drowned."[40] Arpad's redaction of the by-now fifteen-year-old letter from Nicaragua makes some sense if we assume that he genuinely believed it was unlikely that his father had been drawn to his death by an alligator. He may have been persuaded to change his earlier opinion by the "other information" that he cryptically referred to in his 1879 manuscript. What the "other information" was Arpad did not say, though it is reasonable to assume that he had received it from his brother Gaza and his sisters Ida and Otelia when he was finally able to meet them face-to-face and discuss the tragedy that had befallen them.

This latter view is supported by the only other bit of written evidence known to shed any light on the circumstances of Agoston's death. That was a letter that Ida wrote in 1906, thirty-seven years after her father's fatal accident, in response to an inquiry from the well-known Wisconsin historian Reuben Gold Thwaites. In that letter, Ida stated simply that her father had gone to Nicaragua in 1868, where "the government gave him valuable concessions to induce him to remain. And then at Corinto he met his death by drowning in crossing a b[a]you, in 1869."[41] Again, drowning, with no mention of alligators. Ida's statement on this point is entitled to some weight, for she had accompanied Agoston on his final trip to Nicaragua and was there when the search was organized and the telltale footprints were discovered.

It is possible, of course, that both Ida and Arpad decided in their later years to suppress any reference to alligators when speaking or writing of their father's death. Perhaps they thought such a death unseemly, undignified, somehow demeaning, and on that ground not to be repeated. Or perhaps they simply hoped that their father had not actually met his end under such gruesome circumstances. Although Arpad was called upon to supply information concerning Agoston and the Haraszthy family more frequently than any of the other Haraszthy children (and thus had more opportunity to misrepresent the facts of his father's life), both he and Ida did their bit to contribute to the Haraszthy Legend by confusing, misrecollecting, and, in some cases, intentionally misrepresenting, the facts. Although the reasons that might have prompted them to suppress the story of the alligators hardly seem compelling—was drowning any more "dignified" than being eaten by alligators?—the possibility that they made a conscious (or even unconscious) decision to tell only one version of the story deserves at least to be considered.

The available evidence is simply inadequate to establish with any certainty whether Agoston drowned and his body was swept out to sea, whether he was drawn down into the water by one or more alligators, or whether both drowning and marauding sharks played a part in his death. But under any of these circumstances, his death was tragic, and bizarre. He was a relatively young man (seven weeks and six days short of his fifty-seventh birthday) and, so far as the available evidence reveals, still in vigorous good health. In this remote part of the world he had embarked on another great adventure that was as challenging—and gave some hope of being as rewarding—as any of his previous adventures. But we can never know if the Hacienda San Antonio would have been a success, if he could have opened a great market for the products of Nicaragua in California, if he could have recouped his lost fortunes in the Central American jungle and thus added another noteworthy chapter to the already astonishing story of his life.

Another circumstance made Agoston's death both unusual and

poignant. When the bark *Mary Belle Roberts* arrived in San Francisco on August 2, its captain reported that Charles Haraszthy had died aboard that ship somewhere between Corinto and San Francisco.[42] He died on July 22, 1869, of dropsy.[43] His wife was with him at the end, and his body was buried at sea.

Charles Haraszthy's death occurred only sixteen days after Agoston's, and neither man was aware of the other's death. Neither knew that the bonds that had bound them so closely through a long and almost incredible odyssey across the face of two continents had been severed so suddenly not by one, but by two cruel blows. Perhaps, as Agoston believed, Nicaragua had represented a great new opportunity. But that opportunity had turned to agonizing disaster when Eleonora died, and Agoston and Charles both followed her within a year.

Eleonora was buried in Léon. Agoston and Charles were denied the dignity of a Christian burial, though their bodies both found ultimate rest in the sea.

Afterword

The Haraszthy family was devastated by Agoston's sudden death. He left six children and four grandchildren to mourn his passing, but the grandchildren were all so young (Arpad's daughter Agostine was the oldest at four) that in years to come they would have difficulty preserving even the haziest memories of him.

Otelia returned at once to California with news of her father's disappearance. Twenty years old and still unmarried, she went to live in Los Angeles with her sister, Ida Hancock. Major Hancock had acquired a substantial portfolio of properties during the twenty years he lived in California and was frequently in San Francisco on business. Ida was fond of the city by the Golden Gate, and she and Otelia often escaped there from the dusty streets of Los Angeles for rest and rejuvenation.

Gaza Haraszthy remained in Nicaragua. A strapping six-footer, he was thirty-five years old and still unmarried when his father died, and he was anxious to continue the military career he had given up at the end of the Civil War. He accepted a colonel's commission in the Nicaraguan army and served for a time as an aid to the Nicaraguan minister of war. He returned to California to visit his brothers and sisters in the early 1870's, but the Golden State held no allure for him, and he promptly returned to Central America to continue his military career.

Attila Haraszthy was thirty-four years old when his father disappeared, but he did not share his brother's desire to pursue a life of adventure in a tropical jungle. He was a dedicated family man, with a three-year-old son, Mariano, enlivening his Sonoma house, and another baby on its way. On December 26, 1869, Attila's wife, Natalia, gave birth to a second son, named Agoston and affectionately called Guszti in honor of the grandfather he never knew.

Attila continued to make wine with grapes harvested from his vineyard near the Buena Vista estate and, later, on a tract of a hundred acres adjoining General Vallejo's Lachryma Montis property.[1] In 1875 he built a handsome new home for his family on this property. Called Willows Wild, the two-story, frame house was modeled on General Vallejo's own home. Attila made wine for himself and also for his grape-growing neighbors. After a board of trustees was organized to govern the affairs of Sonoma, he became president of the board (the equivalent of mayor) and a trustee and vice president of the Sonoma Valley Bank. As next-door neighbors to General Vallejo, Attila and Natalia Haraszthy raised their children in the shadow of one of the living legends of California history. But the memory of another legend, their Hungarian grandfather-become-pioneer winemaker, was never far from their minds. Soon little Mari and Guszti Haraszthy were joined by two sisters, Natalia (called Tala) and Eleonora (called Lola).

Arpad Haraszthy was twenty-nine years old when Agoston died, but he was well on his way to becoming one of California's most successful winemakers. The chief winemaker at Isidor Landsberger's San Francisco wine cellars since 1866, Arpad became a partner in Landsberger's firm in the early 1870's and began producing sparkling wine under the brand name Eclipse. This "California champagne," first distributed by Landsberger and later by Arpad's own firm of Arpad Haraszthy & Co., became a favorite of wine lovers as far away as Chicago and New York. Buoyed by his champagne success, Arpad bought the large Orleans Hill vineyard northwest of Sacramento and built a large winery and distillery on it. Eclipse champagne was served at the opening of Stanford University, and cases of the wine were shipped to Andrew Carnegie in New York and Robert Louis Stevenson in Samoa.[2]

Arpad took an active role in efforts to organize the California wine industry. He wrote articles in newspapers and magazines, and in 1878 he was elected president of the California State Vinicultural Society. Two years later he was inaugurated as first president of the California State Board of Vinicultural Commissioners, a position he held for eight years. As president of the State Board, he traveled widely, spoke frequently at gatherings of winemakers, and continued to write, all the while cementing his position as leader of the wine industry in California.

Ida was twenty-six years old when her father died, and her three children were all born after her father's passing. Twin sons named George Allan and Henry were born in San Francisco in 1875; a third son, Bertram, was born in 1877. But Henry died at the age of two; Bertram died at the age of fifteen in 1893. When Major Henry Hancock died at his home near Los Angeles in January 1883,[3] Ida was forty and little George Allan (called "Allan") was seven. Ida and her sole surviving son forged a close partnership that was to continue to the end of her life. She held on to the La Brea Rancho that her husband had acquired in the 1850's, continuing to sell asphalt from the tar pits on the property while she looked for opportunities to exploit the property's other natural resources.

Bela Haraszthy was twenty-three years old and the father of a two-year-old son named Charles Ernest when Agoston died in 1869. His wife, Edna Smith, gave birth to a second child, a daughter named Harriet, in 1873. Bela took his little family south from Sonoma to the Los Angeles area some time in the 1870's. There, in the foothills of the San Gabriel Mountains, he became superintendent of the Lake Wine and Vineyard Company established by Benjamin D. Wilson in the 1850's. After eight years at the Wilson property, Bela turned his eyes toward mining. He prospected in the desert hills of Arizona and eventually settled in the town of Yuma, on the Colorado River.[4] Married a second time to a woman named Isabel King, Bela had a third child, a daughter named Gertrude, in 1882.

Agoston's youngest daughter, Otelia, continued to live with Ida Hancock until, at the age of thirty-four, in 1883, she married the

Irish-born Michael Flood in St. Mary's Cathedral in San Francisco. Flood was a fifty-four-year-old widower, and the father of two sons and one daughter. Otelia never had any children of her own.

The Buena Vista Vinicultural Society in Sonoma continued under the management of Emil Dresel after Agoston left the property in 1868. The German winemaker was an energetic superintendent who excited the admiration of nearly all his Sonoma neighbors. He chose not to move into the big house Agoston had built in the middle of the vineyard but remained in his own home nearby, using Agoston's house as the headquarters of the Buena Vista estate. After Agoston left Sonoma in 1868, Dresel continued to remove all traces of the vines Agoston had layered at Buena Vista, firm in his conviction that the faltering health of the vineyard was attributable to Agoston's close planting patterns. But even after all the layers were ripped out of the ground, the vines continued to yellow and wither. Dresel did not have an opportunity to reevaluate his decision, for he died suddenly in January 1869, six months before Agoston disappeared in Nicaragua.

Dresel was followed at Buena Vista by a succession of superintendents who sought to maintain the vineyards much as he had left them and made no serious efforts to expand the plantations. Some very good wines were produced by the Buena Vista Vinicultural Society in the 1870's. They were bottled under a variety of names, including Vin de la Montagne, El Dorado Claret, Buena Vista Golden Hock, National Grape, Sparkling Sonoma, and Pearl of California (the latter a sparkling wine made entirely from Sonoma grapes). Newspapers reported that the vineyard and adjoining cellars were the largest of their kind in America, with a storage capacity of about 400,000 gallons of wine and about 100,000 bottles of champagne. Buena Vista wines and brandies were sold throughout the United States and were exported worldwide, to Mexico, Central and South America, Europe, China, Japan, Australia, and New Zealand. The BVVS mounted a vigorous promotional campaign, and in 1876 at the Centennial Exhibition in Philadelphia presented a special exhibit of wines that introduced Buena Vista to many easterners.

But the BVVS was never profitable.[5] The health of the vines continued to deteriorate long after the last of Agoston's layers were gone, eventually forcing the board of trustees to authorize the replanting of some sections of the vineyard. Soon the same malaise that had settled over Buena Vista was observed in other vineyards nearby, making it increasingly obvious that some cause other than layering was responsible for the withering and dying vines. Attila's vineyards suffered along with the rest. In 1873, Attila reported to the Sonoma Viticultural Club that an important discovery had been made in the vineyards of one of his neighbors. Oliver Craig had dug up one of his sick vines and noted a strange kind of scarring on its roots. Examination with a microscope revealed that the roots were infested with tiny insects. Craig took his vine to Attila, who confirmed his observations. Attila thought the insect must be the destructive *Phylloxera vastatrix*, the parasite that had already been observed in the vineyards of France.

Attila dug up withered vines in his own vineyard and in that of General Vallejo and, to his horror, discovered insects on all the roots. Joining with his Sonoma neighbors, he sought valiantly to discover some means of eradicating the blight. They tried flooding the vines. This seemed to produce some relief, but flooding was feasible only on flat valley land, not on hillsides; and, although flooding might eradicate insects in the flooded area, the pests still lurked in the adjoining vineyards, ready at the first opportunity to mount new and even more destructive invasions of all the surrounding vines. Frustrated, Attila covered the roots of his vines with a compost of stable manure mixed with lime and gypsum, but that treatment was time-consuming and it produced little relief. The only effective way of ridding the vines of the infestation seemed to be to rip them out of the ground. It was a disquieting discovery, analogous to a physician's discovery that the only way to cure a disease was to kill the patient.

Before the phylloxera was brought under control, it took a terrible toll on California's vineyards. By 1880, Attila Haraszthy's Sonoma vineyard was reduced to a single vine that grew behind his house.[6] From Sonoma, the blight spread across the Mayacamas Mountains into Napa Valley and beyond. By the time the spread was checked, the pestilence had destroyed almost all the wine vineyards in the state, much as it had done in Europe.

As the vines of Buena Vista yellowed and died, the trustees of the

BVVS decided to sell the vineyards. The property was still encumbered by large mortgages, and there were few growers bold — or rash — enough to invest large sums of money in an infested plantation, so when the 6,000-acre estate went up for auction in 1878 the best bid received was $46,502 in gold coin.[7] The buyer was Robert Johnson, son of George C. Johnson, the Swedish sea captain who had served a year as president of the BVVS board during Agoston's time. But Robert Johnson and his wife, Kate, apparently had no interest in producing wine at Buena Vista. They built a grand mansion, four stories tall and turreted, not far from Agoston's old ranch headquarters, and used his old wine cellars as carriage houses. They transformed Buena Vista into one of the grandest country estates in California, but wholly abandoned the fight to save the vines. When a vineyardist from Australia visited Sonoma in 1883, he found the vines at Buena Vista had nearly all been ruined by the phylloxera and wrote that the once-great vineyard had "a sad and disheartening appearance."[8]

Kate Johnson continued to occupy the Buena Vista property after Robert Johnson died in 1889. She maintained a fine mansion in San Francisco as well as the looming "Johnson Castle" at Sonoma. But Mrs. Johnson survived her husband by only three years, and for the next generation Buena Vista lingered in a kind of limbo. In 1906, the great earthquake that leveled much of San Francisco struck a heavy blow at Buena Vista, cracking the stone walls of the wine cellars, collapsing the underground tunnels, and, in a few seconds, turning the buildings into ruins.

Attila Haraszthy was fifty-two years old when he died in February 1888.[9] He left his widow, Natalia, four young children, a hundred acres of phylloxera-ravaged vineyards, and a mountain of debts. Natalia Haraszthy remained in Sonoma until about 1910, when she joined her son Guszti at his home in San Francisco. She later moved to Oakland to live with her daughters Lola and Tala, and died there in 1913.

Gaza had preceded Attila in death by eight years. Still unmarried and still living in Nicaragua, he succumbed to diphtheria in December 1878, at the age of forty-five.[10] News of his death was reported in San Francisco and even as far away as New York, where the newspapers remembered that he was the son of the legendary Agoston

Haraszthy and himself one of the most notable pioneers of the early days of California statehood.[11]

Arpad continued to produce Eclipse champagne in San Francisco after the deaths of his two older brothers. Always busy, always urbane, he led a rather lonely life after his wife Jovita's early death in 1878.[12] His son Carlos studied medicine in San Francisco and New York, but gave up his career and went to live in Tahiti, while his daughter Agostine made her home in San Francisco with her husband, George Strickland. The wine industry in California came on hard times in the late 1880's, when a crash in grape prices ripened into a general industry depression, and Arpad joined other California wine producers to transfer his assets to a new corporation called the California Wine Association. In 1896 he sold his Orleans Hill Vineyard and began to look for other opportunities. He joined his brother Bela on a trip to the gold fields of Alaska in the spring of 1900, but soon returned to San Francisco, tired and in poor health. A week after his return, Arpad collapsed on the street and, by the time he was taken to the hospital, was dead of a massive heart attack. He was sixty years old.[13]

A few years before Arpad's death, Ida Haraszthy Hancock began to exploit the oil resources of the La Brea Rancho. She and her son Allan leased out portions of the property for oil drilling, and were delighted when the leases produced incredibly rich gushers. Within a few years, Ida found herself an immensely rich woman. She traveled in Europe, bought a rare cello for Allan, and collected expensive art works with which she furnished a palatial mansion.[14] She became one of Los Angeles's most generous philanthropists, and in 1909 ended her long widowhood by marrying Erskine M. Ross, a judge of the United States Circuit Court and former associate justice of the California Supreme Court. Ida Hancock Ross was seventy-one years old when she died in her Los Angeles mansion on March 15, 1913, leaving a fortune valued at nearly $4 million. It was an enormous sum for the time, and marked her as one of the richest women in California.[15]

Bela Haraszthy gave up his home in Arizona not long after he and Arpad returned from Alaska and moved to Los Angeles to take charge of his sister Ida's oil-drilling operations. He was two weeks short of his sixty-seventh birthday when he died on March 15, 1912, survived by his son, Charles Ernest Haraszthy, and his daughters, Harriet Haraszthy Hunt and Gertrude Haraszthy Meadows.[16]

Otelia Haraszthy Flood joined Ida and Bela in Los Angeles after the death of her husband, Michael Flood, in 1907. She lived with Ida until the latter's death, then moved to the suburb of Colegrove (later part of Hollywood), where she died on June 4, 1916. The youngest of Agoston Haraszthy's six children and the last to die, Otelia was sixty-seven years old at the time of her death.[17]

After Ida's death, Agoston's grandson Allan Hancock took over the La Brea Rancho and its oil properties. He laid out some of the finest residential neighborhoods in Los Angeles and donated ten acres of land surrounding the La Brea tar pits as a public park. Called Hancock Park, the plot became a center of scientific study after a group of university paleontologists began to mine the tar pits for their rich stores of Pleistocene fossils. As scientists uncovered skeletons of woolly mammoths, saber-toothed tigers, and other long-extinct animals, Allan contributed to the erection in Los Angeles's Exposition Park of a special museum dedicated to the exhibition of prehistoric fossils. He became a founder and officer of the California Bank (later part of First Interstate Bank and finally Wells Fargo Bank), president of La Brea Securities Company and the Santa Maria Valley Railroad, founder of Allan Hancock College and the Allan Hancock Foundation for Scientific Research, and a major benefactor of the University of Southern California.

The State of California acquired title to the old Buena Vista estate sometime before 1920, apparently for unpaid taxes, but by that time Agoston's gleaming white house on the hill and the even grander Johnson Castle had both disappeared in flames. By 1943, the property was used only for grazing horses and cattle, and the crumbled walls of Agoston's hillside cellars were the only visible reminder that wine had once been made on the property.

In the latter year Frank H. Bartholomew, vice president of the United Press, bought the 500 acres that were the core of the old estate at a state auction in Sacramento.[18] Surprised to learn that the property had once belonged to Agoston Haraszthy, Bartholomew and his wife, Antonia, made plans to restore the historic Buena Vista cellars and vineyards and again make wine on the property. The phylloxera was controlled now, thanks to the discovery that grafting European vines onto hardy American root stocks would prevent the insects from destroying vines. The Bartholomews' first vintages were produced in the late 1940's with the help of the Russian-born wine consultant André Tchelistcheff. By the 1950's, wine lovers in California and beyond were again enjoying wines made in Sonoma from grapes grown on Agoston Haraszthy's vineyards and bearing the name Buena Vista.[19]

By the late 1960's, Bartholomew had become chairman of the board of United Press International. Justifiably satisfied with his contribution to the rebirth of the California wine industry, he sold the restored Buena Vista wine cellars to a Los Angeles company but continued to hold the adjoining vineyard property. After his death in 1985, his widow rebuilt Agoston's columned home in the midst of the vineyards he had once cultivated with such enthusiasm. Completed in 1989, the rebuilt house became the centerpiece of a 500-acre park owned by the Frank H. Bartholomew Foundation.

Almost from the day of his death, Agoston was remembered as the preeminent winemaker of California's pioneer days. In the laudatory obituary that Arpad wrote for the *Alta* in San Francisco, he described Agoston as the "Father of Viniculture in California."[20] This obituary was widely copied in other newspapers, and formed the basis for a long article that appeared in the *New York Times* under the heading, "A Remarkable Career."[21] Arpad's appraisal of his father's life and work owed much to filial affection, of course, although his portrait was not much more flattering than any newspaper reporter who had known him well would have painted. Those who knew how the California wine industry had mushroomed after Agoston moved to Sonoma in 1857 could not really doubt that he had done more for the development of the industry than any other man—more, in fact, than any dozen other men.[22] Perhaps this is why there was general acquiescence in Arpad's encomiums, and why writers who reviewed the early history of the California wine industry were so uniform in seconding his praise. For the next century, whenever Agoston's name was mentioned in discussions of early wine production in California, he was almost uniformly described as the "Father of California Viticulture," the "Father of California Winemaking," the "Father of Modern Viticulture in California," or in similar words.[23]

But by the 1970's dissenting voices were heard. Wine historian Charles L. Sullivan reviewed the evidence surrounding Arpad's claim that Agoston was the first to introduce the Zinfandel into California and determined that there was absolutely no evidence to support it.[24] Relying largely on the recollections of one of Agoston's neighbors recorded nearly a century before, Sullivan concluded that Agoston had had virtually nothing to do with the early cultivation of the Zinfandel in California.[25] Not long after Sullivan's conclusions were published, a professor of English named Thomas Pinney essayed an ambitious history of winemaking throughout the United States, in the course of which he not only endorsed Sullivan's conclusions about the lack of any evidence tying Agoston to the Zinfandel, but went a step further by asserting that Agoston "was not the 'father' of California winegrowing; he was not the man who first brought superior varieties of grapes to California; and he was not the man who introduced the Zinfandel" into the state. "He certainly was an energetic and flamboyant promoter," Pinney concluded, "combining the idealist and the self-regarding opportunist in proportions that we can now only guess at. He will remain an interesting and highly dubious figure, of the kind that always attracts historians; but we should no longer take seriously the legend that has grown up about him."[26]

There is no question that the Haraszthy Legend is riddled with misinformation, but the story of Agoston Haraszthy is much bigger than the Legend. He will "always attract historians," for he was too vital a figure to be dismissed out of hand, even by the most determined revisionists. Historians may argue whether he was a positive force in the development of the American frontier, or a "dubious figure" out of a distant past—the "great name in California wine history," or a "self-regarding opportunist" who left behind him a string of intriguing questions, but no satisfactory answers. But there is little doubt that he will ever be forgotten, for the trail he blazed so flamboyantly across Europe and America in the middle of the nineteenth century was too bold to be ignored—and the trail will always invite curious travelers on the frontiers of history to follow its signposts and enjoy its twists and turns.

REFERENCE
MATTER

Notes

Published works are cited by author and short title. Full references appear in the Bibliography. The following abbreviations are used in these notes:

AH	Agoston Haraszthy
ArH	Arpad Haraszthy
BVVS	Buena Vista Vinicultural Society
CH	Charles Haraszthy
CSHSW	Collections of the State Historical Society of Wisconsin
DD	Dane County (Wisconsin) Deeds
DM	Dane County (Wisconsin) Mortgages
JCA	Journal of the California Assembly
JCS	Journal of the California Senate
JWA	Journal of the Wisconsin Assembly
NaD	Napa County (California) Deeds
NaMa	Napa County (California) Marriages
RBVVS	Reports of Board of Trustees, Buena Vista Vinicultural Society
RGLO	Records of the General Land Office (Wisconsin)
SaukD	Sauk County (Wisconsin) Deeds
SaukM	Sauk County (Wisconsin) Mortgages
SC	Statutes of California
SDD	San Diego County (California) Deeds
SDHS	San Diego Historical Society
SFD	San Francisco (California) Deeds
SFMa	San Francisco (California) Maps
SFMo	San Francisco (California) Mortgages

SFP　　　San Francisco (California) Powers

SHSW　　State Historical Society of Wisconsin

SMD　　　San Mateo County (California) Deeds

SoBA　　Sonoma County (California) Bonds & Agreements

SoD　　　Sonoma County (California) Deeds

SoMa　　Sonoma County (California) Marriages

SoMo　　Sonoma County (California) Mortgages

SoSh　　Sonoma County (California) Sheriff's Deeds

INTRODUCTION

1. The correct Hungarian pronunciation of this name is *Aa*-go-shtone *Hoar*-o-stee. In Hungarian, "sz" is always pronounced like the English "s," "s" alone like the English "sh," and "th" like the English "t." The first syllable of every word is *always* stressed. The anglicized pronunciation favored by Haraszthy's own descendants is *Ah*-gus-tun *Harr*is-tee, and this may be accepted as the correct American pronunciation.

2. AH, *Grape Culture.*

3. Before the breakup of the Austro-Hungarian Empire at the end of World War I, the geographical area of Hungary was about three times as large as it is today and included all of what is now Slovakia, a good portion of present-day Romania, all of present-day Serbia north of Belgrade, most of Croatia, and a fringe of territories that are now part of the Ukraine and Austria. These territories had not been recent conquests of the Hungarians, but had formed a part of the historic kingdom for hundreds of years.

4. Baptismal Register, Terézváros parish, Budapest, Aug. 30, 1812.

5. Pre–World War I records of this region are now divided between archives in Hungary and Serbia. However, many of the records have been destroyed or lost, some as an accidental consequence of war, others quite deliberately.

6. McGinty, *Haraszthy at the Mint.*

7. Gärtner.

8. Brainard.

9. AH, *Utazás.*

10. Hungarian is not an Indo-European language (as are all the Germanic, Romance, and Slavic languages), but a member of the small Finno-Ugric linguistic group, which also includes Estonian, Finnish, and Lapp.

11. Senate Joint Resolution No. 30, "Relating to the centennial of modern California viticulture," Mar. 20, 1961, urging citizens of the state to honor AH as the "father of modern California viticulture."

12. Sullivan, "Historian's Account"; Sullivan, "Man Named"; Pinney, *History of Wine*, ch. 10, "The Haraszthy Legend"; Pinney, "Agoston Haraszthy."

13. James A. Beard, "Shopping for California Wines," *House and Garden*, Aug. 1956, 94.

CHAPTER 1 *The Young Noble*

1. Baptismal Register, Terézváros parish, Budapest, Aug. 30, 1812. Although this name is Ágoston in Hungarian, the Americanized version Agoston was used after 1842. In the interests of consistency, I have used the latter throughout this book.

2. Nagy, 5: 51–52; *Révai*, 9: 507; *Pallas*, 8: 675.

3. *Révai*, 9: 507; *Pallas*, 8: 675.

4. The story was recalled by Agoston Haraszthy's son Arpad in ArH, "Haraszthy Family," 1.

5. Paget, 1: 415. In modern Hungarian, *úr* is the equivalent of the English "mister," although both words originally denoted an elevated social rank ("mister" was originally "master").

6. Pronounced *Moak*-cha, this village is now located in the Republic of Slovakia, where I visited it on May 29, 1995. The Slovak name for the village is Lieskova (Hazelnut), but the Hungarians who still live there call it Mokcsamogyoros (Hazelnut Mokcsa).

7. Any Hungarian name that ends in "y" or "i" indicates that the family was once noble and owned estates at the place indicated by the name. Thus, the Haraszthy family once owned estates at a place called Haraszth (a wood or forest). However, virtually every Hungarian noble of the eighteenth and nineteenth centuries also had a "predicate" (or "village" name), which also indicated ownership of an estate or estates: Thus, the Mokcsai Haraszthy family owned property at both Haraszth and Mokcsa (although not necessarily at the same time). Mokcsai is pronounced *Moak*-chye. English has no equivalent to the "i" or "y" suffix, although there are parallels in the German "von" and the French "de." In some of the older sources (both published and unpublished), Haraszthy is spelled with an "i" instead of a "y," or with a "t" instead of a "th," thus becoming Haraszthi, Haraszty, or Haraszti. These are all standard variations of Hungarian spelling and do not indicate that the underlying name is distinct or that it represents a different branch of the family. When AH was baptized, his family name was inscribed in the church register as Haraszti, although the family preferred the Haraszthy spelling and always used it in the United States.

8. ArH, "Colonel Agoston Haraszthy"; Siebmacher, 223.

9. Antal Haraszthy was 64 years old when he died in Pest on Jan. 30, 1825. Register of deaths, Terézváros parish, Budapest.

10. Latin was the "official" language of the country, and the language favored not only by church authorities but also by the royal ministries and chancelleries.

11. Baptismal Register, Belváros parish, Szeged, Nov. 19, 1789. Latin spelling varied widely in both church and state records. For example, *Carolus* was sometimes rendered as *Caroli* and *Vilhelmus* as *Vilhelmi*.

12. In a manuscript prepared in 1879 for Lyman C. Draper, corresponding secretary of the SHSW, Arpad Haraszthy wrote that Károly was three months short of his eightieth birthday when he died on July 22, 1870. He actually died

on July 22, 1869 (Arpad merely had the year wrong) at the age of 79. If Arpad's calculation was correct, Károly was born on October 22, 1789.

13. Baptismal Register, Belváros parish, Szeged, Oct. 13, 1785, and May 18, 1787.

14. Ibid., Nov. 19, 1789. The accuracy and clarity of the Latin used in church records varied greatly. Many entries are difficult to read because they were written hurriedly, and the ink has faded with time.

15. Marriage Register, Belváros parish, Pest, Oct. 15, 1811.

16. Baptismal Register, Roman Catholic parish of Óbuda, Apr. 19, 1791.

17. Marriage Register, Belváros parish, Pest, Oct. 15, 1811.

18. Szinnyei, 1040–41.

19. Baláz Dercsényi et al., *Catholic Churches in Hungary* (Budapest: Hegyi & Company, 1991), 269.

20. See, e.g., Mészáros, 69. This name was pronounced *Goo*-stee.

21. Kossuth's ancestry, including his German descent on his mother's side, is traced in Deak, 9–11.

22. Baptismal Register, Terézváros parish, Pest, Aug. 30, 1812.

23. ArH, "Haraszthy Family," 14.

24. *San Diego Herald,* July 3, 1851, 2 (article by "our friend 'C. H.' "); ibid., June 5, 1851, 2, says: "We have received a communication from our esteemed friend, Judge Heraszthy [*sic*], which we shall try to find room for as soon as possible."

25. Inama, 11: 451.

26. Old Settlers' Association, 8.

27. ArH, "Haraszthy Family," 14.

28. Cole, 207. Anna Mária Haraszthy's nephew, Károly Fischer (later Charles Halasz), recalled that Károly Haraszthy was "an excellent chemist." Canfield, 62.

29. ArH, "Haraszthy Family," 14.

30. CH, "Vine Culture," 1.

31. Ibid.

32. Paget, 1: 297–300, explains the rights and obligations of the Hungarian peasants as defined in the Urbarium of Maria Theresa (1767).

33. Comitatus Pestiensis Cum Pilis et Solt, Acta Nobilitaria 9: 1817–19, folios 1–196, pp. 39 (in second series), 160–64.

34. Ibid.   35. Paget, 1: 417, 418.

36. Ibid., 410.   37. Ibid., 416.

38. Sztáray, 26, thinks that AH must have studied at least some law, or he could not have occupied the official positions he later occupied in Bács County.

39. In January 1850, AH told Benjamin Hayes that he entered the Bodyguard (called the "life-guard") at the age of 16. Hayes, 174. ArH, "Haraszthy Family," 2, says that AH entered the Bodyguard at 18.

40. Raimund Sebetic, *A Magyar királyi testőrség, I, Névjegyzék 1760-tól 1850-ig* (The Hungarian Royal Guard, I, register of names 1760–1850) (Bécs [Vienna]: A Szerző Kiadása, 1898); Kálmán Hellebronth, *A magyar testőrségek névkönyve,*

1760–1918 (Namebook of the Hungarian Bodyguard, 1760–1918) (Budapest: Stádium Ny., 1939).

41. This possibility was suggested to me in May 1995 by Dr. Tamás Magyarics.

42. Sztáray, 26, cites Sebetic as authority that AH was *not* a member of the Bodyguard and says Sebetic's list should be "conceded as authentic."

43. Sztáray, 26.

44. Hayes, 174.

45. Ibid.

46. Paget, 1: 165–66 describes the Hungarian efforts to help the Poles.

47. Hayes, 174.

48. The number of "captains," "majors," "colonels," and "generals" that crowded the Western frontier in the nineteenth century demonstrates the ease with which men of little or no military experience could attain commanding military ranks. Although the "Kentucky colonel" later became a cartoon figure, such "colonelcies" were originally marks of respect rather than derision. Explaining how attorneys in Illinois and California came to be called "colonel" and "general" despite their lack of military experience, Oscar T. Shuck, *Bench and Bar in California* (San Francisco: Occident Printing House, 1889), 39, writes: "It seems that plain 'Mr.' is too common a title for a man of fame, even in a Republican-Democratic country. The tendency is to distinguish by some higher style those who have won our special regard."

49. I wish to express my appreciation to Melinda Kovács, who searched the records of the Diet in the Library of Parliament in Budapest in the summer of 1995.

50. Paget, 1: 165.

51. Kossuth was not an elected deputy but a kind of proxy (*ablegatus absentium*) sent to take the place of a magnate who chose not to attend. See Deak, 23–24.

52. This information was conveyed to me by Melinda Kovács, who searched for records of the "Dietal Youth" at the Library of Parliament in Budapest in the summer of 1995.

53. Barany, 222.   54. Halász, 44.

55. Barany, 403, 429.   56. Ibid., 2, 3, 4.

57. I wish to express my appreciation to Dr. George Barany of the University of Denver, who first alerted me to Széchenyi's influence on AH. Fenyő, 174–75, comments on similarities between AH and Széchenyi.

58. A precise physical description of AH was recorded when he received a U.S. passport to return to Europe in 1861. See Passport Letters from July 1 to July 20, 1861, MS, National Archives, Passport issued to A. Haraszthy by Mr. Hunter, Chief Clerk, July 6, 1861.

59. Paget, 1: 463, describes the typical Hungarian mustache. AH writes about his own mustache in AH, *Utazás*, 1: 38.

60. Paget, 1: 419–21 describes the Hungarian uniform.

61. This sword, together with two other swords owned by the Haraszthys, was

kept for many years by AH's grandson G. Allan Hancock at his home in Santa Maria, California. I wish to express my appreciation to Sue J. Sword, president of the Santa Maria Valley Railroad and cotrustee of the Marian Mullin Hancock Charitable Trust, for allowing me to inspect the swords in August 1995.

CHAPTER 2 *A Little Estate in the South*

1. After World War I, most of the Bácska was incorporated into the Serbian-dominated Kingdom of the Serbs, Croats, and Slovenes, which later became Yugoslavia, and Serbian names were attached to towns, villages, and other places. The Serbian name for the Bácska is Bačka.

2. Fiume is now a part of the Republic of Croatia and is called Rijeka.

3. *Futtak* and *Futak* are both acceptable Hungarian spellings; the former is used here because it appears in Hungarian maps and parish registers of the early nineteenth century. The Serbian spelling is Futog; the Serbian name for Újvidék is Novi Sad.

4. See Alexander Wheelock Thayer, *Thayer's Life of Beethoven*, rev. and ed. Elliott Forbes (Princeton, N.J.: Princeton University Press, 1967), 1: 234–36; 2: 1088–93.

5. Dudás, 21; Kempelen, 2: 447.

6. Nagy, 3: 270.

7. Brief descriptions of Ófuttak and Újfuttak in AH's time appear in Fényes, *Magyar Országnak*, 53, 60. Borovszky, 2: 410–12, describes the estate as it was in the first decade of the twentieth century. A good map is in the map room of the National Széchényi Library in Budapest.

8. I wish to express my appreciation to Mr. Negovan Laušev of Novi Sad, who searched for these records in the Historical Archives of the Northern Bačka and Subotica in Subotica and in the Cadastral Archives in Bačka Topola in the summer of 1995.

9. Dudás, 9: 87. The Serbian name for Szenttamás is Srbobran; Pacsér is Pačir.

10. Marriage Register, Parish of Futtak, Jan. 6, 1833; Baptismal Register, Parish of Kishegyes, Jan. 2, 1834; Baptismal Register, Parish of Szenttamás, May 11, 1839.

11. I viewed these hills on May 26, 1995. The Serbian name for the village of Kishegyes is Mali Idjoš.

12. Fényes, *Magyarország*, 4: 119.

13. Register of deaths, Terézváros parish, Budapest, Jan. 30, 1825.

14. Marriage Register, Parish of Futtak, Jan. 6, 1833. Although AH's age was given in the register as 21, he was only 20. Eleonóra is the correct Hungarian spelling. After 1842, this name was anglicized to Eleonora. In the interests of consistency, I have followed the latter spelling throughout this book.

15. Marriage Register, Parish of Futtak, Jan. 6, 1833.

16. The family tradition has always been that the Dedinszkys were Polish. In 1906, AH's daughter Ida recalled that Ferencz Dedinszky was of Polish descent.

Ida Hancock. However, published genealogical studies (and family trees) make it clear that the Dedinszkys were members of the Hungarian nobility. See, e.g., Nagy, 3: 269–70; 8: 190–92.

17. Nagy, 3: 269–70; 8: 190–92.

18. Ibid.

19. Ida Hancock.

20. Kálmán Hellebronth, *A magyar testőrségek névkönyve, 1760–1918* (Namebook of the Hungarian Bodyguard, 1760–1918) (Budapest: Stádium Ny., 1939), 128.

21. Old Settlers' Association, 6; Clark, 321, remembered that both AH and Eleonora were "exceedingly good looking."

22. Baptismal Register, Parish of Kishegyes (also known as Hegyes), Jan. 2, 1834.

23. The spelling was anglicized to Gaza after the family emigrated to the United States.

24. Baptismal Register, Parish of Kishegyes (also known as Hegyes), Jan. 2, 1834.

25. Paget, 1: 539 states that there are "few positions in society more honorable, or more to be coveted" than that of the Hungarian *alispán*. *Vice-comes* is the Latin equivalent of *alispán*.

26. I wish to express my appreciation to Mr. and Mrs. Gyula Lelbach of Budapest, who on May 15, 1995, shared with me their insights into the social and political traditions of the old Bács County nobility.

27. Baptismal Register, Parish of Szenttamás, Apr. 20, 1835.

28. Paget, 1: 540.

29. AH, *Utazás*, 1: 16. In Hungarian, this is "kis birtok." "Kis" ordinarily means "little," although it may also be translated as "modest."

30. AH, *Grape Culture*, 95.

31. Magyar Kancellária Levéltár, Acta Generalia, 1837: 198, 611; 1837: 2258; 1837, 11961, 11963; Sztáray, 25.

32. A lengthy description of the agricultural production of the county is in *Bács-Bodrogh Vármegye*, 1: 426–41.

33. AH, *Grape Culture*, 95.   34. *Bács-Bodrogh Vármegye*, 1: 429.

35. Fényes, *Magyarország*, 4: 119.   36. Halász, 72.

37. József Katona and József Dömötör, *Magyar borok-borvidékek* (Hungarian wines and wine regions) (Budapest: Mezőgazdasági Kiadó, 1963), 69, 115–16; Halász, 75.

38. Halász, 77.

39. AH, "Report on Grapes and Wines," 319–20, 323; see "Farm of Colonel A. Haraszthy," in *Transactions* (1858), 243 ("choice Tokay" wine made at Sonoma, California, in 1857).

40. Although this comment is often attributed to Louis XIV, Halász, 110–11, thinks it was actually made by Louis XV. AH himself described Tokaj as "the world-renowned King of Wines." AH, "Report on Grapes and Wines," 319.

41. CH, "Vine Culture," 1.

42. Report of speech delivered by Arpad Haraszthy, May 27, 1885, at San Jose, Calif., in *San Francisco Merchant,* July 3, 1885, 82.

43. Ibid.

44. George Husmann, *Grape Culture and Wine-Making in California* (San Francisco: Payot, Upham & Co., 1888), 152.

45. Lóránd Benkő, ed. *A magyar nyelv történelmi-etimológiai szotárá* (Historical-etymological dictionary of the Hungarian language) (Budapest: Akadémiai, 1967), 1:.446.

46. Ibid.; Count Alexandre Pierre Odart, *Ampélographie Universelle ou Traité des Cépages les Plus Estimés Dans Tous les Vignobles de Quelque Renom* (Universal ampelography, or treatise on the most valuable wine varieties found in all the principal vineyard regions) (Paris: Librairie Agricole; Tours: Chez les Principaux Librairies, 1874), 314; Charles A. Wetmore, *Propagation of the Wine* (San Francisco: San Francisco Merchant, 1880), 1 (referring to writings of Count Odart).

47. Benkő, *A magyar nyelv történelmi-etimológiai szotárá,* 1: 446.

48. Although "Sylvaner" and "Zierfandler" are today applied to white grapes, both names have been applied to red wine varieties over the centuries. Odart, *Ampélographie Universelle,* 313–14, noted that, in Hungary, a red grape known variously as the *Barát* ("friend"), *Tszin Szőlő* ("colored grape"), and *Raisin couleur de Robe de Moine* ("raisin with the color of a monk's robe"), was the same as the *Klein Roth Szirifandli* ("Small Red Sylvaner") of Rust and the *Rother Tokayer* (Red Tokay) of the Rhine districts. Odart equated the "Roth Szirifandl" or "Zierfahnl" with the vine known in France as the *Silvaner Rouge* ("Red Sylvaner") and said that the grape had proved to be good both for making raisins and for wine. The catalog of vines prepared by AH after his return from Europe in 1861 includes a "red Silvaner" from Germany, a "red Szilványi" from Hungary, and a "red Zierfandler" from Germany. See app. I to the "Supplementary Report of Charles A. Wetmore, Chief Executive Viticultural Officer and Commissioner for the State at Large," part of the "First Annual Report of the Board of State Viticultural Commissioners," 2d ed., in *Appendix to the Journals of the Senate and Assembly of the Twenty-fourth Session of the Legislature of the State of California,* vol. 2 (Sacramento: J. D. Young, Supt. State Printing, 1881), 188. Although the viticulture of Europe was confusing and often contradictory, the same could be said for California well into the nineteenth century. In 1888, Husmann, *Grape Culture and Wine-Making in California,* 152, noted that the names applied to grape varieties in California varied widely from valley to valley and even vineyard to vineyard. Wetmore, *Ampelography of California,* 4–5, noted that many varieties were cultivated in California under different names from those they were known by in Europe.

49. In the 1960's, a grape called the Primitivo was found growing in the Puglia region of southeastern Italy. DNA testing at the University of California at Davis later established that it was genetically identical to the Zinfandel. Despite widespread reports that this discovery proved that the grape "originated" in Italy, historical research established that the Primitivo was in fact brought to Italy sometime in the late nineteenth century from an unidentified place. Later, it was claimed that the Plavac Mali, a red wine grape grown along the Dalmatian coast of Croatia (on the opposite side of the Adriatic from Puglia), was the

same as the Zinfandel. DNA testing has thus far failed to confirm this claim. See Carole Meredith, "Plavac Mali: An Academic View," *Wine Enthusiast* (Oct. 1996). It may be significant that the Italian name Primitivo ("Primitive") approximates the meaning of the Hungarian "Cirfandli" ("growing in the woods"). In the United States, the "Zinfandel" was usually described as a Hungarian grape. During the nineteenth century, Croatia was a part of the Kingdom of Hungary and a grape found growing in Dalmatia might well have been identified as Hungarian. It is possible, even likely, that in AH's time the grape grew in various central European localities, and under different names. It could have been taken to Puglia from Croatia, Hungary, or even California.

50. Halász, 21, cites a comment from an old Hungarian chronicle, "Every kind of activity leads to the drinking of wine."

51. Paget 2: 547.

52. Ibid., 534.

53. "Haraszthy's Letters," *San Francisco Alta California,* June 21, 1868, 3.

54. Ibid.

55. In 1818, Thomas Jefferson wrote: "No nation is drunken where wine is cheap; and none sober, where the dearness of wine substitutes ardent spirits as the common beverage. It is, in truth, the only antidote to the bane of whiskey." James M. Gabler, *Passions: The Wines and Travels of Thomas Jefferson* (Baltimore: Bacchus Press, 1995), 225.

56. Increasing awareness of the health dangers of smoking has aroused in many wine lovers a revulsion against tobacco. However, this is largely a phenomenon of the late twentieth century and was certainly not known in Europe in the nineteenth century. Long after smoking lost favor in the United States, European wine drinkers (and even professional wine tasters) continued to smoke.

57. AH, *Utazás,* 1: 209.

58. The game of the Bácska is described in *Bács-Bodrogh Vármegye,* 1: 97.

59. Paget, 1: 90–93.

60. Magyar Kancellária Levéltár, Acta Generalia, 1837: 198, 611; 1837: 2258; 1837: 11961, 11963; Sztáray, 25; *Bács-Bodrogh Vármegye,* 1: 510–11; Borovszky, 2: 194.

61. On May 7, 1839, Eleonora and AH appeared as godparents in the parish church in Szenttamás. AH, who was acting in place of Ódry, was identified in the parish record as the chief justice of Bács County. Baptismal register, Parish of Szenttamás, May 7, 1839.

62. AH, *Utazás,* 1: 97; Paget, 1: 521 records a similar comment: "Not even my grandfather ever heard of such a thing!"

63. AH comments on the ostentation and idleness of the Hungarian nobility in AH, *Utazás,* 1: 3–5.

64. He also referred to the monopolists as "parasites" and "monsters." Ibid., 3, 97.

65. Ibid., 16.

66. AH identifies these men in his Hungarian text as K. Benet, Witlok, and Hislip. Ibid., 15–16. Since these names are not characteristically English or American, I have tried to anglicize them.

67. Sándor Bölöni Farkas, *Utazás Észak Amerikában* (Travels in North America) (Kolozsvár Ifjabb Tilsch János, 1834).

68. AH, *Utazás*, 1: 16.

69. Gärtner, 145.

70. Hayes, 174.

71. This story was recalled by AH's son Arpad in 1886. ArH, "Haraszthy Family," 2–4. Although Arpad may have embellished this story, it seems improbable that he would have invented it, and it must have been told to him by his father.

72. In fact, there was no such official as "the Hungarian Minister at the Court of Vienna."

CHAPTER 3 *To America*

1. AH, *Utazás*. Except as otherwise noted, all details of AH's journey, and all quotations from him, are from this source.

2. AH states that the voyage lasted 42 days. Since the *Samson* arrived in New York on June 11, 1840, the departure date would have been April 30.

3. Recollections of Charles Halasz (formerly Károly Fischer) as recorded in Canfield, 59.

4. Frederick Marryat, *A Diary in America, With Remarks on Its Institutions*, 2 vols. (London: Longman, Orme, Brown, Green & Longmans, 1839), 2: 72.

5. Ibid., 63.

6. *Burke's Presidential Families of the United States of America*, 2d ed. (London: Burke's Peerage Limited, 1981), 167.

7. *Longworth's American Almanac, New York Register and City Directory for 1839–40* (New York: Thomas Longworth, 1839) lists a Hamilton H. Jackson and gives his address as 113 Chambers. The same directory for 1841–42 gives Jackson's address as 559 Broadway.

8. Robert C. Nesbit, *Wisconsin: A History* (Madison: University of Wisconsin Press, 1973), 150.

9. Canfield, 59.

10. Pease, 228, notes that this area "was famous for soil fertility and also as a breeding place for a great variety of mosquitoes."

11. Canfield, 60.

12. Ibid.

13. Ibid., 61.

14. Recollections of William H. Clark in Old Settlers' Association, 7. These words are repeated, almost verbatim, by the fictional Count Augustin Karanszcy in Schorer, 6.

CHAPTER 4 *A "City" on the Frontier*

1. For descriptions of Sauk Prairie, see *Madison Express*, Sept. 19, 1840, 3; I. A. Lapham, *Wisconsin: Its Geography and Topography* (Milwaukee: I. A. Hop-

kins, 1846), 168; Donald McLeod, *History of Wiskonsan* (Buffalo: Steele's Press, 1846), 274.

2. Canfield, 64–75.

3. Inama, 11: 450.

4. AH, *Utazás*, 1: 130; for general descriptions of the river, see Derleth, *The Wisconsin*.

5. AH, *Utazás*, 1: 131.

6. Gregory, 1137–41.

7. AH, *Utazás*, 1: 131. AH does not explain how he happened to have tradable woolen goods at the end of a long journey on horseback through the woods of Wisconsin. He may have brought the goods with him by ship to Milwaukee, stored them there, then brought them on to Sauk Prairie when a trading opportunity arose.

8. Canfield, 61. Thirty rods equal 495 feet.

9. Since land on the prairie was not yet open to government purchase, no public records were made of this first transaction.

10. AH, *Utazás*, 1: 133.

11. In 1861 or shortly before, Károly Fischer told William H. Canfield that they arrived in July 1840. Canfield, 61. Some time before 1872, he recalled that they arrived in June 1840. Old Settlers' Association, 3.

12. Edmond Rendtorff recalled that Agoston had already built a cabin by the time he arrived in the fall of 1840. Canfield, 65.

13. Ibid., 61.

14. Ibid., 64–65; Ragatz, 214.

15. Canfield, 65–66; Ragatz, 216.

16. Ragatz, 204 n. 38.

17. Pease, 237.

18. Canfield, 63–64.

19. *Madison Express*, Sept. 19, 1840, 3.

20. Fischer recalled that AH met Bryant in Milwaukee in the fall of 1840, and that he was "an Englishman of rank and wealth." Canfield, 62.

21. AH, *Utazás*, 1: 134–35.

22. The original records of the Land Office at Mineral Point are in the Archives Division of the SHSW, Madison. The earliest records for Sauk County are dated Oct. 26, 1843.

23. Gregory, 1202.

24. For a vivid description of the winter of 1842–43 on Sauk Prairie, see Ragatz, 209–12.

25. Gregory, 1140.

26. Derleth, *The Wisconsin*, 118.

27. Jonathan Carver, *Travels Through the Interior Parts of North-America in the Years 1766, 1767, and 1768* (London: Printed for the Author, 1778), 46.

28. SaukD, A: 117.

29. Before Baxter's plat was recorded in 1845, the names of James K. Polk and Alexander Dallas (vice president under Polk) were added to the street names, but those obviously cannot have been bestowed as early as 1841.

30. Canfield, 69.

31. DM, 1: 166.

32. Gärtner, 32, locates the house on lot 6 of Block 27.

33. The original photograph is in the collections of the SHSW, Madison.

34. Canfield, 69.

35. Old Settlers' Association, 12. Bryant was credited as the builder of the mill, perhaps because he and not AH held title to the land on which it was built, but it owed as much in inspiration and planning, if not in capital, to AH as to his partner. The dam was built near the base of a limestone bluff that rises more than 200 feet above the prairie. In later years, it was run by a family named Loddes and called Loddes Mill. August Derleth (1909–71) in his *Return to Walden West* (New York: Candlelight Press, 1970), 83–85, remembers the mill and millpond as they were in his youth.

36. AH, *Utazás*, 1: 127.

37. "Steam-Boat on the Upper Rock River," *Madison Express*, Jan. 2, 1841, 2: "Rock River Steamboat," ibid., 3; "Wisconsin—Steam Navigation," ibid., June 2, 1841, 2 (reporting that the keel was 101 feet long).

38. "Rock River Steamboat," *Madison Express*, Jan. 2, 1841, 3; "Wisconsin—Steam Navigation," ibid., June 2, 1841, 2; *History of Rock County, Wisconsin* (Chicago: Western Historical Company, 1879), 360.

39. "Wisconsin—Steam Navigation," *Madison Express*, June 2, 1841, 2.

40. "The N. P. Hawks," ibid., July 28, 1841, 3.

41. While traveling down the Rock River on his way to Lake Koshkonong, AH noted that the Rock River had a rocky bottom in places, and that in times of low water the rocks hindered navigation by steamboats. *Utazás* 1: 118.

42. Ibid., 136–37. In "The Scrapbook," MS, Hawks' Inn Historical Society, Delafield, Wisconsin, p. 33, N. P. Hawks's son, Nelson Crocker Hawks, records that his father sold the boat to AH.

43. Canfield, 71.

44. Ibid.   45. AH, *Utazás*, 2: 14.

46. Pease, 235.   47. Ibid., 238.

48. For a description of breaking land on Sauk Prairie, see Ragatz, 214–16.

49. Pease, 238, says "this incident was related to me by one who witnessed it, as an illustration of the energy and resourcefulness of Agoston Haraszthy."

50. Ibid., 241, quotes AH as saying "You damned *Cod*," but it is likely that he meant to say "You damned *cad*."

51. Old Settlers' Association, 11.

52. Ibid.

53. Pivány, 34.

54. Written answers by Charles Naffz to questions by Verne Seth Pease, MS, SHSW, Madison. In a letter to Pease of Mar. 3, 1906, Bertha Lachmund, daughter of Károly Fischer (then called Charles Halasz) wrote that she had "never heard any remark as to doubt the nobility of A. Haraszthy" (MS, SHSW, Madison).

55. Pease, 225.

56. ArH, "Haraszthy Family," 14, states that AH's mother was "Anna Halasz." Americans often misspelled this name, rendering it as Hallasz, Hallaz, Halas, Halis, or Hollis.

1. *Utazás*, chs. 13–15. Unless otherwise noted, all details of AH's visit to the Indian country, and all quotations from AH in this chapter, are from this source, as recorded in the (unpublished) English translation of Theodore and Helen Benedek Schoenman.

2. One of the rivers that flows through Milwaukee is the "Kinnickinnic."

3. In *Utazás*, 1: 74, AH refers to "the famous stories of Cooper, which have been translated into almost every language."

4. Sztáray, 76.

5. Ibid., 76–77.

6. Daniel Defoe, *Robinson Crusoe* (New York: Signet Classic of Penguin Books, 1980), 286–89.

7. In 1862, AH admitted he had read *Robinson Crusoe*, asking, "Who has read 'Robinson Crusoe,' and has not desired to travel and see the world?" AH, *Grape Culture*, 80.

8. AH says he met "the secretary of the interior, John Clye." However, there was no secretary of the interior until 1849, and there was no "John Clye" in any prominent office in Washington in 1841. In Hungarian, the name "Clay" would be pronounced much as "Cly" would be pronounced in English. Henry Clay was a United States senator in 1841, and may have been the man to whom the reference to "John Clye" was intended to apply.

9. ArH, "Haraszthy Family," 5.

10. Lewis Cass was minister to France from 1836 to 1842. He did not return to the United States from Paris until December 6, 1842, almost a year after Agoston arrived back in Hungary. See Frank B. Woodward, *Lewis Cass: The Last Jeffersonian* (New Brunswick, N.J.: Rutgers University Press, 1950), 217.

11. See *New York Herald*, Dec. 6, 1841, 4.

12. Baptismal register, Parish of Futtak, June 28, 1840.

13. ArH, "European Vines," *San Francisco Evening Bulletin*, May 15, 1885, 4; condensed and reprinted *St. Helena Star*, May 21, 1885, 2.

14. Kenyeres, 1: 691; advertisements in *Pesti Hirlap* (Pest Gazette), Apr. 15, Apr. 25, May 20, 1845.

15. ArH, "Haraszthy Family," 5.

16. For a thoughtful analysis of the differences between Farkas's views and those of AH, see Katona, 43–51.

17. Ibid., 5.

18. I own a copy of the two-volume set bound in a single book. The National Széchényi Library in Budapest has copies of the two-volume bindings in both the hardcover and softcover versions.

19. *Pesti Hirlap* (Pest Gazette), no. 422, Jan. 16, 1845, 36.

20. Ibid., no. 423, Jan. 19, 1845.

21. Ibid.

22. *Vasárnapi Újság* (Sunday Journal), vol. 16, no. 42 (Oct. 17, 1869), 57; Szinnyei, 4: 456.

23. Fenyő, 171.

24. AH, *Tizenöt hét.*

25. An excerpt from AH's Indian tales was reprinted in 1986 in Lázár, 106–11.

CHAPTER 6 *A Home on the Prairie*

1. Ellet, 374–75; this source is unclear as to whether the fortune-teller was consulted by Anna or by Eleonora, although the forbidding prediction is clear.

2. Passenger list of ship *Philadelphia,* in *Passenger Lists of Vessels Arriving at New York 1820–1897, National Archives Microfilm Publications* (Washington, D.C.: National Archives, National Archives and Records Service, 1957), microcopy no. 237, reel 50, Aug. 1–Oct. 25, 1842; "Passengers Arrived," *New York Herald,* Sept. 28, 1842, 3. The servant's name is not mentioned.

3. "Passengers Arrived," *New York Herald,* Sept. 28, 1842, 3.

4. Ragatz, 210.

5. Gärtner, 145.

6. Ibid., 9.

7. Meredith, 247, gives her full name as Ida Helena. The Hungarian pronunciation is *Ee*-da, not *Eye*-da.

8. I have searched for records of this birth in the oldest Catholic parishes in northwestern Illinois and southwestern Wisconsin, but without success. No baptismal records were kept in Haraszthy Town before 1846.

9. Ida's son remembered that she was born in Imperial, Illinois, on Oct. 5, 1843. G. Allan Hancock, 53; Meredith, 247. Her brother Arpad remembered that she was born in Peoria, although he did not state the date. ArH, "Colonel Agoston Haraszthy," 7. Current records do not reveal the location of any place called "Imperial," but it could have been a settlement that was later absorbed into the city of Peoria.

10. Old Settlers' Association, 7–8.

11. Gärtner, 53.

12. Old Settlers' Association, 8.

13. RGLO, Local Office Tract Group, Wisconsin, 23: 160, SHSW, Madison; SaukD, B: 4, 5, 6, 7, 8, etc.

14. According to Ellet, 374–75, Eliza Bull visited Madison in 1846 or 1847. Although her recollections mention Sauk Prairie, it is not clear whether she visited there or merely talked with Eleonora Haraszthy in Madison. Some errors in the printed version of Mrs. Bull's recollections (including the statement that the Haraszthy home on Sauk Prairie stood beside one of the four lakes of Madison) suggest that she may not have actually visited the prairie.

15. Gärtner, 54.

16. SaukD: B:1, 5–6; DD, 4: 424–25.

17. ArH, "Haraszthy Family," 14; ArH, "Colonel Agoston Haraszthy," 6.

18. Gärtner, 53.

19. See, e.g., Canfield, 62; Old Settlers' Association, 7; Gärtner, 205; Inama, 11: 451–52; Canfield to Verne Seth Pease, July 4, 1906, SHSW, Madison.

20. Ragatz, 213.

21. Canfield to Verne Seth Pease, July 4, 1906, SHSW, Madison.

22. Canfield, 62, 72; Gärtner, 53; Cole, 1: 207; Charles Naffz to Reuben Gold Thwaites, Sept. 12, 1913, SHSW, Madison.

23. William H. Clark recalled that Agoston was both the owner and the captain of the steamboat. Old Settlers' Association, 7.

24. Lafayette H. Bunnell, who took a trip on the *Rock River* in 1842, wrote that it was the first steamer on the Mississippi "to venture into the unchartered trade," i.e., the first to make trips on a regular schedule. Bunnell, 646. Merrick, 287, states that the trips were made between Galena and St. Peters (Minneapolis) once every two weeks.

25. Canfield, 71.

26. Canfield to Verne Seth Pease, July 4, 1906, SHSW, Madison.

27. Richards; John C. Hawley to Verne Seth Pease, Jan. 2, 1906, SHSW, Madison.

28. Richards.

29. Ibid.

30. John C. Hawley to Vern Seth Pease, Jan. 2, 1906, SHSW, Madison.

31. DD, 4: 168–71.

32. Ibid.

33. RGLO, Local Office Tract Book, Wisconsin, 23: 160, SHSW, Madison.

34. SaukD, A: 117.

35. Bates's headstone in the Sauk City cemetery says that he died on Sept. 24, 1845, at the age of 72; *Madison Express*, Sept. 18, 1845, 3, reports that he died at his residence on Sauk Prairie on Sept. 3, 1845, at the age of 73.

36. *Annual Report, American Institute*, 290.

37. The soil, topography, climate, and elevation of AH's vineyard site are described in a Treasury Decision dated Nov. 24, 1993, establishing the Lake Wisconsin Viticultural Area in Columbia and Dane counties. T.D. ATF-352, published in the Federal Register, Jan. 5, 1994.

38. This note appears among others as a kind of appendix to ArH, "Haraszthy Family," but because these notes do not appear to be in Arpad's own handwriting, it is possible that they were transcribed by a researcher for Bancroft from materials supplied by Arpad. The notes refer to specific pages of Agoston's lost account book.

39. Gärtner, 152, 153.

40. The hillsides were located in what was then called the Town of Roxbury. "All over the town," the 1870's observer wrote, "may be found sunny slopes where, in the proper season, hang thousands of rich clusters." *Madison, Dane*, 496.

41. Canfield, 45.

42. Elisha W. Keyes, *History of Dane County* (Madison: Western Historical Association, 1906), 36.

43. DD, 9: 153.

44. SaukD, B: 217–18. Kehl may have been employed in AH's brickyard.

45. I wish to express my appreciation to Robert Wollersheim, proprietor of the Wollersheim Winery and current owner of the vineyard property that once belonged to AH. Mr. Wollersheim conducted me on a tour of his vineyards and winery in August 1991, at which time I inspected the tunnel.

46. See ArH, "Wine-Making in California," 23, with wood engraving illustrating at least two stages in the construction of the Sonoma cellars. One stone winery has already been completed and another is in the process of construction. The entrances to three tunnels are still exposed to the weather.

47. Conversation with Robert Wollersheim, Aug. 1991.

48. John Hawley, who worked on Agoston's ferry over the Wisconsin River, reported that he "always wore a stovepipe hat and carried a walking stick." Hawley to Verne Seth Pease, Jan. 2, 1906, SHSW, Madison.

49. Recollections of the Rev. S. A. Dwinnell as recorded in *History of Sauk County* (1880), 456.

50. Clark, 321, reports AH and Eleonora were frequently in Madison, where they "had a large number of friends and acquaintances, by whom they were much respected."

51. *History of Sauk County* (1880), 350.

52. Ibid., 336.

53. *Madison Express*, Apr. 25, 1844, 3.

54. "An act to provide for re-locating the seat of justice of Sauk county, and for other purposes," approved Jan. 27, 1846. *Laws of the Territory of Wisconsin, Together with the Joint Resolutions and Memorials Passed by the Fifth Legislative Assembly, at the Annual Session, Commencing on the Fifth Day of January, and Ending on the Third Day of February* (Madison: Simeon Mills, Territorial Printer, 1846), 52–53.

55. Canfield, Fifth Sketch, "Baraboo," 19.

56. Ibid. A large bas-relief, installed on one wall of the Sauk County Courthouse in the 1960's, commemorates AH's role in fixing the county seat in Baraboo.

57. SaukD, A: 209.

58. Canfield, Fifth Sketch, "Baraboo," 8, says the store was built by AH and J. C. Grapel.

59. Old Settlers' Association, 7; see SaukM, A: 293–94.

60. SaukD, A: 101–2.

61. Ibid., A: 135–36.

62. Ibid., A: 101–2, 135–36; DD, 5: 359–60.

63. SaukM, A: 41–42.

64. *Madison City Express*, June 22, 1843; Robert Rood Buell, *Sauk County Marriages, 1844–1852* (N.p.: Wisconsin State Genealogical Society, n.d.), 1: 1.

65. Buell, *Sauk County Marriages*, 1: 1.

66. Gärtner, 53.

67. SaukD, A: 208–9.

68. Many years later, Clark's recollections of both Agoston and Charles were highly complimentary. Old Settlers' Association, 6–8.

CHAPTER 7 *An American Cincinnatus*

1. Inama, 11: 348; Gärtner, 8–9.
2. Quoted in Inama, 11: 451n. 90.
3. *Dictionary of Wisconsin Biography* (Madison: State Historical Society of Wisconsin, 1960), 168; Henni and Urbanek, 67n. 1.
4. Inama, 11: 450–51.
5. Ibid., 451–52.
6. Ibid., 348–49. Although the printed English translation of this letter says literally "I received your gracious letter of July 15 of last year," this clearly seems to be an error, since the letter must have been in reply to a letter sent the previous month. The version given here seems most likely to approximate the original (probably in German).
7. Ibid., 351, 353.
8. Gärtner, 24; RGLO, Local Office Tract Book, Wisconsin, vol. 19, SHSW, Madison. The purchase was registered on Dec. 16, 1845.
9. DD, 6: 108–9; SaukD, A: 269.   10. Henni and Urbanek, 74.
11. Gärtner, 18.   12. Ibid.
13. Ibid., 18–20.   14. Inama, 12: 67.
15. *The Old, the New: St. Aloysius Congregation*, n. p.
16. Baptismal register, St. Aloysius Parish, Sauk City. In Hungarian, the name is spelled Béla and pronounced *Bay*-la. Although the accent over the "e" was never used in the United States, the name was always pronounced in the Hungarian style.
17. Gärtner, 130–36.   18. Inama, 12: 69, 73.
19. Gärtner, 145.   20. Ibid., 163–64.
21. Ibid., 164.   22. Inama, 12: 82.
23. Gärtner, 187, 192.   24. Ibid., 57–58.
25. Jennie Wright English, "Those Early Days in Wisconsin," in Elizabeth Steele Wright Papers, MS, Library of Congress, Washington, D.C.; microfilm copies in SHSW, Madison.
26. Gärtner, 57–58.   27. Ibid., 55.
28. Bunnell, 646.   29. Canfield, 71–72.
30. Gärtner, 43.
31. Merrick, 287, suggests that the boat "ran on some lower river tributary" of the Mississippi.
32. Gärtner, 55.
33. Pease, 239 (recollections of Charles Naffz); Monroe, 153–54 (recollections of Edmund Jussen).
34. SaukM, A: 206.   35. Monroe, 151–52.
36. Ibid., 152.   37. Ibid., 152–53.
38. Ibid., 153–54.   39. Ibid., 152–53.

CHAPTER 8 *News from Far Away*

1. ArH, "Haraszthy Family," 6.
2. Gärtner, 205.
3. Ibid., 218.
4. Charles Naffz to Verne Seth Pease, Oct. 25, 1905, MS, SHSW, Madison. The naturalization records for Reiner and Totto both show that they entered the United States at New York in July 1848. Naturalization Records, 1844–1955, Declarations of Intention, 1844–71, Sauk County, Wisconsin, SHSW, Madison.
5. Charles Naffz to Verne Seth Pease, Oct. 25, 1905, MS, SHSW, Madison.
6. Gärtner, 55–56.
7. Naffz says that conversation in the Haraszthy home was carried on in four languages: Hungarian, German, French, and English. Naffz to Reuben Gold Thwaites Sept. 12, 1913, MS, SHSW, Madison.

8. Pease, 242. 9. Gärtner, 56, 241.
10. Ibid. 11. Ibid., 57.

12. Great Register, Sonoma County, California, for 1867. Galena was (and still is) the county seat of Jo Daviess County. Despite repeated efforts, I have been unable to find any original naturalization records for Jo Daviess County, Illinois, for this period.
13. *History of Sauk County* (1880), 332.
14. Gärtner, 54. The *Wisconsin Democrat* reported in November 1848: "We have stirring news from the North. Col. Haraszthy is haranguing the Germans in his most eloquent vein. His influence is known in all the Wisconsin River Country." *Wisconsin Democrat* (Madison), Nov. 11, 1848, 3.
15. *Utazás*, 2: 269–70.
16. Charles Naffz to Verne Seth Pease, Oct. 25, 1905, MS, SHSW, Madison.
17. DD, 9: 37, 49.
18. Baptismal Register, St. Norbert Parish, Dec. 14, 1848; Gärtner, 59, 242–43.
19. *Wisconsin Democrat*, Feb. 3, 1849, 3, "Early Records of the Society, 1849–54," in CSHSW (Madison: Published by the Society, 1903), 1: xxxi–xxxvi.
20. SaukM, A: 238.
21. *Wisconsin Democrat*, Dec. 16, 1848, 3.
22. JWA (1849), 169, 260.
23. "An Act to incorporate the Wisconsin Bridge Company," approved Mar. 2, 1849, in *Acts and Resolves Passed by the Legislature of Wisconsin, in the Year 1849: Together with Memorials to Congress* (Madison: David T. Dickson, Printer to the State, 1849), 40–41.
24. *Wisconsin Democrat*, Dec. 30, 1848, 3.
25. *Wisconsin Argus* (Madison), Jan. 2, 1849, 3.
26. ArH, "Haraszthy Family," 6; Ida Hancock, handwritten reply written on typewritten letter to Madame Ida C. Hancock, Los Angeles, California, dated June 13, 1906, from Reuben Gold Thwaites, MS, SHSW, Madison.
27. ArH, "Haraszthy Family," 6.

28. Pease, 236, suggests that at the end of 1847 Agoston's affairs reached a "crisis, which culminated that year in practical bankruptcy."

29. Hayes, 172, 174.

30. Gärtner, 58, says: "At the beginning of the winter of 1848, a very cold one, cracks were visible in the uncovered gravel walls of the villa, and in the following spring they broke down altogether." Jennie Wright English says that her father, John Wright, bought the property in 1852, tore the cement walls down, and replaced it with a smaller house of red brick. Jennie Wright English, "Those Early Days in Wisconsin," in Elizabeth Steele Wright Papers, MS, Library of Congress, Washington, D.C.; microfilm copies in SHSW, Madison.

31. *History of Sauk County* (1880), 605. Goc, 41, says work on the bridge was begun in 1856 and not finished until 1860.

32. "An act to change the name of the village of Haraszthy, in Sauk county, to Westfield," approved Mar. 17, 1849, in *Acts and Resolves Passed by the Legislature of Wisconsin, in the Year 1849: Together With Memorials to Congress* (Madison: David T. Dickson, Printer to the State, 1849), 72.

33. Gärtner thought Haraszthy was an "impressive, though harsh-toned name" that sounded "very strange to American ears." Gärtner, 29.

34. *History of Sauk County* (1880), 597, says the name was changed because "Westfield" was "more short and appropriate."

35. "An Act to change the name of the Village of Westfield in Sauk County," approved Apr. 14, 1852, in *Acts and Resolves Passed by the Legislature of Wisconsin in the Year Eighteen Hundred and Fifty-Two, Together With Memorials to Congress* (Madison: Chas. T. Wakeley, State Printer, 1852), 444.

36. See DD, 9: 37, 49, 64–65, 153; SaukD, B: 214–17, 239, 269–70; SaukM, A: 286–87, 293–94.

37. *Wisconsin Argus*, Mar. 30, 1849, 3.

38. Testimony of Joseph Reiner, *San Francisco Alta California*, Mar. 17, 1858, 2.

39. Gärtner, 59.

40. Richards.

CHAPTER 9 *Across the Plains*

1. Gärtner, 59.

2. ArH, "Haraszthy Family," 16.

3. Brainard, 16.

4. Lucius Fairchild, who accompanied the Haraszthys as far as St. Joseph, wrote from the latter city on April 24, 1849, that Charles Haraszthy "will be here soon[.] [W]e left him in St. Louis. He is going to C—having left his wife for ever. He sold every thing and gave her half and is agoing [*sic*] to keep away from her." Fairchild, 14. In the census of 1850, Frances Haraszthy was listed as a resident of the Village of Adams (later Baraboo) in Wisconsin. She lived with her daughter, Matilda Clark, and her son-in-law, William H. Clark. Charles Haraszthy lived in San Diego at the time of the 1850 census.

5. Fairchild, 3.

6. In August 1991 I retraced the route followed by the Haraszthy family from Madison, Wisconsin, to San Diego, California. Descriptions of the landscape along the way are derived in part from my own observations.

7. Brainard, 16. The exact location of the "Lyn Grove" noted by Brainard cannot be determined today, but it is likely that it was in Sheridan Township in what later became part of the city of Davenport.

8. In this chapter, all details of the journey to California, and all quotations from David Brainard, are from his journal, unless otherwise noted.

9. William H. Emory, *Notes of a Military Reconnaissance from Ft. Leavenworth in Missouri to San Diego in California* (Washington, D.C.: Wendcell and Van Benthuysen, 1848), 126.

10. ArH, "Haraszthy Family," 16.   11. Fairchild, 24.

12. Ida Hancock.   13. Hayes, 174.

14. Ibid., 201; letter from Thomas W. Sutherland dated Council Grove, Indian Territory, June 4, 1859, originally published in *Philadelphia Inquirer*, republished July 29, 1849, in *New York Tribune*, and reprinted in *Kansas Historical Quarterly* 8 (1938): 205.

15. Marc Simmons, *Following the Santa Fe Trail: A Guide for Modern Travelers* (Santa Fe, N.M.: Ancient City Press, 1986), 75.

16. Gregory M. Franzwa, *The Santa Fe Trail Revisited* (St. Louis: Patrice Press, 1989), 72.

17. Brainard, 24–25.

18. Clover, 8.

19. Thelma S. Guild and Harvey L. Carter, *Kit Carson: A Pattern for Heroes* (Lincoln: University of Nebraska Press, 1984), 185–87.

20. Simmons, *Following the Santa Fe Trail*, 151.

21. *Register of Enlistments in the United States Army 1798–1914*, vol. 45, July 1846–May 1848. National Archives Microfilm Publications, microcopy no. 233. National Archives, Washington, D.C., 1958; ArH, "Haraszthy Family," 16.

CHAPTER 10 *And On to the Promised Land*

1. In this, as in the preceding chapter, all details of the journey and all quotations from David Brainard are from Brainard's journal, unless otherwise noted.

2. *Register of Enlistments in the United States Army 1798–1914*, vol. 45, July 1846–May 1848. National Archives Microfilm Publications, microcopy no. 233. National Archives, Washington, D.C., 1958. The date of the enlistment was recorded as July 21, 1849, but it must have been July 29, because Brainard's journal clearly shows that the Haraszthys could not have been in Albuquerque until the later date. The enlistment record reveals that at the time of his enlistment Gaza was sixteen years old and stood five feet six inches tall. ArH, "Haraszthy Family," 16, reports the essential facts of the enlistment.

3. Brainard, 64; Hayes, 174.

4. Letter to editors of *Daily Missouri Republican* (St. Louis), dated Nov. 14, 1849; first published Jan. 28, 1850; reprinted in Ralph B. Bieber, ed., *Southern*

Trails to California in 1849 (Glendale, Calif.: Arthur H. Clark Company, 1937), 379–83.

5. Hayes, 177, quotes Agoston as referring to the "Illinois river," but this was probably an error; it is much more likely that Agoston would have referred to the Wisconsin.

6. Ibid., 174.

7. Ibid.

CHAPTER 11 *A Genial Climate*

1. The Federal Census taken on Feb. 26, 1850, fixed the town's population at 650.

2. Hayes, 172–73.

3. Ibid., 174–76.

4. Powell, 205.

5. Handwritten notes attached to ArH, "Haraszthy Family."

6. P. 1 of MS in handwriting of Arpad Haraszthy, attached to typescript of ArH, "Haraszthy Family."

7. The tax assessor found them in the house on Calhoun Street in November 1850. Auditor's Office, 1850—First Assessment, San Diego County (no. 47, "Augusto Harassithy" [*sic*]; no. 56 "Josefa de Fitch"), Archives of the San Diego Historical Society, San Diego.

8. This lot is identified as Lot 3 of Poole's Survey of Mission Valley on p. 1 of 4-page handwritten MS attached to ArH, "Haraszthy Family."

9. Handwritten notes attached to ArH, "Haraszthy Family."

10. Ibid. The notes include the following statement: "It is more than likely, however, that this plantation, begun on the 4th of March 1850, was made only with Mission grape vine[s]. His *first* importation of foreign or European vines not arriving till the end of 1850, or the first months of 1851." In 1864, AH recalled that his first European importations were made in 1850. *Annual Report, American Institute,* 285.

11. Handwritten notes attached to ArH, "Haraszthy Family." Opposite the date of Feb. 17, 1851, and the notation "pp 18," the following appears: "Note plantation of grape vines, trees &c. Peach & Cherry trees from New York."

12. ArH, "Early Viticulture," 77, asserts that AH imported his first Zinfandels in February 1852. However, this was a month after he left San Diego to attend the legislature; and, if he in fact received Zinfandels in that month, it was not in San Diego. Two years earlier, Arpad asserted that AH imported his first Zinfandels sometime before March 1854, by which time they were all in the ground at Crystal Springs. P. 2 of 4-page MS in handwriting of Arpad Haraszthy, attached to typewritten script of ArH, "Haraszthy Family." Although Arpad's statements were not entirely consistent, he never claimed that AH received Zinfandels while at San Diego, despite suggestions to the contrary. See Sullivan, "Zinfandel," 88n. 4; "Viticultural Mystery," 128n. 4.

13. P. 1 of 4-page MS in handwriting of Arpad Haraszthy, attached to type-

script of ArH, "Haraszthy Family," states that AH's vineyard in Mission Valley was "conducted by Joseph Reiner" after AH left San Diego. SDD, D: 381–82, reveals that AH conveyed his interest in several parcels of land in and around San Diego to his San Francisco business partners, Charles Uznay and Sámuel Wass, on June 10, 1854. This conveyance included Lot 3 in the 160-acre range of Mission Valley, which almost certainly embraced vineyard property managed by Reiner and visited by Hayes in 1856. See note 8.

14. Benjamin Hayes, *Pioneer Notes from the Diaries of Judge Benjamin Hayes, 1849–1875* (Los Angeles: Privately printed, 1929), 130–31.

15. In 1858, Joseph Reiner testified that the coaches ran from "the bay to the city of San Diego." *San Francisco Bulletin,* Mar. 17, 1858, 2.

16. Handwritten notes attached to ArH, "Haraszthy Family."

17. Ibid.

18. Reiner set the number of cattle at 300 and the horses at 100. Testimony of Joseph Reiner, *San Francisco Bulletin,* Mar. 17, 1858, 3.

19. For brief biographies of Robinson, see Smythe, 1: 286–87, and Leland G. Stanford, *Tracks on the Trial Trail in San Diego* (San Diego: Law Library Justice Foundation, 1963), 15–17.

20. Ronald Quinn, "James W. Robinson and the Development of Old Town San Diego," *Journal of San Diego History* 31 (1985): 158.

21. *San Diego Herald,* Aug. 21, 1851, 3.

22. Ibid., Oct. 2, 1851, 2.

23. Letter from William P. Toler to William Heath Davis, in William Heath Davis Letters, MS, San Diego Pioneers, 1850–55, San Diego Public Library.

24. San Antonio, in Baja California, was an old silver mining center that had a resurgence when foreign capitalists became interested in it in the 1860's. However, it is more than 750 miles south of San Diego, probably too far for AH and Johnson to have traveled there overland in 1851.

CHAPTER 12 *Pillars of the Community*

1. Smythe, 1: 230–32.

2. Ibid., 230. There were only 157 qualified voters (white males over 21 who had resided in the state for at least 6 months and the county for at least 30 days).

3. Ibid., 233; "Proceedings," 1.

4. Smythe, 1: 723.

5. *San Francisco Bulletin,* Mar. 17, 1858, 3.

6. "Proceedings," 35–39, 73–74, 85–86.

7. Ibid., 73–74.

8. SDD, B: 75.

9. SDD, B: 76, 110–11.

10. Legal advertisement in *San Diego Herald,* Jan. 7, 1854, 2.

11. The Middletown Tract and Clayton's map are described in Neal Harlow, *Maps of the Pueblo Lands of San Diego, 1602–1874* (Los Angeles: Dawson's Book Shop, 1987), 109.

12. Letter of attorney dated June 17, 1850, SDD, B: 116–17.

13. "Proceedings," 9–10

14. See San Diego Tax Assessor's Book, p. 47 (Archives of SDHS, San Diego).

15. Handwritten notes attached to ArH, "Haraszthy Family."

16. "Proceedings," 108. 17. Ibid., 116.

18. Ibid., 114. 19. Ibid., 135.

20. Ibid., 119–20. 21. Ibid.

22. Ibid., 83–84. 23. Ibid., 85–88.

24. Ibid., 95–96. 25. Ibid., 20.

26. Ibid., 45. 27. Ibid., 1.

28. Ibid., 46–47. 29. Ibid., 61.

30. A copy of the contract is in the complaint in D. B. Kurtz v. Louis Rose, E. W. Morse, and George Lyons, as Trustees of the City of San Diego, filed Dec. 8, 1853, in the District Court of the First Judicial District in and for the County of San Diego (Archives of SDHS, San Diego).

31. Smythe, 1: 262.

32. Ibid., 234–35. This story has been accepted without question by later writers. See Leland G. Stanford, *Footprints of Justice . . . in San Diego and Profiles of Senior Members of the Bench and Bar* (San Diego: San Diego County Law Library, 1960), 12; Henry Schwartz, *Tales of Old Town* (San Diego: San Miguel Press, 1980), 35–38.

33. *San Diego Union,* June 1, 1900, 6.

34. Smythe, 1: 264, says the bid of $3,000 was submitted by "Israel Brothers," presumably a partnership composed of Robert Israel and his brother Joseph.

35. "Proceedings," 100.

36. Ibid., 103. The minutes reveal no opposition to the increased payment.

37. Ibid., 119. 38. Ibid., 126.

39. Ibid., 133. 40. Ibid.

41. Ibid., 149. 42. Bell, 226.

43. Ibid., 227–28.

44. See Smythe, 1: 264; "Old Town Items," *San Diego Daily Union,* Aug. 31, 1872, 3; Harr Wagner, "North San Diego and Its Development," *Golden Era,* Nov. 1888, 561.

45. "Proceedings," 160, 166, 182, 198–99.

46. Ibid., 152. As sheriff, AH paid the city $75 per month for the use of half of the jail.

47. Phillips, 89. For an account of the Indian uprising, see Ch. 14.

48. "Proceedings," 215.

49. "Horse Thief," *San Diego Herald,* Mar. 6, 1852.

50. "Presentment of the Grand Jury," ibid., Apr. 17, 1852, 3.

51. On Mar. 28, 1851, the council authorized the issuance of scrip in the total amount of $3,495. "Proceedings," 152–53. (Charles Haraszthy was not then a member of the council.) The scrip was issued in denominations of $100 each (with one certificate in the amount of $95) and was payable to AH or bearer. A copy of one of the scrip certificates was later printed in the *San Diego Union,*

Oct. 3, 1871, 3. In 1900, a pioneer named Ephraim W. Morse recalled that 8 percent per month was "the ordinary rate of interest at that time." *San Diego Union,* June 1, 1900, 6.

52. Order approving compromise, entered in D. B. Kurtz v. Louis Rose, E. W. Morse, and George Lyon, Trustees of the City of San Diego, District Court of the First Judicial District in and for the County of San Diego, Aug. Term, 1854 (Archives of SDHS, San Diego).

53. Order of dismissal in Agoston Haraszthy v. J. C. Bogert, W. W. Ware, and James Donohoe, President and Trustees of the City of San Diego, entered Jan. 21, 1860, in District Court of the First Judicial District, State of California, County of San Diego (Archives of SDHS, San Diego). The order does not state the grounds on which it was based, but merely recites that the defendants' motion for dismissal was "sustained."

54. Smythe, 1: 264.

55. *San Diego Union,* Oct. 3, 1871, 3. The scrip bore AH's endorsement on the reverse.

56. In 1858, a committee of the California State Agricultural Society visited San Diego and reported as follows: "Seven years ago we saw this town in all the hum and bustle and activity of an embryo City, full of life and animate with nervous hope. But now all is still. The hand of death seems upon the place." *Transactions* (1858), 272.

57. See Wagner, "North San Diego and Its Development," *Golden Era,* Nov. 1888, 557, 561, for a description and a drawing of the jail as it appeared in the late 1880's.

CHAPTER 13 *Drawing a Line*

1. *San Diego Herald,* Aug. 14, 1851, 3.

2. Bancroft, 6: 653-55.

3. AH, *Utazás,* 2: 252. AH specifically mentions Pope Leo X's 16th-century encyclical against slavery. For a fuller discussion of traditional Catholic views on slavery, see Madeleine Hooke Rice, *American Catholic Opinion in the Slavery Controversy* (Gloucester, Mass.: Peter Smith, 1964), and Herbert S. Klein, "Anglicanism, Catholicism, and the Negro Slave" in Ann J. Lane, ed., *The Debate Over Slavery: Stanley Elkins and His Critics* (Urbana: University of Illinois Press, 1971), 137–90.

4. AH, *Utazás,* 1: 226.

5. Gerald Stanley, "Senator William Gwin: Moderate or Racist?" *California Historical Quarterly* 50 (1971): 245–49.

6. J. Ross Browne, *Report of the Debates in the Convention of California on the Formation of the State Constitution in September and October, 1849* (Washington, D.C.: John T. Towers, 1850), 169, 197, 198.

7. Lately Thomas, *Between Two Empires: The Life Story of California's First Senator, William McKendree Gwin* (Boston: Houghton Mifflin, 1969), 44–49.

8. "Loyalty of the State Agricultural Society's Officers: Letter from the President," *California Farmer,* Aug. 29, 1862, 177.

9. There were many similarities between black slavery in the American South

and oppressive treatments of Indians in Spanish and Mexican California. See James J. Rawls, *Indians of California: The Changing Image* (Norman: University of Oklahoma Press, 1984), 35, 37, 38, 55, 58, 60, 74.

10. Ibid., 96.

11. See David Alan Johnson, *Founding the Far West: California, Oregon, and Nevada, 1840–1890* (Berkeley: University of California Press, 1992), 122, 134.

12. *Congressional Globe*, May 11, 1850, 967.

13. Ibid.   14. SC (1849–50), ch. 17; ch. 52, §1.

15. Ibid., ch. 17; ch. 52, §2.   16. Cal. Const. (1849), Art. XI, §13.

17. Address of Gov. John McDougal to State Legislature, Jan. 7, 1852, JCA (1852), 12–13.

18. Smythe, 1: 295–98.   19. *San Diego Herald*, July 24, 1851, 2.

20. Ibid., July 31, 1851, 2.   21. Ibid., Aug. 28, 1851, 2.

CHAPTER 14 *An Indian "War"*

1. SC (1851), ch. 6, §34.

2. SC (1849–50), ch. 17; ch. 52, §1.

3. AH to editor, Dec. 22, 1851, *Los Angeles Star*, Dec. 27, 1851.

4. Ibid.

5. *San Diego Herald*, Dec. 18, 1851, 2.

6. AH to editor, Dec. 22, 1851, *Los Angeles Star*, Dec. 27, 1851.

7. *Los Angeles Star*, quoted in *San Francisco Alta California*, Jan. 6, 1852, 2.

8. *Los Angeles Star*, Dec. 27, 1851.

9. Ibid., Nov. 29, 1851.

10. *San Diego Herald*, Dec. 27, 1851, 2.

11. *San Francisco Alta California*, Jan. 16, 1852, 6, quoting from *Los Angeles Star*.

12. *San Francisco Alta California*, Dec. 3, 1851, 2.

13. *San Diego Herald*, Dec. 27, 1851, 2.

14. Ibid., Dec. 11, 1851, 2.

15. Ibid.; see also Phillips, 89.   16. *San Diego Herald*, Dec. 18, 1851, 2.

17. Ibid.   18. Ibid.

19. *Los Angeles Star*, Dec. 27, 1851.

20. *Los Angeles Star*, quoted in *San Francisco Alta California*, Jan. 6, 1852, 6.

21. Phillips, 164–71.

22. *San Francisco Alta California*, Dec. 14, 1851, 2.

23. Ibid., Jan. 15, 1852, 2.

CHAPTER 15 *The Legislature*

1. *San Diego Herald*, Aug. 14, 1851.

2. Ibid., Sept. 11, 1851, 2.

3. Ibid.

4. Leon O. Whitsell, *One Hundred Years of Freemasonry in California* (San Francisco: Grand Lodge, Free and Accepted Masons of California, 1950), 4: 1625–26.

5. "A Remarkable Career," *New York Times*, Feb. 27, 1870, 3.

6. ArH, "Haraszthy Family," 4.

7. *San Diego Herald*, Jan. 1, 1852, p. 2, col. 3, marked "Second Edition, Monday morning, Jan. 5, 1852."

8. Ibid., June 26, 1851, 2; July 24, 1851, 2; Edward C. Kemble, *A History of California Newspapers, 1846–1858* (Los Gatos, Calif.: Talisman Press, 1962), 109.

9. Davis, 11; Bancroft, 6: 648–49n. 14.

10. Brian McGinty, "Could One of These Have Been 'The City'?" *California History* 64 (1985): 136.

11. *San Francisco Alta California*, Jan. 7, 1852, 2; Jan. 16, 1852, 3.

12. JCA (1852), 3.   13. Cal. Const. 1849, Art. XI, §13.

14. JCA (1852), 13.   15. Ibid., 27–31.

16. Ibid., 51.   17. Ibid.

18. Ibid., 38.   19. Ibid., 41, 166–74.

20. "Proceedings," 198–99.   21. *San Diego Herald*, May 29, 1851, 2.

22. SC (1852), ch. 139.

23. See card for Weller and Sutherland, Attorneys and Counsellors at Law, in *San Francisco Daily Herald*, Nov. 1, 1851, 1.

24. JCA (1852), 120–21.   25. Ibid., 135.

26. Ibid., 282.   27. Ibid., 223.

28. SC (1852), ch. 65.   29. *San Diego Herald*, May 22, 1852, 3.

30. An amendment could be proposed by majority vote in both houses of the legislature. If a majority of all members in the next legislature concurred, the amendment would be submitted to the people for their approval. Cal. Const. (1849), Art. X, §1.

31. JCA (1852), 174.

32. William Henry Ellison, *A Self-Governing Dominion: California, 1849–1860* (Berkeley: University of California Press, 1950), 178.

33. JCA (1852), 258.

34. Davis, 17–19.

35. SC (1850), ch. 99, §14 (criminal cases); SC (1851), ch. 5, §394 (civil cases).

36. SC (1852), ch. 33.   37. JCA (1852), 146–47.

38. SC (1852), ch. 33.   39. JCA (1852), 395–96.

40. Theodore H. Hittell, *History of California* (San Francisco: N. J. Stone, 1897), 1: 105–6.

41. Ibid., 85.   42. SC (1850), ch. 97.

43. SC (1851), ch. 108.   44. SC (1852), ch. 37.

45. Ibid., 768.   46. Ibid., 800.

47. *San Diego Herald*, Sept. 11, 1851, 2.

CHAPTER 16 *Las Flores and Crystal Springs*

1. "Proceedings," 159, 160.   2. *San Diego Herald*, Sept. 18, 1851, 3.

3. SFD, 9: 620.   4. Ibid., 621.

5. Handwritten notes attached to ArH, "Haraszthy Family"; testimony of Joseph Reiner, *San Francisco Alta California*, Mar. 17, 1858, 1.

6. Handwritten notes attached to ArH, "Haraszthy Family."

7. Ibid. The original account books are apparently no longer in existence.

8. Testimony of Joseph Reiner, *San Francisco Alta California*, Mar. 17, 1858, 1.

9. On Nov. 10, 1852, AH returned to San Francisco on the coastal steamer *Sea Bird* after a voyage of four days from San Diego, bringing a shipment of "668 packages of grapes." *San Francisco Alta California*, Nov. 10, 1852, 2.

10. ArH, "Wine-Making in California," 491–92.

11. Handwritten notes attached to ArH, "Haraszthy Family."

12. P. 1 of 4-page manuscript in handwriting of Arpad Haraszthy, attached to ArH, "Haraszthy Family."

13. Ibid.

14. Handwritten notes attached to ArH, "Haraszthy Family."

15. *San Francisco Business Directory*, 11, lists the store under the name of "Haraszthy & Noltner." Noltner was apparently Attila's partner. Harris, Bogardus, 59, lists the store under "Haraszthy, A. F., hay and grain." Colville, 93, lists the store as "Haraszthy & Co., dealers in hay and grain," and it lists "Haraszthy A. F. of Haraszthy & Co."

16. See William Heath Davis, *Seventy-five Years in California*, ed. Harold A. Small (San Francisco: John Howell—Books, 1967), 5.

17. SFD, 28: 100. This transfer was for 108 acres. Andrew McDuffie and Charles Hunter, who were apparently mortgage holders, joined AH as grantors.

18. On Aug. 1, 1853, he gave Sutherland his power of attorney. SFP, 3: 374.

19. *San Francisco Bulletin*, Oct. 2, 1856, 2; Harris, Bogardus, 130, describes the society's facilities and the results of the election of Oct. 1, 1856.

20. Kenyeres, 2: 65.

21. Wass arrived in San Francisco on the steamer *Sarah Sands* from Panama. Louis J. Rasmussen, *San Francisco Ship Passenger Lists*, vol. 2 (Colma, Calif.: San Francisco Historic Records, 1966).

22. Ibid.

23. See Henry H. Clifford, "Pioneer Gold Coinage in the West—1846–1861," in *The Westerners Brand Book, Book Nine* (Los Angeles: Los Angeles Westerners, 1961).

24. Advertisement in *San Francisco Herald*, Nov. 1, 1851, 1; Nov. 25, 1851, 1.

25. *San Francisco Herald*, Nov. 19, 1851, quoted in Edgar H. Adams, *Private Gold Coinage of California, 1849–55, Its History and Its Issues* (Brooklyn, N.Y.: Edgar H. Adams, 1913), 77–78.

26. See Adams, *Private Gold Coinage of California*, 77–82; Clifford, "Pioneer Gold Coinage in the West," 226; Donald H. Kagin, *Private Gold Coins and Patterns of the United States* (New York: Arco, 1981), 167–70. Wass and Molitor also contributed to the literature of gold mining and refining. See, e.g., A. P. Molitor, "Essay on California Gold," *San Francisco Alta California*, Sept. 30, 1859, 4, reprinted in part as "California Gold," *Hutchings' California Magazine* 4 (1859): 212–17; A. P. Molitor, "Russian Gold-Mines," *Overland Monthly* (Old series) 15 (1875): 71–75.

27. Statutes of California (1852), ch. 4.

28. Ibid.

29. SFMa, 1: 26, refers to claims "located 3d September 1853." An earlier

reference to a "preemption" made by AH on Aug. 6, 1853, appears in the Grantor Index with a reference to Book B of Miscellaneous, 668. However, this book cannot now be located and the property to which this preemption applied cannot be determined. Many of the San Francisco real estate records for this period were destroyed by fire in 1906.

30. Gaza was discharged June 6, 1852, after not quite three years of service. National Archives Microfilm Publications, microcopy no. 233, *Register of Enlistments in the United States Army 1798–1914*, roll 22, vols. 45–48, July 1846–Oct. 1850 (Washington, D.C.: National Archives, 1958), vol. 45, July 1846–May 1848. He arrived in San Francisco on the coastal steamer *Sea Bird* on Oct. 26, 1852. *San Francisco Alta California*, Oct. 27, 1852, 2.

31. See SFMa, 1: 26.

32. In 1857, J. Ross Browne called AH's San Mateo property "Redwood land." J. Ross Browne to Howell Cobb, June 4, 1857, in "Letters and Reports," 1: no. 404. In 1858, Reiner described it as "Pulgas." *San Francisco Alta California*, Mar. 17, 1858, 1. In 1886, Arpad Haraszthy described it as "Crystal Springs." ArH, "Haraszthy Family," 7.

33. Testimony of Joseph Reiner, *San Francisco Alta California*, Mar. 17, 1858, 1; *San Francisco Bulletin*, Mar. 17, 1858, 2.

34. Testimony of John Felix, *San Francisco Alta California*, Apr. 15, 1858, 1; Apr. 21, 1858, 1.

35. *LeCount & Strong's*, 81; Harris, Bogardus, 70 (brewery).

36. *California Farmer*, Jan. 5, 1854, 2.

37. Ibid.

38. P. 2 of 4-page manuscript in handwriting of Arpad Haraszthy, attached to ArH, "Haraszthy Family," 2.

39. Kenyeres, 2: 197. I am indebted to Mr. Gyula Lelbach of Budapest who gave me access to his unpublished monograph on the Mészáros family, compiled in 1993.

40. Lázár Mészáros to Amália Szutsics, Dec. 7, 1852, in Mészáros, 18–19.

41. LM to Antal Mészáros, Mar. 12, 1854, in ibid., 53–54.

42. LM to Antal Mészáros, Apr. 14, and Sept. 14, 1854, in ibid., 54, 69.

43. LM to Antal Mészáros, Nov. 20, 1854, in ibid., 75–76.

44. LM to Antal Mészáros, Apr. 14, 1854, in ibid., 57.

45. LM to Antal Mészáros, Sept. 14, 1854, in ibid., 68–69.

46. LM to Antal Mészáros, Dec. 17, 1857, in ibid., 132.

47. Four-page manuscript in handwriting of Arpad Haraszthy, attached to ArH, "Haraszthy Family."

48. *California Farmer*, Dec. 9, 1859, 138.

49. Prince, 343; Maynard A. Amerine to editor, *Wines & Vines*, Mar. 1982, 64.

50. "California Viniculture," in *San Francisco Bulletin*, Jan. 20, 1877, 4.

51. P. 1 of 4-page manuscript in handwriting of Arpad Haraszthy, attached to ArH, "Haraszthy Family." Although this manuscript is not dated, it was written sometime before 1882, probably for John S. Hittell, whose article on AH in his *Commerce and Industries of the Pacific Coast* (San Francisco: A. L. Bancroft, 1882), 245–47, is obviously based on it.

52. ArH to editor, May 11, 1885, *San Francisco Bulletin*, May 14, 1885, 4, re-printed in *St. Helena Star*, May 21, 1885, 2; reports of discussions in viticultural convention in *San Jose Daily Herald*, May 28, 1885, 3, and *San Francisco Merchant*, July 3, 1885, 82–83; ArH, "Early Viticulture," 77.

53. When William M. Boggs challenged Arpad's recollections about the origins of the Zinfandel in California, he pointed out that Arpad was outside California during this critical period and thus in no position to know what his father was doing. Boggs to editor, *St. Helena Star*, June 8, 1885, 1, 4. See discussion of Boggs and his challenge in Ch. 19. This argument was later stressed in Sullivan, "Historian's account," 18; "Viticultural Mystery," 116–17; "Zinfandel," 73–74. But Arpad was in a good position to know what was happening in New Jersey, and he was in California for two critical months in 1857, at the time when AH's foreign grapes were being moved from Crystal Springs to Sonoma.

54. J. Fisk Allen, *A Practical Treatise on the Culture and Treatment of the Grape Vine*, 3d ed. (New York: C. M. Saxton, 1855), 308, states that the "Zinfindal" grown under glass in Massachusetts "may be the same" as the "Zinfardel" listed by Prince. Allen was a prominent Massachusetts horticulturist.

55. Testimony of Joseph Reiner, *San Francisco Alta California*, Mar. 17, 1858, 1; *San Francisco Bulletin*, Mar. 17, 1858, 2.

56. J. Ross Browne to Howell Cobb, June 4, 1857, in "Letters and Reports," 1: no. 404.

57. ArH, "Early Viticulture," 77. Although Arpad did not see the Crystal Springs property when it was being planted, he did see it when he returned to California in 1857 at the time that his father was in the process of transferring his vines from there to Sonoma.

58. In 1858, some 14,000 foreign grapevines, representing 165 different varieties, were in the ground at Sonoma. A visiting committee of inspectors from the State Agricultural Society reported that these vines were planted in February 1857 and by 1858 were "bearing splendid grapes from one pound up to thirty pounds to a single vine." *Transactions* (1858), 242–43.

59. Records of the U.S. Land Commission, MS, Bancroft Library, University of California, Berkeley. Case no. 148, Northern District. Feliz Rancho Grant, Domingo Feliz, Claimant. For another summary of the Feliz claim and the Commission's decision, see J. N. Bowman, "Index of the Spanish-Mexican Private Land Grant Records and Cases of California," 1958, typescript, Bancroft Library, University of California, Berkeley.

60. The original deed was recorded in SFD, 51: 514. AH gave the sellers a mortgage, which was recorded in SFMo, 25: 448. The original San Francisco records are missing, apparently destroyed by the fire of 1906, but the deed and mortgage are referred to in SMD, 1: 49. The latter record is of a deed given on Oct. 31, 1856, to correct errors in the property description set forth in the earlier deed and mortgage.

61. SMD, 1: 49.

62. Ibid., 51.

63. Ibid., 108.

64. J. Ross Browne to Howell Cobb, June 4, 1857, in "Letters and Reports," 1: no. 404; *San Francisco Herald,* June 13, 1857, 2 (described as "Angelo [*sic*] Tract").

CHAPTER 17 *A House of Gold*

1. James M. Crane, *The Past, the Present, and the Future of the Pacific* (San Francisco: Printed by Sterett & Co., 1856), 32.

2. The mint as it appeared in 1856 is described in "Coining Money," 145–53.

3. Testimony of Jacob R. Snyder, *San Francisco Alta California,* Apr. 2, 1858, 1.

4. John Hewston, Jr., to James Booth, Apr. 15, 1854, in Giffen, 16.

5. *San Francisco Alta California,* Apr. 1, 1854, 2.

6. Ibid., 146.

7. AH to Louis [*sic*] Aiken Birdsall, May 10, 1855, in *San Francisco Business Directory,* advertisement for Justh & Hunter, Assayers.

8. Testimony of Peter Lott, *San Francisco Bulletin,* May 13, 1858, 2; *San Francisco Alta California,* May 13, 1858, 1; testimony of Leopold Kuh, *San Francisco Alta California,* Apr. 9, 1858, 1.

9. Testimony of Lewis Garnett, *San Francisco Alta California,* Mar. 25, 1858, 1.

10. Colville, 93, 225; Harris, Bogardus, 59. This house stood at the northeast corner of Harrison St. and Hampton Pl. The lot is described in SoD, 8:1.

11. Testimony of Henry Fisher, *San Francisco Alta California,* Dec. 6, 1857, 1.

12. Testimony of John Eckfeldt, ibid., Apr. 10, 1858, 1.

13. Testimony of John Felix, ibid., Apr. 15, 1858, 1.

14. Agreement between AH, Lewis Birdsall, James King of William, and Adams & Co., Oct. 9, 1854; AH to James Guthrie, Sept. 17, 1855; C. Mason to AH, Nov. 11, 1854, all in "Letters and Reports," 1:nos. 268, 274, 275.

15. Testimony of James Condon, *San Francisco Alta California,* May 14, 1858, 1. Condon was employed by AH in the Montgomery Block.

16. Jones, *Ark,* 81, 97, 118–21, 142, 180, has much to say about AH's association with the Montgomery Block, although not all of it can be precisely documented.

17. James Ross Snowden to Lewis Birdsall, Feb. 3, 1855, "Letters and Reports," 1:no. 278.

18. Albert Shumate, *The Notorious I. C. Woods of the Adams Express* (Glendale, Calif.: Arthur H. Clarke, 1986), 46–50.

19. *San Francisco Bulletin,* Oct. 13, 1856, 2.

20. See an account in Robert M. Senkewicz, S. J., *Vigilantes in Gold Rush San Francisco* (Stanford, Calif.: Stanford University Press, 1985), 7–8.

21. See advertisement for Justh & Hunter in *San Francisco Business Directory,* ad. section.

22. *LeCount & Strong's,* 86.

23. AH to James Guthrie, Sept. 17, 1855, "Letters and Reports," 1:no. 275.

24. Testimony of Peter Lott, *San Francisco Alta California,* May 14, 1858, 1.

25. Testimony of John Hewston, ibid., Mar. 27, 1858, 1.

26. Testimony of Jacob Snyder, ibid., Apr. 2, 1858, 1.

27. In a technical article published more than two years after AH left the mint, Molitor detailed the many causes of losses in the course of melting gold. See A. P. Molitor, "Essay on California Gold," ibid., Sept. 30, 1859, 4.

28. AH to Peter Lott, Oct. 20, 1856, ibid., May 13, 1858, 1.

29. Testimony of John Hewston, ibid., Mar. 27, 1858, 1.

30. Richard H. Dillon, *J. Ross Browne: Confidential Agent in Old California* (Norman: University of Oklahoma Press, 1965), 3–18.

31. J. Ross Browne to James Guthrie, Sept. 17, 1855, "Letters and Reports," 1:no. 267.

32. Browne to Guthrie, Sept. 19, 1855, ibid., no. 269.

33. Browne to Guthrie, Oct. 2, 1856, ibid., no. 378.

34. Testimony of Joseph Reiner, *San Francisco Alta California*, Mar. 17, 1858, 1; *San Francisco Bulletin*, Mar. 17, 1858, 2.

35. SDD, D: 381–82.

36. Testimony of Peter Lott, *San Francisco Alta California*, May 13, 1858, 1; *San Francisco Bulletin*, May 13, 1858, 2.

37. AH to Peter Lott, Dec. 18, 1856, *San Francisco Alta California*, May 13, 1858, 1.

38. Testimony of John Eckfeldt, ibid., Apr. 10, 1858, 1.

39. AH to Peter Lott, Dec. 18, 1856, ibid., May 13, 1858, 1.

40. Browne to Guthrie, Nov. 19, 1856, "Letters and Reports," 1:no. 384.

41. Testimony of Peter Lott, *San Francisco Alta California*, May 13, 1858, 1.

42. Browne to Guthrie, Oct. 4, 1856, "Letters and Reports," 1:no. 380.

43. In a trust deed drafted by U.S. Dist. Atty. William Blanding and signed by AH on June 10, 1857, the date of the resignation was given as November 1856. SMD, 1: 154. On Jan. 19, 1857, Browne wrote Secretary Guthrie that AH "intends sending on his resignation by this mail." Browne to Guthrie, Jan. 19, 1857, "Letters and Reports," 2: no. 2.

44. Browne to Guthrie, Jan. 19, 1857, "Letters and Reports," 2:no. 2.

45. Harris was later renamed Seventh Street.

46. The San Francisco Directory for 1858 (probably written in 1857) noted that the California Metallurgical Works had been "in successful operation during the past eighteen months" (Langley, 42). If this is correct, it probably opened in 1856. For a description, see Langley, 42, and Xántus, 191.

47. On June 4, 1857, Browne noted that AH held a mortgage of $15,000 "on metallurgical works." J. Ross Browne to Howell Cobb, June 4, 1857, "Letters and Reports," 1:no. 404. The mortgage was from John Warwick and was recorded in SFMo, 35: 99. See description of this mortgage in SMD, 1: 154. AH had sold his interests in both the metallurgical works and refinery at the end of May 1857.

48. Langley, 43.

49. Xántus, 187.

50. For services performed in the California Metallurgical Works, see advertisement for Wass, Uznay & Warwick in Langley, 199.

51. Langley, 43.

52. Xántus, 187. Xántus was a refugee from the Hungarian Revolution of

1848–49 who enlisted in the U.S. Army dragoons soon after his arrival in the United States and, between 1854 and 1857, wrote a large number of letters from the United States to his family in Hungary. The letters were collected in two widely read books published in Budapest. However, later scholarship revealed that the letters were composed in about equal parts of actual observations, rank fictionalization, and shameless plagiarism. Although a charlatan, Xántus cannot be totally dismissed from serious consideration, for he was also an expert naturalist who contributed significantly to the botanical and zoological collections of the Smithsonian Institution in Washington. For background, see Henry Miller Madden, *Xántus, Hungarian Naturalist in the Pioneer West* (Palo Alto, Calif.: Books of the West, 1949). Given his penchant for fabrication, it is possible that Xántus's description of the Eureka Gold and Silver Refinery was exaggerated, though its basic facts are corroborated by other information.

53. Xántus, 188.

54. Ibid.

55. Madden, 130. The Schoenmans translate this phrase as "our countryman, the famous adventurer, Augustin [*sic*] Haraszthy." Xántus, 191.

56. Xántus, 192.

57. Browne to Guthrie, Mar. 5, 1857, "Letters and Reports," 1:no. 398.

58. An original of this letterhead, with handwritten notations dated June 4, 1857, is in the Archives of the SDHS, San Diego.

59. Donald H. Kagin, *Private Gold Coins and Patterns of the United States* (New York: Arco Publishing, Inc., 1981), 170. For a photograph of one of the gold ingots produced by the firm of Haraszthy, Uznay & Co., see Henry H. Clifford, "Pioneer Gold Coinage in the West—1846–1861," in *The Westerners Brand Book, Book Nine* (Los Angeles: Los Angeles Westerners, 1961), 254.

60. *San Francisco Herald*, June 7, 1857, 1.

61. Langley, 199.

62. On May 28, 1857, Emmanuel Justh gave AH a mortgage for $20,000, which was recorded in SFMo, 35: 96. On May 29, Warwick gave AH a mortgage for $15,000, which was recorded in SFMo, 35: 99. These records were apparently destroyed in the fire of 1906 and cannot now be found, but the mortgages are described in SMD, 1: 154. Browne noted that the mortgage for $15,000 was on the metallurgical works and that for $20,000 was on the refinery. J. Ross Browne to Howell Cobb, June 4, 1857, "Letters and Reports," 1: no. 404.

CHAPTER 18 *Called to Account*

1. J. Ross Browne to James Guthrie, Mar. 5, 1857, "Letters and Reports," 1: no. 398.

2. Ibid.

3. Accounts of Melter and Refiner, Oct. 1, 1856, through Apr. 23, 1857, in U.S. v. Haraszthy, Wass, and Uznay, U.S. Circuit Court, No. Dist. California, National Archives and Records Service, San Bruno, Calif.

4. J. Ross Browne to Howell Cobb, June 4, 1857, "Letters and Reports," 1:no. 404.

5. Accounts of Melter and Refiner, Oct. 1, 1856, through Apr. 23, 1857, in U.S. v. Haraszthy, Wass, and Uznay, U.S. Circuit Court for Northern District of California, National Archives and Records Service, San Bruno, Calif.

6. J. Ross Browne to Howell Cobb, June 4, 1857, "Letters and Reports," 1:no. 404.

7. SMD, 1: 154. The original deed of trust is in Snyder, "Major Jacob Rink Snyder Collection."

8. J. Ross Browne to Howell Cobb, June 4, 1857, "Letters and Reports," 1:no. 404.

9. *San Francisco Alta California*, June 5, 1857, 1.

10. *San Francisco Bulletin*, June 2, 1857, 2.

11. *San Francisco Herald*, June 7, 1857, 2.

12. *San Francisco Bulletin*, June 4, 1857, 2.

13. See "New Phases in the Mint Robberies," ibid., Sept. 14, 1857, 2; the examination of the storekeepers in the police court was extensively reported in the San Francisco papers beginning Sept. 17, 1857.

14. *San Francisco Morning Call*, Sept. 15, 1857.

15. *San Francisco Bulletin*, Sept. 12, 1857, 2; Sept. 17, 1857, 2.

16. For reports of this trial, see *San Francisco Alta California*, Dec. 4, 1857, 1; Dec. 6, 1857, 1.

17. *San Francisco Bulletin*, Aug. 4, 1857, 2, 3; *San Francisco Herald*, Aug. 4, 1857, 2.

18. Presentment filed Sept. 19, 1857, in U.S. v. Agostin [*sic*] Haraszthy, U.S. Circuit Court, No. Dist. California, National Archives and Records Service, San Bruno, Calif.

19. *San Francisco Herald*, Sept. 20, 1857, 2; *San Francisco Bulletin*, Sept. 21, 1857, 3.

20. *San Francisco Herald*, Sept. 5, 1857, 2; Sept. 9, 1857, 2.

21. Affidavit for continuance filed Nov. 19, 1857, in U.S. v. Agostin [*sic*] Haraszthy.

22. *San Francisco Alta California*, Nov. 20, 1857, 2.

23. Order of reference filed Mar. 16, 1858, in U.S. v. Agostin [*sic*] Haraszthy.

24. Testimony of Lewis A. Garnett, *San Francisco Alta California*, Mar. 25, 1858, 1; Mar. 26, 1858, 1; Mar. 27, 1858, 1.

25. Testimony of Peter Lott, *San Francisco Bulletin*, May 13, 1858, 2; *San Francisco Alta California*, May 13, 1858, 1.

26. Testimony of Jacob R. Snyder, *San Francisco Alta California*, Apr. 2, 1858, 1.

27. Testimony of John Felix, ibid., Apr. 15, 1858, 1; Apr. 21, 1858, 1.

28. Testimony of Joseph Harmstead, ibid., Apr. 30, 1858, 1.

29. Testimony of James Condon, ibid., May 14, 1858, 1; *San Francisco Bulletin*, May 14, 1858, 2.

30. Testimony of John Short, *San Francisco Alta California*, May 18, 1858, 1; testimony of James Curtis, ibid., May 18, 1858, 1; testimony of Charles Uznay, ibid., May 22, 1858, 1.

31. Testimony of Henry Johnson, ibid., May 19, 1858, 1.

32. Clerk's file in U.S. v. Agostin [*sic*] Haraszthy (civil action), U.S. Circuit

Court, No. Dist. California, Action No. 63, National Archives and Records Service, San Bruno, Calif.

33. Clerk's file in U.S. v. Agostin [sic] Haraszthy, Samuel C. Wass, and Charles Uznay, U.S. Circuit Court, No. Dist. California, Action No. 65, National Archives and Records Service, San Bruno, Calif.

34. Order to enter *nolle prosequi* filed Nov. 27, 1860, in U.S. v. Agostin [sic] Haraszthy. See *San Francisco Alta California*, Nov. 28, 1860, 1.

35. Ibid., 2.

36. Testimony of CH, *San Francisco Bulletin*, Mar. 2, 1861, 1.

37. Clerk's file in U.S. v. Agostin [sic] Haraszthy, Samuel C. Wass, and Charles Uznay.

38. Ibid.; *San Francisco Alta California*. Mar. 3, 1861, 1, 2. A copy of the verdict is in Snyder, "Major Jacob Rink Snyder Collection."

39. He gave Stanly two mortgages on his Sonoma property, one dated Feb. 9, 1858, for $3,000 (SoMo, B: 247–50), and a second dated Apr. 28, 1858, for the same amount (SoMo, B: 365–68).

40. SMD, 2: 521–26.

41. ArH, "Haraszthy Family," 8.

42. SMD, 2: 500; 3: 347, 349, 372.

CHAPTER 19 *In the Vineyards*

1. For a general description of Angelica, see Brian McGinty, "Angelica: An Old California Tradition," *Vintage*, Oct. 1975, 33–37, 58.

2. ArH, "Early Viticulture," 77.

3. ArH, "Wine-Making," 23.

4. Munro-Fraser, 458. In 1858, AH fixed the age of the oldest vines at twenty-four years, which would mean they were planted in 1834. AH to O. C. Wheeler, Corresponding Secretary of California State Agricultural Society, Oct. 31, 1858, in *Transactions* (1858), 243.

5. Transcript of the Proceedings in Case No. 611[,] Jacob P. Leese[,] Claimant[,] vs. The United States, Defendant, For the Place Named "Lac," MS, Bancroft Library, University of California, Berkeley.

6. Ibid.

7. SoD, C: 125–26; SoD, H: 96.

8. SoD, M: 47.

9. Testimony of Julius K. Rose, *San Francisco Alta California*, Apr. 29, 1858, 1; "A Visit to the Largest Vineyard in the World," ibid., Aug. 29, 1869, 3.

10. ArH, "Early Viticulture," 77. In Leese's time, the grapes were collected in cowhide bags and trampled on by Indians. Munro-Fraser, 461. Wine was still made in this way in the Napa Valley when Charles Krug arrived there in 1859. *St. Helena Star*, Dec. 19, 1890, 2.

11. Rose won a premium at the first California State Fair in 1854, but it was for the best display of grapes and not wine. *California Farmer*, Jan. 5, 1854, 1.

12. In 1856, a man named James H. Jenkins was living in a house in the

middle of the Lac Rancho and making wine from the grapes on the property. SoD, N: 159. On June 26, 1857, wine "made at the Buena Vista Rancho, Sonoma County, by J. H. Jenkins" was advertised for sale in San Francisco. *San Francisco Herald*, June 26, 1857, 4. Since Jenkins did not own the property, he was probably making the wine under contract with Rose.

13. In a report to the California State Agricultural Society dated Oct. 31, 1858, AH gave the total number of vines on the property and stated their ages. Assuming that all the vines were planted eight feet on center (the usual custom in Sonoma), the 1,312 vines planted in 1834 covered about two acres, the 1,280 vines planted in 1850 covered another two acres, and the 12,714 vines planted in 1855 covered a little more than eighteen acres. *Transactions* (1858), 243.

14. In 1864, an article published in *Harper's New Monthly Magazine* (probably written by Arpad) stated that AH bought the property in 1856. ArH, "Wine-Making," 23. In 1866, AH reported to the trustees of the Buena Vista Vinicultural Society that the severe frost that struck the Sonoma Valley in the spring of that year was "the first frost I have experienced on this domain since 1856." BVVS, *Reports* (1866), 9. This date is consistent with and helps to explain other aspects of the transaction.

15. Testimony of Julius K. Rose, *San Francisco Alta California*, Apr. 29, 1858, 1.

16. SoD, B: 562; SoSh, N: 159–64.

17. ArH, "Early Viticulture," 77; William M. Boggs to editor, May 25, 1885, *St. Helena Star*, June 8, 1885, 1.

18. Testimony of A[ttila] F. Haraszthy, in Private Land Claim Docket Number 502 ("Lac Land Claim"), Record Group 49, Records of the General Land Office, California. Washington, D.C.: National Archives, National Archives and Records Service, General Services Administration, 1967.

19. *California Farmer*, Nov. 7, 1856, 113, which also stated that the wine was being made "under the supervision of an experienced man from Hialbron on the Rhine." The name of this man has not been determined; he may have been one of the German immigrants who had recently settled in Sonoma, or a man whom AH sent up from San Francisco to take charge of the autumn crush. In a speech delivered at Buena Vista in 1980, William F. Heintz expressed the opinion that the name Buena Vista was already in use before AH acquired the property. Heintz draws this inference from the cited article in *California Farmer*. However, Rose called the property the Vineyard Farm when he owned it, and Buena Vista is the kind of picturesque name that AH liked to give to his properties.

20. In January 1857 he was still living in San Francisco. SoD, B: 562. By October of that year, he was a resident of Sonoma. SoD, 6: 264–65.

21. ArH, "Haraszthy Family," 8. The *San Francisco Alta California*, Apr. 30, 1857, Special Supplement, showed that "A. F. Haraszthy" was one of the passengers who arrived in San Francisco on the Pacific Mail steamship *Golden Gate* on Apr. 30, 1857. The Hungarian John Xántus, who arrived in San Francisco on the same ship, said that he traveled from New York with AH's "brother" (Madden, 130), but this is obviously an error for "son," since AH had no brother and Arpad was returning from the East at this time.

22. ArH, "Early Viticulture," 77. Munro-Fraser, 461, reports that Hill bought his first grapevines in 1852 and began his Sonoma plantation in 1855.

23. William M. Boggs to editor, May 25, 1885, *St. Helena Star,* June 8, 1885, 1.

24. ArH, "Early Viticulture," 77.

25. Ibid.

26. AH to O. C. Wheeler, Oct. 31, 1858, *Transactions* (1858), 243–44.

27. Ibid., 244.

28. ArH, "Early Viticulture," 77.

29. Robert A. Thompson to editor, *San Francisco Bulletin,* May 1, 1885, 2; William M. Boggs to editor, ibid., May 5, 1885, 2; see Boggs to editor of *Napa Reporter,* reprinted in *St. Helena Star,* July 10, 1884, 1; Boggs to editor, *St. Helena Star,* June 8, 1885, 1.

30. W. M. Boggs to editor, May 25, 1885, *St. Helena Star,* June 8, 1885, 1, 2.

31. Ibid., 4.

32. *Transactions* (1858), 243.

33. AH to O. C. Wheeler, Oct. 31, 1858, *Transactions* (1858), 243.

34. *California Culturist,* Nov. 15, 1858, advertisement; *California Farmer,* Nov. 26, 1858, 131 (reprinted in subsequent editions through Feb. 25, 1859).

35. For discussion of this importation, see Chs. 22 and 23.

36. A letter to the *St. Helena Star* dated May 4, 1885, signed L. L. P., claimed that a man named Stock had a vineyard of foreign grapes at San Jose in 1858 or 1859 and noted that AH had not gone to Europe for vines until 1861, concluding, "So much for the introduction of foreign vines into the State." *St. Helena Star,* May 18, 1885, 1.

37. In his letter to the editor of the *Bulletin,* Thompson took pains to demonstrate that the Zinfandel was in California before AH's 1862 importation. He was apparently unaware that AH had made extensive importations before 1862. *San Francisco Bulletin,* May 1, 1885, 2. I have found no evidence that Thompson's wine history was ever published.

38. Arpad Haraszthy to editor, May 11, 1885, *San Francisco Bulletin,* May 14, 1885, 4.

39. *San Francisco Merchant,* July 3, 1885, 82.

40. See Ch. 3. In 1864, AH told the Farmers Club of the American Institute in New York City that he had tried several varieties of American grapes, including the Isabella, Catawba, Delaware, and Scuppernong, "but the fruit is not to be compared to the fine imported varieties." "Wines, Almonds," 137.

41. William M. Boggs to editor, May 25, 1885, *St. Helena Star,* June 8, 1885, 1.

42. Ibid.

43. SoD, 6: 264–65.

44. SoD, 8: 1–5. Until the titles were actually exchanged, Larkin had the right to collect rents on the house and Agoston had possession and use of the Huichica land.

45. SoD, 9: 592–93; also NaD, G: 412–13. Larkin died in San Francisco on Oct. 27, 1858.

46. AH to O. C. Wheeler, Oct. 31, 1858, *Transactions* (1858), 242.

47. Ibid., 244.

48. *Transactions* (1858), 243

49. "A Notable Gorham Accession, With a Reason," *San Francisco Examiner,* Sept. 2, 1867, 2.

50. Speech delivered at Petaluma on Aug. 30, 1860, as reported in *San Francisco Alta California,* Sept. 2, 1860, 1.

51. Article in *Sonoma Democrat* as reported in "Col. Haraszthy's Vineyard," ibid., Dec. 6, 1857, 1.

52. AH to O. C. Wheeler, Oct. 31, 1858, in *Transactions* (1858), 242. AH said he planned to increase the second cellar to a depth of 240 feet.

53. Ibid., 242–43.

54. In his October report to the State Agricultural Society, AH noted that all the buildings then standing at Buena Vista were of "cheap construction." This temporary press house was replaced in 1862 with a stone structure.

55. AH, "Report on Grapes and Wine," 322, contains AH's own description of the requirements of a good press house.

56. ArH, "Wine-Making," 28, describes the experiment with redwood barrels and says that it was undertaken in 1859.

57. Although the date when the new house was constructed has not been definitely ascertained, it must have been after Oct. 31, 1858 (when AH described all the structures at Buena Vista as of "cheap construction") and before the summer of 1862, when a picture of the new house was included as the frontispiece in AH, *Grape Culture.* Since it would have been necessary to prepare this picture several months before the book was published, and since AH was absent from Sonoma for most of 1861, it is reasonable to assume that the house was built before 1861, i.e., in either 1859 or 1860.

58. *Transactions* (1858), 311–29.

59. Ibid., 328–29.

60. Wilson Flint, "Pomological Report" to Board of Managers of California State Agricultural Society, *Transactions* (1859), 298.

61. ArH, "Early Viticulture," 77.   62. Darlington, 72.

63. *Transactions* (1858), 246.   64. Carosso, 10.

65. Ibid., 31.

66. "California Wine," *California Farmer,* Oct. 3, 1856, 84.

CHAPTER 20 *Bacchus Loves the Hills*

1. ArH, "Wine-Making in California," 23.

2. Barthélemy [Bertalan] de Szemere, *Notes on Hungarian Wines* (Paris: Printed by E. Brière, 1861), 11, quoted in AH, *Grape Culture,* 154. Szemere wrote: "In Hungary, the vineyards are commonly situated upon elevated hills, I dare even call them mountains. The Hungarians, knowing the old Latin proverb: '*Bacchus colles amat*' (Bacchus loves the hills), have followed the advice; they even now laugh at and despise the wines growing in the low plains, which is the case with most French wines."

3. AH, "Report on Grapes and Wine of California," 314.

4. "Wines, Almonds," 137.

5. ArH, "Wine-Making in California," 23–24.

6. Article in *Sonoma Democrat*, as cited in "Col. Haraszthy's Vineyard," *San Francisco Alta California*, Dec. 6, 1857, 1.

7. "Proposition to Plant Vineyards," *San Francisco Alta California*, Sept. 9, 10, 11, 1859, 2.

8. *California Farmer*, Sept. 7, 1860, 12; Nov. 16, 1860, 89.

9. This method is described in AH, "Report on Grapes and Wine," 321–22.

10. Ibid., 322.   11. *Transactions* (1859), 150.

12. Ibid., 198–99.   13. *California Farmer*, Aug. 31, 1860, 10.

14. *Transactions* (1860), 165.   15. Ibid., 257, 262–64.

16. In 1862 AH copied an extract from Johann Carl Leuchs's description of the methods for making these two classes of Tokay wines in AH, *Grape Culture*, 162. The extract referred to *esszencia* as "Essence" and *aszú* as "Ausbruch."

17. AH, "Report on Grapes and Wine," 323.

18. Ibid.

19. "Sainsevain's Sparkling California," *San Francisco Alta California*, Dec. 12, 1857, 2; Hittell, *Commerce*, 249; Irving McKee, "Jean Louis Vignes: California's Pioneer Wine Grower, Part 2 of a Two-Part Article," *Wine Review*, Sept. 1948, 12. In 1878, the *Alta California* recalled that the wine from which the Sainsevain champagne was made (a white wine produced in Los Angeles) was "so strong that a large proportion of the bottles were burst by the vigor of the fermentation, and it lacked delicacy of flavor." *San Francisco Alta California*, July 22, 1878, 2.

20. *California Farmer*, Sept. 28, 1860, 37.

21. "Cultivation of the Grape in Sonoma Valley," ibid., Oct. 12, 1860, 60.

22. For AH's own description of "botanical or experimental gardens" in Europe, see AH, *Grape Culture*, xviii.

23. *California Farmer*, Apr. 22, 1859, 92.

24. *California Culturist*, July 1860, 41; *California Farmer*, May 20, 1859, 12.

25. *California Farmer*, Sept. 21, 1860, 28.

26. Ibid.

27. "Proposition to Plant Vineyards," *San Francisco Alta California*, Sept. 9, 10, 11, 1859, 2.

28. Anaheim was located in Orange County after that county was formed in 1889.

29. Carosso, 60–63.

30. "Haraszthy's Proposition to Plant Vineyards for other People," *San Francisco Alta California*, Oct. 3, 1859, 1.

31. SoD, 9: 491–93.   32. SoBA, A: 136–38.

33. SoD, 9: 640–41.   34. *California Farmer*, Sept. 21, 1860, 25.

35. William M. Boggs to editor, *St. Helena Star*, June 8, 1885, 1.

36. SoD, 9: 222–23.

37. Ibid., 224, 770.

38. *California Farmer*, Sept. 7, 1861, 12.

39. Book A of Maps, Sonoma County, 6. The map was titled "Plat of Loveall [*sic*] Valley, Agoston Haraszthy." "Lovall" is the modern spelling.

40. SoBA, A: 218–28; SoD, 11: 492–93, 496–97.

41. In the summer of 1863, a writer for the *Alta California* found Attila directing a group of thirty Chinese, who were grubbing oak saplings on a steep hill overlooking Lovall Valley. "A Trip to the Vineyards of Sonoma Valley," *San Francisco Alta California*, July 28, 1863, 1.

42. Ibid., May 6, 1859, 2.   43. SoD, 11: 211–12.

44. ArH, "Haraszthy Family," 17.   45. SoD, 11: 542–45.

46. ArH, "Haraszthy Family," 24–25.

47. *California Farmer*, Oct. 12, 1860, 60.

48. Ibid., Mar. 15, 1861, 20.

49. Ibid., Aug. 24, 1860, 5.

50. *Transactions* (1860), 78.

51. By the summer of 1863, this experimental vineyard was bearing its first fruit. "A Trip to the Vineyards of Sonoma Valley," *San Francisco Alta California*, July 28, 1863, 1.

52. *California Farmer*, June 14, 1861, 124.

53. *An Illustrated History of Sonoma County, California* (Chicago: Lewis, 1889), 178.

54. *San Francisco Alta California*, July 30, 1860, 1.

55. *California Farmer*, Oct. 12, 1860, 52.

56. Ibid., June 14, 1861, 124.

57. Ibid.; for date of meeting, see ibid., June 7, 1861, 117.

CHAPTER 21 *A Bold Proposal*

1. *Transactions* (1860), 17, 20.

2. Ibid., 17–18.

3. Ibid.

4. *San Francisco Alta California*, Sept. 2, 1860, 1; see Ch. 20 for discussion.

5. ArH, "Haraszthy Family," 18, asserts that AH contributed $15,000 to Latham's campaign. However, this amount was almost surely an exaggeration.

6. Theodore H. Hittell, *History of California* (San Francisco: N. J. Stone, 1898), 4: 262.

7. *San Francisco Alta California*, Feb. 15, 1861, 2.

8. *Transactions* (1860), 17–18.

9. "Report of Special Committee on the Culture of the Grape-Vine in California," in *Appendix to Journals of Assembly, of the Twelfth Session of the Legislature, of the State of California* (Sacramento: C. T. Botts, 1861); reprinted in *San Francisco Alta California*, Feb. 26, 1861, 1; *California Farmer*, Mar. 15, 1861, 17. Original in California State Archives.

10. JCA (1861), 300. The original of the resolution is in the State Archives.

11. JCS (1861), 508.

12. "To Wine and Fruit-Growers," *California Farmer*, May 24, 1861, 100.

13. Governor Downey's Message to Legislature, Jan. 8, 1862, JCA (1861), 44; JCS (1862), 43–44.

14. Letter from Ramirez to Price in Senate/Assembly Standing, Special Committee Reports, Committee on Grape Culture in California, California State Archives.

15. "The Importation of Foreign Vines and Fruits," *San Francisco Alta California*, May 26, 1861, 2.

16. AH, *Grape Culture*, xv.

17. "Report of J. J. Warner," *Appendix to Journals of Senate and Assembly, of the Thirteenth Session of the Legislature of the State of California* (Sacramento: Benj. P. Avery, State Printer, 1862), 11.

18. In August 1861, approximately three months after AH's departure, a writer for the *California Farmer* visited Sonoma and, near the mission, "amused myself in the company of the brothers H., who entertained me with a discourse on Vine-culture, reclamation of Swamp-Lands, steam navigation to Sonoma, etc., etc." *California Farmer*, Aug. 23, 1861, 177.

19. See, e.g., ibid., May 24, 1861, 100. This advertisement was repeated in the newspaper on a weekly basis through Sept. 6.

20. Pinney, *History of Wine*, 279, asserts that the "coolness" of AH's offer to bring "every grape variety now in cultivation in the civilized world" "tells us a great deal about the man." This suggests that the offer was disingenuous, but without discussing its factual basis or whether AH might reasonably have believed that he could deliver such a broad selection of cuttings.

21. *San Francisco Alta California*, Mar. 3, 1861, 1, 2.

22. SMD, 2: 521–26.

23. AH, *Grape Culture*, xx.

24. Ibid., 152.

25. "To Wine and Fruit-Growers," *California Farmer*, May 24, 1861, 100. Smyrna was the old name for the Turkish port city of Izmir on the Aegean.

CHAPTER 22 *Mission to Europe*

1. AH, *Grape Culture*, 34.

2. "To the Citizens of Sonoma Valley," *California Farmer*, June 14, 1861, 124.

3. AH, *Grape Culture*, xix; unless otherwise indicated in this chapter, all details of the journey, and all quotations from AH, are from this work.

4. Szemere, 358.

5. Ibid. It would be interesting to speculate whether Arpad's views on slavery at the start of the Civil War reflected his father's views at that time; but there is no evidence upon which this question can be answered. Arpad may have developed those views independently during the several years he was absent from the family, and Szemere may also have exaggerated or misunderstood those views.

6. AH, *Grape Culture*, 56; *San Francisco Alta California*, Apr. 1, 1861, 1.

7. Harry C. Blair and Rebecca Tarshis, *Lincoln's Constant Ally: The Life of Colonel Edward D. Baker* (Portland: Oregon Historical Society, 1960), 159.

8. "Report of A. Haraszthy," in *Appendix to Journals of Senate and Assembly, of the Thirteenth Session of the Legislature of the State of California* (Sacramento: Benj. P. Avery, State Printer, 1862), 9; also in *San Francisco Alta California*, Feb. 11, 1862, 2; *California Farmer*, Feb. 14, 1862, 145.

9. "Wines, Almonds," 137.

CHAPTER 23 *An Official Rebuff*

1. *Sacramento Union*, Jan. 18, 1862, 1.

2. JCS (1862), 123, 125.

3. AH to His Excellency the Governor, dated Feb. 8, 1862, in *California Farmer*, Feb. 21, 1862, 154.

4. JCA (1862), 44; JCS (1862), 43–44; *California Farmer*, Jan. 17, 1862, 114.

5. "Report of J. J. Warner," *Appendix to Journals of Senate and Assembly* (1862), 23, 24; the original of this report is in the California State Archives, Sacramento.

6. "Report of A. Haraszthy," *Appendix to Journals of Senate and Assembly* (1862), 9–10; also in *San Francisco Alta California*, Feb. 11, 1862, 2; *California Farmer*, Feb. 14, 1862, 145; original report in California State Archives, Sacramento.

7. "Report of A. Haraszthy," 10.

8. Ibid., 9.

9. "Letter from Mr. Haraszthy," dated Buena Vista Ranch, Feb. 8, 1862, in *Appendix to Journals of Senate and Assembly* (1862); original in California State Archives, Sacramento.

10. Ibid.

11. Pinney, *History of Wine*, 279.

12. JCA (1861), 300; original resolution in California State Archives, Sacramento.

13. *San Francisco Alta California*, Feb. 15, 1861, 2.

14. *California Farmer*, Feb. 21, 1862, 156.

15. Ibid., Feb. 14, 1862, 148.

16. JCA (1862), 220; *San Francisco Alta California*, Feb. 15, 1862, 2.

17. Assembly Concurrent Resolution No. V was adopted Feb. 14, 1862. See SC (1862), 592.

18. JCS (1862), 276; *San Francisco Alta California*, Feb. 28, 1862, 1.

19. *San Francisco Alta California*, Apr. 4, 1862, 1.

20. JCS (1862), 476.

21. JCA (1862), 552.

22. "Report of the Committee on the Culture and Improvement of the Grape-Vine," Apr. 9, 1862, *Appendix to Journals of Senate and Assembly* (1862).

23. JCA (1862), 552.

24. JCS (1862), 502; reprinted in *San Francisco Alta California*, Apr. 8, 1862, 1; *Sacramento Union*, Apr. 9, 1862, 4.

25. JCS (1862), 502–3; *San Francisco Alta California*, Apr. 8, 1862, 1; *Sacramento Union*, Apr. 9, 1862, 4.

26. *Sacramento Union*, Apr. 9, 1862, 4.

27. *San Francisco Alta California*, Apr. 8, 1862, 2.

28. *Sacramento Union*, Apr. 10, 1862, 2.

29. Ibid., Apr. 18, 1862, 4.

30. *San Francisco Alta California*, Apr. 17, 1862, 1.

31. *Sacramento Union*, Apr. 18, 1862, 4.

32. Ibid.

33. JCS (1862), 570; *San Francisco Alta California*, Apr. 17, 1862, 1; *Sacramento Union*, Apr. 18, 1862, 4.

34. Fredericksen, "Authentic," pt. 4, 18; Carosso, 57; Teiser and Harroun, 38–39.

35. ArH, "Haraszthy Family," 9–10.

36. *San Francisco Alta California*, Feb. 14, 1862, 1.

37. "Report of A. Haraszthy," *Appendix to Journals of Senate and Assembly* (1862), 9; also in *San Francisco Alta California*, Feb. 11, 1862, 2; *California Farmer*, Feb. 14, 1862, 145.

38. Appendix I to the "Supplementary Report of Charles A. Wetmore, Chief Executive Viticultural Officer and Commissioner for the State at Large," part of the "First Annual Report of the Board of State Viticultural Commissioners," 2d ed., in *Appendix to the Journals of the Senate and Assembly* (1881), 2: 184–88.

39. "Wines, Almonds," 137.

40. See, e.g., Pinney, *History of Wine*, 280.

41. Pinney, ibid., characterizes the absence of the Zinfandel from the 1861 catalog as a "sensational omission."

42. For a discussion of the etymology of "Zinfandel" and its probable root in "Silvaner" (or "Sylvaner"), see Ch. 2.

43. Appendix I to the "Supplementary Report of Charles A. Wetmore," 184.

44. Four-page manuscript in handwriting of Arpad Haraszthy, attached to ArH, "Haraszthy Family," 4, 10.

45. Sullivan, "Man Named," pt. 3, 15; Sullivan, *Napa Wine*, 36, argues that "Haraszthy's imports never had much effect on California winegrowing." This statement is broad enough to include not just the 1862 importations but also those made in earlier years.

46. Pinney, *History of Wine*, 280.

47. [John S. Hittell,] *The Alta California Almanac and Book of Facts, 1869* (San Francisco: F. MacCrellish & Co., 1869), 75 [the catalog in the Bancroft Library attributes this work to Hittell, although his name does not appear on the title page].

48. Nordhoff, 219.

49. Munro-Fraser, 74.

50. "California Viniculture," *San Francisco Bulletin*, Jan. 20, 1877, 4.

51. Charles Wetmore, *Second Annual Report to the Board of State Viticultural Commissioners, For the Years 1882–3 and 1883–4* (Sacramento: James J. Ayres, Supt. State Printing, 1884), 38.

52. This idea, which seems patently fallacious to people familiar with the development of the California wine industry in the twentieth century, was remark-

ably persistent in the nineteenth. For example, one Joel Clayton wrote to the *Alta California* from Contra Costa County in February 1862, "There is not much science needed in planting grapes, and I doubt the assertion that the grape is a criterion in making good wine, having traveled through our State and seen that locality always tells in its own favor." *California Farmer*, Feb. 21, 1862, 154.

53. *Statutes of California* (1880), Ch. 62.

CHAPTER 24 *Taking Stock*

1. *Transactions* (1861), 16–17.
2. An Act donating Public Lands to the several States and Territories which may provide Colleges for the Benefit of Agriculture and the Mechanic Arts, approved July 2, 1860, 37th Congress, Session II, ch. 130, in *Statutes at Large*, vol. 12 (Boston: Little, Brown, 1863). This was popularly known as the Morrill Act.
3. "President's Opening Address," *California Farmer*, Oct. 3, 1862, 25, 28.
4. See Pinney, *History of Wine*, 277; Pinney, "Introduction," xxi.
5. *New York Times*, May 10, 1862, 5.
6. "Literary Notices," *Harper's New Monthly Magazine*, Dec. 1862, 133.
7. "Haraszthy's Book on Wine-Growing," *San Francisco Alta California*, Feb. 2, 1863, 2.
8. "Premiums at Sonoma Fair," *California Farmer*, Oct. 24, 1862, 50.
9. *Transactions* (1863), 129–31.
10. *San Francisco Alta California*, June 25, 1863, 2.
11. *Annual Report, American Institute*, 193.
12. "Sonoma County Fair—No. 2," *San Francisco Alta California*, Oct. 16, 1862, 1.
13. An Act to provide Internal Revenue to support the Government and to pay Interest on the Public Debt, approved July 1, 1862, ch. 119, sec. 75, 37th Congress, Session II, 1862, in *Statutes at Large*, vol. 12 (Boston: Little, Brown, 1863).
14. "Memorial of the Wine-Growers of California," *San Francisco Alta California*, Dec. 10, 1862, 1.
15. "A Wine-Growers' Convention," ibid., Nov. 18, 1862, 2.
16. An Act to provide Internal Revenue to support the Government and to pay Interest on the Public Debt approved July 1, 1862, ch. 119, sec. 41.
17. See "A Wine-Growers' Convention," *San Francisco Alta California*, Nov. 18, 1862, 2.
18. *San Francisco Alta California*, Nov. 20, 1862, 1; *California Farmer*, Nov. 21, 1862, 84.
19. Ibid.
20. *San Francisco Alta California*, Dec. 10, 1862, 1; *California Farmer*, Dec. 12, 1862, 105; *California Wine and Wool Register*, Jan. 1863, 2–6.
21. Ibid.
22. See Davis, 188–91.
23. "The State Agricultural Society," *California Farmer*, Aug. 15, 1862, 164.

24. Ibid.

25. "Loyalty of the State Agricultural Society's Officers: Letter from the President," ibid., Aug. 29, 1862, 177.

26. ArH, "Haraszthy Family," 18–19.

27. SoD, 13:736.

28. Muster Roll, Company B, 18th N.Y. Cavalry, National Archives Microfilm Publications, Compiled Records Showing Service of Military Units in Volunteer Union Organizations (Washington, D.C.: National Archives, National Archives and Records Service, General Services Administration, 1964), roll 110; Phisterer, 2: 1025, 1026, 1034; Edmund Vasvary, *Lincoln's Hungarian Heroes: The Participation of Hungarians in the Civil War, 1861–1865* (Washington, D.C.: Hungarian Reformed Federation of America, 1939), 56.

29. ArH to editor, *San Francisco Bulletin*, May 14, 1885, 4.

30. The Sonoma Steam Navigation Company was incorporated January 30, 1863, with authorized stock of $30,000. A copy of the articles of incorporation, showing the incorporators to be AH, William Hayes, Lewis Tichener, Jacob Gundlach, and Martin Flynn, is in the California State Archives, Sacramento. The *Princess* was in regular operation as early as October 1862, when a writer for the *Alta California* saw AH on one of the San Francisco–Sonoma runs. "Sonoma County Fair," *San Francisco Alta California*, Oct. 10, 1862, 1. The operation of the boat is described in "A Trip to Sonoma Valley," *California Wine, Wool, and Stock Journal*, May 1863, 78.

31. This third tunnel was being dug when a writer for the *California Farmer* visited Buena Vista in the late summer of 1860. "Great Vineyards in Sonoma," *California Farmer*, Sept. 7, 1860, 12.

32. Various published sources give different dimensions for the tunnels. These differences are perhaps evidence that the widths and heights of the tunnels were changed over a period of years or simply that the published figures were not always checked carefully. The depths of the tunnels were, of course, changed, in some cases by deepening them, and in other cases by walling off the ends.

33. The old wooden press house was probably razed before the third tunnel was dug. This would have greatly facilitated the excavation, since both the old and the new press houses stood directly in front of the tunnel entrances. Years later, Arpad recalled that the press house (he called it a "fermenting house") was built in 1862. ArH, "Early Viticulture," 78. Arpad's recollection is confirmed by other evidence. For example, the prospectus of the BVVS (dated Mar. 27, 1863) describes "a most substantial wine press-house, a powerful press steam engine, grape crushers, mammoth tanks for fermentation," and other new facilities on the property. BVVS, *By-Laws*, 15. Further, a detailed description of the new press house and its equipment was published in *California Wine, Wool, and Stock Journal*, May 1863, 79. Before AH's tour of Europe in 1861, there was no mention of such a structure at Buena Vista, and it is unlikely that he would have authorized the construction of so large a project during his absence.

34. ArH, "Early Viticulture," 78; "A Trip to Sonoma Valley," *California Wine, Wool, and Stock Journal*, May 1863, 79.

35. The building was described in the spring of 1863 as "a large two story building, 54 by 64 feet . . . a most substantial structure." "A Trip to Sonoma Valley," *California Wine, Wool, and Stock Journal,* May 1863, 79.

36. Ibid.; "A Trip to the Vineyards of Sonoma Valley," *San Francisco Alta California,* July 28, 1863, 1.

37. For a description of the process of steaming redwood barrels, see ArH, "Wine-Making in California," 23; see also discussion in Ch. 19.

38. "A Trip to Sonoma Valley," *California Wine, Wool, and Stock Journal,* May 1863, 79; ArH, "Wine Presses—No. 2," 113–16, describes a variety of wine presses, including the type of screw press used at Buena Vista.

39. "A Trip to Sonoma Valley," *California Wine, Wool, and Stock Journal,* May 1863, 79.

40. Ibid.

41. Emparan, 304–5.

42. SoMa, A: 335; Register of Marriages, St. Francis Solano Church, Sonoma, June 1, 1863; "Married," *San Francisco Alta California,* June 6, 1863, 4. The marriage certificate was filed for record by Gaza Haraszthy June 2, 1863.

43. Emparan, 311, 353.

44. In the fall of 1862, the *Alta* reported that there were "no less than 2,000 acres of all varieties of vines, planted and in bearing, within a circuit of ten miles about Sonoma." "Sonoma County Fair—No. 2," *San Francisco Alta California,* Oct. 16, 1862, 1.

45. ArH, "Early Viticulture," 78.

46. On Nov. 8, 1860, Krug sold his Sonoma property of 35.61 acres to Edward R. Highton for $5,000. SoD, 11: 95. He moved to Napa Valley in the fall of 1860. Charles Krug to editor, *St. Helena Star,* Dec. 19, 1890, 2.

47. Charles Krug and Caroline (originally Carolina) Bale were married in Napa Valley by Fr. Peter Deyaert Dec. 26, 1860. NaMa, A: 67.

48. Charles Krug to editor, *St. Helena Star,* Dec. 19, 1890, 2.

49. Ibid.; "Viticulture in Napa County," *St. Helena Star,* May 18, 1885, 1.

50. This point was made by many early reporters, including a writer for the *California Wine, Wool, and Stock Journal,* who wrote: "The improvement of the valley is dated from the time of Col. Haraszthy, whose untiring energy and perseverance has been the means of inducing others to come and locate in the valley, plant vineyards, and build their future homes." "A Trip to Sonoma Valley," *California Wine, Wool, and Stock Journal,* May 1863, 108.

51. Mortgage dated May 15, 1862, to Charles G. Zaehnsdorf, in SoMo, E: 477–81; mortgage dated Mar. 13, 1863, to William Blanding, in SoMo, F: 72–79; mortgage dated Apr. 20, 1863, to Charles G. Zaehnsdorf, in SoMo, F: 138–45.

CHAPTER 25 *The Largest Vineyard in the World*

1. Szemere; see Ch. 22.

2. Mortgage from AH to Charles G. Zaehnsdorf of St.-Cloud in the Empire of France, SoMo, E: 477–81.

3. Cal. Const., 1849, art. IV, sec. 35; SC (1850), ch. 128, authorized corporations for certain purposes, not including agriculture.

4. SC (1858), ch. 181, sec. 1.

5. SC (1863), ch. 248.

6. See, e.g., Pinney, *History of Wine*, 283; Teiser and Harroun, 39; Fredericksen, "Authentic," pt. 5, 22.

7. BVVS, *By-Laws*, 5. A handwritten copy of the original certificate of incorporation is in the California State Archives, Sacramento.

8. AH, *Grape Culture*, 64–65; see Ch. 22.

9. BVVS, *By-Laws*, 5; "Buena Vista Vinicultural Society," *California Farmer*, Apr. 3, 1863, 41.

10. SoD,13: 772–76.

11. SoMo, E: 477–81; F: 72–79, 138–45; SoD, 13: 734–35.

12. BVVS, *By-Laws*, 15.

13. Ibid.; BVVS, *Reports* (1864), 5, 7.

14. BVVS, *Reports* (1864), 8.

15. A woodcut showing the building in its one-story form appears in ArH, "Wine-Making in California," 23.

16. ArH, "Haraszthy Family," 25.

17. Appendix, "Production of Wine in California," in William P. Blake, ed., *Reports of the United States Commissioners to the Paris Universal Exposition, 1867* (Washington, D.C.: Government Printing Office, 1870), 5: 26.

18. ArH, "Haraszthy Family," 25.

19. Register of Baptisms, Parish of St. Francis Solano, Sonoma, Feb. 26, 1865.

20. Emparan, 309.

21. Muster Roll, Company B, 18th N.Y. Cavalry, National Archives Microfilm Publications, Compiled Records Showing Service of Military Units in Volunteer Union Organizations (Washington, D.C.: National Archives, 1964), roll 110.

22. See "A Californian Captured," *San Francisco Alta California*, July 19, 1864, 1, referring to article in *Star*.

23. "The Napa Fair," *California Farmer*, Oct. 14, 1864, 89.

24. "The Industrial Exhibition," ibid., Oct. 7, 1864, 80.

25. *San Francisco Alta California*, Mar. 27, 1865, 2; Apr. 13, 1865, 2.

26. Ibid., Apr. 13, 1865, 1.   27. BVVS, *Reports*, (1864), 6.

28. Ibid., 9.   29. Ibid., 16.

30. *Annual Report, American Institute*, 284–90; "Wines, Almonds," 137–38.

31. *Annual Report, American Institute*, 288–90.

32. "Matter of A. Haraszthy," Schedule A. See Ch. 27.

33. "California as Vineland," 600–604; ArH, "Wine-Making in California," 22–30.

34. "California as Vineland," 602.

35. ArH, "Wine-Making in California," 22.

36. Pinney, *History of Wine*, 281, calls the *Harper's* piece "an article of unashamed advertising" for AH's Buena Vista property and its wines.

37. AH, *Grape Culture*, 142.

38. "Notes on Sonoma Valley—No. 3," *San Francisco Alta California,* Feb. 21, 1865, 1; "The Great Vineyard of California," ibid., July 2, 1869, 4; Hyatt, 74. In 1869, when the BVVS was not appreciably larger than it was in 1864, the *Alta* stated that it was "undeniably" the largest vineyard in the world and compared it to typical European vineyards of the time. "A Visit to the Largest Vineyard in the World," *San Francisco Alta California,* Aug. 29, 1869, 5. [John S. Hittell], *The Alta California Almanac and Book of Facts, 1871* (San Francisco: F. MacCrellish & Co., Publishers "Alta California" Newspaper, 1871), 113, stated that the vineyard was "second in size to no other in the United States, if indeed, in the world."

39. An original invitation to this ball is in the collections of the California Historical Society in San Francisco. A photograph of an invitation to the same ball, addressed to "Mr. & Mrs. Auger & Family," is in *Count Found,* 2.

40. The Augers' surviving daughters gave the invitation to Frank Bartholomew, then the owner of Buena Vista, in the 1940's.

CHAPTER 26 *Restless Again*

1. Victoria Post Ranney, Gerard J. Rauluk, and Carolyn F. Hoffman, eds., *The Papers of Frederick Law Olmsted,* vol. 5, *The California Frontier, 1863–1865* (Baltimore: Johns Hopkins University Press, 1990), 30, 31.

2. Ibid., 338.   3. Olmsted, 3.
4. Ibid., 8.   5. BVVS, *Reports* (1865), 4.
6. BVVS, *Reports* (1864), 9.   7. BVVS, *Reports* (1865), 4.
8. Ibid., 6.   9. Ibid., 7–8.

10. In June 1865, Attila Haraszthy reported that vines that were layered the previous fall at Buena Vista had "made immense growth of wood and are now equal in size, to three years [*sic*] old vines, and have as many grapes on them." Ibid., 6.

11. This method of planting a vineyard is described in AH, "Best Modes."

12. BVVS, *Reports* (1865), 4, 7.

13. "California Viniculture," *San Francisco Bulletin,* Jan. 20, 1877, 4.

14. AH, "Best Modes," 146; *Transactions* (1864–65), 290–94; Hyatt, 74–79.

15. AH, "Best Modes," 294.

16. "Notes on Sonoma Valley—No. 2. The Distance Between the Vines," *San Francisco Alta California,* Feb. 16, 1865, 1.

17. "Grape Growing in California," *California Rural Home Journal,* Feb. 15, 1866, 146.

18. John S. Hittell, "The Wines of California," *Pacific Monthly,* Sept. 1863, 202.

19. "Letter from Sonoma," *San Francisco Alta California,* Mar. 26, 1866, 1.

20. "A Visit to the Largest Vineyard in the World," ibid., Aug. 29, 1869, 5.

21. "Col. Haraszthy's Letters. No. 1," ibid., Sept. 30, 1865, 1.

22. Ibid.

23. "The Vineyards," ibid., Mar. 26, 1866, 1.

24. Carosso, 81.

25. "Col. Haraszthy's Letters. No. 1," *San Francisco Alta California,* Sept. 30, 1865, 1.

26. These articles are known only because of AH's own statement that they were written. The actual publications have not been located.

27. The Philadelphia and California Petroleum Company was formed in Pennsylvania on Dec. 15, 1864, under the leadership of the Pennsylvania railroad executive and oil investor, Thomas A. Scott. W. H. Hutchinson, *Oil, Land and Politics: The California Career of Thomas Robert Bard* (Norman: University of Oklahoma Press, 1965), 1: 78. A file of corporate documents is preserved in the California State Archives, Sacramento.

28. "Col. Haraszthy's Letters. No. 1," *San Francisco Alta California,* Sept. 30, 1865, 1.

29. "Col. Haraszthy's Letters on the California Wine Interest—No. 2," ibid., Oct. 12, 1865, 1.

30. Ibid.

31. Ibid.

32. Hutchinson, *Oil, Land and Politics,* 1:112.

33. "The Vine Growers Ahead," *California Rural Home Journal,* Jan. 1, 1866, 134.

34. "Col. Haraszthy's Letters. No. 1," *San Francisco Alta California,* Sept. 30, 1865, 1.

35. Pauly, "J. Ross Browne: Wine Lobbyist," 105.

36. J. Ross Browne to Benjamin Wilson, Apr. 5, 1866, MS, Huntington Library, San Marino, California; copy in Pauly, "J. Ross Browne: Wine Lobbyist," 113–14.

37. [J. Ross Browne], *Letter from J. Ross Browne, to the Committee on Finance of the Senate, in Relation to the Proposed Tax on Native Wines* (Washington, D.C.: Printed by William H. Moore, 1866), 2–4; Browne to James A. Garfield, June 20, 1866; MS, Library of Congress; copy in Pauly, "J. Ross Browne: An Opportunity."

38. An Act to reduce Internal Taxation, etc., ch. 184, 39th Congress, approved July 13, 1866, in *Statutes at Large* (Boston: Little, Brown, 1868), 150.

39. "Wine Convention in Napa," *San Francisco Alta California,* Sept. 23, 1866, 1.

40. "City Items. The Wine-Growers' Convention," ibid., Nov. 2, 1866, 1.

41. "The Wine-Growers' State Convention. Third Day," ibid., Nov. 4, 1866, 1.

42. Ibid.

43. "City Items. The Wine-Growers' Convention," ibid., Nov. 2, 1866, 1.

44. "The Wine-Growers' State Convention. Third Day," ibid., Nov. 4, 1866, 1.

CHAPTER 27 *Tangled Vines*

1. SoMa, B: 110, fixes the correct date of this wedding, which has often been given as 1863.

2. *An Illustrated History of Los Angeles County[,] California* (Chicago: Lewis, 1889), 496, and Rockwell D. Hunt, *California and Californians* (Chicago: Lewis, 1926), 253, both give Hancock's birth date as Feb. 22, 1822. G. Allan Hancock, 53–56; Meredith, 3–15; and Clover, 1–40 record Hancock family recollections.

Although the family tradition was that Henry Hancock was a graduate of Harvard Law School, in fact he attended classes there for less than a year, entering May 8, 1848, and leaving in the same year, presumably to join the Gold Rush to California. *Harvard Law Quinquennial, 1817–1934*, 35–142; letters to author from Danielle Green, Curatorial Assistant, Harvard University Archives, Aug. 28, 1995, and Annie C. Bombard, Associate Registrar, Harvard Law School, Feb. 26, 1996.

3. On Jan. 31, 1850, a federal census taker recorded Hancock as a resident of the Middle Bar of the American River in El Dorado County. His age was 29 and his occupation miner. Population Schedules of the Seventh Census of the United States, 1850.

4. *Map of the city of Los Angeles showing the confirmed limits surveyed in August 1857 by Henry Hancock* (Los Angeles: Bancroft and Thayer, 1857).

5. Peninou and Greenleaf, *Directory*, 17.

6. Register of Baptisms, Parish of St. Francis Solano, Sonoma, July 8, 1866.

7. Phisterer, 1034.

8. Arpad referred to this firm in the debates of the winegrowers' convention held in San Francisco in December 1866. "City Items. The Wine-Growers' Convention," *San Francisco Alta California*, Nov. 3, 1866, 1. It is also listed as proprietor in 1867 of a vineyard located near the center of Sonoma. Cronise, 170.

9. Landsberger was listed as a trustee in the original prospectus of 1863 and in the annual reports for 1864 and 1865. His name does not appear in the annual report for 1866.

10. In an article quoted in Brace, 267, the *San Francisco Bulletin* reported that the firm was formed in January 1866. Peninou, *History of the Orleans Hill Vineyard*, 13, states that Arpad moved to San Francisco to join Landsberger in late 1865. The earliest city directory entries for Landsberger and Co. appear in 1867.

11. BVVS, *Reports* (1866), 7.

12. Ibid., 8.

13. Ibid. The financial statement does not give a separate figure for the expenses of the trip, but lumps them together with legal expenses and reports the total amount as $3,967.23.

14. Alonzo Phelps, *Contemporary Biography of California's Representative Men* (San Francisco: A. L. Bancroft, 1882), 2: 199–200; "Deserved Promotion," *San Francisco Alta California*, Sept. 21, 1866, 1; "Death of Geo. C. Johnson," *San Francisco Alta California*, May 20, 1872, 1; "The Late George C. Johnson's Will," *San Francisco Alta California*, May 25, 1872, 1.

15. BVVS, *Reports* (1866), 6.

16. Ibid., 10.

17. These symptoms were later described by Attila Haraszthy and E. P. Cutter. H. Appleton, "The Phylloxera-Vastatrix and its Ravages in Sonoma Valley," *Appendix to the Journals of the Senate and Assembly of the Twenty-Fourth Session of the Legislature of the State of California* (Sacramento, 1881), 2: 110.

18. In the spring of 1866, Buena Vista suffered severe leaf wilt, which reduced the crop for the year by one third; this was attributed to frost ("A Flying

Visit to Sonoma," *San Francisco Alta California*, Sept. 12, 1866, 1), but the damage was almost certainly aggravated by the phylloxera.

19. The Australian Thomas Hardy toured the California vineyards in the summer of 1883, when the phylloxera epidemic was raging, talked with Attila Haraszthy and other winemakers, and then concluded that Buena Vista was "the first place where it [the phylloxera] was observed." Hardy, 16.

20. Although it is not technically true that the phylloxera "sucks" the life out of grapevines, the "sucking" promotes the formation of galls that impede the physiology of the roots and eventually result in the death of the plant.

21. Ordish, 168–69, thinks it more likely that the phylloxera came directly from the eastern states, since reports of its appearance in California predate 1863, the year in which it was first noticed in Europe.

22. As noted in Ch. 19, there were some Catawbas on the Buena Vista property when AH arrived there, but he promptly dug them up. See William M. Boggs to editor, May 25, 1885, *St. Helena Star*, June 8, 1885, 1. It is possible that these vines were infested with the phylloxera and the pest spread from them to the *vinifera* vines at Buena Vista.

23. Ordish, 19–20, 44.

24. AH executed a promissory note in favor of Guy on Sept. 29, 1863. Transcript on Appeal in Dussol v. Bruguiere, 50 California Supreme Court Reports 456 (1875).

25. Opinion of Supreme Court of California in Dussol v. Bruguiere, 50 California Supreme Court Reports 456, 457–58 (1875).

26. "Matter of A. Haraszthy," Schedule A.

27. Fredericksen, "Authentic," pt. 5, 41, writes that in 1867 AH "guessed wrong with investments"; I have been unable to find any evidence supporting this statement.

28. Transcript on Appeal, p. 8, in Dussol v. Bruguiere, 50 California Supreme Court Reports 456 (1875).

29. See Ch. 18.

30. "Matter of A. Haraszthy," Schedule A.

31. Ibid.

32. SoD, 18: 738–41.

33. For description of mortgage, see "Matter of A. Haraszthy," Schedule A.

34. SoD, 19: 53–54.

35. "A Flying Visit to Sonoma," *San Francisco Alta California*, Sept. 12, 1866, 1.

36. "Accident at the Buena Vista Vineyard," ibid., Dec. 11, 1866, 1.

37. BVVS, *Reports* (1867), 9.

38. Charles Loring Brace visited Buena Vista soon after Dresel took over and observed that Dresel had "been obliged to take up thousands of his vines, to the great loss of the Society," because Agoston's new plan for spacing the vines "cost so much in hand-labor, and diminished so much the product." Brace, 261.

39. "California Viniculture," *San Francisco Bulletin*, Jan. 20, 1877, 4.

CHAPTER 28 *A Very Sad Place*

1. Emparan, 354.
2. SoD, 20: 428–29.
3. Register of Marriages, Parish of St. John the Baptist, Napa, Calif., May 18, 1867; SoMa, B: 474; "Married," *San Francisco Alta California*, May 23, 1867, 4.
4. Emparan, 355.
5. "Haraszthy on Immigration," *San Francisco Alta California*, May 4, 1867, 5.
6. "A Notable Gorham Accession, With a Reason," *San Francisco Examiner*, Sept. 2, 1867, 2.
7. "A Mongrel Gathering," ibid., Sept. 3, 1867, 1.
8. Menefee, 324.
9. Article 1, Section 8, of the U.S. Constitution gives Congress the power to establish uniforms laws on the subject of bankruptcies throughout the United States.
10. "Matter of A. Haraszthy," petition filed Sept. 17, 1869.
11. Ibid., Schedules A and B.
12. "Matter of A. Haraszthy," Schedule B.
13. Ibid., Certificate of Final Discharge.

CHAPTER 29 *The Final Frontier*

1. "Brandy Production," *Pacific Wine & Spirit Review*, Mar. 21, 1892, 30.
2. "Statement of Isidor Landsberger, of San Francisco, for the Wine Interest," in *Transactions* (1866–67), 223–24.
3. Appendix, "Production of Wine in California," in *Reports of the United States Commissioners to the Paris Universal Exposition, 1867* (Washington, D.C.: Government Printing Office, 1870), 27.
4. *San Francisco Alta California*, Nov. 29, 1867, 1.
5. *Petaluma Journal and Argus*, Jan. 23, 1868.
6. "Letter from Nicaragua," *San Francisco Alta California*, supp., Apr. 26, 1868, 3.
7. Ibid.
8. Ibid. The letter refers to "Major J. H.," which is almost certainly a typographical error. The reference should be to "Major G. H." and refer to Gaza Haraszthy.
9. Ibid.
10. "Haraszthy's Letters from Nicaragua," ibid., June 7, 1868, 1.
11. Ibid.
12. Ibid.
13. Ibid.
14. "Haraszthy's Letters," ibid., June 21, 1868, 3.
15. Ibid.
16. Ibid.

17. Hubert Howe Bancroft, *History of the Pacific States of North America, Central America* (San Francisco: History Company, 1887), 3: 471–71.

18. "Struck a Good Thing," *San Francisco Alta California,* July 16, 1868, 1.

19. ArH, "Haraszthy Family," 12; ArH, "Colonel Agoston Haraszthy," 1.

20. ArH to John Codman Hurd, Mar. 3, 1870, Papers of John Russell Hurd and Family, Library of the Boston Athenaeum, Boston.

21. Ibid.

22. Ibid.

23. Ibid.

24. "Arrival of the 'Oregonian,' " *San Francisco Alta California,* Aug. 14, 1868, 1.

25. "Died," ibid., 4; "Deaths," *San Francisco Bulletin,* Aug. 14, 1868, 3.

26. ArH, "The Vintage in Sonoma," *San Francisco Alta California,* Nov. 21, 1868, 2.

27. In his report dated June 21, 1867, Emil Dresel reported that "a temporary press-house was built on the roof of the new cellar building" in October 1866, and that he proposed "to build on the press cellar building two more stories in stone, which would give sufficient room for storage and wine making for several years to come." He added that 158,000 gallons of wine could be stored in the entire building and the three adjoining tunnels, and that it would cost $5,300 to make the addition to the building. BVVS, *Reports* (1867), 9, 11.

28. "A Visit to the Largest Vineyard in the World," *San Francisco Alta California,* Aug. 29, 1869, 3.

29. ArH to John Codman Hurd, Mar. 3, 1870, Papers of John Russell Hurd and Family, Library of the Boston Athenaeum, Boston.

30. SoD, 25: 496.

31. ArH, "Haraszthy Family," 15.

32. "Probable Death of Colonel Haraszthy," *San Francisco Alta California,* Aug. 6, 1869, 1.

33. ArH to John Codman Hurd, Mar. 3, 1870, Papers of John Russell Hurd and Family, Library of the Boston Athenaeum, Boston.

34. Bancroft, 3: 470–73.

35. "Family of Colonel Haraszthy," *California Farmer,* Aug. 5, 1869, 21.

36. "Probable Death of Colonel Haraszthy," *San Francisco Alta California,* Aug. 6, 1869, 1.

37. "Sad News," ibid., Aug. 26, 1869, 1.

38. "Colonel Auguston [*sic*] Haraszthy," ibid., Aug. 27, 1869, 2.

39. ArH, "Colonel Agoston Haraszthy," 3.

40. ArH, "Haraszthy Family," 13.

41. Ida Hancock.

42. "Death of General Charles Haraszthy," *San Francisco Alta California,* Aug. 3, 1869, 1; "Death of General Chas. Haraszthy," *San Diego Union,* July 22, 1869, 3.

43. ArH, "Haraszthy Family," 15.

AFTERWORD

1. SoD, 42: 29.

2. In the 1870's, Eclipse won medals in San Francisco, Los Angeles, New York, Philadelphia, New South Wales, Chile, and Antwerp, Belgium. Wait, 94–95. For an overview of Arpad Haraszthy's champagne-making career, see Ruth Teiser and Catherine Harroun, "Introduction" to Arpad Haraszthy, *Wine-Making in California* (San Francisco: Book Club of California, 1978); see also McGinty, "Toast to Eclipse."

3. File in Estate of Henry Hancock, Deceased, Superior Court, Los Angeles County, Probate no. 2036.

4. Guinn, 1: 820–23.

5. "Industrial Condition of the Slope," *San Francisco Alta California*, July 22, 1878, 2.

6. Charles A. Wetmore, *Propagation of the Vine* (San Francisco: San Francisco Merchant, 1880), 2.

7. SoD, 71: 336–44.

8. Hardy, 16.

9. "Death of A. F. Haraszthy," *San Francisco Call*, Feb. 8, 1888, 8.

10. ArH, "Haraszthy Family," 22, sets Gaza's death at Dec. 17, 1878; the *San Francisco Call*, Jan. 28, 1879, 4, gave the date as Dec. 27, 1878, which happened to be Gaza's forty-fifth birthday.

11. "Death of Major Gaza Haraszthy," *San Francisco Alta California*, Jan. 28, 1879, 1; "Death of Major Gaza Haraszthy," *New York Times*, May 10, 1879, 5.

12. "Died," *San Francisco Examiner*, May 6, 1878, 3; *San Francisco Call*, May 7, 1878, 4; *San Francisco Call*, July 14, 1879, 4.

13. "Arpad Haraszthy's Death a Shock," *San Francisco Bulletin*, Nov. 16, 1900, 2; "Sudden Death of Arpad Haraszthy," *San Francisco Chronicle*, Nov. 17, 1900, 4; "Death Strikes Arpad Haraszthy," *Pacific Wine and Spirit Review*, Nov. 30, 1900, 29.

14. G. Allan Hancock, 53–56.

15. "Remarkable Woman's Career at an End," *Los Angeles Times*, Mar. 16, 1913, pt. 2, 1. "Last Testament," *Los Angeles Daily Times*, Mar. 20, 1913, pt. 2, 1; file in Estate of Ida Hancock Ross, Deceased, Superior Court, Los Angeles County, Probate no. 23295; Estate of Ross (1915), California Supreme Court Reports 64; Hancock v. Hunt (1917), 34 California Appellate Reports 530.

16. "Deaths," *Los Angeles Sunday Times*, Mar. 17, 1912, pt. 1, 12; file in Estate of B. A. Haraszthy, Deceased, Superior Court, Los Angeles County, Probate no. 20705.

17. "Deaths," *Los Angeles Daily Times*, June 5, 1916, pt. 1, 10; "Funeral of Mrs. Flood," ibid., June 14, 1916, pt. 2, 8; file in Estate of Otelia Flood, Deceased, Superior Court, Los Angeles County, Probate no. 32666.

18. Frank H. Bartholomew, *Bart: Memoirs of Frank H. Bartholomew* (Sonoma, Calif.: Vine Brook Press, 1983), 113; Official Records, Sonoma County, 611: 223.

19. Bartholomew, *Bart*, 118–19.

20. "Colonel Auguston [*sic*] Haraszthy," *San Francisco Alta California*, Aug. 27, 1869, 2. Although the author of this article was not identified, the words "written for the Alta California" appeared just below the title. The contents, which include generous helpings of the Haraszthy Legend, suggest that it was written by Arpad.

21. "A Remarkable Career: Story of a Hungarian Emigrant's Adventures in America," *New York Times*, Feb. 27, 1870, 3.

22. Hittell, 247, says, "Certainly no one had more confidence in the future of California wine, or expressed it with more enthusiasm, or did more to promote its interests" than AH.

23. See, e.g., Nordhoff, 217 ("father of wine-culture in this State"); Hittell, 247 ("father of the vine in California"); Wait, 91 ("father of the wine industry in this state"); Bancroft, 7: 44 ("father of viniculture in California"); Emerson, 225 ("father of the wine industry as it is in California to-day"); Jones, *Vines in the Sun*, 84 ("father of modern California viticulture"); Carosso, 38 ("father of the modern California wine industry"); Leon D. Adams, *The Commonsense Book of Wine* (New York: David McKay, 1958), 126 ("father of modern California viticulture"); Schoonmaker, 162 ("often and quite fairly called the 'father of California viticulture'"); Lichine, 78, ("father of California viticulture"); Paul, 24 ("the 'father' of the wine industry").

24. Sullivan, "Viticultural Mystery," 114–29.

25. William M. Boggs to editor, *San Francisco Bulletin*, May 4, 1885, 2; Boggs to editor, *Napa Reporter*, reprinted in *St. Helena Star*, July 10, 1884, 1; Boggs to editor, *St. Helena Star*, June 8, 1885, 4, all discussed in Ch. 19.

26. Pinney, *History of Wine*, 284.

Bibliography

Hundreds of printed references to Agoston Haraszthy and his winemaking career have appeared over the years in the United States, Hungary, and other countries. Although this Bibliography makes no effort to list them all, it does include the most important sources relied on in the preparation of this book, as well as a selection of less important but still interesting publications. Each entry is accompanied by a brief description designed to help the reader evaluate its importance.

Adams, Leon D. *The Wines of America.* 3d ed. New York: McGraw-Hill, 1985. Overview of winemaking in California and other states. Many references to AH.

Agárdi, Ferenc. *Régi Magyar Világjárók* (Old Hungarian world travelers). Assembled by Béla Borsody Bevilaqua. Budapest: Művelt Nép Könyvkiadó, 1954. Article on AH at pp. 129–41.

———. *Régi Magyar Világjárók* (Old Hungarian world travelers). 2d ed, assembled by Béla Borsody Bevilaqua. Budapest: Művelt Nép Tudományos és Ismeretterjesztő Kiadó, 1955. Article on AH at pp. 144–56.

"Agoston Haraszthy." MS, State Historical Society of Wisconsin, Madison. Typewritten biography of 17 pages, with 179 footnotes. Author not identified.

Amerine, Maynard A. "The Importance of Agoston Haraszthy's Activities for the Development of Viticulture in California." *Congressional Record,* 91st Cong., 1st sess., 1969, 115, pt. 12: 16559–60. Assessment of AH's viticultural achievements by professor at University of California, Davis.

Annual Report of the American Institute, of the City of New York, for the Years 1863, '64. Albany, N.Y.: Comstock & Cassidy, 1864. Pp. 284–90 contain a report of AH's February 1864 appearance before the Institute's Farmer's Club, at which time he expounded on his views on vines, vineyards, and wines.

Appendix to the Journals of the Senate and Assembly of the Twenty-Fourth Session of the Legislature of the State of California, vol. 2. Sacramento: State Office: J. D. Young, State Printing. 1881. Includes (at 184–88) "Appendix I to the Supplementary Report of Charles A. Wetmore, Chief Executive Viticultural Officer, etc., being a reproduced copy of an original catalogue of the vines, etc., introduced in 1861 by Colonel Agostin [*sic*] Haraszthy." Copy of catalog prepared by AH to advertise grapevines and fruit trees he offered for sale after his return from Europe in 1861, probably obtained by Wetmore from Arpad Haraszthy. Original catalog has not been discovered.

Bács-Bodrogh Vármegye Egyetemes Monográfiája (Universal monography of Bács-Bodrogh County). Zombor: Bitterman Nándor és Fia Könyv és Könyomdája, 1896. Interesting information about agriculture, game, natural resources, and similar matters; no references to AH.

Bako, Elemer. "Agoston Haraszthy's Hungarian Background." *Congressional Record*, 91st Cong., 1st sess., 1969, 115, pt. 10: 13492–93. Essay on Haraszthy family and AH's life in Hungary and U.S. by Finno-Ugrian Area Specialist at Library of Congress.

Balzer, Robert Lawrence. *California's Best Wines*. Los Angeles: Ward Ritchie Press, 1948. Veteran wine journalist's description of his visits to California wineries, with liberal dose of history. Short essay on AH at pp. 53–55.

————. *The Pleasures of Wine*. Indianapolis, Ind.: Bobbs-Merrill, 1964. AH features prominently in this panegyric to wine in California and Europe. Interesting descriptions of Buena Vista Vineyards at Sonoma during the time they were owned by Frank and Antonia Bartholomew. Includes many references to 1951 European wine tour made by Balzer with AH's *Grape Culture, Wines, and Wine Making* (1862) "never beyond arm's distance."

————. *Wines of California*. New York: Harry N. Abrams, 1978. Lavishly illustrated introduction to California wines and wineries, with many references to AH. Revised and updated in 1984 as *The Los Angeles Times Book of California Wines*.

Bancroft, Hubert Howe. *History of California*, 7 vols. San Francisco: History Company, 1886–90. Although outdated in many respects, this landmark history remains a useful tool for historians. References to AH in vol. 6 at pp. 349, 610, 657; vol. 7 at pp. 44–49, 167, 744, 745.

Barany, George. *Stephen Széchenyi and the Awakening of Hungarian Nationalism, 1791–1841*. Princeton, N.J.: Princeton University Press, 1968. Standard English-language source on the great Hungarian who inspired much of AH's life and work; no references to AH.

Bede, Piroska, and Sándor Somogyi, eds. *Magyar utazók, földrajzi felfedezők* (Hungarian travelers and geographical explorers). Budapest: Tankönyvkiadó, 1973. Includes chapter by Tibor Nagy titled "Az utazó és tájalakító Haraszthy Ágoston (1812–1869) (Agoston Haraszthy the traveler and landscape architect [1812–1869])" (237–40), in which author says: "There is no doubt that he [AH] was the first globe-trotting Hungarian to exert a lasting effect on the character of the New World with his cultural and economic initiatives."

Bell, Horace. *On the Old West Coast: Being Further Reminiscences of a Ranger, Major Horace Bell*. Ed. Lanier Bartlett. New York: William Morrow, 1930. Western history filtered through lenses of personal recollection and legend. Ch. 21 contains much information (most inaccurate) about Roy Bean's escape from San Diego City jail built by AH.

Blair, Harry C., and Rebecca Tarshis. *Lincoln's Constant Ally: The Life of Colonel Edward D. Baker.* Portland: Oregon Historical Society, 1960. Describes (pp. 159–60) AH's role as member of committee appointed to accompany remains of U.S. Senator Edward D. Baker from New York to San Francisco after Baker's death in Civil War battle of Leesburg.

Borovszky, Samu. *Bács-Bodrog Vármegye* (Bács-Bodrog County). Budapest: Országos Monográfia Társaság, n.d. One volume in two books, part of series published c. 1910 under general title *Magyarország Vármegyéi és Városai* (The counties and cities of Hungary). Typical "county history," with most information supplied by local residents; some references to early Haraszthys, but little about AH.

Bowles, Samuel. *Across the Continent: A Summer's Journal to the Rocky Mountains, the Mormons, and the Pacific States, with Speaker Colfax.* Springfield, Mass.: Samuel Bowles, 1866. Travel letters written in summer of 1865 by editor of *Springfield Republican.* Includes interesting impressions of Buena Vista and its wines.

Brace, Charles Loring. *The New West: or, California in 1867–1868.* New York: G. P. Putnam and Son, 1869. Description of California by New Yorker with special interest in wine. Ch. 21 is devoted to Sonoma vineyards.

Brainard, David. "Journal of the Walworth Co. Mutual Mining Company, Commencing March the 20th, 1849. By David Brainard." MS, Bancroft Library, University of California, Berkeley. Typewritten copy in State Historical Society of Wisconsin, Madison. Brainard was one of a company of Wisconsinites who joined AH's California-bound party at Lyn Grove (near Davenport), Iowa, Apr. 11, 1849. His diary makes it possible to follow the Haraszthy party from that date until Nov. 30, 1849.

Brown, Madie. *California's Valley of the Moon: Historic Places and People in the Valley of Sonoma.* Sonoma, Calif., 1961. Pamphlet with short descriptions of historic places in Sonoma Valley. Includes description of Buena Vista Winery and references to AH.

Buena Vista Vinicultural Society. *By-Laws and Prospectus of the Buena Vista Vinicultural Society.* San Francisco: Alta California Book and Job Printing Office, 1863. Prepared at time of incorporation of BVVS in 1863.

———. *Buena Vista Vinicultural Society, Prospectus: Incorporée le 27 Mars 1863.* San Francisco: Imprimée par l'Office de l'Alta California, 1863. French-language version of original prospectus.

———. *Reports of the Board of Trustees and Officers of the Buena Vista Vinicultural Society.* Annual reports, 1864–?. Valuable sources of information for business activities of the BVVS.

Bunnell, Lafayette Houghton, M.D. *Winona and Its Environs on the Mississippi in Ancient and Modern Days.* Winona, Minn.: Jones and Kroeger, 1897. Bunnell was a sometime passenger on AH's steamboat, *Rock River.* Although his description of the boat and its fate (pp. 202, 646–47) is replete with errors, it nonetheless contains some useful information. The vessel is included in list of early steamboats on the Mississippi (p. 673).

"California as a Vineland." *Atlantic Monthly* 13 (1864): 600–604. Description of viticulture and winemaking in California in the early 1860's. Many statistics, most supplied by AH.

"California Private Land Claim Docket Number 502." MS, National Archives and Records Administration, Regional Center, San Bruno, Calif. Part of Record Group 49, Records of the General Land Office. Includes letters, maps, and sworn testimony given in 1870's to settle northern boundary of Pueblo of Sonoma; frequent references to Lac Rancho, which formed core of AH's Buena Vista property.

Canfield, William H. *Outline Sketches of Sauk County; Including Its History from the First Marks of Man's Hand to 1861, and Its Topography.* Baraboo, Wis.: A. N. Kellogg, Printer, Republic Office, 1861. Recollections of early Sauk County pioneers, including AH's cousin Charles Halasz (Károly Fischer) (pp. 58–62), and Edmond Rendtorff, who joined AH at Sauk Prairie in the fall of 1840 (pp. 63–72).

Carosso, Vincent P. *The California Wine Industry: A Study of the Formative Years, 1830–1895.* Berkeley: University of California Press, 1951. Early history of California wine industry by a careful scholar. Ch. 2 is "The Pre-Haraszthian Fifties," ch. 4, "The Age of Haraszthy."

Chroman, Nathan. *The Treasury of American Wines.* New York: Crown, 1973. General survey of American wines by wine columnist for the *Los Angeles Times.* Many references to AH.

Clark, Satterlee. "Early Times at Fort Winebago." *Collections of the State Historical Society of Wisconsin* (1908) 7: 320–21. Brief but interesting personal recollections of AH and his family in Wisconsin, recorded by army sutler at Fort Winnebago.

Clover, Sam T. *A Pioneer Heritage.* Los Angeles: Saturday Night Publishing Company, 1932. About AH's accomplished grandson George Allan Hancock, with many references to Hancock's mother, Ida Haraszthy. Ch. 1, "California Gets a Recruit," tells AH's story from the perspective of Hancock family tradition.

"Coining Money at the San Francisco Branch Mint." *Hutchings' California Magazine* 1 (Oct. 1856): 145–53. Detailed description of operations of U.S. Branch Mint in San Francisco during the time AH was melter and refiner. Illustrated with woodcuts.

Cole, Harry Ellsworth. *A Standard History of Sauk County, Wisconsin.* Chicago: Lewis Publishing Company, 1918. Good source of information about early history of Haraszthy Town (later Sauk City) and its founder.

"Colonel Agoston Haraszthy." *California—Magazine of the Pacific* 36, no. 9 (1946): 16. Describes dedication ceremonies held in Sonoma June 15, 1946, for monument honoring AH as Father of California Viticulture.

Colville, Samuel. *Colville's San Francisco Directory for the Year Commencing October,*

1856. San Francisco: Commercial Steam Presses: Monson, Valentine & Co., 1856. References to AH and his business associates.

The Count Found a Valley. Sonoma, Calif.: Rancho Buena Vista. 1947. Booklet prepared under the direction of Frank Bartholomew, newspaperman who purchased Buena Vista in 1940's, restored old Haraszthy wine cellars, and reintroduced Buena Vista wines to market. Based mostly on Haraszthy Legend, but contains interesting photographs, prints, and information supplied by Haraszthy descendants.

Cronise, Titus Fey. *The Natural Wealth of California.* San Francisco: H. H. Bancroft, 1868. Description of Sonoma Valley and list of its principal vineyards (pp. 169–70).

Darlington, David. *Angels' Visits: An Inquiry into the Mystery of Zinfandel.* New York: Henry Holt, 1991. Absorbing account of author's efforts to learn "the truth" about Zinfandel and its origins. Although much of the book describes modern-day Zinfandel wines and their makers, a good part is devoted to "an epic romantic triangle: the story of Haraszthy, nineteenth-century California, and Zinfandel."

Davis, Winfield J. *History of Political Conventions in California, 1849–1892.* Sacramento: California State Library, 1893. Describes early political conventions in which AH was a participant.

Deak, Istvan. *The Lawful Revolution: Louis Kossuth and the Hungarians, 1848–1849.* New York: Columbia University Press, 1979. Standard authority on central event in nineteenth-century Hungarian history; no references to AH.

Derleth, August. *The Heritage of Sauk City.* Sauk City, Wis.: Pioneer Press, 1931. Pamphlet published without author's name, but later claimed by him. Reprinted (without date or place) about 1976. Many references to AH.

———. *Restless is the River.* New York: Charles Scribner's Sons, 1939. Roman à clef based on AH's experiences in Wisconsin. Hero is "Count Augustin Brogmar," political refugee from Hungary. A Sauk City native, Derleth was an accomplished and prolific writer of fiction and nonfiction.

———. *The Wisconsin, River of a Thousand Isles.* Rivers of America Series. New York: Farrar and Rinehart, 1942. Reprint Madison: University of Wisconsin Press, 1985. Popular history, with many references to AH. Adheres closely to Haraszthy Legend.

Dictionary of Wisconsin Biography. Madison: State Historical Society of Wisconsin, 1960. Article on AH at p. 158.

Dillon, Richard H. "Colonel Haraszthy and His Puzzling Legacy." *Westways*, Nov. 1957, 30–31. Speculation about origins of Zinfandel.

———. *J. Ross Browne: Confidential Agent in Old California.* Norman: University of Oklahoma Press, 1965. Account of Browne's years as agent for the U.S. Treasury Department, during which time he investigated mint in San Francisco and recommended that AH be prosecuted for embezzlement.

Dojcsák, Győző. *Amerikai magyar történetek* (American Hungarian stories). Budapest: Ifjúsági Lap és Könyvkiadó, 1985. Historical stories for young people. Numerous references to AH, all based on the Haraszthy Legend.

————. *Arany Kaliforniában* (Gold in California). Budapest: A szerző kiadása (published by the author), 1992. This Hungarian "biography" of AH combines Haraszthy Legend with a lot of guessing, most of it wrong.

Donohoe, Joan Marie, S.N.D. "Agostin [*sic*] Haraszthy: A Study in Creativity." *California Historical Society Quarterly* 48 (1969): 153–63. Admiring overview of AH's career.

Dorozynski, Alexander, and Bibiane Bell. *The Wine Book: Wines and Wine Making Around the World.* New York: Golden Press, 1969. References to AH at pp. 249–50, 255, 275.

Dudás, Gyula. *A bácskai nemes családok* (Noble families of the Bácska). Zombor, Hungary: Bitterman Nándor Könyv és Könyomdájából, 1893. Vol. 9, p. 87, includes short article about Haraszty [*sic*] family.

Dunlap, Carol. *California People.* Salt Lake City: Gibbs M. Smith, 1982. Short biographies of notable figures from California's past and present. AH's story at pp. 83–84.

Ellet, Mrs. Elizabeth F. *The Pioneer Women of the West.* Philadelphia: Porter and Coates, 1852. Also New York: Charles Scribner, 1852. Early accounts of pioneer experiences from woman's viewpoint. Short account of AH's mother and wife in Wisconsin at pp. 374–75.

Emerson, Edward R. *The Story of the Vine.* New York: G. P. Putnam's Sons, 1902. Short summary of AH's winemaking career at pp. 225–27.

Emparan, Madie Brown. *The Vallejos of California.* San Francisco: Gleeson Library Associates, University of San Francisco, 1968. Meticulously researched history of Vallejo family in California. Includes biographies of M. G. Vallejo, his wife, and children. Biographies of Natalia Vallejo, who married AH's son Attila, and Jovita Vallejo, who married AH's son Arpad, contain interesting information about Vallejo-Haraszthy family connection.

Encyclopedia Americana. International ed. Vol. 13. Danbury, Conn.: Americana Corporation, 1980. Short biography of AH by Prof. Maynard Amerine of University of California, Davis, at p. 782.

Evans, William Edward. "The Garra Uprising: Conflict Between San Diego Indians and Settlers in 1851." *California Historical Society Quarterly* 45 (1966): 339–49. Description of 1851 Indian uprising in which AH played prominent role.

Fadiman, Clifton, and Sam Aaron. *The New Joys of Wine.* Ed. Darlene Geis. New York: Harry N. Abrams, 1990. "Coffee table book" with contributions by noted writers and wine authorities. References to AH at pp. 57, 82, 94, 103, 148.

Fairchild, Lucius. *California Letters of Lucius Fairchild.* Ed. Joseph Schafer. Madison: State Historical Society of Wisconsin, 1931. Later noted as Civil War general, governor of Wisconsin, and U.S. minister to Spain, Fairchild was seventeen years old when he encountered AH, Charles Haraszthy, and their traveling companions on the trail to California in 1849. His California letters help to establish their route from Wisconsin to St. Joseph, Missouri.

Fényes, Elek. *Magyar Országnak, 's a Hozzá kapcsolt tartományoknak mostani állapotja statistikai és geographiai tekintetben* (Descriptive views of present-day Hungary

and its connected territories, with statistical and geographic considerations).
2d ed. Pest: Trattner Károlyi Nyomtatása, 1837. Brief descriptions of Bács
County as it appeared in AH's time at pp. 53, 60, 67.

———. *Magyarország geographiai szótára* (Geographical dictionary of Hungary).
Pest: Nyomatott Kozma Vazulnál, 1851. Brief descriptions of counties, villages, and other places of interest in mid-nineteenth-century Hungary.

Fenyő, Mario D. "Haraszthy: A Hungarian Pioneer in the American West." In
Society in Change: Studies in Honor of Béla K. Király, ed. Steven Béla Várdy and
Agnes Huszar Várdy, 169–87. Boulder, Colo.: East European Monographs;
distributed by Columbia University Press, 1983. AH's life as seen in broader
context of early-nineteenth-century American immigration.

Fisher, M. F. K. *The Story of Wine in California.* Berkeley: University of California Press, 1962. Gracefully written volume by one of the world's best-known
writers on food and drink. Dedicated to AH.

Fougner, G. Selmer. *Along the Wine Trail: An Anthology of Wines and Spirits.* Boston:
Stratford, 1935. Short summary of AH's winemaking career at pp. 89–90.

Fredericksen, Paul. "The Authentic Haraszthy Story." *Wines and Vines,* pt. 1, June
1947, 25–26, 42; pt. 2, July 1947, 15–16, 30; pt. 3, Aug. 1947, 17–18, 37–
38; pt. 4, Sept. 1947, 17–18, 34; pt. 5, Oct. 1947, 21–22, 41–42. Pioneering
series of articles by public relations officer of Wine Institute in San Francisco.
Notes and photographs.

———. "One Hundred Years of American Champagne." *Wine Review,* June 1947,
22, 24; July 1947, 14, 16. Good summary of early efforts to produce sparkling
wine in California and other states; discusses efforts of AH and his son Arpad.

———. "One More River: The many lives of Agoston Haraszthy, father of California wine-growing, who dared greatly on two continents." MS, Frank H.
Bartholomew Foundation, Sonoma, Calif. Nearly 600-page typescript of full-
length biography completed before 1954. Based on years of research, this
heroic effort to tell the full story of AH's life fails because of the author's
unswervingly adulatory attitude toward his subject and because he did not
recognize the obstacles presented by the Haraszthy Legend.

———. "Utazás Éjszakamerikában (Travels in North America) by Agoston Haraszthy de Mokcsa." MS, State Historical Society of Wisconsin, Madison.
Fourteen-page digest and English translation of AH's original work in Hungarian. Prepared with assistance of George J. Ratty, publisher of San Francisco *Hungarian News.* Introductory note states: "Only those parts of the two
volumes thought likely to be of interest to the general reader were translated,
and then not necessarily either in full or literally."

Fuller, Theodore W. *San Diego Originals: Profiles of the Movers and Shakers of California's First Community.* Pleasant Hill, Calif.: California Profiles Publications,
1987. Biographical sketches in popular style. "Agoston Haraszthy, the Un-
lucky Innovator" (reprinted from *PGandE Progress,* Oct. 1980), at pp. 161–65.

Gabler, James M. *Wine into Words: A History and Bibliography of Wine Books in the
English Language.* Baltimore: Bacchus Press, 1985. Short biographical article

on AH and good review of *Grape Culture, Wines, and Wine-Making* (1862) at pp. 119–20.

Gál, István. *Magyarország, Anglia és Amerika: különös tekintettel a szláv világra* (Hungary, England, and America: With special reference to the Slavic world). Budapest: Officina Budapest, 1945. References to AH at pp. 168, 185.

Gärtner, Maximilian. "Tagebuch der röm. katholischen Missionen in Nord-America für Joh. Stef. Maximilian Gärtner[,] regul. Chorherrn des Praemonstrat. Stiftes Wilten in Tirol, A.D. 1846 (Diary of the Roman Catholic missions in North America by Johann Stefan Maximilian Gärtner, Canon Regular of the Praemonstratensian Abby of Wilten in Tyrol, A. D. 1846)." MS, St. Norbert Abbey, De Pere, Wis. English translation by Stephan Klopfer in Archive of Archdiocese of Milwaukee, Milwaukee, Wis. Film copy of English translation in Stiftsarchiv Wilten, Wilten Abbey, Innsbruck, Austria. Norbertine missionary Gärtner was a frequent guest in the Haraszthy home in Wisconsin. His diary, handwritten in German, offers valuable insights into the business activities, home life, and character of AH in Wisconsin.

Giffen, Helen S., ed. "Letters of John C. Hewston, Jr., on the Establishing of the U.S. Branch Mint in San Francisco." In *Publications for the Year 1952 of the Society of California Pioneers*. San Francisco: Society of California Pioneers, 1952. Contains firsthand observations on early operations at San Francisco mint, of which AH was an officer.

Goc, Michael J. *Lives Lived Here: A Walk Through the History of Sauk City*. Written by Michael J. Goc and compiled by Myrtle Wilhelm Cushing. Friendship, Wis.: New Past Press, 1992. Traces history of important houses, stores, and other places in Sauk City (originally Haraszthy Town). Many references to AH.

———. *Many a Fine Harvest: Sauk County, 1840–1990*. Friendship, Wis.: New Past Press, 1990. Local history; some references to AH.

Goodman, David Michael. *A Western Panorama 1849–1875: The Travels, Writings and Influence of J. Ross Browne on the Pacific Coast, and in Texas, Nevada, Arizona, and Baja California, as the first Mining Commissioner, and Minister to China*. Glendale, Calif.: Arthur H. Clark, 1966. Account of Browne's work in various government posts. Includes material on San Francisco mint, which Browne investigated for Treasury Department, and some references (not uniformly accurate) to AH.

Gracza, Rezsoe and Margaret. *The Hungarians in America*. Minneapolis: Lerner Publications, 1969. "A Versatile Pioneer," a brief summary of AH's story, at p. 15.

Gregory, John G. *Southwestern Wisconsin: A History of Old Crawford County*. Chicago: S. J. Clarke, 1932. Local history, with many references to AH.

Guinn, J. M. *A History of California and an Extended History of Its Southern Coast Counties, also Containing Biographies of Well-Known Citizens of the Past and Present*, vol. 1. Los Angeles: Historic Record Company, 1907. Includes biography of AH's son Bela at pp. 820–23.

Halász, Zoltán. *The Book of Hungarian Wines*. Budapest: Corvina Kiadó, 1981.

Good survey of Hungarian wines and winemaking, with historical perspectives; no references to AH

Hancock, G. Allan. "Madam Ida Hancock Ross, With Views of her home, 'Villa Madonna.'" *Historical Society of Southern California Quarterly* 34 (1952): 53–56. Short reminiscence of AH's daughter by her son, G. Allan Hancock.

Hancock, Ida (Haraszthy). Handwritten reply to typewritten letter dated June 13, 1906, from Reuben Gold Thwaites, Secretary and Superintendent of State Historical Society of Wisconsin. MS, State Historical Society of Wisconsin, Madison. Written on original letter, briefly responds to questions about AH propounded by Thwaites.

Haraszthy, Agoston. "Address of Col. Haraszthy, at the Second Annual Fair of the Sonoma County Agricultural and Mechanical Society, August 31." *California Farmer*, Aug. 31, 1860, 10. Lengthy dissertation in which AH explains his views on Chinese labor in California and advocates establishment of government-sponsored agricultural schools.

———. "Best Modes of Cultivating the Grape in California—as Established by Observations Made in Europe, and Practical Experiments in California, by Col. A. Haraszthy, Manager of the Buena Vista Vinicultural Society's Vineyards in Sonoma." *California Rural Home Journal*, Feb. 15, 1866, 145. Reprinted in *Transactions of the California State Agricultural Society, during the Years 1864 and 1865* (Sacramento, 1866), at pp. 290–95, and in *Hyatt's Hand-Book of Grape Culture* (San Francisco, 1867) at pp. 74–79. AH explains his reasons for planting new vines four rather than eight feet apart and urges farmers of modest means to cultivate grapes.

———. *Father of California Wine: Agoston Haraszthy.* Ed. Theodore Schoenman. Santa Barbara, Calif.: Capra Press, 1979. Facsimile reprint of travel narrative portion of *Grape Culture, Wines, and Wine-Making* (1862), with biographical introduction by Schoenman.

———. *Grape Culture, Wines, and Wine-Making, with Notes Upon Agriculture and Horticulture.* New York: Harper & Brothers, 1862 (Booknoll Reprints, Hopewell, N.J., 1971). Historic book, generally recognized as first important work of California wine literature. Opens with reprint of AH's report to State Legislature on his 1861 mission to Europe, followed by engaging account of his tour through Europe. Ch. 9 consists of extracts from AH's "Report on Grapes and Wine of California" (1858), with comments on points on which his opinions had since changed. Concludes with reprints of technical texts on winegrowing and other agricultural subjects.

———. "Loyalty of the State Agricultural Society's Officers. Letter from the President." *California Farmer*, Aug. 29, 1862, 177. AH responds with vigorous defense to newspaper articles challenging his loyalty to the Union.

———. "President's Opening Address." *California Farmer*, Oct. 3, 1862, 25, 28. Address delivered at opening session of 1862 California State Fair.

———. "Report of A. Haraszthy." In *Report of Commissioners on the Culture of the Grape-Vine in California.* San Francisco: Benj. P. Avery State Printer, 1862.

Pamphlet version of fifteen-page, handwritten report submitted to California Legislature after AH's return from Europe in 1861. Included in bound
collection of 26 pamphlets preserved in the Bancroft Library, University of
California, Berkeley, under the general title, *Wines and Viniculture of California*. Also includes contemporaneous "Report of J. J. Warner," "Letter from
Mr. Haraszthy" to governor dated Feb. 8, 1862, and undated letter of trans-
mittal from Gov. Leland Stanford to California Senate. Same material in
*Appendix to Journals of Senate and Assembly, of the Thirteenth Session of the Legisla-
ture of the State of California* (Sacramento: Benj. P. Avery, State Printer, 1862).
AH's own report also reprinted in *Grape Culture, Wines, and Wine-Making* (New
York, 1862), pp. xv–xxii.

———. "Report on Grapes and Wine of California." In *Transactions of the California State Agricultural Society During the Year 1858*. Sacramento: John O'Meara,
State Printer, 1859 (at 311–29). Dated at Buena Vista, Feb. 21, 1858, this early
manual of practical viticultural and enological techniques has been called
"the first American explication of traditional European winemaking practices" (Darlington, *Angels' Visits: An Inquiry into the Mystery of Zinfandel*, p. 72).
Widely read by winegrowers and would-be winegrowers in California. Portions reprinted in ch. 9 of *Grape Culture, Wines, and Wine-Making* (1862).

———. "Report to the Honorable the Senate and Assembly of the State of
California." MS, California State Archives, Sacramento. Handwritten report
dated Feb. 8, 1862, addressed to "His Excellency the Governor," in which AH
reports that he has taken charge of fruit trees and grapevines he purchased
in Europe and requests payment for same in amount of $12,000.

———. *Tizenöt hét indiánok közt* (Fifteen weeks among the Indians). Budapest:
Pallas Irodalmi és Nyomdai Rt., 1926. Paperback reprint of Indian chapters from *Utazás Éjszakamerikában*, vol. 7 in the publisher's Ifjúsági Könyvtár
(Library for Young People). Illustrated with line drawings. Includes short
biography of AH.

———. "To the Honorable the Senate and Assembly of the State of California."
MS, California State Archives, Sacramento. Handwritten report on AH's mission to Europe in 1861 and vines he collected there. Reprinted in pamphlet
form by State of California and in *Grape Culture, Wines, and Wine-Making* (New
York, 1862).

———. *Utazás Éjszakamerikában* (Travels in North America). Irta Mokcsai Haraszthy Ágoston. Pest: Heckenast Gusztáv. 2d popular ed. Pest: Heckenast
Gusztáv, 1850. 2-volume journal of AH's travels through United States in
1840 and 1841. In popular edition, volumes were bound together as one.

Haraszthy, Arpad. "Bottling Red Wine." *California Farmer*, June 21, 1861, 129. Description of French methods of bottling red wine, written from Paris; based
on author's studies in Champagne country.

———. "The Castle of Johannisberg, and the Famed Johannisberg Wine." *California Farmer*, Dec. 27, 1861, 89. Description of visit made with AH to one of
Europe's most celebrated wine cellars.

———. "Colonel Agoston Haraszthy." MS, State Historical Society of Wisconsin,

Madison. Manuscript in handwriting of Arpad Haraszthy, apparently written in 1879 in response to request from Lyman C. Draper, Secretary of State Historical Society. Includes clipping from San Francisco *Daily Alta California*, Aug. 25, 1870, sketching AH's life story.

———. "Drawing Off Wine." *California Farmer*, July 4, 1862, 114. Describes French method of *soutirage*.

———. "Early Viticulture in Sonoma." In *Sonoma County and Russian River Valley Illustrated*. San Francisco: Bell and Heymans, 1888, 77–79. Reprinted in *San Francisco Merchant* 20 (1888): 113–14. Contains some valuable historical statistics and personal recollections, but its assertions about how and when AH brought Zinfandel to California have been vigorously challenged by later historians.

———. "Fermenting Vats." *California Wine, Wool, and Stock Journal* 1 (1863): 93–96. Practical discourse on fermenting vats, describing advantages of redwood.

———. "Frost in the Vineyards of France." *California Farmer*, Sept. 6, 1861, 4. Describes late frost in France and urges California winemakers to take advantage of unfavorable weather conditions in Europe to redouble their efforts.

———. "The Haraszthy Family." MS, Bancroft Library, University of California, Berkeley. Prepared by Arpad Haraszthy for Hubert Howe Bancroft with assistance of unnamed Bancroft researcher. Includes 48 pages of typescript with handwritten corrections by Arpad; 4 pages of handwritten manuscript in Arpad's hand; 10 pages of handwritten notes extracted from account book of AH. Although this MS is source of much of Haraszthy Legend, it is also indispensable source of data about AH and his family.

———. "Letter No. 4 from Our Paris Correspondent." *California Farmer*, Sept. 6, 1861, 193. Argues against irrigation of vineyards.

———. "Make Pure Wine—No Imitations." *California Farmer*, July 18, 1862, 129. Warns against adulteration of wine.

———. "Monpellier [*sic*]—One of the Wine-Presses." *California Farmer*, Nov. 8, 1861, 54. Describes unusual winepress observed in Montpellier, France.

———. "Our Parisian Correspondence." *California Farmer*, June 14, 1861, 121. First in series of letters written by author to *California Farmer*.

———. "Vine Cultivation, Demand for Wine, Etc." *California Farmer*, Dec. 20, 1861, 81. Argues that there is good market for well-made California wine.

———. "Vineyards on the Rhine." *California Farmer*, Oct. 18, 1861, 41. Dated at Ems, Aug. 27, 1861, covers part of AH's European tour.

———. "Visit to the 'Clos de Vougeot.'" *California Farmer*, Feb. 7, 1862, 137. Describes visit with AH to one of Burgundy's most celebrated vineyards.

———. "Wine Cellars—No. 3." *California Wine, Wool, and Stock Journal* 1 (1863): 137–39. Practical discussion of wine cellars and their construction.

———. "Wine-Making—Clearing, Etc!" *California Farmer*, Mar. 21, 1862, 185. Eleventh in series of letters from France.

———. "Wine-Making. Diseases and Treatment of Casks, Barrels, etc." *Califor-*

nia Farmer, May 8, 1863, 81. Discusses proper treatment of wine barrels and other containers.

———. "Wine Making—Drawing off the Wine." *California Farmer*, Feb. 27, 1863, 1. Practical instructions for beginners in art of winemaking.

———. "Wine-Making in California." *Harper's New Monthly Magazine* 29 (1864): 22–30. Important article that includes good descriptions of vineyards and wine cellars at Buena Vista in 1864. Illustrated with four engravings. Although table of contents credits "A. Haraszthy" as author, text repeatedly refers to "Mr. Haraszthy" in third person. This fact, and style of article, strongly suggest that Arpad Haraszthy was author.

———. "Wine-Making in California." *Overland Monthly* 7 (1871): 489–97; 8 (1872): 34–41, 105–9, 393–98. Series of four articles containing wide-ranging discussion of vinegrowing and winemaking in California, with many historical insights.

———. *Wine-Making in California*. San Francisco: Book Club of California, 1978. Reprint of articles from *Overland Monthly* for 1871 and 1872, with biographical introduction by Ruth Teiser and Catherine Harroun.

———. "Wine-Making in France." *California Farmer*, Aug. 20, 1861, 161. Compares European and California winemaking conditions, giving advantage to latter.

———. "Wine Making No. 4." *California Wine, Wool, and Stock Journal* 1 (1863): 161–64. Practical discussion of winemaking techniques, with emphasis on red wine.

———. "Wine Making No. 5." *California Wine, Wool, and Stock Journal* 1 (1863): 193–96. Practical discussion of winemaking techniques, with emphasis on white wine.

———. "Wine Making No. 6." *California Wine, Wool, and Stock Journal* 1 (1863): 241–44. Practical discussion of winemaking techniques, with emphasis on dessert wines.

———. "Wine Making No. 7." *California Wine, Wool, and Stock Journal* 2 (1864): 13–15. Interesting insights into problems of California wine industry in 1863.

———. "Wine Making No. 8." *California Wine, Wool, and Stock Journal* 2 (1864): 44–45. Describes distillery of Buena Vista Vinicultural Society.

———. "Wine Making No. 9." *California Wine, Wool, and Stock Journal* 2 (1864): 53–54. Discusses choice of grapevines for California vineyards; expresses dissatisfaction with Mission grape but fails to suggest logical successor.

———. "Wine Making No. 10." *California Wine, Wool, and Stock Journal* 2 (1864): 77–79. Continued discussion of choice of grapevines for California vineyards, focusing on grapes for white wines.

———. "Wine Making No. 11." *California Wine, Wool, and Stock Journal* 2 (1864): 113–15. Condemns adulteration of wine.

———. "Wine Making No. 12." *California Wine, Wool, and Stock Journal* 2 (1864): 137–38. Decries practice of passing off adulterated *piquette* as claret.

———. "Wine-Making on the Clos de Vougeot." *California Farmer*, Feb. 14, 1862, 145. Describes winemaking in Burgundian cellar.

————. "Wine Presses—No. 2." *California Wine, Wool, and Stock Journal* 1 (1863): 113–16. Practical discussion of different types of winepresses and their uses.

Haraszthy, Charles. "Vine Culture" by "C. H." *San Francisco Daily Alta California,* Nov. 18, 1856, 1. While living in San Francisco in 1856, AH's father published this proposal for planting vineyards for others in California, in the course of which he briefly sketched his own viticultural background in Europe.

"Haraszthy Family Biographical Sketch." MS, State Historical Society of Wisconsin, Madison. Handwritten letter dated June 10, 1879, addressed to Lyman C. Draper, Corresponding Secretary of the State Historical Society, including short description of visit to AH's Wisconsin home in 1840's. Author not identified.

"Haraszthy, Uznay & Co's, Gold and Silver Refinery, Cor. Brannan & Harris Sts." MS, San Diego Historical Society, San Diego. Lithograph by Kuchel and Dresel, 176 Clay St., San Francisco. With handwritten invoice by Wass, Uznay, and Howard, dated June 4, 1857. Indexed under name of Charles Haraszthy.

Hardy, Thomas. *The Vineyards and Wine Cellars of California.* Ed. Thomas Pinney. San Francisco: Book Club of California. A prominent Australian vineyardist, Hardy toured the California vineyards in the summer of 1883. Among other things, he talked with Attila Haraszthy about the phylloxera (p. 16).

Harris, Bogardus and Labatt. *San Francisco City Directory for the Year Commencing October, 1856.* San Francisco: Whitton, Towne & Co., Printers, Excelsior Steam Power Presses, 1858. References to AH and his business associates.

Hart, James D. *A Companion to California.* New ed. Berkeley: University of California Press, 1987. Standard reference work. Includes short biography of AH at p. 206.

Hayes, Benjamin. "Diary of Judge Benjamin Hayes' Journey Overland from Socorro to Warner's Ranch from October 31, 1849, to January 14, 1850." MS, Bancroft Library, University of California, Berkeley. An Indiana lawyer who was destined to become a prominent judge and historical chronicler in southern California, Hayes met AH on trail east of San Diego in January 1850 and left some revealing recollections of their campfire conversations.

Heintz, William F. "Heintz on History: The woes of early champagne making." *Wines and Vines,* June 1979, 93–94. Includes notes about Arpad Haraszthy's manufacture of Eclipse champagne.

————. "Is the Buena Vista–Haraszthy riddle unraveling after more than 100 years?" *Wines and Vines,* Feb. 1981, 59. Results of author's research into winemaking activities on site of Buena Vista before AH's arrival.

————. "The Role of Chinese Labor in Viticulture and Wine Making in Nineteenth Century California." Master's thesis, Sonoma State College, 1977. Good source of research materials. Many references to AH.

————. *Wine Country: A History of Napa Valley: The Early Years: 1838–1920.* Santa Barbara, Calif.: Capra Press, 1990. History of wine industry in Napa Valley, based mostly on original newspaper accounts. Although AH does not figure directly in the Napa story, there are many references to his contemporary efforts in nearby Sonoma Valley.

Helble, John J. "Wisconsin's Wollersheim Vines Successful: Local Markets Absorb All Their Wines." *Vinifera Wine Growers Journal,* Summer 1987, 81–83. Short history of Wollersheim vineyard near Sauk City, Wisconsin, located on property owned by AH in 1840's.

Henni, John Martin, and Anthony Urbanek. "Letters of the Right Reverend John Martin Henni and the Reverend Anthony Urbanek." *Wisconsin Magazine of History* 10 (1926): 66–94. Henni was the Roman Catholic Bishop of Milwaukee when AH lived on Sauk Prairie. His letters to the Archbishop of Vienna include some interesting references to AH.

Herbst, Ron, and Sharon Tyler Herbst. *Wine Lover's Companion.* Hauppauge, N.Y.: Barron's, 1995. Short article on AH at p. 249.

Hinkle, Richard Paul, and Dan Berger. *Beyond the Grapes: An Inside Look at Sonoma County.* Wilmington, Del.: Atomium Books, 1991. Many references to AH.

The History of Sauk County, Wisconsin. Chicago: Western Historical Company. 1880. Many references to AH and Haraszthy Town (later Sauk City).

Hittell, John S. *The Commerce and Industries of the Pacific Coast of North America.* 2d ed. San Francisco: A. L. Bancroft, 1882. Articles on AH (pp. 245–47) and Arpad Haraszthy (pp. 250–52). Although Hittell was best known as one of nineteenth-century California's most prolific journalists, he was also a viticulturist and participant with AH in efforts to organize the California Wine Association.

———. *Hittell's Hand-Book of Pacific Coast Travel.* San Francisco: A. L. Bancroft, 1885. Short description of Sonoma Valley and Buena Vista Vineyards at pp. 124–25.

———. *The Resources of California.* San Francisco: A. Roman, 1863. Many revised editions. Many references to viticulture, including short descriptions of vineyards at Sonoma and AH's wine cellars at Buena Vista.

Hunt, Rockwell D., ed. *California and Californians,* vol. 3. Chicago: Lewis Publishing, 1926. Biographies of AH (pp. 254–57) and his daughter Ida Hancock Ross (pp. 252–54).

Hutchison, John N. "The Astonishing Hungarian." *Wine and Food* (London), Spring 1968, 68–69. Admiring appraisal of AH by veteran wine journalist.

———. "Drinking in America." Ch. 10 in *Gods, Men, and Wine* by William Younger. Cleveland, Ohio: Wine and Food Society in association with World Publishing Company, 1966. Brief outline of AH's career and accomplishments at pp. 454–56.

———. "A letter to Agoston Haraszthy: Buena Vista Winery revisited." *Wines and Vines,* June 1980, 71. Recent developments at Buena Vista described in letter to winery's founder.

———. "The Wines of the Americas." In *Wines of the World,* ed. André L. Simon. New York: McGraw-Hill, 1967. Long and intelligent survey of viticulture and winemaking in North and South America at pp. 661–98. AH's story at pp. 680–85.

Hyams, Edward. *Dionysus: A Social History of the Wine Vine.* New York: Macmillan,

1965. Many references to AH and Jean Louis Vignes, "than whom very few men have served Dionysius better" (p. 291).

Hyatt, T. Hart. *Hyatt's Hand-Book of Grape Culture.* San Francisco: H. H. Bancroft, 1867. First book on wine published in California; second edition published by A. L. Bancroft, 1876. Hyatt was a viticulturist and editor of *California Rural Home Journal.* AH is cited as authority throughout. Includes reprint (pp. 74–79) of AH's article, "Best Modes of Cultivating the Grape in California," originally published in *California Rural Home Journal,* Feb. 15, 1866.

Inama, Adalbert. "Letters of the Reverend Adelbert [*sic*] Inama, O. Praem." *Wisconsin Magazine of History* 11 (1927–28): 77–95, 197–217; (1928): 328–54, 437–58; 12 (1928–29): 58–96. A Norbertine missionary, Inama came to Wisconsin at the end of 1845 and, on land donated by AH, built two churches. His published letters provide interesting details of AH's business life and business affairs in Wisconsin.

Jackson, Joseph Henry, and James D. Hart, eds. *The Vine in Early California.* San Francisco: Book Club of California, 1955. Series of unbound folders containing reproductions of early items relating to wine. No. 5 is "Buena Vista" by Harold H. Price.

Jacobs, Julius L. "California's Pioneer Wine Families." *California Historical Quarterly* 54 (1975): 139–74. Discussion of Haraszthys at pp. 144–46.

Johnson, Allen, and Dumas Malone, eds. *Dictionary of American Biography.* Vol. 4. New York: Charles Scribner's Sons, 1932. Author's ed. Vol. 8., 1937. Biography of AH by Charles Feleky at pp. 236–37.

Johnson, Hugh. *Vintage: The Story of Wine.* New York: Simon & Schuster, 1989. World history of wine by best-known wine writer of his time. Many references to AH.

Jones, Idwal. *Ark of Empire: San Francisco's Montgomery Block.* Garden City, N.Y.: Doubleday, 1951. Popular history of one of San Francisco's most celebrated Gold Rush buildings. Many references to AH, who worked in building.

———. *Vines in the Sun: A Journey Through the California Vineyards.* New York: William Morrow, 1949. A graceful writer but not a careful historian, Jones added a thick layer of gloss to the Haraszthy Legend in this popular history of California wine. Ch. 4 is devoted to AH and Buena Vista.

Kalapis, Zoltán. *Régi bácskai és bánáti utazók* (Old travelers of the Bácska and the Bánát). Újvidék (Novi Sad), Yugoslavia: Forum Könyvkiadó, 1987. Interesting essay on AH at pp. 11–15, followed by short excerpt from his *Utazás Éjszakamerikában.*

Katona, Anna. "Sándor Farkas Bölöni, 1795–1842, and Ágoston Mokcsai Haraszthy, 1812–1869." In *Abroad in America: Visitors to the New Nation, 1776–1914,* ed. Marc Pachter and Frances Wein. Reading, Mass.: Addison-Wesley, in association with National Portrait Gallery, Smithsonian Institution, 1976. 43–51. Scholarly analysis of two early books about U.S. published in Hungary.

Kempelen, Béla. *Magyar Nemes Családok* (Hungarian noble families). Budapest: Grill Károly Könyvkiadóvállalata, 1912–13. Multivolume encyclopedia of noble families of Hungary. Includes articles on Dedinszky family (vol. 3), Haraszthy family (vol. 4), and Mokcsai family (vol. 7).

Kende, Géza. *Magyarok Amerikában: az amerikai magyarság története, 1583–1926* (Hungarians in America: The history of the Hungarian Americans, 1583–1926). Cleveland, Ohio: A Szabadság Kiadása, 1927. Ch. 7 is "Haraszthy Ágoston, az amerikai magyar honalapító (Agoston Haraszthy, the first Hungarian settler in America)." Written in popular style.

Kenyeres, Ágnes, ed. *Magyar Életrajzi Lexikon* (Hungarian biographical dictionary). Budapest: Akadémiai Kiadó, 1967. Articles on AH and his ancestor, Ferenc Haraszthy, appear in vol. 1 at p. 675.

Kőszeghi, Sándor. *Nemes Családok Pestvármegyében* (Noble families in Pest County). Budapest: Hungária Könyvnyomda, 1899. Genealogical work by chief archivist of Pest County; includes references (p. 120) to Antal Haraszty de Makcsa [*sic*] and his son, Károly.

Lamb, Richard, and Ernest Mittelberger. *In Celebration of Wine and Life*. New York: Drake, 1974. Rev. ed. San Francisco: Wine Appreciation Guild, 1980. Well-illustrated exploration of wine and wine history, with many references to AH.

Lambert-Gócs, Miles [pseud.]. "On the Trail of the Zinfandel." *Journal of Gastronomy* 2 (1986): 5–15. Interesting speculation on origins of Zinfandel by wine scholar and agricultural economist for U.S. government.

Láng, Dezső. "Ágoston Haraszthy." *Hírek a magyar népi demokráciából* (News from the Hungarian People's Democracy), May 29, 1954, 16–18. Short but tantalizing article purporting to describe AH's return to Hungary from Wisconsin and lecture he gave in Budapest in May 1844 [*sic*], describing his impressions of United States. Replete with obvious errors that strongly suggest it is work of fiction rather than fact.

Lange, Kenneth I. *A County Called Sauk: A Human History of Sauk County, Wisconsin*. Baraboo, Wis.: Sauk County Historical Society, 1976. Somewhat disjointed county history, with scattered references to AH.

Langley, Henry G. *The San Francisco Directory for the Year 1858* (San Francisco: Commercial Steam Presses: S.D. Valentine & Son, 1858). Many references to AH and his business associates.

Lázár, István. *Világjárok-világlátók: Régi magyar utazók antológiája* (Globetrotters-travelers: An anthology of early Hungarian travelers). Budapest: Móra Ferenc Könyvkiadó, 1986. Includes interesting essay on Indian chapters in AH's *Utazás Éjszakamerikában.*

LeCount & Strong's San Francisco Directory for the Year 1854. San Francisco: San Francisco Herald Office, 1854. References to AH and his business associates.

Leedom, William S. *The Vintage Wine Book*. New York: Vintage Books, 1963. Short summary of AH's winemaking career at pp. 212–14.

Leggett, Herbert B. "Early History of Wine Production in California." Master's thesis, University of California, Berkeley, 1939. Early effort to summarize history of California viticulture and winemaking in pioneer days. Ch. 4 is devoted to AH.

Lengyel, Emil. *Americans from Hungary*. Philadelphia: J. B. Lippincott, 1948.

Mentions AH at pp. 33–35. Author commits novel error of supposing that there were two men named Agoston Haraszthy, father and son; father was author of *Utazás Éjszakamerikában* (Travels in North America), while son was the founder of Sauk City, Wisconsin, and pioneer California winegrower.

"Letters and Reports Received by the Secretary of the Treasury From Special Agents, 1854–1861." Washington, D.C.: National Archives, Record Group 36. Microfilm. Includes letters written to Secretary of Treasury by J. Ross Browne during time he was investigating affairs at San Francisco mint, of which AH was officer.

Lichine, Alexis, with William Fifield, Jonathan Bartlett, and Jane Stockwood. *Alexis Lichine's Encyclopedia of Wines and Spirits.* New York: Alfred A. Knopf, 1967. Interesting references to AH, whom author describes as "extraordinary." Many later editions.

"Literary Notices: Grape Culture, Wines, and Wine-Making, by A. Haraszthy." *Harper's New Monthly Magazine* 26 (1862): 133. Book review.

Lukinich, Imre. "American Democracy As Seen by the Hungarians of the Age of Reform (1830–1848)," *Journal of Central European Affairs* 8 (1948): 270–81. Professor at University of Budapest discusses AH, his *Utazás Éjszakamerikában*, and its effect on Hungarian readers (pp. 279–80).

Madden, Henry Miller. "California for Hungarian Readers: Letters of János Xántus, 1857 and 1859." *California Historical Society Quarterly* 28 (1949): 125–42. Excerpts from letters written by Hungarian emigrant who visited California in 1850's. Describes gold refinery operated in San Francisco by AH, Sámuel Wass, and Károly Uznay.

Madison, Dane County and Surrounding Towns. Madison, Wis.: William J. Park, 1877. Local history; includes interesting descriptions of land owned by AH on east side of Wisconsin River in 1840's.

"Magyar Kancellária Leveltár, Acta Generalia (Archives of the Hungarian Chancellery, General Acts)." MS, Magyar Országos Levéltár (Hungarian National Archives), Budapest. Voluminous records relating, among other things, to Hungarian nobility. Records (in Latin) of investigation of government of Bács County, in which AH was one of subjects, in archives for 1837 at leaves 611, 2258, 11961, 11963.

Márki, Sándor. "Amerika s a magyarság" (America and the Hungarian People). *Földrajzi közlemények* (Geographical review) (Budapest, 1893). Discusses AH's *Utazás Éjszakamerikában* (Travels in North America) at pp. 69–70.

Martin, Andrew. "Third time is the charm at Sauk City." *Wines and Vines*, Sept. 1978, 66–68. Describes Wollersheim Winery and vineyards near Sauk City, Wisconsin, and AH's efforts to make wine there in 1840's.

———. "Wine history or mythology." *Wines and Vines*, July 1979, 26. Account of speech by William F. Heintz at California History Institute's Conference on Wines and Grapes, in which he traces some erroneous history of AH to "innocent embellishment" of Arpad Haraszthy.

"In the Matter of A. Haraszthy of Sonoma, Sonoma County, California." MS, National Archives and Records Administration, Regional Center, San Bruno,

Calif. Petition (filed Sept. 17, 1867), schedules, and other documents in bankruptcy proceedings in U.S. District Court, District of California.

McGinty, Brian. *Haraszthy at the Mint.* Famous California Trials, vol. 10. Los Angeles: Dawson's Book Shop, 1975. AH's career at U.S. Mint in San Francisco and his subsequent prosecution for embezzlement; based on original research in court documents and contemporary newspaper accounts.

———. "The Legacy of Buena Vista." *American West* 10, no. 3 (1973): 17–23. Story of AH, with focus on Buena Vista vineyards and cellars. Relies excessively on Haraszthy Legend.

———. "A Toast to Eclipse." *Wine World*, Sept.–Oct., 1974, 41–43, 46. Overview of Arpad Haraszthy's career as a champagne-maker in San Francisco.

———. "A Vintage Life." *Historical Society of Southern California Quarterly* 41 (1959): 375–83. Sketch of AH's life; based on Haraszthy Legend.

McKee, Irving. "Early California Wine Growers." *California—Magazine of the Pacific* 37, no. 9 (1947): 16, 34–37. Survey of California wine producers before AH, with emphasis on Los Angeles County.

———. "Historic Sonoma County Winegrowers." *California—Magazine of the Pacific* 45, no. 9 (1955): 17, 33–34. References to many winemakers, including AH.

Melville, John. *Guide to California Wines.* San Carlos, Calif.: Nourse, 1955. Includes discussion of AH and Buena Vista.

Menefee, C. A. *Historical and Descriptive Sketch Book of Napa, Sonoma, Lake, and Mendocino.* Napa City, Calif.: Reporter Publishing House, 1873. Early guidebook, with good descriptions of vineyards. Article on AH at pp. 287–90.

Meredith, DeWitt. *G. Allan Hancock: A Pictorial Account of One Man's Score in Fourscore Years.* San Jose, Calif.: Paramount Printing, 1964. Written for Hancock, one of southern California's best-known financiers and philanthropists. Many references to his father (California pioneer Henry Hancock), mother (Ida Haraszthy Hancock), and grandfather (AH).

Merrick, George Byron. *Old Times on the Upper Mississippi.* Cleveland, Ohio: Arthur H. Clark, 1909. Short history of AH's *Rock River* at p. 287; contains some obvious errors, but includes revealing and mostly plausible details.

Mészáros, Lázár. *Külföldi levelei és életirata* (The foreign letters and autobiography of Lázár Mészáros). Pest: Ráth Mór, 1867. Mészáros was minister of war in the Hungarian government formed by Lajos Kossuth in 1848. Forced into exile after the Austrians ousted Kossuth, he arrived in New Jersey in 1853 and became friendly with Eleonora Haraszthy, then living in Plainfield with her youngest children. He was an avid horticulturist, and probably sent vine cuttings from New Jersey to Agoston Haraszthy in California. Letters he wrote in New Jersey include some interesting references to AH and Eleonora.

Monroe, Marie Jussen. "Biographical Sketch of Edmund Jussen." *Wisconsin Magazine of History* 12 (1928): 146–54. Based on recollections of Edmund Jussen, young German immigrant who was befriended by AH on Sauk Prairie in 1848.

Munro-Fraser, J. P. *History of Sonoma County.* San Francisco: Alley, Bowen, 1880.

Includes valuable information on early-day viticulture in Sonoma County supplied by surviving pioneers. Article about AH at pp. 74–75; Buena Vista described at pp. 459–60.

Muscatine, Doris, Maynard A. Amerine, and Bob Thompson, eds. *The University of California/Sotheby Book of California Wine.* Berkeley: University of California Press/Sotheby Publications, 1984. Rich source of historical, economic, political, legal, literary, and technical information about California wine. Includes chapters titled "Northern California from Haraszthy to the Beginning of Prohibition" by John N. Hutchison and "Zinfandel" by Paul Draper. Many references to AH.

Nagy, Iván. *Magyarország Családai Czimerekkel és Nemzékrendi Táblákkal* (Hungarian families with their coats of arms and genealogical tables). Pest: Ráth Mór, 1857–68. Multivolume encyclopedia of Hungarian families, their coats of arms, and genealogies. Includes articles on Dedinszky family (vol. 3), Haraszthy family (vol. 5), and Mokcsai family (vol. 7).

Nehéz, Ferenc. "Tizenhárom szőlővessző" (Thirteen vinestalks). *California Magyarság* 62, nos. 37, 39, 41, 43, 44, 45, 46, 48; 63, no. 63 (1985). Frankly fictionalized version of Haraszthy Legend.

Nordhoff, Charles. *California for Health, Pleasure, and Residence: A Book for Travellers and Settlers.* New York: Harper & Brothers, 1872. Enormously popular book in its time, based on author's visit to California in 1871. Ch. 13 is devoted to winegrowing. Author describes AH (p. 217) as "the father of wine-culture in this State."

Old Settlers' Association of Sauk County, Wisconsin. *Transactions of the Old Settlers' Association of Sauk County, Wisconsin, Held June 20th, 1872.* N.p., n.d. Includes reminiscences of Sauk City pioneers William H. Clark (pp. 5–9) and Charles Halasz, originally Károly Fischer (p. 17).

[Olmsted, Frederick Law.] *The Production of Wine in California: Particularly Referring to the Establishment of the Buena Vista Vinicultural Society.* San Francisco: Printed by Towne and Bacon, 1865. Prospectus for investors in BVVS, written by Olmsted at request of William C. Ralston. Pamphlet included in bound collection of 26 pamphlets preserved in Bancroft Library, University of California, Berkeley, under general title of *Wines and Viniculture of California.* Text reprinted in *The Papers of Frederick Law Olmsted,* vol. 5, *The California Frontier,* ed. Victoria Post Ranney, Gerard J. Rauluk, and Carolyn F. Hoffman. Baltimore: Johns Hopkins University Press, 1990, at pp. 332–38.

The 100th Anniversary of [the] Death of Agoston Haraszthy. Washington, D.C.: U.S. Government Printing Office, 1969. Reprint of proceedings reported in *Congressional Record,* 91st Cong., 1st sess., 1969, 115, pt. 12, commemorating centennial of death of AH. Includes remarks of U.S. Senators George Murphy and Alan Cranston; message from Gov. Ronald Reagan; address by AH's great-grandson Jan Haraszthy; and statement on importance of AH's viticultural activities in California by Prof. Maynard A. Amerine of University of California, Davis.

Ordish, George. *The Great Wine Blight.* New York: Charles Scribner's Sons, 1972.

Scholarly study of the phylloxera and the devastation it wrought in fine wine vineyards around the world; no references to AH.

Ortutay, Gyula, ed., *Messzi népek magyar kutatói: Az egyetemes néprajz magyar előfutárai és művelői* (Hungarian research into faraway peoples: Works and influence of the forerunners of Hungarian ethnography). In *A magyar néprajz klasszikusai* (Classics of Hungarian ethnography), vol. 1. Budapest: Gondolat, 1978. Short introductory biography of AH, followed by reprint from Indian adventures in his *Utazás Éjszakamerikában* (Travels in North America).

Paget, John, Esq. *Hungary & Transylvania.* New ed. 2 vols. London: John Murray, 1855. (1st ed. London, 1839.) An English gentleman who married a daughter of Baron Miklós Wesseléyni, Paget traveled through Hungary and Transylvania during the late 1830's. His perceptive observations of Hungarian life and customs are invaluable; no references to AH.

Pallas Nagy Lexikona az Összes Ismeretek Enciklopédiája (Great Pallas dictionary and encyclopedia of collected knowledge). Budapest: Pallas Irodalmi és Nyomdai Részvénytársság, 1893–1904. Multivolume Hungarian encyclopedia. Short article on AH in vol. 8, p. 675.

Paul, Rodman W. "The Beginnings of Agriculture in California: Innovation *vs.* Continuity." *California Historical Quarterly* 42 (1973): 24. This essay by a distinguished professor of history at the California Institute of Technology includes a reasoned and logical explanation of why AH is entitled to be known as the Father of California Viticulture.

Pauly, Thomas H. "J. Ross Browne: An Opportunity and a Bottle of Wine." MS, Bancroft Library, University of California, Berkeley. Discusses wine-lobbying efforts of California Wine Growers' Association, undertaken by Browne at urging of AH, and copies letter sent by Browne to Congressman James A. Garfield.

———. "J. Ross Browne: Wine Lobbyist and Frontier Opportunist." *California Historical Quarterly* 51 (Summer 1972): 99–116. Additional discussion of Browne's wine-lobbying efforts, in which AH was involved.

Pease, Verne Seth. "Agoston Haraszthy." In *Proceedings of the State Historical Society of Wisconsin at its Fifty-Fourth Annual Meeting, Held October 18, 1906.* Madison: State Historical Society of Wisconsin, 1907. Valuable summary of AH's career, with emphasis on his Wisconsin years (pp. 224–45); largely based on personal recollections of Sauk Prairie pioneers.

Peninou, Ernest P. *A History of the Orleans Hill Vineyard and Winery of Arpad Haraszthy and Company.* Winters, Calif.: Winters Express, 1983. Interesting booklet based on original research into local and other records.

Peninou, Ernest P., and Sidney S. Greenleaf. *A Directory of Wine Growers and Wine Makers in 1860, With Biographical and Historical Notes and Index.* Berkeley, Calif.: Tamalpais Press, 1967. Article on AH at pp. 63–65.

———. *Winemaking in California. I. How Wine Is Made. II. From the Missions to 1894.* San Francisco: Peregrine Press, 1954. References to AH and Arpad at pp. 24–26, 28.

———. *Winemaking in California. III. The California Wine Association.* San Francisco: Porpoise Bookshop, 1954. Sketch of Arpad Haraszthy and Company at pp. 8–12.

Phillips, George Harwood. *Chiefs and Challengers: Indian Resistance and Cooperation in Southern California.* Berkeley: University of California Press, 1975. Includes scholarly study of the Indian insurrection (often called the "Garra Uprising") in which AH played a prominent role in his capacity as sheriff of San Diego County.

Phisterer, Frederick. *New York in the War of the Rebellion 1861 to 1865.* 3d ed. Albany, N.Y.: J. B. Lyon Company, State Printers. 1912. Multivolume compendium of regimental histories. Vol. 2 contains history of 18th Regiment of Cavalry (also known as Corning Light Cavalry) and brief biography of Gaza Haraszthy, who served as captain of Company B and was elevated to rank of major July 4, 1865.

Pinney, Thomas. "Agoston Haraszthy." In *The Oxford Companion to Wine,* ed. Jancis Robinson. Oxford: Oxford University Press, 1994. Short biography (p. 479) stating that AH is "frequently but wrongly identified as the 'father of California wine'" and that story that has grown up around him "has become legendary and difficult to dislodge."

———. *A History of Wine in America: From the Beginnings to Prohibition.* Berkeley: University of California Press, 1989. AH is the only figure who merits an entire chapter (Ch. 10, "The Haraszthy Legend") in this ambitious history of vinegrowing and winemaking in U.S. Although the author describes AH as "remarkable," he argues that his viticultural achievements are more mythical than real.

———. "Introduction" to Thomas Hardy, *The Vineyards and Wine Cellars of California.* San Francisco: Book Club of California, 1994. Hardy was an important Australian viticulturist who visited California in 1883 and left interesting descriptions of its vineyards and wineries.

Pivány, Eugene [Jenő]. *Hungarian-American Historical Connections From Pre-Columbian Times to the End of the American Civil War.* Budapest: Royal Hungarian University Press, 1927. Summary of AH's career at pp. 33–37.

———. *Magyarok Északamerikában* (Hungarians in North America). Budapest: Officina Budapest, 1944. Short book, includes brief references to AH (at pp. 15, 16) and picture of Buena Vista Ranch House in Sonoma.

Powell, H. M. T. *The Santa Fé Trail to California, 1849–1852: The Journal and Drawings of H. M. T. Powell.* Ed. Douglas S. Watson. San Francisco: Book Club of California, 1931. A traveling artist, Powell encountered AH at Mission San Luis Rey on Mar. 12, 1850 (p. 205).

Preston, Wheeler. *American Biographies.* New York: Harper, 1940. Encyclopedia of notable Americans. AH at p. 441.

Prince, William Robert, assisted by William Prince. *A Treatise on the Vine.* New York: T. & J. Swords, 1830. Pioneer work that includes detailed descriptions and classification of European and American grape varieties, including the "Black Zinfardel [*sic*] of Hungary" (p. 468), which may have been the same as California's Zinfandel; no references to AH.

"Proceedings of the Council of San Diego, Commencing with its organization June 17th, 1850." MS, in Book A of City Records, Office of City Clerk, City of San Diego. Typewritten copy in San Diego Historical Society, San Diego. Invaluable source of information about public activities in San Diego during time AH served as city marshal and county sheriff.

Ragatz, Oswald. "Memoirs of a Sauk Swiss," *Wisconsin Magazine of History* 19 (1935): 182–227. The Swiss-born Ragatz was a schoolmate of Gaza and Attila Haraszthy in Haraszthy Town. His memoir preserves interesting details of life on Sauk Prairie during the time the Haraszthys lived there.

"Records of the General Land Office, Local Office Tract Book, Wisconsin. Record Group 49, Vol. 23." MS, State Historical Society of Wisconsin, Madison. Contains records of United States Land Office at Mineral Point, California, during time the Haraszthys lived in Wisconsin. Many Haraszthy entries.

Report of the Committee on Culture of the Grape on the Cultivation of the Grape, and the Production of Wines and Brandies in California. Sacramento: D. W. Gelwicks, State Printer, 1870. Appendix D is a letter from I. Landsberger and Co., dated Mar. 23, 1870, explaining method for making champagne from Haraszthy grapes and AH's experiments with layering of grapevines in Sonoma. Arpad Haraszthy was champagne maker for Landsberger and later partner in Landsberger company.

Révai Nagy Lexikona az Ismeretek Enciklopédiája (Great Révai dictionary and encyclopedia of knowledge). Budapest: Révai Testvérek Irodalmi Intézet Részvénytársaság, 1911–35. Multivolume Hungarian encyclopedia. Short article on AH in vol. 9, p. 507.

Richards, Robert, Jr. "Recollections." MS, State Historical Society of Wisconsin, Madison. Four-page statement made about 1923 for unnamed newspaper reporter. Photocopy of typescript made in 1976 by John J. Waldmer, Milwaukee. Richards was 80 years of age and living in Riverton, Kansas, at the time of this statement. His father operated AH's Wisconsin River ferry in 1840's.

Roper, William L. "Sheriff Haraszthy's Great Legacy." *California Highway Patrolman* 20, no. 3 (1966): 15, 37, 47–48, 54–56. Story of AH's career as sheriff in San Diego, with considerable information about AH's grandson G. Allan Hancock.

Rossigneux, Paul. *Where Wine History Was Made.* Sonoma, Calif.: Napa and Sonoma Wine Co., 1949. Booklet by president of Napa and Sonoma Wine Co., which held lease on one of AH's wine cellars at Buena Vista in late 1940's and early 1950's.

Ruhl, Karl. *Californien.* New York: Verlag von E. Steiger, 1867. References to California vineyards and AH at pp. 238–49.

San Francisco Business Directory for the Year Commencing January 1, 1856. San Francisco: Baggett, Joseph & Co., 1856. References to AH and his business associates.

Schoenman, Theodore. "Agoston Haraszthy, The Father of Californian Viticulture." *New Hungarian Quarterly* 24 (1983): 141–46. Retelling of Haraszthy

Legend, with some insights into AH's early life in Hungary and career in Wisconsin.

Schoonmaker, Frank. *Frank Schoonmaker's Encyclopedia of Wine*. New York: Hastings House, 1964. The first seven editions of this standard reference work declared that AH was "often and quite fairly called the 'father of California viticulture.'" After the author's death in 1976, *The New Frank Schoonmaker Encyclopedia of Wine* (revised by Alexis Bespaloff) deleted the words "and quite fairly" but repeated the rest of the original assessment.

Schoonmaker, Frank, and Tom Marvel. *American Wines*. New York: Duell, Sloan and Pearce. 1941. Ch. 4 includes short account of career of AH, whom authors call "an extraordinary individual."

Schorer, Mark. *A House Too Old*. New York: Reynal and Hitchcock, 1935. Novel loosely based on AH, here renamed Count Augustin Karanszcy. Born and raised in Sauk City, Wisconsin, Schorer is best known for his 1961 biography of Sinclair Lewis.

Schwartz, Henry. *Tales of Old Town*. San Diego: San Miguel Press, 1980. Stories of early-day San Diego, written in popular style. Ch. titled "El Dorado" reprises story of AH. Other references to AH in "The Garra Uprising" and "Roy Bean's Duel on Horseback." "Without Benefit of Blackstone" recalls Charles Haraszthy's service as judge of San Diego's first Court of Sessions.

Siebmacher, J. *Die Wappen des Adels in Ungarn, J. Siebmacher's grosses Wappenbuch Band 33* (Coats of arms of the Hungarian nobility, Volume 33 of J. Siebmacher's Great Book of Coats of Arms). Neustadt an der Aisch: Bauer & Rapse, Inhaber Gerhard Gessner, 1982. Standard work; describes noble arms of Haraszthy Mokcsai family at p. 223.

Smythe, William E. *History of San Diego, 1542–1908*. 2 vols. San Diego: History Company, 1908. Early history of San Diego, with references to AH. Some of author's conclusions are inconsistent with modern research.

Snyder, Jacob Rink. "Major Jacob Rink Snyder Collection." MS, Society of California Pioneers, San Francisco. Large collection of letters, accounts, deeds, contracts, and other original documents donated to Society in 1931 and 1932 by Snyder's widow. Includes original deed of trust dated June 10, 1857, from AH to Snyder as trustee for United States, given to secure government against any losses for which AH might be held responsible as melter and refiner of mint in San Francisco, and copies of several important documents in mint litigation, apparently made for Snyder from court originals.

Stanford, Leland. "To the Honorable The Senate of California." MS, California State Archives, Sacramento. One-page, handwritten letter dated Feb. 10, 1862, in which Stanford, as governor, transmits Official Reports of two of three commissioners appointed to report on ways and means best adapted to promote improvement and growth of grapevine in California.

Stark, William F. *Wisconsin, River of History*. Nashotah, Wis.: William F. Stark, 1988. Local history by longtime admirer of Wisconsin River; many references to AH.

Starr, Kevin. *Inventing the Dream: California Through the Progressive Era.* New York: Oxford University Press, 1985. Part of Starr's widely read "Americans and the California Dream" series, this book includes a chapter on the early development of California agriculture and a short but interesting summary of AH's life and achievements (pp. 147–49).

Stevenson, Tom. *Sotheby's World Wine Encyclopedia: A Comprehensive Reference Guide to the Wines of the World.* New York and Boston: New York Graphic Society and Little, Brown, 1988. "The Amazing Haraszthy" (pp. 361–62) briefly summarizes AH's career, describing him as "a colourful, flamboyant entrepreneur in the mould of Barnum or Champagne Charlie."

Stoll, Horatio F. "Agostin [*sic*] Haraszthy's Eventful Career." *Wines and Vines,* Jan. 1937, 16–17. Short sketch of AH's career, recommending that monument be erected to his memory in Sonoma.

Stuller, Jay, and Glen Martin. *Through the Grapevine: The Business of Wine in America.* New York: Wynwood Press, 1989. Reprinted, San Francisco: Harper San Francisco, 1994, as *Through the Grapevine: The Real Story Behind America's Billion Dollar Wine Industry.* Study of business of winemaking and wine selling in California in 1980's, with historical references, many to AH.

Sullivan, Charles L. "By the late 1880's, Arpad Haraszthy was producing 250,000 bottles of Eclipse." *California Winelands,* Jan. 11, 1986, 6. Short summary of Arpad Haraszthy's career as a producer of fine champagne in San Francisco.

———. "*The Father of California Wine: Agoston Haraszthy. Theodore Schoenman (ed.).*" *Vintage Magazine,* Dec. 1979, 43–44. Scathing review of 1979 reprint of AH's *Grape Culture, Wines, and Wine-Making* (1862). Argues that AH's reputation as viticultural pioneer should be based not on vines he introduced into California but on "what he was able to induce others to do."

———. "A Historian's Account of Zinfandel in California." *Wines and Vines,* Feb. 1977, 18–20. Argues that AH was not first to introduce Zinfandel to California. Contains much material included in author's later articles in *California History* (1978) and *Vinifera Wine Growers Journal* (1982).

———. "A Man Named Agoston Haraszthy," Parts. 1–3. *Vintage Magazine,* Feb. 1980, 13–19; Mar. 1980, 23–25; Apr. 1980, 11–17. Ambitious reassessment of AH's contributions to early development of California viticulture. While the author would deny him the title "Father of California Viticulture," he would accord him recognition as "the most important individual to affect the course of California wine history in its pioneer years."

———. *Napa Wine: A History from Mission Days to Present.* San Francisco: Wine Appreciation Guild, 1994. Although AH was not directly involved in the viticultural development of Napa Valley, his influence was felt there, and he is mentioned frequently (and not always favorably) in this ambitious and widely read history.

———. "A Viticultural Mystery Solved: The Historical Origins of Zinfandel in California." *California History* 57 (1978): 114–29. Demonstrates that grape called "Zinfindal" was grown in hothouses in New England as early as the 1830's and imported into California by several horticulturists in the early

1850's; argues that this was the same grape that was later known as "Zinfan del" in California; charges that Árpad Haraszthy manufactured the story that AH imported the grape in the early 1850's; no effort to trace Zinfandel to its European source.

———. "Zinfandel: A True Vinifera." *Vinifera Wine Growers Journal,* Summer 1982, 71–86. Updated version of author's earlier *California History* article on origins of Zinfandel in California.

Szemere, Bertalan. *Naplóm: Számüzetésében* (My diary: In exile). Pest: Ráth Mór, 1869. Premier in Hungarian government formed by Lajos Kossuth in 1848, Szemere was living in exile when he met AH in Paris in 1861. His diary contains interesting (and not altogether favorable) impressions of AH and his "visionary" business activities.

Szente, Péter. "Egy elfelejtett amerikás magyar—Haraszthy Ágoston (Agoston Haraszthy—A forgotten Hungarian-American)." *Századok* (Budapest) 112, no. 1 (1978): 110–24. This interesting attempt to separate the Haraszthy Legend from the factual story of AH's life fails because the author relies on secondary works to the exclusion of original sources.

Széplaki, Joseph. *The Hungarians in America 1583–1974: A Chronology and Fact Book.* Dobbs Ferry, N.Y.: Oceana Publications, 1975. AH mentioned at pp. 4–5.

Szinnyei, József. *Hazai és Külföldi Folyóiratok Magyar Tudományos Repertóriuma* (Hungarian scientific bibliography of domestic and foreign periodicals). Budapest: Magyar Tudományos Akadémia, 1874–85. Bibliographical references to articles in Hungarian journals from 1731 to 1880 by chief keeper of Budapest University Library. References to AH in vol. 5, cols. 464, 868.

———. *Magyar Írók Élete és Munkái* (The lives and works of Hungarian writers). A Magyar Tudományos Akadémia megbízásából írta Szinnyei József. Budapest: Hornyánszky Viktor Könyvkiadóhivatala, 1896. Basic reference work on Hungarian writers prepared for Hungarian Academy of Sciences. Article on AH in vol. 4, cols. 456–58.

Sztáray, Zoltán. *Haraszthy Ágoston, A kalifornia szőlőkultúra atyja* (Agoston Haraszthy, the father of California viticulture). New York: Püski, 1986. First book-length biography of AH in Hungarian. A serious work of scholarship which is disappointing only because the author could find little hard evidence of AH's early life in Hungary.

Teiser, Ruth, and Catherine Harroun. *Winemaking in California.* New York: McGraw-Hill, 1983. Carefully researched history of wines and wineries of California. Many references to AH.

Titus, W. A. "Historic Spots in Wisconsin: Sauk City and Prairie du Sac, Twin Villages with an Historic Background." *Wisconsin Magazine of History* 9 (1926): 333–39. Contains interesting information about the Sauk Indians, brief biography of AH, and a quotation about AH from Satterlee Clark.

Transactions of the California State Agricultural Society. Annual volumes, published at Sacramento, 1858–67. 1858 includes "Farm of Colonel A. Haraszthy" (pp. 242–46) and AH's "Report on Grapes and Wine of California" (pp. 311–29);

1860 includes the resolution proposed by AH requesting that the legislature send a commissioner to Europe to collect vines for the benefit of the state (pp. 17–18); a short description of AH's vineyards at Sonoma (p. 78); and a list of wines entered in the State Fair for 1860 (pp. 165–66); 1864–65 includes AH's essay titled "Best Modes of Cultivating the Grape in California" (pp. 290–95).

Turner, Andrew Jackson. "The History of Fort Winnebago." *Collections of the State Historical Society of Wisconsin* 15 (1898): 65–102. Includes short description of AH's contract to supply fuel to Fort Winnebago and a short biography of AH in a footnote by Reuben Gold Thwaites, ed.

Várdy, Steven Béla. *The Hungarian Americans: The Hungarian Experience in North America.* The Peoples of North America, consult. ed. Daniel Patrick Moynihan. New York: Chelsea House, 1990. Includes short summary of AH's American experience (pp. 38–39).

Vasvary, Edmund. *Lincoln's Hungarian Heroes: The Participation of Hungarians in the Civil War 1861–1865.* Washington, D.C.: Hungarian Reformed Federation of America, 1939. Biographical note on "Géza Haraszthy" (p. 56).

Vine, Richard P. *Wine Appreciation: A Comprehensive User's Guide to the World's Wines and Vineyards.* New York: Facts on File, 1988. Many references to AH and his winemaking efforts in Wisconsin and California.

Voigt, Vilmos. "Hungarian Ethnography in American Studies." *Artes Populares* (Yearbook of the Department of Folklore, Eötvös Lóránd University, Budapest) 9: 281–304. Survey of early Hungarian contacts with North and South America as reflected in Hungarian literature. AH and his *Utazás Éjszakamerikában* (Travels in North America) are discussed at pp. 284–85. This yearbook was dedicated to the memory of AH (see p. 298 n. 6).

Wagner, Philip M. *American Wines and Wine-Making.* New York: Alfred A. Knopf, 1956. Intelligent survey of wines and winemaking techniques, based on Wagner's *American Wines and How to Make Them* (1933). Interesting references to AH (p. 43), "who almost singlehanded planted the seeds of California's present-day viticultural industry."

Wait, Frona Eunice. *Wines and Vines of California: A Treatise on the Ethics of Wine-Drinking.* San Francisco: Bancroft Company, 1889. First comprehensive description of California wine industry for general readers, with many references to AH. Ch. 4 is "How to Drink Wine," by Arpad Haraszthy.

Wetmore, Charles A. *Ampelography of California.* San Francisco: Merchant Publishing Co., 1884. Booklet consisting of revised versions of articles originally published in *San Francisco Merchant,* Jan. 4 and 11, 1884. Wetmore was Chief Executive Viticultural Officer of California State Vinicultural Society and a close student of vines and viticulture in California. Many references to AH, plus article on Zinfandel, whose origin is "veiled in mystery."

Wilson, James Grant, and John Fiske. *Appleton's Cyclopaedia of American Biography,* vol. 3. New York: D. Appleton, 1898. Biography of AH (p. 76).

"Wines, Almonds, and Olives in California." *Scientific American* 10 (1864): 137–38. Short but valuable report on AH's appearance before American Institute of City of New York in February 1864. Includes partial transcript of remarks he made on cultivating vineyards, choosing wine grapes, and similar subjects.

Wisconsin, A Guide to the Badger State. American Guide Series. New York: Duell, Sloan and Pearce, 1941. Compiled by Writers' Program of Works Projects Administration in Wisconsin. References to AH and Sauk City at pp. 492–94.

Woodward, Arthur. "The Garra Revolt of 1851." In *The Westerners Brand Book: Los Angeles Corral . . . 1947.* Los Angeles: The Los Angeles Westerners, 1948. Pro-Indian account of the Garra Affair that takes some liberties with facts.

Xántus, John. *Letters from North America.* Trans. and ed. Theodore and Helen Benedek Schoenman. Detroit, Mich.: Wayne State University Press, 1975. The author was a Hungarian who came to the U.S. in 1851 and wrote letters back home about his American experiences; includes descriptions of AH's private gold and silver refinery in San Francisco.

———. *Travels in Southern California.* Trans. and ed. Theodore and Helen Benedek Schoenman. Detroit, Mich.: Wayne State University Press, 1976. Further letters from Hungarian immigrant of the 1850's, with peripheral references to AH.

Závodszky, Géza. *American Effects on Hungarian Imagination and Political Thought, 1559–1848.* Translated from the Hungarian by Amy Módly. Highland Lakes, N.J.: Atlantic Research and Publications, 1995. Demonstrates influence that political, economic, and social developments in U.S. had on Hungarian political ideas before 1848–49; includes interesting discussion of AH's *Utazás Éjszakamerikában* (1844) and its influence in Hungary.

Index

Library of Congress Cataloging-in-Publication Data

McGinty, Brian.
  Strong wine : the life and legend of Agoston
  Haraszthy / Brian McGinty.
      p. cm.
  Includes bibliographical references and index.
  ISBN 0-8047-3145-4 (cl.)
  ISBN 0-8047-3146-2 (pbk.)
  1. Haraszthy, Agoston, 1812–1869. 2. Vintners
  —California—Biography. 3. Viticulturists—
  California—Biography. I. Title.
  TP547.H37M33 1998
  641.2'2'092—dc21
  [B]   97-48454

⊗ This book is printed on acid-free paper.

Original printing 1998
Last figure below indicates year of this printing:
06 05 04 03 02 01 00 99 98